INNOVATIVE HEALTH PARTNERSHIPS

The Diplomacy of Diversity

GLOBAL HEALTH DIPLOMACY – Vol. 1

INNOVATIVE HEALTH PARTNERSHIPS

The Diplomacy of Diversity

Edited by

Daniel Low-Beer

Switzerland

World Scientific

NEW JERSEY • LONDON • SINGAPORE • BEIJING • SHANGHAI • HONG KONG • TAIPEI • CHENNAI

Published by

World Scientific Publishing Co. Pte. Ltd.
5 Toh Tuck Link, Singapore 596224
USA office: 27 Warren Street, Suite 401-402, Hackensack, NJ 07601
UK office: 57 Shelton Street, Covent Garden, London WC2H 9HE

British Library Cataloguing-in-Publication Data
A catalogue record for this book is available from the British Library.

Front cover images by John Rae.

Global Health Diplomacy — Vol. 1
INNOVATIVE HEALTH PARTNERSHIPS
The Diplomacy of Diversity

ISBN-13 978-981-4366-14-4
ISBN-10 981-4366-14-5

Typeset by Stallion Press
Email: enquiries@stallionpress.com

Printed by FuIsland Offset Printing (S) Pte Ltd Singapore

Contents

List of Authors[1]

Daniel Low-Beer — is Director of Performance, Impact & Effectiveness at the Global Fund to Fight AIDS, TB and Malaria. He has worked with WHO, ministries of health and NGOs.

Richard Manning — was Chair of the OECD Development Assistance Committee, Director General of Policy at DFID and chair of the Replenishment of the Global Fund. He has played a leading role in development, health and the replenishments of World Bank and Innovative Health Partnerships.

Paul Isenman — is an independent consultant on aid architecture and effectiveness. He held senior positions in the World Bank and OECD. He was one of the principal architects of the Paris Declaration on aid effectiveness.

Alexander Shakow — has spent over 50 years working on development issues. He held senior positions in the US Peace Corps, USAID and the World Bank. Now retired, he is an occasional independent consultant for international agencies.

Minister Tedros Adhanom Ghebreyesus — is Minister of Health, Federal Democratic Republic of Ethiopia and has been chair of the Roll Back Malaria Partnerships and the Global Fund. He has been a major voice in strengthening the country ownership of development aid.

---

[1] The findings and views are those of the authors and do not necessarily represent those of the affiliate institution.

Hareya Fassil — is international affairs advisor to the Minister of Health of Ethiopia.

Dean Shuey — has worked for both non-governmental organizations and the World Health Organization at field, national and regional level in both Africa and Asia.

Rebecca Dodd — works at the Western Pacific Regional Office of the World Health Organisation in Manila, She previously worked at WHO country office in Vietnam, and has written extensively on health partnerships and health governance.

Margret Thalwitz — was director of Global Programs and Partnerships for the World Bank. She helped lead the World Bank's work with innovative health partnerships and the Accra Action Agenda.

Prerna Banati — is Takemi Fellow in Global Health and Population at Harvard University.

Bernard Nahlen — is deputy coordinator of the United States President's Malaria Initiative (PMI).

Richard Stekete — is responsible for the malaria control and evaluation partnership in Africa (MACEPA), for Path. He was chair of the Monitoring, Evaluation, Reference Group of RBM.

Bjorg Sandkjaer — is senior programme officer, Public Policy, GAVI Alliance.

Kathy Marconi — was director of Strategic Information at PEPFAR. She is Professor and Director of Health Care Administration at University of Maryland University College.

Paul Bouey — is director of Strategic Information at PEPFAR and leads their approach to results.

Mark Dybul — was the US Global AIDS Coordinator in charge of PEPFAR and works in HIV, malaria, and global health as co-director at Georgetown's Institute for National and Global Health Law.

Nina Ingenkamp — is technical officer at the Global Fund for AIDS, TB and malaria.

Dida Connor — is a senior private-sector officer at the Global Fund for AIDS, TB and malaria.

David Evans — is manager, private-sector resource mobilisation at the Global Fund.

Brian Brink — is chief medical officer of Anglo-American plc. and lives in South Africa.

Josh Galjour — is Program Officer at the Global Fund to Fight AIDS, Tuberculosis and Malaria. He has worked with civil society organizations in the U.S. and sub-Saharan Africa, and his research interests include the governance of global health.

Asia Russell — is Director of International Policy at Health GAP (Global Access Project) and is a leading community activist in AIDS and global health. From 2007–2009, she represented Developed Country NGOs on the Board of Directors of the Global Fund to Fight AIDS, Tuberculosis and Malaria.

Alan Whiteside — is the Director of the Health Economics and HIV/AIDS Research Division at the University of KwaZulu-Natal. He was Commissioner of the UN Commission on HIV/AIDS and Governance in Africa. He has been working on issues of HIV AIDS since 1987. His most recent book 'HIV/AIDS: A very Short Introduction' was published by Oxford University Press in 2008.

Jean-Marc Olivé — is a medical doctor and public health specialist. He spent more than 30 years at the World Health Organization, serving in The Caribbean, Latin America, Africa, Europe and Asia. His last post was as WHO Representative in Vietnam.

Wuleta Lemma (with N. Kedir, G. Azene, B. Abdosh, J. Aliy) — is Assistant Professor, Country Director, Tulane Ethiopia Program and Director, Center for Global Health Equity, Tulane University, USA. N. Kedir is the former Director General, Policy, Planning & Finance (PPF) Directorate, Federal Ministry of Head Ethiopia. G. Azen, B. Abdosh and J. Aliy are Senior Experts and Heads of programs at the Tulane University Technical Assistant Program, Ethiopia.

Aparajita Ramakrishnan (with S. Sgaier, A. Alexander) — is a senior programme officer with the Bill & Melinda Gates Foundation. Sema Sgaier is a programme officer. Ashok Alexander is the head of the India Office of the Bill & Melinda Gates Foundation.

Alexey Bobrik — is director of the Open Health Institute in Russia and pioneer of the NGO response.

Erling Hog — is at the London School of Economics and Political Sciences, specializing in fragile states.

Acknowledgements

This book is dedicated to Ann and Tom Low-Beer, and to their love of health, education, debate and books.

Special thanks to Eve, Louis and Noah Low-Beer for their wonderful support, stimulation and distractions while writing the book, Ann Low-Beer for patiently discussing and shaping the ideas and language, Andrew Cassels for his guidance on several chapters, John Rae for the fitting cover photos, and Elena Nash and V.K. Sanjeed for their excellent editorial support.

Abbreviations

AIDS	acquired immune deficiency syndrome
ART	antiretroviral therapy or treatment
DALY	disability-adjusted life year
DFID	Department for International Development (United Kingdom)
FDI	foreign direct investment
G8	group of eight nations (Canada, France, Germany, Italy, Japan, the United Kingdom, the United States and Russia)
G20	group of twenty nations (G8 and Argentina, Australia, Brazil, China, India, Indonesia, Mexico, Saudi Arabia, South Korea and Turkey)
GAVI Alliance	Global Alliance for Vaccines and Immunisation
GDP	gross domestic product
HIV	human immunodeficiency virus
IAVI	International AIDS Vaccine Initiative
IMF	International Monetary Fund
MDG	Millennium Development Goal
MSF	Medecins Sans Frontieres
NGO	nongovernmental organisation
ODA	official development assistance
OECD	Organisation for Economic Co-operation and Development

PEPFAR	United States President's Emergency Plan for AIDS Relief
TB	tuberculosis
UNAIDS	Joint United Nations Programme on HIV/AIDS
UNDP	United Nations Development Programme
UNICEF	United Nations International Children's Fund
USAID	United States Agency for International Development
WHA	World Health Assembly
WHO	World Health Organisation

Introduction and… The Health Diplomacy of Diversity

Daniel Low-Beer

The last decade has seen an innovative, almost tectonic, period in global health governance. Fissures have formed in the old structures, health has grown into a wider development and diplomatic issue, the G8 has expanded into the G20 and international health governance has opened up within nations and beyond the United Nations (Buse *et al.* 2009; Lee 2003). There has been an eruption of new partners — private foundations, northern and southern non-governmental organisations (NGOs), pop stars and private companies have all become stakeholders in global health. With this has come innovative ways of putting these partners together to focus on health goals — from the Global Fund to Fight AIDS, TB and Malaria to the International Health Partnership. However, these partnerships have also faced many of the traditional challenges of development: coordination, alignment with country plans and accountability for health results (Cohen 2006; Garrett 2007; Richter 2004). The overall focus of this book is to open up this diplomacy of diversity to discuss frankly how health partners can work together more effectively, globally and in countries.

Fifteen years ago, it would have been difficult to predict some of these changes: Bill Gates programming global health rather than software; NGOs and people living with AIDS formally governing a US$20 billion Global Fund to Fight AIDS, TB and Malaria; the World Health Organisation

(WHO) convening a wide range of partnerships on TB, malaria, health metrics and the health workforce; financial markets launching bonds to support vaccines; President Bush announcing an emergency US$15 billion global programme on AIDS; Bono selling RED products, including iPods and sunglasses for global health, alongside his music. The increasing scope and range of new partners and partnerships since then suggest that it is time to assess the landscape that is forming. This is the first aim of this book — to review the new diversity of partners and how these partners can contribute effectively to health outcomes.

Yet how do we make sense of these new partnerships? How does an African minister of health negotiate support for the country health plan with such a diverse set of partners? How does a European Development Minister decide to whom to give funding to achieve international health goals? How does someone living with AIDS represent all others in the governance of a global programme? How does an activist who has worked in clinics in New York support health workers in Uganda and on the Board of a Global Program? How do these innovative partnerships work in Swaziland, Russia, Vietnam, or Sudan? This requires a new, frank, direct health diplomacy, critical yet constructive, between diverse partners, and so that countries are not overwhelmed. This is the second aim of the book — to assess how these partners work together globally, in countries and communities and learn lessons on how this may be improved.

There has been action and reaction; each of these partners has altered health governance and have themselves changed. Civil society now raises its hand to speak within board meetings, as well as raises its placards outside. The WHO hosts a range of new partnerships going beyond the "United Nations," which can extend or undermine its core functions (Brown *et al.* 2006). Businessmen launch global health programmes and others defend drug prices in African courts.[1] The millennium brought together a surprising synchrony of partners for global health — activists rallying for universal access to health, private foundations catalyzing

[1] For example, the South African legal case on patents and drug access for HIV treatment (Buse *et al.* 2009).

funding, politicians committing financing, companies reducing drug prices and the UN in its Millennium Declaration formalising and universalising the goals. There were a number of characteristics:

1. **Social movement for development and health:** based on the dividends of development which still come from social investments to educate a new generation and remove the diseases of poverty. It brought together diverse partners, which went beyond traditional health institutions.
2. **Creation of global health partnerships to address global risks:** this movement created innovative health partnerships. They reflected a new partnership between the public, private sector, civil society, private foundations, and multilaterals to provide global not fragmented responses to global risks.
3. **New constituency model of governance:** the new actors have evolved beyond just innovative partners. They have become constituencies in global health, and "claimed a space" in health diplomacy and decision making. This is changing governance mechanisms, globally and in countries.

With the increased commitment to global health, a period of creation of innovative health partnerships occurred since 2000 (Figure 1).This has been followed by a period of consolidation and common actions to improve their effectiveness — to deliver better health aid, improve health systems, partner in country and extend achievements to mother and child health (Greco *et al.* 2008; Oliveira-Cruz *et al.* 2003). This is the third aim of the book — to assess how these partners have changed health governance, how they have been changed themselves and how they may need to improve to accelerate health development.

Each chapter assesses the innovations of new partners and provides practical recommendations to improve their effectiveness. These are provided from different perspectives: from activists, private sector, country ministers of health, district health workers, multilaterals and those working in these partnerships, including authors of the Paris Declaration on aid effectiveness, and in communities delivering health services. This frank discussion on innovations and challenges is at the heart of the diplomacy of diversity and improving health partnerships.

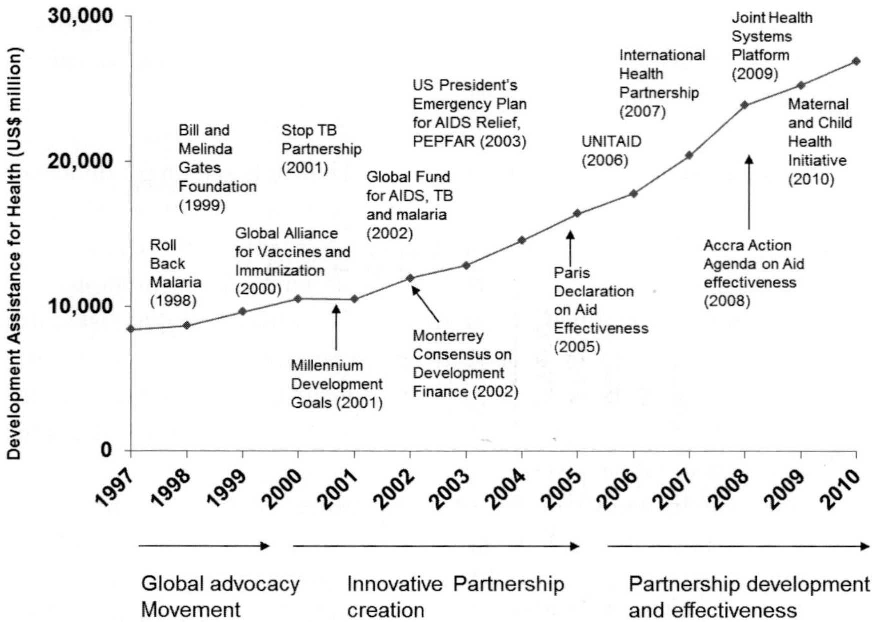

Figure 1. Development assistance for health in US$ million by year and key events in innovative partnerships.

This "partnership period" in global health changed the balance of power in health governance, internationally and in countries. This is seen in the role of Ministers of Health in countries and their negotiations with Ministers of Finance, and the WHO internationally in its use of disease and health partnerships. Yet, it also opened up a governance and coordination gap. Decisions were being made across a network of boards and agencies, loosely linked by a shifting set of constituencies. Increasingly, new partners needed to take common actions to strengthen health systems, reduce transaction costs and show their overall impact. This raises the challenge of collective action and the health diplomacy required to support it.

If the period 2000–2006 created new health partnerships, from 2007 initiatives were created to tackle collective actions on health systems and aid effectiveness. Yet some argue there is more talk of coordination and improved effectiveness than action. The financial crisis has given sudden impetus to this subsequent period of partnership effectiveness (Marmot and Bell 2009). A recent review stressed this "era of consolidation not expansion" characterised by a shift from emergency to sustainability, and a

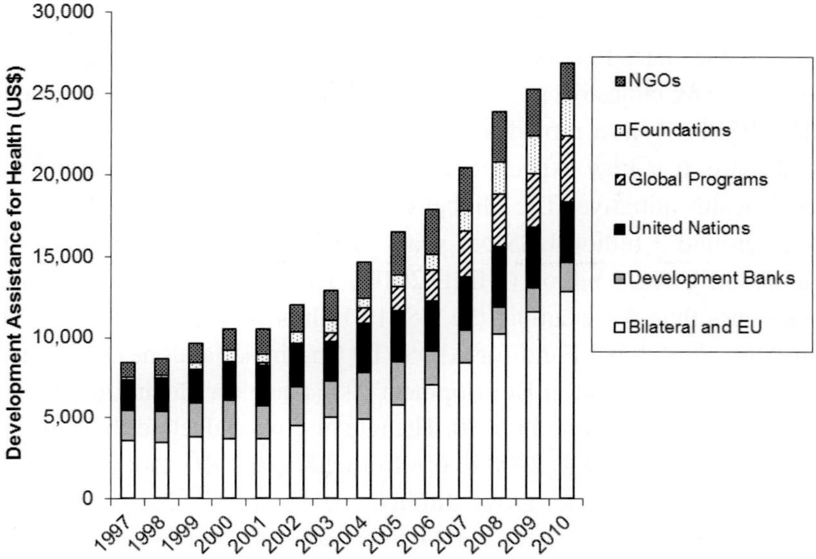

Figure 2. Development Assistance for Health by channel of assistance, 1997–2010. (*Datasource*: IHME 2010 Statistical Annex. 2009 and 2010 are preliminary estimates).

relentless focus on effectiveness (High Level Independent Review Panel, 2011). This emphasises the focus of the book on this second period of effectiveness, recognised in health before the financial crisis but reinforced by it. The new diversity has been an important source of innovation, if it goes with the diplomacy to forge strong collective actions to manage common risks (Burris *et al.* 2005; Kickbusch *et al.* 2007). The book puts these governance and effectiveness issues in real contexts and situations with contributions by the people involved in partnerships globally and in countries.

1. A New Diversity of Health Partners

The twenty-first century started with a renewed commitment and movement for development and global health. Official development aid (ODA) for health stagnated in the 1980s and 1990s. From 2000 to 2006, it increased at 15% per year (OECD 2008) and the health share of ODA increased additionally from 12% to 15%.[2] An overall total of US$23.9 billion was provided for health in 2008 (Figure 2), using a wider definition of

[2] Health share of bilateral sector-allocable aid, 2005–2006 compared to 2001–2002.

Development Assistance for Health to include public and private institutions like the Gates Foundation (IHME 2010). There were some significant and surprising milestones. The US President's Emergency Program for AIDS (PEPFAR) now provides 6 billion US$ per year, from one country for one disease. It is now expanded to cover TB and malaria and with a new global health initiative. The Global Fund for AIDS, TB and malaria disburses around 3 billion US$ per year, GAVI US$1 billion and the Gates Foundation US$1.8 billion (IHME 2010). The new funds are substantial, though less than for example the US$10 billion per year originally envisioned for the Global Fund for AIDS, TB and malaria alone. Preliminary estimates show growth in Development Assistance for Health to a total of US$26.87 billion per year in 2010. The rate of growth declines by half from 13% per year from 2004–2008 to 6% from 2008 to 2010, though estimates suggest it continued to grow through 2011 (IHME 2010). However, UNAIDS estimates suggest donor AIDS spending declined for the first time by 10 percent in 2010. The financial crisis has reemphasised the need to look further than a financial contribution of these new players. We need to assess their innovations, challenges and how they contribute to the improved effectiveness of aid (Lane and Glassman 2007; Piva and Dodd 2009).

None of these major innovative partners disbursed significant funds, and many did not exist before the start of the new millennium. They account for a large part of the increase in development aid to health. The share of the World Bank and regional banks declined from 23 to 7% from 2000 to 2008 and of the United Nations from 23 to 15% from 2000 to 2008 (largely due to increases in other sources, rather than absolute declines in funding). Bilateral aid declined from 46.8% in 1990 to 34% in 2001. Largely due to PEPFAR, it then increased to 43% in 2008. At the same time, the percentage channelled through the Global Fund and GAVI increased to 13.5%, through NGOs to 13% and through the Gates Foundation to 6% by 2008. Overall, the share of Global Programs, Foundations and NGOs of Development Assistance for Health has increased from 13% in 2000 to 35% in 2008. However, there has also been a significant increase in overall health funding, including relatively unexpected increases from Gates and US government. This suggests Global Programs did contribute extra funding, but there was wider additionality with new sources emerging for health and aid more generally (Macro 2009).

Traditional bilateral and multilaterals still play a strong role in these partnerships, WHO and the World Bank sit on the board of the Global Fund even if they do not have full voting rights, provide technical support to the programmes and UNDP implements Global Fund financing in some countries. Many innovative partnerships could not implement or develop common standards without these traditional partners. They do not replace but play an additional role in global governance and diplomacy, sometimes in unpredictable ways. Some have argued "the upsurge of global nonstate actors has led to the emergence of a new global public domain" with "the end of a state-centred system of world governance, and its replacement by one which is dominated by loosely coupled networks of governance" (Bull and McNeill 2007). However multilateral and state actors anchor and are very much part of the models of many new partnerships.

What is new is the diversity of partners negotiating in health — bilaterals, private foundations, private sector, global programmes and civil society. Previously global health diplomacy was largely between nations and could be focused in specific fora like the World Health Assembly of WHO. When the Global Program on AIDS was created in the 1980s, diplomatic issues arose from a new, powerful department within WHO. UNAIDS coordinated diplomacy largely across its member international and UN organisations. The new partnerships bring together very different partners, who are not aligned politically, and where many automatic trade-offs cannot occur. They present a new landscape for negotiation, coordination and health diplomacy internationally and in countries. As Sigrun Mogedal, HIV ambassador for Norway, comments, they are "*not only the place where we create partnerships, but where we have actually been able to do that differently — to set the pattern and learn. Maybe it's the place where we, more than anything, have learned to listen.*"

2. Innovative Partnerships — How Do these Partners Work Together Effectively?

The stage of partnership creation was quickly followed by the movement to develop and improve the effectiveness of these partnerships. This is the second major theme of the book, with which each chapter and innovative partnership is challenged. Working together effectively requires an increased focus on diplomacy among partners alongside diversity and innovation. How can these new and traditional partners negotiate to improve their overall effectiveness and tackle common challenges? A framework for improving aid effectiveness was provided by the principles of the Paris Declaration (Figure 3). This focus on effectiveness between partners has been increasingly important since 2005 and more recently since the financial crisis.

In 2015, a few short years in the future, this eventful stage in health development will be held to account. The Millennium Development Goals target significant reductions in HIV, TB, malaria, infectious diseases, child and maternal mortality by 2015 (Figure 4). They also call for a new global partnership for development, of which health provides some of the most innovative examples and may act as a "tracer" sector. The new financing and partnerships were created not for the sake of partnership but to achieve meaningful health results.

There is increasing evidence of progress towards achieving Millennium Development Goal (MDG) 6 and decreasing TB incidence globally (though not in Africa), evidence of declines in HIV prevalence (WHO 2009) and reductions in malaria incidence by 50% in 10 high-burden countries (WHO 2009). Where integrated childhood interventions including immunisations and malaria are implemented, there are substantial declines in child mortality (MDG 4). Where AIDS treatment is made widely accessible in Africa, the mortality of women of child-bearing age declines for the first time in twenty years. However, significant challenges remain to achieve MDG 5 on maternal mortality, MDG 4, and to sustain progress against MDG 6. Despite the challenges, the progress catalysed by new financing and partners should

The Paris Declaration defines *five principles* to improve the effectiveness of aid, signed by over one hundred ministers and officials from countries and donors in 2005	
Ownership	*Developing countries set their own strategies for poverty reduction, improve their institutions and tackle corruption*
Alignment	*Donor countries align behind these objectives and use local systems*
Harmonisation	*Donor countries coordinate, simplify procedures and share information to avoid duplication*
Managing for Results	*Developing countries and donors shift focus to development results and results get measured*
Mutual Accountability	*Donors and partners are accountable for development results*

Figure 3. Table of Aid effectiveness principles.

Source: OECD 2005.

Millennium Development Goals		
Goals		**Targets**
1	Eradicate extreme poverty and hunger	Halve between 1990 and 2015, the proportion of people whose income is less than $1 a day
		Halve, between 1990 and 2015, the proportion of people who suffer from hunger
2	Achieve universal primary education	Ensure that, by 2015, children everywhere, boys and girls alive, will be able to complete a full course of primary schooling
3	Promote gender equality and empower women	Eliminate gender disparity in primary and secondary education, preferably by 2005, and in all levels of education no later than 2015
4	Reduce child mortality	Reduce by two-thirds, between 1990 and 2015, the under-five mortality rate
5	Improve maternal health	Reduce by three-quarters, between 1990 and 2015, the maternal mortality rate
6	Combat HIV/AIDS, malaria and other diseases	Have halted by 2015 and begun to reverse the spread of HIV/AIDS
		Have halted by 2015 and begun to reverse the incidence of malaria and other major diseases
7	Ensure environmental sustainability	Integrate the principles of sustainable development into country policies and programs and reverse the loss of environmental resources
		Halve, by 2015, the proportion of people without sustainable access to safe drinking water and basic sanitation
		Have achieved by 2020 a significant improvement in the lives of at least 100 million slum dwellers
8	Develop a global partnership for development	Which includes: In cooperation with pharmaceutical companies, provide access to affordable, essential drugs in developing countries

Figure 4. Millennium development goals and targets for 2015.

not be underestimated. As the Minister of Health of Botswana comments, "*You go to a medical ward and now half of the beds are not occupied, before they were mushrooming. A manager came to me as Minister of Health and said 'You are bad for business, our funeral business is going down.' There was a time when every weekend we were burying four to eight people, now weeks go by without a funeral.*"

Yet only in the last two to three years are health services in Africa being scaled up "to the population level" to impact adult and child mortality (e.g. insecticide-treated bednets distributed for 60% of the population at risk from malaria, or over 50% of those in need of HIV treatment receiving it). There are also critical system-wide challenges — the need to renew health systems to extend health gains to rural and remote areas and to widen the response to neglected health issues (Biesma *et al.* 2009). There are collective challenges to improve aid effectiveness — reduce missions, parallel reporting, build the capacity of local institutions and develop a coherent partner approach to support country health strategies. This requires a new health diplomacy and cannot be achieved by any one health partner alone.

However, much discussion on aid effectiveness is focused at global level and on principles rather than practice. The main sections of the book look at how partners can work effectively together in real contexts, globally and in countries. This includes the progress and challenges within global partnerships and in different country contexts in Africa, Eastern Europe and Asia. Different views and recommendations are also provided from Ministers of Health, Heads of Development Cooperation, Coordinators of PEPFAR and the US President's malaria initiative, civil society activists, private sector, planners in countries, multilaterals and academics to those working in innovative partnerships. Each author was encouraged to provide practical recommendations on this theme of how partners can work together more effectively in practice.

3. Changing Health Governance — Innovative Partners, Traditional Challenges

The third aim of the book is to assess how these partners have changed health governance and how they have been changed themselves. The Millennium Development Goals explicitly aim for renewed partnerships, with goal 8 to "develop a global partnership for development". Partnership underlies the push for the MDGs, which overall aims to draw in a wide range of public and private partners to focus on development. As well as mentioning trade and debt, pharmaceutical companies are specifically mentioned to ensure access to affordable essential drugs in developing countries (target 17), as are new technologies and communications. Partnerships are defined by the United Nations as "voluntary and collaborative relationships between various parties, both state and non-state, in which all participants agree to work together to achieve a common purpose or undertake a specific task and to share risks and responsibilities, resources and benefits" (UN General Assembly 2005).

There are many such partnerships, for research, to develop technologies, for advocacy and networking or to finance and implement programmes.

However, the MDGs call for more innovative partnerships across health, education and financing in all their goals. The Accra Agenda for Action (AAA) on aid effectiveness signed in 2008, by donors and countries, recognises a change in governance to integrate more inclusive partnerships (as shown by selected commitments in Figure 5). It states quite explicitly "*Aid is about building partnerships for development. Such partnerships are most effective when they fully harness the energy, skills and experiences of all development actors — bilateral and multilateral donors, global funds, CSOs, and the private sector ... we resolve to create partnerships that will include all these actors.*" This is the spirit and challenge of innovative health partnerships in this book.

Accra Agenda for Action on Partnerships — agreed by donor and country ministers and officials in 2008
Building More Effective and Inclusive Partnerships for Development 16. Aid is about building partnerships for development. Such partnerships are most effective when they fully harness the energy, skills and experience of all development actors — bilateral and multilateral donors, global funds, CSOs, and the private sector. To support developing countries' efforts to build for the future, we resolve to create partnerships that will include all these actors. ***We will reduce costly fragmentation of aid*** 17. The effectiveness of aid is reduced when there are too many duplicating initiatives, especially at country and sector levels. We will reduce the fragmentation of aid by improving the complementarity of donors' efforts and the division of labour among donors, through improved allocation of resources within sectors, within countries, and across countries. ***We will increase aid's value for money*** 18. Since the Paris Declaration was agreed in 2005, OECD-DAC donors have made progress in untying their aid. A number of donors have already fully untied their aid, and we encourage others to do so. We will pursue, and accelerate, these efforts. ***We welcome and will work with all development actors*** 19. The contributions of all development actors are more effective when developing countries are in a position to manage and coordinate them. We welcome the role of new contributors and will improve the way all development actors work together by taking the following actions: ***We will deepen our engagement with civil society organisations*** 20. We will deepen our engagement with CSOs as independent development actors in their own right whose efforts complement those of governments and the private sector. We share an interest in ensuring that CSO contributions to development reach their full potential. ***We will adapt aid policies for countries in fragile situations*** 21. In the Paris Declaration, we agreed that aid effectiveness principles apply equally to development cooperation in situations of fragility, including countries emerging from conflict, but that these principles need to be adapted to environments of weak ownership or capacity.

Figure 5. AAA: Selected actions on partnerships (OECD 2008).

Innovative health partnerships combine in new ways major health constituencies (bilateral and multilateral donors, developing countries, civil society, private sector, private foundations and people affected by health issues) to achieve an agreed health purpose. They should be innovative in their governance in the way they bring together new constituencies, and in how these partners implement to achieve the health purpose. This can be through board structures, country coordination and implementation arrangements which include partners from different constituencies in new ways.

The partnership can be internal to the organisation (e.g. global programmes defined as programmes providing substantial assistance focused on a restricted purpose to a wide variety of countries). The partnerships can also exist externally in the way a particular partner works with other partners in countries to achieve focused health goals, for example through the International Health Partnership, the Avahan programme in India or civil society in many health programmes.

However, most existing innovative health partnerships combine traditional features, for example a reliance on traditional donor funds, with innovative aspects of governance, financing and implementation. The US President's Emergency Plan for AIDS (PEPFAR) is also included in this book. It falls between a bilateral and a global health programme. However, PEPFAR is the "elephant in the room" as the largest component of new health financing. It is essential to engage with PEPFAR in discussing innovative health partnerships in the country. In addition, PEPFAR brings together innovation in bilateral aid (between different agencies), in private sector and civil society implementation and in its recent transition to country partnerships. PEPFAR also highlights the mixed nature of many innovative health partnerships.

The year 2012 is therefore an important time to understand the new health landscape, the partners that have emerged and the health diplomacy that can guide us towards the MDGs in 2015. The book describes the new forces beneath the surface and the innovative partnerships created as a result. It assesses the way partnerships are being shaped within countries and by many traditional development challenges. Finally, it provides guidance on how to achieve greater results from these partnerships in different contexts.

Some have talked of health architecture, a structure we build according to a master plan, adding extensions to house new members, coordinating rooms and redesigning the living spaces (Godal 2005). Watt *et al.* (2009) have argued this analogy may constrain our thinking "because 'architecture' is usually defined in terms of solid or permanent structures, rather than the changing, fluid interests and interrelations between architects, investors, builders, and building users." The analogy used in this book is of a landscape shaped and negotiated by many actors: with many traditional features, yet with new forces, mountain ranges thrown up, shaped and eroded in relation to the basic gravitational forces of improving the effectiveness of aid. Gaps form in this landscape, and periods of creation are often followed by consolidation. Rather than an architect who can put the pieces together, the skills of health diplomacy are required to negotiate the terrain. The diplomacy of diversity aims to incorporate new opportunities and partners into global health while shaping collective actions to face system-wide risks.

4. Overview of the Book

This book does not aim to fit all the elements together like jigsaw pieces, or bricks in a building. It takes two perspectives — the first is global describing the new partners and innovative partnerships they have formed. This covers global health programmes, private foundations, the private sector and civil society in general. It also covers specific analysis of PEPFAR and GAVI, as well as partnerships in malaria. It brings out innovations they have contributed, together with the challenges of negotiating effective aid. The second perspective is to focus at country level to assess the issues of incorporating new partnerships in country contexts. This covers examples from Africa, Asia and Eastern Europe and specific issues of governance, state fragility and health systems. Together, these two perspectives allow us to challenge innovative partnerships and connect the arguments in principle and in practice, globally and in countries.

Introductory chapters cover the common themes. The book aims to capture the diversity of views from different partners and the critiques and recommendation on improving the effectiveness of innovative partnerships, while basing discussion on case studies and country examples. It presents these views side by side around common themes at global and country level. This reflects the diplomacy of diversity focusing on new partner opportunities and risks — health systems, aid effectiveness and meaningful partnerships for the twenty-first century.

4.1 Common themes

The book has three sections: common themes, innovative partners globally and integrating partners in countries. The common themes that bind together the book are developed in the first section — the origins and diversity of health partnerships, negotiating aid effectiveness among these partners, the limits of partnerships, managing programmes for results, health systems and country strategies for managing innovative health partnerships. These themes are presented in detail and then developed in real global, country and community contexts through the book.

The first chapter provides the historical context to the origins and diversity of health partnerships. Innovative Health Partnerships have a long history from the role of the Rockefeller Foundation in supporting the WHO in its early stages to the new set of partnerships formed around the millennium. The history is punctuated by periods of creation and consolidation. The chapter identifies three periods of creativity: the inter- and postwar period leading to the creation of the WHO, the late 1950s and early 1960s with decolonisation and the establishment of development agencies and the new millennium with the creation of new global health partnerships. The historical perspectives suggest that these periods are not just the rebottling of "old wine in new bottles," discussed elsewhere (see Chapter 5 and Chapter 6; Berridge *et al.* 2009). They do set off long waves of innovation in health aid, which take time to settle. Each creative period generates innovative partnerships, yet is usually followed by periods of consolidation "when participants sought to rationalise the architecture that they had created" (Chapter 1). This balance of creativity and consolidation lays out clearly the tone of the book.

The second chapter puts us squarely in the present. How do development agencies make sense of these new partners? Who should they fund to achieve health outcomes? The chapter is written as a staff report to the Director-General of a development agency (and was presented to and influenced the UK multilateral aid review in 2011). It is based on extensive interviews with decision makers globally, asking them how to negotiate with new partners to increase the effectiveness and volume of aid. It lays out the "difficult decisions" in typically frank yet engaging fashion. The chapter discusses how a Director-General "confronts some difficult decisions, analytical and political, on how to allocate aid to ensure that it is used to maximum effect." It discusses the creation of new global funds and whether we should "think twice" before doing so. The chapter assesses how aid effectiveness principles may be negotiated into these funds, and the importance of the incentives that drive behaviour in key institutions. It discusses the balance of fund allocation needed between global funds and other multilateral programmes. Moreover, it calls on aid donors to assume responsibility for their own role, in establishing and in participating in governance structures and in addressing issues of aid effectiveness that they criticise in global funds. This pragmatic diplomacy uses "the soft power of negotiations, networks, and incentives" to improve aid effectiveness. Thus, this chapter presents one important element of the call for a new health diplomacy to negotiate with diverse partners that is at the heart of this book.

In this book, the test of the diplomacy of diversity is in countries. The next chapter focuses on health diplomacy from a country perspective. The Minister of Health of Ethiopia has played an important dual role — as chair of the Roll Back Malaria Partnership and the Global Fund and as health minister in his country. He believes in a "direct diplomacy" based on candid dialogue with partners, often using bold requests for support to challenge partners to break bureaucratic barriers. When AIDS funds were proposed to train AIDS health workers, TB to train TB health workers and immunisation to train immunisation workers, he challenged donors to support 30,000 community health workers to support all health services. He describes approaches to harmonise partners at country level, while keeping a "healthy and manageable diversity" of sources of support. This basic diversity is necessary to ensure the predictability of funding from a portfolio of health donors.

The key ingredients of national policy frameworks are identified to ensure country ownership of health objectives. This provides a springboard to understand, learn and shape innovative health partnerships. The minister then describes how to steer and leverage partnerships at country level to benefit from opportunities while managing risks. Finally, the types of country governance which can best engage innovative partners are presented. He describes the basic innovations in "results-based partnerships" and the strategies and tactics of the diplomacy of diversity at country level. Throughout the chapter is a belief in direct health diplomacy — exerting peer pressure on partners, "tough love," openness to change and using the bottom line of results as a common currency for diplomacy.

The next chapters tackle three key themes of the book: (1) the results agenda, managing and coordinating partners not for partnership sake but for health results, (2) coherent approaches to strengthen health systems and (3) innovative partnerships and different partnership models.

The fourth chapter focuses on results in health and development. Innovative partnerships are not created for partnerships sake, but to achieve health results. They do not have the formal legitimacy of multilaterals, for example WHO, and depend on their continual ability to achieve health results. Managing for results has emerged as an "overarching principle" (OECD 2005) of aid effectiveness as shown in the Accra Action Agenda and a defining feature of global programmes. Yet there is scepticism as to the ability of partners to measure compelling development results, and to manage and coordinate diverse partners for results. This chapter assesses the origins of the results agenda and the contribution of innovative health partnerships. Alongside results measurement, it identifies a more radical results agenda to use common results to coordinate development partners. It assesses to what extent innovative health partnerships have been able to build results into their business models. Furthermore, the chapter investigates whether results provide a basis or "common currency" for coordination of diverse partners. It argues that, lacking the political alignment of traditional donors, diverse partners may have little else in common, except their comparative roles in achieving health results.

The next chapter on health systems cuts across different health partnerships, for example for immunisation, AIDS, TB, malaria, maternal health or the health workforce. Considerable health diplomacy is required for countries to ensure different goals contribute to strengthening health systems generally. The chapter notes "GHPs (global health partnerships) have clearly brought new energy and new partners into the sector. But ... the scale of GHP resources means that the scale of challenges has increased." Many of the traditional issues of "good donor practice" and "effective aid" apply to innovative health partnerships as they do to traditional donors. The challenges and adaptations described based on widespread country consultations are "an example of global health diplomacy in action." The chapter provides practical recommendations on "what are the challenges, how to think about them, and what to do differently."

The last chapter of this section is on partnerships and looks at the history, different forms and limits of the concept. It describes key characteristics of health partnerships. It raises the issue of whether new partnerships are innovative or are becoming new multilaterals with similar structures and constraints. The chapter emphasises the importance of a coherent policy framework, the integration of new research and knowledge and funding with implementation support, to make the most of innovative partnerships. It assesses models of partnerships, and more general platforms and networks, which may contribute to improved aid effectiveness.

4.2 Integrating new partnerships at global level

The second section takes apart the components of innovative health partnerships at global level. It assesses the characteristics and contributions of global health programmes, private foundations, private sector and civil society — their governance, added value and challenges. The section also describes wider partnerships around a health issue — for example the Roll Back Malaria Partnership. There is an underlying aim across the chapters to assess to what extent a coherent yet diverse approach to health can be negotiated among these partners. Each chapter is therefore challenged with the common themes of the first section to identify practical recommendations to improve overall aid effectiveness.

The case studies on partnerships are not exhaustive, but are chosen to illustrate important aspects of innovative partnerships. There are many hundreds of new health partnerships, in research, financing, coordination and implementation support. Many interesting and innovative partnerships have not been given full chapters, for example UNITAID that aims to make medicines affordable by raising truly additional financing from direct air ticket taxes, the Global Business Alliance, the HIV/AIDS Alliance that has

Common Definitions and Terms		
Term	**Definition**	**Comments**
Innovative health partnerships	Health partnerships that combine in new ways major health constituencies (bilateral, multilaterals, developing countries, civil society, private sector, private foundations, people affected by health issues) to achieve an agreed health purpose	They should be innovative in their governance in the way they bring together new constituencies, and in how these partners implement to achieve health outcomes
Global programs	Programmes providing substantial assistance focused on a restricted health purpose to a wide variety of countries	Definition follows Accra Action Agenda. They have a restricted purpose (though see arguments for a global fund for health), but can implement vertically (through parallel implementation units) or horizontally through existing health systems
Aid effectiveness	The movement to improve the delivery of development aid and its support of development outcomes. Suggested, agreed principles and actions to achieve this are further defined in the Paris Declaration (2005) and the Accra Action Agenda (2008)	It is increasingly recognised that aid is only one factor in the complex process of human development. To achieve the MDGs it was agreed that "more and better aid" was needed. Aid effectiveness refers to efforts to secure "better aid"
Health systems	A health system is the sum of all organisations, institutions and resources, whose primary purpose is to improve health	This is the WHO definition, five key components to allow it to work as a system are identified: Policy and Governance, Financing, Human Resources, Procurement & Supply, Information Systems
Health diplomacy	Health diplomacy is the method of negotiation between different stakeholders in public health and politics to achieve health goals	It recognises the importance of the quality of political relationships and partnerships in achieving health goals, and negotiations with an increasing diversity of partners
Global governance	The steering through institutions, authority, networks and collaboration of global partners to achieve common goals	Stems from the Greek word "to steer." Although it can rely on political authority, at the global level its source is not clear. Common actions therefore require "soft" negotiations as well as hard rules to coordinate partner actions and behaviours

Figure 6. Table of key definition used in the book.

been a force in bringing together civil society, the International Health Partnership, the Medicines for Malaria Venture and the International AIDS Vaccine Initiative, to name just a very few. There are also many important actors within and outside these new partnerships, including Medicins Sans Frontieres (MSF), OXFAM, Rockefeller Foundation and South Africa's

Treatment Action Campaign. Many are addressed within chapters and have contributed importantly to new partnerships.

The first chapter in this section begins with an analysis of Global Health Programs defined as programmes providing substantial assistance focused on a restricted health purpose to a wide variety of countries (following the AAA). It describes their evolution, their differences in terms of governance and implementation arrangements. The chapter describes the challenges of negotiating aid effectiveness into new partnerships — their capacity to learn, adapt and engage in health diplomacy. The chapter assesses the stages of negotiation with recommendations on how to improve aid effectiveness.

The next three chapters assess how partnerships have been formed around a global health issue — malaria, immunisation and AIDS. The chapters provide concrete examples of the new stage of "health partnership" in tackling these issues, the progress and challenges. Of all the major health issues, malaria has moved from a disease neglected in terms of financing to one that is "fashionable" and has attracted a diverse range of partners in the last few years. The historical development of malaria partnerships is combined with a view to 2015 of how to combine partners to achieve the common goals of reducing child mortality. The chapter on the Global Alliance for Vaccines and Immunisation (GAVI) highlights the innovations in financing globally and at country level that have been possible with a new mix of partners.

The next chapter assesses PEPFAR, its genesis, evolution and the new partnership models developed — for bilateral assistance and within countries. It describes its "innovation in country leadership, results-driven programming, and partnerships," while recognising the controversy around its approach. A large part of the increase in global health financing is due to this one programme which reached US$6 billion per annum within five years (twice the multilateral Global Fund which covers three diseases). The chapter describes the evolution of PEPFAR from its origins in coordinated US bilateral aid to a wide view of partnership in the recent Global Health Initiative under President Obama.

The following three chapters assess innovative constituencies that contribute to health partnerships: private foundations, the private sector and civil society. Private foundations have brought new finance and innovations; yet their role in global governance has not always kept pace with their increasing involvement. There has been a long historical involvement of private foundations in global health, from the role of the Rockefeller Foundation in supporting WHO in its early years to the recent prominence of the Gates Foundation in catalyzing new global partnerships. They have worked at the edges of "the United Nations" provoking and extending health governance. Critiques of their own governance and engagement in improving overall aid effectiveness are reviewed alongside their new contributions.

Similarly the private sector has provided "new ways of doing business" in financing health and implementing health programmes. Innovative Health partnerships are often termed "public private partnerships," although private sources have contributed a minority of their finances. The private sector chapter brings out innovations in financing and implementation, as well as the challenges. The civil society chapter shows how civil society has increasingly "claimed its space" in Global Health, from AIDS treatment in USA to Africa, and global issues of AIDS, TB, malaria and health systems. This has transformed global health governance as well as civil society.

In sum, this global section describes some of the new constituents of innovative partnerships — civil society, private sector and private foundations — and how they have come together at global level to focus on a health issue. It does not tackle all new partnerships, but opens up different perspectives on health diplomacy and partnerships to address some common questions:

- To what extent have "innovative health partnerships" been an important or defining characteristic of the period in global health governance since 2000?
- What are the "new ways of doing business" that these partners have contributed to tackle health issues?
- What are the common challenges of aid effectiveness, system-wide risks and governance?
- What recommendations are there for making these partnerships more effective?

4.3 Integrating new partnerships at country level

The final section of the book moves to real country contexts to assess how new partners can be put together to achieve country health goals. Much discussion on health governance has focused at global level, yet the biggest challenges are at country and even community level. How do countries negotiate with the new range of partners to contribute to health results? How do innovative partnerships work in contexts of state fragility and health system weakness? What general recommendations can be provided by those negotiating with new partners in country? In this section, the common themes of the book are assessed in different disease, economic and political contexts in East and Southern Africa, Asia and Eastern Europe. The first country studies assess issues of governance and national leadership, followed by health systems and state fragility. Then the issues of integrating innovative private and civil society models into country health plans and finally the importance of partnerships at community level are assessed.

The first chapter of this section begins with central issues of governance and sustainable financing in the AIDS response in Southern Africa. The chapter uses the examples of countries like Swaziland, which are overwhelmed by AIDS as well as by the number of partners in the AIDS response. "The impact of AIDS on governance is central to both lack of response and its failure to be fully effective." The dependency of countries on international support, the difficult issues of "AIDS exceptionalism" and distinctions between lower- and middle-income countries are assessed. The chapter concludes with a Kiswahili saying, "when elephants fight, it is the grass that suffers," stressing the need for reform and coordination among partners in country.

The next chapter shifts context to Vietnam to assess policy-making processes in the health sector to improve aid effectiveness. It provides detailed qualitative and quantitative analysis of the country policy context, showing "overlapping 'policy networks' which cut across the traditional donors — government divide." It describes how coalitions can be formed to overcome individual and institutional incentives, showing clearly the diplomacy and political processes involved. The principle of "country ownership" is unpacked and shown to be too simplistic to describe the diversity of actors and incentives in real country contexts (as well as within donors). The different actors in "policy networks" and "policy communities" need to be understood as a basis for "the diplomacy of diversity" and to improve aid effectiveness in county.

The following chapter looks at how county leadership can align stakeholders behind national health plans. It assesses the politics and negotiations in establishing health plans and using national results to coordinate partner activities. In particular, it shows the importance of planning and tracking results at district and local level to coordinate donor activities. When these are successful, they provide a critical foundation to the more usual discussions of national governance. They also allow follow up and accountability of partner and country commitments. The chapter provides evidence of the integration of disease and general health services, which has been the backbone of the Ethiopian response.

The Gates Foundation has supported one of the largest and most innovative HIV prevention programmes in India — Avahan meaning "Call to Action." The chapter describes the challenges of rooting HIV in a community response, scaling up these activities and combining business and public health approaches. This approach has brought considerable innovation and scale to the HIV-prevention response in India. The challenge is nevertheless one of partnership to negotiate the transfer of this innovation to the national programme to ensure its sustainability. As Bill Gates comments "Through Avahan, we have learned how important it is to get local communities involved in delivering effective public health interventions at a large scale. The next challenge will be passing on all that we've learned and transitioning Avahan to the government and other partners."

In Russia, the Soros Foundation has played a key role in supporting HIV prevention focused on difficult to reach populations — Intravenous drug users (IDUs), prisoners and sex workers. The development of a consortium within the NGO response allowed it to shift from advocacy to wide scale support to these populations. This also triggered changes and professionalisation of the NGO response including the development of assertive leadership, procedures and broad partnerships. However, the health response reflects the development of civil society and is an unfinished agenda. While it has catalysed a national AIDS response, a sustainable partnership between government and NGO responses will take time and persistent health diplomacy.

Many of the previous chapters have assumed the importance of country ownership and the capacity to negotiate with new partners. However, there are limits to country ownership, particularly in situations of fragile and failed states. The Accra Agenda emphasises that partners "will adapt aid policies for countries in fragile situations" and that general aid effectiveness principles apply in these situations. This chapter discusses "some of the most delicate issues of how to engage in partnerships with fragile and failed states" reviewing Somalia, Sudan and Democratic Republic of Congo compared to Mozambique. It highlights many of the challenges for health diplomacy of "difficult partnerships."

The final chapter shifts to the community level and the importance of mobilising community responses. It shows that successful HIV prevention has occurred where health governance and programmes have built on community responses — in the gay community in USA, Uganda, Thailand, Kenya and Malawi. It compares to situations where coordination has not occurred, and relatively fragile community responses have often been confused and smothered. In these situations, despite the delivery of financial and technical resources, HIV prevention has been much less successful. Our understanding of coordinating new partners needs to go deep into communities to support effective health prevention.

5. Conclusions: Health Diplomacy in Real Global and Country Contexts

In sum, a major trend since 2000 has been a shift to a wider "partnership approach" to delivering health aid, bringing together governments, private sector, civil society, private foundations and multilaterals, sometimes shouting and sometimes kicking. The brief period since 2000 has been innovative in how these partners have been put together in global and country governance. These partnerships have also been challenged with traditional development issues — aid effectiveness, coordination, health systems and the need to show results.

Diplomacy involves listening to the arguments, evidence and the different voices and constituencies. The book aims to connect these arguments in principal and in practice, globally and in countries. Diplomacy also involves shaping directions, incentives, common actions and at times challenging interests, however undiplomatically. The authors are pushed to make recommendations on how to improve the effectiveness of innovative partnerships, to make the most of their opportunities while identifying the risks.

The book raises a series of important questions about how to make this broader approach more effective and integrate better in-country contexts in Asia, Africa, Eastern Europe, middle income, poor and fragile states. How does a country make sense of new partners in Swaziland, Vietnam and Russia? What are the opportunities and risks of this new partnership model? How do civil society, private foundations and global programmes learn and adapt to their new roles?

There are a number of directions identified, discussed and challenged in the chapters:

1. **Innovative "partnership period" in global health**: Since 2000 health aid has gone through a creative period, characterised by new initiatives, recognition of diverse constituencies and new ways of putting them together into partnerships, but significant work is needed so they become most effective on the ground.
2. **Diverse constituencies in health governance**: There has been a focus on the number of partners, yet health finance has also concentrated upstream among a few global partnerships. What is most distinctive is the diversity of constituencies recognised in global health governance, as increasingly "having a vote": civil society, private companies, people affected by diseases, private foundations as well as government. This results in a shift from single to multiparty coalitions of governance, and issues of representation within constituencies.
3. **Partnership challenge of collective actions to address risks**: Innovative partnerships have provided new ways to bring these constituencies together in governance and implementation of programmes. Yet, there is a major partnership challenge to help these constituencies work together more effectively. They bring considerable innovations, as well as challenges of coordination, alignment with country plans and system-wide risks.
4. **Network model of health governance:** The diversity in partners has changed the balance of power globally and in countries. Decisions are

being made across a network of boards and agencies, loosely linked by a shifting set of constituencies. As well as a closed or club model of membership (for example of the World Health Assembly or the OECD), we need to harness this network model to negotiate collective and inclusive actions. This network model extends and is an addition to the role of states and multilaterals whose role and decision power still remains at its core.
5. **Managing partners for results:** There is a developing model of health aid which is results based, inclusive of diversity, and represents a wider partnership to implement programmes. It coexists with a more explicitly politically aligned model of aid dominant during the Cold War. However, there are critiques of the ability of partners to measure collective results and to use results for a more radical agenda to coordinate diverse partners.
6. **New "diplomacy of diversity"**: Many of our skills and approaches have not changed to this new health landscape. Previously global health diplomacy was largely between nations and could be focused in specific fora like the World Health Assembly of WHO. Coordination is too weak a term for the coherence in steering required from global and national level to community level. Yet there is a new diplomacy emerging in some countries to harness the opportunities from a "manageable diversity" of partners.

Achievement of the MDGs calls for a new "global partnership for development." The actions in the Accra Agenda also promote innovative partnerships "Aid is about building partnerships for development. Such partnerships are most effective when they fully harness the energy, skills and experiences of all development actors — bilateral and multilateral donors, global funds, CSOs, and the private sector … we resolve to create partnerships that will include all these actors." In these negotiations, health was seen as a "tracer sector" given the new and innovative way partnerships had been created, as well as some of the challenges. The year 2012 is therefore an important time to review these partnerships, and how partners can effectively work together to contribute to the MDGs in 2015.

Forging strong collective actions among these diverse partners requires a new health diplomacy. This has implications for global governance, country tactics and negotiation, and how this can be extended into communities. It requires a change in perspective, to open up the debate on the range of partners contributing to global health and the common challenges. It also requires a change in mentality to acknowledge and address new partners and partnerships, the opportunities and risks. From the outside, health has had unprecedented support, finance and partner interest in the last ten years. It has also achieved significant results in AIDS, TB, malaria, vaccines, adult and child mortality. Yet from within health, the mindset on partnerships has often not kept up — to openly discuss challenges, work as a team and recommend actions to improve health partnerships to achieve better results both on their own mandates and on better health overall.

The diplomacy of diversity is an unfinished agenda, aiming to open and not close the questions in this area. The chapters are engaged, critical and constructive in equal doses. This direct diplomacy is required to realise the immense opportunities in global health since 2000, and the system-wide actions needed to tackle the risks. This stage of health 2000–2015 will be reviewed in five short years as part of the Millennium Development Goals and will succeed or fail on the strengths of the partnerships created to achieve collective results.

References

Berridge V, Loughlin K, Herring R (2009) "Historical Dimensions of Global Health Governance," in Buse *et al.* ed (2009) *Making Sense of Global Health Governance*.

Biesma R, Brugha R, *et al.* (2009) "The Effects of Global Health Initiatives on Country Health Systems: A Review of the Evidence from HIV/AIDS Control," *Health Policy and Planning* 24(4):16–24.

Brown T, Cueto M, Fee E (2006) "The World Health Organisation and the Transition from International to Global Public Health," *American Journal of Public Health* 96:62–72.

Bull B, McNeill D (2007) "Development Issues in Global Governance: Market Multilateralism and Public Private Partnerships," Routledge, New York.

Burris S, Drahos P, Shearing C (2005) "Nodal Governance," *Australian Journal of Legal Philosophy* 20:20–58.

Buse K, Hein W, Drager N eds (2009) *Making Sense of Global Health Governance*, Basingstoke, Palgrave.

Cohen J (2006) "The New World of Global Health," *Science* 311:162–67.

Fidler DP (2007) "Architecture Amidst Anarchy: Global Health's Quest for Governance," *Global Health Governance* 1(1):1–17.

Garrett L (2007) "Do no Harm: The Challenge of Global Health," *Foreign Affairs*, 86(1):14–38.

Godal T (2005) "Do We Have the Architecture for Health Aid Right? Increasing Global Aid Effectiveness," *Nature Reviews Microbiology* 3:899–903.

Greco G, Powell-Jackson T, Borghi J, Mills A (2008) "Countdown to 2015: Assessment of Donor Assistance to Maternal, Newborn and Child Health between 2003 and 2006," *Lancet* 271:1268–75.

(High Level Independent Review Panel (2011), *Final Report on Fiduciary Controls and Oversight Mechanisms of the Global Fund: Turning the Page from Emergency to Sustainability*, The Global Fund for AIDS, TB and Malaria, Geneva. http://www.theglobalfund.org/en/highlevelpanel/)

IHME (Institute for Health Metrics and Evaluation) (2009) *Financing Global Health 2009: Tracking Development Assistance for Health*, Seattle, USA.

IHME (Institute for Health Metrics and Evaluation) (2010) *Financing Global Health 2010*: *Development Assistance and Country Spending in Economic Uncertainty*, Seattle, USA.

Kickbusch I, Silberschmidt G, Buss P (2007) "Global Health Diplomacy: The Need for New Perspectives, Strategic Approaches and Skills in Global Health," *Bulletin of the WHO* 85(3):230–32.

Lane C, Glassman A (2007) "Bigger and Better? Scaling Up and Innovation in Health Aid," *Health Affairs* 26(4):935–48.

Lee K ed (2003) *Health Impacts of Globalization: Towards Global Governance*, Basingstoke, Palgrave.

Macro (2009) "The Five-Year Evaluation of the Global Fund to Fight AIDS, Tuberculosis, and Malaria — Synthesis Report," Macro (accessible at www.theglobalfund.org).

Marmot M, Bell R (2009) "How Will the Financial Crisis Affect Health?" *BMJ* 338:1314.

OECD (2005) *Paris Declaration on Aid Effectiveness*, Paris, OECD.

OECD (2008) *Measuring Aid to Health*, Paris, OECD.

OECD (2008) *Accra Action Agenda on Aid Effectiveness*, Paris, OECD.

Oliveira-Cruz V, Kurowski C *et al.* (2003) "Delivery of Priority Health Services: Searching for Synergies Within the Vertical Versus Horizontal Debate," *Journal of International Development* 15(1):67–86.

Piva P, Dodd R (2009) "Where Did all the Aid Go? An In-Depth Analysis of Increased Health Aid Flows over the Last 10 Years," *Bulletin of the World Health Organization* 87(12):930–39.

Poku N, Whiteside A, Sandkjaer B, eds (2007) *AIDS and Governance*, Aldershot: Ashgate.

Richter J (2004) "Public–Private Partnerships for Health: A Trend with no Alternatives?" *Development* 47(2):43–48.

Watt G, Spicer N, Buse K (2009) "Mapping the Global Health Architecture," in Buse *et al.* ed (2009) *Making Sense of Global Health Governance*.

World Health Organisation (2009) "World Malaria Report," WHO, Geneva.

World Health Organisation (2009) "Towards Universal Access: Scaling up Priority HIV/AIDS Interventions in the Health Sector," WHO, Geneva.

Section 1

Common Themes

1

Origins and Diversity of Health Partnerships

Richard Manning

Summary

This chapter provides the historical context to the origins and diversity of health partnerships. Innovative Health Partnerships have a long history from the role of the Rockefeller Foundation in supporting the World Health Organisation (WHO) in its early stages to the new set of partnerships formed around the millennium. The history is punctuated by periods of creation and consolidation. The chapter identifies three periods of creativity: the inter- and postwar period leading to the creation of the WHO, the late 1950s and early 1960s with decolonisation and the establishment of development agencies and the new millennium with the creation of new global health partnerships. Each creative period generates innovative partnerships; yet it is usually followed by periods of consolidation "when participants sought to rationalize the architecture that they had created." They set off long waves of innovation in health aid, which take time to settle. This balance of creativity and consolidation lays out clearly the tone of the book.

1. Introduction: The Rise of International Cooperation and Its Implications for Global Health

This chapter argues that the concept and practice of international cooperation for better health outcomes has developed through a number of periods of creativity, each of which has added to the machinery for such cooperation, usually followed by periods of consolidation as participants sought to rationalise the architecture that they had created. A feature of the creative periods is the innovative nature of the partnerships on which they were based. The challenge in the periods of consolidation (of which the present may be one) is to sustain momentum in helping to improve health outcomes while addressing the tensions produced by the periods of creativity. The background to all this is that health outcomes at the country level normally depend more on local effort than on international cooperation; but that international cooperation has contributed to these outcomes and in some cases (particularly for specific health problems and in countries highly dependent on aid) has been central to their achievement.[1]

International concern about health status has a long history, but for most of this the concerns were very limited, the focus being on the risks posed to the citizens of better-off countries by diseases for which national systems were poorly prepared to cope. Thus, a first International Sanitary Conference, attended by 12 nations, was held in Paris in 1851 as countries struggled to cope with imported infectious diseases such as cholera.[2] Similarly, all the main colonial powers set up institutes of tropical medicine, which started research on diseases that affected not least colonial officials, traders and missionaries with no inherited immunity. The Spanish influenza pandemic of 1919 broadened the agenda by demonstrating starkly the need for cooperation to tackle easily spread infectious diseases. The Pan-American Health Organisation was already in existence

[1] Particular thanks are due to Andrew Cassels, Paul Isenman, Daniel Low-Beer and Alex Shakow for their comments on drafts of this chapter. I have drawn on many of their insights, but the responsibility for the observations in the chapter is mine alone.

[2] Historical Dimensions of Global Health Governance, Virginia Berridge, Kelly Loughlin and Rachel Herring in 'Making Sense of Global Health Governance' edited by Kent Buse, Hein and Drage.

over a century ago as an early example of crossborder collaboration to tackle health problems.

After the World War I, the new League of Nations established a Health Organisation in Geneva, in parallel with the International Labour Office. This did a good deal of basic work, not least in making possible the compilation of comparable health statistics, and on appropriate basic standards in areas such as nutrition.[3] Interestingly, the LNHO was funded to a significant extent (between a third and a half) by the Rockefeller Foundation despite the US not being a member of the League of Nations.

2. The Postwar Architecture and the "Independence Period" to the End of the Cold War

The post-World War II settlement brought a new impetus to international cooperation in many fields, with the setting up of the United Nations and of the Bretton Woods Institutions. As part of this highly creative period, the WHO was established in 1948 as the Specialised Agency of the UN with a global mandate to address health issues, bringing together the various regional health institutions that had been developed. UNICEF, the first model of a special-purpose fund, had already been created by the UN as early as 1946 initially for postwar relief for children in Europe.

A second creative period for the international system took place in the late 1950s and early 1960s as large numbers of countries gained their independence. This period saw the establishment of key development institutions such as the UNDP, IDA (the soft-loan arm of the World Bank, which became the largest multilateral concessional fund) and the main Regional Development Banks. The newly founded European Economic Community embarked on its own aid programmes and bilateral donors set up the Development Assistance Committee which established the basic definition of official development assistance and a system of peer review of its members. This "architecture" of the international cooperation system, in which the official aid donors of the OECD/DAC played in many ways the strongest role, was to remain unchanged in substance for over

[3] Op. cit.

thirty years, until the establishment of major global funds for the environment and for health (and a more modest one for education) in the 1990s and early 2000s.

Resources for development increased in this period, driven in part by the Cold War competition between the West and the Soviet Bloc, and by the emergence of major donors among the oil-producing countries. The "Green Revolution" demonstrated the value of applying research to development problems, and the eradication of smallpox, launched by WHO in 1967, showed the potential of collective action in health.

Donors' support for health programmes in this period was almost exclusively through bilateral agencies, which financed both research into specific diseases and bilateral projects (the latter often with a focus on family planning or on hospital-based services). As Figure 1 shows, multilateral aid for health was extremely small at this time.

What little multilateral aid existed was largely through the UN system. The UNDP was seen as the major channel for channelling operational funds into the UN system, with the Specialised Agencies, such as WHO,

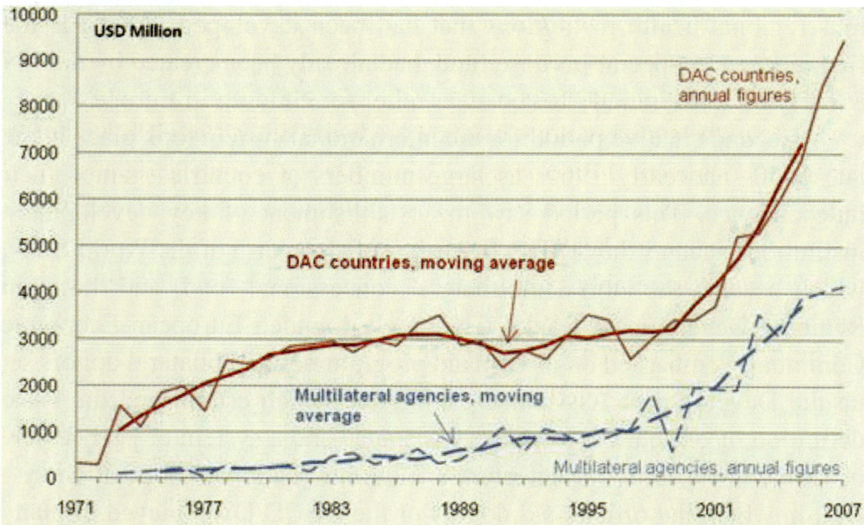

Figure 1. Trends in aid to health.

1973–2007, five-year moving averages and annual figures, constant 2006 prices

(*Source*: OECD/DAC).

acting more as sources of expertise and norm setting than as operational bodies in their own right, except where executing projects were financed by UNDP. UNICEF and, from 1967, the UN Fund for Population Activities (UNFPA) were the two main special-purpose funds, both of them quite small (funding for smallpox eradication and for malaria did not involve new institutions). The World Bank and Regional Development Banks were not major actors in the social sectors at this stage. Figure 1 relates only to official development assistance and does not cover private voluntary flows, which of course provided a significant further channel of assistance.

Concerns grew, however, that despite aid, conditions for poor people had only very modestly improved. The 1970s saw a new stress by many donors, including the World Bank, on meeting what were called the "basic needs." As a result, the Bank, and to a lesser extent the Regional Development Banks, began to embark on lending for health (and for education). However, despite the positive statements in the 1980 World Development Report on Basic Needs, Poverty and Human Development, this emphasis on the social sectors was limited by a renewed focus on growth and on structural adjustment because of the oil crisis that started in 1979. There was some resistance to addressing education and health until the supposedly temporary balance of payments crisis had been dealt with; there was not much focus on the cost of waiting. Re-emphasis on poverty and the social sectors resumed gradually in the mid-1980s, shortly before "Adjustment with a Human Face" came out, and gave it a good push, in 1987. As shown in Figure 1, this was reflected in some increase in multilateral aid for health from about 1980 onwards, while bilateral aid, though still considerably larger in aggregate, stagnated at similar real levels from 1980 to the mid-1990s.

Within the health sector, greater attention was placed on primary health care, as highlighted by the Alma Ata Declaration of 1978, which called for all governments to "formulate national policies, strategies and plans of action to launch and sustain primary health care as part of a comprehensive national health system and in coordination with other sectors."

This concern for radically changing the lives of the poor was effectively promoted by UNICEF under the leadership of Jim Grant in the 1980s through the aggressive use of targets for such key interventions as vaccination and oral rehydration therapy — an early and successful example of results-based aid through a high-impact and cost-effective vertical programme within a UN Agency, but also one seen by proponents of comprehensive primary health care as an overselective "vertical" programme that risked detracting from system-wide horizontal approaches. The results-based approach was emphasised further at the Children's Summit of 1990 in the form of seven "Major Goals for Children and Development in the 1990s," six of them quantified, and supported by no fewer than 26 supporting/sectoral goals, for example in women's health and education, nutrition and water and sanitation. It was supported by the UNDP's "Human Development Reports" from 1990 onwards. These reports, initiated by Mahbub ul Haq with advice from distinguished economists including Amartya Sen, provided a sharp focus on poverty reduction. One important innovation was the Human Development Index, which combined life expectancy, basic education and income to focus attention on the multidimensional nature of poverty. It demonstrated that even poor countries could have significant achievements in the social sectors and that economic development alone was not an adequate guarantee of social progress.

3. Pressures for Change

The end of the Cold War presented both opportunities and challenges for international cooperation to improve the health conditions for the poor. Aid was no longer so dominated by political considerations — but political considerations necessitated a whole new arena for assistance in relation to countries of Central and Eastern Europe, and countries emerging from the former Soviet Union. Aid to developing countries outside the "transition economies," far from benefiting from a "peace dividend," declined for much of the 1990s, partly because of those competing needs and partly because the end of the Cold War had reduced the political incentive to "buy" the support of developing countries for one side or another.

At the same time, however, the share of aid allocated for health-related purposes began to rise. Several factors contributed to this. The seriousness of the HIV/AIDS pandemic was now evident, and the need for a more coordinated approach was underscored by the establishment of

UNAIDS by ECOSOC in 1994. Health was also an area which public opinion and advocacy nongovernmental organisations (NGOs) in donor countries tended to support. At the same time, aid for industry and economic infrastructure declined for several reasons: an increased donor focus on poverty, with which health resonated well; strong pressures from public opinion and NGOs on environment and resettlement issues, which made the multilateral development banks and some bilateral donors more reluctant to support large infrastructure projects; and OECD agreements restricting tying which made it harder to use aid to win commercially attractive contracts in industry or in economic infrastructure. Moreover, new advances in research gave hope that some major diseases could be eradicated (polio) or tackled much more effectively (e.g. malaria, which after promising progress had been a major failure of the previous 20 years[4] and TB). At this stage, the cost of antiretroviral treatment for HIV/AIDS was generally held to be beyond the scope of international assistance, though this was soon to change.

On the other hand, attention to family planning declined, as world population growth rates continued to fall, even in South Asia, previously a major area of assistance for family planning programmes. Levels of population growth in Africa remained high, but did not attract equivalent donor attention.

Within the UN system, most specialised agencies, including WHO, were now receiving relatively substantial operational funds from bilateral donors directly, and the role of UNDP was slimmed down to concentrate on a limited number of issues. In other respects, funding channels were largely unchanged from the 1970s.

The World Bank was the largest multilateral provider of support to the health sector in aggregate. Its 1993 World Development Report "Investing in Health" espoused a case for a significant increase in the priority given to health as well as a mixture of growth policies that benefit the poor, more education for girls, re-direction of government spending to more cost-effective interventions of high value to the poor and diversity and competition in service delivery. The successful joint programme to

---

[4] See the chapter by Stekete and Nahlen in this volume.

control onchocerciasis in West Africa showed the value of cooperation between agencies, though there was no clear framework for routine cooperation even between WHO and the World Bank (a contrast to the Bank's relations with FAO).

A series of major thematic summits, such as the Children's Summit already referred to, put forward strong cases to increase investment in the social sectors and raised increasingly urgent concerns about the consequences for such investment of structural adjustment and of the debt crisis, particularly for the heavily indebted poor countries.

Donors reacted to the pressures on aid budgets by agreeing, in 1996, a set of International Development Goals, mainly drawn from these thematic summits and including goals for maternal and infant and child mortality and for access to reproductive health services, to be achieved by 2015. This initiative, initially conceived as a basis for justifying investment in aid programmes, led in turn to the establishment of the Millennium Development Goals, most of them highlighted in the UN Millennium Declaration, and brought together formally by the UN Secretary-General in 2001. Of the eight goals, three were health related: child mortality, maternal health and combating HIV/AIDS and other infectious diseases.

A further important input to thinking was the Commission on Macroeconomics and Health, set up by Gro Harlem Bruntland as Director-General of WHO and chaired by Jeffrey Sachs, which reported in 2001. Its key messages were that better health would contribute positively to both growth and poverty reduction, and that major strides in improving health status of poor and lower-middle income countries were possible, but only if there was a major increase in both aid and domestic resources. In addition to financing, the Report of the Commission also supported new forms of delivery including public/private partnerships (to which WHO had been opposed in the 1980s).

4. A New Creative Period, Late 1990s and Early 2000s

The tantalising possibility that the health status of the poor could be radically and quickly improved, and the evidence that in the 1990s rates of reduction in indicators such as infant and child mortality had fallen well short of hopes, encouraged questioning of the existing architecture for delivering international support to the health sector, which had changed little over the previous couple of decades. A key catalyst for change was the arrival of the Bill & Melinda Gates Foundation as a new entity with a clear vision, an extremely strong focus on results and on the need for evidence and the funding to back its vision. However, the Foundation seldom acted alone, and its impetus was carried forward through a set of different partnerships. Three main types of such partnerships can be distinguished.

One type of partnership was a financing entity. One of the first of these was the Global Alliance for Vaccines and Immunisation (GAVI), established in 2000 with a grant of $750 million from the Gates Foundation, but also with the key support of the Government of Norway and the Norwegian Director-General of WHO, Gro-Harlem Bruntland. Funds for immunisation were not new — UNICEF had long devoted resources to support immunisation, and concerted vaccination programmes against smallpox and measles dated back to the 1960s and were being pursued energetically in the case of polio under the auspices of WHO. GAVI provided, however, a distinctively different approach as an independent organisation with an independent Board including civil society and private-sector participants as well as government representatives, not part of the UN system (though with its programmatic arm in Geneva "hosted" by UNICEF), with a strong "vertical" focus on specific interventions and a correspondingly strong focus on results. It had the characteristic research grant or "Foundation" approach of proceeding by calling for proposals, to be scrutinised by an independent expert group, as the basis for its financing. It also decided against setting up of an in-country administrative presence, in favour of using a variety of local agents. The speed with which it garnered support from other donors (20 bilateral donors now support it financially) showed that this was a model with significant attractions.

It was not long before the G8 agreed (at the Genoa Summit in 2001) to join the UN Secretary-General in calling for the establishment of an even larger such fund, based on a concept very similar to that of GAVI, but this time aimed at the three large infectious diseases of HIV/AIDS, malaria and tuberculosis. The genesis of the new fund was complex. There was tension between those — including Northern AIDS activists — arguing for an international AIDS fund with a focus on making antiretroviral therapy, the costs of which had now fallen while still very substantial in relation to health budgets, available to AIDS sufferers in developing countries as a basic human right, and those, including WHO, who were in favour of a more broadly based fund to support action on a range of communicable diseases. The EC played a seminal role in hosting in 2000 a high-profile conference on "diseases of poverty" which they defined to be HIV/AIDS, TB and malaria. Following difficult negotiations, the concentration on the "three diseases" made it possible to go into the Special Session of the UN General Assembly in June 2000 and the subsequent G8 Summits in Okinawa and Genoa with a compromise that kept the health lobby on Board while providing sufficient visibility for AIDS. The GFATM quickly built up its operations, and by 2007, it was already disbursing nearly $2 billion a year.

Just as GAVI had been set up independently of the UN system, but using the facilities of UNICEF, so the new Global Fund had its own Board, including seats for the private sector, for Northern and Southern Civil Society and — uniquely — for representatives of affected communities, but was hosted by the WHO, using WHO financial, personnel and IT systems.[5]

These financing partnerships have radically changed the landscape of international assistance for health and are discussed further below.

A second type of partnership was aimed at tackling specific diseases and other specific issues, with the focus on advocacy and stronger networking of those concerned with the diseases or issues, rather than on funding as such. Here the major examples were the founding in 1998/99 of Roll Back Malaria and STOP TB,[6] both originally "Cabinet Projects" put in place by Mrs Brundtland in order to inject a sense of priority into WHO and to cross organisational boundaries, and both hosted by that organisation.

[5] Both GAVI and the Global Fund have now separated themselves from their original host organisations, and are now established an independent charitable entities.

[6] The aim of STOP TB, for example, is "to realize the goal of eliminating TB as a public health problem and, ultimately, to obtain a world free of TB. It comprises a network of international organizations, countries, donors from the public and private sectors, governmental and nongovernmental organizations and individuals that have expressed an interest in working together to achieve this goal" (STOP TB website).

A second wave of single-purpose WHO-hosted partnerships of similar type was to follow a few years later. Examples included the Health Metrics Network (2005), the Partnership for Maternal, Newborn and Child Health (2005) and the Global Health Workforce Alliance (2006). Each of these similarly brought in alliances of bilateral and multilateral donor agencies, developing country governments and interested civil society in support of advocacy and networking for a particular area of international health.

These partnerships have had varied success. Where successful, they have served (as in STOP TB) to broker strong international consensus on what needs to be done and how to do it. They have a good potential "fit" with the funding partnerships, for example in helping countries draft technically sound proposals.

A third type of partnership was focused on product development and R&D, which market forces alone were failing to stimulate adequately in diseases of particular significance to poor countries. Again, the Bill & Melinda Gates Foundation played an important role in encouraging and supporting such initiatives as the International AIDS Vaccine Initiative and the Medicines for Malaria Venture. The latter was among the first public–private partnership established to tackle a major global disease. The initiative arose from discussions between the WHO and the representative body of the pharmaceutical industry, the International Federation of Pharmaceutical Manufacturers Associations (IFPMA). Early partners in these exploratory discussions were the Global Forum for Health Research, the Rockefeller Foundation, the World Bank, the Swiss Agency for Development and Cooperation, the Association of the British Pharmaceutical Industry and the Wellcome Trust. At the product-marketing end of the spectrum, the Clinton Foundation's HIV/AIDS Initiative (CHAI) has worked to reduce the costs of anti-retroviral (ARV) and other treatments.

The potential of these partnerships is very significant, and they have certainly stimulated a major upturn in research and development activity in their areas of focus.

Innovation was not confined to the multilateral level. The US Administration set up the President's Emergency Program for AIDS Relief (PEPFAR) in 2003. This was also an innovative, lightly staffed, financing organisation, in this case designed to coordinate US bilateral support across the main official agencies (USAID, the Center for Disease Control and the National Institutes for Health) and to bring in private-sector and community organisations (including faith based).

PEPFAR accounted for a large percentage of the increase in donor health financing. It swiftly became the largest funding source for assistance to the HIV/AIDS pandemic (including the US contribution to GFATM) and in many African countries became the predominant expression of US aid. PEPFAR was followed by a further presidential initiative for malaria and for global health. The Obama Administration developed this family of programmes further in its Global Health Initiative, which also includes a related agricultural initiative, 'Feed the Future'.

Three further initiatives by groups of bilaterals came into effect between 2006 and 2008. The International Financing Facility for Immunisation, supported by the UK, France, Italy, Spain, Sweden, Norway and South Africa, successfully launched a bond on the international markets in 2006 (and further bonds subsequently) which have so far produced over $3 billion in resources for GAVI, more or less doubling its annual level of expenditure. A new tax on air travel, introduced by France and, initially, four other countries (now seven in total using air taxes and 22 others making financial contributions) in 2006, generated an annual income stream of some $300 million for specific malaria and HIV treatments, administered by a new purpose-built vehicle, UNITAID, which has also partnered with the Clinton Foundation to reduce drug prices. Moreover, Canada, Italy, Norway, Russia, the UK, the Bill & Melinda Gates Foundation, GAVI and the World Bank combined to test the long-discussed concept of a "pull" mechanism for research, by establishing a $1.5 billion Advanced Market Commitment (AMC) for a new antipneumococcal vaccine. It should be noted that the three initiatives had very different financial models: thus IFFIm drew its funds from the international bond market, effectively enabling expenditure to take place earlier than would have otherwise been possible; the air ticket levy provided an additional source of development assistance contributed by the travelling public; and the AMC involved donors putting money into escrow year by year with a view to actual disbursements to successful drug developers at a later date.

The last few years of the twentieth century and the early years of the twenty-first century, therefore, witnessed an increase in the sources of concessional finance for health (Foundations, notably Gates, new and emerging donors, such as China and India, the bond market and air ticket levies, all at a time when many traditional donors were also scaling up assistance for health and major diseases such as HIV/AIDS and NGOs, continued to give high priority to health-related interventions) and an even larger increase in the channels for providing assistance in the form of finance (as with GAVI, the Global Fund for AIDS, TB and malaria), advice and advocacy (Roll Back Malaria, STOP TB etc) or for R&D. Annex 1 documents some of the changes.

This led to increasing concerns that:

- Large-scale special-purpose funds would put in question the ability of recipient countries to set their own priorities;
- The substantial resources now available to the major "vertical" funds would attract resources (not least trained staff) from other health services to an extent that would damage the latter and put in question the sustainability of the "vertical" interventions themselves;
- The system was becoming overcomplex, not least from the point of view of recipient countries.

The first issue was most visible in relatively small countries where special-purpose funding (typically for HIV/AIDS) appeared to lead to funds being spent in ways that were suboptimal for the actual burden of disease in the country concerned. A counter-argument was that effective special-purpose interventions would have positive consequences for the overall health system as well as for the specific beneficiaries (thus effective programmes of treatment for HIV/AIDS should free up many beds in national hospitals and reduce mortality among health workers). Nevertheless, the figures were striking. In 2007,[7] out of development assistance for health (DAH) of nearly $22 billion, $5 billion was for HIV/AIDS alone, compared to less than $1 billion apiece for health systems, for malaria or for TB. Nor was it clear that at country level such programmes were routinely aligned in support of a credible national health policy.

---

[7] Financing Global Health 2009: Tracking Development Assistance for Health, Institute for Health Metrics and Evaluation, 2009.

The second problem was not new — the respective virtues of "vertical" (i.e. single-purpose) and "horizontal" (i.e. system-wide) approaches to health having been debated for many years — but now acquired greater focus because of the rapid increase of vertical funding to a level that had potential systemic consequences. A study for the GFATM by McKinsey (2005) highlighted in particular the problem of sustainability of major single-purpose interventions, and its findings were a major piece of evidence looked at by a "High Level Forum on Health," which met between 2003 and 2005. The Forum, in which the World Bank and WHO were heavily engaged along with the major global funds and key funders, sought to encourage greater coherence among the many health-related initiatives. Several of the ideas canvassed by this group were to be taken up later in the "International Health Partnership" and associated initiatives discussed below. Recognising the limits to "pure" vertical programmes, both GAVI and the GFATM began to finance broader health system development in areas linked to their mandates. This in turn led to questions over the most appropriate international architecture for assisting the development of health systems, and the roles of special-purpose funds and institutions like the World Bank. A report of 2006 by Alex Shakow for the Global Fund and the World Bank[8] (see Chapter 2) proposed a division of labour between the special-purpose funds concentrating on their core programmes and a health systems focus for the Bank, but in the immediate future, the tendency was rather to build the health system windows of GAVI and GFATM.

The third issue was by no means limited to the field of health, and successive High Level Forums in Rome (2003), Paris (2005) and Accra (2008) developed an agenda around the concepts of Ownership, Alignment, Harmonisation, Results and Mutual Accountability in an attempt to encourage greater coherence among the large number of actors at country level. Particular efforts were made to secure coherence in

---

[8] Shakow A *Global Fund-World Bank HIV/Aids Programs: Comparative Advantage Study*, January 19, 2006, prepared for the Global Fund and the World Bank, http://www.theglobalfund.org/documents/library/studies/position_papers/GFWBReportFinalVersion.pdf or http://siteresources.worldbank.org/INTHIVAIDS/Resources/375798-1103037153392/GFWBReportFinalVersion.pdf.

HIV/AIDS programmes through the "Three Ones" initiative of 2004, which called for a single national strategy, a single national implementing body and a single monitoring and evaluation plan. In a separate but related initiative, several special-purpose funds (including GAVI and GFATM, but also the Fast Track Initiative on Education, the Global Environment Facility and the Cities' Alliance) established a "Learning Group on Aid Effectiveness," which in particular addressed practical issues of good practice highlighted in the Paris Declaration of 2005, such as aligning decision-making timetables of such funds more closely to local budget cycles and harmonising reporting requirements where relevant.

None of these issues, important though they were, put in question the value of special-purpose funds in terms of a close link to results, "saleability" to donor public opinion and relatively light styles of governance. An important round of replenishments in 2007 confirmed that donors were ready to continue to invest both in special-purpose funds such as GFATM and in funds with a broader remit such as IDA or the soft fund of the African Development Bank. PEPFAR was also given a renewed mandate by Congress, with an extra amount for global health more generally.

A study of special-purpose funds (covering the environment and education as well as health) was undertaken in 2007–2008 by the World Bank and concluded that in countries with relatively low dependence on aid, such funds posed few problems of local management or priority setting, but that in more aid-dependent countries, where finance from such funds was relatively large in relation to local budgets, these issues had to be addressed carefully.

This study was one important input into a Roundtable on Aid Architecture that was convened at the Accra High Level Forum on Aid Effectiveness in September 2008 and provided an opportunity for a large number of stakeholders to give their views on the role of what were termed "Global Program Funds." A consensus was reached at this Round Table that:

"Global Program Funds had many positive achievements. However, particularly where such funds were large and had a tight focus there were some 'side-effects' of earmarking. These needed to be addressed by a good balance between earmarked funds and funds that responded to local needs across the Board, and by more integrated approaches, in line with the Paris Declaration. The aim must be balanced funding within and across sectors and sustainable development at country level (though full sustainability would take an extended period in poorer countries). When new global concerns arose, such as climate change or the food and energy crises, there was a call to 'think twice' before creating new global funds or separate aid channels and to give priority to reforming existing institutions to take on new challenges. There was a danger that new global funds would simply re-route existing aid, rather than deliver real additionality."

Fuller details of the Roundtable's messages to key stakeholders are given in Annex 2 to this chapter.

Already in 2007, a year before the Accra Forum, further health initiatives had been announced by Norway (in favour of MDGs 4 and 5 — child and maternal mortality), Canada and the UK (the "International Health Partnership," which was ostensibly about increased support for health systems, drawing on the concepts in the Paris Declaration of 2005). An intensive period of intradonor negotiation led to the establishment of a more formal "IHP+," which brought in more donors and promulgated the concept of coordinated donor support for stronger country-led health system initiatives. Together with the formalisation of coordination among key agencies through the "H8" process (the eight agencies being WHO, the World Bank, GAVI, GFATM, UNICEF, UNAIDS, UNDP and the Gates Foundation), this demonstrated the wish of many players to get a better balance between diversity and coherence in the international system for supporting better health for the poor.

This search for coherence with forward momentum was taken further in 2009 by two important reports sponsored by a High Level Task Force on Innovative International Financing for Health Systems co-chaired by UK Prime Minister Gordon Brown and the World Bank President Robert Zoellick. The focus on health systems was central to this initiative, and in September 2009 the sponsors were able to announce a number of additional financing initiatives, including an expansion of the IFFIm in support of health systems, financed by Australia, Netherlands, Norway and the UK; additional finance for "buy-downs" of loans for health systems strengthening from Australia,

Norway and the UK; a scheme for voluntary contributions by the public on travel products; and a pilot project in Italy for redirecting a portion of VAT receipts for development. What was significant about this seemingly disparate set of initiatives was the common intention to build a stronger and more coordinated approach to health systems as a whole. Significantly, the Global Fund, GAVI and the World Bank announced in the same context their intention to work together on a "common platform" for health systems strengthening.

It seems therefore that there is at least on paper a strong consensus among the external financiers of support for health activities in favour of combining the strengths of the special-purpose "vertical" interventions with the need to build competent and sustainable health systems.

It is noteworthy that a major boost to maternal and child health by the G8 and the United Nations did not invlove a new special-purpose fund. A new round of replenishments in 2010 and 2011, conducted in a much more challenging international economic environment than in 2007, encouragingly delivered increased funding again for both the key 'general purpose' multilateral fund, IDA, and for the two largest health funds, the Global Fund securing a 17% increase over its previous replenishment, and GAVI raising more than it had sought. The design characteristics of an effective and sustainable "international health support" model are clear enough. Such a model should:

- Be built on country ownership and, over time, decreasing dependence on external financing
- Recognise the need to make the best use of all local channels (state, civil society, private sector)
- Draw on the strengths of both vertical and "system" approaches, and on the insights and resources of private as well as public funders
- Deliver real benefits for the poor and excluded
- Enable external assistance to be increasingly coordinated by host country and aligned to local priorities (with alignment prioritised over harmonisation)
- Incorporate strong and coordinated monitoring and independent evaluation of results, based on competent, locally owned health information systems.

Where, as in some countries, there is good local capacity and where external finance is complementary to a locally financed system that is already sustainable at a worthwhile level, this model is not too hard to implement. The government is likely to be able to coordinate donors behind an agreed local strategy for health improvement drawing on both public and private resources; requests to donors for both unallocated sector support and targeted interventions to tackle leading causes of morbidity and mortality can be coordinated and made complementary; the country rather than the donors can call the shots. Even here, however, given that health costs typically increase as wealth increases, issues of sustainability will need to be given attention, particularly in circumstances of international financial stringency.

However, where donor finance is large in relation to local resources and in the case of what are often termed "fragile states," the position is much harder. Here, there should be a greater premium than is generally given on the alignment of donor policies and interventions to local strategies and to use of local systems, which will probably need significant strengthening.[9] In the case of particularly fragile states, it may not be feasible to align to local strategies and systems. Rather the emphasis may need to be on harmonising among donors behind the delivery of assistance which may in the short term need to bypass government institutions that cannot absorb large flows of external resources. Given the large number of both sources and channels of health-related assistance, this poses problems. The direction of travel is nevertheless clear. It should be:

- From individual "doing good" interventions to collaboration in helping a country develop a set of policies and institutions (public and/or private) that can deliver health services effectively. This will require a positive impetus among the various donors to collaborate, even in the absence of a strong push from the country concerned;

[9] The signifiance of this point is underlined by the concerns of many donars over alleged misuse of Global Fund resources in some African countries, which came to light in 2010/11, and which led to the establishment of an independent panel in March 2011 to review the Fund's financial safeguards.

- From donor-led to country-led approaches, which necessarily implies a major and sustained effort to build local capacity, rather than to rely indefinitely on external technical assistance;
- From donor-oriented to locally relevant M&E systems; and, in the longer term,
- From reliance on donors and on out-of-pocket expenses for health service delivery by citizens to a gradually more predictable and locally led set of financing arrangements that address the needs of the poor.

Many of these challenges are not unique to the health sector; but the number and variety of channels of assistance to health makes them particularly challenging to tackle in this sector.

> Chapter 2 reflects further on how such a desirable outcome could be promoted, specifically as between the special-purpose funds and donors which operate broader financial support for health systems.
>
> Chapters 7 and 8 further develop the history and diversity of global programmes and partnerships for malaria, respectively.

Annex 1: International Health Assistance Architecture: A Changing Picture

In 2009, the new Institute for Health Metrics and Evaluation at the University of Washington published the first in what was promised to be a series of annual reports detailing what it termed DAH.[10] This provided in particular a detailed time series for all the main sources and channels of international health assistance, whether official or private, concessional or non-concessional, and whether in kind or in cash. While any such attempt faces major challenges of accessing truly comparable data, the IHME report provides an extremely useful basis for describing the rapid changes

[10] See footnote 4.

that have taken place in the global health assistance architecture in the last two decades, and particularly since 2000.

These changes have taken place against the background of a very significant increase in DAH. According to the IHME report, in constant 2007 US dollars, DAH rose from $5.6 billion in 1990 to $21.8 billion in 2007, a remarkable example of scaling up of international assistance.

The sources of DAH changed moderately over this period. In 1990, DAC member governments accounted for over three-quarters of the total, and they remained collectively by far the largest source (some two-thirds) in 2007. Within this group, the US has consistently been the largest contributor (though as the report points out, not on a per capita basis), accounting for 23.5% of total DAH in 1990 and 26% in 2007 (and thus becoming a significantly larger proportion of total DAC assistance). In 1990, France, Sweden, Japan and Italy were the next largest DAC contributors; in 2007, the comparable list was UK, France, Germany and Japan. The report was unable to estimate the amount of official DAH from donors outside the DAC: the amount is likely to be relatively modest, given the weight that aid for infrastructure has in the programmes of some of the largest such donors, such as China or the Middle East Funds.

The fastest growing contributions came from the private sector: in-kind donations from private companies (mostly the major pharmaceutical firms) rose from about $250 million (4%) to $2.5 billion (11%). The report points out however that valuing such contributions is difficult, and their real value may be significantly overstated. US NGOs and Foundations increased their contributions from a little under $500 million (8%) to $3.3 billion (15%). Of the latter figure, the Bill & Melinda Gates Foundation accounted for $1.1 billion or 5% of total DAH. Clearly, there would be also be significant (but probably in aggregate considerably smaller) additional contributions from NGOs based outside the US, which the report was unable to estimate fully, and from non-US Foundations. Other smaller sources included repayments to the IFIs and miscellaneous categories. The latter presumably includes the contribution of innovative finance, which was just getting underway in 2007. The figures for GAVI do incorporate the contribution of IFFIm, but this is not singled out in the table on sources of finance, and there is no specific mention of air-ticket levies, UNITAID or AMC. For subsequent years, these sources will become increasingly important, though still modest in relation to total DAH.

The period thus saw major absolute increases from all sources, but a disproportionate increase from US NGOs and Foundations (with Bill and Melinda Gates Foundation (BMGF) being an outstandingly large single contributor, considerably larger than any DAC member apart from the US and the UK), and in the form of private-sector in-kind donations. Nevertheless, DAC governments remained by far the largest sources of DAH in aggregate.

However, in general, the channels of DAH have changed much more significantly than the sources. The report shows some striking developments between 1990 and 2007. In the former year, of the $5.6 billion of DAH, about 47% was channelled to developing countries by bilateral official agencies, 32% by the UN system (WHO, UNICEF and UNFPA), 15% by US NGOs and Foundations and 5% by the World Bank and Regional Development Banks. By 2007, the bilateral share (including the EC, which became a more important channel over the period) had dropped to 36% and the UN share (including also UNAIDS) to a mere 14%. The main increases in share were from US NGOs and Foundations, which had doubled to 30%, factors in this including the use by the US Government (USAID and PEPFAR) of NGOs as a channel of assistance, the rise of the Bill & Melinda Gates Foundation, and a quadrupling in the money raised by NGOs over the period. There was a smaller rise in share of the development banks to a little over 7%. Moreover, a further 12% or so was accounted for by the two major new international funding initiatives, the Global Fund and GAVI.

It should be noted that the report does not capture the full institutional complexity of the institutional architecture for DAH. There is thus no specific mention of partnerships such as Roll Back Malaria, or STOP TB, or, as noted above, innovations such as UNITAID.

Another way of looking at the changes in channels of assistance is that multilateral channels (UN system, development banks and GF/GAVI) have remained a fairly stable share of the total (around one-third), though with major changes between agencies, and that NGOs and BMGF have increased their share as channels of assistance remarkably, while the traditional bilateral government-to-government assistance in health has declined from nearly one-half to just over a third. On the ground, the effect is that a rising share of the rapidly increasing DAH (including a significant share of Global Fund finance, for example) is being delivered through non-government channels.

Within the multilateral "system," key changes have been the rise of the two major special-purpose funds, GAVI and GFATM, a very large increase in World Bank finance (from under $100 million for IDA and IBRD together in 1990 to some $2 billion in 2004) and to a lesser extent Regional Development Bank financing (both of which appeared however to go into reverse from 2005–2007), and a consistent but less spectacular rise in spending by WHO, UNICEF, UNFPA and UNAIDS.

Annex 2: Conclusions of Accra Roundtable Discussion on Global Program Funds, September 2008

1) **Global Program Funds**
   a) **Funders of existing and potential global program funds are invited to:**
      - *Consider carefully the balance between funding for targeted global initiatives and funding for aid institutions with a broader remit, able to accommodate local priorities across the Board.*
      - *"Think twice" before establishing new funds, applying a clear test of value added. Learn lessons from the experience of existing global programme funds. In accordance with the Accra Agenda for Action (AAA), as new global challenges arise, ensure that existing channels are used and if necessary strengthened before creating separate new ones which would tend to increase fragmentation at the country level.*
      - *Ensure consistency between their overall commitment to the principles of aid effectiveness and the line that their representatives take in the Boards of Global Program Funds.*

   b) **The boards of global program funds are invited to:**
      - *Recognise that focused interventions will normally require also the strengthening of overall systems, however financed.*

- *In accordance with the AAA, ensure that the principles of ownership, alignment, harmonisation and mutual accountability are given support along with the focus on achieving results.*
- *Align decision-making timetables to local planning and budget cycles.*
- *Ensure timely reporting of commitments and disbursements to feed into partner countries' budget and planning processes.*
- *Encourage greater coordination with central ministries in recipient countries.*
- *Give high priority to sustainability, particularly where funding recurrent costs, while recognising that this can often be achieved only over a considerable period.*
- *Invest in capacity development and avoid policies that drain capacity from other parts of the national system.*
- *Recognise the broad links between outputs and outcomes, which are typically the product of relevant activities by many actors often in many sectors, when monitoring results.*
- *Actively engage in a learning process to improve effectiveness, through sharing of best practices, such as in the Global Programs Learning Group.*

c) Countries receiving assistance from global program funds are invited to:

- *Strengthen national and sectoral policies in order to provide a robust framework for the uptake of Global Program Funds on a sustainable basis including working with IMF to adjust financial envelopes to better include predictable spending by such Funds.*
- *Ensure close coordination between sector and central Ministries, especially the Ministry of Finance, under existing budget and planning processes.*
- *Ensure that global programme funds take full account of local policies for decentralisation.*
- *Strengthen national results monitoring frameworks for public expenditure that Global Program Funds and others can use to monitor the impact of their interventions.*

- *Address systemic issues that inhibit the development of capacity (as opposed to bidding staff away from other activities by special inducements).*
- *Promote domestic resource mobilisation in order to contribute to sustainable financing of high-priority interventions over the longer term.*
- *Build on the opportunities that Global Program Funds provide for greater engagement with non-state actors.*

d) Nongovernment partners of global program funds are invited to:

- *Recognise the need for appropriate coordination with government policies and interventions in the area concerned.*
- *Report transparently about receipt and expenditure of funds.*

e) The OECD/DAC is invited to:

- *Improve the reporting of the flow of funds from the original sources (e.g. taxpayers, voluntary contributors) through all the intermediate channels to the country level.*
- *Continue to encourage active learning and sharing on aid effectiveness among existing and new global programmes and consider providing a forum to facilitate monitoring, discussion and action, through support of a formalised relationship between the OECD–DAC and the Global Programs Learning Group.*

f) All parties are invited to:

- *Promote an evidence-based culture by continuing joint learning and by regular joint evaluation of the activities financed by Global Program Funds.*
- *Consider whether the appropriate response to the growing concern about effective systems at sector level is best addressed by broadening the mandate of Global Program Funds or by adjusting the balance between these initiatives and broader-based programmes.*

2

Negotiating with New Partners to Increase the Effectiveness and Volume of Aid: The Role of Global Funds

Paul Isenman and Alexander Shakow[1]

Memorandum for the Director-General

Introduction and Summary

This report responds to your request for an analysis of policy choices raised by the growing importance of global funds, particularly in the health sector. The report draws on our agency's experience working with these funds and on interviews with knowledgeable people, including in global funds, as well as on published sources. It aims to help you confront some difficult decisions, analytical and political, on how to allocate our aid and how to ensure that it is used to the maximum effect. (Global fund is used in this report, as in the Accra Agenda for Action (AAA), to refer to global programmes that provide substantial assistance earmarked for a limited set of purposes to a wide variety of countries.)

We start from our objective of managing our total aid portfolio, bilateral and multilateral, in a way that maximises poverty reduction, the

---

[1] We would particularly like to thank Masood Ahmed, Keith Bezanson, Andrew Cassels, Mukesh Chawla, Helen Evans, Daniel Low-Beer, Richard Manning, Andrew Rogerson, Jean-Louis Sarbib and Andrew Steer for their advice and comments on drafts of this chapter. Responsibility, including for recommendations and errors, remains ours.

Note: This chapter is written as a report from advisers to the senior managers of a representative bilateral development agency facing issues common to all donors.

achievement of the MDGs and, more generally, development impact. This then raises some tough issues regarding global funds: whether and when to set up new funds; whether and when to use existing institutions when we do so; how aid effectiveness principles can be built into new funds and retrofitted into existing ones; how to allocate funds between global funds and other multilateral programmes — some of which (including most UN agencies) are themselves earmarked by sector; the implications of global funds for the overall balance between our bilateral and multilateral assistance and how we can encourage better coordination and more joint action between global funds and more "horizontal" aid programmes. Our focus is on the negotiation with other key stakeholders, taking account of their incentive systems, with the objective of increasing development impact.

The report stresses the importance of understanding the incentives that drive major stakeholders, including our own, and the challenges and opportunities for change that these incentives suggest. We recognise that on the most important issues regarding global funds, our agency's influence, even within our own government, is limited. We cannot give "orders" either to our ministers or to global funds on their policies or funding levels. A new type of diplomacy is needed which uses the "soft power" of negotiations, networks and incentives — taking account of our role as funders — to deal more effectively with global funds. We concentrate on the two biggest global health funds — the GAVI Alliance and the Global Fund to fight AIDS, TB and malaria. Our key recommendations are, however, broadly applicable beyond the health sector, including global funds for climate and food security.

Our staff's views on global funds vary widely, as do those of senior policy makers from developing countries. Some of our colleagues, particularly those involved in country programmes, have been highly critical of global funds, calling them inconsistent with the Paris Declaration's (PD's) emphasis on supporting overall government development strategies and priorities. Some others, including us, understand these weaknesses but recognise that global funds are a reality and a growing one, that they are producing tangible results on the ground and that they are important to our efforts to help increase both the effectiveness and volume of aid. Moreover, sector specialists are often strong champions of global funds as a way to address chronic underfunding of their own (sub)sectors, including through supporting advocacy work designed to generate even more funding.

Moreover, we need to recognise that we, as one of the initial funders — and not the global funds themselves — have determined their number, funding, mandates and broad policies. To the extent there are problems, we need to be at least as proactive in addressing them as we were in causing them. To some extent, we have been trying, recognising that since we have set up inclusive governance structures, we as funders cannot make unilateral decisions. However, we can do better, much better. The challenge we face is how to bring closer together the earmarked approach of global funds and the non-earmarked approach of the PD and the AAA (Paris-Accra).

Here are our main recommendations for action:

- *Clarify our strategy for multilateral aid, of which support for global funds is a major part, taking account of the issues in the attached background report.* Recognise the limits of strategies *per se*, however, and focus on how to bring about real-world change. Involve ministers and other parliamentarians as well as civil society — so we do not become what one observer referred to as the "butter in their sandwich." Consult developing countries and the private sector.
- *Set ourselves a challenge of working effectively with other donors and private foundations on the range of policy issues regarding the role and effectiveness of global funds.* Interests may differ in part, but they overlap substantially and progress requires joint action. The Development Assistance Committee (DAC) offers a basis for high-level informal joint efforts, but this would require reaching beyond the DAC to other donors and foundations.
- *Get more serious about "thinking twice" before establishing new earmarked funds and use existing institutions where possible to implement them.* Our ministers and representatives at international meetings on sectoral issues should avoid open-ended and exaggerated promises to meet all needs in a given subsector when — as is almost always the case — this would lead to an adding-up problem of intra- or inter-sectoral distortions. Take a lead in building sound principles of aid effectiveness in new global funds and retrofit them to existing ones.

- *Use a portfolio approach in allocations, taking account of evidence on cost-effectiveness, as part of that strategy.* Increase the share of multilateral aid, and within that increase the share of "horizontal" multilateral aid relative to that of global funds. Moreover, give more attention to evidence-based cost-effectiveness. In the case of health, this can lead in quite surprising directions, such as including support for country nutrition strategies or for raising tobacco taxes as "defaults" in health systems.
- *Be less schizophrenic and more proactive in helping resolve problems that we were a party to creating.* Speak with a consistent voice in relevant fora — including governing boards and committees of global funds, replenishments, the DAC Working Party on Aid Effectiveness (WP-EFF) and at the country level. Encourage champions of change in global funds, as well as the WP-EFF's "Global Programmes Learning Group" in this effort.
- *Do not underestimate the importance of the issues discussed here for aid-dependent countries with weak capacity. On the other hand, do not exaggerate their importance, particularly in countries where global funds account for a relatively small share of relevant overall public financing.*
- *Learn from, and be better partners with, global funds.* They have much to offer, including the focus on results, constructive involvement of civil society and the private sector, transparency and capacity for adaptation and innovation. We may criticise how they have achieved these objectives, but we ourselves need to do more and better in these areas. Moreover, there is plausible evidence that the sharp focus of their programmes has led to substantial reductions in mortality and morbidity, even if it is also plausible that some of their funds could have had a bigger impact elsewhere in health systems. The competition from global funds is constructive in making all donors raise their game. Recognise that staff of global funds, like staff of multilateral and bilateral agencies, are doing their best to respond to their mandates, incentives and accountability systems. Recognise also, though, that they are strong advocates for their mandates and that mission creep becomes a strong temptation for their staff and governance structures alike. Treat global

fund staff, at the country and global levels, as the valued partners they are.

- *Recognise and support the changes global funds are making to respond to the PD and the AAA. These changes have come through a combination of field experience, changes in incentives from external pressures and peer learning, and from internal champions.*However, recognise that much more is needed and "follow the incentives" to help bring about that change. Give more priority in our work on aid effectiveness to climate change and the environment, where there has been the fastest growth in the number of funds and volume of funding.
- *Face up squarely to the incentives of key stakeholders of global funds that make it likely that "raising money vertically and spending it horizontally" will instead end up both raising and spending it vertically, particularly as funding gets tighter.* Some "diagonalism" is probably necessary, given the stronger political support for specific activities that capture the popular political mind. However, be discerning diagonalists, going in with our eyes open and recognising that added political support does not at all mean full additionality — i.e. that increased flows to a global fund would increase aid by a similar amount overall.
- *Give more attention to the sustainability of funding for programmes that we have encouraged that entail strong moral and political commitments to financing ongoing costs — particularly given the uncertain environment for growth in overall aid.*

These are our recommendations in brief. However, knowing you will ask searching questions about the analysis behind them, we attach an in-depth background report structured as follows:

1. New models for increasing aid effectiveness: Paris-Accra and global funds, weakness of the two models and lessons from global funds.
2. Turning the spotlight on ourselves and other donors: incentives, progress and challenges.
3. GFATM and GAVI: incentives of key stakeholders and progress to date.

4. Selected remaining issues: health systems, sustainability, allocations, GFATM's country co-ordinating mechanisms (CCMs) and mutual accountability.
5. Conclusion.

MAIN REPORT

Negotiating With New Partners to Increase the Effectiveness and Volume of Aid: The Role of Global Funds

I. New Models for Increasing Aid Effectiveness: Paris-Accra and Global Funds

In the past decade, our agency has been a major contributor to the emergence of two new approaches, or models, of aid effectiveness that have from the start travelled in quite different and, in part, contradictory directions. The Paris-Accra model concentrates on the "how": improving the effectiveness of how aid is provided, with a focus on support for government-"owned" programmes. The global funds model combines "what" and "how," with sector- and subsector-specific objectives and a focus on applying global best practice at country level. We deal with both on a daily basis. However, it is worthwhile to step back and reflect on their relative strengths and weaknesses.

The Paris-Accra model

This model, embodied in the Paris Declaration (2005) and the AAA (2008), is based on the recognition that, especially in the longer run, it is what countries, not donors, do that matters. Donors can create hothouse programmes that bloom brilliantly for a time and then wither away. Thus, the emphasis is on country ownership, alignment of development assistance in support of country programmes, a complementary harmonisation of aid among donors and reduction in transaction costs, and more focus on results and accountability of donors as well as of developing countries. This approach emerged from lessons of decades of experience that showed the weaknesses of the prevalent approach, which was, in over-simplified terms, the "principal-agent" model: development would succeed only if aid agencies (the principals) could find effective incentives (persuasion, conditionality and the power of the purse) to get poor countries (the agents) to implement the programmes and policies that donors knew were needed. Experience, particularly in countries with the most rapid progress in economic growth and human development, has demonstrated that sustainable progress depends rather on the countries' own commitment and implementation capacity.

The Paris-Accra approach recognised that the power imbalance between donors and recipients was more a hindrance than a help in achieving development results. It represents a move away from a principal-agent model towards a "network model," emphasising mutual accountability for achieving development goals based on shared objectives and greater voice for developing countries and, to some extent, for civil society as well. It turned out that the long-standing "club model" of the OECD-DAC, which relied on shared objectives and peer pressure, was well adapted to encouraging this shift at the global level — in part through its WP-EFF. A 2008 evaluation of the Paris Declaration found that in just three years it had had a significant impact on behaviour of both donors and developing countries (Wood *et al.* 2008). This conclusion was further developed and re-enforced in the follow-up evaluation in 2011 (Wood *et al.* 2011)

The global funds' model

Since 2000, we and other donors have created a number of global funds, particularly for the environment and health. There are about 90 global programmes (often referred to as "partnerships") in health alone, including research, technical assistance, advocacy and financing entities. Only a small number fall into the last category and only two provide financing at the country level in amounts that are significant sector wide: the Global Fund to Fight AIDS, TB and Malaria (GFATM) and the GAVI Alliance. They disbursed nearly $3 billion in 2010, over 15 percent of total ODA for health. These amounts are dwarfed, however, by the U.S. President's Emergency Fund for AIDS Relief (PEPFAR), with annual disbursements over $7.3 billion in 2008, or about 30 percent of the sectoral total (Financing Global Health 2010). Although it is funded bilaterally, PEPFAR otherwise behaves like a global fund and is struggling with essentially the same aid effectiveness issues as GAVI and GFATM.

We participated in the creation of GAVI and GFATM and other so-called "vertical funds" for a number of reasons. There was a view, particularly among our civil society organisations (CSOs), that there was a need to break the mould of development orthodoxy. Existing international institutions were seen — depending on whether it was the World Bank, UNICEF or WHO — as some combination of too bureaucratic and slow, powerful and arrogant and unwilling to give a seat at the table to CSOs. As Paul Farmer put it more recently, "A first principle for the emerging global health movement, in fact, might well be 'Do not emulate the mainstream aid industry'" (Farmer and Garrett 2007). Thus, something new and different was needed. In the case of GAVI and GFATM, the objectives were, respectively, to deliver newly available vaccines and to address, on an urgent basis, the prevention and treatment needs of the many millions suffering from these three diseases. Both had great global appeal to publics, CSOs and political leaders.

The model was, like that of Paris-Accra, intended to be a sharp break from the past, but in quite different ways. It was to:

- be evidence based, sharing cutting-edge technology and good practice globally;
- incorporate scientific review panels to pass on or rank the quality of proposals submitted;
- pool funds at the global level that donors might otherwise be providing bilaterally;
- give a key governance role to civil society and the private sector;
- show quantifiable results (if more on outputs than outcomes) and, more recently, provide performance-based financing to help achieve them;
- have the ability to bring off massive short-term change unlikely to be achievable otherwise (e.g. insecticide-treated bednets for malaria);
- create "financing" rather than "implementing" agencies, thereby requiring fewer staff (though in practice many times more than initially anticipated) which would rely on partner agencies for help in-country;

- be nimble and adaptable, not weighed down by the baggage of accumulated rules and perceived political interference found in the World Bank or UN agencies;
- set a high standard of transparency, putting documents on their websites that donor agencies would normally consider internal or confidential and
- address issues that had, to varying extents, characteristics of global public goods, and that appealed to the moral sensitivities of civil society and political leadership in donor countries.

Both these new approaches, or models, have much to commend them. Not surprisingly, their weaknesses are in large part mirror images of their strengths. Our agency has on different occasions strongly supported both these models without sufficient thought to inconsistencies between them and how they might be reconciled. The appeal of global funds to civil society and world-famous public figures and artists, and to political leaders, has led to explosive growth in their financing, initially in health and, more recently, in attention to climate change, where there were 24 funds with pledged funding of nearly $32 billion as of June 2011 (Climate Fund Update 2011). In contrast, we have had much more difficulty gaining public or political understanding of the longer-run benefits of the Paris-Accra approach. Nevertheless, it is encouraging how much support there was in Accra in 2008 for recommitment to the Paris Declaration and for carrying it forward in the AAA. One person we interviewed characterised Accra as a "coup of the (aid) technocrats."

Weaknesses of the two models

Global funds

Global funds have significant disadvantages when viewed from the perspective of the health sector as a whole. These disadvantages are the flip side of their strengths — particularly that they focus on specific issues rather than taking a sector-wide approach, that they receive disproportionate increases in funds relative to other sectoral needs and that there is insufficient involvement at the country level. Moreover, we were, again, a party to establishing each of these features.

GAVI and GFATM grants are made on a research-based model of rounds of proposals reviewed by external panels. This essentially one-off competitive approach is an excellent way to promote research and innovation. However, it is ill-suited to long-term support and system strengthening and so creates internal tensions within the global fund model. It creates incentives to tailor proposals to take account of the generally known preferences of external review panels with limited country knowledge rather than of what the country needs and "owns." Another source of tension is between relatively short-term financing and the "moral mortgage" of long-term obligations for recurrent cost financing of staff, medicines and vaccines. (Financing of anti-retroviral therapy by GFATM is the extreme example.) That tension is exacerbated by the risk that a country's follow-on proposal may not make the cut, raising severe financial and political risks. In addition, the rounds approach has meant that global funds have set up their own processes, including calendars for proposals and for reporting. This has meant that governments need to "align" with the systems of global funds, while Paris-Accra calls for the contrary. The widely admired leanness of their staffs (at least initially) has meant less capacity to work with developing countries or donors on strengthening or overseeing programmes on the ground. In addition, the lack of country staff has made collaboration harder for governments and donors.

There has been a good deal of debate about the extent to which global funds have a distortionary effect within sectors. Disease-specific programmes, mostly for HIV/AIDS, accounted for half of aid to health — and about three quarters of the increase in aid to health — from 2002 to 2006 (Financing Global Health 2009). The implicit basis of global funds is an updated version of the traditional principal-agent model of aid, although one reflecting more of "global best practice knows best" than "donor knows best" and without conditionality except that implicit in the award process. Note that the issue is not whether a given programme is vertical at the country level. It is rather whether the vertical earmarking is done at the global or country level.

If the question is whether governments would have spent the same amount of funding differently, the answer would generally be yes. The rapid expansion in the programmes the global funds financed created a great many new jobs for skilled health staff and higher salaries in their programme countries — either directly or as top-ups to government salaries. They attracted a significant share of the best staff from elsewhere in the sector (Biesma *et al.* 2009). Whether the rest of the health sector would have been better off in the absence of global fund support, though, depends on the extent to which: that funding was additional; there was direct funding for the rest of the sector (as recently in the case of funding by GFATM and GAVI for health systems); there were positive spillovers (externalities) on the sector as a whole and governments have found ways to restore partial fungibility — itself determined by the importance of global funds in total financing for the sector as well on government ingenuity. A further complication comes from the varying (and often overstated) extent to which what is financed by global funds is for "global public goods"; to the extent that benefits are global rather than national, donors would be justified in an earmarking that reflected those global benefits. These same points apply to distortions between sectors. Understandably, this complexity makes empirical analysis of distortions difficult.[2]

Paris declaration

Despite its overall highly positive assessment, the evaluation of the Paris Declaration prepared for the Accra conference made it clear that there were also issues to address (Wood *et al.* 2008). One was the need for greater emphasis on civil society and parliaments as part of "country ownership" and for not equating country ownership simply with whatever finance ministries say even in countries with weak governance and commitment to development. There were also questions about the high transaction costs of harmonisation to both developing countries and donors, whether overall or at the sectoral or project levels. Some of

---

[2] Problems of distortion of priorities and of obliging countries to respond to global fund processes have been amply documented at the field level in evaluations and reviews, initially in a path-breaking cross-country study by McKinsey commissioned by the Gates Foundation in 2005 (McKinseyand Company 2005). Also, for a debate on distortions versus positive spillover effects see Garret(2007) and Farmer and Garrett (2007).

these high costs were recognised as a necessary initial investment to be recouped in future higher development impact and lower costs. The recognised need to reduce those costs lies behind the emphasis, particularly among European donors, on "division of labour," primarily through reducing the number of donors in each sector to reduce donor fragmentation (OECD 2009). The evaluation, like the "2008 Survey on Monitoring of the Paris Declaration," also pointed to the lack of progress on mutual accountability. There is also concern in some countries about the principle of "harmonisation" being carried so far that developing countries are faced with "ganging up" from a unified donor monopoly supplier. The monitoring survey confirms strongly that the problem remains one of more fragmentation and, for example, inability to pool funds, than of "excessive" progress on harmonisation.

Some development agency staff — on occasion even our own — forget that Paris-Accra deals essentially only with process and not with the substance of what needs to be done. They at times focus so heavily on a literalist view of country ownership and alignment that important issues such as quality, voice of civil society or severe risk of corruption are neglected. They seem to forget that modalities, dialogue and allocations should be adapted to the needs and institutional capacities of individual developing countries and that the objective is not better processes *per se* but better sustainable development outcomes. We should be wary of taking to an extreme any reasonable approach, whether the Paris-Accra or global fund models or the MDGs.

The key challenge we face is how to bring closer together the approaches of Paris-Accra and of global funds — in a way that draws the best lessons from each. In doing so, we need to see them, like aid in general, as only a small part of the complex socio-economic and political process that determines development outcomes. There is growing, if still far from universal, recognition that the two approaches are not "good versus evil" but can even be complementary. The issue is partly how and in what dosages they should be applied, at the country and global levels, and partly how they can enrich each other. An example is how to achieve better results over time by combining the focus of global funds on measurable (and so essentially short term) results with the focus of Paris-Accra on longer-term systems and capacity. In the past several years, a number of important steps have been taken, discussed below, to bring greater consistency between the two approaches. There is still a long way to go. We shall start by looking at what donors, especially ourselves, need to do, and then focus on the global funds themselves.

Box 1 — Selected lessons from global funds

Focus on results

All donors are giving increased priority to managing for results. Global funds have, to varying extents, been at the vanguard of this effort. There is now need for joint work on linking disbursements more directly to results, on moving further along the results chain and on difficult issues like "moving from attribution to contribution" and balancing short-run results against the longer-run results that come from strengthening systems and capacity.

A broader concept of "ownership"

We have a good deal to learn from the positive experience of GAVI and GFATM in integrating CSOs and the private sector into governance structures. The main advantage is greater inclusiveness of ownership and voice, leading to better results as well as to broader ownership. The main disadvantages are increased cost, difficulty in bringing about change, more complex governance decisionmaking and conflicts of interest regarding grants. Our dialogue with governments of developing countries should, in keeping with the AAA, encourage greater "voice" for civil society and parliaments as well.

A hybrid country-based and global model

The experience of global funds suggests that good results can be obtained by a hybrid model that combines support of country strategies with global knowledge and objective external validation. It is important that any such validation be done early enough to influence programme design rather than result in unexpected last-minute turn-downs; it is also important that the validation system draws on substantial country knowledge rather than just on technocratic criteria or, worse yet, simply on the proficiency with which someone, too often a consultant, has drafted the proposal.

Transparency

Here GFATM in particular has set a high standard for transparency in posting on its website material on its operations as well as on the deliberations of its board. GFATM and GAVI have only recently recognised, though, the need for the same transparency at the country level, including proactively informing Finance Ministries of support they are providing.

II. Turning the Spotlight on Ourselves and Other Donors

Looking objectively at our own incentives

Understanding the incentive structures — in practice and not just on paper — of major stakeholders is crucial to encouraging changed behaviour, including our own. Our own house is more divided than we like to think. We are pushed by political pressures — i.e. incentives to act — from our ministers and from CSOs, including the media, to support global funds even though our official policy strongly supports the Paris-Accra approach. Our sectoral staff are often supporters of expanding the number and size of global funds in an effort to get earmarked resources for their (sub)sector(s). A well-informed commentator, Owen Barder, puts it more strongly: "Within many aid agencies there is a permanent state of low intensity bureaucratic warfare for resources, sucking up the time and attention of staff as they fight to defend and expand funding for the causes they work on.They deliberately stoke up pressure in private alliances with CSOs — many of whom they fund — to raise the political stakes through conferences, international declarations and publications with the aim of committing funders to spend a larger share of aid resources on their issue. Territory is captured and held by way of international commitments in summit communiqués" (Barder 2009). Barder goes on to say: "…we should, as a development community, heap scorn and opprobrium on anyone caught advocating for more resources in their sector." This goes too far. Competition in ideas, including advocacy for them, can help advance development. However, he is right in calling for "social norms" to govern this donor- and foundation-funded globalised "market." Moreover, we should see that our internal policies and incentives reflect sensible social norms to govern that market.

Our policy and field staff are most worried about the proliferation and size of funding of global funds, a concern consistent with our policy statements. We have yet to set clear accountability guidelines for our country-based staff in working constructively with global funds, helping them and, at the same time, pushing them to do the most they can within their own rules to increase their effectiveness. Some policy staff, though, are tiring of being the "butter in the sandwich" between political leaders and CSOs and so are tempted to subscribe to the idea that "funds have to be raised vertically, but should be spent horizontally." This "diagonal approach" is in part a necessity for both political and fund-raising reasons, but also a risky one. Those who are most closely involved with global funds are sincerely and deeply committed to their objectives and internal incentive systems. This applies to their staff and, if anything, more strongly to CSOs who sit on their boards or who otherwise support them.

When funding is growing rapidly, there may appear to be enough slack for both vertical and horizontal objectives. Even then, it seems odd for donor countries to be saying implicitly to developing countries: "We are politically unable to provide aid in the highly fungible and aligned manner called for in Paris-Accra. We hope that you have the capacity and institutional structure to do what we have been unable to do and set this right. In other words, do as we say rather than as we do. However, we have to warn you that we will have to criticise your efforts to increase the inter- and intra-sectorial fungibility of our funding, sometimes even calling this a diversion of funding."

When growth in funding slows relative to growing needs to meet core mandates, the consequences are likely to be more severe, and the result could well be that funding intended to be spent horizontally ends up being spent more and more vertically. We have an insufficient idea of the net additionality that global funds bring to our and other-donor overall aid levels. We know that even in countries like ours that have commitments to reaching given GDP targets, delivering on those commitments over time is far from assured. Moreover, we can see the political and popular push behind global funds — particularly, for example, when they are identified as key development initiatives of a G8 presidency. What is more diffuse and harder to see is what the impact is on direct mobilisation of horizontal funding, including for future replenishments of IDA and concessional loan windows of regional banks. *Thus, if we are to be in-part diagonalists, let us be discerning diagonalists, going in with our eyes open and recognising that added political support does not at all mean full additionality.*

We must engage our political leadership in a strategic process in which they take on some ownership. If not, we are likely to be condemned to continue making decisions one by one, responding to the political attractiveness of the proposal at hand. The task is difficult, but it is important that we find a way to get through to our ministers more convincingly. They, not we, make the political decisions. We hope that as the G8 gives way to the G20 and its more diverse membership, there will be greater appreciation for the importance of working together to promote sustainable growth and human development — a strong argument for greater attention to country-focussed "horizontal" programmes. There is a risk to be resisted, though, of decreased focus on problems of low-income countries.

Paris-accra principles — donor challenges

Like other donors, our own behaviour, reflecting our own incentives, has been far from a model of consistency. Others, speaking less diplomatically, have talked of donor schizophrenia about global funds.

Box 2 — How are we doing on responding to Accra?

Donor responses to the recommendations of the Accra Roundtable on Aid Architecture (RT) and the AAA OECD (2008Ab).

- *"Think twice" before establishing new funds, applying a clear test of value added (RT):* Our record is not good. The AAA has been followed by a profusion of new funds, with emphasis moving from health to climate change and now to food security and agriculture. We badly need to find politically viable processes for "thinking twice."

- *As new global challenges emerge, donors will ensure that existing channels for aid delivery are used and, if necessary, strengthened before creating separate new channels that risk further fragmentation and complicate co-ordination at country level.* Here our record is much better and we should strive to keep it that way. New funds post-Accra are thus far being implemented through existing institutions.
- *Consider carefully the balance between funding for targeted global initiatives and funding for aid institutions with a broader remit, able to accommodate local priorities across the board.* Global health funds have accounted for three-quarters of the total increase in health funding, not a good sign of this balance. With the profusion of global funds for the environment, there is a strong danger of repeating the same pattern. *Yet in the spirit of Paris-Accra, we should be increasing the share of multilateral aid. While Paris-Accra does not explicitly call for more multilateral aid, that is the logical implication of its focus on harmonisation, including minimising fragmentation and transaction costs. (Why not do harmonisation on a "wholesale" basis rather than "retail" by country and sector?) We should also be increasing the share of "horizontal" aid, where developing countries get to decide their own sectoral priorities, relative to "vertical" aid, of which global funds are the biggest part. As part of our decisionmaking, we should invest more, with other donors, to bring evidence to bear on the contentious question of when and to what extent funding for global funds is additional.*
- *Ensure consistency between their overall commitment to the principles of aid effectiveness and the line that their representatives take in the Boards of Global Program Funds.* The positions taken on global fund boards by our representatives are too often not consistent with those taken by our representatives elsewhere, such as at the MDBs. We need to be more consistent.

Our challenge is to sharpen our strategy on multilateral aid, including support of global funds, so that it provides clear guidance on the major policy choices we face; to get that strategy accepted government wide and, most difficult, to move from an agreed piece of paper to consistent implementation. Given that we are talking about collective action to fund global institutions and that all donors face a mix of policy and politics, we should — in the spirit of Paris-Accra — work closely with other donors. We could start with the "like minded group" of more progressive donors but also be working DAC wide, encouraging the DAC in its recent efforts to involve emerging donors and foundations as well. *We should set ourselves the challenge of being a major catalyst for working effectively at the highest levels with other donors and private foundations on the range of policy issues regarding the role and effectiveness of global funds.* Here at home, we should involve our ministers and parliamentarians, as well as CSOs — especially those not limited to specific sectoral issues — in our strategy; this will bring in their ideas and help build the needed political support.

III. GFATM and GAVI: Incentives and Progress to Date

Understanding the incentives of other key stakeholders

As in our own agency, we need to understand the funds' incentive structures if we and other donors want to have a significant impact on increasing their effectiveness. The issue is not "good guys" and "bad guys." Rather, we need to take greater account of what drives behaviour of global funds and their key stakeholders (as described below), including the axiom in public administration that "where you stand depends on where you sit" (Miles' law). People are usually behaving rationally according to their incentive and accountability systems — the real, *de facto* ones more than those implicit in announced policies.

Foundations

The Gates Foundation has been by far the lead foundation in global funds (Financing Global Health 2010). The incentive system of the Gates

Foundation emphasises measurable results, evidence, evaluation and, importantly, meeting disbursement objectives. While Gates is supportive of the work of the World Bank and to some extent other multilateral organisations in health, it wants the global health funds it supports to guard their independence and different way of doing things. Its focus on global funds has meant some ambivalence in practice about relative priority given to Paris-Accra principles. *It is important for us and other bilateral donors to continue to reach out to Gates and other major foundations on aid effectiveness issues*(see Chapter 11 for further analysis).

Private sector

GFATM and GAVI, even more so, have broken new ground in partnerships with the private sector. These partnerships are vital for research and production of pharmaceutical products important for developing countries, as well as for raising funds, through innovative financing. GAVI and GFATM are, however, well aware that in some cases there are tensions between social objectives and obligations to shareholders for profit maximisation (see Chapter 12).

Developing country governments

Developing country governments are represented on the boards of global programmes, but they have had little role in determining how the funds were set up or the rules by which they function. It is hard for most governments not to seek such funds, even though they might much prefer unearmarked assistance.

A World Bank study for Accra in 2008 (World Bank 2008a) found that the extent of concern about distortion in country programmes caused by earmarked funds depended largely on two things: how important such funding was as a share of the country's overall health budget, itself determined substantially by the country's income level, and the general capacity of the country to manage donors. While this, too, is influenced by income level, countries like Ethiopia, Rwanda and Vietnam show that poor countries can effectively manage donors. *To further strengthen the hand of governments, we should encourage more consistent involvement with global funds of finance ministries and other central coordinating agencies of government.More generally, let us not underestimate the importance of the issues discussed here for aid-dependent countries with weak capacity. However, by the same token, let us not exaggerate their importance in countries where global funds account for a relatively small share of relevant overall public financing and where capacity to manage donors — and global funds — is high.*

Civil society

Understandably, CSOs on the boards of global funds, or otherwise active in promoting them, tend to be those with a similar focus.[3] They tend to be key supporters of increased funding for their issues and "their" global funds, and also tend to argue forcefully for the role of CSOs in country programmes. They were influential in getting the GFATM Board to put through its "dual-track" approach of encouraging separate grants to government and CSOs — rather than encouraging joint proposals that would provide incentives for governments and CSOs to work more closely together. However, CSOs increasingly recognise the need to deal with broader health issues. The Roundtable on Civil Society in Accra reflected an increased recognition by CSOs of the importance of government programmes and of the need for CSOs to hold themselves, as well as others, accountable.[4] Some major CSOs with a broad (rather than sector-specific) focus on poverty-reduction have become strong advocates of Paris-Accra. *We, like other donors, can play an important role in informal dialogue with CSOs, particularly those based in their own countries, on issues of aid effectiveness* (see Chapter 13).

[3] The GFATM Board (20 members) has representatives from the communities suffering from the diseases as well as a representative from both a developing and a developed country NGO. The GAVI Board has 27 members, one of whom is a developing country NGO, but it also has nine "unaffiliated" persons from a wide variety of backgrounds.

[4] The summary of the Roundtable on civil society took account of "the importance of CSO accountability as a key topic that CSO partnerships could and should address," although this was not a major theme of the Roundtable (OECD 2009).

The World Bank

Multilateral incentives differ by institution. While our multilateral strategy should cover all major multilaterals, including those of the United Nations as well as the regional development banks, the focus here is on the World Bank, by far the largest source of multilateral "horizontal" aid.

The World Bank places strong emphasis on overall country development plans, or Poverty Reduction Strategies in the case of the poorest countries eligible for highly concessional credits from the World Bank's International Development Association (IDA), so its field and central policy and fund-raising staffs tend to have sharply negative views on (sub)sectoral earmarking. Where there is such earmarking, the World Bank much prefers that it take the form of otherwise completely fungible add-ons to IDA. At the same time, the World Bank is in aggregate by far the biggest implementer (and even more so financial trustee) of such earmarked "trust funds." This is partly because bilateral donors have confidence in the World Bank and partly because World Bank sectoral-staff have been highly entrepreneurial in encouraging and raising trust funds.

The World Bank incentive structure includes a sharp focus on meeting targets for lending and other "deliverables." So, like those in global funds, World Bank staff are concerned about the opportunity cost of time spent working with other donors, including global funds (whose staff are generally not present on the ground during World Bank missions). World Bank incentives also include a heightened risk aversion in response to strong pressure from its Board and President for strict observance of its "fiduciary" (procurement and public financial management) and safeguard (environment and resettlement) policies. This has occurred in part due to reactions to some much-discussed cases of corruption in World Bank-financed projects (World Bank 2008b).

The combination of the concerns about opportunity costs and World Bank policies reduces incentives for the World Bank to focus on sector-wide programmes, even though such programmes are its comparative advantage. There are clear implications for our close dialogue with the World Bank at various levels, but by no means limited to our representation on its board. We share the World Bank's concern about corruption.

However,we should urge it — and fellow Board members — to put more emphasis on strengthening country systems relative to that put on following World Bank rules. The World Bank's current stance is quite a change from the period leading up to the Paris Declaration when it was at the forefront of urging recalcitrant donors to change. We should also urge the World Bank to give more emphasis to working with global funds and other donors — and to be less risk averse — even if it means higher costs or, because of multiple donors, a somewhat higher chance of difficulties in implementation. We should also encourage our bilateral partners to press the Bank on these matters as well. (For a specific current area of concern see the discussion of health systems below.)

Global funds

Those of us who have worked with global fund staff know that they are generally highly capable, stretched and hard-working. Their management, staff and governance structures are fully committed to carrying out their mandates, in part because they have been selected on the basis of past experience and commitment to those mandates. They face strong pressures (incentives) to commit, and then to disburse, with relatively few staff (though increasing fast[5]) and with none on the ground. Time spent on harmonisation, or on country visits to attend major donor meetings with government, come at the expense of time spent on commitments and disbursements and monitoring their rapidly growing portfolios. These pressures suggest we should show some sympathy for their requests for further increases in staff — rather than seeing this as a betrayal of their original design. This implies recognition by our staff on the ground of the constraints that staff of global funds face.

It does not, however, mean accepting the status quo. We need to recognise that their internal incentives, as well as Miles' law, drive global funds to become strong advocates for their mandates. We need also to recognise that mission creep is a common issue for global funds as it is for other organisations. So is staff creep. Sorting out well-justified need for

---

[5] The Global Fund staff, originally intended to be no more than an unrealistic 75, now totals just over 600 (Global Fund 2009b).

more staff from that related to mission creep or territorial imperative requires a well-informed strategic view. We should be proactive in encouraging and assisting change, and we should pursue this encouragement and support consistently — including on governing boards and their committees, and in replenishments, as well as at the country level. To take the example of replenishments, the report of the Chair of the mid-term review of GFATM's second replenishment in March, 2009, shows clearly their relevance for issues of aid effectiveness — in that case alignment, harmonisation, the role of CCMs and sustainability (Global Fund 2009c).

Progress of GFATM and GAVI in applying Paris-Accra principles at the country level

Both GFATM and GAVI have made important progress in their programmes to respond to Paris-Accra principles. They are both active participants in the International Health Partnership (IHP+), as well as in the development of the "common platform for joint health systems strengthening funding and programming." Both are monitoring Paris indicators. Their overall, if gradual, positive trend has resulted from a variety of factors reflecting increasing knowledge and changes in incentives. The knowledge has been important, as increasing experience at the country level and in-depth evaluations of the major global funds have provided clear evidence of where there is need for change — particularly on alignment to country priorities and systems. In response to these, and to what both partner countries and donor staff see on the ground, they have put increasing pressure on global funds to adapt. There has also been increasing "ownership" of the need for change within the global funds, facilitated by champions of change and increasingly supported by top management. That internal ownership has been reinforced by participation of global funds in informal peer groups linked to the WP-EFF. Given the diversity of governing boards, there has not surprisingly been mixed reaction to this effort to erode differences between the externally determined sharp focus of the global fund model and the Paris-Accra principles. However, the direction of change, if at times slow and hesitant, is clear and should be strongly encouraged.

GAVI has implemented the first International Finance Facility for Immunisation (IFFIm), which provided innovative financing to front-load the scale-up of immunisation. It is playing a lead role in the expansion of IFFIm, which will include health services. GAVI has a novel programme for performance-based financing for the take-up of new vaccines that disburses according to the annual increase in the number of vaccinations achieved (GAVI 2009). Its policy is to move towards greater use of country systems, including shifting from its fixed annual date for proposals to a system more aligned to country budget cycles.

GFATM has carried out a series of policy changes to take a more programmatic approach. These include support for national strategies for the diseases it covers, rather than just support for specific project proposals; moving towards consolidation of existing grants into a single stream, at least for each disease and a liberalised and clarified policy on financing of health worker salaries (mitigating salary differentials and encouraging the hiring of needed staff in the programmes they support).

PEPFAR has also made recent progress on aid effectiveness, building on its good record in moving towards its performance targets. In reauthorising the programme in 2008, the U.S. Congress gave PEPFAR a new, much more unfettered mandate (and increased funding) which *inter alia* emphasises "improving harmonization of United States efforts with national strategies of partner governments and other public and private entities" (PEPFAR 2008). Partly as a result, PEPFAR has demonstrated increasing recognition of the importance of broader issues of aid effectiveness, including partnership agreements with countries, more attention to health systems and closer collaboration with the Global Fund and other donors (see Chapter 10 for a fuller analysis of PEPFAR).

The internal change process was facilitated by participation of global funds in two related informal peer groups explicitly focussed on adaptation to Paris-Accra principles. One, the Global Programmes Learning Group, has played a modest but useful role in the reform process. It is a multisectoral forum, convened by GFATM, for global funds — GFATM, GAVI, Fast Track Initiative (FTI) and Global Environment Facility (GEF) — and other global programmes (including the Consultative Group on International Agricultural Research and the Cities Alliance), to compare experience among peers in implementing Paris-Accra. PEPFAR also joined in 2009. As a "learning" group, its intent is not to bring about major policy change, which depends on the accountability structure of each participating global programme. Rather, it works through a peer process to spread good practice and encourage increased commitment to policy change. The Learning Group is closely linked to the DAC WP-EFF, and GFATM represents it on the WP-EFF Steering Committee. To strengthen this link, the WP-EFF secretariat also participates in the Learning Group.

Global health programmes have also participated in a related effort, also linked to the WP-EFF, "health as a tracer sector." This group, in which GAVI and the Global Fund participated with WHO and the World Bank and others, is interested in seeing how the principles of Paris-Accra could be applied at a sectoral level. Thus, it has looked at the intersection of the specific mandates of global funds and of the broader needs of the health sector, identifying areas for change and for common effort.

Both these groups played an active role in Roundtables in Accra. Their main objectives were contributing to change among the global funds themselves as well as informing others of progress made and issues faced.

IV. Selected Current Issues

There remain a range of issues on which more attention is needed, of which several are discussed below. There are others as well, including use of country systems, encouraging more collaboration between governments and CSOs and moving further along the results chain to outcomes. In keeping with the Paris-Accra lessons, the most effective changes are likely to come from encouraging ownership of the change process within the global funds, including support to champions of reform in management, staffs and on boards.

Health Systems[6]

There is broad agreement that strengthening of health systems poses a major challenge for the "architecture" of aid to health. The report of

[6] The term health system refers here to the overall functioning of the health sector. It is sometimes used more narrowly to mean the "glue" or central services that hold disease-specific programmes together. And it is sometimes used more broadly to refer to everything that affects health status, from water and sanitation to girls' education. The latter concept is useful in adding a health dimension to the setting of intersectoral priorities but is so ambitious that it is less useful in determining priorities within the health sector.

Working Group 1 of the High Level Task Force on Innovative International Financing for Health Systems put it powerfully:

"The problems of fragmentation, unpredictability and targeting of development assistance to the delivery of specific technologies have become so visible that they have resulted in a universal call for a coordinated effort to support the country health systems that all disease and programme-specific efforts must ultimately rely on" (High Level Task Force 2009a:12).

The "Shakow report" (Shakow 2006) recommended in 2006 a clear delineation between the World Bank and GFATM (and global health funds in general) according to their respective comparative advantages. This was in response to the financing by GFATM (and GAVI) of health systems, but with lack of clarity on how much or for what. There was broad agreement that the World Bank should take a leadership role in strengthening health systems, working closely with WHO, the global funds and others.

The World Bank, however, faced a number of obstacles in assuming the leadership role on health systems one might have expected from its cross-sectoral comparative advantage. It had an initial slow start, now being redressed, in implementing its 2007 health strategy to focus on health systems. World Bank leadership of pooled funding for health systems has been made more difficult because of the complexity of World Bank fiduciary policies, which GFATM and GAVI — as well as bilateral donors — have been reluctant to follow. In addition, GFATM and GAVI operate in countries where either the World Bank does not lend or its borrowers, which determine the intersectoral use of IDA or IBRD resources in consultation with the Bank, have not requested support for health. GFATM and GAVI have increasingly recognised the need — in order to avoid distortions in priorities and to have the supporting services they need to achieve their objectives — for support of strengthened health systems. The rapid increase in their resources until 2009 made funding of health systems more feasible.

To help overcome problems caused by the large numbers of players in the health sector, we and others encouraged the creation of the IHP+. It aims to accelerate scaling-up of support for health in a manner consistent with the Paris Declaration by getting partners to work more closely together. The IHP+ led in 2009 to the High Level Task Force on Innovative International Financing, which has launched IFFIm2 and made recommendations for expansion of innovative financing (High Level Task Force 2009b:8). It has also led to the development of a "common platform" to provide a "common framework for proposal, approval and implementation processes for joint HSS programming and funding" from the World Bank, GAVI and GFATM (World Bank 2009a,b).

We should continue to strongly support this effort, including encouraging flexibility from boards and managements on all sides, recognising the major differences in their business models. This flexibility should permit pooled financing where the developing country so requests. We should urge the IHP+ process to give priority to evidence-based cost-effectiveness (in terms of life years or DALYs saved), as we should in our own allocations.

Applying this criterion can lead to some surprising results. Health systems would go beyond communicable diseases to include support for country nutrition strategies, with a focus on children under two and on micronutrients; they would include tobacco control as well, with a focus on encouraging increases in tobacco taxes, which both decrease its consumption and generate substantial revenues for scaling up health systems. However, we cannot forget that we already knew that some costly treatments, particularly antiretroviral therapy (ART), did not rank high on cost per DALY when we committed to support them. In planning ahead for the "common platform" and for support for health systems, we should keep in mind that when funding gets tight, as is likely, the share of GAVI and GFATM funding for health systems risks declining sharply. This is a major reason for caution on "raising money vertically to spend it horizontally"(see Chapter 5 for further analysis on health systems).

Sustainability

As the size and impact of GFATM and GAVI, and PEPFAR, funding grow, it becomes increasingly important to address issues of longer-term sustainability. Again, this is an issue we helped to create in the case of GFATM and GAVI, since we recognised the "moral mortgage" involved. Much of the solution to the problem of these ever-larger costs over the medium term must come from increased domestic resource mobilisation. However, this alone will not suffice, except in middle-income countries. It is increasingly uncertain whether these global funds, despite their strong public support and the moral obligation involved, will continue to see rapid increases in funding, particularly as donors face the need to reduce budget deficits. In addition, as funding for them increases, there will be increasing issues of distortions of staff and funding in the rest of the health sector, unless the growth primarily takes the form of support for health systems.

Sustainability is not simply a problem for these institutions. It is one also for the funders who set them up and gave them their funding and ambitious mandates. There is a need for in-depth analysis of likely growth in financing needs, net of domestic resources, and for options for meeting the gap. The need for sustainability reinforces the need to match up long-term commitments to long-term financing, underlining the importance of the work of the High Level Task Force on Innovative International Financing of Health Systems.

Allocations

As the size of GFATM and GAVI financing grows, it becomes increasingly important that they — like other global funds — look at priorities for the highest-impact use of funds across programmes and countries. For GFATM, there are choices among and within (e.g. prevention vs. treatment) its three diseases. For GAVI, there are choices between development and greater use of increasingly expensive vaccines. For both, there is the share going to health systems. Like other global funds, both also face questions of whether their financing should be limited to low-income countries. GFATM has adopted a constructive policy of continuing its support but requiring offsetting contributions from relatively better-off countries.

This then leads to the question of how the global funds should allocate their monies among eligible countries. According to a GEF evaluation, its "resource allocation framework" showed that advance indications to countries of likely allocation envelopes increased country ownership (GEF 2009). It has been relatively easy for GAVI to estimate rough funding levels based on needs across countries, since it provides a largely standardised set of products and services (except in the case of health systems). This becomes harder as funding growth slows and demand shifts in part to more expensive vaccines.

Country allocations are more difficult to determine in the case of GFATM because a given country's request could vary widely, depending in part on the level of programme ambition or on its (or its consultant's) educated guess of the maximum GFATM would be likely to provide. There has been reluctance in the case of GFATM, as in the case of the FTI in Education, to use any cross-country guidelines for allocations. For both, the reluctance comes from a desire to respond to country proposals and because donors had undertaken in principle to let no sound programme go unfunded, although with no means of ensuring that this funding would be available, and if so additional. Indeed, accepting a consistent approach for allocating a given amount of money can be seen as weakening or giving up on that open-ended donor undertaking. Evidence suggests, though, that in the absence of explicit guidelines, the result is a substantial bias by country size, for example, with much higher per capita allocations for less populous countries, or inconsistent treatment of the balance between need and expected cost-effectiveness (Beynon 2003). In addition, indicative country envelopes increase predictability, as called for in the AAA. The FTI is now in the process of installing a system of normative but flexible indicative country envelopes that addresses these issues. It adapts the GEF framework to education and provides increased support to "donor orphans" relative to that of "donor darlings."

We should urge both GFATM and GAVI to consider an approach of indicative country envelopes. That approach could include a policy on financing of programmes in middle- and upper-income countries, up to full cost recovery in some cases. This permits these countries to benefit from the encouragement of improved programmes that can come through global funds without significantly reducing funding available for lower-income countries. Russia has had such an arrangement of full cost recovery with GFATM. The approach could also include reserving some share of funding, aimed at innovation and learning rather than on sustainability of programmes, where a pure competitive model across countries would still apply. (For a more extensive discussion of this topic see Isenman *et al.*, 2010.)

GFATM's country co-ordinating mechanisms

There are strongly held views, pro and con, on the role of CCMs, country co-ordinating mechanisms set up at the behest of GFATM. This is part of a broader debate on issues of country ownership involving the role of external technical assistance in preparing proposals, technical review panels lacking direct country knowledge and the use of Local Funding Agents (Global Fund 2009a). CCMs do not appear to be as well suited as government-led co-ordination mechanisms if they are to be the GFATM counterpart in support of health systems or of national strategies for single diseases. Such government-led mechanisms are explicitly called for in UNAIDS "Three Ones"[7] and implicitly in Paris-Accra. While CCMs set a standard for inclusiveness, they also raise problems of oversight because some of their grants go to their own members, inevitably so since these members represent the leading groups in the fight against its three diseases. At a minimum, we should support GFATM's efforts to encourage mergers of CCMs with existing national coordination mechanisms in a manner that preserves more voice for civil society than is often the case in those mechanisms.

Mutual accountability

Participation in mutual accountability mechanisms at country level — as called for explicitly in the AAA — is a difficult one for global funds, since by design they do not have local staff. While GAVI can draw on help from UNICEF and WHO staff on the ground, these intermediaries have difficulty in speaking to governments on their behalf or in being held accountable for delays or other problems in implementation. Neither CCMs nor Local Fund Agents (LFAs) can play this role on behalf of GFATM. Yet as GAVI and GFATM become more deeply involved in financing health systems, it becomes more important that they participate

[7] The Three Ones are "one agreed framework that provides the basis for coordinating the work of all partners; one national coordinating authority, with a broad multisectoral mandate and one agreed national monitoring and evaluation system (http://data.unaids.org/UNA-docs/Three-Ones_KeyPrinciples_en.pdf).

in key meetings on coordination and mutual accountability between government and health donors. We should also urge all global funds to participate in international initiatives for increased transparency of information regarding current and — to the extent that there are indicative country envelopes — future financing.

V. Conclusion

The conclusion of this report is clear. Global funds are an important, legitimate and growing part of our assistance portfolio. They have strengths and weaknesses — weaknesses that are in part the unintended consequences of our own decisions. We need to help them increase their effectiveness. We need also to strike a better balance between global funds and "horizontal" assistance, and between bilateral and multilateral aid, if we are to increase the impact of our development portfolio as a whole. To do so, we will need to develop and implement, with the involvement of our political authorities, a clearer strategy that takes account of the incentives facing key stakeholders.

> Chapter 5 further assesses the issues of health systems. Chapter 3 provides a country perspective of many of the issues in this chapter. Chapter 7 further develops the themes of negotiating aid effectiveness into new partnerships.

References

Accra Agenda for Action (2008) 3rd High Level Forum on Aid Effectiveness, Accra, Ghana. Accessible at www.oecd.org.

Barder O (2009) "The Lethal Effects of Development Advocacy," November, http://www.owen.org/blog/2717.

Beynon J (2003) *Poverty-Efficient Aid Allocations, Collier-Dollar Revisited*, ESAU Working Paper 2, Overseas Development Institute, November 2003, http://www.odi.org.uk/resources/download/1861.pdf.

Biesma RG, Brugha R, Harmer A, Walsh A, Spicer N, Walt G (2009) "The Effects of Global Health Initiatives on Country Health Systems: A Review of Evidence from HIV/AIDS Control," *Health Policy and Planning*, 24(4):239–52.

Climate Fund Update (2011) http://www.climatefundsupdate.org/listing.

Education for All Fast Track Initiative (2009)*Mid-Term Evaluation*, http://wwwcambed.com/fasttrackinitiative/.

Farmer P, Garrett L (2007) "From 'Marvelous Momentum' to Health Care for All: Success Is Possible With the Right Programs," Foreign Affairs, March/April, http://www.foreignaffairs.com/articles/62458/paul-farmer-and-laurie-garrett/from-marvelous-momentum-to-health-care-for-all-success-is-possib.

Financing Global Health (2010) Financing Global Health 2010: Development Assistance and Country Spending in Economic Uncertainty, Institute for Health Metrics and Evaluation, 2010, http://www.healthmetricsandevaluation.org/publications/policy-report/financing-global-health-2010-de

Garrett A (2007) "The Challenge of Global Health," Foreign Affairs, January/February, http://www.foreignaffairs.com/articles/62268/laurie-garrett/the-challenge-of-global-health.

GAVI Alliance (2000–2005) *Evaluation of the GAVI Phase 1 Performance,* Abt Associates, Inc., Cambridge, MA, http://www.gavialliance.org/resources/GAVI_Phase1_Report_FINAL_to_SC_Oct21.pdf.

——— (2008) Strengthening Technical Support, Prepared by McKinsey and Co., http://www.gavialliance.org/resources/20090116_GAVI_Technical_Support_Report_Final.pdf.

——— (2009) Final Summary Report of GAVI Board Meeting, 2/3 June 2009, http://www.gavialliance.org/resources/Jun09_FINAL_Summary_Report_pdf_version.pdf.

———, *Evaluation of the First Five Years of GAVI Immunization Services Support Funding*, Abt Associates Inc, Cambridge, MA, http://www.gavialliance.org/resources/GAVI_Consolidated_Report_FINAL_to_SC_Sep28.pdf.

——— (2009) *Secretariat Response, Phase I Evaluation*, http://www.gavialliance.org/resources/6._gavi_phase_1_evaluation___secretariat_response.pdf.

Global Environment Facility (2009) "Midterm Review of the GEF Resource Allocation Framework," http://www.thegef.org/uploadedFiles/Evaluation_Office/RAF/raf%208x11%20-%20english.pdf.

——— (2009) "Midterm Review of the GEF Resource Allocation Framework," www.thegef.org/gef/sites/thegef.org/files/documents/GEFME-C34.2-RAF_MTR.pdf.

Global Fund (2009a) *The Five-Year Evaluation of the Global Fund to Fight AIDS, Tuberculosis and Malaria, Synthesis of Study Areas 1, 2 and 3*, Geneva, Submitted by Macro International Inc., March 2009, Geneva.

——— (2009b) Report of the Executive Director to the May 2009 GFATM Board Meeting, http://www.theglobalfund.org/documents/board/19/GF-B19–03_EDReport.pdf.

——— (2009c) Sven Sandstrom, Report of the Chair, The Global Fund's Second Replenishment (2008–2010), April 1, 2009, http://www.theglobalfund.org/documents/replenishment/caceres/Chair_Summary_Caceres_2009.pdf.

High Level Task Force on Innovative International Financing for Health Systems (2009a) Report of Working Group I, http://www.internationalhealthpartnership.net//CMS_files/documents/working_group_1_-_report_EN.pdf.

——— (2009b) Report of Working Group 2, "Raising and Channeling Funds," http://www.internationalhealthpartnership.net//CMS_files/documents/working_group_2_-_report_EN.pdf.

Isenman, Paul; Wathne, Cecilie and Baudienville, Geraldine: Global Funds: Allocation Strategies and Aid Effectiveness, Overseas Development Institute, July 2010.

McKinsey and Company (2005) "Global Health Partnerships: Assessing Health Consequences," for the Gates Foundation.

OECD (2005) The Paris Declaration, http://www.oecd.org/dataoecd/30/63/43911948.pdf.

——— (2008a) Accra Agenda for Action at http://www.oecd.org/dataoecd/58/16/41202012.pdf.

——— (2008b) High Level Forum on Aid Effectiveness, Roundtable 9 Summary Post-Accra, http://siteresources.worldbank.org/ACCRAEXT/Resources/4700790–1225142330310/RT9-AidArchitecture.pdf.

——— (2009) "International Good Practice Principles for Country-Led Division of Labour and Complementarity," DAC Working Party on Aid Effectiveness, March 2009, www.oecd.org.

PEPFAR (2008) Tom Lantos and Henry J. Hyde United States Global Leadership Against HIV/AIDS, Tuberculosis, and Malaria Reauthorization Act of 2008 H.R. 5501.

Shakow A (2006) *Global Fund-World Bank HIV/Aids Programs: Comparative Advantage Study*, January 19, prepared for the Global Fund and the World Bank.

UNAIDS Three Ones Key Principles, http://data.unaids.org/UNA-docs/ThreeOnes_KeyPrinciples_en.pdf.

WHO (2009) "An Assessment of Interactions Between Global Health Initiatives and Country Health Systems," *The Lancet* 173(9681):2137–69.

Wood B, Kabell D, Sagasti F, Muwanga N (2008) *Synthesis Report on the First Phase of the Evaluation of the Implementation of the Paris Declaration*, Copenhagen, July 2008, http://www.diis.dk/graphics/Subweb/paris_evaluation_web/files/pdf/eng/ENG-Report-chap1–5.pdf.

Wood B, Betts J, Etta F, Gayfer J, Kabell D, Ngwira N, Sagasti F, Samaranayake M (2011) The Evaluation of the Paris Declaration, Final Report, Danish Insitute for International Studies, Copenhagen, May 2011, http://www.oecd.org/dataoecd/4/56/48113888.pdf

World Bank (2008a) "Global Program Funds at Country Level: What have we learned?" World Bank Global Programs and Partnership Group, July 2008, "Global Programs and Country Linkages," http://siteresources.worldbank.org/CFPEXT/Resources/GPF_Synthesis_Paper_Final.pdf.

——— (2008b) "Government of India and World Bank Join Forces to Stamp out Corruption in Health Sector Projects," press release 11 January 2008, http://go.worldbank.org/YVLEFEQKZ0.

——— (2009a) "Principles Guiding Joint Programming and a Funding Platform for Health System Strengthening: Notes from the World Bank, GAVI, Global Fund and WHO Geneva Meeting, August 20–21, 2009," http://go.worldbank.org/IODHXHFOB0.

——— (2009b) "Notes from the World Bank, GAVI, Global Fund and WHO: Recent Progress Towards a Joint Programming and Funding Platform for Health System Strengthening, http://go.worldbank.org/IODHXHFOB0.

3

Managing Health Partnerships At Country Level

Hareya Fassil[1] *and Tedros Adhanom Ghebreyesus*[2]

"Where there is ownership, ownership leads to commitment. I cannot commit to something I do not own. You develop a commitment to results. Moreover, when we say ownership in Ethiopia, it goes all the way to the grassroots. The best ownership is when it is owned by the community. In the last five years, we have built over 14,000 health posts and trained 34,000 health extension workers — two per village. If there is ownership, there is scale. If there is no ownership, you will see fragments of things."

Tedros Adhanom Ghebreyesus (PhD)
Minister of Health, Federal Democratic Republic of Ethiopia, October, 2010

Summary

This chapter assesses health partnerships from a country perspective, with reflections and recommendations from the Minister of Health of Ethiopia. The chapter is organised into five sections. The first section provides background to health funding in Ethiopia, the increasing prominence of health as a development issue and the significant results achieved over the last decade. The second section reviews Ethiopia's tough journey over several

---

[1]Dr. Hareya Fassil is the International Affairs Advisor to the Minister of Health of Ethiopia.
[2] H.E. Dr.Tedros AdhanomGhebreyesus is the Minster of Health of the Federal Democratic Republic of Ethiopia and Board Chair of the Global Fund to Fight AIDS, TB and Malaria (July, 2009–May, 2011).

years in consolidating its public health sector and building effective country partnerships. Section three distils practical recommendations for other countries drawing on Ethiopia's experiences. The fourth section focuses on country ownership, viewed as the linchpin of the significant progress Ethiopia has made in building strong country partnerships. Four steps to asserting country ownership are elaborated from the Ethiopian perspective, making the case that the country is not simply one partner among many, but needs to lead the process of planning, implementation as well as resource mobilisation and allocation, while holding itself and partners accountable for results. Finally, the concluding section presents a candid dialogue with the Minister of Health on some tactics and principles that have helped Ethiopia to get the most from its health partners at country level.

1. Introduction: From Fragments to Cohesive Country Partnerships

Over the past decade, the global community has joined together like never before to improve health conditions in the developing world. Health has come to be regarded not just as an outcome of economic progress, but as a critical prerequisite to development. As such, health concerns and investments in the health sector have been assigned high priority on the global political agenda since the beginning of the new century. The centrality of health is well-reflected in the Millennium Development Goals (MDGs), with three of the MDGs focusing specifically on health (MDGs 4, 5 and 6: reducing child mortality by two-thirds; reducing maternal mortality by three-fourths and halting and beginning to reverse the spread of HIV/AIDS, malaria, TB and other diseases, respectively). In addition, health concerns transcend all the other MDGs.

This heightened commitment to health led to significantly more international funding for public health programmes. With the subsequent mobilisation of unprecedented levels of resources and the deployment of effective new technologies for combating the major health problems and pandemics, global health has rapidly evolved into a key foreign policy priority, particularly in developed countries. This has been accompanied by the proliferation of a wide array of actors involved in global health efforts. In addition to governmental efforts, the engagement of a multiplicity of bilateral and multilateral agencies and non-governmental organisations (NGOs), including faith-based, private-sector and civil society resource groups, has resulted in an increasingly complex global health architecture and international policy environment. The emergence of major global health initiatives, with different business models and objectives, has also had a significant influence on the rapidly changing global health landscape. These changes were even more acutely felt at country level. The challenge for countries has been on how best to negotiate this changing landscape to make the most of the great opportunities which come with it.

In the broader context of international development, a new paradigm of development cooperation was also evolving. Developed and developing countries had been deliberating on ways to improve the effectiveness of development aid as whole, with a view to better assisting countries to achieve the MDGs. The traditional "donor–recipient" relationship was giving way to a new paradigm of partnership. The 2005 Paris Declaration of Aid Effectiveness set out a comprehensive framework for improving the way donor and developing countries work together, based on principles of partnership. This sharpened recognition of the challenges countries were facing in managing the country-level impacts of the rapidly changing global health architecture. The Declaration's five core principles, "country ownership," "alignment," "harmonisation," "managing for results" and "mutual accountability," offered countries a blueprint for forging and managing effective partnerships among the myriad of development agencies operating at the country level. Over the ensuing years, these principles have come to constitute the watchwords of the evolving field of global health and have led to the formation of new international coalitions and initiatives aimed at simplifying the increasingly complex global architecture and translating it into manageable collaborative relationships at the country level.

Yet, different countries have navigated the increasing complexity of the global health architecture and the divergent agendas, strategies and *modus operandi* of various development partners with varying degrees of effectiveness. Ethiopia has been among those which have had a particularly positive experience in doing so, in large part because this heightened international momentum and commitment coincided with a renewed national resolve to act on health. Since 1997, the Government of Ethiopia has been implementing a comprehensive Health Sector Development Program (HSDP). This 20-year health sector strategic roadmap designed to be implemented through a series of five-year investment plans has evolved into a robust and comprehensive national planning instrument. The fact that the core priorities of the latter phase of the HSDP have been directly aligned with the health MDGs has also proven to be an advantage. In recent years, the country has registered considerable success in making the major global health initiatives and funding streams (including, the GAVI Alliance, the Global Fund to Fight AIDS, TB and Malaria; PEPFAR; PMI and the World Bank Multi-Sectoral HIV/AIDS Program and others) complement each other, both to achieve the country's disease-specific objectives and to build its health system. At the same time, Ethiopia has been effectively leveraging the support of other major bilateral and multilateral initiatives in complementary ways.

In this chapter, we have two aims. The first aim is to review the development of the country's public health sector over the past years, with a view to providing Ethiopia's perspective on the key ingredients for an effective country partnership for health development. This perspective places country ownership at the core but also argues for a "manageable diversity" of partners focused on results. The second aim is to distil key lessons and practical recommendations which other countries can apply in forging and strengthening effective country partnerships for advancing their efforts to build their health systems and improve health outcomes. These range from the use of "direct diplomacy" and "candid dialogue" with partners in asserting country ownership, as well as in leveraging "peer pressure" among partners in positive ways.

The remainder of this chapter is organised into four sections. The next section reviews Ethiopia's tough journey over several years in consolidating its public health sector and building effective country partnerships. The third section distils practical recommendations for other countries drawing on Ethiopia's experiences. The fourth section focuses on country ownership, viewed as the linchpin of the significant progress Ethiopia has made in building strong country partnerships. Four steps to asserting country ownership are elaborated from the Ethiopian perspective, making the case that the country is not simply one partner among many, but needs to lead the process of planning, implementation as well as resource mobilisation and allocation, while holding itself and partners accountable for results. The concluding section which is presented in the form of questions and answers with the Minister of Health illustrates some of these effective strategies and tactics that have been key to Ethiopia's success in asserting its country ownership and advancing harmonisation among its diverse partners.

2. Building Effective Country Partnerships: Ethiopia's Experience

Today, Ethiopia is often cited among countries where strong national leadership is leveraging the best from a range of health partnerships. How did this come about? A brief review of the evolution of Ethiopia's public health sector over the last couple of decades reveals three clear advantages that have had bearing on the country's capacities in navigating the increasingly complex health partnership environment: (a) the early establishment and gradual refinement of sound national health policy, planning and governance frameworks; (b) timely diagnosis of poor coordination and fragmentation of investments as the main constraints to progress in the health and allied sectors; and (c) clear demonstration of country commitment through increased domestic investments and the delivery of results. The following section reviews the tough journey Ethiopia has made over several years to build effective country partnerships for health, with a view to distilling some of the key ingredients that have enabled this progress.

A. A sound policy framework

The current overarching National Health Policy of Ethiopia was issued by the Government of Ethiopia in 1993 (see Box 1). This policy which still serves as the main framework of the public health sector's programmatic operations is grounded in the Government's commitment to democracy and decentralisation. It is also firmly focused on local realities and the most critical health problems faced by the country's largely rural population. As such, it places strong emphasis on priority interventions and strategies for meeting the pressing health needs — largely attributable to a host of preventable communicable diseases. Although developed almost two decades ago, the main pillars of this policy remain remarkably pertinent to local realities in Ethiopia today.

Box 1: Key Principles of the National Health Policy of Ethiopia (1993)

- Democratisation and decentralisation of the health system;
- Development of the preventive and promotive components of the health service;
- Expanding access to health care to the whole population;
- Promoting intersectoral collaboration, including engagement of NGOs and the private sector; and
- Promoting and enhancing national self-reliance in health development by mobilising and efficiently utilising internal and external resources.

Despite the soundness of this policy framework, its actual implementation took some time. The commitment and capacities needed to translate these policy directives into concrete transformative action had to be built at every level. Further, at the time this national health policy was articulated, Ethiopia was a country undergoing a major political transition. These were the early days of democratisation, when the country's main priority was the establishment and consolidation of democratic systems of governance and administration through a strong focus on decentralisation, which required considerable investments in institutional and capacity building at all levels. Decentralisation served as an important instrument for advancing the democratisation process, broadening participation in development and achieving the full realisation of the rights and powers of Ethiopia's diverse population.[3]

[3] The constitution of the Federal Democratic Republic of Ethiopia (FDRE), which was adopted in December 1994, assigned extensive power to Regional States in establishing their own governments and democracy. Under this new political system, Ethiopia was organized into nine ethnicallybased administrative regions and two chartered cities — Addis Ababa and Dire Dawa.

B. The tough road towards one national health plan

The HSDP, the health sector's 20-year strategic roadmap initiated by the Federal Ministry of Health in 1997, was originally envisaged as the main vehicle for implementing the overarching national health policy. However, it took some time before this vision was fully realised. The effectiveness of HSDP as a cohesive and inclusive national health planning and implementation instrument is something that developed over time.

Indeed, since its inception, the HSDP has evolved considerably, both in the process of its formulation and its scope, in response to developments both in the domestic political environment and in major external influences. The introduction of major global health initiatives, mobilisation of substantial resources and the proliferation of international health partners have all had an impact on the HSDP's development and its implementation over three phases. A brief review of this evolution can shed light on the process by which Ethiopia came to be one of the earliest adopters of concrete measures to improve harmonisation among its multiple health and development partners.

The early days: HSDP-I

The Government's efforts in the years following the establishment of the new constitution were focused on consolidating an effective decentralised system of administration and ensuring political stability. The first five-year phase, HSDP-I (1997/8–2001/2), coincided with the early years of Ethiopia's major push towards political decentralisation. During this period, the main emphasis in all spheres, including the health sector, was on the creation of an enabling environment for regional states to exercise their constitutional autonomy in developing and implementing their own economic development plans, including formulating their own budgets. This entailed a great deal of capacity and institution building at the regional, district and local levels.

(*Continued*) Each Regional State is governed by a regional council where members are directly elected to represent the districts or*weredas*. These regional councils have the legislative and executive power to direct the internal affairs of their regions.

As such, while a clearly articulated national health policy had been in existence for a number of years, and the HSDP was introduced as the official mechanism for translating this policy into concrete plans and actions, considerable work had yet to be done. Striking a balance between the salient objectives of guaranteeing administrative autonomy to the regional states while at the same time, ensuring national coherence of their sectoral plans and a unifying vision for the country's development proved to be a major challenge.

With the Government firmly focused on decentralisation and capacity building, this period saw a multitude of development partners pursuing their own specific interests and health projects, including specifying the particular regional states and areas where they wished to invest their support, with little coordination efforts among themselves at the national level. External funding support from both bilateral and multilateral partners was fragmented and largely project-based. At the federal level, the Ministry of Health grappled with the challenge of coordinating the multitude of projects initiated by a growing number of development partners. Attempts were made to coordinate these disparate activities by designating Ministry staff to serve as focal points for a discrete number of projects led by UN agencies and bilateral partners. These focal persons acted as liaisons between these sponsoring agencies and the regional and local health authorities where the projects were based.

These early coordination efforts proved insufficient however, and many recall this period as a time where there were as many separate plans and projects as there were partners engaged in a given area of public health intervention. Reporting burdens on federal, regional, zonal and *wereda* level staff working with these partners were extremely high and approaching unmanageable levels. Scarce human resources, and much time and energy which ought to have been focused on promoting coherence between regional plans and actually improving health service delivery, were being consumed by the demands of preparing separate budgets and reports for disparate donor-driven projects with little appreciable impact. At one time, Ministry staff are said to have gathered hundreds of pages of different project reporting formats with a total of over a thousand different indicator variables, which were being used by development partners operating in just one of the country's 11 regional states (pers. comm., N. Kedir, May, 2009).

These challenges notwithstanding, it is important to note that the health sector's federal-level governance structures, which have since evolved into effective and inclusive mechanisms of coordination and programme oversight, were actually already in place during the HSDP-I period. These include:

- the Central Joint Steering Committee (CJSC) — a high-level policy dialogue forum comprising representatives of both FMOH and bilateral and multilateral partners, envisaged as the highest governance body with oversight over HSDP;
- the Joint Consultative Meeting (JCM) — which brings together all health sector partners; and
- Joint Core Coordinating Committee — technical arm of the CJSC.

These groups have been meeting regularly since 2000/1. Mechanisms for conducting joint monitoring, reviews and evaluations of the HSDP through annual Joint Review Missions (JRMs) and Annual Review Meetings (ARMs) had also been established. However, in just the way the HSDP mechanism itself matured over successive phases, so too did these consultative forums evolve over time to become more and more effective and inclusive bodies of coordination and governance.

In sum, while decentralisation was a necessary and desirable process for advancing democratisation and broadening participation in the country's development, it was increasingly recognised that a clear and comprehensive "national vision" for the country's development was sorely needed. What made the difference was the timely recognition of this challenge and the Government's resolve to address it squarely. This led to a major push to advance a form of "internal alignment" of sectoral planning processes across regions, to promote cross-sectoral collaboration and a comprehensive 'bottom-up-top-down' planning process, linking the federal, regional and *wereda* levels of administration. The Government also spearheaded Ethiopia's first cross-sectoral Sustainable Development and Poverty Reduction Programme (SDPRP: 2002/3–2004/5) which had considerable influence in shaping the development of the next phase of the HSDP.

A number of policy shifts at the global level and their subsequent translation at country level helped further accelerate the Government's efforts. The late 1990s saw the expansion of sector-wide approaches (SWAps) to development. In Ethiopia, SWAps were being introduced in the education, water and infrastructure sectors. Further, the year 2000 saw the adoption of the MDGs, which led to the translation of global community's commitment to the mobilisation of unprecedented levels of international resources to help countries reach the ambitious MDG targets.

HSDP-II: consolidating internal alignment

With the launch of the five-year SDRP(2002/3–2004/5), ending poverty was clearly articulated as the country's central development objective. In recognition of the centrality of improved health outcomes for reducing poverty and accelerating the country's development, SDRP assigned the highest priority to health. As SDPRP was designed to include all the MDG-relevant sectors, it served as an effective framework for promoting alignment of sectoral planning processes and programmes. With a view to aligning the health sector programme with this overarching development plan, the second phase, HSDP-II, was deliberately designed to span three years (2002/3–2004/5) rather than five as was originally conceived. This also facilitated the subsequent alignment of HSDP-III with the health MDG targets. The comprehensive development vision set out in the SDRP also helped to promote greater coordination and alignment of planning processes across regions and clearer definition of the respective roles and responsibilities of government agencies at the federal and regional levels, including in the health sector.

This broad-based "internal alignment" paved the way for promoting coordination of partners around consolidated national sectoral plans. However, in the health sector, this challenge was further compounded with the appearance of major new players on the scene. The introduction of major global health initiatives, including the Global Alliance for Vaccine Initiatives (GAVI), the World Bank Multisectoral HIV/AIDS Program, the Global Fund to Fight AIDS, TB and Malaria and the United States President's Emergency Plan for AIDS (PEPFAR). Ethiopia received its first Global Fund Grant in 2003 and was also selected as one of the countries chosen to benefit from PEPFAR. This led to substantially increased resource flows into the health sector. The pressing need for much greater coordination in order to ensure the most effective use of these funding streams was now even more acutely felt.

HSDP-III: The turning point

The years following 2005 represented an important turning point for Ethiopia's health sector. In 2005, SDRP was succeeded by its next phase — the "Plan for Accelerated and Sustained Development to End Poverty" (PASDEP, 2005–2010). HSDP-III was recognised as the country's comprehensive national health plan and constituted as a core component of PASDEP. This firmly placed health at the centre of the country's comprehensive development vision. The question of aid effectiveness through increased harmonisation was given highest priority in the implementation of HSDP-III. The country-wide community-based Health Extension Programme (HEP) was established as the driver of HSDP-III and the foundation of the country's decentralised healthcare delivery system.

At the global level, 2005 also saw the coming into force of the Paris Declaration. The Declaration's core principles — "country ownership," "alignment," "harmonisation," "managing for results" and "mutual accountability," resonated with the challenges that Ethiopia was facing in coordinating different sources of support towards all the health MDGs. In effect, the global ascendancy of the harmonisation and alignment agenda simply provided a framework for what was already clearly seen by the Ethiopian Government as the only way forward in advancing its national development objectives (Abebe 2005). The country's ongoing experience of promoting internal alignment and coordination between regional states and across sectoral planning processes also helped spur proactive efforts to identify effective mechanisms for promoting coordination among health partners.

The urgency of much greater coordination in the health sector was most acutely felt when in the same year, the Global Fund came close to suspending Ethiopia's grant for malaria and gave the country six months to show that its national procurement system could deliver malaria bednets and treatment. At the same time, while PEPFAR had become a major funder, the services it was funding were not adequately coordinated with the Global Fund-supported country programme. In some cases, this led to a situation in which the same facilities would provide different antiretroviral (ARV) drugs to different patients. This was clearly not an effective mode of country partnership, and critically not owned by the country. How did Ethiopia develop a position in a few years, to manage country partnerships more effectively? The following sections summarize the Minister's perspectives regarding what made the difference.

First, this critical situation provoked us to challenge ourselves as well as our partners. By promptly taking responsibility to rectify these problems, we were able to clearly demonstrate and assert our commitment and ownership. This required candid dialogue and a very direct, challenging form of diplomacy.

Second, we needed to formalise this ownership through a cohesive country plan and clear strategic roadmaps for particular areas. HSDP-III provided the broader framework for this and given that its priorities were now aligned with the MDGs, it served as an effective tool for aligning the support of our partners. Moreover, with the launch of HSDP-III, we had started aggressively pursuing the "one plan, one budget and one report" principle of the harmonisation and alignment agenda. Concrete efforts to this end began with the launch of a *Harmonization Action Plan* in cooperation with development partners. A major output of this action plan was Ethiopia's groundbreaking *Code of Conduct to Promote Harmonization* in the Health Sector which came into effect in September, 2005. Our leadership on this showed our commitment to make this work better and earned us increased bargaining power. We now had a clear framework with which to hold ourselves and our partners accountable.

In line with this Code of Conduct, we also recognised that a specific harmonisation roadmap for HIV/AIDS support was sorely needed. We gave this highest priority and urged our partners to put together a joint coordination action plan that was developed in six months in 2005 to deal with the fragmentation in this area. We forged a breakthrough agreement between the Global Fund and PEPFAR to combine their support across all health centres throughout the country. This allowed much greater effectiveness, with the Global Fund providing cheaper first-line drugs to all facilities, and PEPFAR covering more expensive, second-line drugs and on-site laboratory and technical support. It was important to challenge donors to organise their support around the country health system and goals, and to think outside their limited project boxes. The *Code of Conduct* was later bolstered by much more practical and measurable procedures contained in the *Harmonization Manual* (HHM) which we developed together with our partners and published in 2007 to guide the alignment of external support and partners' initiatives with our HSDP.

Third, we needed to translate our collective commitment into a clear focus on results. The Global Fund malaria grant crisis served as an important spur to this demonstration of ownership and results focus. After two years, the programme had not delivered the 2 million ITNs targeted, and there were delays in the procurement of new, more effective malaria treatment (ACTs). After a performance review, we were given six months to deliver the ITNs and treatment before the next malaria season, or funding would be stopped. This allowed us to focus on the main problem — procurement bottlenecks which were hindering mobilization of the necessary support for delivering the bednets and treatments. We were in the "red zone" with a clear warning that we could lose our money if we did not deliver results. In essence, performance-based funding allowed us to think through implementation. We delivered the results on time, and the Global Fund was then very flexible in accelerating funding to allow us to go further with results. This was a remarkable breakthrough for us. We could clearly see how our commitment not only helped us achieve the results we needed but these results in turn secured us the support of the Global Fund and other partners. Once this spirit of partnership is created, considerable flexibilities can be found. For example, similar to the Global Fund, the World Bank has shown considerable flexibility by front-loading funding support when we had critical resource shortages to achieve specific results. From then on, we used results as the "common currency" to focus our partners on country needs and the challenges of implementation.

In sum, by 2005 the basic elements of "direct diplomacy" were in place. This approach helped us foster a healthy and manageable diversity of partners, bringing innovative approaches and funding and focusing on delivering results in the priority areas of our national health plan.

3. Healthy Partnerships: Distilling the Key Ingredients

In the ensuing years, we increasingly saw that it also pays off to challenge partners, occasionally with bold requests, to put the country and its health system at the centre of their funding considerations. We persistently challenged our partners to support our national plan, with particular emphasis on the two vital and interrelated components of our national health policy which were given particular priority in HSDP-III.

First, is the need to invest in building up our health system at every level, in line with the evaluation findings of the first two phases of the HSDP which had identified critical system weaknesses and insufficient capacities to meet the health needs of our largely rural population.

Second, is the objective of achieving universal access to primary health care services through the HEP, which we view as the foundation of the strong decentralised health system we are trying to build. The World Health Organization's six health system building blocks provided us with a practical framework for organising our health system strengthening efforts which have been further bolstered by the sector-wide reform of our processes which we initiated in 2008/2009.

Despite their vertical focus on specific diseases, the Global Fund and the GAVI Alliance were, in fact, among the earliest supporters of our health systems strengthening efforts. These two partners could clearly appreciate the fundamental system bottlenecks that countries such as ours face in scaling up effective services for AIDS, TB and malaria and broadening immunisation coverage. The flexibility of the Global Fund business model enabled us to make increased investments in system strengthening efforts. Indeed, we have used both Global Fund and PEPFAR to strengthen the capacities of our newly consolidated national Pharmaceutical Fund and Supply Agency. This included the purchase of warehouses and trucks and the construction of cold-rooms which benefitted the supply chain processes of the whole health system. Global Fund and PEPFAR financing have also helped to improve our national Health Management Information System.

Likewise, in 2007, following consultations with developing countries, GAVI introduced a health systems support programme to help countries expand immunisation services by addressing critical system constraints but to do this is in an integrated way that benefits other service delivery components. Ethiopia was one of the first countries to apply and successfully receive a grant under this scheme.

A. Strengthening country ownership through stronger global engagement

Ethiopia's increasingly active engagement and representation in relevant international forums also helped sharpen appreciation of the rapidly evolving international aid and global health architecture. The MDGs and the Paris Declaration provided useful common frameworks. We used the latter in particular to challenge partners to improve the effectiveness of their support. We increasingly recognised the importance of keeping abreast and contributing to policy developments at the global level by getting engaged in international health forums and governance structures. Stronger engagement through representation on the Boards of major global health agencies (including the Partnership for Maternal and Newborn and Child Health, the Roll Back Malaria Partnership, the GAVI Alliance, the Institute of Health Metrics and Evaluation, UNAIDS and the Global Fund to Fight AIDS, TB and Malaria) helped us to better appreciate their policy priorities and internal workings.

This strong international engagement enabled us to contribute to the rules of the development game and to help shape health governance at the global level by representing perspectives shared by developing countries. As a result, when the International Health Partnership and related initiatives (IHP+) was launched in 2007, our decision to sign up to it was straightforward. We could see clearly how improving coordination and harmonisation among our diverse partners and aligning their contributions with our HSDP could enable us to scale up our efforts for greater impact. Ethiopia thus became the first country to conclude an IHP+ Country Compact. The Compact which was signed by the Government of Ethiopia and its development partners in August, 2008 now serves as the overarching framework for coordinating all funding support to Ethiopia's health sector. Negotiating the Compact with our diverse partners was not easy, but we were determined to make it work. The initial implementation steps involved jointly reviewing and re-costing our existing plans and identifying our funding gaps. The

Compact provided the framework for establishing our "Millennium Development Goal Performance Fund" or "MDG Fund," an innovative pooled funding mechanism designed to allow both for greater predictability in the flow of resources and for optimal flexibility in their allocation.

In 2009, following further hard negotiations with our development partners, we launched the Joint Financing Arrangement (JFA) which has, to date, been endorsed by nine of our partners. The JFA which clearly sets out the purpose and scope of the MDG Fund is viewed as key milestone in our efforts to advance harmonisation. It stipulates the respective roles and responsibilities of our Government and signatory development partners and outlines the relevant rules, procedures and institutional arrangements for channelling resources through our MDG Fund and clearly outlines priority interventions eligible for financing through this pooled mechanism. A key lesson has been that implementation of the IHP Compact and all our efforts to advance harmonisation require constant follow up and negotiations. Partners need to be continually challenged to provide greater flexibilities and align with country priorities. In 2010, we sent letters to our development partners requesting them to put the Paris principles into practice and align their funding with our HSDP. We challenged them to live up to their commitments to accelerate implementation of our IHP+ Country Compact. Today, all recognise that implementation of the Compact requires significant behaviour change in the way we do business, not only on the Government side but also among our partners. In 2010 Ethiopia became among the first group of countries to conduct a Joint Assessment of National Strategy (JANS) of the next fourth phase of our health sector plan (HSDP IV) using tools developed under the IHP+ to help countries move towards "one plan." This exercise has helped to further bolster and maintain the positive momentum and progress we have made over the past few years and renewed our collective commitment to advance harmonisation.

In summary, a manageable but diverse partnership has been the bedrock of Ethiopia's progress on health. The Government is not one partner among many, but must take primary responsibility. This requires a very open and candid diplomacy, where the country and partners challenge each other to achieve results. The five major ingredients that have been the key to Ethiopia's success in fostering effective country partnerships for health are summarised below.

(i) *Conducive national political environment:* The most basic prerequisite is strong government commitment to development and health at the highest political level. This includes a clear national vision and well-articulated priorities, strategies and plans. In Ethiopia, the Government's focus on the basics has been key, i.e. addressing the root causes of poverty and poor health through expanded access to cost-effective, high impact primary health care interventions and building the health system from the bottom up. Our Government's clear commitment to ending poverty and bringing development, health and ownership into local communities through democratisation and decentralisation helped create a conducive environment for positive and participatory change.

(ii) *Effective leadership and country ownership:* Our experience in Ethiopia has shown that strong country ownership is indisputably the centrepiece of effective partnerships. Perhaps most importantly, the ultimate proof of country ownership is the demonstrated commitment and capacity to deliver results. Country ownership must be asserted in very practical ways and at all stages of the development process. It should start with the development of a cohesive national strategic plan, followed by the effective resourcing of that plan (including developing mechanisms to align and pool different funding streams and improving value for money by reducing overheads and transaction costs), through to actual implementation and monitoring and evaluation. The importance of strong country leadership and engagement in all of these stages is elaborated in *Section IV* below.

(iii) *Strong international engagement:* Getting involved in international forums, through representation on major task forces as well as the governance structures of leading global health agencies, has proved to be a crucial way for countries to keep abreast of the rapidly evolving global health landscape. Such engagement is vital for countries to improve their understanding of the mandates, business models, strengths and comparative advantages of different development partners and to align them with country-identified needs. Strong international engagement also allows developing countries a vital opportunity to contribute to the shaping of health policies at the global level.

(iv) *Steering and leveraging partnerships:* Challenging ourselves as well as our partners to break bureaucratic barriers and "think outside the box" in order to harmonise our efforts around specific country priorities requires both strong country ownership and a sound appreciation of the global health architecture and the modus operandi of different partners. By aiming to strike a balance between harmonisation and maintaining a "healthy diversity" of partners and funding approaches, countries can improve overall predictability of funding flows. Securing support from different sources can increase the negotiation power of countries. This requires a range of tactics, including regular networking, communication of progress, formal recognition of partners' positive contributions to country priorities, reinforcing strategies that work, as well as pressing for advice and joint solutions to challenges. Further, countries and partners must all commit to be in a "permanent learning mode" in order to rise to new challenges and learn from best practices in other countries. Establishing effective participatory governance processes which involve all country partners, is also key to strengthening partnerships and building mutual accountability. In Ethiopia, the early establishment and gradual refinement of formal health sector governance mechanisms has proven to be a clear advantage. Our experiences with the Global Fund's uniquely composed country coordinating mechanism (CCM) is also positively influencing our governance structures and partnerships in the health sector.

(vi) *Direct diplomacy for results: candid dialogue with partners:* Formal coordination forums need to be matched with direct diplomacy and less formal approaches for continual exchange in order to create and reinforce a sense of community among country partners. In Ethiopia, we have learned that regular informal exchanges with partners can often help build trust, foster cooperation and lead to greater openness to change. A culture of candid dialogue with country partners is also necessary to jointly address challenges as they arise and leverage positive peer pressure on partners to keep promises. All sides need to be constantly challenged to live up to their commitments to country-identified priorities. Moreover, all partners must be willing to depart from 'business as usual' and show greater flexibility at critical times in order to deliver results. Delivery of the jointly agreed result should be the clear bottom line on which all efforts and support should be focused. Clearly defined targets provide the basis for an effective diplomacy focused on results and a common monitoring system for showing and sharing recognition for joint achievements.

These ingredients all require strong country ownership throughout all phases of the development process — from planning and resourcing through to actual implementation and effective monitoring and evaluation of results.

4. Country Ownership: Consolidating the Centerpiece

Our experience in Ethiopia over the last decade has clearly shown that country ownership is the essential centrepiece needed to drive and animate effective country health partnerships at country level. This is particularly the case as we begin the "final push" to the 2015 MDGs. Drawing Ethiopia's experiences, four key steps for making country ownership a reality are elaborated below.

Planning: The first and most decisive step towards real country ownership is ownership of the national planning process. To this end, countries must start with a clear and unifying vision for their development and a detailed roadmap for realising that vision. In Ethiopia, our vision is to end poverty and become a middle-income country over the next ten to fifteen years. Moreover, our Government has clearly articulated concrete strategies for how to get there. For country ownership to be realised, development partners must allow countries the space to identify their own needs and priorities and develop their own national plans as they see fit. In doing so, countries should draw on best practices from around the world and tailor proven approaches to their own particular needs and circumstances. Once countries have a clear national plan in place, partners need to accept and support that plan in order for genuine country ownership to thrive. In Ethiopia, we stayed open to ideas throughout the planning process. We invited our diverse partners to contribute ideas and also benchmarked best practices from other countries.

Resourcing: As a second step, countries must also assume a leading role in resourcing the plan. As resources are invariably limited, careful prioritisation will be crucial. Flexible and predictable funding flows foster accountability and ownership by allowing countries greater leverage in responsibly managing and directing resources to areas of critical need. Given the enhanced flexibility and leverage it allows for countries, our experience in Ethiopia indicates that direct budget support is the most effective way of fostering country ownership. In cases where the funding mechanism chosen by our partners is not budgetary support, then, in line with our country plan, we try to negotiate ways in which the funds provided can be used to benefit the health system as a whole. Even "vertically raised funds," channelled primarily for expanding services for specific diseases have been used in ways to benefit the entire health system.

In order to make prudent and efficient use of limited resources, countries must also be able to set clear priorities as part of their plan. In developing our national health plan in Ethiopia, we have learned to define two alternative versions: "Plan A" and "Plan B." In the event that, due to resource constraints, we are unable to achieve "Plan A," the broader and more ambitious scenario, then "Plan B," which focuses on the most pressing priorities, serves as our contingency.

Implementation: The third key step in country ownership is implementation. It should be the country that implements health programmes. Partners should refrain from setting up parallel health structures in a country. Some have argued that countries lack the capacity to implement. However, the response to this should be to strengthen existing capacities and systems rather than weakening them by setting up parallel structures. Further, all development partners should adhere to the same operational procedures and policies as the country does. If these systems and procedures are inadequate, partners should work with countries to fix them. Strengthening country implementation capacities is a more efficient and sustainable use of resources than setting up parallel systems.

Monitoring and evaluation: Finally, countries must have the ability to track their performance through effective monitoring and evaluation systems. It is important for partners and governments to agree on a clear result-based framework in order to hold each other accountable. Accountability should be based on specific outcomes that we can all agree to work towards. The goals, outcomes and indicators should be agreed from the outset during the planning stage.

If countries truly own their health plans, then they are committed to them. We are seeing that steadfast commitment is what yields results and guarantees the long-term sustainability of programmes. In Ethiopia, we would not have registered the encouraging progress we are seeing in our health sector without this type of genuine ownership.

The link between commitment and results: Over the past years, government health expenditure in Ethiopia has increased from 7 to 11% of total budget, showing the commitment of the country to health. This commitment has been critical to show that the country is leading and investing in the process of development and health. We have focused on high impact, low-cost interventions and building our primary health care delivery system at the community level. To this end, we have been making strategic use of support from a wide range of sources. Key to the progress we have made to date have been, our strong country-led strategy and the range of effective negotiation tactics we have used to challenge our partners and ourselves to use funding more flexibly, efficiently and effectively.

In line with the overarching national health policy, priority was given to an "integrated health system approach" to expanding health services, the overall aim of which is to accelerate expansion of services to achieve greater disease-specific results while also at the same time, building the national health system. Underpinning this approach is a firm commitment to a community-centred effort aimed at ensuring universal access to primary health care. This central objective is being driven by our community-based HEP which has rapidly trained and deployed over 34,000 health extension workers throughout the country — two for every village, almost doubling Ethiopia's health workforce in only three years. Using social mobilisation and an innovative "model family" approach, our health extension workers are propagating healthy behaviours among their communities and improving utilisation of basic health services. The broad-based health information and referral system that HEP is establishing at the local level is also helping to improve access to a continuum of care at secondary and tertiary levels.

At the same time, the Ethiopian Government has been investing heavily in an accelerated infrastructure development effort which aims to put in place 15,000 health posts and 3,200 health centres around the country, the bulk of which have already been completed. The returns on these investments have been greatly encouraging. We have used funding from AIDS, TB, malaria, vaccines and general health support to progressively strengthen our health system and scale up key health interventions. With expanded immunisation and access to services, under-five mortality has decreased from 204 per 1000 live births in 1990 to 101 per 1000 in 2008.

A combination of interventions have helped reduce maternal mortality from 1068 in 1990 to 470 in 2008. Expanded access to key HIV-related interventions has resulted in declining HIV prevalence in recent years; and the distribution of 36 million bednets and scale-up of other key malaria control interventions have led to dramatic declines in malaria cases and deaths. We have also achieved full geographical coverage of tuberculosis treatment with good treatment success rates.

In addition, we are building our procurement capacities and streamlining our health information management as well as our commodity procurement and supply chain systems. The comprehensive health insurance system we are developing is also expected to improve access to healthcare.

As a result of these gains, we are beginning to see the positive economic effects of a healthier population. All of this progress has been possible because we were able to direct the available resources towards our most critical areas of need. We are committed to meeting these needs, because they are essentially ours. Moreover, as the owners, we feel the urgency perhaps even more than any of our partners could.

5. Conclusion: Tactics for the Diplomacy of Diversity

We have described some of the key ingredients of effective country partnerships and the steps needed to assert country ownership, drawing on our experiences in Ethiopia. However, country ownership cannot simply be proclaimed. Ethiopia's experiences suggest that there is a particular type of diplomacy needed to draw diverse partners to support a country's plan. This section summarises illustrative examples cited by the Minister of Health which provide some insight into the tactics of building diverse country partnerships by consistently asserting ownership.

Why have so few countries exerted country ownership like Ethiopia? What recommendations do you have for other countries?

I believe two things are key — commitment and results, and more importantly the link between the two. You cannot expect real country ownership in any meaningful way without a unifying national vision and strong commitment for change starting at the highest level of government all the way down. Moreover, for ownership to really take root it is important for countries to be in the driver's seat and to know exactly where they want to go and how to get there. The Government must be fully engaged in leading at every stage of the development process — from planning to implementation, through to measuring and monitoring results and impact.

Does country ownership go beyond the government, what is the role of civil society, private sector and communities themselves?

Ownership of the development process most definitely must extend to every segment of society. We know we cannot hope to achieve the health MDGs in Ethiopia without genuine engagement of communities themselves. We firmly believe in the transformative power of social mobilisation. However, you also cannot hope to have meaningful engagement of civil society without real government commitment and leadership. Only when the Government takes the lead and shows a real commitment to change, can you expect civil society and the private sector to take part and contribute to the development process.

What will be the effect of the financial crisis on country partnerships? What will happen if health financing declines?

Enhancing predictability and sustainability of external resource flows to support the health sector is one of the key objectives of the IHP+ and our Country Compact. I believe the efficiency gains that can be made through the full implementation of our Country Compact can offset the impacts of any overall reduction in external funding flows over the short to medium term. Ensuring that both domestic and external resources are well-aligned with costed national strategies and delivered through country-led procedures will greatly reduce transaction costs and enable clear priority setting. In Ethiopia, we are working to advance harmonisation at the same time as cultivating a healthy diversity of partners with different approaches and comparative advantages. This is particularly important for funding predictability as individual contributions or pooled resources have their own funding constraints. In terms of contingency planning, we are trying to make greater use of domestic resources for health. We have increased government contributions to health and are developing a comprehensive health insurance system. We are now working on the establishment of Ethiopia's very first national health insurance agency which will focus on the formal sector. At the same time, we are piloting a community-based insurance mechanism tailored to our vast an diverse informal sector. With the introduction of these two complementary schemes in the near future, we expect to remove the financial barriers to health care access through risk-pooling among the poor and better-off as well as the sick and healthy. However, the way in which world leaders came together to address the global economic downturn inspires optimism that we can continue to count on global solidarity to support investments in health. As we have shown in Ethiopia, it is often from difficult situations, with fronts dialogue that strong partnerships can be created.

What have been the most challenging situations you have faced with partners? How did you resolve them?

Getting partners with divergent interests to support our national plan is always a challenge. Asserting country ownership requires a persistent focus on country-identified priorities and confidence in the strategies devised to achieve the results we want. It is about knowing what you want to achieve and having done your homework well enough to know that you have selected the most viable way of attaining it. In Ethiopia, we always stay open to ideas throughout the planning process and make every effort to also research and benchmark best practices from other countries. Despite this we have often encountered situations in which partners are reluctant to support our chosen strategy for a variety of reasons. Broadly speaking, there are at least three types of situations where we face such challenges from our partners, and I can give several examples to illustrate each.

"'Too ambitious": First, is the "too ambitious" response. There have been many instances when various partners have looked at our proposed strategy for achieving a particular outcome and said they could not support it because they felt it was too grand, beyond our means and hence, unlikely to be implemented in full. Often, this is because they have underestimated our commitment and determination. A good example is the initial reactions we got from some partners when we launched our flagship HEP and proposed to train and deploy 30,000 health extension workers throughout the country. A number of partners expressed strong reservations regarding our "flood and retain" approach for dealing with the severe health worker shortage in our country. They worried that we could not possibly train that many health workers within such a limited time, and that even if we did, this would end up distorting our labour

market and possibly lead to large-scale unemployment. But of course we had already thought through these concerns and taken them into consideration in developing our plan. So we insisted on moving ahead as we were confident that the approach we had chosen was best suited to our specific needs and circumstances. Our target was developed through a systematic population-based needs assessment. We were also convinced that we had to move away from the volunteerism model by engaging Health Extension Workers (HEW) as salaried civil servants. This, in fact, turned out to be HEP's key success factor. In the end, we actually met our target on schedule. By the end of December 2008, the training of a total of 30,190 HEWs had been completed and all of those trained were deployed to health posts throughout the country. However, once we achieved this target and partners saw that we were seriously focused on delivering results through this programme, even those who were reluctant to lend their support have gone to lengths to mobilise all types of resources to help us go further.

*Special projects:*The second type of challenge is when partners approach us with their own special project ideas and offer to commit substantial resources for programmes focused on specific diseases or particular causes which they regard as priorities. We find ourselves in a very difficult situation when the focus of such projects is not aligned with the most pressing needs prioritised in our country plan, especially in cases when we are still working to secure resources to fill critical resource gaps. In such situations, we have asserted ownership by explaining to our partners what our core priorities are and persuaded them to redirect their investments. We have found that being candid and firm about our priorities pays off. For example, on one occasion we were approached by our Carter Center partners who were prepared to make a substantial investment in projects focusing on neglected tropical diseases. We could clearly appreciate their commitment and concern about these diseases. But at that time, we also happened to be facing a critical shortage of resources for purchasing additional malaria bednets. We discussed this candidly with them and asked them if they would consider starting by using their funding to help us procure more bednets instead. They agreed, and in fact the Carter Center ended up being among the top investors in our largest ever malaria bednets procurement and distribution effort. Further, the Carter Center's engagement in our malaria control efforts led to an innovative approach whereby they could address other vector-borne tropical diseases, such as Guinea worm in tandem.

'Tough love': Perhaps the most pervasive challenge we face is making our Compact actually work and achieve its ultimate objectives. The strength of our commitment is the key to the progress we have made — from the challenging process of negotiating the Country Compact to the establishment of the MDG Pooled Fund and the development the Joint Financing Agreement to which an increasing number of partners are now contributing. However, what we have seen is that the signing of agreements does not mean that the job is done and implementation will be automatic. Partners have a wide range of interests that hinder them from fully embracing country-led processes. Harmonisation and alignment requires constant dialogue and tough and candid negotiations. Some have called it "tough love," referring to the real behaviour change that must occur both on the part of the government and among partners if the resources available are to be used in the most effective and efficient way to save lives and build up a strong health system. Our ultimate success will depend on sustaining the genuine partnerships we have built up thus far and the willingness of all of us to make the difficult departure from "business as usual." The bottom line for all of us should be the results. We should expect partners to be tough in holding countries accountable for the returns on their investments, and to trust countries entirely to lead on the process. In turn, countries must exercise full ownership and vigilantly follow up with partners to ensure that they live up to their commitments. If the 2015 MDG targets are to be met, developing country governments must exercise true ownership and commit to changing the health conditions of their people once and for all. Development partners must also move forward with a new spirit of candour and true commitment to make country ownership a reality.

Chapter 16 provides further analysis of aligning stakeholders behind national health plans in Ethiopia. The next chapter further develops the themes of managing partners for results.

Acknowledgements: The authors wish to acknowledge the comments and perspectives provided by the following individuals who had first-hand involvement in supporting the development of Ethiopia's health sector and country partnerships in various capacities: Dr. Nejmudin Kedir Bilal, Dr. Medhin Zewdu, Ms. Marion Kelly and Dr Catorina Waddington.

References

Abebe A (2005) *Bilateral Donor Coordination Experience of the Federal Government of Ethiopia.* Ministry of Finance and Economic Development. Addis Ababa. January 11, 2005.

Accra Agenda for Action (2008) Toaccelerate and deepen implementation of the Paris Declaration on AID effectiveness. Accra. September 4, 2008.

FMOH (2005) Code of Conduct to Promote Harmonization in the Health Sector. Federal Ministry of Health, Addis Ababa. September, 2005.

FMOH (2007) The Health Sector Development Program (HSDP) Harmonization Manual (HHM). September, 2005 (EFY 1997). First Edition. Federal Ministry of Health, Addis Ababa.

MOFED (2006) Ethiopia: Building on Progress: A Plan for Accelerated and Sustained Development to End Poverty (PASDEP 2005/06–2009/10) Volume I: Main Text Ministry of Finance and Economic Development (MoFED), September 2006.

Paris Declaration on Aid Effectiveness (2005) Ownership; Harmonization; Alignment; Results & Mutual Accountability. February 28–March 2, 2005. Paris.

4

Managing for Results: A "Common Currency" to Coordinate Health Development

Daniel Low-Beer[1]

Summary

There has been an increasing movement to put results at the centre of the agenda for development programmes and improved aid effectiveness. This is reflected in the Millennium Development Goals (MDGs), the business models of global programmes and the movement to improve the effectiveness of aid with "managing for results as an overarching principle" (OECD 2005). Yet there is scepticism as to the ability of partners to measure compelling development results, and to manage and coordinate their activities for results. This chapter assesses the origins of the results agenda, and the contribution of innovative health partnerships. Alongside results measurement, it identifies a more radical results agenda to use results to manage diverse partners and improve aid effectiveness. The chapter provides examples, and criticisms, of how different innovative partnerships and countries have managed health development for results. The final section identifies some key principles for the results agenda among innovative health partnerships.

[1] The findings are those of the author and do not necessarily represent those of the affiliate institution.

1. Introduction — Coordinating Partners for Results

In 2004, the Global Fund to Fight AIDS, TB and Malaria and PEPFAR had emerged as the two largest funders of the Ethiopian AIDS Program. As financing for the AIDS programme increased from a few to several hundred million US dollars per annum, they each brought their own way of doing health development. They supported separate health centres in the country ("PEPFAR" and "Global Fund" clinics), which would get different types of drugs, laboratory and testing equipment and report results separately.

The Ethiopian government decided to coordinate the donors behind national results and a country roadmap in 2005. It did not start by harmonising and aligning procedures, and then adding a monitoring and evaluation framework. It started with results, laying out the national results it wanted to achieve. It then asked donors to coordinate their activities to achieve them. There were very few working groups, just an overall roadmap with clear results, agreed by partners within six months.

This national results framework pushed donors to coordinate their programmes, consistent with their respective comparative advantages, to achieve results. Partners kept separate procedures but the Global Fund supported cheaper generic, first-line HIV treatment across all health centres while PEPFAR supported more expensive, patented second-line HIV drugs. PEPFAR also provided direct technical assistance to all sites, including laboratory and testing support, which the Global. Fund could not provide. Global Fund and PEPFAR "sites" in Ethiopia soon no longer existed. The efficiencies were significant — targets for reaching people with HIV treatment increased 50%, from 20,000 to 30,000, with the same funding. Politically and procedurally the organisations were diverse, but could coordinate closely around a "common currency" of results.

In a number of countries, results have been used not only to measure but to manage diverse health partnerships. In Russia, the NGO network has a joint internet-based results system to share information and coordinate activities across the diverse set of organisations responding to AIDS (see Chapter 18). In Malawi, a common results framework is used as a basis to coordinate partner activities contributing to pooled financing under the SWAp (Low-Beer *et al.* 2007). In Rwanda, performance-based funding is used to coordinate service provision across partners to the clinic and community level (Rusa *et al.* 2009).

There are also criticisms, however, that this focus has resulted in an epidemic of indicators, a stress on short-term, measurable activities, and led to an "M&E industry" (Attaran 2005; Fidler 2007). In many countries, separate reporting is required by new health initiatives from the Global Fund, GAVI, PEPFAR, bilateral and multilaterals agencies (OECD 2008). Rwanda is in many ways an effective country in managing donors by results, ensuring funding has contributed to a wide range of health outcomes (Binagwaho and Ratnayake 2009). However they claim that they need to report on several hundred indicators, produce dozens of reports and support multiple missions. The independent Five-Year Evaluation of the Global Fund found more generally "fragmentation in information flows as different donors track information on their own activities and services with a lack of standardised, transparent and joint reporting systems" (Macro 2009). If results provide an important basis to improve aid effectiveness, equally, improved coordination is essential to realise the results agenda.

"Managing for Results" has been a defining goal of new health partnerships, emphasised by private foundations like the Gates and Packard Foundations, and core to the business models of GAVI and the Global Fund, as well as PEPFAR (Low-Beer *et al.* 2007). The diverse stakeholders brought together in these partnerships — government, civil society, private sector, multilaterals and bilaterals — are not coordinated politically or procedurally but in their commitment to specific health results.

To what extent have innovative health partnerships been able to build results into their business models? Has this focus on results provided a "common currency" to coordinate the diverse partners they bring together? To what extent has the results agenda contributed to aid effectiveness and improved health governance? These three questions are the focus of this chapter. The chapter first assesses the origins of the results agenda and provides examples of how innovative partnerships have incorporated the results agenda into their business models. The chapter then critically reviews a more radical results agenda, which uses results to coordinate diverse health actors and better manage aid. Diverse partnerships may have very little else in common, except their contributions to health results.

2. A Recent History of the Results Agenda

In the last ten years, a results agenda which had been largely technical has emerged as a political and management discourse on how to better manage aid. Results have become prominent to measure aid, to manage aid programmes and to improve the overall effectiveness of aid. The Paris Declaration added a prominent commitment to "Managing for Results" alongside the more traditional "Alignment and Harmonization" agenda (for example the Rome Declaration on Harmonization of 2003) (OECD 2005). As important as the monitoring of results was the component of "managing for." Results were not just a monitoring issue to measure the outcomes of development generally at the end of a project. Results were an important input and focus to how aid was managed. The results movement was further developed with the Accra Action Agenda agreed by countries and partners in 2008 which stated: "Achieving development results — and openly accounting for them — must be at the heart of all we do. More than ever, citizens and taxpayers of all countries expect to see the tangible results of development efforts" (OECD 2008).

They were two sides to this statement. First, a number of new partners, specifically private foundations, were building results into the business models "and the heart of" innovative partnerships. This included performance-based funding for GAVI and the Global Fund. At the same time, the second part of the quote on the expectations of "tangible results" was a response to a critique of development. This questioned whether social investments and aid can show compelling results demanded by citizens, taxpayers and those in need of services (Moyo 2009). The chapter will come back to these critiques.

2.1 Measuring and managing for results

The results agenda in health has a longer history that crystallised as part of the development movement from 2000 (with the MDGs and the Paris Declaration on aid effectiveness). Two agendas "measuring" and "managing" programmes for results came together during this period.

Measurement and results had become increasingly important in health programmes and in new measures of development. From the 1980s,

UNICEF had used a results focus to guide key health interventions in vaccination and oral rehydration therapy — an early example within a UN agency. The UNDP's Human Development reports in the 1990s tracked poverty reduction developing the Human Development index which explicitly combined measures of health, education and income. Furthermore, the collaboration of WHO and the World Bank led to the comprehensive measurement of the Global Burden of disease in the 1990s. This provided for a first time "a consistent and comparative description of the burden of diseases and the risk factors that cause them as an important input to health decision-making" (Murray and Lopez 1997, 1998).

The burden of disease estimates featured prominently in the World Bank report on "Investing in Health" (World Bank 1993), which marked the integration of health and development issues (health as a contributor as well as an outcome of economic development). The evidence base supported the case for the development benefits of health, and the prominence of health as part of human development. As Sen noted "At all levels of development the three essential capabilities are for people to lead a long and healthy life, to be knowledgeable, and to have access to the resources needed for a decent standard of living" (Sen 1999). The measurement initiatives were influential in putting health and measurement at the heart of the International Development Goals of 1996 and the MDGs in 2001.

There is also a second history on the management side of "managing for results," largely outside mainstream development. This comes from innovations particularly in the public sector in education and health, and from private foundations on returns on social investments (Jongbloed and Vossensteyn 2001; Low-Beer *et al.* 2007). In particular, performance-based funding and rewards were introduced in the public sector in the United States in the 1970s, starting in Tennessee and becoming widespread in the 1990s in education and health. The managing for results agenda developed with the increasing prominence of venture philanthropy and socially responsible investing in the private sector in the mid-1990s. These trends were incorporated into mainstream financial indices in the Dow Jones Sustainability Index in 1999 and the FTSE4 Good index launched in 2001. In development, the World Bank's 1993 World Development Report — Investing in Health — promoted results and performance-based funding

Selected Key Developments in Managing for Development Results	
Measurement Agenda	Management Agenda
1993: World Development Report – Investing in Health (World Bank). Describes agenda for investing in health for development based on results	1970–1980s: Performance-based funding developed in US education sector in late 1970s and 1980s, starting in Tennessee. 1990s, introduced in health
1996: Global Burden of Disease Project by WHO and World Bank. Quantifies and compares burden of disease for different conditions and causes	1990s: Developments in venture philanthropy and inclusion in mainstream financial indexes, the Dow Jones Sustainability Index in 1999
2000: The World Health Report – health systems: improving performance. Measures and ranks the performance of overall country health systems	2000: The influence of new private foundations, for example the Gates Foundation focusing on global health, and help establish innovative partnerships
Managing for Development Results	
2000–2001: Millennium Development Goals including MDGs 4,5 and 6 on health, building on the international development goals of 1996	
Managing for results in global programmes	
2000: GAVI launched using performance-based funding	
2001: Global Fund established using performance-based funding	
2004: Millennium Challenge Account launched using results-based management	
International platforms for managing for results	
2002, 4, 7: International Roundtables on Managing for Development Results	
2005: Paris Declaration with "Managing for Results" one of five key principles of aid effectiveness, extended and emphasised in the Accra Action Agenda (2008)	
2007: International Health Partnership and Joint Health Systems Platform (2009) launched to support system-wide platforms for health and results in countries	

Figure 1. Selected key events in managing for development results.

(World Bank 1993). The World Bank increasingly built performance incentives into its programmes and helped convene the International Roundtables on Managing for Results in 2002 and 2004, feeding directly into the Paris Declaration on aid effectiveness. New health partnerships brought together the two agendas — technical partners working on measuring results and partners pursuing new management approaches from the private sector and private foundations.

2.2 The MDGs — a global results-based movement

The MDGs and the new health partnerships after 2000 brought together the two agendas of measurement and management for results. At the overall level of aid, the MDGs were proposed as "the most broadly supported, comprehensive, and specific poverty reduction targets the world has ever established" (Millennium Project p.2). Building on a set of International Development Goals agreed in 1996, with their specific commitments, goals and targets, the MDGs provided a collective focus on development results from 2000 to 2015.

Critics have argued that despite becoming "the zeitgeist of the global development enterprise," the MDGs "suffer from a worrying lack of scientifically valid data" particularly for health (Attaran 2005). Alongside raising and spending finance, the MDGs rely on mechanisms to ensure accountability in the management and measurement of this finance. Attaran argues this second element has not received adequate attention to provide sufficient accountability behind the global targets. His critique ultimately argues that this shortcoming is not only a technical measurement issue, but an ethical issue of accountability to the world's poor.

The results challenge of the MDGs is two-fold — to measure progress at the global level and to ensure development finance is managed for results in programmes. New health partnerships convened many of the partners who had brought innovation into the results agenda (multilaterals, foundations, private sector and civil society) in their governance. The influence of new partners, like the Gates Foundation, was important in establishing performance-based funding as integral to the business models of GAVI and the Global Fund. Instead of just measuring results to track the MDGs, they were faced with the accountability challenge of using results as a basis for their financing to countries. In addition, most global programmes, such as GAVI and the Global Fund, did not have country offices, and so relied on transparent information on results as a basis for their management decisions. They needed transparency in results to operate at a distance.

At the same time, the World Bank invested heavily in results-based financing with a focus on health. The results and targets focus were also reflected in the targets of PEPFAR (to treat 2 million people, prevent 7 million HIV infections and provide care for 10 million adults and orphans), the Millennium Challenge Account in 2004, the 3 by 5 AIDS initiative of WHO (to treat 3 million people for HIV by 2005) and Stop TB and Roll Back Malaria. In the period 2000–2010, most of these organisations separately set targets and measured results. Increasingly, however, they are challenged to show contributions to the collective targets of the MDGs. This requires a "shareholder" approach to results, where a partner is only one contributor to these global targets. The approaching 2015 targets have been an important force in developing common approaches to managing for results. This is the second challenge of the results agenda since

2000 — to develop common partner approaches to results to show clearly their contributions.

2.3 Collective challenges — aid effectiveness and "managing for results"

"Managing for results" became an increasingly important component of the wider aid effectiveness agenda. Similarly, coordination among partners has taken on greater importance in the results agenda. Individual partners can show results, but impact and the MDGs require collective efforts. The international focus on development results developed rapidly with successive partner roundtables on managing for development results (2002, 2004, 2007). However with different organisations pursuing separate results agendas, the system-wide issues of supporting common country measurement for health results became a pressing issue. The "Three Ones" principles of coordination for AIDS announced in 2004 reflected this concern, which included "one agreed country-level monitoring and evaluation system" (UNAIDS 2004). The support of system-wide platforms for health was made explicit in the International Health Partnership (IHP) launched in 2007 (WHO 2008). This emphasised "improved results through better use of existing funds" and the use of "one results monitoring framework" in countries. The Three Ones (based on AIDS) was being extended to the three diseases (AIDS, TB and malaria) and to health.

The IHP, including GAVI and the Global Fund, has worked towards setting common frameworks for monitoring performance and evaluation of the scale-up for better health (WHO 2008). This includes a strong focus on "common results," alignment with country reviews and building country measurement capacity, as shown in their basic principles below:

- *Collective action*: the primary focus should be on the contribution for the collective efforts to scale up the health sector response in countries.
- *Alignment with country processes*: monitoring performance and evaluation should build upon national processes that countries have established to evaluate and review progress in the implementation of national health sector plans.

- *Balance between country participation and independence*: evaluation processes should be driven by country needs but conducted in a manner that maintains their independence.
- *Harmonised approaches to performance assessment*: evaluations of the scale-up should use common protocols and standardised outcome indicators and measurement tools, with appropriate country adaptations and leadership, minimising the separate evaluation efforts of individual initiatives, grants and programmes.
- *Capacity building and health information system (HIS) strengthening*: systematic involvement of country institutions in performance monitoring and evaluation is necessary to strengthen HIS and promote local capacity for analysis and application of information and evidence.
- *Adequate funding*: as a general guide, between 5 and 10% of the overall scale-up funds need to be set aside for monitoring performance, evaluation, operational research and strengthening HIS.

Similarly, "managing for results" became formally embedded as one of the five principles of aid effectiveness (in the Paris Agenda) and one of the three major challenges (in the Accra Action Agenda), illustrated below (OECD 2005, 2008). The basic principle combined measurement and management defined as "Managing for results means managing and implementing aid in a way that focuses on the desired results and uses information to improve decision-making," together with the action that "Donors will align their monitoring with country information systems."

The increasing use of results-based financing has led to some critical governance issues — how to align with country systems and assessments of health performance. In addition, many of the weaknesses in country monitoring and evaluation systems have become apparent. This highlights the enhanced focus in the Accra Action Agenda on country capacity building. To further pursue this technical agenda, the Gates Foundation financed the Health Metrics Network (HMN) to coordinate country support around an agreed common results framework (HMN 2008).

Given this prominence, results increasingly became a political as well as a technical issue. Results have become the focus of country health diplomacy, as to who defines them, assesses them and how the basic surveys

The Paris Declaration 2005	Accra Action Agenda 2008
Managing for Results (One of Five Principles) *Managing resources and improving decisionmaking for results*	**Results (One of Three Major Challenges)**
Managing for results means managing and implementing aid in a way that focuses on the desired results and uses information to improve decisionmaking	Evidence shows that we will need to address three major challenges to accelerate progress on aid effectiveness:
*Partner countries*commit to: • Strengthen the linkages between national development strategies and annual and multiannual budget processes • Endeavour to establish results-oriented reporting and assessment frameworks that monitor progress against key dimensions of the national and sector development strategies; and that these frameworks should track a manageable number of indicators for which data are cost-effectively available *Donors*commit to: • Link country programming and resources to results and align them with effective partner country performance assessment frameworks, refraining from requesting the introduction of performance indicators that are not consistent with partners' national development strategies • Work with partner countries to rely, as far as possible, on partner countries' results-oriented reporting and monitoring frameworks • Harmonise their monitoring and reporting requirements, and, until they can rely more extensively on partner countries' statistical, monitoring and evaluation systems, with partner countries to the maximum extent possible on joint formats for periodic reporting Partner countries and donorsjointly commit to: • Work together in a participatory approach to strengthen country capacities and demand for results based management	1. *Country ownership is key.* Developing country governments will take stronger leadership of their own development policies and will engage with their parliaments and citizens in shaping those policies. Donors will support them by respecting countries' priorities, investing in their human resources and institutions, making greater use of their systems to deliver aid and increasing the predictability of aid flows 2. *Building more effective and inclusive partnerships.* In recent years, more development actors – middle-income countries, global funds, the private sector and civil society organisations – have been increasing their contributions and bringing valuable experience to the table. This also creates management and co-ordination challenges. Together, all development actors will work in more inclusive partnerships so that all our efforts have greater impact on reducing poverty 3. *Achieving development results – and openly accounting for them – must be at the heart of all we do.* More than ever, citizens and taxpayers of all countries expect to see the tangible results of development efforts. We will demonstrate that our actions translate into positive impacts on people's lives. We will be accountable to each other and to our respective parliaments and governing bodies for these outcomes
Managing for results: Indicators of progress and target for 2010	**We will improve our management for results by taking the following actions:**
Results-oriented frameworks – Number of countries with transparent and monitorable performance assessment frameworks to assess progress against	(a) Developing countries will strengthen the quality of policy design, implementation and assessment by improving information systems, including, as

Figure 2. "Managing for results" from the Paris declaration (2005) to the accra agenda for action (2008)(OECD 2005, 2008).

(a) the national development strategies and (b) sector programmes *Reduce the gap by one-third*– Reduce the proportion of countries without transparent and monitorable performance assessment frameworks by one-third by 2010	appropriate, disaggregating data by sex, region and socioeconomic status (b) Developing countries and donors will work to develop cost-effective results management instruments to assess the impact of development policies and adjust them as necessary (c) Donors will align their monitoring with country information systems We will be more accountable and transparent to our publics for results
Other important links to Managing for Results	**Other important links to results**
Principle of Ownership: "Partner countries commit to translate national development strategies into prioritized results-oriented operational programmes" *Principle of Alignment*: "Donors commit to adopt harmonized performance assessment frameworks for country systems so as to avoid presenting partner countries with an excessive number of potentially conflicting targets"	*Country systems*: Donors agree to use country systems as the first option for aid programmes in support of activities managed by the public sector *Global Funds*: We call upon all global funds to support country ownership, to align and harmonise their assistance proactively and to make good use of mutual accountability frameworks, while continuing their emphasis on achieving results

Figure 2. (*Continued*)

and surveillance will be undertaken. Some countries have successfully defined their results and targets, and used these to coordinate external partners and financing. Others have become overwhelmed by separate reporting requirements. A multitude of reporting forms can appear in remote African health centres, reporting primarily to Geneva or Washington, and only nominally through the national system. This has led to critiques of results-based financing, technically and politically. It has also led to a more radical and political agenda which regards results as a basis for coordinating diverse partners in country.

3. Innovative Health Partnerships — Building Results into Their Business Models

Nowhere have the governance issues of managing for results been more apparent than in innovative health partnerships, such as GAVI or the Global Fund. At the highest level, their creation was framed by the MDGs, the legitimacy of new partners based on their contribution to its indicators and targets. Generally innovative health partnerships were not treaty based (for example, like UN organisations). As in the description of the Global Fund model "raise it, invest it, prove it," their "raison d'etre" depended on their ability to prove results. The replenishment of these Funds focused on the results the programmes they support could achieve and progress towards international goals.

Second, innovative partnerships brought together in their governance a new range of partners representing different strands of the results agenda. This included private foundations, like the Gates Foundation, the private sector, civil society and multilaterals, particularly WHO and the World Bank. The twin components of measuring and managing for results came together and were negotiated in the founding principles and frameworks of these innovative health partnerships. At key moments, private foundations and the private sector insisted on a "business-like" focus on results, civil society demanded that accountability went beyond national programmes to ensure real people received services and WHO and technical agencies provided the guidance on measurement (for example in contributions to their initial M&E toolkits for AIDS, TB, malaria and later health systems). Without this balance between normative-, political- and business-focussed stakeholders many of the difficult decisions would not have occurred, such as the decision to stop the first programmes in the Global Fund which did not produce the desired results.

Third, these innovative partnerships did not have country offices, and needed to manage financing of country programmes "remotely" relying on performance data. For this to occur, targets needed to be explicit and achievements transparent, as continually stressed by the Gates Foundation. This was a different model of development to that of "country presence" supported by a network of regional and country representatives. They needed the "invisible hand" of measurable results to coordinate partners, rather than a structure of coordination meetings. The results focus was also the basis of the country partnership, bringing together an innovative mix of partners in country, often with little in common except a commitment (or legal agreement) to achieve the results of the programme. The distance between the financing organisation and the programmes they support required a different business model which could manage primarily on results. GAVI and the Global Fund both developed performance-based funding to measure, but most importantly, to manage by results (Plowman 2008).

	Selected results approaches	**Key Characteristics**	**Challenges**
GAVI	Performance-based funding	Strong use of incentives and rewards for good performance. Use partner estimates and country reporting. Define baselines for support	Unintended effects of incentives on reporting, data quality issues. Incentives to improve less-performing grants
Global Fund	Performance-based funding	Explicit performance ratings for each disbursement. Actions defined for each level of performance. Transparent M&E frameworks defined for all countries	Five-Year Evaluation pointed to the burden of reporting and country data quality. Challenge to balance impact and quality with numbers of services delivered
PEPFAR	Target-based financing	Overall programme targets set and reported to Congress. Strong building of M&E capacity to report on key indicators in country	Alignment of M&E with national reporting, explicit policies to use results as a basis for subsequent financing. Challenges in showing HIV prevention impact
World Bank	Results-based financing and output-based aid	Performance incentives actively decentralised to local and health worker level. Results included in conditional loans	Evaluation showed the need to explicitly measure goals of programmes during implementation. Results-based financing used in selected projects

Figure 3. Selected managing for results approaches among health partners.

Both performance- and results-based funding use results as a primary basis for decisions about funding. They shift funding decisions to outputs and outcomes rather than inputs. Results-based funding is a more direct, conditionality of funding on results (or outputs in output-based aid). Results are often directly bought, for example US$10 is reimbursed for every person treated above a baseline. Performance-based funding involves an overall review of results against targets (performance rather than just results) and reasons for deviation (context). Funding decisions are often based on a performance rating (for example A-well performing, B-adequate, C-inadequate) rather than directly on results. This is the basis for funding amounts. Results-based funding has more, direct conditionality and incentives, performance-based funding is adaptable to different contexts and incentivises improvements at all levels of performance. Plowman (2008) describes six features that commonly characterise performance-based funding systems:

1. General goals reflecting the interests of main stakeholders
2. Performance indicators that are measurable and related to the goals; such indicators may include inputs, processes, outputs, outcomes and impact

3. Targets established for each indicator
4. Performance data to measure achievement relative to targets
5. Funds allocated according to a uniformly applied, easily understood mechanism relating funding to attainment of targets
6. Evaluation and adjustment to respond to the changing goals of the performance-based funding system, and to refine and correct operational problems in its application

Innovative health partnerships did not, however, avoid many of the traditional problems of development and the results agenda. They needed to invest in measurement systems in countries if they were to use their results. Measurement of outcomes and impact required coordination between several partners (for example to finance Demographic and Health surveys, or develop vital registration). They needed to balance results information required for twice yearly financing decisions with the longer term outcome focus of the MDGs. They faced issues of attribution of their financing to results from country programmes which had inputs from many domestic and international organisations. There was a partnership or shareholder model of financing countries.

Finally, as their financing grew and they developed separate performance systems, they faced common aid effectiveness issues. Separate reporting requirements needed to align if country transaction costs were to be managed and for the necessary systematic capacity building (for surveys, disease surveillance, vital registration, independent evaluations and country analytical capacity to produce health and disease reviews). Health partnerships bring to the surface many of the innovations and challenges of creating common country systems to manage for results.

3.1 GAVI: the innovative use of performance incentives

GAVI has introduced one of the most innovative models of performance-based funding. It is outcome based, actively uses incentives and is relatively light on requirements relying on technical partners in country.

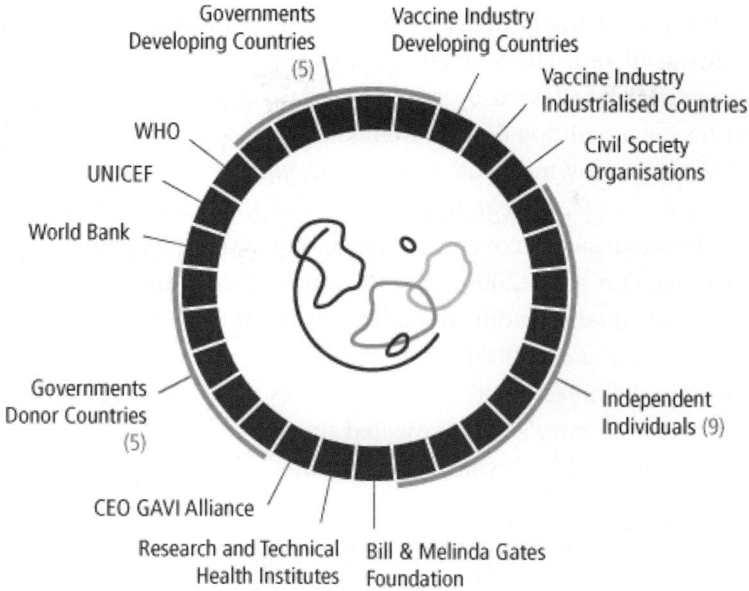

Figure 4. GAVI alliance partnership (the numbers show seats on the board).

GAVI is made up of a distinctive alliance, bringing together technical organisations (particularly WHO and UNICEF), private foundations (with a leading role of the Gates Foundation), bilaterals and private members of its board. The Gates Foundation was important in the establishment of GAVI and in promoting performance-based funding in its business model.

The guiding principles of GAVI include results and transparency: "delivering results with the resources we have been given is of the utmost importance — and we seek and share information about these results" (GAVI 2006). At the same time, GAVI embodies a partnership approach to measuring and managing results, reflecting strongly the influence of DFID, Norway, WHO and UNICEF on its board. The interaction of these partners has influenced a number of initiatives, including the Norwegian support to the World Bank for results-based financing, and DFID support for the partnership and results focus of the IHP. This unique balance of partners has strongly influenced the GAVI model of performance-based funding.

The GAVI Alliance developed a results-based window of support for partner country national immunisation programmes in 1999. It combines a predictable investment phase of support, with a reward phase based on the results achieved. The investment phase involves two years of flexible support, which is followed by a reward phase in which countries receive US$20 for each additional child immunised above an agreed-upon target level. The reward payments are true rewards in that they are not earmarked to programme costs. Research suggested that the results programme has improved immunisation coverage, especially in countries with lower baseline coverage (Lu *et al.* 2006). Results are verified through partners, and additional data quality audits, though there are limitations to the quality of country data (Lu *et al.* 2006).

The initial "investment" phase involves funding over three years, based on each country's self-projected number of children to be immunised. Thereafter, the "reward" phase pays a reward amount for each additional child immunised above the projected first-year targets. Reward funding requires both increasing the number of children immunised and achieving a verification factor of greater than 80% in the independent data quality audit.

The active use of incentives and of the partnership approach for measurement are two innovative elements of the GAVI approach. The use of incentives aligns the interests of the donor and the programme without requiring micromanagement of the programme or heavy reporting. Countries have considerable flexibility in the use of funds, but are rewarded directly for their results. As the first GAVI evaluation concluded "flexibility of GAVI funding, and the minimal reporting burden at country level, were important advantages of GAVI support" (Chee *et al.* 2007).

GAVI uses partners for oversight and reporting on results, and funds staff in WHO and UNICEF. This has brought greater alignment in its results reporting and potentially creates partner buy-in to the goals and results. Country results can be focused on a single indicator, increases in coverage or number of children immunised with GAVI support (compared to a baseline, pre-GAVI year). These are provided by WHO which reports these indicators on an annual basis. Nevertheless, there have been challenges in using these partners for the more routine verification of results. They are also not independent from the programmes they are supporting. The systems have therefore also relied on independent data quality audits, implemented outside these partners.

The approach has led to increases in immunisation coverage, flexibility in supporting country programming and goals, but can lead to distortions. The first evaluation of GAVI found it rewarded countries with higher population growth (which alone predicts whether a country receives rewards in 76% of countries). There were also issues with data quality which were explicitly recognised by GAVI; two-thirds of the countries that did not initially qualify for rewards (15 did not qualify out of 51) did not pass their data quality audit. The Phase 1 evaluation of GAVI also suggested improved approaches "for facilitating support to underperforming countries" were needed. The incentives were focused on countries which overperformed, rather than incentivising actions at all levels of performance. More recent reviews (Lim *et al.* 2008) have also pointed to the differences between officially reported and survey estimates, and the distortions incentives may provide for country reporting.

Overall, GAVI was one of the first innovative health partnerships to routinely apply performance-based financing approaches. Its most distinctive aspects are the active use of incentives, partnership measurement (by WHO and UNICEF) and flexible support of country-based priorities and programming. It also shows some of the challenges of the potential distortions of incentives, the need to aggressively build country measurement capacity and develop approaches and incentives to improve poorer performing countries.

3.2 Global fund: performance-based decisions

The Global Fund provides one of the most comprehensive applications of performance-based funding for management decisions as well as for measurement. It uses performance-based funding for all decisions to release financing to its programmes in 140 countries (Low-Beer *et al.* 2007). This has brought many of the challenges to the surface from the experience of managing for results across three diseases, health systems and in very different contexts. Challenges include aligning reporting with countries and other partners, building country capacity and balancing shorter term services with outcomes and the MDGs. One of the distinguishing factors of the Global Fund is its decision focus — to base all financing decisions at each grant stage on a review and explicit rating of performance. Performance-based funding needs to work in very different contexts and not penalise poorer countries and those with weaker health systems.

Performance-based funding has applied two of the Global Fund's core principles –a results focus and country ownership. The Global Fund does not have its own indicators but has collected indicators recommended by technical partners in its M&E toolkit. The country proposes indicators and targets as part of its proposal which is reviewed independently and competitively by a technical review panel. The country is also meant to set aside 5–10% of programme funds to strengthen country systems which measure results (in 2009, 4.9% of finance or US$280 million were allocated for M&E strengthening) (Global Fund 2010).

Performance is measured against targets that are owned and feasible within a country context. Performance does not compare the absolute performance of, for example, Russia against Zambia or China against Malawi. Performance is relative to country context and targets, rather than to other countries. The country ownership of targets is open to distortions — such as by setting low initial targets or changing them during implementation. This flexibility is important, however, for performance-based funding to work in very different country situations in over 140 countries. Due to this approach, as of end 2009, the poorest third of Global Fund-supported countries had no worse performance than the mean, and slightly less funding was removed in these countries at programme reviews (Global Fund 2010).

Results are used to make management decisions at each stage of financing. The Global Fund makes all disbursements (quarterly, six monthly or annually) in tranches based on progress in results. In addition, progress against impact and overall programme goals are reviewed to renew programme funding every two to three years. The Global Fund has implemented the Paris Declaration indicator of "transparent and monitorable performance assessment frameworks" in all its programmes. These are published on the Fund's website together with all results updates for over 600 programmes in all participating countries (at http://www.theglobalfund.org). Each grant is given an explicit performance rating (A-exceeding targets, B1-adequate performance, B2-inadequate performance but potential demonstrated, C-unacceptable performance) which guides financing decisions. Local Fund Agents (local representatives paid directly by the Global Fund) verify results with on-site checks at the point of service delivery each year. The performance rating takes into account explanations of performance by the implementer and actions to improve performance. Actions to improve performance, at all levels of performance, are central to the model.

Decisions can be made to adjust funding based on progress and results at each stage of implementation. The aim is to adjust funding to the underlying rate of implementation, rather than just to disburse according to the passing of calendar time. Programmes can be accelerated if they exceed targets — for example, the Ethiopia malaria programme brought forward its year 5 budget into year 3. If implementation is slower than expected, funding can be reduced or additional strengthening measures added to improve results. In extreme situations, funding is stopped, with safeguards to ensure continuity of life-saving services (for example HIV treatment). Instead of money remaining in programmes which are delayed, almost US$1 billion of unused funds has been reallocated so far to fund new programmes.

In addition, performance-based funding aims to promote management decisions to improve programmes at all stages of performance, by providing incentives for acceleration in those performing well, incentives for strengthening actions in those performing less well and promoting restructuring (with relevant safeguards) in those with unacceptable performance (see Figure 5). Even in the majority of programmes that have stopped (with No Go Recommendations), this has led to much better proposals and performance in subsequent years (for example the Senegal malaria, Nigeria HIV or Honduras HIV programmes). Overall, at programme reviews (after year 2), 78% of programmes were performing against their targets (rated A or B1), while 19% showed inadequate performance but demonstrated potential (B2) and 3% reflected unacceptable performance (C).

The importance of "Managing for Results" and taking decisions to improve programmes at all levels of performance is shown in the country examples below in Figure 5. The Niger malaria programme had achieved its targets; however targets were increased by more effectively using local partners and linking the programme to the International Red Crescent activities. Programmes which are consistently A-rated can access additional finances to those in their grant without going through a new application. Performance-based funding should also benefit less well-performing programmes. The

Performance	Country and Programme	Decisions and Adjustments made
A	Niger Malaria	Used local partners and International Red Crescent to further Accelerate ITN delivery
B1	Malawi HIV	HIV treatment – human resources bottleneck, reallocated US$40 million to support this in the middle of implementation. The transparent identification of the performance issue allowed partners to coordinate their support
B2	Mali HIV	Procurement bottleneck identified, UNDP supported country to build local capacity to improve performance
	Ethiopia Malaria	B2 rated, identified bottleneck as part of the review. Given 6 months to deliver the 2 million ITNs which had not been delivered. The country invited UNICEF to build capacity, revised its treatment and prevention procedures, delivered the ITNs and is now A-rated
C	Senegal, Nigeria	Grant stopped, reformed coordination and M&E, signed new effective grants

Figure 5. Performance ratings and adjustments made for country programmes.

Malawi HIV programme was rated B1 at its review. As part of this review, a major bottleneck in human resources was identified. This explicit performance review allowed US$40 million to be reallocated to the human resources budget (not included in the original strategy) to improve performance. As this was a transparent performance review, these changes could be coordinated with DFID support to tackle human resources. Similarly, the performance reviews in the Mali HIV and Ethiopia malaria programmes transparently identified the issues and allowed country system strengthening to occur (with the support of UNICEF and UNDP). Even the stopping of grants due to performance (No Go decisions) in countries like Senegal precipitated the reform of coordination mechanisms and the M&E system, rapidly improving the performance of the programme. Judgements on poor performance have been some of the most effective triggers of improvement (supported by technical assistance, for which there is suddenly a demand).

Much of the most effective capacity building has been in programmes rated poor in terms of performance. Only recently has the Global Fund provided incentives to reward the best performing programmes by allocating additional funding on top of their approved amounts. This in part was in response to innovations in GAVI.

Many partners support results measurement, but fewer use results to make the more difficult management and performance decisions. The unique partnership in the Global Fund Board was critical to many of its most difficult performance decisions. The first programmes recommended for discontinued funding took over six months to pass through its Board. Many partners wanted to do performance-based funding in principle (discuss indicators and measurement frameworks) but not in practice (make performance-based decisions). Board representatives from communities living with the diseases were the first to vote to end financing which did not benefit their constituents. For many other partners, there were important political reasons "to turn a blind eye." However communities living with the diseases changed the political dynamic on the Board, refocusing the debate directly on the needs of people receiving services. This returns to Attaran's comments that ultimately managing for results is not only a technical or measurement issue, but an ethical one of accountability to those in need of health services (Attaran 2005). There are many measurement, management and partnership hurdles to achieve management for results.

The Independent Five-Year Evaluation of the Global Fund highlighted some of the challenges of implementing performance-based funding (Macro 2009). It recognised performance-based funding as one of "two of the stronger achievements in *[the Global Fund's] first five years of operations"* and pointed to "the management benefits and health systems contributions made through the Global Fund's commitment to PBF." At the same time, both this and other evaluations identified the following challenges:

- A more systematic partner approach is needed to invest in strengthening weak country HIS.
- Simplification and streamlining of performance-based funding, particularly at country level, to increase alignment and reduce transaction costs.

- A greater emphasis on impact and outcome indicators and quality of services in performance-based funding decisions.
- Communication issues in coordinating various actors to support programme performance, and a more differentiated approach for countries with weaker capacities in M&E.

The Global Fund has taken actions to respond within its programmes. It is consolidating its grants into a "single stream of funding" for each disease to streamline and align its programmes. It is also separating a review of outcomes and impact every three years from ongoing reporting on services. It is introducing an explicit component of quality of services (which will affect all ratings and result in conditions for continued funding). In addition, it has reduced the number of indicators to an average of 14 per programme and introduced joint M&E strengthening assessments with partners across 80% of its programmes. The benefits and challenges of implementing managing for results are nevertheless apparent in these evaluations.

The evaluation presents a wider partner challenge — to develop an aligned results approach in countries to coordinate capacity strengthening and measure impact. Even if the Global Fund requests 14 indicators, if the indicators and reporting schedules are not aligned with other partners and ultimately the country, this can lead collectively to a significant reporting burden. The Five-Year Evaluation pointed to actions beyond Global Fund-supported programmes: "The Global Fund should urgently seek a more coordinated approach and the more systematic investment of partners to strengthen the country HIS which are needed as the basis for monitoring overall progress, enabling performance based funding, and conducting ongoing evaluations" (Macro 2009). As the number of programmes and partners using performance-based funding increases, this leads to the wider aid effectiveness challenge internationally and in countries. It also raises the possibility of a more radical results agenda, where common results can coordinate financing among diverse partners — a results-based partnership.

3.3 Coordinating partners behind country results

The last decade has been a period of innovation in managing for results — in its development and application in varied settings and health programmes.

As often occurs after a period of innovation, the need for consolidation and to tackle system-wide issues soon becomes apparent. The major challenge has been to move from a donor project to a national programme or shareholder approach to managing for results. This has required considerable country and international diplomacy.

(a) *Country leadership in coordinating partners for results*

A number of countries have taken strong actions to coordinate partners around a common platform for national results. Ethiopia is described in some detail in other chapters. It has combined political leadership with a clear results focus to coordinate diverse donors — including World Bank, GAVI, PEPFAR, Global Fund and bilaterals. This has been particularly beneficial for health systems strengthening actions. Despite separate immunisation, AIDS, TB, malaria and other health goals, donors support the common deployment of 30,000 community health workers and over 1000 health centres to deliver these services. This is "diagonal funding" where disease-specific programmes also finance crosscutting horizontal health systems components (Low-Beer *et al.* 2007). Previously, the AIDS programme had separate health worker goals and targets. This led to stigma and a reluctance of those in the community to visit an "AIDS health worker". The common results approach has led to more effective delivery of AIDS, TB and malaria services together with contributions to the delivery of other health services by these workers. The diverse partners (with different disease goals) contribute financing to the same targets for deployment of community health workers and health centres. They have moved to "shareholder reporting" on the country's progress.

Ethiopia has also been able to use the separate funds from donors for capacity building for results-based management. It has combined PEPFAR, World Bank, Global Fund and national funding to pay for crosscutting surveys and to improve disease surveillance. Most importantly, it has strengthened its national analytical capacity to be able to produce the reports and analysis to manage the programme (and to an extent its donors) by results. Instead of filling in indicator sheets and reporting forms, the Ethiopians now have a strong national M&E capacity (funding with a budget of over US$50 million) to produce their own analysis, interpretation and reports. The system has also been strengthened at regional and community level to support managing for results and basic health decisions at all levels. They have built capacity to take country control of the results agenda. Countries generally have access to much better data than global partners (though they do not always realise this) but need to match this with the capacity to analyse and use their results.

Most recently, the Ethiopians have established an MDG fund. They use the IHP and aid effectiveness agenda to push partners to coordinate around national outcomes. They have also ensured M&E is a key component of health systems strengthening. The recent GF proposal for health systems strengthening focused particularly on M&E strengthening across all health programmes (and beyond HIV, TB and malaria) with a budget of over US$20 million. This has nevertheless been a process over several years. It is based on a firm national commitment to provide results and build the national capacity to own the management of results. They have created a country partnership for results.

Rwanda was initially presented as an example of unbalanced health aid. A large proportion of funding to health came from AIDS programmes (particularly PEPFAR, World Bank and the Global Fund). Rwanda has used a common results framework to overcome some of these aid effectiveness and allocation issues. It has defined a basic package of health services and results and ensured their delivery is the backbone of the health system. They are built into contracts from the government down to health clinics and local mayors. This has allowed Rwanda to use specific funding to fit into wide-reaching health goals, including progress against MDGs 4,5 and 6.

By focusing partners on the results of the health service, Rwanda can use resources from diverse partners more flexibly. By having a clear results framework for AIDS, TB and malaria services, Global Fund financing has been able to contribute to the health insurance package directly. This has resulted in AIDS, TB, malaria and all health services (visits for all health services have more than doubled with this additional funding focused on HIV) increasing in the country. Similarly antenatal services have been improved generally through HIV funding to preventing mother to child HIV transmission (PMTCT). Their results approach has led to significant synergies and improvements in all the health-related MDGs 4, 5 and 6. Although the inputs have been focused on HIV, the results have been distributed more evenly across health conditions. Rwanda provides an example of how a results focus can be effective in coordinating diverse partners. Nevertheless, there were significant transaction costs, and Rwandan authorities want to significantly harmonise the number of indicators and reports requested by donors.

Two other examples highlight further elements of this more radical results agenda. First, Malawi has gone through an extensive process to develop an agreed national results framework for its pooled health financing for all partners. This has allowed disease-specific funding and pooled health financing in the SWAp to coordinate closely in implementation. While tensions remain, the results focus has improved the functioning of the SWAp, and the SWAp has brought benefits of alignment and harmonisation to disease focused health partnerships like the Global Fund. If the results focus of global health partnerships and the benefits of pooled financing can be combined, it can lead to significant increases in aid effectiveness.

Second, the Russian NGO coalition shows the important role of transparent results in coordinating the very diverse partners involved in the NGO response. Despite initial concerns, NGOs have risen to the challenge of performance-based funding in the Global Fund. They have been able to establish systems to report results, and their performance is at least as good as government implementers (84% are rated well performing compared to 76%) for all programmes. The Russian NGOs (see Chapter 18) have used results to coordinate activities of diverse NGOs within the country. They have established an internet-based results portal where partners can view the activities and results of other implementers (at http://www.symona.mednet.ru). The portal shows the activities and updated results and performance of each NGO, from national to local level. Such an approach has helped show the results transparently of NGO activities, as well as coordinate their implementation among widely dispersed and diverse partners (who cannot meet regularly). It is results rather than meeting based coordination. Cambodia has used a similar approach to show all the development programmes in the country, though focused on programmes and financial inputs (http://cdc.khmer.biz/).

These country examples have been highlighted first deliberately. They show the possibility of a more radical country agenda where results can be used to manage programmes and diverse partners. It requires leadership to coordinate investments and country capacity (in surveys, health surveillance, vital registration and particularly for analysis), considerable health diplomacy and a transparent focus on country results.

(b) *International leadership in coordinating partners for results*

There have also been increasing efforts at the international level to coordinate partners behind national results. The Paris Declaration (OECD 2005) is relatively clear that donors commit to "Link country programming and resources to results and align them with effective partner country performance assessment frameworks." Following the initial challenges to establish operational systems for managing for results across over a hundred countries, the challenge has shifted to how to coordinate donor results reporting within countries.

The World Bank did significant initial work to support "Results Based management." It has focused on the results conditions of its funding to countries (output-based aid). More recently it has developed results-based financing to build incentives into programmes from national to health worker level. The World Bank has investigated the use of cash payment of non-monetary transfers made to a national or sub-national government, manager, provider, payer or consumer of health services after predefined results have been achieved and verified. With the strong support of the Norwegians and British, they have established a specific trust fund to pilot and introduce these approaches. This has been applied in countries as diverse as Argentina, Haiti, Lesotho and Rwanda, combining incentives with results. It has developed some of the more innovative approaches in a wide range of areas, provider payment incentives, vouchers, contracting linked to targets and conditional cash payments and transfer to households.

The WHO has also developed global level common frameworks for monitoring and evaluation, health systems strengthening, under the IHP and CHESS (Country Health Systems Surveillance) (WHO 2009). It has increasingly focused its technical role in supporting countries to coordinate partners around common results frameworks. This has built on the prominent role of its disease programmes in TB, malaria, HIV and the role

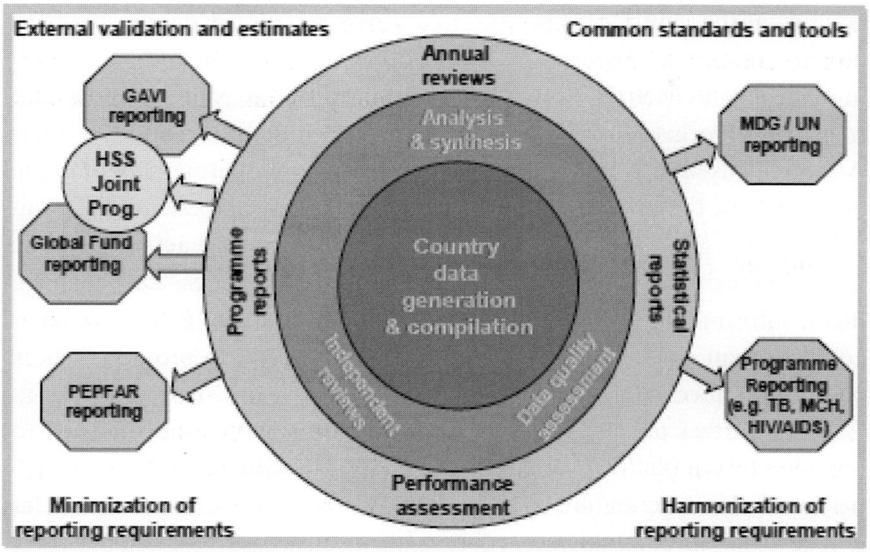

Figure 6. Country health systems surveillance (CHESS) platform.

Source: WHO 2009.

of UNAIDS (in promoting the Three Ones principles of coordination, one country action framework, one coordinating body, one country monitoring and evaluation system). Increasingly, WHO is working to put these disease components together in support for an overall results framework for health. Countries are inviting WHO to play this role, to coordinate partners around results, most recently in Nepal, Mozambique, Sierra Leone and Benin in 2011.

The CHESS framework states "a national country health systems surveillance (CHESS) platform is needed to bring together the monitoring and evaluation work in disease-specific programmes, such as TB, HIV and immunisation, with cross-cutting efforts such as tracking human resources, logistics and procurement, and health service delivery." The aim is to form "the platform for subnational, national and global reporting, aligning partners at country and global levels around a common approach to country support and reporting requirements." This is illustrated in Figure 6, which aims to use country results, analysis and review as a platform to coordinate diverse partners. These approaches place the country at the centre of reporting and analysis, and the donors as shareholders in their results.

The Health Metrics Network has also catalysed support behind a common framework for strengthening country Health Information systems. Although based in WHO, it aims to mobilise a wider partnership of global programmes, the private sector, private foundations and countries to support country HIS. The HMN framework focuses partner activities on six key components: HIS resources, indicators, data sources, data management, information products and dissemination and use. It has supported countries and partners to implement this framework, to provide a single country platform to manage for results.

Two further developments in health diplomacy have also pushed for common health platforms focused on results. The IHP+ aims to coordinate partners behind a common country strategy and performance review. It has helped develop common procedures, for example for assessing national health plans (JANS) and for monitoring and evaluation. The Joint Health Systems Strengthening Platform has built on this work and was initiated by the heads of GAVI and the Global Fund, the World Bank, WHO and other partners to coordinate their activities. Following a period of consultation and health diplomacy, criteria for common partner approaches to managing for results have been agreed by partners and countries:

1. **Country-owned reporting and health reviews, which include:**
   — Explicit indicators and time-bound targets
   — Joint guidance on common health systems strengthening indicators
   — Providing results on health systems strengthening and for immunisation, AIDS, TB and malaria services and outcomes
   — M&E plan for measurement including necessary investments

2. **Explicit, transparent, performance ratings**
   — Based on an initial country review of performance (as part of the health review process)
   — These should include explanations of deviations between results and targets, including catch-up plans
   — Common guidance to be provided on ratings and how they are adjusted by contextual factors

3. **Use of clear performance incentives**
   — To accelerate funding to grants related to activities that are supported
   — Invest in systems strengthening for those which do not fully perform but show potential
   — Reduce funding where it is not used, and exceptionally to stop funding
4. **Alignment of reporting between partners and with country cycles**
   — Align reviews to an annual cycle, with mid-year triggers where necessary
   — Align performance reviews to a common timing between participating partners
   — Align the timing of performance reviews and funding decisions to the underlying country results and budget cycles
   — Coordinate performance reviews as a basis of continued partner funding
5. **Joint system strengthening for performance reviews**
   — The approach will require investments to build the capacity of countries in reporting, data quality and analysis, as to improve performance reviews
   — Partners agree to commit 5–10% of health funding to these activities
   — Partners to coordinate data quality assessments to ensure regular on-site data verification and sampled, detailed audits. This will either involve joint tools or cross-accreditation and recognition of partner tools

The major challenge at present is to create common country results systems, which see donors as shareholders or stakeholders. This more radical results agenda focuses on aligning and coordinating donors not around political conditionality but around results. The diversity of partners operating in health requires a "common currency" of health results as a basis for coordination. To achieve this requires considerable health diplomacy to align interests, measurement and management of development results. This is an emerging agenda, supported by an increasing coalition of partners and countries across diseases and health, but an unfinished agenda.

4. Conclusions and Critiques — Can Development be Managed for Results?

Results are often seen as a technical issue, of defining indicators, and agreeing a monitoring and evaluation framework to return to after a programme has been implemented. Despite the prominence of "Managing for Results' as a core principle of aid effectiveness, efforts have often reverted to measurement rather than managing programmes for results. Attempts are made to harmonise each component of implementation (procurement, finance and management) with working groups of partners. Countries are often overwhelmed by harmonisation or technical assistance. Yet since 2000 a more radical results agenda has emerged to use results actively to manage programmes, and in some countries to manage donors. It aims to focus partners on results and to create space for countries to own the process of implementation.

This more radical results agenda has been shown in a number of countries and NGOs as illustrated in this chapter. Yet for every Ethiopia, Rwanda and Malawi which have managed programmes and donors for results, many countries still have results defined from outside and their reporting fragmented. Initially, the challenges of the results agenda were to build performance-based funding into the business models of individual partnerships, like the Global Fund and GAVI. Increasingly the challenges have shifted to coordinate a common country platform to report to the country and all donors. This has culminated in a shift to seeing global programmes as shareholders in country results, rather than with their separate results chains and lines of accountability.

The chapter has stressed the dual traditions of measurement and management for results — and how a diversity of partners brought these together in innovative health partnerships. The chapter showed the challenges of building results-based financing into the business models of innovative partnerships. Financing initially occurred with limited agreement on indicators, country applications with few explicit targets and limited policies for reporting and review. Yet the accountability demands were high, and the "raison d'etre" of new health partnerships was their ability to show and communicate results. The mandates of global programmes did not refer to agreed treaties, and they needed to prove themselves with results in new ways. The chapter showed some of the innovations these partnerships brought — in using incentives to reward performance- and results-based decision making and introducing these approaches into countries. Rapidly the challenges became apparent and the limitations of separate results-based financing systems is increasingly evident. The final section reviewed the country and international initiatives to support common country platforms to manage programmes for results.

Common results reporting and decisions have been captured by the Results TRAIN principles:

- **T**ransparency: of results and targets, methods, data, and results reports
- **R**esults-based decisions: using results as the basis for funding and policy decisions, so partners manage for as well as measure results
- **A**lignment with country reporting: donor reporting should align to the extent possible with country systems, timing and common indictors
- **I**nvestment in country results systems: invest in the country data, results systems and evaluations to manage for results (5–10% of donor funding as guidance)
- **N**ational results rather than attribute to donors: donors should clearly show their financial and technical contribution and share, but base programmatic results on country national results and outcomes to the extent possible."

Yet there are continuing criticisms of the results agenda — the ability of partners to measure compelling development results and to manage and coordinate their activities for results. In addition, countries can become overwhelmed by external reporting and technical advice from the growing "M&E industry." The second set of very important criticisms are the distortions that results and incentives can place on country programmes. Yet some of the most important results have been shown in the health MDGs 4,5 and 6. Scepticism cannot be avoided, but as even Attaran concludes results involve a basic accountability of the MDGs to the world's poor (Attaran 2005).

Despite this degree of healthy scepticism, a results agenda has been one of the most innovative elements of development since 2000. New health partnerships have contributed significantly as they have built performance-based funding into their individual models. There is now a major challenge for health diplomacy to move to a shareholder approach behind country results. This involves the more radical results agenda, where results provide a "common currency" to coordinate diverse partners. It will require a much closer combination of the aid effectiveness principles with the MDGs — to form a development partnership which can measure and manage itself for collective health results.

Managing for results is further illustrated with examples in Chapter 16 on Ethiopia and in Chapter 10 on PEPFAR.

References

Attaran A (2005) "An Immeasurable Crisis? A Criticism of the Millennium Development Goals and Why They Cannot be Measured," *PLoS Med* 2(10):955–61.

Binagwaho A, Ratnayake N (2009) "The Role of Social Capital in Successful Adherence to Antiretroviral Therapy in Africa," *PLoS Medicine* 6(1):10–11.

Buse K, Hein W, Drager N eds (2009) *Making Sense of Global Health Governance*, Basingstoke, Palgrave.

Chee G, His N, Carlson K, Chankova S, Taylor P (2007) *Evaluation of the First Five Years of GAVI Immunization Services Support Funding*, Bethseda MD, Abt Associates Inc.

Eichler R, Levine R (2009) *Performance Incentives for Global Health: Potential and Pitfalls*, Centre for Global Development, Washington.

Fidler DP (2007) "Architecture Amidst Anarchy: Global Health's Quest for Governance", *Global Health Governance* 1(1):1–17.

GAVI (2006) *GAVI Alliance Strategy, 2007–10*, GAVI Alliance, Geneva (http://www.gavialliance.org).

Global Fund to Fight AIDS, Tuberculosis and Malaria (2007) *Partners in Impact: Results Report*, Global Fund, Geneva (http://www.theglobalfund.org).

Global Fund to Fight AIDS, Tuberculosis and Malaria (2010) *Innovation and Impact: Results Report*, Global Fund, Geneva (http://www.theglobalfund.org).

Health Metrics Framework (HMN) (2008) *Framework and Standards for Country Health Information Systems*, HMN, WHO, Geneva.

Jongbloed B, Vossensteyn H (2001) "*Keeping up Performances: An International Survey of Performance-Based Funding in Higher Education,*" *Journal of Higher Education Policy and Management* 23(2):127–45.

Lim S, Stein D, Charrow A, Murray C (2008) "Tracking Progress towards Universal Childhood Immunisation and the Impact of Global Initiatives: A Systematic Analysis of Three-Dose Diphtheria, Tetanus, and Pertussis Immunisation Coverage," *Lancet* 372(9655):2031–46.

Low-Beer D, Afkhami H, Komatsu R, Banati P, Sempala M, Katz I, Cutler J, Schumacher P, Tran-Ba-Huy R, Schwartlander B (2007) "Making Performance-Based Funding Work for Health," *PLoS Med* 4(8):1308–11.

Lu CL, Michaud CM, Gakidou E, Khan K, Murray CJL (2006) "Effect of the Global Alliance for Vaccines and Immunisation on Diphtheria, Tetanus, and Pertussis Vaccine Coverage: An Independent Assessment," *Lancet* 368:1088–95.

Murray C, Lopez A (1996) *The Global Burden of Disease*, Geneva, Switzerland: World Health Organisation.

Murray C, Lopez A (1997) "Mortality by Cause for Eight Regions of the World: Global Burden of Disease Study," *Lancet* 349:1269–76.

Macro (2009) "The Five-Year Evaluation of the Global Fund to Fight AIDS, Tuberculosis, and Malaria — Synthesis Report", Macro (accessible at http://www.theglobalfund.org).

Moyo D (2009) *Dead Aid: Why Aid Is Not Working and Why There Is Another Way for Africa*, Penguin, London, UK.

Murray C, Lopez A (1998) Health Dimensions of sex and reproduction, Harvard University Press, Cambridge.

OECD (2005) *Paris Declaration on Aid Effectiveness*, Paris, OECD.

OECD (2008) *Accra Action Agenda on Aid Effectiveness*, Paris, OECD.

Plowman B (2008) *How the Big Three AIDS Donors Define and Use Performance to Inform Funding Decisions*, Background Paper, Center for Global Development, Washington.

Rusa L, Schneidman M, Fritsche G, Musango L (2009) "Rwanda: Performance-Based Financing in the Public Sector" in Eichler R, Levine R *Performance Incentives for Global Health: Potential and Pitfalls*, Centre for Global Development, Washington.

Sen A (1999) *Development as Freedom*, Oxford, Oxford University Press.

UNAIDS (2004) *The Three Ones: Key Principles*, UNAIDS, Geneva.

World Bank (1993) *Investing in Health: World Development Report 1993*, World Bank, Washington.

World Health Organisation (2008) *A Common Framework for Monitoring Performance and Evaluation of the Scale-Up for Better Health*, WHO, Geneva.

World Health Organisation (2009) *Monitoring and Evaluation of Health Systems Strengthening, an Operational Framework*, WHO, Geneva (http://www.who.int).

5

Country Health Systems and Global Health Partnerships: What are the Challenges, How to Think about Them and What to Do Differently

Dean Shuey and Rebecca Dodd[1]

Summary

This chapter looks at the challenges and opportunities associated with the global health partnerships (GHPs) and building country health systems. Part one synthesises findings from country case studies on GHPs and health systems development. It presents existing evidence — "what we know" — in terms of how the operations of GHPs can help or hinder various aspects of systems development. Part two explores possible reasons for these challenges from a governance perspective. It will look at broader health sector co-ordination processes at country level and discuss how these have been affected by the emergence of GHPs — often with large budgets but typically operating without a country presence. Stronger health sector co-ordination processes can in turn strengthen sector planning and budgeting processes, creating a mutually reinforcing cycle. This is the basis for a

[1] Division of Health Services, Western Pacific Regional Office of the World Health Organization: shueyd@wpro.who.int; doddr@wpro.who.int.

more effective contribution from GHPs to health systems development, yet it is challenging to achieve in practice. We also need more practical advice and recommendations from staff working on health development at county level about entry points and mechanisms for engaging GHPs in health systems development. These concrete recommendations form the final section of the chapter.

1. Introduction

Global health partnerships (GHPs) are often described as a "new phenomenon" in international health. In many respects, this is true: the scale of their funding is unprecedented; their close links with civil society have channelled the activism and energy of single-issue campaigns into mainstream development and, their partnership approach brings together developing and developed countries, the private sector and NGOs in common cause.

However, from a country perspective, particularly the perspective of those who deliver services, the newness is less obvious. For the most part, GHPs fund discrete sets of activities to be implemented according to a project plan. While this plan is developed and approved at country level, widespread use of consultants combined with a proposal-development process concentrated in senior levels of government mean that in practice it is often developed with minimal input from those who carry out the tasks it outlines, and typically with little regard to the entire spectrum of tasks they perform. Equally, while linking funding to results (or indicators) is often presented as innovative, it has been a feature of most health development projects for the last three decades through instruments such as logical frameworks. What is different, particularly with regard to the Global Fund to Fight AIDS, TB and Malaria (GFATM), is the *scale* of support: an entire nation may depend on a single organisation for provision of a critical intervention. This creates efficiency gains, but also presents risks.

In this chapter, we consider the impact of GHPs, including GAVI, Global Fund, PEPFAR and others working in health, on health systems development from the perspective of those who work at country level — whether for government or for development partners. Our views have been shaped by direct experience of working with GHP processes in countries, as well as by discussions with multiple stakeholders; we recognise that partiality and bias may be associated with our particular perspective.

By placing GHPs in their historical context, we show that much about the way they work, the challenges they encounter, even the critique of their operations by others, is familiar. It follows that the lessons learnt by other development partners operating in health may also be relevant to GHPs. In reviewing these lessons and considering their applicability to GHPs, we hope to provide insights into how GHPs can become more effective supporters of health systems in future.

2. Development Assistance in Health — A Short History

The second half of the 20th century was a tumultuous time in large parts of the developing world. In the 1950s and 1960s, there was much optimism as political independence was progressively realised. Combined with new financing on offer in the form of aid, it was hoped that this would catalyse an era of sustained economic growth, finance the expansion of public services, including health, and lead to an ever-increasing standard of living (see Chapter 1 for further historical context).

During the 1970s and 1980s, a different reality asserted itself. Global stagflation, often combined with conflict and economic mismanagement, led to the collapse of public health budgets at the same time that populations, and population demands, were growing rapidly. Salaries in the public sector were progressively devalued leaving many public sector employees — including health workers — below the poverty line.

A new model of development — structural adjustment — emerged, which prioritised investment in "productive" sectors over social sectors (Lundberg and Wang 2006). At the same time, privatisation was introduced or expanded, either through the establishment of a stand-alone private health sector or through the introduction of private-sector practices within the public institutions. Though privatisation was often poorly regulated and monitored, and did not always produce the expected results, it was seen as a necessity given that no alternative sources of funds were available.

The declining priority to publicly funded health care persuaded many that the vision of comprehensive primary health care as outlined in Alma Ata in 1978 was no longer viable. "Selective" primary health care — which had emerged immediately following Alma Ata, as an alternative, less aspirational and more pragmatic approach suited to low-income environments — became increasingly dominant, and judgments about cost-effectiveness took on a new level of importance. It is worth noting that Walsh and Warren's seminal article on selective PHC refers to it as an *interim* strategy necessitated by the lack of resources and that comprehensive PHC should remain the ultimate goal (Walsh and Warren 1979).

During the 1990s, ideologies shifted again as greater emphasis was given to human development alongside economic growth. There was recognition that health is a precondition for, not just a result of, economic development and therefore requires sustained investment (World Bank 1993; WHO 2001). New international commitments such as the Millennium Declaration (United Nations 2000) led to an increasing share of health in ODA (Piva and Dodd 2009). Much of this increase was derived from and/or channelled through new GHPs, such as the Global Alliance for Vaccines and Immunization (GAVI) and the GFATM (WHO 2008). Other important new funding sources included the US President's Emergency Plan for AIDS Relief (PEPFAR) which is part of the US bilateral aid programme, with country-level staff, but which also shares some of the same characteristics of GHPs.

The large increase in funding for health was significant, but new resources still fell short of needs. Even so, issues of absorptive capacity were encountered. Country health systems that had been designed to cope with an extreme shortage of resources were now being asked to manage a massive influx of new funds. Systems that were used to a trickle were suddenly faced with a flood. It is not surprising that the GHPs quickly encountered health system bottlenecks.

3. Country Operations of GHPs: Old Wine in New Bottles?

Although GHPs are a new type of funding organisation, their ways of working in-country hold much in common with the project approach favoured by "traditional" donors. Stand-alone project proposals with project-specific goals, targets, logical frameworks and distinct budgets are — with some important exceptions — the norm.

Equally, many countries establish dedicated managerial teams to handle GHP reporting and monitoring requirements (even though these are not a formal requirement of GHPs) in the mode of traditional project management units (PMUs). Now, as in the past, the push to establish PMUs comes not only from donors but also from recipient governments, who use them as a mechanism to provide higher salaries and thus attract good staff, and to bypass their own, poorly-functioning bureaucracies. This is a long-recognised catch-22 of project approaches, which has continued with the advent of GHPs.

GHPs often encourage (or mandate) countries to form new governing bodies to represent their interests at country level, e.g. the Interagency Coordinating Committee (ICC) for GAVI and the country coordinating mechanism (CCM) for GFATM, even when more general donor coordination mechanisms are in place. In many respects, these mechanisms are not unlike the project-steering committees used by bilateral- and multilateral-funded projects for decades. A key difference, though, is that CCMs (in particular) are more diverse. This has both positive and negative implications. On the one hand, civil society groups previously excluded from policy-level discussions now have a seat at the table. On the other, diversity may be difficult to manage and lead to gridlock in decision-making processes.

4. Global Health Partnerships and Health Systems — General Issues

The impact of GHPs on health systems has been a topic of heated discussion almost from their inception (Oliveira-Cruz *et al.* 2003). Much of this critique has historical roots in the long-standing "vertical" versus "horizontal" debate which is often at the centre of discussions about health systems strengthening and primary health care. The range of opinion is large: at one extreme the idea that GHP work on specific health issues is an effective entry point to support health systems, at the other the view that the presence of GHPs "undermines progress towards the long-term goal of an effective, high-quality, inclusive health system" (Bennett and Fairbank 2003; Marchal *et al.* 2009).

More balanced critiques recognise the complexity of judging "impact" and the importance of local context. Unsurprisingly, many studies on the impact of GHPs on health systems find both positive and negative effects, depending on the local realities and the implementation methods chosen. Positives include rapid scale-up of the coverage of interventions and greater stakeholder participation, particularly from non-government stakeholders, improved data on (targeted) diseases and wider promotion of standardised guidelines for targeted services (TERG 2009). Negative effects include a distortion of country policies (Travis *et al.* 2004; Caines 2005; Lane 2007), distraction from coordinated efforts to strengthen health systems, and a re-verticalisation of planning, management and monitoring and evaluation systems (Biesma *et al.* 2009).

One of the most common criticisms of GHPs by countries is their "one size fits all" approach: deadlines for the submission of funding proposals that cannot be adjusted to country planning and budgeting cycles; global budgeting and reporting formats that are standardised globally and do not map onto local systems and so on. Again, though, these criticisms are not new: similar complaints have been made (and still are) of bilateral donors, and recommendations on how to address these problems have been around for years (Unger *et al.* 2003; Buse *et al.* 2007).

In assessing the impact of GHPs on health systems, it is important to emphasise that there is nothing inherently wrong with either vertical funding or the setting of targeted priorities. Resources are always finite — even when they are plentiful — so priorities are always needed. The issue is *how* priorities are set and by whom, and how to ensure fairness, equity and balance in the process. The decision to establish GHPs to tackle particular health challenges such as HIV and immunisation was taken at the global level. It was not, primarily, a technical decision based on the resource needs and priorities of individual countries. From the service delivery perspective — and from the perspective of those who need care — the practical result is that ill-health associated with some diseases appears to be more important (i.e. more likely to be prevented or treated) than ill-health associated with other diseases. This is true even when the neglected conditions are more prevalent, and/or cheaper to address. That said, the success of social movements around HIV and child health has prompted activism in other areas resulting in a growing list of issue-specific funds and programmes offering support at country level.

Equally, vertical or project funding (to support globally-agreed priorities) is not in and of itself a problem: all health systems have both vertical disease programmes and horizontal components, for example human resources, and very few interventions are either completely stand-alone or completely integrated (Atun *et al.* 2010). The question is how vertical and horizontal components relate to each other and the balance of resources between them. Indeed, a well-designed and -targeted disease project that does not distort the system and is sustainable will be more beneficial than a poorly-designed and implemented cross-cutting intervention.

In summary, the problem is not that GHPs prioritise, but that providing resources for one set of priorities while ignoring others creates imbalance and inequities at local level which undermine the credibility and the integrity (in a managerial sense) of the health system. To their credit, both GAVI and GFATM are acutely aware of many of these issues and are seeking to improve their practice to better support health systems (GAVI 2008; GFATM 2009). However, experience suggests that this is easier to say than to do: and while there has been a clear and important shift in the *intentions* of GHPs to be more systems' friendly, this has not yet translated into significantly different ways of doing business in countries. "The devil is in the detail" — in the next section we try to tease out some of the specific challenges and offer recommendations on what can be done.

5. GHPs and Health Systems — Specific Issues and Examples

This section will examine the impact of GHPs on specific aspects of health systems and make recommendations. As the peer reviewed literature on this subject is notoriously limited (WHO Positive Synergies Collaborative Group 2009), we have drawn on a variety of sources, including grey literature and our own knowledge of countries. This is not a comprehensive analysis: experience suggests that there are wide variations between countries and even within countries, making generalisation difficult. Equally, many of the recommendations we make have been made before in relation to other donors. We hope that what they lack in originality they make up for in common sense.

Health systems have been described as "dynamic complex systems amidst complex systems [which are] relentlessly subject to negotiation, resistance, adaptation, leak and borrow, bloom and fade" (Pawson *et al.* 2005). This interconnectedness means that interventions in one part of the system are likely to have ripple effects elsewhere: sometimes intended, but often not. A classic example would be an increase in efforts to address water-borne illnesses associated with an expansion of irrigation without sufficient attention to hygiene and sanitation. *All health systems interventions should therefore be analysed for their likely effects on the overall system, not just the effects on the problem being directly addressed.*

Different frameworks have been proposed to make sense of the complexity of health systems. WHO's framework identifies six "building blocks" (service delivery, information, human resources, financing, drugs and technology and leadership/governance) which lead to four types of health systems outcomes (level of health, financial protection, responsiveness and efficiency) (WHO 2008).

Other frameworks cover similar ground. For example, the World Bank framework highlights financing, payment, organisation, regulation and behaviour as the five "control knobs" of the system (Roberts *et al.* 2003; World Bank HNP Strategy 2007) while USAID-funded research on this topic highlights the causative pathways and interactions between these different components (Bennett and Fairbank 2003). Other variations use the same categories as the WHO building blocks, but combine them differently or give them different labels (Atun *et al.* 2004; Atun *et al.* 2010). The point is not to argue that one framework is better than another, but to show that most frameworks share common characteristics and all agree that, even when we focus on the impact of interventions on particular aspects of the system — as we do below — we should never lose sight of the "whole."

THE WHO HEALTH SYSTEMS FRAMEWORK

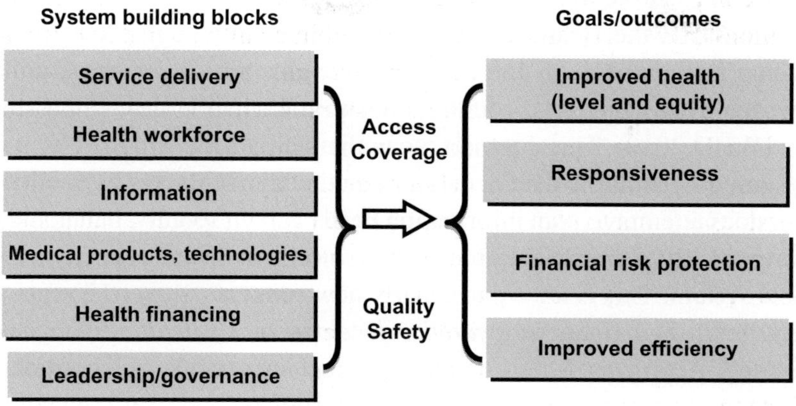

Information

The renewed emphasis on results-based financing associated with GHP funding has increased demands on health information systems, which are often already overburdened and functioning poorly. Increased demand has also meant increased attention, though Boerma and Stansfield note that efforts to strengthen monitoring and evaluation have been uncoordinated, resulting in a proliferation of indicators. They suggest that poorly-targeted and fragmented investments in information have not necessarily improved data quality, that a preoccupation with MDG- (and GHP-) related monitoring has contributed to the neglect of equally important topics such as non-communicable disease. Further, a proliferation of household surveys that are also often not coordinated nor comparable have consumed large amounts of valuable resources, both financial and human (Boerma and Stansfield 2007). In addition, there is evidence from some countries that the emphasis on results-based financing may be skewing incentives for reporting of data, leading to uncertainty about the accuracy and adequacy of health statistics (Lim *et al.* 2008).

Faced with inadequate data from the "routine" system, development partners often design new monitoring forms or commission new surveys. From the perspective of individual programmes, this is a rational solution.

However, when multiple programmes all respond in this way, the risk of duplication, distraction and distortion is clear.

One GHP, the Health Metrics Network, is encouraging countries to develop National Health Information Strategies which present a unified approach to meeting all a country's health information needs in a single plan (WHO 2010). This does not mean that all data are supplied by a single source — multiple data generation methods will always be needed — but it does attempt to plan information needs in their totality, balancing the desires of different programmes and projects with the capacity of the whole system. This is not a particularly new concept — over 15 years ago WHO published *Guidelines for the development of health management information systems* which emphasised the importance of coordinating and integrating health information (WHO 1993) — but from the country perspective it seems to be one that must be re-learned every few years.

Medical products and technologies

A large amount of GHP money has been used to purchase medical supplies and commodities. The GFATM reports that up to 45% of its total expenditure is on drugs, commodities and products, compared to 9% on infrastructure and equipment (GFATM 2010). The scale of this funding has overwhelmed many weak and vulnerable procurement and distribution systems, systems that were already suspected of mismanagement, abuse and in some cases fraud. As a result, many GHPs do not use them. This is not a new phenomenon: the World Bank, the UN and many bilateral donors also routinely bypass national procurement systems. A related issue is that GHPs have at times bypassed national procedures for introducing new drugs and technologies — we know of three countries in the Asia Pacific region where this has happened — in the process undermining essential drug systems that have taken years to develop.

As with health information needs, what makes sense for a single entity creates fragmentation from a system's perspective. It is not unusual for the same rural health facility to be supplied by literally dozens of different procurement systems (Global Health Forecasting Working Group 2007). This leads to both gaps and duplications. Stories of multiple microscopes from different donors — or sometimes even from different programmes of the same donor — are common. Equally, the rapid scaling up of funding for some commodities is acknowledged to have created imbalances in access to diagnostic services, the availability of guidelines and medicines (TERG 2009); while the availability of HIV, TB and malaria diagnostics has increased with earmarked GHPs resources, other effective medicines remain unavailable. A common example cited by countries is that HIV tests are now more easily available than haemoglobin measurements.

The exceptions to these trends are the ones that suggest the way forward. For example, in Cambodia, the HIV programme is spearheading a more coordinated approach to laboratory and reproductive health services in operational districts.

Health workforce

There is a worldwide shortage of skilled health workers, which is most acute in the least developed world where the burden of disease is highest (WHO 2006). Within developing countries, rural and poor areas are most severely affected, lacking both absolute numbers of and adequately trained staff. Even when health facilities have staff, they may see relatively few patients because they lack the basic infrastructure, equipment and supplies. In addition, staff may be poorly motivated because they are badly paid and/or there is a lack of supervision and support.

In this context, health systems have struggled to provide sufficient numbers of health workers to implement rapidly expanding GHP programmes. This is particularly so in countries where the health workforce has suffered high levels of attrition due to death and disability from AIDS. In some countries, the roll-out of GHP initiatives has been most successful in the higher-capacity settings, further exacerbating existing equity issues (WHO Positive Synergies Collaborating Group 2009). On the other hand, GHPs have provided many HIV-positive health workers with access to treatment, a good thing in its own right but also of benefit to the system as a whole as it slows down health worker attrition due to death and illness.

There have been several responses to the shortage of health workers. One is to *shift tasks* traditionally performed by doctors to health workers who have lower levels of basic training. This is not a new response, but the current scale of implementation is probably unprecedented. Another is to update or improve the skills of health workers through short training courses. A well-known but little-mentioned side effect of such training is that it can create perverse incentives for health workers to be away from their facilities, through provision of per diems and allowances (Dodd *et al.* 2009). In one country that we know of, the donor budget for short courses for health workers exceeded the entire salary budget of the Ministry of Health.

Similarly, donor-funded projects often provide financial incentives (euphemistically labelled as "compensation," "top ups" or "performance allowances") for those who deliver the services and activities they fund. The justification is that these health workers — or Ministry of Health staff working in PMUs — have increased levels of responsibility and a greater work load. The result is that staff doing similar jobs may receive vastly different levels of remuneration — for example nurses working in the same hospital, but one in an HIV ward and the other in a general ward; or civil servants in the same department but affiliated with different donor programmes. Such practices have a distorting impact on the overall health sector, attracting staff away from routine duties towards donor-funded priorities and skewing service delivery in favour of particular types of treatment. These problems have always existed and are not only associated with GHPs, but the massive scale up of GHP resources combined with decades of neglect in health systems has magnified the impact. There are some important examples of GHP funds being used to address overall health worker shortages — such as Global Fund support for 30,000 community health workers in Ethiopia. At present these are the exception rather than the rule, but they provide encouraging indication of what is possible.

Many of the efforts described above attempt to *build capacity* of the health workforce. In reality, they may simply *capture capacity*. Systems, especially those that depend on resources such as health workers and institutions, can expand only at the rate that these resources can be produced. Expanding a service faster than new resources can be built inevitably means that either there is surplus capacity in the system or that there is some way of rapidly increasing capacity without affecting the rest of the system, or — most commonly — that rapid expansion borrows capacity from other parts of the system. While improvements in health worker productivity may be possible (for example by providing HIV-positive staff with access to medicines), many health projects capture capacity rather than build it. Programmes that invest in continuing education or short courses without investing in basic preservice education, or pay allowances for disease specific activities, are at particular risk of doing this.

Health financing

Health systems suffer from long-term problems rooted in decades of under-investment. Rebuilding the system — expanding the health workforce, reforming planning and budgeting processes and strengthening monitoring systems — requires sustained, predictable, multiyear support. By contrast development assistance is often volatile and unpredictable, undermining its effectiveness in relation to health systems strengthening (Lane and Glassman 2007).

Early analysis suggests that GHPs have more flexibility than traditional donors to make long-term commitments — up to ten years in the case of GAVI and five years for the Global Fund — and thus the *potential* to contribute positively to systems building (Dodd and Lane 2009). To date, though GHP funds have been channelled primarily through projects and there has been limited engagement in other, more sustainable health financing mechanisms such as social health insurance [The GFATM's support to community-based social health insurance in Rwanda is a notable exception (GFATM 2009)].

A related issue is that GHP support to non-government stakeholders may not be captured in either the national expenditure frameworks or national health accounts, undermining the capacity of ministries to plan effectively. Equally, when programmes are well funded by external partners, there is less incentive to participate in national planning processes, and as a result their contribution to overall health systems strengthening may be limited.

An associated risk is that if Ministries of Finance consider that "health is taken care of by donors," they may be reluctant to increase the national health budget, threatening the sustainability of donor programmes. This risk is particularly serious when the programmes in question are those with long-term funding implications, such as provision of anti-retroviral therapy which requires life-long support.

An additional financing issue frequently raised by country staff is that GHPs may have increased the cost of development work in countries. Anecdotal reports suggest that a large influx of funds chasing a relatively small pool of human and physical resources has led to rising costs for training venues, per diem rates, staff incentives, and even vehicles.

Despite these constraints, short-term financing *can* contribute to long-term systems strengthening if projects are designed and implemented appropriately. A guiding principle is that actions taken to meet short-term targets should not be an obstacle to long-term implementation and sustainability.

Service delivery

If the other building blocks of a health system make a difference to health outcomes, it is through the medium of service delivery. It is also through *delivery of services* — AIDS treatment, bednets and immunisations — that GHPs make an impact. Many analyses of the impact of GHPs on health systems therefore focus on service delivery.

The history and mission of GHPs means that it is impossible to simply shift their resources from one health priority to another — their *raison d'être* is issue specific. Yet, from a country perspective, it is fair to ask: why are funds available for one condition and not another, particularly if that other condition represents a larger share of the burden of disease and is equally amenable to treatment, perhaps at lower costs? (It is important to remember though that when GHPs were first established the diseases they tackled were often under-funded). There are clear ethical dilemmas here, as well as questions of efficiency. Most health systems frameworks regard efficiency as a health systems goal. At one level, this is about value for money: resources better spent means more lives saved. However, it is also about equity: the underlying principle is that the preventable loss of life is equivalent, no matter the cause, and thus certain diseases and conditions should not be privileged over others.

The challenge is to locate GHP support within a comprehensive and balanced package of services that is appropriate to the local context and burden of disease. This does not require that GHPs work beyond their mandate or lose focus, but rather that they seek synergies with other health programmes. Most programmes and projects share common elements. These include supportive supervision, upgrading of managerial skills, laboratory development, continuous education, procurement and supply and so on. Linking and integrating interventions to support these functions can strengthen the system without weakening individual programmes, and indeed may make individual programmes stronger. HIV and reproductive health, immunisation and maternal health, TB and HIV, are all examples of programmes that have been successfully integrated at service delivery level in many countries. However, in reality the pursuit of such synergies with GHP funds is difficult and is likely to remain so unless it becomes a proactive part of the GHP agenda.

Leadership and governance

The leadership and governance function of the health system is arguably the most important, but also the most difficult to assess and influence. There is considerable consensus at international level that if development assistance is to play its part in strengthening leadership and improving governance then it needs to follow the Paris Principles of harmonisation, alignment, country ownership, managing for results and mutual accountability (OECD 2005). These are accepted in principle by almost all global health actors and countries as organising principles for ODA. Not surprisingly, practice lags behind intentions. However, no degree of aid effectiveness or aid coordination can make up for an absolute lack of resources. Thus, at country level, GHPs — and particularly those with significant resources — tend to be welcomed even when their resources are not fully "Paris compliant."

From a country perspective, GHPs have a mixed record on aid effectiveness. They have helped to broaden the notion of "country ownership" to include non-government partners and brought new actors into the development dialogue. Equally, because GHPs do not have staff on-the-ground, nationals of the respective countries tend to have a larger managerial role in running projects than is the case for other donors — an indication of country ownership. However, the complexity of the application process — for both GAVI and GFATM — has led to a high dependence on external technical assistance. This has in turn created a mini-industry of consultants who work almost exclusively on GHP applications.

GHPs are also criticised for not engaging in country-level co-ordination mechanisms. They have constraints in harmonising and aligning because their procedures are often driven by global deadlines rather than local planning cycles. There is some evidence that GHPs may even be undermining established co-ordination mechanisms by working outside of agreed processes for procurement, reporting, joint missions and so on, causing existing, fragile agreements to unravel (Martínez 2008).

It is important to recognise that GHPs are aware of these criticisms and working to change them. Yet, as with aid effectiveness measures more broadly (OECD 2008) global and HQ-level intention do not always filter down to change country-level practice.

6. Recommendations: How GHPs can Better Support Health Systems in Countries

Global Health Partnerships are a feature of the landscape of ODA in health and are likely to remain so. Countries that face a shortage of resources need to access their funds.

Growing recognition of the challenges associated with GHP's *modus operandi* in countries is leading to an evolution of their business model — and an increasing focus on how GHPs can better support systems. In our view, there are actions that can be taken *now*, within existing structures and funding mechanisms, that would improve the quality of GHP support to the overall health systems development. Taking such actions requires goodwill, an acceptance that other health problems deserve attention, and time and patience to make things work.

Below we summarise recommendations for GHPs. Many of these ideas are not new — where they have been previously suggested by others a reference has been provided. We make these recommendations in full recognition that most health systems interventions are *not* based on detailed evidence or data about "what works" — coming to such firm conclusions is extremely difficult given the complexity and context-specificity of health systems (Mays *et al.* 2005; Lavis 2009). Rather, we urge partners to act on their experience and their local knowledge, and to work in a more joined-up and a coherent way when it makes sense.

Summary of recommendation for global health partnerships

Information

- Support the development of a unified health information strategy for a country that includes GHP needs, but also others.
- Develop joint monitoring and evaluation plans that extend beyond one project, one disease or one donor.

Medical products and technologies

- Bypass national procurement, supply and distribution systems as a last resort. If the systems are weak, work with others to strengthen them.
- Use national essential drug policy mechanisms.
- Support the development of national strategies for laboratory and technology and their use.
- Attempt to unify and consolidate laboratory interventions across different projects, a point particularly important for the GFATM.

Health workforce

- Incentives for staff should follow the guidelines agreed by the government and other donors if they exist.
- Capacity building and training should take into account the other demands on health worker time.
- Consider shared training and continuing education. The largest cost of many trainings is the transport and time away from work. That could be shared.

- Invest in preservice education also.
- Avoid using training as an income incentive.

Health financing

- Avoid inflating the cost of doing business. Follow agreed norms and standards that have been negotiated jointly with government. The short-term benefits of paying more often dissipate.
- Avoid the fragmentation of funding sources. Unify the grant financing structures as much as possible.
- Support strengthened financial management, not just within the project but in the system — national health accounting and accountability for expenditure.
- Ensure that GHP funds get into the books so they enter national health account processes, even if the implementers are non-governmental.

Service delivery

- Work with all programmes in defining an agreed-upon service delivery package and service delivery model. The model should recognise that other conditions are also important.
- Consider joint or integrated supportive supervision as well as joint monitoring and evaluation. The biggest cost of supervision is the transport. It makes sense to unify that.
- Actively look for places where you can share resources — laboratories, transport and infrastructure — initially within GHP-funded programmes, but over time throughout the entire sector.

Leadership/Governance

- Participate fully in existing donor coordination and aid effectiveness mechanisms. When there is not an in-country presence of the GHP, then the CCM and ICC need to be formally linked to other forums for donor coordination.
- GHP-supported activities need to be a part of the national health planning (NHP) process. Programmes supported well by external funds still need to be part of NHPs.

- Continue to work to unify grants and simplify the application process.
- Try to use existing coordination mechanisms and be less reliant on the separate CCMs and ICCs. In some settings, they should perhaps be phased out.
- Assess all new projects and interventions for their impact on the health system, using one of the several, comprehensive frameworks that currently exist.

7. Conclusion

Taking a dogmatic position on the pros and cons of GHPs may be ideologically appealing, but it is of little practical use on the ground. GHPs are a reality, and national health systems must learn how optimise the benefits of their resources, just as GHPs must learn how to interact with the complexity of national systems.

GHPs are a new phenomenon in global health and have clearly brought new energy and new partners into the sector. However, the way they operate at country level and the challenges they create are the same as those previously associated with project funding. The scale of GHP resources means that the scale of challenges has increased — but the problems are fundamentally the same. It follows that lessons learned about what makes "good donor practice" and "effective aid" also apply to GHPs.

It is important to acknowledge that GHPs are evolving. If we were to continue the brief history of health aid begun at the beginning of this chapter it would show an important shift in the expressed priorities of GHPs. GAVI and Global Fund, for example, have both endorsed the Paris Declaration and measure progress towards Paris targets. Importantly, these commitments are filtering down to operational level, and leading to adaptations of GHP funding instruments: GAVI now has a dedicated funding window for health systems, although still having to show a link to immunisation coverage, and the Global Fund has launched the National Strategy Application (NSA) process that will allow countries to submit entire national disease strategies for funding. These changes are an example of global health diplomacy in action, an indication that GHPs are "listening" to their critiques and — most significantly — that they have the flexibility to adapt fairly fast.

With the exception of GAVI, though, the changes have not yet had a widespread impact at country level. At the time of writing, few NSA have yet been funded and examples of the Global Fund supporting systems strengthening interventions are (albeit important) exceptions to a predominantly projectised way of working. The responsibility for overcoming this trend lies with countries as well as with donors. Many country applicants do not want to take the risk of asking for systems strengthening funding, when they believe that stand-alone disease-oriented grants are more likely to be successful.

The active diplomacy that is happening at global level — between systems and programmes advocates — now needs to take root in countries. To date, both sides have often been more comfortable with working independently, avoiding the difficult and time-consuming negotiations associated with integration. However, there is now an onus on all players to co-operate more closely. Different country contexts will require different actions, which will present a challenge to the globally standardised approach of GHPs. Nevertheless, providing GHPs with the flexibility to adapt their country operations according to local contexts is essential if their activities are to contribute to the strengthening of health systems and the sustainable improvement of health outcomes. If this is to happen, pressure and recommendations need to come from "below" from national practice as well as from internationally agreed principles.

References

Atun R, de Jongh T, *et al.* (2010) "A Systematic Review of the Evidence on Integration of Targeted Health Interventions into Health Systems," *Health Policy and Planning* 25:1–14.

Atun R, Lennox-Chhugani N, *et al.* (2004) "A Framework and Toolkit for Capturing the Communicable Disease Programmes within Health Systems: Tuberculosis Control as an Illustrative Example," *Eur J Public Health* 14(3):267–73.

Bennett S, Fairbank A (2003) *The System-Wide Effects of The Global Fund to Fight AIDS, Tuberculosis and Malaria: A Conceptual Framework*, The Partners for Health Reformsplus Project, 031.

Biesma R, Brugha R, *et al.* (2009) "The Effects of Global Health Initiatives on Country Health Systems: A Review of the Evidence from HIV/AIDS Control," *Health Policy and Planning* 24(4):239–52.

Boerma J, Stansfield S (2007) "Health Statistics Now: Are We Making the Right Investments?" *Lancet* 369(9563):779–86.

Buse K, Harmer AM, *et al.* (2007) "Seven Habits of Highly Effective Global Public–Private Health Partnerships: Practice and Potential," *Social Science & Medicine* 64(2):259–71.

Caines K (2005) *Key Evidence from Major Studies of Selected Global Health Partnerships: Background Paper Prepared for the High-Level Forum on the Health MDGs*. London, DFID Health Resource Centre.

Dodd R, Hill PS, *et al.* (2009) "Paris on the Mekong: Using the Aid Effectiveness Agenda to Support Human Resources for Health in the Lao People's Democratic Republic,"*Human Resources for Health* 7(16):1–7.

Dodd R, Lane C (2009) "Improving the Long-Term Sustainability of Health Aid — Are Global Health Partnerships Leading the Way?" *Health Policy and Planning* 25(5):363–71.

GAVI (2008) *Good Examples from Country Proposals to GAVI for HSS Support.* Geneva, Global Alliance for Vaccines and Immunisation.

GFATM (2009) *Technical Evaluation Reference Group Summary Paper Study Area 3: Health Impact of Scaling Up Against HIV, Tuberculosis and Malaria: Evaluation of the Current Situation and Trends in 18 Countries*, The Global Fund to Fight AIDS, TB and Malaria.

GFATM (2010) "The Global Fund to Fight AIDS, Tuberculosis and Malaria: Distribution of Funding After 7 Rounds." Retrieved 10 January 2010, from http://www.theglobalfund.org/en/distributionfunding/.

Global Health Forecasting Working Group (2007) *A Risky Business: Saving Money and Improving Global Health Through Better Demand Forecasts.* Washington DC, Center for Global Development.

Lane C (2007) *Scaling Up for Better Health in Cambodia WHO/HDS/2007.1.* Phnom Penh, World Health Organization & Ministry of Health, Cambodia.

Lane C, Glassman A (2007) "Bigger and Better? Scaling Up and Innovation in Health Aid," *Health Affairs* 26(4):935–48.

Lavis JN (2009) "How Can We Support the Use of Systematic Reviews in Policymaking?" *PLoS Med* 6(11):e1000141.

Lim S, Stein D, *et al.* (2008) "Tracking Progress Towards Universal Childhood Immunisation and the Impact of Global Initiatives: A Systematic Analysis of Three-Dose Diphtheria, Tetanus, and Pertussis Immunisation Coverage," *Lancet* 372(9655):2031–46.

Lundberg M, Wang L (2006) *Health Sector Reforms. Analyzing the Distributional Impact of Reforms: A Practitioner's Guide to Pension, Health, Labor Markets, Public Sector Downsizing, Taxation, Decentralization, and Macroeconomic Modeling*. A Coudouel, S Paternostro. Washington, DC 20433, USA, World Bank. 2:43–110.

Marchal B, Cavalli B, *et al.* (2009) "Global Health Actors Claim to Support Health System Strengthening — Is This Reality or Rhetoric," *PLOS Medicine* 6(4):1–5.

Martínez J (2008) *Sector Wide Approaches at Critical Times: The Case of Bangladesh* (Technial Approach Paper). London, HLSP Institute.

Mays N, Pope C, *et al.* (2005) "Systematically Reviewing Qualitative and Quantitative Evidence to Inform Management and Policy-Making in the Health Field," *Journal of Health Services & Research Policy* 10(Suppl 1):6–20.

OECD (2005) *Paris Declaration on Aid Effectiveness*. Paris, OECD.

OECD (2008) *Aid Effectiveness: A Progress Report on Implementation of the Paris Declaration. Third High-Level Forum on Aid Effectiveness*, 2–4 September 2008. Accra, OECD.

Oliveira-Cruz V, Kurowski C, *et al.* (2003) "Delivery of Priority Health Services: Searching for Synergies within the Vertical Versus Horizontal Debate," *Journal of International Development* 15(1):67–86.

Pawson R, Greenhalgh T, *et al.* (2005) "Realist Review — a New Method of Systematic Review Designed for Complex Policy Interventions," *Journal of Health Services & Research Policy* 10(Suppl 1):21–34.

Piva P, Dodd R (2009) "Where Did all the Aid Go? An In-Depth Analysis of Increased Health Aid Flows Over the Last 10 Years," *Bulletin of the World Health Organization* 87(12):930–9.

Roberts M, Hsiao W, *et al.* (2003) *Getting Health Reform Right: A Guide to Improving Performance and Equity*. USA, Oxford University Press.

Technical Evaluation Reference Group (TERG) (2009) TERG Summary Paper Study Area 3: Health Impact of Scaling Up Against HIV, Tuberculosis and Malaria: Evaluation of the Current Situation and Trends in 18 Countries, The Global Fund to Fight AIDS, Tuberculosis and Malaria.

Travis P, Bennett S, *et al.* (2004) "Overcoming Health-Systems Constraints to Achieve the Millennium Development Goals." *Lancet* 364(9437):900–6.

Unger J, De Paepe P, *et al.* (2003) "A Code of Best Practice for Disease Control Programmes to Avoid Damaging Health Care Services in Developing Countries." *Int J Health Plann Manage* 18(Suppl 1):S27–S39.

United Nations (2000) United Nations Millennium Declaration, General Assembly Resolution A/RES/55/2 New York, United Nations.

Walsh J, Warren K (1979) "Selective Primary Health Care: An Interim Strategy for Disease Control in Developing Countries." *The New England Journal Medicine* 301(18):967–74.

WHO (1978) *Alma Ata Declaration on Primary Health Care*. International Conference on Primary Health Care, USSR.

WHO (1993) *Guidelines for the Development of Health Management Information Systems*. Manila, WHO Regional Office for the Western Pacific.

WHO (2001) *Macroeconomics and Health: Investing in Health for Economic Development*. Report of the Commission on Macroeconomics and Health. Geneva, WHO.

WHO (2006) *The World Health Report: 2006: Working Together for Health*. Geneva, World Health Organization.

WHO (2008) *Effective Aid — Better Health. Report Prepared for the Accra High Level Forum on Aid Effectiveness*, 2–4 September 2008. Geneva, WHO.

WHO (2008) *Everybody's Business: Strengthening Health Systems to Improve Health Outcomes: WHO's Framework for Action*. Geneva, World Health Organization.

WHO (2010) "Health Metrics Network." Retrieved 3 February 2010, from http://www.who.int/healthmetrics/en/.

WHO Positive Synergies Collaborative Group (2009) "An Assessment of Interactions Between Global Health Initiatives and Country Health Systems." *The Lancet* 373(9681):2137–69, 20 June 2009.

World Bank (1993) *World Development Report: Investing in Health*. Washington, DC, The World Bank.

World Bank (2008) Strategy for Health, Nutrition, and Population Results, World Bank, Washington DC.

6

Limitations of Partnerships: Taking the Agenda Forward

Margret Thalwitz

Summary

Today, global health rests on a cascading system of partnerships, from global to country level. Health partnerships date back decades and initially focused on research results and the provision of critical inputs in the fight against particular diseases. In the past ten years, the spectrum of partnerships has been broadened by shifting the focus from research to general health finance contributing to global health goals. In assessing the concept of partnerships in achieving better results, the chapter identifies limits to the concept of partnerships, embedded in narrow institutional mandates and a limited ability to flexibly react to changing priorities. Are financing partnerships well adapted to use the opportunities to facilitate the key elements of effective assistance: the integration of research and knowledge, global and local, funding and implementation support within a nationally and regionally driven, coherent policy framework? Are there important additional models of partnerships, platforms and networks which may contribute to improved health effectiveness? While challenging the traditional system of international support for health, the new partnerships' effectiveness in the long run may well be determined by the way the international community restructures its approach to global health. After reviewing the contributions and limitations of existing partnerships, the chapter concludes with a proposal to that effect.

1. Introduction

Spurred by a widespread concern for the devastating effects of certain diseases on human development, global health has received much attention in the past twenty years. International funding for health from official and private sources has risen from about US$5.5 billion to almost US$22 billion annually between 1990 and 2007.[1] New financing instruments are being developed to offer incentives for research and development of drugs and vaccines affordable to low-income countries, and billions have been committed to fight a select number of diseases, in particular HIV/AIDS, malaria and tuberculosis.[2] Health has been a primary target among the Millennium Development Goals (MDGs).

Accompanying these developments has been a surge in new initiatives and formal partnerships. Health partnerships have a long history and can point to outstanding achievements, such as the eradication of smallpox and the control of river blindness in West Africa. Never before, however, has health in developing countries, and particularly Africa, been so much in the forefront of official donors, NGOs, philanthropists, corporations and multilateral institutions eager to form new structures and search for new funding instruments. Today, "innovative partnerships" have become the preferred instrument of funding health programmes in developing countries. The majority of donor resources for health, public and private, flow through such relatively young institutions as the Global Alliance for Vaccines and Immunization (GAVI) and the Global Fund to Fight HIV/AIDS, Tuberculosis and Malaria (henceforth called the Global Fund) and PEPFAR, the President's Emergency Plan for AIDS Relief, a U.S. bilateral programme. They were created to target global public policy concerns setting them apart from development assistance that includes health as one of many sectors.

---

[1] N. Ravishankar, P. Gibbins, R. Cooley, K. Leach-Kemon, C. Michaud, D. Jamison, C. Murray (June 2009) "Financing of Global Health: Tracking Development Assistance for Health From 1990–2007," *The Lancet*, 373(9681):2113–2124.

[2] HIV/AIDS is estimated to equal about 25% of all development assistance for health in 2007, ibid, pp. 2113.

2. Have Partnerships a Role to Play?

To assess this question, let's first try to define "partnerships," since they play an increasingly important role in public policy, whether nationally, regionally or globally. The literature uses words like "global governance," "global programmes," "transnational public–private partnerships" or "networks," often synonymously.[3] In the most general interpretation, partnerships express consent to cooperate with others in the pursuit of a common goal. Partnerships have an organisational structure of some sort, ranging from professional and political networks (e.g. an international professional association, or the finance ministers forum of the G20[4]) to highly regulated governance structures that detail the roles and functions of various bodies of the partnership — boards, steering committees, technical advisory groups, executing institutions, trustees, etc. The partnerships that will be discussed in this paper fall into this latter category.

Formally structured partnerships fall into three distinct categories: (i) research-driven partnerships that enhance and enable application of knowledge. The Tropical Disease Research Program (TDR), the Consultative Group for International Agricultural Research (CGIAR) and special drug research initiatives fall into this category; (ii) partnerships that aim at mobilising resources for a common cause. Examples here include IAVI and MMV, partnerships that mobilise resources to finance research into vaccines for HIV/AIDS, malaria and other high-priority diseases; or the Global Environment Facility (GEF) that mobilises funding to protect against environmental threats and (iii) partnerships that bring the application of new knowledge to scale. Among these, the Global Fund and GAVI stand out as the largest of such partnerships, but they also include the rule setting EITI (Extractive Industry Transparency Initiative), CGAP (the Consultative Group to Assist the Poor), EFA/FTI and other major initiatives. Ideally, these three different orientations of partnerships interact to bring innovation and knowledge to where they are most needed. It is only in that combination that

---

[3] Diane Stone (2009) "Global Public Policy, Transnational Policy Communities and the Shaping of Governance," in *Governance and the Depoliticisation of Development*, WilHout and Richard Robinson, eds., Routledge, p. 65.

[4] Martinez Dias J, Woods N (eds) (2009) *Networks of Influence*, Oxford University Press.

the transition from knowledge to the provision of a public good, such as the affordable and widespread use of a new vaccine, can be achieved. Moreover, in a development context, results — measured in improved health of a rising share of population — would be further enhanced if local experience were to be filtered back into research and policy to reach increasingly higher levels of innovation and outreach.

Successful partnerships have taken full account of this cycle. The Onchocerciasis Program is one example. Created in 1974 jointly by WHO, UN agencies, the World Bank and USAID, it has fought the spread of river blindness across countries in West Africa. Starting with localised interventions in treating the disease, new findings in research and treatment devices and financial support from private and public sources allowed a rapid regional expansion of the programme, sustaining success and reaching out beyond the original focus area of West Africa, covering much more than just disease control today. Building on these developments, TDR created in 1975 has filled important gaps in understanding the epidemiology of neglected diseases that are of particular relevance to developing countries.

These are examples of partnerships that led to an ever-rising number of initiatives worldwide addressing the needs of select diseases. Common to all of them is the aim to enhance scientific and commercial knowledge to enable the transition from treatment, to prevention, and possibly even eradication. These partnerships have brought together scientific research, pharmaceutical companies, development agencies and developing countries to connect the dots between an idea, a discovery and the launch of a programme. Every link within this chain is essential to bring the original idea to scale at the most local level. The eradication of smallpox has set a fine example with its detailed attention to surveillance, to community participation, to political commitment, to funding, to research and to a central point of accountability.[5]

Contributions to these endeavours come from many sources, including private companies, philanthropic institutions and specialised funding partnerships. Today, global health rests on a cascading system of

---

[5] Fenner F, Henderson DA, AritaI, Jezek Z, Ladnyi ID "Smallpox and its Eradication," WHO 1988.

partnerships, where a partner in one such venture may represent a partnership in its own right, for example GAVI brings together an alliance of partners to vaccines and immunisation.

These partnerships are crucial to advancements in global health, and in fighting diseases that affect predominantly the poor or have the ability to spread globally. Concerning the latter, the response to the outbreak of the H5N1 virus in 2004/5 is an example of how rapidly the global community can be engaged in collective action when the stakes are thought to be very high.[6] Driven by the fear of a global pandemic, it was possible to organise an institutional structure and mobilise US$1 billion in funding for a concerted approach to scaling back the risk of an animal to human transmission of the virus.

Fighting individual diseases has dominated the global health agenda and global health governance for a long time. This has advanced research and proven that external funds can bring together science, product development and the launch of new products[7]; it has shown the powerful impact of well-designed, well-implemented and broadly supported global efforts and it has shown the capacity of the global governance system to respond when threats of diseases on a global scale become real. These are respectable accomplishments that attest that partnerships can fill gaps in knowledge, policy, finance and implementation.

3. Health — a Global Concern

Notwithstanding the successes of early partnerships, in the global debate on development health has not always been a central concern. It has been WHO's mandate to monitor and safeguard global health standards, UNICEF has been the lead agency in immunising children and UNFPA

[6] The partnership had unique features as under the overall patronage of the U.S. Government and the European Commission it used the multilateral system (FAO, WHO, OIE and development banks) as the principal fundraising, surveying and coordinating agencies at global and country level. All parties concerned, including affected countries and bilateral donors, agreed to this partnership framework in record time.

[7] See, for example, BIO Ventures for Global Health: "Global Health Innovators — A Collection of Case Studies", 2009.

for maternal health. Among the multilateral development banks, the World Bank was the first to create a Department for Health in the early 1980s.[8]

The 1982 summit in Lyon was the first for the G8 to refer to health as a major factor in human wellbeing. Although a start,[9] it was not until 1996 when AIDS had become a major public concern that the G8 devoted increasing attention to health in general and to health in developing countries in particular. Recognising that these concerns had to go beyond an individual disease and had to assess and address the socio-economic determinants of health, the 2000 Okinawa summit called for a "new global partnership." However, the common thread throughout all G8 statements is the attention to HIV/AIDS culminating in the creation of the Global Fund to Fight Aids, Tuberculosis and Malaria at the Genoa summit in 2001. This in turn caused a surge in new activities facilitated in part through the emergence of large philanthropic donors. Research into immunisation against these priority diseases accelerated, PEPFAR became a large player and development banks were asked to increase lending for health to achieve the MDGs. In parallel, GAVI was launched in early 2000, another large global initiative specialising in immunisation in developing countries. There is no doubt that political factors were now weighing heavily on the course of action in global health, in the governance that emerged and in the results that have been attained. This included the interest of the G8 nations and externally pressure from civil society.

---

[8] Robert McNamara's speech at the University of Notre Dame on the issue of population growth set the stage for the World Bank's engagement in health addressing the issue first through the reproductive side of this multifaceted sector. Regional development banks followed suit, but health did not become a large segment of their portfolio.

[9] For a detailed review of the role of the G8 in shaping the global health debate see Kirton, John and JenevieveMannell (2007) "Explaining G8 Health Governance," in Cooper, Andrew F., John J. Kirton, and Ted Schrecker, eds (2007) *Governing Global Health: Challenge, Response, Innovation*. Aldershot: Ashgate., also Kirton, John (2006) "The G8 and Global Health Governance: The Case for a Eurasian AIDS Extension," Paper prepared for presentation at the International Parliamentary Conference in Conjunction with Russia's G8 Presidency, on "HIV/AIDS in Eurasia and the Role of the G8," sponsored by the Transatlantic Partners Against AIDS, at the State Duma of the Federal Assembly of the Russian Federation, Moscow, Russia, June 8.

3.1 The New financing partnerships

With the creation of GAVI and the Global Fund, resource mobilisation for health became a focal point of attention in health partnerships. Combined, these two institutions alone control over $40 billion todate (including pledges made in 2011) and disbursed jointly just about $6 billion in 2010, roughly 5 percent of total 2010 ODA aid flows. These are net disbursement since both institutions only provide grants.

It was a conscious move to create these new health partnerships apart from the multilateral development banks and other international organisations, which were judged to have failed to tackle the rising threat of HIV/AIDS and other health needs. The founders of GAVI and GFATM expected to create new capacities to act fast and transfer resources quickly: both institutions are conduits to disburse funds for their designated purposes relying on local governments, other multilateral agencies, NGOs and the private sector to provide complementary services. Upstream they depend on academia, think tanks, the UN System, the Bretton Woods Institutions, *et al.* for research, policy expertise, resource mobilisation and treasury functions; downstream they operate through public and private institutions to implement programmes at country level.

Their governance structures include the voices of all relevant players in global health (as described in more detail in other chapters): knowledge (research, policy and private sector), funding (private and public donors) and implementation (governments, private sector and NGOs). Accountability for institutional policy rests on the Executive Boards, chaired by an elected board member, and on the CEO for the implementation of Executive Board decisions and management of the institution. The appointment of the CEO follows competitive procedures to be chosen by double majority (GFATM). The voting power among executive board members is not proportionate to the institution's financial contribution. In several ways, these partnerships set an example of what the governance of a modern multilateral institution could look like. Their governance has internalised the major constituency groups in health, though this can also be a constraint on effective decision-making (see Chapter 7 and Chapter 9 for a further discussion of Global Programs and GAVI governance respectively).

Notwithstanding the strong participatory elements in the structure of the large financial health partnerships, in the last instance the sharing of risks of their activities and finances remains in the public domain (with the exception of the major role of the Gates Foundation). The countries in which they operate and the donors who make commitments through pledges and guarantees are ultimately absorbing the risks incurred through the activities of these new institutions, just as they do in the traditional multilateral system.

3.2 Innovative resource mobilisation and partnerships

To execute their role as financing instruments, both the Global Fund and GAVI are dependent on substantial resource mobilisation. They follow different models. The Global Fund has adopted the traditional replenishment model as its principal mode while GAVI has relied to a much greater extent on "innovative" schemes executed by third parties. From the start, they were given considerable flexibility in meeting demand for funds, able to rely on private and public sources alike. These span large contributions from private foundations, specialised international agencies such as IFFIm (the International Finance Facility for Immunization), the AMC (Advanced Market Commitment), the Global Fund's RED Campaign, Debt2 Health swaps and other ideas still being explored.

There are several explanations for these innovations in resource mobilisation: (i) access to market instruments for special-purpose use, backed by sovereign guarantees, has expanded the scope for tapping into global savings (e.g. IFFIm); (ii) the emergence of very wealthy private foundations has brought philanthropy to development at unprecedented scale; (iii) civil society's call for social corporate responsibility has opened new avenues for the private sector to engage in aid and last but not least, (iv) advocacy from think tanks to NGOs to wealthy individuals for the plight of the poor has become a central factor in generating greater solidarity for certain aid initiatives, such as UNITAID. Increasingly developing countries have become supporters of these special-purpose vehicles, too. There may also be an increased realisation that health connects the rich and the poor countries in a different way than agriculture, education or infrastructure. As the span of "donors" and other external aid interests broadens, so does the web of partnerships that sustains their support.

Among all these initiatives and reasoning, it is difficult to find a common thread that leads to a systematic approach in addressing global health and its long-term financing requirements and instruments. A Brookings' study on Innovative Financing concluded the challenge well by pointing out: "We do not claim to have found an answer through this exercise. However, we do think that any discussion of Innovative Financing tools for development, in health or other areas, would benefit from a structured approach that first tries to identify the nature of the problem, systematically scans for instruments that could address the problem and finally assesses the instruments against reasonable criteria that would help to prioritise them."[10]

No partnership or global initiative ever before had access to such large increases in resources as the Global Fund and GAVI while operating within a mandate that only allows a limited focus and a narrow agenda. Achieving the high expectations on results and outcomes that donors expect may become increasingly difficult for both institutions, if there is little attention to the underlying constraints in service delivery beyond drugs, bednets or vaccines. Structural issues within the sector, limited capacities among the users to absorb a growing share of dedicated funds and fiscal constraints on the part of governments to sustain these externally driven efforts are all factors signalling that there may be limitations to the effectiveness of ever-expanding "vertical" interventions. Sooner or later, the question may need to be addressed, whether these partnerships created to "scale up" and achieve tangible results within their limited mandates are not becoming or should not become true global health agencies covering all aspects of health delivery, systems and diseases, prevention and treatment, drawing on a partnership which is public and private.

4. Is There a Case for Change?

Change is already underway. GAVI's sizeable allocations to health systems development and the Global Fund's initial contributions to SWAps mark a turn towards a larger agenda increasingly blurring the distinction between the "specialised" and "country-based" funding. Simultaneously, the reliance on others to meet the institutions' upstream and downstream needs is a growing burden on these providers and the countries that

[10] Brookings Global Development Program, Working Paper 2, August 2008, Global Health Initiative.

receive assistance. The partnership model becomes strained as the objectives and activities get closer between "old" and "new" multilaterals, while their individual mandates and institutional policies, though not fully compatible, remain largely unchanged. The fundamental differences in governance contribute further to operational fragmentation and overlap among the various players, reducing efficiency and aid effectiveness.

Many see partnerships in countries as the level where coherence should be achieved, notwithstanding the multifaceted institutional set up of development assistance. However, if the global governance system in health is complicated and not as effective as it could be, how could the system work better at country level? It is there where the fundamental differences in approach and priorities become most tangible and the potential tensions between domestic priorities, resource availability and external priorities most visible. When all large development institutions, including the Global Fund, GAVI and PEPFAR fit their activities into a government-led priority framework for the economy at large, the prospects for partnership at country level could be greatly enhanced. The Paris Declaration principles of "ownership" and "accountability" should be interpreted along those lines.

However, among the poorest countries not all have taken, or have been in a position to take, the lead in setting clear parameters for donors on the deployment of their grants. The plethora of external interventions makes this an exceedingly difficult task. The Accra High Level Forum addressed this issue in several sessions, but stricter adherence to the Paris Declaration on Aid Effectiveness alone might not help overcome some of today's constraints.[11]

4.1 The international health partnership plus (IHP+)

The creation of the IHP+ in the fall of 2007 was to be a step toward more effective collaboration among the many agencies supporting health in developing countries. Earlier attempts to enhance complementarities within the multilateral health system[12] had failed.

[11] For a detailed review of fragmentation and proliferation of aid and the limitations of the Paris Declaration see JM Severino and Olivier Ray: *The End of ODA (II): The Birth of Hypercollective Action.*" Center for Global Development, Working Paper 218, June 2010.

[12] Shakow A (2006) *Global Fund — World Bank HIV/AIDS Programs: Comparative Advantage Study*, The Global Fund.

IHP+ is a partnership umbrella, bringing together the key donors and a select number of African countries. Like the Paris Declaration, it demands adjustments in the way individual institutions operate and cooperate at country level and it has signed a number of agreements with countries and participating donors to support a mutually agreed longer term health strategy built on close cooperation among donors and between donors and countries. It mirrors aspects of the Education for All/Fast Track Initiative, a partnership to accelerate primary education enrolments, though the IHP+ does not provide funding. For the 2008 independent evaluation of IHP+, it was too early to assess results, but the review drew attention to the slowness among key players, including the World Bank and the Global Fund, in adjusting their operating procedures to deliver on the agreements signed at the IHP constituting meeting. This finding is not surprising asthe path from declaring the need for cooperation to effective collaboration is long, demanding concessions that need to be approved by the very different governance systems and interests of the key players and to be implanted in large institutions. The joint health systems platform involving the Global Fund, GAVI, World Bank, WHO and other partners has recently attempted to further accelerate common funding. There will always be protagonists calling for fast action, but the system at large is not well prepared to respond swiftly and effectively.

5. How Could Health Partnerships Evolve?

Several studies in recent years have questioned the impact and long-term results orientation at country level of global assistance for health. A World Bank-led effort in preparation of the 2008 Accra meetings, conducted jointly with several large global partnerships and in close consultation with developing countries, highlighted the risk of allocation distortions when narrowly defined programmes amount to a large share of a country's budget for a sector, potentially drawing fiscal and human resources away from other equally important development priorities.[13] The call for on-budget foreign assistance has been uniform across the developing world

[13] "Global Program Funds — What Have we Learned" at www.worldbank.org/cfp.

as an important tool to trace and evaluate impact, latent fiscal liabilities and overall assessment of progress.[14]

The 2009 article in the Lancet[15] echoes many of these findings while equally highlighting the urgency to invest in data collection to enhance monitoring and evaluation systems at country level, to better track the impact of the changes pursued over the past 10 years and to identify critical gaps in domestic health systems. A serious lack of data is a major obstacle today to effectively evaluate the past ten years of global health governance.[16]

It is widely accepted that global health has reached a critical juncture and the lessons of the past ten years point to important next steps:

- First, health has significant differences to other sectors. The fight against individual diseases can only be won if a wide partnership of scientists, businesses, local institutions, communities and multilateral institutions join forces to bring innovation to scale and make it sustainable. Sustainability involves knowledge to fight the disease, systems that can deliver essential services and infrastructure that makes access possible.
- Second, though of global concern, achieving better health is a very local challenge, inseparable from the economic and social context of a country and a region.
- Third, engagement of local communities, NGOs and the domestic private sector offers opportunities to integrate local knowledge and capacities into programme design.

To raise partnerships to a higher level, the global community may want to aim at better harnessing the multi-stakeholder and multi-disciplinary knowledge needed in the pursuit of the common goal. Contrary to other challenges such as protection against climate change, the global debate on health does not suffer from fundamental differences on the overarching goal. All the trade-offs are in the approach to achieve the goal and in the fallacy that there are choices between fighting diseases and building systems. Offering a

[14] see www.CDG.com.

[15] "An Assessment of Interactions between Global Health Initiatives and Country Health Systems", prepared by Synergies Collaborative Group, published in *The Lancet*, Vol. 373, June 2009, pp. 2137–69. The World Health Organization Maximizing Positive.

[16] see also Severino/Ray, op.cit p. 26.

platform where multi-stakeholder knowledge covering all aspects of this debate could be brought together and enhanced through research, policy analysis and implementation experience, the debate on global health may move from advocacy and more aid to a long-term strategy in support to reducing avoidable and/or premature morbidity and mortality.

Creating such an overall platform could generate crucial insights into the not yet well-understood or disputed challenges for global health. It would be *a framework for collaboration among a tightly defined group of diverse stakeholders to address the long-term, transformational issues in global health.* To meet these outstanding goals, the platform should meet a few distinctive requirements:

- Establish the relevance of global health beyond select diseases for political decision making at truly global level, such as the G20, the G24 and the G77.
- Work in a multidisciplinary environment with representation of the most relevant knowledge stakeholders.
- Generate information that is widely considered to be trustworthy.
- Use processes that are unbiased in substance, that follow a strategic path and are open and accountable to the global community.
- Be forward looking with a focus on the long term.
- Ensure visibility and present options for engagement where collective action is most needed and most difficult to get.
- Use a light and flexible partnership framework.

6. What Might Emerge?

Elements of these principles exist in the multiplicity of health partnerships, but their fragmentation, operational overlaps and gaps have not created structures and instruments that can be governed effectively through international cooperation in pursuit of the common goal. Current partnerships do not go far enough in fostering global governance of health, except in their specific areas. The current system is reactive, suffering from a lack of vision and a broad-based operational strategy in support of this vision. IHP+, H8 and other attempts exist in part to compensate for these shortcomings, but it is not evident whether these initiatives will contribute to further proliferation rather than consolidation. What might a different system then look like?

The creation of a shared global vision on health demands an agreement among the many stakeholders on a credible definition of what constitutes "progress" and indicators to trace such progress. Traditionally, the health status of a population has been measured in life expectancy and infant mortality, and the MDGs have expanded that definition by specifically targeting communicable diseases and maternal and child health. Progress is measured by the success achieved through specific interventions such as immunisation, access to drugs or other preventive measures. The emphasis is on short-term results, and less on addressing the long-term factors that could make the short-term results sustainable — from improvements in health systems and delivery capacities to access to clean water or nutrition security.

WHO is the institution charged with setting and monitoring global standards. It can draw on a large global knowledge base in setting these standards, but where countries rely on external support to follow these standards they are faced with a vast set of institutions whose respective roles are very difficult to delineate: WHO, UNICEF, UNFPA, UNAIDS, UNITAID, GAVI, the Global Fund, multilateral development banks, NGOs, private companies, etc. A first step could be to delineate at least the roles of those institutions that are publicly governed and where essentially the same set of members control the multilaterals policies and actions. Clarification of core mandates would, thus, seem a more important challenge than harmonisation of processes and policies, which is the focus of the Paris Declaration on Aid Effectiveness.

Formal partnerships and informal networks could replace the short-term-oriented, competitive attitude that characterises the behaviour of the large multilaterals today. Informal networks could facilitate extensive knowledge exchange drawing on research and scientific progress globally; they could facilitate policy exchanges among countries at different levels of development; they could provide a platform for health professionals to discuss specific health system issues from basic organisational questions, training and brain drain. These networks could be ad-hoc, formal events, virtual, large or small in scale.

Formal partnerships might be suitable for cooperation among the key leading global health institutions. They rely on the support of the same constituencies, set different priorities, have comparative advantages in prioritising certain diseases and some specialise in particular regions and/or knowledge that others don't have, such as expertise in financial products. Bringing to bear these specific advantages could lead to a different "division of labour" among these "giants." "Stress tests" might well reveal major gaps in knowledge and coverage, such as the much-discussed question of "who provides assistance for health systems?" This critical issue can't be left to ad hoc decisions, actions by default and no accountability among those who provide assistance. A division of labour will need to tackle the vested interests of donors and institutions.

Out of such a debate might emerge the need for a global health funding organisation, one that helps WHO to achieve its objectives; one that can help translate research, science, standards and indicators into actions at country level. It might be an umbrella organisation that partners up-stream with specialised agencies, from universities to development banks and downstream with countries and regions on implementation. The Global Fund and GAVI have elements of this vision already embedded in their constitutions: GAVI upstream through its link to innovative financing for health and the Global Fund through its network approach to implementation. A merger of the two institutions and a fundamental change in the respective mandates might turn the two into one global health agency.

The institutional implications of such a move would be enormous and would need widespread support to gain legitimacy and be practical. There may also be drawbacks, for example of concentrating financing in one institution and not leveraging fully other partners. However, the platform and convening functions they could fulfil and the guidance to global health they could provide should offset at least some of the pain that inevitably would accompany a major restructuring of the global health governance. A 10-year horizon might be the way to think about it, approximately the time it took to create the proliferation and fragmentation the world faces today.

For WHO, a new role could emerge, one fundamental to the success of global collective action in health: accompanying changes through independent and data-based evaluation. The lack of data is widely assessed to be one of the main shortcomings,[17] making objective evaluation and progress management hazardous.[18]

---

[17] *Lancet* study, op.cit.

[18] Severino/Ray, op.cit., p. 26.

Partnerships centred around a key, legitimate, operationally oriented global health institution might address the shortcomings in global health governance in two important ways:

- there would be a point of accountability to which all, countries, donors and private sector could turn with ideas and for guidance.
- there would be a platform that ties together research, policy, implementation and evaluation aligning as much as possible the "production function" of health of developing countries with the "utility functions" of donors.

7. Conclusions

Health has undergone an enormous change in the past decade. New large funding mechanisms have been created to accelerate investments in specialised health services in developing countries. Constructed initially as "partnerships" relying on upstream and downstream partners to deliver on their mandate, these institutions have grown so large so fast that the "partnership" model can no longer be considered the panacea to dealing with global health issues. While knowledge-based partnerships have and should continue to play a very important role in advancing understanding of the epidemiology, prevention and treatment of diseases, partnership principles are also to be applied in the management of disease control and eradication. On the large-scale health financing side, however, the Paris Declaration principles on ownership and accountability point to a reshuffling in the roles of large international agencies to offer policy makers in developing country a less fragmented, more transparent and more coherent model of choices. The "innovative partnerships" have moved to the ranks of independent multilateral health institutions. They need to be allowed to operate at that level.

Chapter 9 provides further analysis of innovative financing and Chapter 5 of health systems issues.

Section 2

Integrating New Partnerships at Global Level

7

Global Health Programmes: Negotiating Aid Effectiveness into New Partnerships

Prerna Banati and Daniel Low-Beer

Summary

This chapter assesses the evolution of global programmes and partnerships, discusses their role and rationale and their progressive engagement with aid effectiveness. The responses of global programmes to aid effectiveness challenges, and how this has been negotiated among global programmes, are highlighted. The reader is taken through the stages of negotiation: dialogue, assessment, consolidation and engagement. The actions generated through the learning and peer network of global programmes provide an innovative model for partnership and change. This network model of governance has key characteristics including inclusive membership and a focus on internal dialogue, evaluations, monitoring and is centred on learning and peer pressure. Behind the Paris Declaration, it is easy to underestimate the negotiation and diplomacy required to build collective actions. The final part of the chapter concludes with recognition of progress and limitations of the two-way negotiations on aid effectiveness among diverse global programmes.

Introduction

In 2005, Global health programmes, such as GAVI and the Global Fund, were largely seen as outside the structure of aid.[1] Many of the traditional multilaterals and bilaterals saw them at best to be tolerated in-country. At worst, they interfered with established ways of delivering aid, shaking up tried coordination approaches and complicating "business as usual." The Paris Declaration on aid effectiveness saw global programmes as one of the major challenges to the aid architecture, alongside corruption and weak country systems. Yet at the same time, it defined some broad principles that provided a framework for global programmes to negotiate with other partners. These principles appealed to important elements of the global programmes model, including managing for results and a wider country ownership which included civil society and the private sector. At the same time, it framed negotiations among global programmes and partners to tackle some of the challenges of alignment and harmonisation at country level.

The Paris Declaration did not always provide concrete solutions; indeed they were framed at the level of principles and depended on partners negotiating solutions. However, they did aim to shift development from an approach based on country by country negotiation and conditionality to one which referred to general principles of ownership, incentives and could be informed by M&E and accountability structures. It necessitated negotiation and diplomacy within a framework of overall rules for aid effectiveness. An important test of the challenges and opportunities of this approach is its ability to provide a framework to incorporate new partners. Global programmes are therefore important "tracers" for the strengths and weaknesses of the Paris Declaration in framing negotiations on improved aid effectiveness.

In the last decade, there has been an intense process of learning from experience, negotiation and diplomacy, and readjustment of global programmes, bilaterals, multilaterals and countries (e.g. World Bank 2004[2];

[1] As reflected in the Paris Declaration (2005).

[2] World Bank (2004) *Addressing the Challenges of Globalization: An Independent Evaluation of the World Bank's Approach to Global Programs.*

McKinsey 2004[3]). This has changed how global programmes and other stakeholders have operated and had a significant impact on management of aid overall. The process has been steered globally during debate and negotiations on aid effectiveness, through learning from evaluations and experience on the ground, replenishments and board meetings. At the country level, country programmes, SWAps and other coordination mechanisms are increasingly incorporating global programmes. At the centre has been the concept of partnerships — opening up bilateral aid to support partnership efforts in countries, adapting the roles of multilateral partners and leading to frank evaluation and learning among global programmes. This process of learning and negotiation has also involved a new role for countries as stewards of this partnership, while coordinating capacity building and country planning (Accra Agenda for Action 2008).

Global programmes are diverse organisations, varying in structure and organisation. However, they share some commonalities and what follows applies broadly and to differing degrees depending on the programme. Global programmes were designed as results-based organisations to provide funding untied to political conditionality, thematically organised around specific MDGs, with no country offices. As compared to bilateral institutions, they were not subject to competing national political or economic interests. Their country coverage and programme amounts were set by international processes and direct country proposals. The lack of country offices meant they had to work through other partners, and rely on an effective development partnership. This brought them close to the Paris Principles, in terms of both their model and their vulnerabilities if partnerships were not effective. Their boards were set up to give substantial voice to developing countries and civil society. In a more fundamental sense, any set of governance and operational arrangements is "political". However, what was accomplished was to introduce a new form of governance that was less dominated by any single donor or by donor groups. At the minimum, donors were forced to negotiate rules for financing and development with recipients, civil society and the private sector, based on a balanced voting structure. Global programmes also provided a common goal across

[3] McKinsey (2004) *Global Health Partnerships — Assessing Country Consequences A report for the Bill and Melinda Gates Foundation.*

countries of improving on results achieved by previous programmes. However, many of their characteristics have only evolved in contact with this engagement and the challenges of increasing their effectiveness, including through interaction with other parts of the aid system or "architecture." This process of negotiation, adjustment and learning is the focus of this chapter.

The chapter highlights the process by which global programmes have responded to aid effectiveness and negotiated with other partners to address challenges and opportunities. In addressing aid effectiveness, global programmes have been led to better define their added value, share their inclusive network models of governance and show evidence of complementarity with other development financers. However, it is a work in progress, and some of the limitations of the Paris Declaration in supporting system-wide rules and negotiations which can change behaviour at country level are also apparent. The negotiations around full inclusion of global programmes in the aid architecture continue to be under discussion as the newly remodelled Working Party on Aid Effectiveness (WP-EFF) clarifies its role in shaping a more inclusive global discourse on development, and as Global Programs learn to be better bridges with partners.

This chapter takes the reader through the four stages of the engagement of global programmes with the aid architecture, highlighting the challenges, adaptations and the central role of partnerships.

The first part provides the context of the aid effectiveness agenda and explores significant shifts between the Paris Declaration and the Accra Agenda for Action, describing an expansion of the aid architecture to include new actors and the shift towards principles-based partnership approaches to development.

The second part looks at the evolution of global programmes and their added value to existing management of aid. It reviews the strengths and weaknesses of the global programme model and how these new models of global governance have increased opportunities for partnership. It assesses to what extent the negotiations on aid effectiveness have compromised their distinctive characteristics or extended them through more effective partnerships.

The third part reviews the process of negotiating within the framework of the Paris Declaration and discusses the scope and expansion of a learning group of global programmes and places it within the broader context of development. It identifies the stages of negotiation through dialogue, assessment, consolidation and engagement in how global programmes are included in global discussions. The actions generated through the learning and peer network of global programmes provide an innovative model for partnership and change. This network model of governance has key characteristics including inclusive membership and a focus on internal dialogue, evaluations and monitoring and centred on learning and sharing.

The final part of the chapter concludes with the recognition of progress and challenges in the incorporation of global programmes and the two-way negotiations and dialogue on aid effectiveness — viewing with cautious optimism the future directions in this evolving partnership.

Part 1. Evolution of the Aid Effectiveness Movement: Towards Inclusion and Partnership

The Paris Declaration in 2005 was the culmination of a decade-long effort to learn lessons of good and bad practice in order to establish principles to frame negotiations between partners on improving aid effectiveness. This process started in the Development Assistance Committee of the OECD but then opened to include developing countries and international organisations and to interact with civil society and with global programmes. This led to negotiation among over one hundred donors and partner countries to produce a set of aid effectiveness principles and a commitment to measure progress in 2010. The principles included targets focused on ownership, alignment, harmonisation, managing for results and mutual accountability. The principles were then summarised into 12 indicators, 11 of which had quantified targets.

This came at a key moment of increased financing and high expectations for aid related to the Millennium Development Goals (MDGs) (Figure 1). With the turn of the century came a focus on consolidating approaches to aid behind the MDGs and country priorities. There were substantial increases in the quantity of development assistance and an accompanying effort on how to improve quality — in order to achieve sustainable development results. Country ownership and accountability

Time	Event	Key outcome
2000	MDGs	Global community agrees on eight Millennium Development Goals for 2015
2002	Monterrey consensus	Successfully raises additional funds for development and calls for concomitant effort to improve the effectiveness of aid
2003	Rome Declaration	Identifies harmonisation, ownership and alignment as key principles
2004	Marrakesh Memorandum	Agreed donor focus for the first time on development results
2005	Paris Declaration	Built on the Rome Declaration with renewed commitment to principles of ownership, alignment and harmonisation, as well as managing for results and accountability as part of a package
2008	Accra Agenda for Action	Strengthened the focus on the need for action on all principles, with emphasis on results, transparency and predictability, civil society and parliaments and a more constructive view of global programmes
	Doha Financing for Development	Further called for increasing aid and improving effectiveness of aid
	UN High Level Event on MDGs	Reaffirmed support for MDGs as critical
2010	UN Development Cooperation Forum; UN Millennium Summit	Emphasis on mutual accountability and governance; Millennium Summit took stock of global progress to the MDGs
2011	High Level Forum in Busan Korea	Upcoming High Level Forum
2015	MDG targets	MDG deadline and formulation for next steps for development aid community

Figure 1. Chronology of key events in aid effectiveness (OECD 2006; United Nations 2009).

formed integral parts of the reform agenda, and in 2008 the Paris Declaration encompassed these shifts as new codes of voluntary conduct.

However, the Paris Declaration did not fully incorporate some of the new players and opportunities in the aid architecture. In particular, the incorporation of civil society and global programmes was initially limited. Global programmes were largely seen as outsiders requiring special rules and guidelines, with little effort made to harness their potential innovations and contributions to aid effectiveness. They were identified as one of the five challenges to the aid architecture, alongside corruption and lack of transparency. In 2005, the Declaration highlighted "*...insufficient integration of global programmes and initiatives into partner countries' broader development agendas, including in critical areas such as HIV/AIDS.*" Second, tensions among the principles (e.g. between alignment and results) and how to implement them as a package was not fully worked through, allowing stakeholders to cherry pick those most appropriate to their existing models.

The Paris Declaration had less traction initially in countries than globally; with action far behind rhetoric of the DAC-hosted, and to a large extent, donor dominated WP-EFF. The Working Party was based on a voluntary "club" approach to membership. It was initially reluctant to reach out to new partners. Additionally, the Working Party did not always prove worthwhile for developing countries to invest scare senior government capacity, in part due to a lack of voice among country participants. There was also insufficient emphasis on robust evaluation and to the radical adjustment and learning required to improve aid effectiveness. Finally its principles were voluntary, leading to engagement and incremental change, but without the accountability and binding decision making that may be required for more radical change in the delivery of aid. There were however significant achievements in establishing a system-wide agenda to reform aid backed up by targets and a measurement process, along with attention to formal and open learning opportunities which were lacking in many other sectors, such as the finance and banking.

Despite the comprehensive nature of the Paris principles, the early implementation and measurement tended to emphasise the traditional principles of alignment and harmonisation over the principles of country ownership, managing for results and mutual accountability. This is apparent in the Paris indicator framework where nine of twelve indicators are focused on the two principles of alignment and harmonisation. Development partners were able to focus on the principles which most suited them, de-emphasising those which were more challenging.

However a more inclusive, results-based aid architecture also gained momentum as country and donor actions were developed in preparation for the Accra Conference held in 2008. In particular, it became clear that civil society and global programmes contributed strengths in managing for results, wider country ownership and accountability alongside the traditional donor focus on alignment and harmonisation. The challenges of aligning global programmes in countries were also highlighted, together with the need to strengthen country systems and the policy environment to make new financing work more effectively.

The Paris Principles framed this process of negotiation between partners, but with a number of limitations. First, the principles of the Paris Declaration are proposed as a package to improve aid effectiveness. They need to be implemented as a package, not used selectively to justify aid arrangements solely on the basis of "alignment and harmonisation" or "to achieve results." The measurement framework also puts a disproportionate focus on alignment and harmonisation (nine out of twelve indicators), and a narrower focus on managing for results (which is represented by solely the existence of an M&E framework, capturing measurement but not managing for results). Similarly at country level, tensions have arisen in assuring that this general framework fully incorporates the strengths of a range of partners, for example, in SWAp contexts, for Global Programs, private sector and civil society. Despite tensions, aid effectiveness requires all aid effectiveness principles to be improved together. Finally, as noted, the aid effectiveness principles are voluntary. They rely essentially on the goodwill of donors, with limited peer pressure (e.g. DAC peer reviews, WP-EFF and UN Development Co-operation Forum).

Aid effectiveness began as a reorientation towards a more inclusive, results-based agenda from the Paris Declaration to the Accra Action Agenda including these excerpts from the AAA:

> A strengthened focus on results as an overarching principle at the heart of aid effectiveness: *"Achieving development results — and openly accounting for them — must be at the heart of all we do"; "we will be judged by the impacts that our collective efforts have on the lives of poor people"; "we will focus on delivering results"; "we will be more accountable and transparent to our publics for results"; "we need to achieve much more if all countries are to meet the Millennium Development Goals (MDGs)."*
>
> Inclusive partnerships for development: *"Aid is about building partnerships for development. Such partnerships are most effective when they full harness the energy, skills, and experience of all development*

actors — bilateral and multilateral donors, global funds, CSOs, and the private sector"; "We welcome and will work with all development actors"; "we will deepen our engagement with civil society organizations"; "We will engage in open and inclusive dialogue on development policies."

A more active engagement with the challenges and opportunities of new players including global programmes: *"Global funds and programs make an important contribution to development. The programs they fund are most effective in conjunction with complementary efforts to improve the policy environment and to strengthen the institutions in the sectors in which they operate. We call upon all global funds to support country ownership, to align and harmonise their assistance proactively, and to make good use of mutual accountability frameworks, while continuing their emphasis on achieving results."*

This evolution marked by the Accra Action Agenda was consistent with a continued commitment to all Paris Principles, and in some ways was more consistent with the spirit of the original Paris Declaration than its early application and measurement. Efforts to improve country capacity were also stressed, together with the recognition of Health as a Tracer Sector for aid effectiveness. The Accra Action Agenda also strengthened the emphasis on a network model of partnership, drawing in many organisations beyond the more formal discussions of the Working Party on aid effectiveness.

This transition has continued in the follow up from the Accra Meeting, with a more active outreach and network approach, rather than donor club model, to future OECD discussions around aid effectiveness. Civil society, the private sector, emerging donors like China and South Africa and global programmes through the Global Programs Learning Group[4] have been more formally included in the aid effectiveness movement. South Korea, which joined the OECD in 1996 and its Development

[4] The Global Programs Learning Group includes the Global Environment Facility, the Global Alliance for Vaccines and Immunizations, the Global Fund to fight AIDS, TB and Malaria, the Education for All-Fast Track Initiative, the Consultative Group for International Agriculture Research and links with the Health Metrics Network, the Presidents Emergency Plan for AIDS Relief and the Gates Foundation.

Assistance Committee in 2009 will host the triannual "High Level Forum on Aid Effectiveness" in 2011. As a member of the G20 group of nations, it also brings in a new perspective on global governance, with a strong role for countries like South Africa, Brazil, India, China and South Korea. There is also an increasing awareness that actions will be needed now in countries, together with the contribution of all partners and donors, if the MDGs are to be reached by 2015. This has provided an increasing results focus to the aid effectiveness movement from inside and outside.

Part 2. The Evolution of Global Programmes

With renewed commitment, the development community at the turn of the millennium set out a series of new resolutions, declarations and mechanisms designed to deliver aid more effectively. These included overall commitments on the MDGs, the creation of GAVI, the Global Fund, PEPFAR and the FTI. They provided opportunities by mobilising substantial funding and a range of partners both globally and in countries to work together to achieve results (DAC and new donors, foundations, civil society, private sector and global programmes). At the same time, this raised tensions at the system or architecture level to deliver aid, where more organisations were needed to ensure the effectiveness of aid delivery. This was recognised in the millennium commitments, where a substantial increase in aid from donors was predicated on demonstrated increases in the effectiveness of the delivery of aid and a new global development partnership (MDG 8). However, the system-wide declarations generally relied on voluntary principles and mechanisms for their application.

Global programmes have been increasingly seen as an innovative model, bringing in new partners and principles to aid, yet also facing many development challenges, both "traditional" challenges applicable to aid in general and some specific to global programmes. Largely, they were designed to be lean, with no or limited county presence, and focused on financing country-owned programmes. It was often assumed that these country programmes and strategies existed, together with an international partnership to support their financing. Since 2000, the number and scope of global programmes has increased, and over the last decade the challenges to their integration into this wider development partnership were noted.[5] Their rapid growth has promoted additional funding through this channel, innovation in leveraging additional funds and aid delivery and is characterised by inclusive ownership of development and a focus on MDG results. Equally, global programmes have been keenly criticised for adding to an already complex development landscape, vertical programming which focuses on specific thematic areas and insufficient integration with country development plans. Largely, global programmes have taken these criticisms, including those in their own independent evaluations, seriously.

Global programmes such as the Global Alliance for Vaccines and Immunizations (GAVI) and the Global Fund to fight AIDS, TB and Malaria are partnerships developed in the last decade to respond to requests for additional and more results-based financing. Without country offices, these organisations were designed with the aim to work with partners, promote ownership and transparency with a focus on achieving health results. They also are organised to leverage a wider range of partners, beyond nation-states to civil society, private sector and others. Global programmes have similarly faced critiques in adopting parallel approaches and paying insufficient attention to national development processes.[5] Although they were often established outside existing aid mechanisms, they are in fact heavily dependent on the effective functioning of an international partnership for development comprised of bilaterals, multilaterals and recipient countries.

In 2005, the Global Fund and the GAVI Alliance began exploring ways to improve harmonisation between these two health agencies, conducting joint visits to review country coordination, and to improve shared arrangements, particularly for collective support in health systems strengthening. This informal coordination effort in its early stages presented a useful opportunity for information sharing across the agencies and focused practices towards a coordinated approach, consistent with the ideas of the new International Health Partnership (IHP+), to which both GAVI and the Global Fund are signatories.

---

[5] World Bank (2006) *Integrating Global Partnership Programs with Country-led National Programs: Synthesis and Findings*. Presented at the Policy Workshop on "Global Programs and the Paris Agenda" December 2006.

At the same time, the deliberations of the Paris Declaration in 2005 also highlighted the insufficient integration of global programmes with overall aid programmes at the country level. In response in 2006, global programmes in health, agriculture, environment, education and urban affairs met at the margins of the OECD's Working Party on Aid Effectiveness to discuss how best to respond and how to integrate better within global discussions. There were reservations: some global programmes voiced concerns around the suitability of this forum to engage in the distinctive modality of the global programme; whether donor groupings would allow a meaningful expression of their concerns and whether existing in country processes could sufficiently capture global programmes.

After deliberation, the groups settled on an innovative independent network structure, which was sufficiently connected to the Working Party on Aid Effectiveness, hosted by the OECD-DAC, to ensure a fair exchange of ideas and information and to maintain accountability to global processes, but also permitted independence from control by donors or from DAC processes. The idea was to have a neutral space in which global programmes, as a peer group, could discuss common issues — their own as well as relations with donors and how they fit into the overall structure of aid. This was seen as a complement to each global programme's own policy and accountability structures, adding, though, "soft" accountability as a peer network and through annual reporting to the Working Party.

The Global Programmes Learning Group has stressed the importance of engagement from within and across the Global Programmes and their partners, to the broader development community. This was followed by consolidation of the Global Programmes Learning Group, development and publication of a joint work plan (Figure 2) and a more defined relationship with the OECD-DAC's Working Party on Aid Effectiveness. A direct line with the OECD-DAC's WP-EFF provided an opportunity to respond to its participants on progress and problems, and to make requests — particularly towards better integration and improved coordination. This initiated an important stage of peer learning and adaptation within global programmes and two-way discussions with the Working Party on aid effectiveness and the Learning Group. However, adjustments for the aid

5 PRIORITY AREAS	ACTIONS
I. Promote transparency & predictability	1. Provide transparent reporting, including to OECD of global programs finances to countries and improve predictability
	2. Prepare brief report on actions taken to improve predictable and transparent financing
II. Monitoring	3. Improve Paris Declaration monitoring survey, increasing coverage and quality
	4. Provide a forum for shared learning of aid effectiveness among Global Programs and others through joint meetings and bilateral discussions
	5. Integrate aid effectiveness as part of routine monitoring and evaluation of Global Programs
III. Results and Impact	6. Exchanging information and documenting innovation on managing for development results, including linkages with MfDR Cluster
	7. Strengthen the case for management for results in the Paris process
IV. Broaden ownership and improve alignment	8. Actions to improve support for and links to country strategies & programs
	9. Taking steps to make ownership more inclusive by incorporating CSOs, private sector and fragile states into Global Programs
	10. Actions to align Global Program funds to country reporting and fiscal cycles
V. Innovation	11. Exchange of information on innovative financing, including contributing best practices to innovative financing task team

Figure 2. Summary of priority areas and actions from the joint Global Programmes learning group workplan, 2009–2010.[6]

system to accommodate global programme funding have proven to have both transaction and transition costs, for both countries and Global Programmes.

Part 3. Negotiating Aid Effectiveness and Fostering Partnerships Through the Network Model

As noted, at the time of the Paris Declaration, global programmes were seen as a significant challenge to the established aid architecture, contributing to fragmentation and working outside existing development strategies. Their engagement in monitoring and commitment to reform of their own institutions, as well as peer learning and sharing, has substantially changed the international community's understanding and acceptance of global programmes. The Accra Agenda for Action described them as making an "important contribution to development" as well as identifying challenges going forward. With this recognition have come responsibilities to change and adapt to challenges — on the basis of two-way dialogue and negotiation needed to improve the overall aid partnership.

At the global level, this has signalled a change in the discourse around these programmes on aid effectiveness and the aid architecture.

[6] Available at: http://www.oecd.org/dataoecd/32/6/43947784.pdf.

The innovation of active incorporation of civil society as board members, implementers and decision makers reflects a broadened ownership of health and development. Global programmes are pioneering mechanisms for new directions in development, as illustrated by initiatives such as the Innovative Financing Facility for Immunizations (IFFIm), the Affordable Medicines for Malaria venture (AMfM), the airline tax levy and Product (RED), a programme in which private firms contribute a share of revenues of specified products to the Global Fund.

The network model employed by global programmes in launching the Learning Group is a response to the need for mutual adjustment by global programmes and by the broader aid structure generated by the advent of these new models for development assistance, with the aim of increasing effectiveness of both. The global programmes exemplify inclusive network governance through their boards and councils, incorporating civil society, private sectors, developing and developed countries, donors and NGOs. The Learning Group provided a voice in global discussions on development and an opportunity to negotiate within the wider development infrastructure. This "global action network"[7] consolidates its engagement with international structures and forms a complementary extension of the internal governance arrangements of participating global programmes (Figure 3).[8]

The diversity of global health constituencies in global programmes allows varying viewpoints, decisions and politics to reach the table. The discourse is messy and the dynamics of reaching consensus can be

---

[7] Sridhar, Khagram and Pang (2008) "Are Existing Governance Structures Equipped to Deal with Today's Global Health Challenges? Towards Systemic Coherence and Scaling Up,"*Global Health Governance*II(2).

[8] PEPFAR is a bilateral, rather than global, program with a specific mandate. While many donors have specific programs of this type, PEPFAR is unique in its overall scale and the extent of its operations at country level. Its governance and accountability is reflective of that seen in bilateral agencies. The position of "US Global AIDS Coordinator" is a presidential appointment requiring senate confirmation and reporting directly to the Secretary of State. PEPFAR's first authorisation consolidated US bilateral and multilateral activities and resources for HIV/AIDS through a "whole of government" response. In country, agreements between PEPFAR, governments and in-country partners are formed as Partnership Frameworks which lay out a five-year country strategy and implementation plan.

GAVI Alliance Created in 2000 to increase access to vaccine products and immunisation services in developing countries	▪ GAVI is an alliance of developing countries, donors, the vaccine industry, the Gates Foundation, WHO, UNICEF, civil society and private individuals ▪ The GAVI Alliance Board, constituted by these members, oversees and monitors policy development and implementation in all programme areas ▪ In addition to the GAVI Alliance Board, GAVI relies upon two other boards –the IFFIm Board and the GAVI Fund Affiliate Board– who administer the International Finance Facility for Immunisation (IFFIm), an innovative financing mechanism established to fund GAVI programmes ▪ Recommendations to the Board are made by Independent Review Committees (IRCs) ▪ The GAVI Secretariat, with offices in Geneva and Washington, is responsible for day-to-day operations, including: resource mobilisation; coordinating programme approvals and disbursements; developing policy and implementing strategic initiatives; monitoring and evaluation; legal and financial management and administration for the GAVI Alliance Board and Committees. Regional working groups operate through WHO regional offices and typically coordinate TA and review proposals for the region ▪ Country governance by Immunization Coordination Committees (ICCs)
The Global Fund to Fight AIDS, TB and Malaria The Global Fund to Fight AIDS, Tuberculosis and Malaria was created in 2002 to increase resources to fight the three diseases in less developed countries	▪ The Global Fund Board is composed of donor and recipient governments, civil society, private sector, private foundations and communities living with and affected by the diseases. The board is responsible for the organisation's governance, establishing strategies and policies, making funding decisions and setting budgets, as well as advocating for the mobilisation of resources ▪ Key partners include the WHO, UNAIDS and public–private partnerships such as Roll Back Malaria, Stop TB & UNITAID and the World Bank ▪ In countries, the country coordinating mechanism (CCM) is a partnership composed of all key stakeholders in a country's response to the three diseases. The CCM submits proposals, nominates those accountable for administering the funding and oversees the grants ▪ The Geneva-based secretariat manages the grant portfolio, screens proposals, issues disbursements and implements performance-based funding of grants. They also execute Board policies and undertake resource mobilisation, providing strategic, policy, financial, legal and administrative support and oversees monitoring and evaluation ▪ The Technical Review Panel (TRP) is an independent group of international experts. It reviews proposals based on technical criteria and provide funding recommendations to the Board

Figure 3. Descriptive governance arrangements of key global programmes in health, environment and education.[9]

[9] All information from respective Global Program websites, including www.theglobalfund.org; www.educationfasttrack.org; www.gavialliance.org and www.thegef.org.

Global Environment Facility Established in 1991, the GEF is today the largest funder of projects to improve the global environment. 10,000 small grants directly to nongovernmental and community organisations	▪ The Global Environment Facility (GEF) is a partnership of 182 member governments, international institutions, nongovernmental organisations and the private sector ▪ The GEF Council is the main governing body, with 32 constituencies – 16 from developing countries, 14 from developed countries and two from countries with transitional economies. It functions as an independent board of directors, with responsibility for developing, adopting and evaluating GEF programmes ▪ All member countries participate in the GEF Assembly. It meets every three to four years and is responsible for reviewing and evaluating the GEF's general policies, the operation of the GEF and its membership ▪ The GEF partnership includes ten agencies: UNDP, UNEP, the World Bank, FAO UNIDO, AfDB, AsDB, EBRD, IADB and IFAD ▪ The Scientific and Technical Advisory Panel provides technical and scientific advice on the GEF's policies and projects. The panel consists of six members who are internationally recognised experts
Education for All – Fast Track Initiative (FTI) The Education for All –FTI is a global partnership between donor and developing countries to ensure accelerated progress towards universal primary education by 2015	▪ The strategic decisions for the FTI are made at biennial Partnership Meetings. The partnership approves the basic policies, goals, principles and working methods of the initiative and reviews and approves the objectives as a reflection of FTI goals ▪ The Board of Directors provides overall policy guidance to the partnership, gives direction to the Secretariat, oversees the work of the various task teams and working groups and helps ensure overall coordination. It includes donors, multilateral agencies, developing countries and civil society representatives ▪ The Secretariat handles technical and administrative support of the initiative. It comprises staff from the various partners. It is responsible for managing the FTI trust funds on behalf of the donor partners ▪ Discussions and decisions around a country's education sector plan take place in country with the group of local stakeholders (government, bilateral and multilateral agencies and civil society) ▪ A Coordinating Agency is designated among the local donor representatives. It has a decisive role during the development and endorsement of the education sector plan of the country and also during the implementation of the plan ▪ Civil society organisations support progress towards EFA goals through advocacy and dialogue with governments and local donor groups

Figure 3. (*Continued*)

challenging. The outcomes are secured and owned by constituents and spread through further independent networks. A key example is seen among the Boards of Global Health programmes such as the Global Fund or GAVI. These institutions have representatives from developing countries, donors and civil society, including NGOs from the South.

Elements of "good governance" in development are noted to include greater transparency, strategic vision, equitable allocation of resources, broad participation from stakeholders and sustainable and efficient

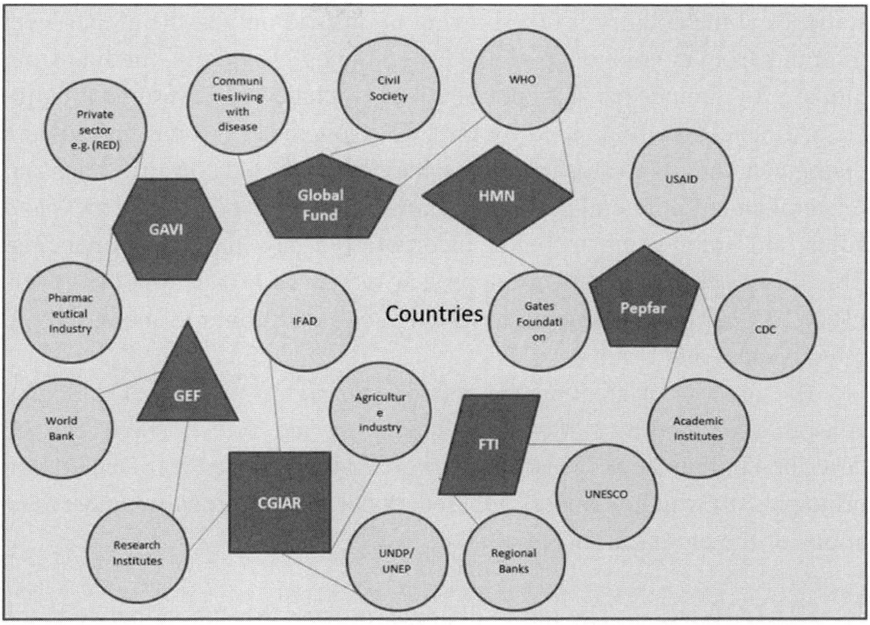

Figure 4. Constellation of networks of global programmes (diagram is suggestive of the breadth and diversity of their interactions).

functioning.[10] These principles could be used to apply, to take the example of the Global Fund, to support health systems strengthening and direct funding of national strategies in the Global Fund Board. Additional elements may include managing for results, normative rules and standards for development assistance and opportunities for adjudication among the different constituents in their governance (such as seen in the human rights violations through the International Criminal Court or trade disputes through the World Trade Organizations' Appellate Body). These latter broad principles of governance have not been explored much in health literature to date and could include negotiations across constituencies (Figure 4).

This network has facilitated improved practices and monitoring of aid effectiveness in countries. For example, finances from these global programmes have not been routinely captured in official OECD aid

[10] UNDP (1997) *Five Principles of Good Governance*; Kaufman (1999) *Governance Measures*, The World Bank.

statistics at the country level (showing up instead only at the global level as grants from donors to the global programmes). Similarly, funding from global programmes has not been routinely included in government budgets or financial ceilings used by the IMF. Nonetheless, it has promoted a dialogue among global programmes, their broad-based constituencies and bilateral and multilateral partners on how to improve aid effectiveness and adjust aid architecture to better incorporate a new model of financing. This illustrates how a network approach, as part of broadening the governance of global development assistance, can contribute to increased aid effectiveness and results.

The process of creating the network through a process of dialogue, consolidation and two-way engagement on aid effectiveness can be described in four steps. These stages were framed by the Paris Declaration principles, to which members adhered, and a series of reviews and evaluations of the organisations involved.

1. **DIALOGUE** — The initial dialogue process, beginning between the Global Fund and GAVI, was expanded and stressed the importance of engagement within and across the global programmes and their partners, including donors, and to the broader development community. The first interactions provided an opportunity for global programmes to network and discuss bilaterally and collectively how aid effectiveness could be incorporated into their policies and practices.
2. **ASSESSMENT** — A focus on learning and sharing through monitoring and evaluation has been a critical part of the inclusion. There have been external evaluations for a number of global programmes, as well as case studies at country level by the World Bank. A joint assessment of global programmes on aid effectiveness identified strengths and weaknesses and made recommendations for improvement. In response, global programmes have developed a joint work plan for 2009–2010 with actions for improvement.
3. **CONSOLIDATION** — This was followed by consolidation of the Global Programmes Learning Group, development of a joint work plan and definition of the relationship with the WP-EFF. This has allowed space for a discussion to occur between the Working Party and the Learning Group (Figure 5).

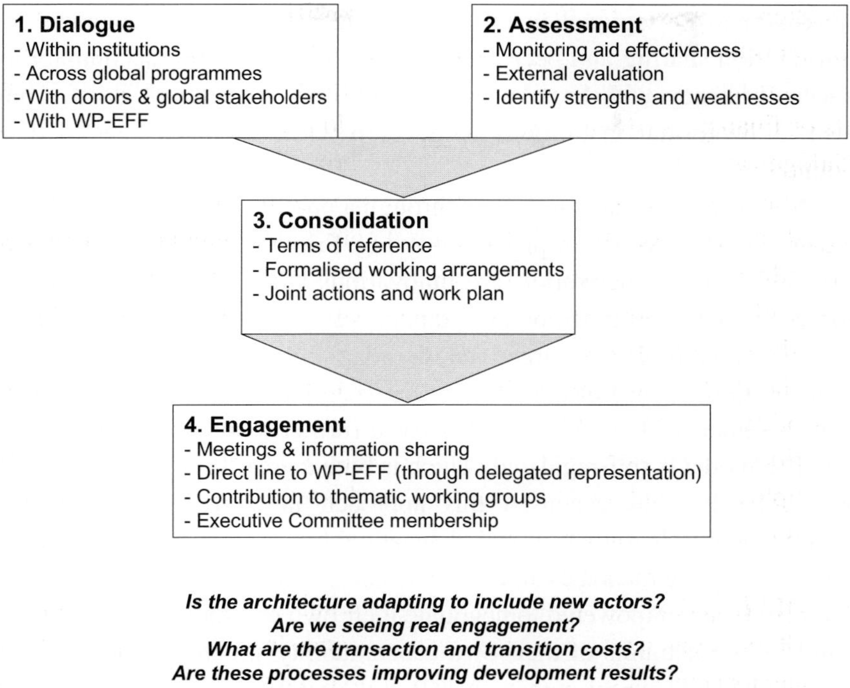

Figure 5. Creating a global programmes network.

4. **ENGAGEMENT** — The network was titled the Global Programmes Learning Group, reflecting the spirit of continued learning and the effort to share best practice and experience. It has a direct line to the OECD-DACs WP-EFF, allowing a formal engagement with aid partners to report progress and discuss actions needed to improve the partnership for development.

Dedeurwaerdere (2005)[11] notes that the aim of network governance is to "create a synergy between different competencies and sources of knowledge in order to deal with complex or interlinked problems." This mode of governance is typically accomplished through decentralised networks of public and private constituencies that retain links with national,

[11] Dedeurwaerdere (2005) The contribution of network governance to sustainable development. Les séminaires de l'Iddri, No 13, Feb 2005.

international or regional institutions. These links provide channels for information sharing and peer learning and serve to ensure accountability and consistency with broader agendas beyond the network itself. They also allow formal institutions to develop wider linkages beyond their boundaries.

Network legitimacy is gained through a process of peer oversight and a common framework for problem solving. Sridar *et al.* (2008-2009) note that global action networks "are innovations whose legitimacy is being forged by optimizing democratic imperatives (transparency, participation and accountability) and effectiveness (adaptability, efficiency and scalability).[12] Governance of the linkages between these mechanisms and how they facilitate scaling up for results merit further work.

The model is self-regulated, which is both a great strength and a weakness. The EC has espoused this approach in some of its work on development.[13] It allows global delegation for a broader set of actions (beyond existing mandates and competencies) to networks of self-regulated actors who are empowered to negotiate their own common solutions, albeit within the constraints of their own accountability structures, including, in the case of global programmes, their Boards and the donors that fund them.

There are acknowledged limitations of such self-regulating network models of governance, including network opportunism (the priority or agenda is set by global elites); the network no longer addresses the interests of its constituents or is captured by a minority of them; and the network operates outside established norms and standards. Additionally, one limitation of the network approach for global programmes is that members are accountable to their own accountability mechanisms (e.g. Boards). The challenge of a network such as the Global Programmes Learning Group is to complement and add value while respecting the accountability of each organisation's own accountability mechanism. Here, the changes apply two fold — first to the global programmes themselves, seen through behaviour change facilitated by the network, and

---

[12] Sridhar, Khagram and Pang (2008–2009) "Are Existing Governance Structures Equipped to Deal With Today's Global Health Challenges? Towards Systemic Coherence and Scaling Up," *Global Health Governance*II(2).

[13] European Commission White paper on governance 2001.

second to the aid architecture including how donors deal with global programmes.

There are advantages to self-regulated autonomous networks. Remaining connected yet outside bureaucratic constraints allows development and support of flexible solutions to complex problems. The network model of peer oversight is in the spirit of learning not judging, though pressure is exerted through peers. Comparative standards are relaxed and accountability is transferred to within the institutions.

Networks allow institutions to steer a wider and more diverse group of partners, than is reached with their more formal membership. Additionally, evidence from the Global Programme Learning Group suggests that participation in the network model has contributed to organisational learning and support for monitoring with peer support. Schout and Jordan (2003) suggest self-regulated networks should be steered by institutions that can facilitate in their design, auditing, management practices and coordination and ensure objectives are integrated across the network and goals are met. There remain questions if these are sufficiently provided by the DAC's Working Party or if the UN or G-20 may provide a more suitable forum.

Questions remain in the effort to broaden global governance in development through a network approach as applied to global programmes: are we seeing real engagement? Is the architecture adapting to include new actors? What are the transaction and transition costs? Moreover, to what extent are these processes improving development outcomes? These questions need to be considered in the context of the broader systems of accountability and incentives driving the behaviour of global programmes. Expectations for the network should not be set — in this case as in most networks — too high. The Global Program Learning Group was recognised at the start as a complementary element in those broader systems.

The expansion of global governance to incorporate new and innovative actors has been met with degrees of resistance and challenges. This has not been so much due to the increasing number of partners. Funding for AIDS, malaria and vaccines for example has in some ways become more concentrated than ever in a few partners, including GAVI, PEPFAR and the Global Fund. However, the types of donors have gone beyond the normal club of partners. They now include important non-DAC donors, for example China, South Africa and India, foundations, civil society, private sector and global programmes. Coordination and mutual learning among these diverse funding sources requires more of a network model, going beyond nation-states alone, to provide fora globally and in countries to promote dialogue, good practice and norms related to aid effectiveness.

MDG 8 identifies the need for a global partnership to deliver on development (United Nations 2008). How global programmes, and even more the other non-DAC funders, fit into the architecture of health and development is as yet undefined and lacks clear rules of engagement. In contrast (for the most part) to global programmes, other newer donors are reluctant to various extents to participate in joint work with DAC donors, partly because of concerns about being dominated and partly to preserve maximum freedom of action — much as today's DAC donors did in earlier days of their own evolution.

In broadening governance arrangements, there have been some concerns regarding structural limitations. The OECD Development Assistance Committee, the principal body through which OECD donors deal with issues related to co-operation with developing countries and the most well-established platform for considering issues of development aid, has shown strength in defining standards and policy guidelines. It has been criticised both for expanding too far beyond its mandate to focus on leveraging international development cooperation and for the opposite — remaining too much a club of bilateral donors. The WP-EFF is the key vehicle through which such issues are brought on to the table. This is a wide consultation group including donors, countries and civil society. New members have gradually been added, but concerns remain about the donor-driven nature of the agenda, very recent civil society engagement and whether partner country representation has been meaningful.

Finally, the recent financial crisis has brought greater global attention to system-wide political and financial risks. The global health community will need to look at innovative ways to incorporate and attract new donors and sources of finance. Countries wish to avoid fragmentation of aid, with its high transaction costs. They also seek a manageable diversity of donors to safeguard against risks, rather than rely on single sources or pooling of funds. The necessary improvements in aid effectiveness may require going beyond the voluntary commitments and self-regulation of the Paris

Declaration to develop more binding "rules of the game," setting parameters for engagement.

In summary, the Global Programmes Learning Group has generated actions for joint implementation. The legitimacy and flexibility afforded through a peer network approach has allowed the group to promote the underserved principles of managing for results and share their lessons in monitoring and evaluation, transparency and accountability and widened country ownership.

This network model of governance has key drivers centred on learning and sharing, including (i) a focus on monitoring and evaluation, (ii) support for internal dialogue and reform.

(i) Monitoring and evaluation

Global programmes have been proactively involved in the monitoring process for the Paris Declaration indicators and some global programmes have internalised these as measures of corporate performance (e.g. The Global Fund and GAVI), while others have adapted the measures to appreciate the suitability of the sector in which they work (e.g. EFA/FTI). The monitoring exercise for the Paris Declaration showcased the variation in the country operations of Global Programs as compared with those of traditional bilateral and multilateral partners. While the challenges of using national systems for reporting and recording results were evident, there was a greater focus on strengthening national M&E systems, building capacity for reporting through developing in country tools and systems support. The formal process of monitoring and evaluation was important to ensure accountability of network models of governance (Figure 6).

	Strengths	Weaknesses	Actionable recommendations
Ownership	Country led proposals and implementation, usually strongly inclusive of civil society & private sector.	Overall ownership by government, particularly Finance Ministries – necessary for sustainability.	Pro-active approach – direct or via principal intermediaries – to involve Finance Ministries; the gain in sustainability outweighs the increased transaction cost.
Alignment	Alignment to varying degrees at subsectoral level.	Tendency to use systems (e.g. timing, auditing) that make sense for crosscountry comparison by global program. Focus needed to use and strengthen country systems.	Steps, varying by program, include: support for national strategies; pooling funding; pro-actively putting funding onbudget; and pro-active effort to follow country, rather than global program, systems, and budget cycles. Donors should: provide more sustainable and innovative financing (e.g. the airline ticket tax); give strong support on GP boards and at country level for better alignment of global programs; increase the share of core funding relative to earmarked contributions; "think twice" before starting new global programs; and build alignment, and harmonization, into program design within a thought-out sectoral "architecture".
Harmonization	Donor financing of GPs is a form of upstream harmonization.	Limited country presence limits involvement with other donors.	Participation, directly or by delegation, in harmonization and streamlining at country level. Make fuller use of existing flexibility and get more from Boards and management.
Managing for results	Results frameworks in place. Innovation in performance based financing and incentives. Internal and external evaluation culture built in from start	Varying attention to results, including varying quality of results frameworks. Use of own results and M&E framework, rather than governments.	More attention to using and strengthening national M&E systems. Consistent focus on managing for results, with reasonable balance among outcomes, intermediate outputs and implementation processes. Monitor each global programs implementation of the Paris Declaration. Emphasis on results can be a major contribution of global programs to SWAps and country programs.
Mutual accountability	Accountability to international constituencies as well as local accountability through involvement of CSOs and private sector. Transparency of documentation & processes.	Country level accountability.	Participation, directly or through delegation, in country mutualaccountability related structures, including annual sectoral mutual reviews. Encourage improved local accountability systems (e.g. role of beneficiaries or expenditure tracking.)
Cross-cutting issues	Wide support of Paris Declaration.	Mostly not signatories of the Paris Declaration. Weak incentives for emphasis on Paris Declaration, especially harmonization & alignment by overstretched staff. Inadequate communication among global programs & "culture gap" between global programs & country based assistance.	Sign by sending letter to DAC Chair. Set clear management priorities and incentives, with support from Boards, and communicate them effectively to country intermediaries and implementing agencies. Build bridges of dialogue and joint learning, with support from the top. Focus on and monitor behavior change in each global program.

Figure 6. Joint evaluation of global programmes to improve aid effectiveness, 2008.[14]

[14] This synthesis of good practices, adjustments and learning is a broad summary across diverse programs, including items that apply to many but not all. The Learning Group of Global Programs — Actions for Aid Effectiveness, 2008. Available at: http://www.theglobalfund.org/documents/aideffectiveness/2008_Global_Programs_Learning_Group_Actions_for_Aid_Effectiveness.pdf.

(ii) Internal dialogue and reform

Continued learning and adapting has been a critical part of model development. At times, tensions built into the global programme model have limited the rapid or complete internalisation of adjustments. In some areas (such as donor harmonisation), reform has been slow, given the differences in adaptability of global programmes. Despite this, there has been dialogue internally and within the broader development context about how global programmes adjust and some promising advances have been made. This dialogue has allowed the sharing of best practices, helped develop joint agendas and supported the process of change management required in each institution.

Part 4. Conclusion — Adaptation and Change, Ways Forward

Global programmes have played an increasing role in development and in so doing have had to adapt to other partners and the agreed principles of the Paris Declaration. This chapter has described this process of adaptation and change. It has also assessed to what extent the Paris Declaration principles have been valuable in framing adaptation and providing a common engagement for diverse global programmes. The chapter has shown the stages of this engagement and the network model developed to promote learning among global programmes. It has also highlighted some of the limitation to change among global programmes, and for the wider change process foreseen by the Paris Declaration. There has been considerable progress, but building an effective global partnership for development (MDG 8) remains an unfinished agenda. It needs to be a major priority, among global programmes and other partners, in the build up to 2015, as a major contributor and outcome of the MDGs.

There have been a number of forms of change and adaptation under the framework of the Paris Declaration, highlighted in this chapter. The Boards of global programmes have also enabled formal policy engagement across the diversity of partners now active in providing health assistance (including China, South Africa and Brazil). However, strategies now need to be developed and sustained across an increasing number of constituencies involved in global health governance. More binding rules (beyond the voluntarism of the Paris Principles) may be required to promote consistency across this network governance.

In addition, many of these constituencies need to reach out to wider groups to ensure effective deliberation, representation and legitimacy. This has promoted the form of network governance described in the chapter, which is not intended to replace existing formal governance, but so far it has worked to increase the scope and reach of more traditional mechanisms. Thus, the OECD has broadened the aid effectiveness agenda by reaching out to civil society, private sector and global programmes through these new networks. There have been limitations to the ability of this mix of formal and network governance to systematically increase aid effectiveness, as shown by the results of the Paris indicators.

Behind the Paris Declaration and principles and formal measurement, it is easy to underestimate the negotiation and diplomacy required to build system-wide approaches and networks to improve aid effectiveness. Network governance does not emerge from thin air, but from extensive alliances, engagement and negotiation. This involves aligning objectives through global programme Boards and finding common interests (e.g. health systems strengthening common to both the Global Fund and GAVI). Without such an approach, formal governance is very limited in its ability to steer a diversity of partners beyond its more restricted "club members" — albeit even there in a limited fashion. The chapter has shown the wider process of adaptation and network governance that the Paris Declaration has initiated. It has also highlighted some of its limitations.

In the case of global programmes, the network model and its ability to leverage a wide variety of partners has created space for innovation in dealing with development challenges. Importantly, they seek to monitor and promote change management, based on evidence from monitoring, peer learning and independent evaluations. The five-year evaluation of the Global Fund and the evaluation of GAVI had extensive sections on aid effectiveness and partnerships, which provided an important evidence base for the working of the Global Programme Learning Group. This group was a forum to respond to such evidence, in a way that could frame peer learning and an indirect form of negotiations within the Paris Principles and the evidence base these principles initiated. This internal process of change management, negotiation and diplomacy is often neglected in governance discourse, beyond the agreement and monitoring of principles and their indicators. The next step to realise the full benefits of the model is to associate the formal Paris Declaration process with a stronger network model to promote the learning, adaptation and negotiation required to accelerate change.

There is also a wider challenge beyond global programmes, as to how development partners respond as a system to incorporate innovations and address collective risks. Many of these partners are represented on the Boards of global programmes and so can act more consistently in framing their activities either when global programmes are created or as their policies are reviewed. These can be responses to the emergence of new partners, for example global programmes, new donors such as China or India, or to new health issues and risks. Without this responsiveness to change and innovation, it is unlikely that the MDG of a new partnership for development, mentioned above, can be achieved.

The chapter has stressed the wider negotiation and coordinated actions which need to accompany governance rules and principles like the Paris Declaration. These principles help frame the negotiation of change and may need to be strengthened to provide fora to resolve disputes, review accountability and renew these "rules of the game." System-wide rules are often promoted and extended by more open governance. Innovative partnerships will require creative governance, which combines traditional and new partners, the G8 and the G20, new and older donors, and critically places partner countries at its centre. The changes illustrated in this chapter suggest we can conclude with cautious optimism that a substantial change process has been initiated among global programmes framed by the Paris Declaration principles. Aid in some ways had its crisis in the 1990s, ten years before the current financial crisis. Out of this developed new partnerships and rules to improve system-wide effectiveness. This and the evidence of adaptation across all partners is the basis for optimism. Caution is due as this engagement, learning and negotiation needs to be intensified and deepened to affect practice at country level, if we are to make the case for more and better aid during the brief period from 2000 to 2015.

The aid industry has incorporated new opportunities while defining common actions to manage risks in the last decade, with open eyes to new models of delivery and organisation of aid. The new landscape has better focused players, with common goals and shared interests. An extensive change and negotiation process has been initiated on the basis of the agreed Paris principles, involving formal boards and network governance which can extend change to a wider group of constituencies. The shift to a results focus in the wake of the MDG deadline in 2015 has been further consolidated by addressing critical challenges through partnership and negotiation on the basis of common principles for effective development. The global programmes and the learning group that they established provides one example of progress and the unfinished agenda, to negotiate, evaluate and learn how to improve the effectiveness of aid. This unfinished agenda should provide the basis for a firm push towards a new global development partnership, which is a major contributor as well as objective (in MDG 8) of the MDG process to 2015.

Chapter 2 provides further assessment of negotiations on aid effectiveness among global programmes. Chapter 15 and Chapter 16 provide country examples in Vietnam and Ethiopia.

8

Malaria: Partnerships in Malaria Control

Bernard L. Nahlen, and Richard W. Steketee†*

**United States President's Malaria Initiative, USAID, Washington DC*

†Malaria Control and Evaluation Partnership in Africa (MACEPA), PATH, France

Summary

Of all major health issues, malaria has moved from a disease neglected in terms of financing to one that has attracted interest and a diverse range of partners: multilaterals, global health programmes, private sector, NGOs, foundations and donors. Coordination and governance of these partners has also developed rapidly, with a focus on targets and tracking meaningful results contributing the Millennium Development Goal (MDG) of reduced child mortality. This chapter describes the history of partnerships to fight malaria. It then analyses how partnerships have developed and shifted from a scientific disease investigation mode to a disease intervention and control model. This has not been an easy transition, and the communications and coordination between different potential partners remains critical to its success.

1. Introduction

As we complete the first decade of the new millennium, the emphasis on partnerships is now pervasive in public health. It wasn't always that way. Past disease control programme advances have often been run centrally and produced good results: the Smallpox Eradication Program is perhaps the best known example of this, but many others exist and some were not as successful. The move in the mid-1970s to primary health care and "Health for All" was apparently a struggle against the central management and the single disease control approach;[1] but limited clarity about what was to be done, constrained resources and little documented impact led to some disillusionment in this approach. The discussion of "disease control priorities"[2] was developed in the late 1970s and persists to the present in various iterations.[3,4] The global public health community most recently has focused particular attention on immunisation programmes, HIV-AIDS, TB and malaria. One view of this is that the global public health community transitioned during the past decades to focus on those disease control programmes that could forge broad partnerships and then use the partnerships to both move science to programme and advocate for and justify the required resources to make the programmes function.

To truly embody a "disease control programme," the thinking and work among the participants must evolve from a scientific disease investigation mode (where the disease burden and disease mechanisms are primary) to a disease intervention and control mode (where reducing the burden, containing transmission and tracking progress are primary). This is never an easy transition. The competencies in one area do not always transfer to the other area, and the communications and coordination between the different potential partners is critical to success.

This transition from pilot investigative projects to disease control partnerships can certainly occur. One excellent example for the malaria control community is the series of randomised controlled trials of insecticide-treated mosquito nets (ITNs)[5] that led to global policy changes that were then picked up by a variety of partners including national governments, global donors, scientific and technical agencies, non-governmental implementation support agencies and private sector insecticide and mosquito net manufacturers. While not without different opinions of the best programming methods,[6,7] over time these partners have developed highly effective interventions, advocated for substantial domestic and global resources and delivered an unprecedented (at least for the malaria community) amount of product to rural households in malaria-endemic communities around the world and particularly in difficult-to-reach places in Africa. The formation of a wider, global partnership has supported the required scale to move from an investigation mode to a partnership which targets sufficient coverage to affect population level disease trends.

Malaria control was not always characterised by partnerships. Approximately fifty years after the key scientific discoveries in malaria (e.g. the identification of the parasite and mosquito vectors and the characterisation of their critical interactions),[8–10] the Malaria Eradication Program (MEP) was developed at WHO.[11] This programme relied on pesticides [indoor residual spraying (IRS) of long-lasting insecticide] and treatment of cases (using chloroquine and other effective drugs of the time). This was described[12] more as a military campaign approach with highly centralised management and decision making and limited "partnerships." Despite a number of successes, the Malaria Eradication Program was disbanded in the mid-1970s, and this ushered in a period (the mid-1970s to the late 1990s) of greatly limited resources and a shift to scientific investigation rather than disease control programming. As the malaria community once again approached a major disease control programme effort in the late 1990s (Roll Back Malaria [RBM])[13] the larger public health community was increasingly invested in partnerships as a way of addressing the multi-faceted responsibilities of disease control programming and attracting the necessary global commitment and financing. The evolving RBM Partnership thus emerged as a partnership between endemic countries, the donor community, the science community, non-governmental agencies and public–private relationships. The financial resources did not precede the decision making; in fact the surge of resources came relatively late in the partnership process. The decade from 2000 to 2010 saw a truly complex web of partners lead a growing documented success in malaria control programming.

The beginning of our current millennium represents a "creative period"[14] in which malaria control emerged as a visible success in the commitment to country ownership and results. It has also created a powerful and diverse partnership focused on a disease issue. Here we summarise the timing, events and content of the malaria partnership. We

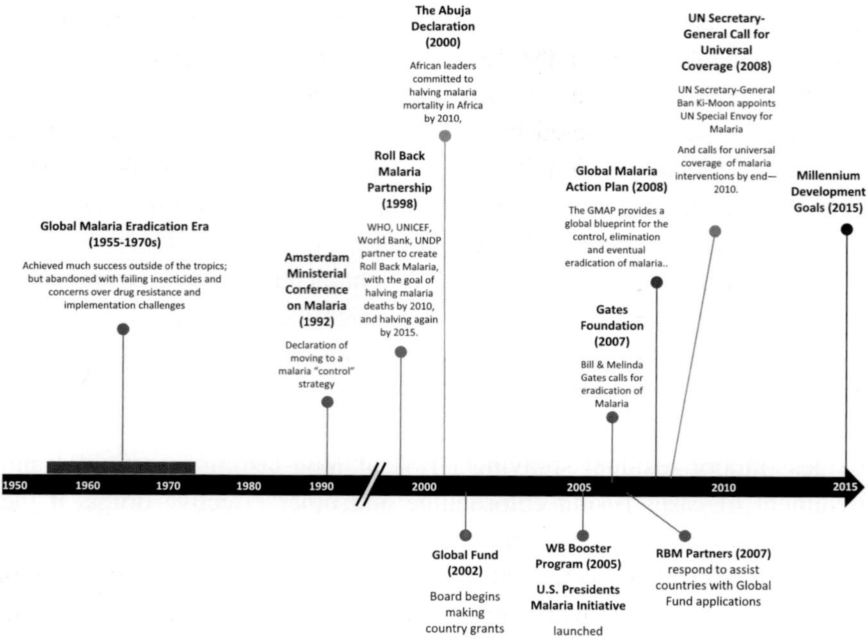

Figure 1. Major events in malaria control over the past 50+ years.

have taken a chronologic approach as this allows a characterisation of what has or has not changed with time, and an opportunity to compare and contrast these approaches over time (see Figure 1).

2. Early Years in Malaria

Arguably, the early years of malaria began with oral and then written history of several millennia.[15] However, the discovery at the end of the 1890s and early 1900s of the malaria parasite[8] and the mosquito vector[9] and the biologic interactions between parasite, mosquito vector and human host[15,16] represented a watershed period of scientific exploration and advancement. Like many such science breakthroughs, there was intrigue and credit grabbing amidst the collaboration and competition. Ultimately, the discovery of prevention measures including the use of inexpensive, highly effective long-lasting spray with dichloro-diphenyl-trichloroethane (DDT), and the understanding of effective treatment with the aminoquinoline drugs (chloroquine, amodiaquine, primaquine and others), during and after the second world war in the 1940s, led to an opportunity to move to an "assault" on malaria.

This assault, embodied by the Malaria Eradication Program at the World Health Organisation (WHO) from the 1950s, has been described in detail[12] and its components cannot be fully recounted here. The relevant consideration is that for the time and the context (World War II had just ended and public health infrastructures had developed importantly in this war time environment), the disease control effort had an "assault"-like quality and a highly centralised command structure, management style and deployment methods. Guidance for malaria eradication was written and standard operating procedures were defined. These were much more "vertical" than present-day approaches, with para-governmental units established in countries with staff selected internationally according to standard terms of reference. However, none of the accounts offer much insight into what today would be considered "partnerships" of different organisations and entities bringing different expertise to a common problem. The Rockefeller Foundation and the League of Nations were described as "godfathers" of the Malaria Eradication Program and the United Nations International Children Emergency Fund (UNICEF) was noted as recognising that investment in malaria control would give particular benefits for mothers and children. However, the "assault" was led by WHO under the auspices of its constitution stating that it should "act as the directing and coordinating authority on international health work." Countries and WHO regional offices were recognised as having a critical role, but there is relatively little mention of other partners (donors, researchers, NGOs, private sector, etc.). The technical and normative agencies were in control, and any balance that might come with other partners with more adaptive regional and local experience would also come with broader governance that would be more challenging to manage. The natural tension became increasingly apparent between the focused disease control approach and the growth of primary health care, and it is little surprise that the end of the Malaria Eradication Program coincided with the advent of "primary health care" and "health for all." The assault on malaria had nevertheless achieved important results, with eradication in many countries, not matched in the several decades that followed. It had nevertheless reached important limits, political, technical and in terms of health partnerships.

The ending of the Malaria Eradication Program in the mid-1970s did not leave a wake of partnerships undone. Rather it was a relatively clean break and a reversion to getting the science right, identifying better interventions and addressing the problems of insecticide and drug resistance that were seen as the undoing of the eradication effort.

3. Post-Malaria Eradication Program and the 1980s

By the 1980s, the optimism of the eradication campaign had been replaced by a belief that malaria, particularly in highly endemic Africa, could not be eliminated but it could possibly be controlled. The systems set up for eradication, leadership that was centrally organised and directed, were discredited, and while it was said that malaria control should be integrated into the general health systems instead of being a vertical programme, the means to do this were neglected.

With the emphasis on primary health care developing in the late 1970s (Alma Ata declaration[a]), malaria control efforts began working in the context of child survival initiatives with programmes jointly focused on immunisations, diarrhoeal diseases, respiratory diseases and malaria.[17] The changing emphasis brought in a shift in the partnership, and the increasing role of UNICEF. This was a time of re-examining the burden of malaria and rebuilding the science around the available and possible new or evolved malaria control interventions. The relatively small malaria science community had modest support, and programmes were often pilot efforts and did not take on a national scope. This decade was characterised by:

- Many high-burden countries, with a predominance in sub-Saharan Africa; few countries with systematic full deployment prevention efforts; much reliance on treatment of febrile illness; deteriorating health systems that were often unable to provide access to effective case management;
- Emergence and spread of CQ-resistant *P. falciparum* globally, particularly in Africa;

- Numerous studies providing further evidence of the tremendous negative impact of malaria on maternal and child health;
- Most external funding targeted to research, and very little money was available for programme support — everyone was "waiting for the vaccine";[18]
- Sense of lethargy despite the tremendous burden of malaria — few national malaria control programmes in Africa were adequately supported either by their own governments or by financing partners; "business as usual" remained the approach in the face of increased threats from drug-resistance malaria and deteriorating health systems;
- The scientific community was busy because it was a great time to study malaria because there was a lot of it;
- Despite the huge burden, malaria was not high on health priority lists of endemic countries or the global public health constituency; and malaria became overshadowed by other partnership approaches, e.g. HIV/AIDS, which mobilised civil society, private sector and others, and linked itself to economics and development more generally.

4. The 1990s

At the end of the 1980s and in the early 1990s, WHO worked with all malarious countries to develop a global strategy for malaria control. This strategy was adopted at a Global Ministerial Conference on Malaria in Amsterdam in 1992. The strategy had four elements: (1) to provide early diagnosis and prompt treatment; (2) to plan and implement selective and sustainable preventive measures, including vector control; (3) to detect early, contain or prevent epidemics; (4) to strengthen local capacities in basic and applied research. The strategy was widely endorsed, and efforts to implement it have shaped the development of malaria control in most malarious countries. The strategy was adapted to the needs of different regions; however, again the necessary funding for this effort never materialised.

Emphasis was placed on the scientific endeavours to find new and better interventions. This included continued work on developing malaria vaccines, research on ITNs and other preventive strategies for malaria including intermittent preventive treatment in pregnancy (IPTp) and better drugs for treatment, including artemisinin-based combination therapy (ACTs).

It is hard to suggest that "partnerships" were a strong feature of this decade. However, the limited programming that did occur was done with linkages to the Expanded Programme on Immunisation (EPI), Diarrheal Disease Control and the Integrated Management of Childhood Illnesses (IMCI). Malaria treatment figured prominently in the IMCI guidance for management of febrile illness in young children.[19] There was a growing understanding that a disease control programme must be established on firm scientific grounds with effective interventions and reasonable partnerships with other groups with similar public health interests.

The simultaneous effort to develop an effective global HIV/AIDS prevention programme provided opportunities for the malaria community. With HIV as an expanding lethal infection, there was no shortage of partners interested in tackling the myriad of problems faced by HIV-at-risk populations and HIV-infected persons. Moreover, the global community was responding with resources. This momentum in the HIV/AIDS control partnership likely had a major, if undocumented, impact on the malaria community. There were known biologic links between HIV and malaria.[20–22] However, there was more interest in the similarities between two expanding diseases with a major health burden where HIV was attracting attention that the smaller and less well-organised malaria community was trying to understand and emulate.

5. The Most Recent Decade[1] — Malaria Programming Resurgence

Based on the identification of new proven effective measures for both prevention and treatment, public health leaders were in a position to begin anew with expanded malaria control programming. The disease control programming context had evolved as had the scientific and partnership

[1] This describes the interval from the establishment of the Roll Back Malaria Partnership at the end of 1998 through to the publication of this work in 2010 (technically more than the ten years of a decade, but illustrative of the dramatic changes that have taken place in this short interval).

basis. The Alma Atta declaration for the 1970s and the efforts in child survival programming in the 1980s and 1990s had set the stage for a broader set of public health partnerships. The HIV/AIDS prevention and control community had established an absolute requirement for these partnerships. In that context, the African Ministers' effort to place malaria control on the global agenda was met with a rallying of partners around the cause.

In 1998, Dr. Gro Harlem Brundtland, Director General, WHO, launched a Global Roll Back Malaria Initiative against malaria with a set of four UN partners: WHO, UNICEF, World Bank and UNDP. The RBM strategy included early case detection and prompt treatment, integrated vector management, prevention in risk populations such as pregnant women and young children and containment of focal epidemics.

The emphasis was clearly on bringing multiple partners into a common effort because, at the time, there was little new money to truly support malaria control programmes. While it could not have been known fully at the time, this process was fortuitous and preceded the substantial growth in resources that began to occur several years later. Some key events in the chronology are listed below (see Table 1).

Table 1. Key actions achieved in the first decade of roll back malaria.

1998	• Advocacy efforts by African Ministers resulted in the launch of RBM 1998 (WHO, UNICEF, World Bank and UNDP are the four "founding" international partners) • The RBM founding encourages mobilisation for action and resources, but no substantive funding for malaria control scale-up is initially available
2000	• African heads of states pledge to halve malaria mortality by 2010 (Abuja Declaration) • Bill & Melinda Gates Foundation established — initiates major increase in funding for malaria research and development
2001	• Release of report. Macroeconomics and health: Investing in health for economic development report of the Commission on Macroeconomics and Health, Jeffrey D. Sachs *et al.* — Malaria positioned as both a health and a development issue • UN member states adopt Millennium Development Goals (MDGs) — includes specific goals and targets for malaria

(*Continued*)

Table 1. (*Continued*)

2002	• G8 Conference: Creation of the Global Fund to Fight AIDS, Tuberculosis and Malaria
2003	• First external evaluation of RBM — progress identified, but many aspects of the partnership and the work required improvements • First Global Fund malaria grants signed — countries begin to have substantial external funding to scale up malaria prevention and treatment
2005	• World Bank launches Malaria Booster Program • US Government launches President's Malaria Initiative
2005–2009	• Equitorial Guinea (Bioko Island), Eritrea, Ethiopia, Gambia, Lubombo Spatial Development Initiative (Mozambique, Swaziland and South Africa), Rwanda, Sao Tome & Principe, Zambia, Zanzibar begin to demonstrate how increased funding translates into scaling up coverage and reduction in burden. Factors associated with success include robust planning, resourcing (typically with multiple partner sources), implementing a "package" of multiple interventions, documenting progress • October 2007 — Gates Malaria Forum: call for malaria elimination/ eradication • April 2008 — UN Secretary General calls for Universal Coverage with effective malaria interventions by the end of 2010

On the one hand, the partnership development preceded the growing resources, but the growing resources also led to partnerships having clarity on the work to be done. For example, an early mantra of "Raise it, Spend it, Prove it" allowed partners to rally around a simple call and focus on resources, action and evidence. The emphasis on donor support of country actions resulted in both a substantial growth in capability within countries (e.g. malaria programmes increased their staffing in many countries and expanded the malaria work into districts and communities) and a growth in the number and size of organisations (both in-country and external) providing assistance. The growing number of partners have increasingly committed to joint work in support of countries applying for and then effectively using Global Fund grants and the support from US-PMI and the World Bank. The increasing funding and its effective use have recently been described in an RBM report.[23]

6. RBM Partners and Partnerships

At its inception, the RBM "Partnership" was described early in 2000 as a "commitment to coordinated action" and a "global movement" with an evidence-based focus on progress with set goals and targets.[24] There was both an appreciation of the need for resources and global donor commitment and the understanding that the actual progress would be reliant on in-country action. While perhaps not fully articulated at the outset, aspects of the Paris Declaration[25] and the Accra Agenda for Action[26] were already anticipated in the RBM Partnership. In particular, the partnership itself was not a goal — the goal focused on reducing disease and saving lives by achieving high coverage with effective interventions; and the partners were asked to rally around these goals.

An early part of the partnership emphasised agreement on: (1) the prioritisation of populations most at risk of malaria; (2) the package of proven effective interventions and (3) the prioritisation of global funding required to address the burden and deliver the interventions. This work led to the strong focus on Africa, on young children and women of reproductive age and on rural and poor communities. The intervention package addressed key proven prevention interventions (vector control with insecticide treated mosquito nets [ITNs] and indoor residual spraying [IRS], prevention in pregnancy with intermittent preventive treatment [IPTp]) and prompt and effective case management.[27]

The RBM Partnership also was quick to respond to good ideas from other global health partnerships. In April 2004, the HIV/AIDS partnership endorsed the "Three Ones" principles,[28] to achieve the most effective and efficient use of resources and to ensure rapid action and results-based management:

- One agreed Action Framework that provides the basis for coordinating the work of all partners.
- One National Coordinating Authority, with a broad-based multisectoral mandate.
- One agreed country-level Monitoring and Evaluation System.

Shortly thereafter in a September 2005 Paris meeting, the RBM Partnership drew from this work and adopted the "Three Ones" for malaria. This embodies the commitment to coordinated action noted earlier and while it is not always easy for partners to agree on every point, the Three Ones principle allows each partner to encourage their colleagues to seek a common approach.

In the recent Global Malaria Action Plan (RBM 2008),[29] the roles and responsibilities of the RBM Partnership are detailed with a focus on what the countries and the international community can do to ensure that countries scale up control, sustain control and ultimately eliminate malaria. These actions support advocacy, resource mobilisation, policy and regulatory affairs, planning, financing, procurement and supply management, communication and behaviour change, monitoring and evaluation and appropriate research to inform existing work and seek new tools.

Partner roles and responsibilities

Donor Agencies. In 1998 with little money available to support work in malaria control, a major emphasis of the RBM founding was to work with donor agencies to raise resources for country action. Among the founders, WHO, UNICEF and UNDP were not expected to be "donors" to this effort; and while the World Bank had clear responsibilities for financing engagement, its mechanisms were oriented to lending and it had relatively limited experience with direct support for malaria control. The partnership engagement with the G8 (and the inception of the Global Fund for AIDS, Tuberculosis, and Malaria), major bilateral donors and foundations led to rapid resource generation. The development of and complementary nature of the financing from the Bill & Melinda Gates Foundation (2000), the GFATM (2002), the World Bank Malaria Booster Program (2005) and the U.S. President's Malaria Initiative (2005) was rapid and unprecedented (Table 1). While annual malaria funding available in 2000 was close to US$100 million, by 2005 a rapid increase in funding began reaching approximately US$1.5 billion annually by 2009.[23]

Technical Assistance Partners. A variety of multilateral, governmental and non-governmental partners have stepped forward to provide a spectrum of support to the country work, including technical guidance, programme action, tracking progress and helping to continue to raise resources and assure good use of those resources. Increasingly these partners have worked in coordination to support countries. The RBM Partnership has used working groups and sub-regional networks as a formal partnership means to coordinate and communicate in these technical and programme support activities. RBM currently has working groups in the following areas: vector control, case management, malaria in pregnancy, procurement and supply management, monitoring and evaluation, advocacy and communication, resource mobilisation and harmonisation. Sub-regional networks include four in Africa (Eastern, Southern, Central and Western); in addition, there are networks in the Mekong River region and in the South and Central American region. Their work is further described on the RBM website.[30]

In-country Partners. Whether through a country coordinating mechanism (CCM) or direct links between individual donors and the Ministry of Health, there has been a consistent commitment that partners would respect the National Government's responsibility for coordinating the work in malaria prevention and control. That is no small task for a Ministry of Health. In principle, they are being asked to coordinate across other ministries (Agriculture, Education, Community Development, etc.), across the non-governmental organisations (both indigenous and externally based NGOs) and across the public and the private sectors. In some of the small countries where progress has been documented rapidly (e.g. Zanzibar,[31] Sao Tome & Principe,[32] Eritrea,[33] Equatorial Guinea–Bioko Island,[34] Gambia,[35] Rwanda[36]), this coordination may be simpler to achieve just on the basis of having smaller populations, smaller ministries and fewer NGO and private-sector partners. However, as work progresses in larger (both land area and population) countries, the coordination of the many and diverse in-country partners can be a major undertaking.

Partner skill requirements may be many, even for a single intervention. For example, to achieve high national coverage and use of ITNs, it is rare that the government by itself or any single partner can do all the work required. Money must be raised and placed where it can be efficiently used. Tenders, bids and orders must be managed. Delivery to the country must be scheduled, received and further managed. Delivery to households and support to encourage regular use of the ITNs must be done in a timely fashion and through mechanisms that truly reach all at-risk populations. Moreover, monitoring and evaluation of the results will be required. The many partners must align to do this and then be prepared to repeat the work and make improvements to sustain coverage and gain efficiancies.

Partnering models can differ greatly nation by nation. In Zambia, the National Malaria Control Program evolved and was designated as the National Malaria Control "Center" where many partners can participate directly in the day-to-day work; the collaborative work has been credited with achieving much progress during the last five years.[37,38] In Tanzania, a populous nation where in-country and external research groups are many and the Global Fund, US-PMI, World Bank and other bilateral donors all support malaria control activities, the coordination requires a robust effort from the Ministry and the country is achieving progress.[39] In Ethiopia, where national work supports regions for a broad public health measures, even the conduct of an evaluation effort of malaria and malaria control requires many partners.[40] In Kenya as reported for World Malaria Day 2010,[41] the U.S. Ambassador to Kenya, Mr. Ranneberger stated:

> "Together with the Kenyan government, non-government organisations and the private sector, we are committed to stop malaria and its contribution to many Kenyans' cycle of disease, poverty and death. This year's World Malaria Day theme in Kenya is Malaria-Free Kenya possible through Partnerships. We could not agree more. If we are to win the war against this disease we have to do it together. It is not a fight to be fought by health workers alone. All sectors of Kenya's economy and society will have to be actively engaged in this struggle. It will be a victory shared by many partners."

Moreover, in Senegal,[42] the partnership includes leaders in the entertainment industry. Youssou N'Dour, Angelique Kidjo, Malaria No More, the United Nations Foundation, the Roll Back Malaria Partnership and other project partners supported both the concert and the powerful film "Africa Live: The Roll Back Malaria Concert" at the United Nations in Dakar in March 2008. The film reached a global audience when it was premiered on PBS — a testimony to the reach of a partnership.

7. Future Opportunities and Challenges

The malaria community has witnessed unprecedented success, especially in Africa, the region with the worst malaria. The partnership is built on solid ground, including:

1. Common partnership and programme goals, in support of country malaria programmes
2. A proven set of interventions with a strong scientific basis
3. Good and flexible standards for delivering the interventions
4. Common metrics to document results and success
5. Partners willing to take ownership and demonstrate their contribution and not require that all success be attributed to their contribution

The RBM Partnership will ultimately face many of the same pressures that challenged the Malaria Eradication Programme and more recent partnerships (Expanded Programme on Immunization, Global Alliance for Vaccines and Immunisations, UNAIDS and others). Will the success continue and expand to additional countries and regions? Will the success be sufficient to garner sustained interest? Will the money stabilise and be durable in the settings where donors need to attend to new and changing economic and political priorities?

The malaria community would like to advocate for continued financing on the basis of success; this is in contrast to past advocacy on the basis of burden alone. However, the real challenge facing the many partners now will be to see if this advocacy can be done with a common and compelling voice. Moreover, it remains to be seen whether the response during tough economic times will be sufficient to support continued improvement and sustain enthusiasm for the future.

Perhaps a final question for the future is: "Is a global partnership required for initial and then sustained success in disease control programmes such as malaria?" As noted at the outset, the Malaria Eradication Programme was never described as a partnership effort; and it is possible that its demise may have been, in part, due to some of the inflexibility that might arise without the many voices of a partnership. If a partnership approach is critical, it is important to remain clear that it is because of the principles of the partnership — and the partnering itself is not the goal.

The openness to new ideas and the common willingness to learn together will remain fundamental to partnership success.

8. Conclusions

A disease control partnership will never be easy. RBM partners have already battled over core strategies such as ITN delivery methods[6,7] (e.g. subsidised, vouchered, free, a mix of these, or delivered by community outreach, by fixed facilities, by campaigns, etc.). Often the partners have different perspectives and priorities and compete for everything from notoriety to money. However, if certain principles can be imbedded in the partnership (e.g. agreement that: the beneficiary is the nation and its people afflicted with the disease; the programme must be results oriented; the programme progress and success can be shared among all contributors and the beneficiaries), the partnership can bring the needed diversity of experience and advocacy to garner the political will and the often heroic resourcing that is required. However, we live in a time of short attention spans and a pervasive notion that "new and different" is somehow better than the good that has preceded it. The public health community is still young in its efforts to understand the ultimate value of partnerships, and addressing the test of time and the required long-term attention for true and lasting results will be our biggest challenge.

See Chapter 1 for a more general history of health partnerships. Chapter 16 describes partnerships in malaria at country level.

References

1. *Declaration of Alma-Ata.* International Conference on Primary Health Care, Alma-Ata, USSR, 6–12 September, 1978. *www.who.int/hpr/NPH/docs/declaration_almaata.pdf.*
2. Walsh JA, Warren KS (1979) Selective Primary Health Care: An Interim Strategy for Disease Control in Developing Countries. *N Engl J Med* 301:967–74.

3. *Global Burden of Disease and Risk Factors*. Eds. Lopez AD, Mathers CD, Ezzati M, Jamison DT, Murray CJL (2006) The World Bank and Oxford University Press.
4. *Disease Control Priorities in Developing Countries*. Second Edition. Eds. Jamison DT, Breman JG, Measham AR, Alleyne G, Claeson M, Evans DB, Jha P, Mills A, Musgrove P (2006) Oxford University Press and The World Bank.
5. Lengeler C (2004) Insecticide-Treated Bet Nets and Curtains for Preventing Malaria. *Cochrane Database of Systematic Reviews* Issue 2:CD000363.
6. Curtis C, Maxwell C, Lemnge M, Kilama WL, Steketee RW, Hawley WA, Bergevin Y, Campbell CC, Sachs J, Teklehaimanot A, Ochola S, Guyatt H, Snow RW (2003) Scaling-Up Coverage with Insecticide-Treated Nets Against Malaria in Africa: who should pay? *Lancet Infect Dis* 3(5):304–7.
7. Lines J, Lengeler C, Cham K, de Savigny D, Chimumbwa J, Langi P, Carroll D, Mills A, Hanson K, Webster J, Lynch M, Addington W, Hill J, Rowland M, Worrall E, MacDonald M, Kilian A (2003) Scaling-up and Sustaining Iinsecticide-Treated Net Coverage. *Lancet Infect Dis* 3(8):465–6; discussion 467–8.
8. Laveran A (1880) A New Parasite Found in the Blood of Malarial Patients. Parasitic Origin of Malarial Attacks. *Bull MemSoc Med Hosp Paris* 17:158–64.
9. Ross R (1910) *The Prevention of Malaria*. New York.
10. Markham CR (1880) *Peruvian Bark.* London.
11. World Health Organization (1957) Expert Committee on Malaria, Sixth Report, *Techn Rep Ser* 123.
12. Pampana E (1963) *A Textbook of Malaria Eradication.* Oxford University Press.
13. Nabarro D (1999) Roll Back Malaria. *Parassitologia* 41(1–3):501–4.
14. Low-Beer D *et al.* (2011) *Innovative Health Partnerships*. World Scientific Press.
15. Marchiafava E, Bignami A (1901) Malaria, in *Twentieth Century Practice*. vol. 6. New York.
16. Boyd MF (1930). *An Introduction to Malariology*. Harvard University Press, Cambridge Massachusetts.
17. Gove S (1997) Integrated Management of Childhood Illness by Outpatient Health Workers: Technical Basis and Overview. The WHO Working Group on Guidelines for Integrated Management of the Sick Child. *Bull World Health Organ* 75(Suppl 1): 7–24.

18. *Malaria, Waiting for the Vaccine*. Ed. Targett GAT. (1991) John Wiley & Sons, England.
19. WHO and UNICEF. Model IMCI Handbook: Integrated Management of Childhood Illness. (2005) WHO/FCH/CAH/00.12 http://www.who.int/child_adolescent_health/documents/9241546441/en/index.html (accessed July 2010).
20. Greenberg AE (1992) HIV and Malaria: Interactions of HIV and Other Diseases. Eds. Mann J, Tarantola DJM, Netter TW. *AIDS in the World: A Global Report*. Cambridge, MA: Harvard University Press. pp. 143–8.
21. Steketee RW, Wirima JJ, Bloland PB, Chilima B, Mermin JH, Chitsulo L, Breman JG (1996) Impairment of a Pregnant Woman's Acquired Ability to Limit *Plasmodium falciparum* by Infection with Human Immunodeficiencyvirus type 1. *Am J Trop Med Hyg* 55(10):42–9.
22. Kuile FO, Parise ME, Verhoeff FH, Udhayakumar V, Newman RD, van Eijk AM, Rogerson SJ, Steketee RW (2004) The Burden of Co-Infection with Human Immunodeficiency Virus Type 1 and Malaria in Pregnant Women in Sub-Saharan Africa. *Am J Trop Med Hyg* 71(2 Suppl):41–54.
23. RBM Progress and Impact Series (2011) *A Decade of Partnership and Results* Vol 8
24. RBM. Promise for Progress (2000) WHO/CDS/RBM/2000.16 http://rollbackmalaria.org/cmc_upload/0/000/015/146/p4p.pdf (accessed July 2010).
25. OECD (2005) The Paris Declaration for AID Effectiveness http://www.oecd.org/document/18/0,2340,en_2649_3236398_35401554_1_1_1_1,00.html (accessed July 2010).
26. OECD (2008) Accra Agenda for Action at http://www.oecd.org/document/18/0,2340,en_2649_3236398_35401554_1_1_1_1,00.html (accessed July 2010).
27. http://rollbackmalaria.org/cmc_upload/0/000/014/813/malaria_at_a_glance.pdf (accessed July 2010).
28. UNAIDS declaration of the "Three Ones": http://www.unaids.org/en/CountryResponses/MakingTheMoneyWork/ThreeOnes/default.asp (accessed July 2010).
29. Roll Back Malaria (RBM) (2008) *Global Malaria Action Plan*. Geneva, RBM, (http://www.rollbackmalaria.org/gmap) (accessed July 2010).
30. RBM Mechanisms. http://rollbackmalaria.org/mechanisms/index.html (accessed July 2010).

31. Bhattarai A, Ali AS, Kachur SP, Martensson A, Abbas AK, Khatib R, Al-mafazy A-w, Ramsan M, Rotllant G, Gerstenmaier JF, Molteni F, Abdulla S, Montgomery SM, Kaneko A, Bjorkman A (2007) Impact of Artemisinin-Based Combination Therapy and Insecticide-Treated Nets on Malaria Burden in Zanzibar. *PLoS Medicine* 4:e309:1784–90.
32. Teklehaimanot HD, Teklehaimanot A, Kiszewski A, Rampao HS, Sachs JD (2009) Malaria in Sao Tome and Principe: On the Brink of Elimination After Three Years of Effective Antimalarial Measures. *Am J Trop Med Hyg* 80:133–40.
33. Nyarango PM, Gebremeskel T, Mebrahtu G, *et al.* (2006) A Steep Decline of Malaria Morbidity and Mortality Trends in Eritrea Between 2000 and 2004: The Effect of Combination of Control Methods. *Malar J* 5:e33.
34. Kleinschmidt I, Schwabe C, Benavente L, *et al.* (2009) Marked Increase in Child Survival After Four Years of Intensive Malaria Control. *Am J Trop Med Hyg* 80:882–8.
35. Ceesay SJ, Casals-Pascual C, Erskine J, *et al.* (2008) Changes in Malaria Indices Between 1999 and 2007 in The Gambia: A Retrospective Analysis. *Lancet* 372:1545–54.
36. Sievers AC, Lewey J, Musafiri P, Franke MF, Bucyibaruta BJ, Stulac SN, Rich ML, Karema C, Daily JP (2008) Reduced Paediatric Hospitalizations for Malaria and Febrile Illness Patterns Following Implementation of Community-Based Malaria Control Programme in Rural Rwanda. *Malaria Journal* 7:167. doi:10.1186/1475-2875-7-167.
37. Steketee RW, Sipilanyambe N, Chimumbwa J, Banda JJ, Mohamed A, Miller J, Basu S, Miti SK, Campbell CC (2008) National Malaria Control and Scaling up for Impact: The Zambia Experience Through 2006. *Am J Trop Med Hyg* 79(1):45–52.
38. Chizema-Kawesha E. Miller JM, Steketee RW, Mukonka VM, Mukuka C, Mohamed AD, Miti SK, Campbell CC (2010) Scaling up Malaria Control in Zambia: Progress and Impact 2005–2008. *Am J Trop Med Hyg* 83(3): 480–8.
39. Smithson P. Down but not out. The Impact of Malaria Control in Tanzania. Ifakara Health Institute Spotlight May 2009, Issue 2. http://www.ihi.or.tz/docs/Spotlight%20Issue%20No2%20-%20Down%20but%20not%20out.pdf (accessed July 2010).
40. Jima D, Getachew A, Bilak H, Steketee RW, Emerson PM, Graves PM, Gebre T, Reithinger R, Hwang J (2010) Malaria Indicator Survey Working

Group Ethiopia. Malaria Indicator Survey 2007, Ethiopia: Coverage and Use of Major Malaria Prevention and Control Interventions. *Malar J* 9(1):58.

41. Daily Nation Web News. Kenya: Partnerships Key in Fighting Disease 24 April 2010 Ref: http://allafrica.com/stories/201004260814.html (accessed July 2010).
42. "Africa Live: The Roll Back Malaria Concert" http://www.afropop.org/multi/feature/ID/587 (accessed July 2010).

9

Innovative Approaches to Financing Development: The GAVI Alliance

Bjorg Sandkjaer

Senior Programme Officer, Public Policy, GAVI Alliance
b.sandkjaer@gmail.com[1]

Summary

An important attraction to establish public–private partnerships has been innovative financing. Public–private partnerships are seen as contributing new sources of financing and innovative methods on how it is mobilised and scheduled. There are limitations to public-sector models of resource mobilisation and reliance on the budget funding cycles. GAVI is a new public–private partnership, which has made significant contributions to innovative financing based on its partners. This chapter describes GAVI, its contributions to innovative financing and the challenges in the current context of financial uncertainty. The chapter assesses the experiences of innovative financing, the role of innovative partnerships and the limits of public and private models.

[1] Thanks to several colleagues who helped me with this paper. I am particularly indebted to Geoff Adlide, who helped shape the concepts and structure the paper. The views expressed in the paper are those of the author.

1. Introduction

The Global Alliance for Vaccines and Immunisation — the GAVI Alliance — was launched at the World Economic Forum in Davos, Switzerland, in early 2000. A partnership of developing countries, international development and finance organisations, philanthropic groups, civil society, the vaccine industry and others, the GAVI Alliance has focused on innovative financing from the start. By the end of 2009, GAVI had committed US$4 billion through to 2015 for immunisation and health programmes in the poorest countries. This represents a strong contribution to redressing the inequity in children of the developing world previously only receiving six antigens, while children in the developed world are vaccinated with at least twice as many.[2]

Vaccines are among the most cost-effective health interventions for developing countries (WHO/UNICEF/World Bank 2009). In the 1990s, immunisation coverage declined, and GAVI was established to address the urgent need to "save children's lives and protect people's health by increasing access to immunisation in poor countries." The United Nations defines partnerships as "voluntary and collaborative relationships between various parties, both State and non-State, in which all participants agree to work together to achieve a common purpose or undertake a specific task and to share risks and responsibilities, resources and benefits." (UN General Assembly 2005, p. 4.) In the same spirit, GAVI was not set up to compete, and rather, in setting up the new initiative, GAVI partners chose an alliance model in recognition that the distribution of new and underused vaccines to the poorest countries depends on strong partnerships. In setting up GAVI as a partnership, the Alliance partners created a space where donor and implementing countries, technical and academic institutions, private foundations, civil society and the vaccine industry could negotiate how to best ensure adequate supply and demand of life-saving vaccines. The GAVI Alliance can therefore be said to represent a new model of health diplomacy, where "no longer do diplomats just

[2] The exact number of antigens varies by individual country immunisation schedule, see overview of immunisation schedules at http://www.who.int/immunization_monitoring/data/data_subject/en/index.html.

talk to other diplomats — they need to interact with the private sector, nongovernmental organisations, scientists, activists and the media, to name but a few, since all these actors are part and parcel of the negotiating process" (Kickbush *et al.* 2007, p. 161).

2. GAVI at Work: Results, Challenges and Learning

Since inception, the World Health Organisation (WHO) estimates that GAVI funds have enabled the vaccination of an additional 257 million children by end 2009 through routine immunisation programmes in implementing countries, preventing four million premature deaths. An estimated 233.2 million children have been immunised against hepatitis B; 59.7 million children have received *Haemophilusinfluenzae* type B (Hib) vaccine and 41.6 million are protected against yellow fever (WHO 2009). The increasingly available and preferred 5-in-1 pentavalent vaccine, a combination of Hib and Hepatitis B with the standard diphtheria, tetanus, pertussis (DTP) formula, is helping to boost immunisation coverage against Hib and hepatitis B without adding to the number of shots children receive. In addition, GAVI funds flowing through disease-specific initiatives against measles, maternal and neonatal tetanus, yellow fever and polio have prevented over one million premature deaths, bringing the total number of deaths prevented by GAVI-funded vaccines in its first 10 years up to 5.4 million.

The GAVI model also seeks to be catalytic and flexible to existing country programmes. The 2002–2007 "China Ministry of Health/GAVI Hepatitis B Vaccination Projects" supported the introduction of hepatitis B vaccine in selected provinces. The US$76 million project, equally co-funded by the GAVI Alliance and the Chinese Government, with technical support from WHO and UNICEF, achieved a 60% increase in hepatitis B coverage in targeted provinces — translating into 11.1 million additional children vaccinated. With the additional demand generated, Chinese vaccine manufacturers stepped up vaccine production. Another component of the project was injection safety, and as a result all vaccines in the project area are delivered using safe auto-disable syringes. GAVI funds were catalytic in that central and provincial governments were ready to assume the cost of vaccinating children against hepatitis B at the end of the project period and helped strengthen vaccine supply through collaboration with Chinese vaccine manufacturers (GAVI Alliance 2006).

There have also been challenges. At the start of GAVI, partners predicted that the increased demand for vaccines (in particular, the 5-in-1 pentavalent vaccine) would rapidly bring the price down to a level where developing countries were able to cover the cost themselves. However, at the time there was only one manufacturer of pentavalent vaccine that was prequalified by WHO.[3] With increased demand, but limited supply, the vaccine price initially increased, creating the exact opposite of the desired effect (Lydon *et al.* 2008). Over time, however, more suppliers have invested in pentavalent vaccine production. Currently there are four prequalified pentavalent vaccine suppliers, two in the North and two in emerging markets. As a result of increased competition, the pentavalent price has dropped from US$3.65 per dose to US$2.94 per dose in 2010. Further price declines are expected (UNICEF 2010).

Increased demand is a direct result of increasing vaccine coverage at the country level. From the start, one way that GAVI sought to increase demand was to provide Immunisation Services Support (ISS), an incentive-based support where countries receive a reward per additional child vaccinated, following an initial investment phase. Countries report year on year on the number of children vaccinated, in order for the Independent Review Committee to review and approve any rewards due. The approach was adopted not only to increase immunisation coverage, but also with a view to "strengthening the capacity of governmental data systems and not creating parallel processes" (Lob-Levyt 2008). In addition, in adopting the ISS model in March 2000, the Board members commented that "DTP3 coverage would be used to measure immunisation rates; while an imperfect measure, it is widely recognised as the best tool that is available at this time. Improvements in indicators are envisioned as implementation proceeds" (GAVI Alliance Board 2000).

In recent years, the ISS model has been criticised for providing incentives for countries to inflate the number of children vaccinated, meaning

[3] For GAVI funds to be spent on procuring a vaccine, the vaccine must be "prequalified" by the World Health Organisation, ensuring that vaccines procured with GAVI funds are of the highest quality.

that the real number of additional children vaccinated may be substantially lower than what has been reported (Lim *et al.* 2008). While the methodology used by Lim *et al.* has been criticised by WHO and UNICEF, these key GAVI Alliance partners concur that it is necessary to "continue to work with partners, national programmes, and independent reviewers in strengthening immunisation monitoring and reporting systems at global, national and local levels" (Burton *et al.* 2008). Previous studies have shown that performance-based systems have a positive effect on immunisation coverage (Lu *et al.* 2006; Chee *et al.* 2007). However, as the 2008 study demonstrated, "results-based financing initiatives in developing countries, and also in developed countries, remain controversial and beset by data issues. It might now be time to revise ISS to meet differing goals, to strengthen checks and balances" (Lob-Levyt 2009, p. 209). As a result, work is being undertaken to delineate new performance-based funding mechanisms for consideration by the GAVI Alliance Board in 2010.

Another challenge has been to find a way to provide support to countries that keeps transaction costs of accessing the support to a minimum. The Alliance model in itself seeks to draw on the comparative advantage of the different partners to achieve GAVI's mission of "saving children's lives and protecting people's health through increasing access to vaccines in poor countries." This means, for example, that rather than setting up a new infrastructure with regional and country offices, the GAVI Alliance is represented at country and regional levels through Alliance partners such as WHO and UNICEF. While this represents a partnership approach to development cooperation, through early experience the GAVI Alliance Board recognised that it also entails challenges at the country level. Already in 2003 the Board remarked that "countries are currently overwhelmed with global initiatives, and it is often the same few people in countries expected to work on these initiatives and attend ICC type of meetings."[4] As part of the same discussion, "many board members noted that advances in immunization coverage in large countries with low coverage are only likely to be achieved if larger systemic problems are

[4] Interagency Coordination Committee, a committee under the Ministry of Health bringing together actors working on immunization in a country.

addressed both within and outside of the health sector" (GAVI Alliance Board 2003). Several studies and consultations at different levels formed the basis for subsequent changes in GAVI policies. Support has become better aligned with the countries' own health and immunisation plans, and the evidence and negotiation process also laid the foundation for GAVI's support for health systems strengthening, available from 2006, and the health system funding platform with the World Bank and the Global Fund to Fight AIDS, TB and Malaria, to be rolled out in the first countries during 2010–2011.

As GAVI increasingly provides cash support to the countries for system strengthening, the partners through the GAVI Alliance Board have also seen a need to strengthen the management of the cash flows, and to that effect instituted a Transparency and Accountability Policy (TAP) from 2009. At the October 2008 Board meeting, where the TAP implementation plan was adopted, the Board remarked that "the implementation plan will send a strong signal to donors that GAVI is addressing risk in a proactive manner, without jeopardising the effectiveness of GAVI programmes." The Board also emphasised the use of countries' own systems for financial management as "critical" and stated that "the success of this policy will be judged against the promises that GAVI has made by supporting the Paris Declaration and the Accra Agenda for Action" (GAVI Alliance Board 2008). Aid effectiveness principles, negotiated and agreed by the global development community, have therefore become another important guiding principle of GAVI policy formation as the partners seek to improve provision of support to poor countries.

3. New Vaccines — Accelerating Their Introduction

There is potential to do much more. Every year, close to 24 million children go unvaccinated, and over two million children die from vaccine-preventable diseases (WHO 2009). Pneumonia is the biggest killer of children and is responsible for almost one in four child deaths (Williams *et al.* 2002). Diarrhoeal diseases are the second leading cause of death in children under the age of five. Rotavirus is the most common cause of severe diarrhoea in young children and is responsible for more than half a million child deaths a year (Atherly *et al.* 2009). New pneumococcal and rotavirus vaccines have the potential to prevent a large proportion of these deaths. GAVI supports the introduction of both of these vaccines in poor countries, and the first GAVI countries introduced rotavirus vaccine in 2007 and pneumococcal vaccine in 2008. As both of these vaccines are new, this means that the goal of shortening the time lag between vaccine availability in the rich and poor parts of the world — traditionally 10–20 years — is close to being reached. Together, these two vaccines have the potential to lower child mortality and contribute to global progress towards achieving Millennium Development Goal 4: two-thirds reduction in child mortality by 2015. However, significantly increased funds are required to scale up new vaccine availability in the poorest countries, coupled with increased financial sustainability of immunisation programmes at country level.

4. Innovative Financing

This chapter focuses on innovative financing mechanisms or approaches that have been introduced through the work of partners in the GAVI Alliance. Three examples will be elaborated — all working with different actors and designed to achieve specific objectives in pursuit of GAVI's overall mission of saving children's lives and protecting people's health through expanding immunisation services in poor countries. All speak to innovation and are rooted in forging new partnerships across the public and private sectors and between developing countries and global actors — drawing on the skills and experience of business practices in the private sector to overcome historic limitations to development aid flows and mitigate the risks of scaling up.

A. Leveraging public funds on capital markets: International financing facility for immunisation

Traditionally, donor funds are available as a relatively unpredictable year on year amount. What would happen if this support instead could be "frontloaded" — available as a significant upfront investment to achieve high-level coverage of vaccines? Following the "Financing for

Development" conference in 2002, the idea of an international financing facility that would "frontload" funds for development was launched by then UK Chancellor of the Exchequer Gordon Brown and International Development Secretary Clare Short in 2003 (UK HM Treasury 2003). However, concerns were raised about the value of frontloading funds for general development, and around developing countries' ability to spend the additional funds (Moss 2005). Following the launch, work therefore continued to refine and find appropriate ways to spend the frontloaded funds effectively.

Analysis indicated that frontloading funds for immunisation would increase their value by about 10%, and that making funds more predictable, enabling countries to plan ahead, would add another 11% in terms of reduction in the cost per life-year gained (Barder and Yeh 2006). At the same time, demand for vaccines accelerated in GAVI-eligible countries. The Commission for Africa, chaired by UK Prime Minister Tony Blair, recommended in its March 2005 report "Our Common Interest" that an International Financing Facility for Immunisation (IFFIm) be established. Later the same year, governments present at the G8 summit in Gleneagles pledged support for IFFIm in the context of the summit's overall theme to "Make Poverty History."

IFFIm was formally launched in 2006. The United Kingdom was initially supported by France, Italy, Norway, South Africa, Spain and Sweden. The Netherlands has since also become an IFFIm donor. The donors have pledged a total of US$5.3 billion over up to 20 years, an exceptionally long period for donors to make legally binding commitments to development assistance. IFFIm works by using these long-term government commitments to raise funds in the international capital markets. The IFFIm bonds, underpinned by the pledged funds of governments that themselves receive good ratings, are rated AAA/Aaa/AAA by Fitch Ratings Limited, Moody's Investors Service Inc. and Standard & Poor's Ratings Services, making them an attractive investment.

IFFIm's inaugural bonds were issued in London on 14 November 2006 and raised US$1 billion. The bonds were priced comparably to other sovereign/supranational issuers and were bought by a broad range of investors — both geographically and by investor type — including several central banks, pension funds, fund managers and insurance companies.

Deutsche Bank and Goldman Sachs managed this inaugural bond issue, which was quickly oversubscribed. Since, four bond issuances have taken place in Japan (one in 2008 and three in 2009), and a further bond issuance took place in the UK in May 2009. The frontloading capacity was demonstrated by IFFIm raising US$2.3 billion in bond issuances in the first three years, when during the same period only US$393 million of donors funds had been received in the IFFIm account. This is particularly remarkable considering the global financial climate; however, it seems that in turbulent financial markets the triple-A rated IFFIm bonds offered the kind of security that investors were looking for. The second bond issuance in the UK was lead managed by HSBC, and the bonds were marketed as ethical investments, attracting investments from trusts, charities and individuals who want to see their investments being put to good use.

Two entities make IFFIm operational: the International Finance Facility for Immunisation Company, registered in the UK, and the GAVI Fund Affiliate. Each of these is overseen by a board. IFFIm is managed by its board of directors and has no employees. Principal activities are outsourced: all administrative support functions are provided by the GAVI Secretariat and all treasury functions and related accounting services are provided by the World Bank, in its capacity as IFFIm's Treasury Manager.

GAVI is responsible for the operational activities related to the immunisation, health systems strengthening and vaccine procurement programmes for which IFFIm provides funding. Through GAVI, US$634 million of IFFIm funds went to support new vaccines in developing countries from 2006 through 2009. IFFIm funding has been used to procure the 5-in-1 vaccine to immunise children against the traditional DTP vaccine, hepatitis B and Hib. With the support of IFFIm, GAVI has been able to make a long-term purchase commitment of pentavalent vaccines, of which by 2009 US$177.4 million had been drawn down.

The availability of IFFIm funding until 2015 is supporting security of future supplies. Such secure demand leads manufacturers to enter the market, and four manufacturers now supply WHO-prequalified pentavalent vaccine, up from one in 2006. As a result of increased competition, the pentavalent price has dropped from US$3.65 per dose to US$2.94 per dose in 2010. Further price declines are expected (UNICEF 2010).

An important and controversial issue, within the GAVI board and externally, has been additional support needed to address broader health system issues that currently limit the ability to get vaccines to children. These investments are necessary to deliver vaccines, though some of them argued it may dilute the funding and focus of GAVI. In addition, one global programme cannot "strengthen health systems" without broad cooperation across a range of partners which fund HSS for vaccines, for specific diseases and more general health workforce and governance issues.

Through 2009, US$198.3 million of IFFIm funds went to GAVI's health systems strengthening programme to support immunisation delivery and coverage. This represents a substantial portion — nearly 39% — of GAVI's initial funding estimate of US$500 million for the HSS programme from 2006 to 2015. IFFIm funding has also been deployed in tactical one-off investments to catalyse the progress against specific diseases, channelled through initiatives such as:

- Measles Initiative
- Yellow Fever Initiative
- Global Poliomyelitis Eradication Campaign
- Maternal and Neonatal Tetanus Elimination Campaign

In its 2009 report, the High-Level Task Force on Innovative International Financing for Health Systems made a number of recommendations on how to get "more money for health and more health for the money." Co-chaired by President Robert Zoellick of the World Bank and then UK Prime Minister Gordon Brown commended IFFIm as a mechanism that has helped improve the quality of funds available for development by making available large amounts of predictable funds and funds to finance one-off investments in services and delivery infrastructure. The Task Force (2009) recommended that the IFFIm be expanded, specifically for health systems (though also pointing out it was only one element of HSS, and other sources were needed for components with large recurrent costs like salary support). Subsequently, three countries, the UK, Norway and Australia, announced their financial support for this "expanded IFFIm" at the UN General Assembly in New York in September 2009

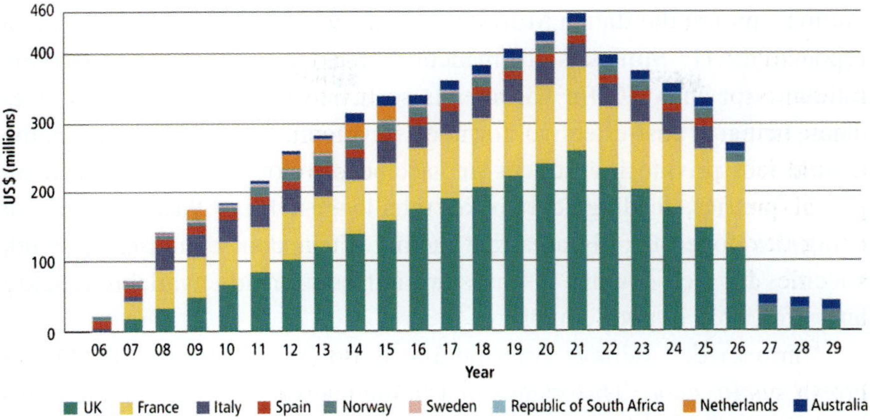

Figure 1. Total donor pledges to IFFIm by November 2009.

Source: GAVI Alliance 2010.

(GAVI Alliance 2009). Following the announcement and also as recommended by the High Level Task Force for Innovative International Financing for Health Systems, discussions are being held to determine how these funds could flow to countries through a common Health Systems Funding Platform, comprising GAVI, The Global Fund to Fight AIDs, TB, and Malaria, the World Bank, WHO and other partners (Figure 1).

B. Shaping markets: Advance market commitment (AMC)

AMCs are a new approach to public health funding designed to stimulate the development and manufacture of vaccines for developing countries. The idea has been raised in different contexts, and the concept was elaborated in a 2005 Center for Global Development Report: "Making Markets for Vaccines." The report is the outcome of a working group of experts, co-chaired by Alice Albright (GAVI), Michael Kremer (Harvard University) and Ruth Levine (Centre for Global Development).[5] In addition, in 2005,

[5] Report is available here: http://www.cgdev.org/doc/books/vaccine/MakingMarkets-complete.pdf.

GulioTremonti, the Italian Minister of Finance, presented the concept in a report to the G7 Ministers of Finance.[6] In the summary of this report, the rationale for an AMC for vaccines is spelt out as a combination of vaccines being a cost-effective form of development assistance, and the insufficient private investment in vaccine development for diseases in poor countries, leading to two key challenges: First, vaccines are not being developed for diseases that mainly affect poor countries. Second, vaccines for rich-country diseases are not being made available quickly and affordably in poor countries.

"Two market failures contribute to these problems. First, R&D is a *global public good.* This means that in the absence of a coordinated policy intervention, either there will be inefficiently little innovation or the resulting products will be inefficiently expensive. Second, policy makers' incentives are *time inconsistent* — once a vaccine is developed, policy makers' interest in creating incentives for R&D are overtaken by the need to ensure affordable and widespread access to the vaccine. Knowing that policy makers' incentives will change in the future, firms have little incentive to invest today" (Tremonti 2005, p. 1).

The AMC approach was also recommended through other processes and reports, including in the report of the WHO Commission on Intellectual Property Rights, Innovation and Public Health (WHO 2006) and the 2009 report of the High Level Task Force on Innovative International Financing for Health Systems.

Following their welcome of Minister Tremonti's report on AMCs, G7 Ministers requested GAVI and the World Bank to convene experts and perform necessary analytical work to develop a proposal for a pilot AMC for their consideration at the World Bank Spring Meetings. To assess the key question of which of the six vaccines included in the Tremonti report would be most suitable for a pilot AMC, an independent Expert Committee was convened, chaired by Dr Ntaba, Minister of Health, Malawi, and comprising developing and industrial country experts in public health, epidemiology, industry economics, vaccine development and law. Following careful review, the expert group recommended the pneumococcal vaccine as the most suitable candidate for a pilot AMC, at a minimum

---

[6] Report is available here: http://www.vaccineamc.org/files/AMC_Tremonti%20Report.pdf.

size of US$1.5 billion, in their February 2006 report. The Committee also drew up a framework document for how the AMC might be structured to achieve the desired objectives.[7]

The AMC was announced in Rome, Italy, in February 2007, by Her Majesty Queen Rania Al-Abdullah of Jordan, and high-level representatives of the World Bank and AMC donors (see below). At the launch, then World Bank President Paul Wolfowitz said that "the key aim is to accelerate the production of viable and urgently needed vaccines for the poorest countries where thousands of children die every day from diseases that can be prevented."[8]

Donors announced their commitments to the AMC (see Table 1).

To develop the concept further, an economic expert group (EEG) was convened to advise on key design decisions for AMC donors, using new information available from industry consultations, demand forecasts and modelling of returns to industry under various demand and price scenarios. The key results, made available in an April 2008 report, were that: the AMC should be integrated with GAVI structures for financing, procurement and vaccine introduction; the $1.5 billion committed is sufficient to achieve the AMC objectives; introducing a supply commitment would

Table 1.

Country	**AMC Contribution in $US**
Italy	$635 million
UK	$485 million
Canada	$200 million
Russia	$80 million
Norway	$50 million
The Bill & Melinda Gates Foundation	$50 million
Total	**$1.5 billion**

[7] Report of the expert group is available here: http://www.vaccineamc.org/files/iec_rec_pilot.pdf.

[8] As quoted in GAVI press release available at: http://www.gavialliance.org/media_centre/press_releases/2007_02_09_en_pr_amc.php.

increase the likelihood of expanded manufacturing capacity; obtaining a supply commitment from firms may require donors to mitigate demand-side risk, probably through either additional frontloading of rewards committing to purchase a specific volume, or a combination of the two approaches; and that a price ceiling (hard or soft) should be considered. Having also evaluated the framework documents that were put together earlier, the group suggested changes in how the AMC would be structured.[9] Negotiating these changes proved to be difficult, but group members deemed it important enough to take the time to get the structure right. The main change made was to modify the terms to ensure that no one manufacturer could collect the full AMC funds (Alliance for Case Studies in Global Health 2009).

Consultations were also held with donor nations, developing countries, multilaterals, civil society organisations and industry. At every step of the process, donors carefully reviewed the advice provided. Following the release of the EEG report, an implementation working group (IWG) was put together, and this provided its recommendations for AMC implementation in a July 2008 report,[10] and the pilot AMC for pneumococcal vaccine was formally activated with the signature of legal documents by Italy, the United Kingdom, Canada, Russia, Norway and the Bill & Melinda Gates Foundation together with GAVI Alliance partners World Bank, UNICEF and the WHO in June 2009.

The objectives of the pilot AMC are:

- Accelerate development of vaccines that meet developing country needs.
- Bring forward the availability of effective pneumococcal vaccines — through scaling up of production capacity.
- Accelerate vaccine uptake — through predictable vaccine pricing for countries and manufacturers.
- Test the AMC concept for potential future applications.

---

[9] Report of the Economic Expert Group is available here: http://www.vaccineamc.org/timeline_media/Expert_Group_Report.pdf.

[10] Available here: http://www.vaccineamc.org/files/AMC_IWG10JULY08_2_.pdf.

In August 2009, a strategic demand forecast was published on the GAVI Alliance website. Twice a year, UNICEF will issue calls for offers for vaccines that meet the specifications: the vaccine must cover at least 60% of the prevalent disease strains in the target region and must include serotypes 1, 5 and 14, i.e. those that are the most frequent in GAVI-eligible countries. The first call for offers was issued in September 2009, and four offers were made. While the identity of the participating manufacturers is confidential, two have announced their offers publicly. Both of these are producers from developing countries.

In practical terms, the AMC will work through manufacturers that take part in the AMC signing legally binding documents to supply their vaccine for 10 years at a price no higher than US$3.50 per dose. This price will be paid for by a combination of regular GAVI funds and country co-financing and is also referred to as the "tail price." In addition, companies receive a top-up payment, bringing their total payment per dose to US$7, for approximately 20% of the doses they provide. This top-up is paid for with the donors' committed AMC funds (see Figure 2). This additional

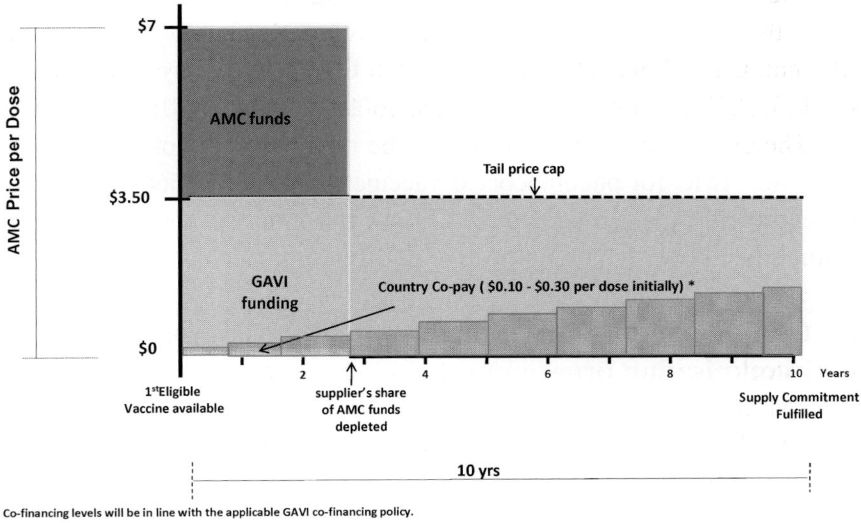

Figure 2. Advanced market commitment support showing GAVI, AMC and country co-funding.

Source: GAVI Alliance 2009.

payment is what is calculated to provide the incentive for industry to make the initial investment to expand their manufacturing capacity to supply the appropriate pneumococcal vaccines tailored to developing country needs.

UNICEF acts as the procurement agent for the pilot AMC and assesses each supply offer. UNICEF can enter into supply agreements only with those manufacturers whose products are prequalified by WHO and are deemed eligible for AMC funding by an Independent Assessment Committee. UNICEF can also decide to enter into provisional supply agreements with those companies whose vaccine is under pre-qualification at WHO. Provisional supply agreements will automatically turn into supply agreements once vaccines are pre-qualified by WHO and are deemed eligible for AMC funding by an Independent Assessment Committee.

The AMC approach is not without its critics. One of the main critical voices has been the civil society organisation Medecins Sans Frontieres, which, following its criticism of the original AMC design, was involved in redesign efforts to ensure that one single manufacturer could not be awarded all the AMC funds (Alliance for Case Studies for Global Health 2009). Fundamentally, the AMC has been criticised for being too expensive, for favouring multinational firms over emerging suppliers and for not encouraging technology transfer to developing country manufacturers (see e.g. Light 2007). These claims have been rebutted by supporters of the mechanism (Levine 2009, Schwalbe and El-Ziq 2010), and also by emerging suppliers being involved in the initial "round" of offers made. The pilot AMC for pneumococcal vaccine is the first of its kind, and as the contracts are awarded and AMC roll-out continues, much is yet to be learnt about how such an innovative pull-funding mechanism will work.

C. Co-financing: Empowering countries to assume cost of immunisation programmes

GAVI provides support for eligible countries' health and immunisation plans, for the duration of the country's planning cycle. This allows countries to plan in the longer term, and to allocate GAVI funds against priorities as laid down in the national planning framework. GAVI support also represents innovation in the way it requires, and provides support for sound financial planning aiming for countries to gradually take over the cost of immunisation programmes.

From the start, GAVI Alliance partners defined financial sustainability of countries' immunisation programmes to be a key objective of GAVI support. To this end, the GAVI proto-Board, which met in 1999, established a Financing Task Force (FTF) of partners and experts to address country capacity to make immunisation programmes financially sustainable (Milstien *et al.* 2008). The FTF represented a space to negotiate, plan and implement support for countries' planning and budgeting of immunisation programmes. The first achievement was to agree a definition of "financial sustainability," enabling development of guidelines and eventual implementation. Following heated debate and extensive consultation among partners — including implementing countries — the FTF agreed and the GAVI Alliance Board approved that "although self-sufficiency is the ultimate goal, in the nearer term sustainable financing is the ability of a country to mobilise and efficiently use domestic and supplementary external resources on a reliable basis to achieve current and future target levels of immunisation performance." (GAVI Alliance Board 2001). Partners then worked together in the FTF to draw up guidelines for financial sustainability planning at the country level, requiring countries to develop financial sustainability plans and providing the technical assistance for countries to do so. A coordinator in the WHO brought the partners together, and regional working groups carried the work forward in regions and countries. Countries were expected to demonstrate in their financial sustainability plans how they intended to continue financing their programme beyond the grant period. The submitted plans provided valuable information, assisting GAVI partners in better understanding financial planning issues at country level, and informing reviews of GAVI policies.

However, the financial sustainability plans were generally not aligned with the overall planning framework and have over time been replaced by the current and aligned costed multi-year plans (cMYP).[11]

GAVI policy, regardless of planning tool, has been to have countries gradually assume the cost of the immunisation programmes as GAVI's

[11] The history of the Financing Task Force is charted in the report: "Financial sustainability for immunisation in the poorest countries: lessons from GAVI 2000–2006," produced under the guidance of the World Health Organisation and available at http://www.gavialliance.org/media_centre/publications/FTF_Task_Force_Report.php.

market shaping effect also meant that prices would come down. GAVI therefore requires countries to contribute a share of the cost of vaccines. Such co-financing became compulsory from 2008, and countries have to co-finance either following completion of the first five years of (fully funded) vaccine support or when introducing a new vaccine in 2008 or later. The level of co-financing depends on the country's expected ability to pay, and the least poor GAVI-eligible countries have to gradually increase their co-financing amounts over time.

To fulfil their co-financing commitments, countries have to spend non-GAVI funds procuring a proportion of the vaccine within the given year, and document the procurement to GAVI. Countries that do not fulfil the co-financing requirement by the end of the year are considered to be in default, triggering a series of interventions to seek to understand the reasons for the non-payment, support to get the country out of the default status and ultimately possible suspension of GAVI support. In 2008, 27 countries co-financed GAVI-supported vaccines, and in 2009, 49 countries were expected to co-finance. Of these, four were in default at the start of 2010, meaning that well over 40 of the world's poorest countries have been able to co-finance GAVI-supported vaccines.

Co-financing requires countries to put immunisation costs on budget, and the required plans ensure that immunisation is included in overall health planning. This enhances programme sustainability and promotes a steady increase in immunisation coverage. GAVI Alliance partners believe that the current approach will enable countries to take ownership of immunisation programmes and form a more solid foundation for subsequent introduction of new vaccines, as opposed to an externally driven immunisation programme which may achieve increased immunisation coverage in the short term, but not be sustainable. Analysis of countries' financial sustainability plans also shows that GAVI funding has indeed been catalytic, in that funding from national governments, multilateral, bilateral and other sources increased during the first years of GAVI support, and there is no indication that GAVI funding has displaced existing financial flows for immunisation; "rather GAVI funding added to growing funding from both national and other external sources." (Lydon *et al.* 2008, p. 6711). Drawing on data from countries own financial sustainability plans for their immunisation programmes, Lydon *et al.* (2008)

found that "the trend in immunization financing is one characterized by increases in both national and external financing for routine immunization." (p. 6711). National government financing was found to have increased from US$3.4 per infant pre-GAVI to US$4.0 per infant with GAVI support, and is projected to increase even further. From non-GAVI donor sources, the funding increased from US$2.6 pre-GAVI to US$3.0 per infant with GAVI. Yet challenges remain to these innovative approaches to financing. Given the financial crisis, both donor and country sources of support are under significant pressure, and the coming years will be critical to sustain innovative and long-term support for vaccines and immunisation.

5. Conclusion

The GAVI Alliance, in its ten years of existence, is an example of a new approach to global health, providing a space for partners to negotiate and roll out innovative approaches to development finance and programme sustainability. In the process, there have been many challenges and partners have learnt lessons that have informed the work. For example, as was mentioned at the start of this chapter, the vaccine manufacturing industry did not respond as rapidly as expected to the increased demand created by GAVI funds. Through dialogue with industry, it became clear that as vaccines are complex to produce and require large investments in equipment and know-how, manufacturers are more reluctant to initiate production of a vaccine, and also need a two-year lead time to supply a vaccine in a given quantity. Efforts were therefore made to improve the quality of demand forecasts, and currently, the UNICEF Supply Division[12] works with countries in the context of the GAVI partnership to provide reliable demand forecasts. In turn, this enables industry to dimension their investments.

However, there are still limitations in supply of new vaccines. Countries have also expressed dissatisfaction with the packaging of new

[12] The UNICEF Supply Division procures most of the vaccines procured with GAVI funds. Such bulk procurement and pooled demand enables more efficient negotiations with the vaccine industry.

vaccines, as current packaging of for example the available Rotavirus vaccine requires a large increase in countries' storage and delivery infrastructure (cold chain) capacity. In 2007, GAVI established a working group with members from WHO and UNICEF and the vaccine industry was set up in the context of the GAVI partnership and is working to resolve the problem.[13]

The space to negotiate and collaborate has also enabled the development and implementation of the three approaches to financing development discussed in this chapter: IFFIm, AMC and country co-financing. All three are recognised as new ways of doing development differently, each with a different aim and approach. The IFFIm, enabling the issuance of bonds underpinned by government guarantees, has proven to be an effective way to frontload funds for development. Donors are currently expressing interest in using the model to frontload funds for certain areas of health systems strengthening, recognising that a large, upfront investment is required to enable developing country health systems to provide immunisation and other critical services. However, the funds committed so far are likely to support only restricted areas of health systems strengthening, and there are questions of whether such an approach is relevant for the recurring costs involved in for example salary support. The pneumococcal AMC, on the other hand, aims to accelerate the availability of the pneumococcal vaccine in poor countries by providing incentives for industry to manufacture this vaccine and sell it at an affordable price. The use of such funding for longer term, recurrent costs compared to restricted, focused vaccine support remains an important and controversial issue of debate.

Country co-financing focuses on countries' ability to achieve sustainability of their immunisation programmes, over time rendering GAVI support obsolete. Again the chapter has stressed the challenges and learning required among partners to achieve a balanced approach. Arriving at the current model of co-financing was not easy, and several approaches were tested before partners and countries agreed that a reasonable approach had

[13] This group is called the Vaccine Presentation and Packaging Advisory Group, and WHO took over the management of the group in 2008 as the mandate was extended to non-GAVI vaccines. More information here: http://sites.google.com/site/vppagp/.

been found. Countries that were early adopters of policies that subsequently changed have expressed frustration with the learning approach taken — resulting in changes and tweaks that in turn require changes in procedures at the country level. At the same time, countries have expressed appreciation of GAVI's willingness to learn and improve approaches that turn out to be less effective than originally envisaged. Emerging evidence indicates that the current co-financing approach does enable countries to strengthen financial planning and take greater ownership of their immunisation programmes. The policy is being reviewed in 2010, and lessons will again be taken on board to improve the approach to supporting financial sustainability of countries' immunisation programmes. However innovation requires considerable flexibility and a learning and negotiation process with countries and a wide range of public and private partners. This illustrates the innovations and challenge of the "diplomacy of diversity" in this book.

All three approaches discussed in this chapter are still being rolled out, and it will be critical for partners to carefully evaluate and learn from each approach. There is a need for formal evaluation and learning built into partners and their innovations, so they can be adapted from a clear evidence base. Additional, frontloaded funds for vaccines and health systems, making vaccines against diseases more prevalent in poor countries more accessible, and furthering financial sustainability at country level, all have the potential to accelerate significant improvements in the health of people in the developing world. They require a diverse and adaptable partnership, which is innovative and able to evaluate and learn from the challenges and benefits these innovations generate.

Chapter 12 also assesses examples of innovative financing from the private sector. Chapter 7 assesses aid effectiveness issues related to GAVI.

References

Alliance for Case Studies for Global Health (2009) *A Marriage of Divergent Interests: Partnership in the Making of the World's First Advance Market Commitment*. Alliance for Case Studies for Global Health.

Atherly D, Dreibelbis R, Parashar UD, Levin C, Wecker J, Rheingans RD (2009) "Rotavirus Vaccination: Cost-Effectiveness and Impact on Child Mortality in Developing Countries," *The Journal of Infectious Diseases* 200:S28–38.

Barder O, Yeh O (2006) *The Costs and Benefits of Front-loading and Predictability of Immunization*. Working Paper Number 80. Washington DC: Centre for Global Development.

Burton T, Neil M, Okwo-Bele J-M, Salama P, Wardlaw T (2008) "Measurement of Immunisation Coverage," *Lancet* 373:210–11.

Chee G, Hsi N, Carlson K, Chankova S, Taylor P (2007) *Evaluation of the First Five Years of GAVI Immunization Services Support Funding*. Bethesda, MD: Abt Associates Inc. Available at: http://www.gavialliance.org/resources/GAVI_Consolidated_Report_FINAL_to_SC_Sep28.pdf (accessed 9 May 2010).

Commission for Africa (2005) *Our Common Interest*. London: Commission for Africa.

GAVI Alliance (2006) *China Immunises Millions of Children Against Hepatitis B in Historic Collaboration between Government and GAVI Alliance. Press release*. Geneva: GAVI Alliance.

——— (2009) *GAVI Alliance Welcomes New Funding to Strengthen Health Systems. Innovative Health Financing Taskforce Set Up by World Leaders Announces Financial Measures Worth US$5.3 Billion. Press release.* Geneva: GAVI Alliance.

GAVI Alliance Board (2000) *GAVI Board Teleconference 31 March 2000.* Geneva, GAVI Alliance. Available at: http://www.gavialliance.org/about/governance/boards/reports/Teleconference_31_March_2000.php (accessed 3 May 2010).

——— (2001) *Report, 5th GAVI Board Meeting*. Geneva, GAVI Alliance. Available at: http://www.gavialliance.org/about/governance/boards/reports/5th_Board_fifth_boardmeeting.php (accessed 10 January 2010).

——— (2003) *Report 10th GAVI Board Meeting*. Geneva, GAVI Alliance. Available at: http://www.gavialliance.org/about/governance/boards/reports/10_board.php (accessed 30th April 2010).

——— (2008) *Report, GAVI Alliance Board Meeting 29&30 October 2008.* Geneva, GAVI Alliance. Available at: http://www.gavialliance.org/about/governance/boards/reports/2008_10_29_gavi_alliance_board_meeting.php (accessed 9 May 2010).

Kickbush I, Silberschmidt G, Buss P (2007) "Global Health Diplomacy: The Need for New Perspectives, Strategic Approaches and Skills in Global Health," *Bulletin of the World Health Organization* 85:230–2.

Levine R, Kremer M, Albright A (2005) *Making Markets for Vaccines. Ideas to action. The Report of the Center for Global Development Advance Market Commitment Group*. Washington DC: Center for Global Development.

Levine R (2009) *Dispute over Penumococcal Vaccine Initiative: A Response*. Washington DC: Center for Global Development (online) (updated 18 December, 2009), available at: http://blogs.cgdev.org/globalhealth/2009/12/dispute-over-pneumococcal-vaccine-initiative-a-response.php (accessed 27 February 2010).

Light D (2007) "Is G8 Putting Profits before the World's Poorest Children?" *The Lancet* 370(9584):297–8.

Lim SS, Stein DB, Charrow A, Murray CJL (2008) "Tracking Progress Towards Universal Childhood Immunisation and the Impact of Global Initiatives: A Systematic Analysis of Three-Dose Diphtheria, Tetanus, and Pertussis Immunisation Coverage," *Lancet* 372:2031–46.

Lob-Levyt (2008) "Tracking Progress in Maternal, Newborn & Child Survival, the 2008 Report," GAVI, Geneva.

Lob-Levyt (2009) Press release "GAVI welcomes WHO report on women and health," GAVI, Geneva.

Lu C, Michaud CM, Gakidou E, Khan K, Murray CJL (2006) "Effect of the Global Alliance for Vaccines and Immunisation on Diphtheria, Tetanus, and Pertussis Vaccine Coverage: An Independent Assessment." *Lancet* 368:1088–95.

Lydon P, Levine R, Makinen M, Brenzel L, Mitchell V, Milstien JB, Kamara L, Landry S (2008) "Introducing New Vaccines in the Poorest Countries: What did we Learn from the GAVI Experience with Financial Sustainability?" *Vaccine* 26:6706–16.

Milstien JB, Kamara L, Lydon P, Mitchell V, Landry S (2008) "The GAVI Financing Task Force: One Model of Partners Collaboration," *Vaccine* 26:6699–705.

Moss TJ (2005) *Ten Myths of the International Finance Facility*. Working Paper Number 60. Washington DC: Center for Global Development.

Schwalbe N, El-Ziq I (2010) "GAVI's Advance Market Commitment," *The Lancet* 375(9715):638–9.

Task Force on Innovative International Financing for Health Systems (2009) *More Money for Health and More Health for the Money*. London/Washington DC: Task Force on Innovative International Financing for Health Systems.

Tremonti G (2005) *Background Papers to Advanced Market Commitments for Vaccines. A New Tool in the Fight Against Disease and Poverty. Report to the G8 Finance Ministers.* London: Italian Ministry of Finance and Economics.

UK HM Treasury (2003) *International Finance Facility. Press release* (online) (updated 14 February 2003), available at: http://www.hm-treasury.gov.uk/press_21_03.htm (accessed 27 February 2010).

UNICEF (2010). Product Menu for Vaccines Supplied by UNICEF for the GAVI Alliance (online) (updated 1 February 2010), Available at: http://www.unicef.org/supply/index_gavi.html (accessed 27 February 2010).

United Nations General Assembly (2005) "The UN and Partnerships: taking stock and sketching a way forward," United Nations, New York. (UN General Assembly 2005, p. 4.)

Williams BG, Gouwe E, Boschi-Pinto C, Bryce J, Dye C (2002) "Estimates of World-wide Distribution of Child Deaths from Acute Respiratory Infections," *Lancet Infect Dis* 2:25–32.

World Health Organization (2006) *Public Health, Innovation and Intellectual Property Rights. Report of the Commission on Intellectual Property Rights, Innovation and Public Health*. Geneva: World Health Organization.

——— (2009) *WHO-UNICEF Coverage Estimates for 1980–2008, as at August 2009.* Geneva: World Health Organization.

World Health Organization, GAVI Alliance (2008) *Financial Sustainability for Immunisation in the Poorest Countries: Lessons from GAVI 2000–2006*. Geneva: WHO/GAVI.

World Health Organization/UNICEF/World Bank (2009) *State of the World's Vaccines and Immunization*. 3rd edition. Geneva: World Health Organization.

10

PEPFAR: A Results-Driven Approach to International HIV Support[1]

Katherine Marconi, Paul Bouey and Mark Dybul

Summary

Since the founding of the Marshall Plan in 1947 and the passage of The Foreign Assistance Act in 1961, US Government involvement in foreign assistance has evolved and changed. The bipartisan support and the passage by the US Congress of the "United States Leadership Against HIV/AIDS, Tuberculosis and Malaria Act of 2003" set the stage for a new and coordinated multi-lateral and bi-lateral approach to foreign assistance. The Act became the first of a family of innovative international partnerships that today include the Millennium Challenge Corporation and The President's Malaria Initiative. In this chapter, we analyse the new coordination model and results-driven framework of The President's Emergency Plan for AIDS Relief (PEPFAR). The Act called for a new government coordinating office with funding authority, which would bring together the HIV activities of US agencies. Additionally, the office was to assure field coordination among governments, non-governmental and faith based organisations and the private sector. The chapter describes and evaluates the formation and implementation of PEPFAR, the lessons learned

[1] The findings and conclusions in this paper are those of the authors and do not necessarily represent the views of the US Department of State.

from its results-based partnerships formed in the first five years and the challenges for the next five years.

Introduction

Since the founding of the Marshall Plan in 1947 and the passage of The Foreign Assistance Act in 1961, United States (US) Government involvement in foreign support has evolved and changed (USAID 2009a). The 2001 United Nations (UN) Declaration of Commitment on HIV/AIDS (UN 2001) and the Millennium Development Goals set high-level objectives for addressing the HIV epidemic, although the Millennium Development Goals did not include HIV treatment. There was a lack of consensus that HIV treatment was possible and that it was too expensive in low- and middle-income countries. However, by 2003, as this epidemic, along with other infectious diseases, was shortening the lives of large groups of people throughout the world (UNAIDS 2004), US foreign health assistance needed to be re-focused. Further progress required an innovative partnership across US agencies and with countries that focused on results.

The Agency for International Development (USAID) had the lead role in foreign assistance, but a number of US government agencies were involved in health, particularly HIV diplomacy, with differing results. Agencies supported bilateral programmes such as the US International Mother and Child HIV Prevention Initiative (PEPFAR 2005a) and multi-lateral programmes such as HIV support for the United Nations family of agencies (PEPFAR 2005a). With each annual US Government funding cycle, resource levels and even the existence of international HIV programmes varied. A systematic and sustained commitment by the United States was needed.

In 2003, President Bush, in his State of the Union address, proposed that the US Congress authorise $15 billion dollars over five years to address HIV, making it the largest international health initiative in history for a single disease (Bush 2003). Bush also called for accountable, measureable results. At that time, using coverage rates adjusted for later revisions in the epidemic, 1.9% or 50,000 people in the focus countries were estimated to be on treatment (USAID *et al.* 2004, pp. 65–6). Incidence, based on past trends, was believed to be rising (UNAIDS 2004). Viewing the high prevalence and lack of treatment as requiring an emergency approach, the US

Congress then introduced and passed "The United States Leadership Against HIV/AIDS, Tuberculosis and Malaria Act of 2003" (The US Leadership Act 2003). Amazingly, in this era of partisan US Congressional politics, the legislation passed by a voice vote in the Senate and a 375-41 vote in the House of Representatives (Govtrack.us 2004).

The Act authorised $15 billion dollars (pending annual appropriations) over five years for both multi-lateral and bi-lateral support for HIV, TB and Malaria in support of the multi-national response (The US Leadership Act 2003, Section 401). The Act called for partnerships among different US agencies, between the public and private sectors and with faith-based organisations and international efforts to reduce the impact of HIV. This 2003 legislation became one of a set of innovative international partnerships initiated by the United States. By 2005, they included the Millennium Challenge Corporation (2010) and The President's Malaria Initiative (USAID 2009b).

In 2008, the Act was reauthorised as The Tom Lantos and Henry J. Hyde United States Global Leadership Against HIV/AIDS, Tuberculosis and Malaria Reauthorization Act (Tom Lantos and Henry Hyde Global Leadership Act 2008), calling for $48 billion over five years. The Act called for thirty-nine billion dollars to be targeted for HIV efforts, $5 billion for malaria and $4 billion for treatment. The 2008 Act built upon the innovative partnerships developed in the first five years while emphasising national system building and related efforts. Its purpose is to further increase US support of HIV prevention, treatment and care while transitioning from an emergency to a sustainable response. Reauthorisation of this programme showed that it survived the political change of government, while adapting to longer-term needs for sustaining the results of the first five years.

This chapter examines the 2003–2009 implementation of The US Leadership Act as a systematic and innovative US partnership that built international health support. After briefly reviewing the enabling legislation, it discusses four characteristics of what came to be called PEPFAR: (1) development of a new health partnership within the federal government, with countries and with multi-lateral donors, especially The Global Fund; (2) use of a common planning and results-driven framework for implementation; (3) standardised results reporting; and (4) continuing transformation of this programme. It concludes with lessons learned and future directions for such an unprecedented US health partnership.

1. Legislative Authority for a Results-Driven Partnership

The 2003 US Leadership Act was based on the assumption that "The United States had the capacity to lead and enhance the effectiveness of the international community's response to HIV" (2003, Section 2, (22)). Throughout the Act, partnerships, such as with countries, the private sector and the international community were highlighted to maximise resources and drive innovation. The Act contained a series of programmatic and financial requirements that were to drive the bi-lateral programmes. Annually, a minimum of 55% of appropriated Emergency Plan funding was to support treatment, 15% for palliative care and 20% for prevention, including 33% of sexual prevention for abstinence and be faithful programmes. Ten percent of all funds allocated to prevention, treatment and care was to support orphans and vulnerable children infected with and affected by HIV (The US Leadership Act 2003, Title IV). Programmes also needed to take into account the specific groups identified by the legislation as high risk. Throughout the legislation, orphans and vulnerable children, women, especially pregnant women, and youth were considered high-priority populations. The legislation emphasised the integration of tuberculosis control and nutrition support with HIV services and the training of health professionals (The US Leadership Act 2003 Sec. 302, 104B, and Sec. 304) to strengthen long-term country capacity.

The Act supported innovative multilateral programmes through active participation in the Global Fund to Fight AIDS, Tuberculosis and Malaria (The Global Fund), international vaccine funds and in other places of the Act, international efforts such as the Joint United Nations Programme on HIV/AIDS (UNAIDS), The United Nations Children's Fund (UNICEF), The World Health Organization (WHO) and the United Nations Development Programme (UNDP) (The US Leadership Act 2003, Title II and Title III, Subtitle A, Section 104A, (C) (3)). The Global Fund section called for reports to Congress including a report by the Controller General and limitations on the transfer of US funding to The Global Fund. Because the US funds were to leverage other contributions to the Fund, the US contribution was not to exceed 33% of funds contributed by all sources

(The US Leadership Act 2003, Title II, Sec. 202).[2] A US Interagency Review Panel was to actively support US involvement in the fund as a "shadow" review of grants (The US Leadership Act 2003, Section 202).

Some of the provisions of the legislation were contentious. Both the Act and the initial policies issued by the Global AIDS Coordinator emphasised a multi-faceted approach to preventing sexual transmission: abstinence, especially that of delaying sexual debut; reducing casual sexual partners and the number of partners through beingfaithful and supporting condoms where appropriate (PEPFAR 2005b). This prevention language combined with the funding requirements for abstinence interventions was controversial, as critics rejected the prescriptive nature of the Act (The US Leadership Act 2003, (Section 402) and The End of the Beginning 2004). The prohibition of funding of organisations that did not have a policy opposing prostitution led to accusations that this new programme was "reducing the effectiveness of our foreign aid, squandering our reputation and alienating our scientifically minded public health allies in Africa" (Tavrow 2005).

A unique aspect of the new approach of PEPFAR was its emphasis on results and accountability, not just financial accountability but social or programmatic accountability. President Bush called for, and the PEPFAR legislation endorsed, results-driven programming. The programme then used the goals established by President Bush. Five-year treatment and care goals and a 2010 prevention goal were identified:

- supporting life-saving antiretroviral treatment for 2 million men, women and children
- preventing 7 million HIV infections
- providing care for 10 million adults and orphans living with and affected by HIV

Thus, PEPFAR became an innovative US approach to supporting international HIV prevention, treatment and care through results-driven partnerships.

[2] Contributions to The Global Fund by International Bank for Reconstruction and development and the International Monetary Fund did not apply to the 33%.

2. Development of New Partnership Models

In October of 2003, Congress confirmed Ambassador Randall Tobias as the first AIDS Coordinator. Joining PEPFAR after a successful private-sector career, Ambassador Tobias brought sound business practices to the programme. As the new Office of the US Global AIDS Coordinator (OGAC) within the US Department of State took shape office, it coordinated and provided oversight of global HIV/AIDS investments, set policy and management direction, and allocated annual budgetary funds for prevention, care and treatment. Ambassador Tobias gave to the office a philosophy that continued through the first phase of PEPFAR: stay focused and aligned with a shared vision, develop a strategy that is translated into programming, and stress the participation of staff in creating the future of an organisation. For example, he maintained the focus on HIV by supporting TB and Malaria services only if they were provided in relation to dedicated HIV prevention, treatment and care programmes. The partnerships that he concentrated on included those among US governmental agencies, with countries and with the international community. Table 1 summarises key PEPFAR implementation milestones, which represents a unique partnership in US health support.

Because of the legislation and the fact that nearly all of the resources were directly controlled by the Coordinator, the AIDS Coordinator was able to empower one US government international approach in this important area of health assistance. Being a US Presidential Initiative with the personal engagement of the President also lent credibility and authority to the new programme. While located in the US Department of State, both Ambassador Tobias and later Ambassador Dybul were able to directly communicate with the White House, which reinforced their legislative authority.

USAID, the Department of Health and Human Services (HHS) including The Centers for Disease Control and Prevention (CDC) and Health Resources and Services Administration (HRSA), The Department of Defense and the Peace Corps along with the State Department assumed major roles in implementing the programme. The Department of Labor, Census Bureau, The Substance Abuse and Mental Health Administration in HHS and the National Institutes of Health (NIH), among other government agencies, also were involved. USAID and CDC garnered the most service

Table 1. 2004–2009 significant PEPFAR milestones.

Date	PEPFAR Milestone
27 May 2003	Signing of P.L. 108-25, the United States Leadership Against Global HIV/AIDS, Tuberculosis and Malaria Act of 2003
October 2003	Congressional Confirmation of Randall Tobias as the first AIDS Ambassador and Global AIDS Coordinator
January 2004	President Bush signs first PEPFAR annual budget and AIDS Coordinator obligates for tranche of funds for services
Spring 2004	Awarding of first PEPFAR bi-lateral funding
December 2004	One-third of Global Fund supported from US Contributions
February 2004	Publication of Five-Year Strategy
March 2004	First country operational plans (COPs) submitted
	HIV/AIDS treatment clinics supported in South Africa and other areas
January 2005	Five-year focus country strategies submitted
	Receipt of the first COPs
December 2004	Receipt of the first annual results reports
March 2005	Engendering Bold Leadership: First Annual Report to Congress
30 July 2008	Signing of the Tom Lantos and Henry J. Hyde United States Global Leadership Against HIV/AIDS, Tuberculosis and Malaria Reauthorisation Act
30 September 2008	Treatment goal reached and care goal reached by 12/2008
May 2009	First Country Partnership Framework signed, Malawi
August 2009	Next-generation indicators published

resources; NIH led the research agenda and largely worked independently of the US AIDS Coordinator. Table 2 summarises US government departmental involvement in PEPFAR. This interagency model was an unusual model for the federal government, given that the programme's locus of authority rested outside of most of the implementing agencies.

In 2003, fourteen countries heavily impacted by HIV were designated as "focus countries" for the bi-lateral efforts. In 2004, because of the requirements of the authorising legislation, Vietnam was added as the fifteenth country (Figure 1). Together, the fifteen focus countries received over 90% of PEPFAR bi-lateral funding and contained over 50% of world HIV infections (PEPFAR 2005b). Most of the multi-lateral resources went to support the Global Fund that served a larger number of countries.

Table 2. United states government PEPFAR implementing agencies.

Agency	**International Mission**
Department of State	Advance freedom for the benefit of the American people and the international community by helping to build and sustain a more democratic, secure and prosperous world composed of well-governed states that respond to the needs of their people, reduce widespread poverty and act responsibly within the international system. Source: http://www.state.gov/s/d/rm/index.htm
United States Agency for International Development (USAID)	Supports long-term and equitable economic growth and advances US foreign policy objectives by supporting: • economic growth, agriculture and trade • global health and, • democracy, conflict prevention and humanitarian assistance Source: http://www.usaid.gov/about_usaid/
Department of Defense (DoD), HIV/AIDS Prevention Program (DHAPP)	DHAPP works with a country and its military plans based on the following process: • Meet with key partners in the country to determine provisional major programme areas and other technical assistance needs • Adapt DHAPP support to a country's need for prevention of its HIV/AIDS situation based on existing plans and assessments • Strengthen the military capacity for ownership and behavioural changes over the long term • Possibly design a programme with other country partners who have had successful prevention efforts • Focus on impact of prevention activities through developing country implementation plans • Implement and monitor programme to ensure sustainability. Source: http://www.med.navy.mil/sites/nhrc/dhapp/proposals/pages/overviewofdhappstrategy.aspx
Department of Commerce (DOC), Census Bureau	The DOC has provided and continues to provide in-kind support to PEPFAR, aimed at furthering private-sector engagement by fostering public–private partnerships. Within the DOC, the Census Bureau's, International Programs Center, conducts demographic and socioeconomic studies and strengthens statistical development around the world through technical assistance, training, and software products. Its work is

(*Continued*)

Table 2. (*Continued*)

Agency	International Mission
	commissioned and funded by federal agencies, international organisations, non-governmental organisations, private businesses, and other governments. Sources: http://www.pepfar.gov/agencies/c19398.htm and http://www.census.gov/ipc/www/aboutintl.html
Department of Labor (DoL)	The DoL's Bureau of International Labor Affairs works to reduce the rate of HIV/AID infection through workplace-based prevention and education programmes and to improve the workplace environment for workers living with HIV/AIDS. Source: http://www.dol.gov/ilab/programs/intlcoop/hivaids/main.htm
Department of Health and Human Services (HHS), CDC	CDC's Global AIDS Program provides critical leadership in the fight against HIV/AIDS in resource-constrained countries assisting to strengthen laboratory, epidemiology, surveillance, public health evaluation and workforce capacity-essential components for strong sustainable public health systems. Source: http://www.cdc.gov/globalaids/about/
HHS, Health Resources and Services Administration (HRSA)	HRSA's HIV/AIDS Bureau's Global HIV/AIDS strategy focuses on supporting health systems strengthening including strengthening clinical, quality, and administrative systems and services to build networks of comprehensive HIV/AIDS care and treatment and human resources for health, supporting training activities and partnerships to develop human and organisational capacity. Source: http://hab.hrsa.gov/special/global.htm
HHS, National Institutes of Health (NIH)	NIH supports a comprehensive programme of basic, clinical and behavioural research on HIV infection and its associated opportunistic infections, co-infections and malignancies. This research will lead to a better understanding of the basic biology of HIV and the development of effective therapies to treat it. It also will foster the design of better counter-measures to prevent new infections, including vaccines and prophylaxis with antiretroviral drugs (ARVs) and microbicides. Source: http://www.pepfar.gov/agencies/c19401.htm

(*Continued*)

Table 2. (*Continued*)

Agency	International Mission
HHS, Food and Drug Administration (FDA)	FDA's Office of International Programs ensures that ARVs produced by manufacturers all over the world can be rapidly reviewed, their quality assessed and their acceptability for purchase with PEPFAR funds supported. The agency reviews applications to the same standards that products must meet to be marketed in the United States and grants "tentative approvals." Source: http://www.fda.gov/ForConsumers/ConsumerUpdates/ucm048558.htm
HHS, Substance Abuse and Mental Health Administration (SAMHSA)	SAMHSA primarily works in Vietnam as part of the PEPFAR country team focusing on substance abusers. Source: http://www.pepfar.gov/agencies/c19401.htm
Department of Treasury	Through the 2008 PEPFAR Legislation, the Department of the Treasury is authorised to provide consultation and technical assistance to countries to strengthen management and financial functions in support of HIV/AIDS programmes. Source: http://www.treas.gov/offices/international-affairs/
Peace Corps	The Peace Corps is a key partner in providing assistance to the countries most affected by the HIV/AIDS pandemic. Peace Corps Volunteers help people affected by HIV/AIDS through work in areas such as public health education, community and nongovernmental organisations and business advising. Source: http://www.peacecorps.gov/teens/ready/takeaction/hivaids.cfm

Innovative US agency partnerships

Lasker *et al.* identify governance as the "key to partnership functioning" (2001, p. 179). Policy and task headquarters' interagency teams became the vehicles for formulating business rules and governing PEPFAR. The policy team (principals), consisting of high-level political appointees from cabinet departments, advised the AIDS Coordinator on key policy issues. Essential to the interagency process was the Deputy Principals group, comprised of the top career officials from each implementing agency. This

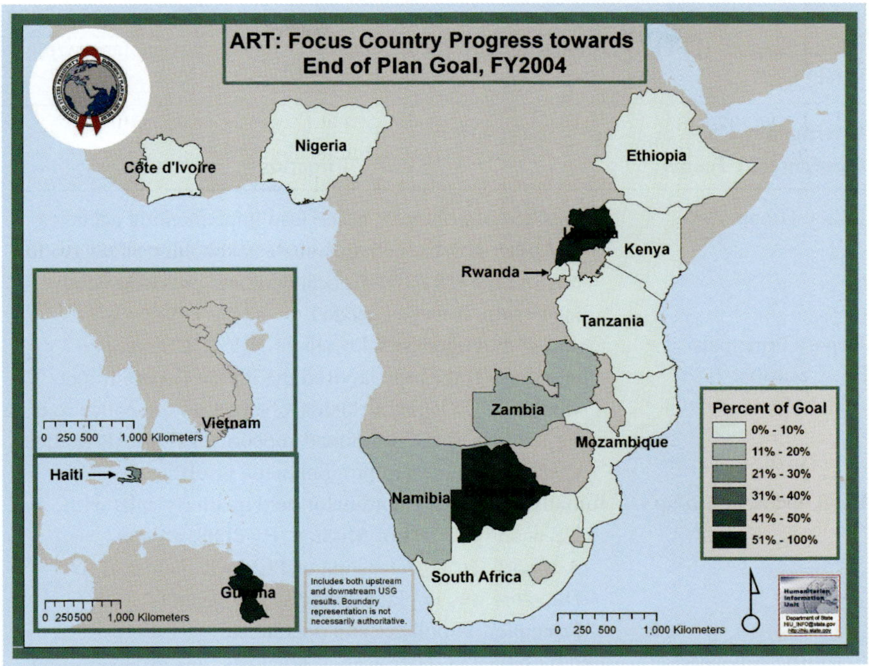

Figure 1. ART: Focus country progress towards the end of plan goal, FY2004.

group developed support for PEPFAR throughout their agencies, helped set the policy agenda for the principals and created programmatic priorities. Other teams ranged in type from technical work groups organised around specific programme and monitoring and evaluation areas, to country support teams and management and budget teams. PEPFAR governance and operations teams are outlined in Table 3. One of the first of the technical interagency teams focused on assuring results-based reporting to measure the legislative goals. These results were to drive the decision making of the other interagency groups.

Because each US government agency participating in PEPFAR brought its own historical business model to the program, developing PEPFAR's approach to international HIV and health assistance became a learning process. For example, Peace Corps volunteers supported community efforts, while CDC physically located its staff in host government

Table 3. PEPFAR US Interagency Governance and Operations Teams 2004–2009. Partial Source: (PEPFAR Annual Report 2006, Chapter 8) http://www.pepfar.gov/press/81042.htm

Interagency US Government Teams	**Function**
Policy Group	Composed of principals at the lead implementing agencies and other key Executive Branch stakeholders. This group advised the US AIDS Coordinator and provided policy leadership. It met as needed
Deputy Principals	Composed of operational heads of HIV/AIDS units in agencies. This group advised the Policy Group. It met weekly. The Deputy Principals helped set the policy agenda for the Principals, developed support for PEPFAR in their agencies and created programmatic priorities
Field Advisory Group	Initially, the AIDS Coordinator held quarterly calls with US country Chiefs of Mission. By 2008, a Field Advisory Group consisting of PEPFAR Field Directors was in place to advise the Deputy Principles on policies and operations
Scientific Advisory Committee	Led by NIH and other agency scientists, this group ensured that PEPFAR programmes were scientifically sound. A Public Health Evaluation Committee operated under this committee to guide field and headquarters evaluations and operations research
Technical Advisory Groups	Technical and Operational Working Groups, co-chaired by OGAC and agency personnel with headquarters and field representation, formulated technical guidance and support implementation in the field
Headquarters Country Core Teams	Headquarters interagency team, led by OGAC staff, advised countries on OGAC policies and programmes and information from headquarters flowed through these country groups
Country Coordinating and Technical Advisory Teams	Depending on the size of country US staff, countries organised interagency country coordinating teams to advise the PEPFAR Country Director and technical work groups

programmes, including surveillance and treatment. USAID provided field support through its many international and local contractors, and their strength in procurement was important. Some US government agencies did not have a field presence. Understanding these structural differences and forming field and headquarters partnerships among USG agencies continually had to be addressed and negotiated.

At its best, this team approach allowed agencies to air differences and to reach consensus, to focus on results. At its worst, consensus on next steps took more time than decision-making by an individual. Within the US Department of State, and given his legislative authority, the AIDS Coordinator made policy and funding decisions, particularly in the absence of consensus.

Forming country partnerships

Expanding a US government HIV field presence in the focus countries was imperative, given the national partnerships needed to quickly allocate large amounts of bilateral funding for services that produced results. A key criterion for the selection of the focus countries was the existing presence of US government personnel dedicated to HIV on the ground. However, the staffing patterns were for one-tenth of the resources and programming needed for scaling up treatment and other programmes. A rapid increase in staff was required.

Lasker *et al.* state that building relationships is one of the most time-consuming tasks of successful partnerships (2001, p. 192). US government teams in the fifteen countries took advantage of American technical skills and technology and provided multiple types of support to governments and country non-governmental agencies (NGOs). However, it took several years for most US Embassies to increase staff and technical contract support to appropriate levels. As the one in-country US authority over US staff, the Ambassador's office could bring order and coordination to the different agency programmes and staff. However, they also had to assure housing, workspace and security for incoming agency staff.

To guide in-country US support for HIV, each US country team was given five-year treatment and care targets. Additionally, the teams had to create their own annual targets for these and other critical services such as prevention-of-maternal-to-child-transmission (PMTCT) and orphan care. Resources were to be allocated in support of these targets. The lack of a method to directly measure the 7 million infections averted meant that mathematical modelling became the only way of estimating total infections averted, including infections averted through PMTCT interventions (PEPFAR 2007). Prevention providers also found it difficult to set and measure prevention targets.

The five-year goals and annual targets for US support of national efforts, along with budget requirements, helped to focus bilateral efforts in the fifteen countries. However, the US targets made it more difficult to negotiate with country governments on how US support fit into their national targets and plans. In 2004, US government country offices began working with governments to define five-year HIV prevention, treatment and control strategies for US investments in each of the focus countries. These strategic efforts along with a growing emphasis on participation in international efforts within countries, such as with The Global Fund grants, began to integrate US targets into national plans.

As coordination with country governments grew, different US strategies and delivery models emerged based on the unique circumstances facing countries and different epidemic models. At the request of governments in Botswana and Uganda, countries with generalised epidemics, USG funding quickly added to the existing government NGO and research facilities for rapid scale-up of HIV treatment and care (PEPFAR 2005b, p. 47). A secondary effect was the positive impact that these services had on health and health systems strengthening. In other countries such as Ethiopia, where the HIV epidemic was more concentrated, the government strategy first emphasised the much needed capacity building of their health system, such as renovating clinics and training health personnel. HIV services could then be delivered through the improved health system.

For example, in Ethiopia, there was an estimated one doctor per 34,000 people in the country and one nurse per every 4,900 people (PEPFAR 2005b, p.67). The US partnership with this government began to address clinical capacity building through new and expanded training programmes. In addition, in Ethiopia, the government brought the Global Fund and PEPFAR together to sign an agreement on formally coordinating bilateral and multilateral services. This agreement became a model for other countries.

Besides "engaging heads of states and other government officials," the 2003 legislation called for "innovative partnerships between governments and organizations in the private sector" (The US Leadership Act, Title II, Section 201). In 2004, direct US funding of NGOs and faith-based organisations began. In countries such as Namibia and Zambia, these groups were critical to the success of prevention efforts (PEPFAR 2006). In many countries, NGO work led to community acceptance of HIV services. However,in all countries, this direct funding of NGOs then had to be coordinated with government strategies.

The 2008–2009 PEPFAR Partnership Framework Guidance shows that integration of PEPFAR within-country HIV/AIDS strategies is a continuing process (PEPFAR 2009b). Conceived as a means to work more closely with country and multilateral partners, these frameworks (formerly Partnership Compacts) are designed to integrate USG efforts into a singular, nationally directed strategy to address the breadth of HIV/AIDS issues and of health systems. The frameworks, such as those with Malawi, Kenya and Swaziland, serve as a road map for USG agencies to shift from direct provision of services to supporting country-led efforts. In 2009–2010, US teams in each of the 33 countries that annually received over $5 million in bilateral HIV funding were encouraged to work with national governments and country donors to develop a partnership framework.

3. Multilateral Partnerships

"To actively become more involved in multilateral forums particularly The Global Fund to Fight AIDS, TB, and Malaria" (The US Leadership Act, Title II, Section 202), the US again used an interagency team approach that emphasised specific reporting and grant review requirements and made recommendations to the Coordinator on US positions on Fund policies and Board resolutions. PEPFAR leaders participated in The Global Fund Board and its committees. In 2003, the HHS Secretary was elected to chair The Global Fund's Board. USG representatives chaired the Global Fund Board's Finance and Audit Committee and the Board's Policy and Strategy Committee at various times. (PEPFAR 2009a). At the headquarters, the US, following the mandate of the 2003 legislation, formed parallel review groups to provide recommendations for grants submitted to the Global Fund and co-sponsored monitoring and evaluation initiatives with the Fund, including their Five-Year Evaluation Framework. Through fiscal year 2010, the US has been the largest contributor to the Global Fund (PEPFAR 2009a).

Policy guidance to US field teams regarding the coordination of bilateral-funded programmes with The Global Fund grants and with other donor support became more directive as PEPFAR developed. The Third Annual Report to Congress cites support for Global Fund grants to upgrade financial management systems, strengthen governance and transparency and improve monitoring and evaluation systems (PEPFAR 2007, p. 1929b). The 2008 and 2009 Partnership Framework Guidance further elaborated on Global Fund support, including one country approach to logistics and commodities, strengthening and participating in Global Fund Country Coordinating Mechanisms (CCM) and strengthening and complementing services delivered through Global Fund grants (PEPFAR 2009b). Annually, approximately $10 million has been allocated for technical assistance in support of Global Fund grantees (PEPFAR 2008). These technical assistance funds are provided to UNAIDS Technical Support Facilities in Africa, Roll Back Malaria and MDR-TB programmes in support of country Global Fund grants.

In addition to the involvement with The Global Fund, support of multilateral coordination has increased. In 2004, an international meeting, co-sponsored by UNAIDS, WHO, the World Bank, the UK and the US, developed the "Three Ones" principles. These principles of "one HIV national plan, one national coordinating authority, and one national monitoring and evaluation system" guided donor strategies for HIV support during the first five years of PEPFAR (2004, p, 84). In 2006–2007, PEPFAR began transforming its annual meeting to co-sponsored international HIV implementers' meetings.

During the development of PEPFAR, the framework for operating bilateral and multilateral HIV support has moved from coordination of emergency efforts to the integration of US programmes into national efforts. Involvement with The Global Fund has increased as PEPFAR focused on support for sustaining the services first created through its emergency approach to treatment.

4. Building a Planning and Results-Driven Framework

PEPFAR success depends upon country-driven partnerships. However,the legislation also stressed accountability; results had to be reported to the US Congress and policy decisions were to be evidence-based (PEPFAR 2004, p.8). Future investments in this international HIV effort depended on reporting results. Ambassador Tobias balanced the country-driven partnership approach and results reporting by creating six threshold measures for partnership success:

- "knowing who PEFAR funding partners and sub-partners are
- what they will be doing with the money they received
- what the goals are to be achieved with the money
- measuring the success of the use of this money
- how the planned activity clearly links to PEPFAR's strategy and
- do the country team's funding proposals adequately bring in new partners and faith-based partners?" (Tobias 2004).

These measurement principles were continued and expanded by Mark Dybul, MD, who became the acting Ambassador in March of 2006 and the permanent replacement for Ambassador Tobias on 11 August 2006.

In 2004, after consultation with the Administration, Congress and The Global Fund, PEPFAR field and headquarters agency staff together designed a web-based Country Operational Planning and Reporting System (COPRS), built on a modified USAID programme reporting software system. Annually, USG teams in focus countries, through the US ambassador, were to submit to The Global AIDS Coordinator one proposed HIV operational plan (COP), including budgetary proposals, for each focus country. In the US funding system, multilateral and bibilateral PEPFAR funding are part of the October 1–September 30 annual budget cycle. First, Congress allocates funds that are then approved by the Coordinator and assigned to US government agencies, mainly through the COP process. Budget obligations are made when a partner signs a grant or contract with a US government agency. Payments are made when the partner submits expenditure records to an agency.

Figure 2 summarises the annual COP planning and reporting cycle. This cycle is a significant innovation in foreign assistance because previously separate plans were submitted by each agency's field team to their own headquarters for separate funding. An unintended consequence of this agency-specific approach was multiple US government agency plans per country.

Through the fiscal year 2010 COP, US field teams have proposed annual targets, activities, potential partners and budget levels, along with a general statement of progress to date, challenges and future plans. Significant support for this planning and reporting process has been provided to country teams by interagency core groups dedicated to each country and by technical working groups. The COP content has been organised around the three HIV programme areas of prevention, treatment and care. The areas are then divided into subareas, which technical work groups

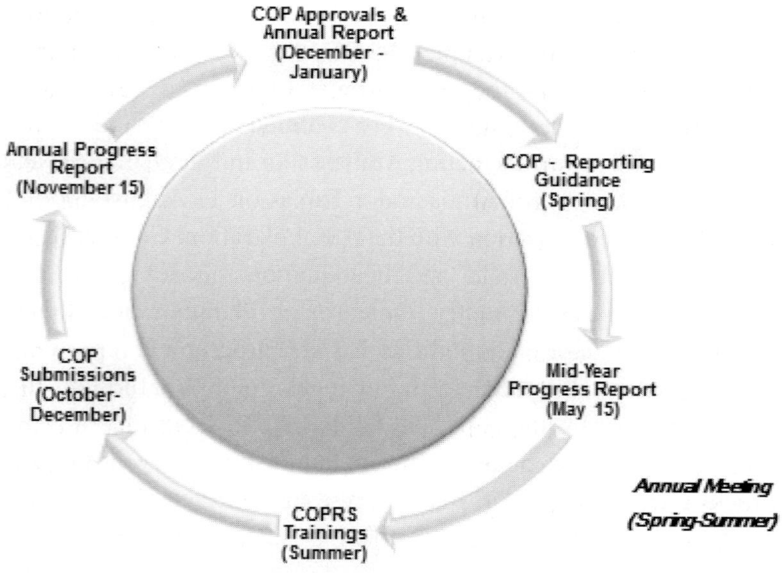

Figure 2. The annual COP planning and reporting cycle.

mirror, such as counselling and testing, PMTCT and laboratory infrastructure. These programme subareas have changed as PEPFAR evolved and are accompanied by management and budget information. The numbers of country teams that complete COPS or smaller versions of the COPS also has grown and changed from the 15 original focus country teams to 33 US country and/or regional teams in 2010.

A lesson learned about partnerships early in the COP planning cycle was that US government teams have to obtain government approval for their funding plans and results. However, the twelve month COP cycle is time consuming for teams, countries and partners, making country negotiations difficult. The amount of information needed and the shortness of the cycle has made country partnerships challenging and detracted from other inherently governmental processes, such as contract oversight and implementation. However,when coordination with a national government did not occur, country ownership of this effort became problematic. In at least one instance, the government quickly brought the lack of transparency of reported results to public attention (Timberg 2005).

Identifying best planning and reporting practices within each country's own political and planning system took much experimentation and learning. In Rwanda, for example, the US staff could negotiate and propose funding using HIV-focused national plans as a guide: Rwanda National HIV/AIDS Strategic Plan, the HIV/AIDS Treatment and Care Plan and the National Prevention Plan (PEPFAR 2009c). Rwanda became known for its adaptation of new reporting technologies and linking accountability for primary health care measures to financing (Rusa *et.al.* 2009).

The government of Vietnam also set specific priorities and indicators for its funding partners and organised HIV and health data collection systems. In contrast, until HIV became a priority of the South African government, it was challenging for the US to receive results information from government-funded sites. Besides variations in country relationships, partner capacity for planning, reporting results and financial tracking also varied. A series of US government Inspector General Reports indicate the weaknesses in partner data collection and in US team monitoring of partners (USAID 2005, 2006).

Similar to the COP design, reaching consensus among US government agencies on a common set of reporting indicators, associated definitions, reporting periods and reporting systems took considerable time. In 2003, each participating agency collected its own set of performance indicators. The number of HIV measures used by each agency varied from a short list of mandated HIV-related performance indicators (USAID 2009b, pp. 57–9) to a hundred-plus reporting indicators (CDC, Global AIDS Program 2004). Internationally, different indicators of the same HIV service existed, and UNGASS measures did not cover all of the PEPFAR priorities, such as the number of children and women currently receiving treatment.

In early 2004, Ambassador Tobias requested initial Country Operational Plans and results six months after funding began to flow to countries. Both updating and simplification of the indicators and reporting of them have evolved over time, such as reducing the amount of mid-year results reporting. In early 2008, PEPFAR undertook with its country, domestic, and international partners a major revision of both COPS and indicators. The 2009 next-generation indicators are a result of this effort (PEPFAR 2009g).

Approved COP documents (minus contract sensitive information) and results now are routinely posted on the PEPFAR website (http://www.pepfar.gov). High-level budget information also is available, but details for expended funds currently are not available because of different US agency financial reporting systems.

5. International Coordination

Shortly after the formation of the Office of the Global AIDS Coordinator, PEPFAR staff from both The Global Fund and PEPFAR began working together to coordinate reporting measures. Later, the UNAIDS Monitoring and Evaluation Reference Group (MERG) took the lead in standardising HIV/AIDS reporting indicators (UNAIDS 2009a). However, differences in reporting still exist, especially in non-clinical areas such as community outreach and health systems support. Differing country government and donor measurement priorities also complicate the standardisation of measures.

Currently, PEPFAR is working with The Global Fund and others on further defining some of the more complex but important planning and reporting areas, such as in health systems strengthening. Health system target setting and measurement will need to take into consideration many different types of support, such as graduate programme training, health worker retention and compensation, the adequacy of facilities and support services, such as nutrition, functioning supply chains, and technology, and population-based health outcomes.

A public example of this spirit of international cooperation was the joint announcement of HIV results at the January 2005 Davos World Economic Forum. WHO, UNAIDS, Global Fund and PEPFAR collaborated in releasing one set of international treatment figures and in recognising The Global Fund and PEPFAR contributions to these national results. Seven hundred thousand people living with AIDS were estimated to be on treatment, and in sub-Saharan Africa it was estimated that since June of 2003 the number of people on treatment had increased from 50,000 to 325,000 (Africa Renewal 2005). This early coordination of results reporting by the international community was part of the foundation for the massive scale up of services that was about to take place.

Another example of international cooperation is the UNAIDS-sponsored joint reviews of National AIDS Responses and other country support activities (UNAIDS 2008). During the final years of the first phase of PEPFAR and the initial years of the current phase, joint national reviews have improved country strategic planning to reduce this epidemic. They have enabled an increased US reliance on country planning.

6. The Components of US Results Reporting

The April 2004, *HIV Indicators, Reporting Requirements, and Guidelines* detailed data collection for the first phase of PEPFAR (PEPFAR 2004). This guidance has been updated annually or biannually and includes UNAIDS and WHO measures, where relevant. The indicators form the basis for estimating infections averted and changes in health events, such as deaths and births. Strategic information, the umbrella term for relevant data, emphasises the use of information, rather than just the gathering of results, and it includes programme monitoring and evaluation, surveillance

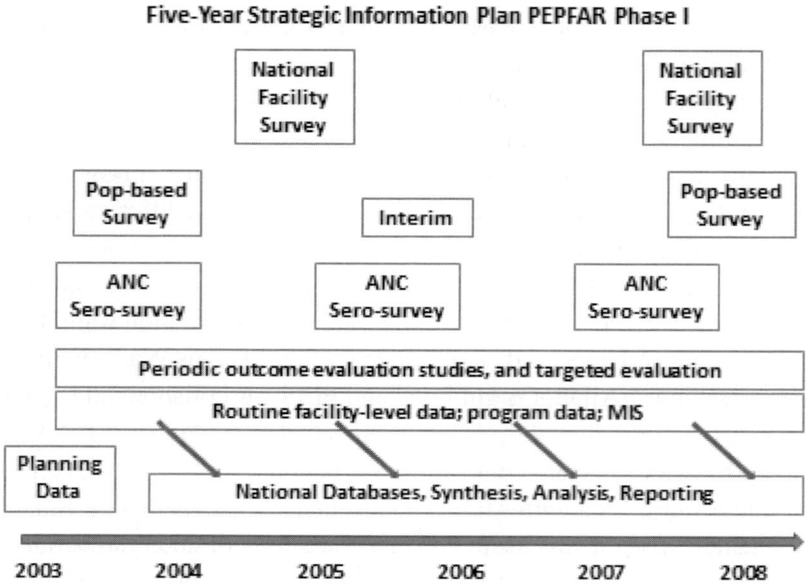

Figure 3. Data collection framework for the first five years of PEPFAR.

for modelling the epidemic and for estimating service coverage and health information management systems (HMIS). Figure 3 summarises the data collection framework for the first five years (Phase 1) of PEPFAR.

These data come from:

- National results. A set of five high-level HIV indicators (two more indicators were later added) address progress in providing treatment including ART and PMTCT, care and orphan support. Initially national counts were divided between direct (downstream) results by funders who delivered services and could actually count clients in their programmes and indirect (upstream) totals where PEPFAR may have provided supportive and technical assistance but not direct service provision. In the 2009 next-generation indicators, there is sole reliance on internationally published national counts.
- Direct programme results. An additional set of approximately 40 prevention, treatment and care indicators, based on the number of funded partners, delivery sites, people served and people trained/retrained is collected annually from USG-funded providers. Results

that may not be collected in national systems, such as service use by gender and paediatric participation in treatment, are measured through these more detailed programme results.

- Pharmaceutical tracking of the specific drugs supplied to countries through US funding is maintained by the lead supply chain contractor, supply chain management services (SCMS), and reported to PEPFAR annually.
- Surveillance and surveys measure HIV-related impact and outcomes and are obtained from governments who use Demographic and Health Surveys (DHS), the AIDS Indicator Surveys (AIS), other population surveys and annual or multiyear ante-natal centre surveillance (ANC) systems. In recent years, the national surveys have included HIV testing. In countries with concentrated epidemics, Behavior Surveillance Surveys (and in some instances Biological Surveillance Surveys) measure HIV prevalence and related behaviours. Surveys and surveillance provide numbers for modelling country epidemics, calculating infections averted and estimating the need for services.
- Evaluation and Operations Research. In 2004, a small number of headquarters and country-driven evaluations were funded and in 2005, the second annual gathering of US field staff working in PEPFAR — the HIV/AIDS Implementers Meeting — focused on evaluated best practices, setting a precedent for all future annual meetings. In 2007, PEPFAR staff designed a headquarters-driven multicountry Public Health Evaluation Effort (2009d) to provide more rigorous best practice information.
- Financing is tracked through agency budget reports and costing studies in such countries as Nigeria, Ethiopia, Uganda, Botswana and Vietnam (CDC 2009). Because US government agencies' accounting systems differ, gathering standard budget information by country has proven challenging. International harmonisation of national HIV budgets is occurring through the use of the UNAIDS National AIDS Spending Accounts (UNAIDS 2009b) and the National Health Accounts (WHO 2009).

At least annually, the Deputy Principals and other interagency teams within PEPFAR review changes in countries' HIV epidemics, treatment and care coverage, and international and US financial resources. This review drives the distribution of the next year's budget allocations to countries. At the country level, US teams in Malawi and Uganda have used geomapping to direct additional service coverage while others analyse cost-per-person reached (CDC 2009). Because trend data for most of the above information is publicly available, there now is a wealth of information that may be used for data mining and programme improvement.

7. PEPFAR Results

After five years, the final US investment in PEPFAR was $18.8 billion (2009 Annual Report) and it continues to be the largest funded health initiative for a single disease. Contributions from the USA account for 55% of HIV resources committed globally by international partners. The results reported during these five years show what has been accomplished and what remains to be accomplished (2009 Annual Report). Table 4 summarises annual US investments from 2004 through 2010.

By the end of US fiscal year 2008, in the fifteen focus countries the US contributed to:

- 2,007,800 people on ARV treatment, a coverage rate estimated to be 38% of the total need. Approximately 63% of all individuals treated in directly funded PEPFAR services were women. Changes in treatment coverage are shown in Table 4 (2007 and 2009 Annual Report).
- 9,693,800 in care with 10 million expected by the end of 2008.
- 4 million orphans and vulnerable children in care.
- 5,859,100 pregnant women receiving HIV counselling and testing services, a coverage rate of approximately 32% in the focus countries.
- 23,751,500 individuals counselled and tested.
- 422,800 pregnant women receiving ARV prophylaxis.

Figure 4 summarises the national progress towards HIV treatment in the fifteen focus countries. Additionally, scaling up HIV services by national programmes with the support of partners has produced results beyond HIV prevention, treatment and care. Infant mortality between 1998 and 2008 fell in 13 of the 15 focus countries, and life expectancy was estimated to increase for the same years in 12 of the focus countries (Table 5).

Table 4. Annual US investments from 2004 through 2010.

Programs*	FY 2004 Enacted	FY 2005 Enacted	FY 2006 Enacted	FY 2007 Enacted	FY 2008 Enacted	FY 2009 Enacted	FY 2010 Enacted
Bilateral HIV/AIDS Programs	1,677	2,278	2,654	3,699	4,979	5,415	5,542
Global Fund	547	347	545	724	840	900	1,000
Bilateral TB Programs	87	94	91	95	162	175	251
Total PEPFAR (without Malaria)	2,311	2,719	3,290	4,518	5,981	6,490	6,991

Source: Making a Difference: Funding.

http://www. pepfar.gov/documents/organisation/80161.p-df.

* Bilateral HIV/AIDS Programs includes funding for bilateral country/regional programs, UNAIDS, IAVI, Microbicides, and NIH HIV/AIDS Research.

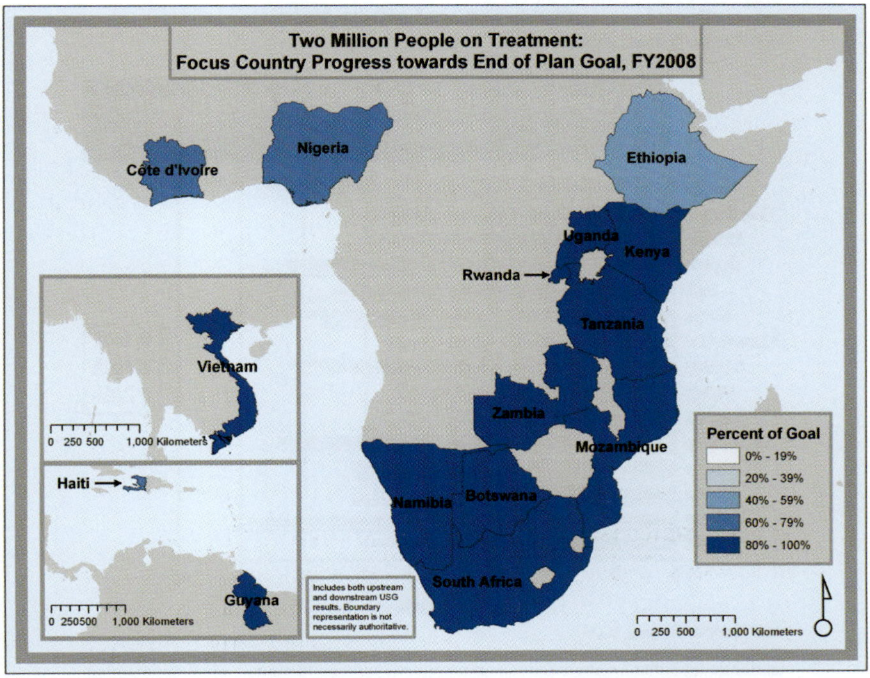

Figure 4. National progress towards HIV treatment in the 15 focus countries.

Table 5. Infant mortality and life expectancy between 1998 and 2008 in PEPFAR focus countries.

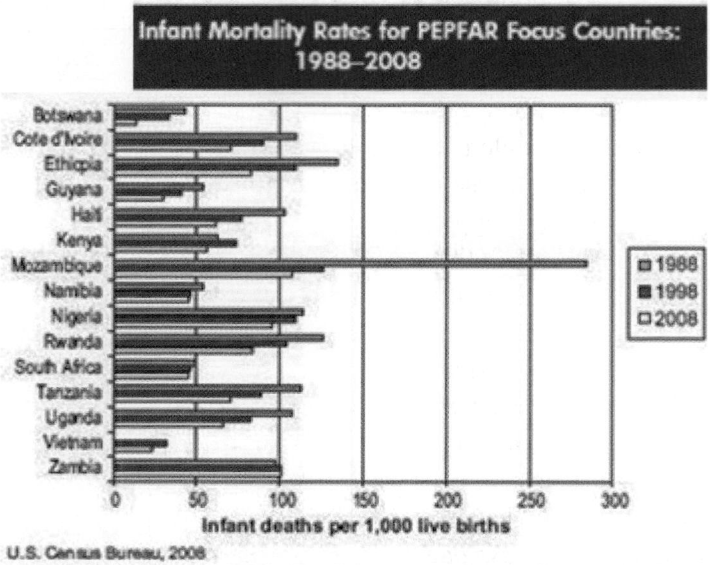

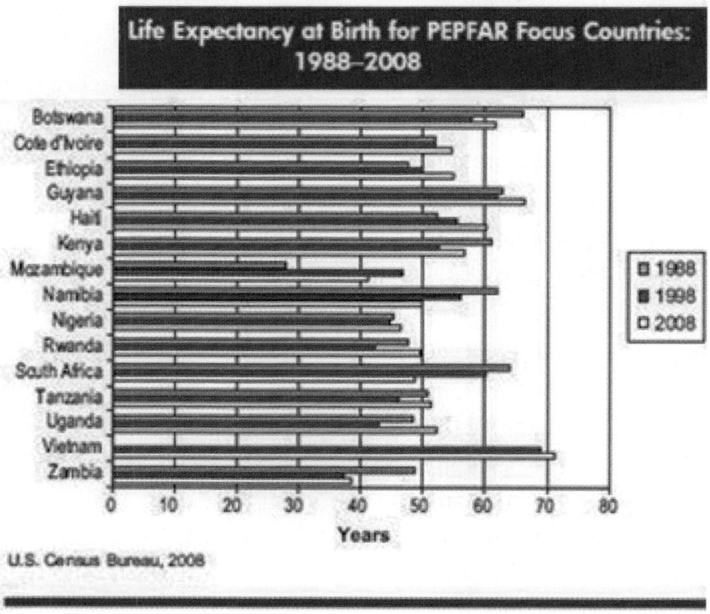

Differing rates of success in PMTCT coverage show how scale-up varied among the focus countries (Table 6). Individual country studies, such as in Rwanda, also show improvements in general health services (Price *et al.* 2009), but the effects seem to differ by country (Biesma *et al.* 2009).

Some progress has been made in preventing new HIV infections (UNAIDS 2008, Chapter 2), but prevention lags behind care and treatment successes, a problem that must be addressed given the resource constraints. Despite internationally shipping 2.2 billion condoms during the first five years and support of national programmes to prevent sexual transmission (PEPFAR 2009e, p. 8), reductions in the incidence of HIV varies by countries and within countries. However,the UNAIDS Report on the Global AIDS Epidemic estimates that by 2007 most national epidemics in sub-Saharan Africa have declining or stabilised prevalence rates (UNAIDS 2008). A recent evaluation showed an impact of PEPFAR on declining incidence in certain focus countries compared to controls (Montaner *et al.* 2010).

Findings of the Institute of Medicine's (IOM) 2007 *PEPFAR Implementation: Progress and Promise*,a report of the multiyear evaluation of PEPFAR's bilateral activities, confirm the successes of international HIV/AIDS efforts supported by PEPFAR, but they also point to the need for continuous learning and change. The report states that increased use of impact measures, such as HIV incidence, to track progress, especially in prevention should be developed. The IOM Study Committee, who authored this report, also called for more transparency of PEPFAR funding plans in country and dissemination of best practices, results and programme evaluations, especially in prevention (IOM 2007).

8. Future Directions — An Evolving Partnership

PEPFAR should be viewed during the first five years of its existence both as an emergency response and as an experiment in the implementation of a USG interagency global health intervention. The basis for innovation is country leadership, results-driven programming and partnerships (Dybul 2009). The international results that PEPFAR contributed to support the US government's leadership role in international AIDS. When calling for re-authorisation of PEPFAR in May 2007, President Bush highlighted the

Table 6. Prevention: Prevention of mother-to-child transmission program[1] with USG support in FY2006-FY2008.

	Estimated coverage of pregnant women receiving HIV counseling and testing								
	Percent Coverage								
Country	**# Pregnant women receiving HIVCT for PMTCT and received test results (FY2006)**	**# Births (2006)**	**# Pregnant women receiving HIVCT for PMTCT and received test results (FY2007)**	**# Births (2007)**	**FY2006**	**FY2007**	**Women**	**# Births (2008)**	**FY2008**
Botswana[2]	43,800	46,000	38,777	42,065	95%	92%	38,849	45,268	86%
Cote d'Ivoi	60,600	661,000	80,832	624,885	9%	13%	154,317	660,478	23%
Ethiopia	47,600	3,064,000	111,513	2,860,779	2%	4%	214,160	3,629,497	6%
Guyana	11,000	16,000	11,367	13,913	69%	82%	12,039	13,759	87%
Haiti	75,200	253,000	106,477	312,302	30%	34%	138,880	261,796	53%
Kenya	549,500	1,322,000	785,840	1,437,420	42%	55%	988,798	1,438,071	69%
Mozambiqu	132,100	769,000	223,591	805,701	17%	28%	453,822	813,288	56%
Namibia	31,900	56,000	36,458	48,335	57%	75%	36,984	48,436	76%
Nigeria	125,800	5,323,000	226,415	5,428,253	2%	4%	637,330	5,445,085	12%
Rwanda	222,000	365,000	243,637	397,886	61%	61%	239,583	407,137	59%
South Africa	563,300	1,093,000	626,863	789,321	52%	79%	834,396	986,875	85%
Tanzania	366,500	1,403,000	535,849	1,415,863	26%	38%	746,993	1,412,286	53%
Uganda	300,000	1,412,000	565,170	1,456,237	21%	39%	830,023	1,510,368	55%
Vietnam	130,600	468,000	159,582	1,417,913	28%	11%	247,202	1,418,340	17%
Zambia	154,800	1,644,000	259,532	468,050	9%	55%	276,738	472,850	59%

Source: Fifth Annual Report to Congress on PEPFAR, 2009.

themes that animated the second half of PEPFAR's initial phase and carried into its current philosophy greater country ownership, an enhanced effort to move from an era of "paternalism" to an "era of partnership in development" and connecting the dots of development for a more integrated approach to the delivery of health services through Partnership Compacts. This same results-driven strategy was reinforced in the 2008 reauthorisation through new five-year HIV/AIDS treatment, care and prevention goals.

President Obama's Global Health Initiative has provided a larger health context for PEPFAR, building on past efforts to create a more coordinated and sustained USG involvement in international health (Obama 2009). This approach still emphasises the interagency PEPFAR model, bringing together historically vertical efforts in HIV/AIDS, TB, malaria, maternal and child health, reproductive health and neglected tropical diseases. Among the goals of this initiative are to advance women-focused health, country ownership, sustainability of health and related support systems and multilateral engagement.

Appointed in June 2009, the new US Global AIDS Coordinator, Ambassador Goosby, brings to PEPFAR an emphasis on high impact interventions and of engaging even more with partner countries to build local capacity to support and expand their health systems (PEPFAR 2009f). His focus is to ensure long-term, enduring local stewardship and control of health systems, not to grow USG or non-indigenous programmes in these countries. There is an increased emphasis on having bilateral activities support multilateral efforts, particularly those of The Global Fund. This direction is consistent with the goals of the partnership compacts envisioned by President Bush, but it is more ambitious in the pace of aligning with country capacity. The current Partnership Frameworks with national governments are viewed as the method for developing integrated strategies and country ownership.

The shift towards country ownership and sustainability begun by the Bush Administration and expanded by President Obama is resulting in new accountability and measurement for tracking global health results that include integration, country ownership and sustainability. Both US government country planning and results reporting are to be fully integrated with national systems and progress is to be measured within this national context. The next-generation indicators should be viewed as the beginning of this process of measurement by the US and its international partners. PEPFAR and The Global Fund also are expanding evaluation and research agendas to strengthen the understanding of programming effectiveness and efficiencies.

Successful coordination and partnerships in health, not just in HIV, TB and Malaria, will not be a simple task. As the types of partners and partner goals broaden and become dissimilar, the ability to successfully collaborate may be threatened. Placing HIV services within global health care has to be done without losing accountability for HIV services or reducing results. President Obama's statement calling for a Global Health Initiative recognises the HIV work begun under President Bush as a key building block for the next phase of US engagement in global health. It recognises that PEPFAR must evolve to meet the changing international needs. The Global Health Initiative builds upon the results-driven partnership begun by PEPFAR, setting numerical targets for US assistance in 80 countries to support HIV prevention and HIV and TB treatment, reductions in child and maternal mortality and child undernutrition, reducing the prevalence of malaria and NTDs and preventing unintended pregnancies. (Retrieved from http://www.ghi.gov/documents/organization/15789.pdf). The emphasis on achieving these targets through partnerships continues.

Chapters 14 and 16 provide country examples which include PEPFAR and issues of their integration into country plans. Chapter 5 looks further at the challenges of health systems.

Acknowledgements

Thanks to the PEPFAR community, particularly the US government staff and their partners who have made PEPFAR a success.

References

Africa Renewal (2005) *Global AIDS Treatment Drive Takes Off*. Available at: http://www.un.org/ecosocdev/geninfo/afrec/vol19no1/191aids.htm [Accessed 20 January 2010].

Biesma RG, Brugha R, Harmer A, Walsh A, Spicer N, Walt G (July 2009) "The Effects of Global Health Initiatives on Country Health Systems: A Review of the Evidence from HIV/AIDS Control," *Health Policy and Planning* 24(4):239–52.

Bush G (2003) *State of the Union Speech.* Available at: http://georgewbush-whitehouse.archives.gov/news/releases/2003/01/20030128-19.html [Accessed 20 January 2010].

Bush G (2007) *Fact Sheet: President Bush Announces Five-Year, $30 Billion HIV/AIDS Plan.* Available at: http://georgewbush-whitehouse.archives.gov/news/releases/2007/05/20070530-5.html [Accessed 4 March 2010].

CDC, Global AIDS Program (2004) *Annual Report Template FY2004 and Country Assistance Plan FY2004.* Available at: http://74.125.113.132/search?q=ache:5zB4sj_Mce8J:www.globalhivmeinfo.org/DigitalLibrary/Digital%2520Library/Country%2520Assistance%2520Plan%2520Template.doc+www.cdc.gol-bal+aids+program+2004+reporting&cd=3&hl=en&ct=clnk&gl=us [Accessed 20 January 2009].

CDC, Global AIDS Program (2009) *Costing Study Helps Ensure Sustainability of Global HIV Care and Treatment Programs.* Available at: http://www.cdc.gov/washington/EGlobalHealthEditions/eGlobalHealth3rd0909.htm#four.

Dybul M (November 2009) "Lessons learned from PEPFAR," *Journal of Acquired Immune Deficiency Syndromes* 52(1):S12–S13.

The End of the Beginning? (Anonymous, 17 July 2004) *Economist* 272(8384): 76–7.

Govtrack.us, 2004. 2003–2004 *HR198.* Available at: http://www.govtrack.us/congress/bill.xpd?bill=h108-1298 [Accessed 20 January 2010].

Institute of Medicine (IOM) (2007) *PEPFAR Implementation: Progress, and Promise* (30 March 2007). Available at: http://www.iom.edu/Reports/2007/PEPFAR-Implementation-Progress-and-Promise.aspx [Accessed 20 January 2010].

Lasker R, Weiss ES, Miller R (2001) "Partnership Synergy: A Practical Framework for Studying and Strengthening the Collaborative Advantage," *The Milbank Quarterly* 79(2):179–204.

Montaner JSG, Lima BD, Williams BG (2010) 19 January. "Evaluating Outcomes of the President's Emergency Plan for AIDS Relief in Africa," *Annals of Internal Medicine* 152:131–2.

Millennium Challenge Corporation (2010) Available at: http://www.mcc.gov/ [Accessed 20 January 2010].

Obama B (2009) *Statement by the President on Global Health Initiative.* 5 May 2009. Available at: http://www.whitehouse.gov/the_press_office/Statement-by-the-President-on-Global-Health-Initiative [Accessed 20 January 2010].

PEPFAR (2004) *Indicators, Reporting Requirements, and Guidelines* [Guidance issued 6 April 2004].

PEPFAR (2005a) *U.S. International Mother and Child HIV Prevention Initiative*. Available at: http://www.pepfar.gov/progress/76906.htm [Accessed 10 October 2009].

PEPFAR (2005b) *Engendering Bold Leadership: The President's Emergency Plan for AIDS Relief First Annual Report to Congress.* Available at: http://www.pepfar.gov/press/c19573.htm [Accessed 20 January 2010].

PEPFAR (2006) *Action Today, a Foundation for Tomorrow, the Second Annual Report to Congress on PEPFAR*. Available at: http://www.pepfar.gov/press/c19573.htm [Accessed 20 January 2010].

PEPFAR (2007) *The Power of Partnerships, The Third Annual Report to Congress*. Available at: http://www.pepfar.gov/press/c19573.htm [Accessed 20 January 2010].

PEPFAR (2008) *Summary Financial Status as of December 31, 2008* (1st Quarter, FY 2009) http://www.pepfar.gov/documents/organization/123761.pdf [Accessed 20 January 2009].

PEPFAR (2009a) *Support for the Global Fund.* Available at: http://www.pepfar.gov/coop/c18962.htm [Accessed 20 January 2010].

PEPFAR (2009b) *PEPFAR Partnership Framework Guidance.*Available at: http://www.pepfar.gov/documents/organization/120510.pdf [Accessed 26 October 2009].

PEPFAR (2009c) *Partnership to Fight HIV/AIDS in Rwanda*. Available at: http://www.pepfar.gov/countries/rwanda/ [Accessed 20 January 2010].

PEPFAR (2009d) *Update on Public Health Evaluations*. Available at: http://www.pepfar.gov/guidance/107686.htm [Accessed 20 January 2010].

PEPFAR (2009e) *Celebrating Life: Fifth Annual Report to Congress on PEPFAR (2009).* Available at: http://www.pepfar.gov/press/c19573.htm [Accessed 20 January 2010].

PEPFAR (2009f) *The US President's Emergency Plan for AIDS Relief Five Year Strategy* (December 2009). Available at: http://www.pepfar.gov/strategy/document/index.htm [Accessed 20 January 2010].

PEPFAR (2009g) *Next Generation Indicators Reference Guide.*August, 2009. Available at: http://www.pepfar.gov/documents/organization/81097.pdf [Accessed 20 January 2010].

Price JE, Leslie JA, Welsh M, *et al.* (2009) "Integrating HIV Clinical Services into Primary Health Care in Rwanda: A Measure of Quantitative Effects," *AIDS Care* 21:608–14.

Rusa L, Schneidman M, Fritsche G, Musango L (2009) *Rwanda: Performance Based Financing in the Public Sector.* Center for Global Development. Available at: http://www.cgdev.org/doc/books/PBI/10_CGD_Eichler_Levine-Ch10.pdf [Accessed 20 January 2010].

Tavrow P (2005) "Bush Administration's Global HIV/AIDS Policies are Undermining Fight Against Pandemic," *Baltimore Sun* 18 October 2005, p. 15A.

Timberg C (2005) "Botswana's Claims Against AIDS Put U.S. Claims to Test," *Washington Post* 1 July 2005. Available at: http://www.washingtonpost.com/wp-dyn/content/article/2005/06/30/AR2005063002158.html [Accessed 20 January 2010].

Tobias R (2004) *Threshold Measures*. [Note] (Personal communication 2004).

The Tom Lantos and Henry J. Hyde United States Global Leadership Against HIV, Tuberculosis, and Malaria Act of 2008 (Tom Lantos and Henry Hyde Global Leadership Act). Pub.L. 110–293 (30 July 2008). Available at: http://www.gov-track.us/congress/billtext.xpd?bill=h110-5501 [Accessed 20 January 2010].

UNAIDS (2001) *2001 Declaration of Commitment on HIV/AIDS.* Available at: http://www.unaids.org/en/AboutUNAIDS/Goals/UNGASS/ [Accessed 20 January 2010].

UNAIDS 2004.*Overcoming AIDS: The 'Next Agenda,' 2004 Report on the Global AIDS Epidemic.* Available at: http://www.unaids.org/bangkok2004/GAR2004_pdf/UNAIDSGlobalReport2004_en.pdf [Accessed 20 January 2010].

UNAIDS (2008) *2008 Report on the Global AIDS Epidemic.* Available at: http://www.unaids.org/en/KnowledgeCentre/HIVData/GlobalReport/2008/2008_Global_report.asp [Accessed 20 January 2010].

UNAIDS (2009a) *New HIV Indicator Registry Improves Access to High Quality Indicators*. Available at: http://www.unaids.org/en/KnowledgeCentre/Resources/FeatureStories/archive/2009/20090313_Propertyright_UNDP.asp [Accessed 20 January 2010].

UNAIDS (2009b) *Guide to Produce National AIDS Spending Accounts (NASA).* Available at: http://data.unaids.org/pub/BaseDocument/2009/20090406_nasa_notebook_en.pdf [Accessed 20 January 20010].

UNDP (2006) *Millennium Development Goals*. Available at: http://www.undp.org/mdg/ [Accessed 20 January 2010].

USAID, UNAIDS, WHO, UNICEF, & The Policy Project (2004) *Coverage of Selected Services for HIV/AIDS Prevention, Care and Support in Low and Middle Income Countries in 2003*. Washington, DC: Policy Project.

USAID (2004)*FY 2004 Performance and Accountability Report*. Accessed at: http://www.usaid.gov/policy/par04/performance.pdf [Accessed 20 January 20=10].

USAID (2005) *Audit of USAID/Uganda's Implementation of the President's Emergency Plan for AIDS Relief 4-617-05-006-P*. 1 August 2005. Available at: http://www.usaid.gov/oig/public/fy05rpts/4-617-05-006-p.pdf [Accessed 20 January 2010].

USAID (2006) *Audit of USAID/Nigeria's Progress in Implementing the President's Emergency Plan for AIDS Relief* 7-620-06-004-P. 31 August 2006. Available at: http://www.usaid.gov/oig/public/fy06rpts/7-620-06-004-p.pdf [Accessed 20 January, 2010].

USAID (2009a) *USAID History*. Available at: http://www.usaid.gov/about_usaid/usaidhist.html [Accessed 10 October 2009].

USAID (2009b).*The President's Malaria Initiative*. Available at: http://www/.fightingmalaria.gov/index.html [Accessed 20 January 2010].

The United States Leadership Against Global HIV/AIDS, Tuberculosis and Malaria Act of 2003 (The US Leadership Act) P.L. 108-25 (27 May 2003). Available at: http://frwebgate.access.gpo.gov/cgi-in/getdoc.cgi?dbname=108_cong_public_laws&docid=f:publ025.108.pdf [Accessed 20 January 2010].

World Health Organisation (WHO) (2009) *National Health Accounts (NHA)*. Available at: http://www.who.int/nha/en/ [Accessed 20 January 2010].

11

Private Foundations: Their Role in Financing and Health Governance

Nina Ingenkamp and Daniel Low-Beer

Summary

Private foundations have been active beyond the borders of their nation-state since the beginning of the nineteenth century. Institutions such as the Rockefeller and the Ford Foundation are older than the United Nations. Private foundations have had a growing influence in terms of financing. They can also use finance flexibly and innovatively to catalyse health governance changes. This role has included support in the early days of the WHO, and a key role in creating global programmes such as GAVI and the Global Fund to Fight AIDS, Tuberculosis and Malaria. Most recently, the Gates Foundation's large volume of financing has significantly increased private foundations' influence in global health. However, their role in global governance has not always kept pace with their increasing involvement in health.

The overall aim of this chapter is to outline the contribution private foundations' have made to global health since the beginning of the century. The chapter starts by defining private foundations and outlines their financial contribution. It then describes some key foundations in more detail, classic foundations, recent twenty-first-century foundations, and emerging foundations such as the Carlos Slim Foundation from Mexico. The chapter then takes a broader perspective on private foundations and presents their positive and negative aspects, discussing in which ways private foundations have brought added value and innovation to global health.

Introduction

'Is the rich world aware of how four billion of the six billion live? If we were aware, we would want to help out, we would want to get involved.' (*Bill Gates*)[1]

'Helping people in need may not be an unsound financial strategy.' (*Melinda Gates*)[2]

Global public health today would look much different without private foundations. WHO programmes, such as polio eradication would probably be underfunded, fewer people would have hope of a malaria vaccine and new technologies. Similarly, health governance would be different. The early disease programmes of the WHO may not have obtained support, important initiatives such as the GAVI or the Global Fund to Fight AIDS, Tuberculosis and Malaria might not exist. New foundations continue to emerge, with the increasing role of the Gates Foundations since the 1990s and of the Carlos Slim Foundation more recently. Although their overall financing is still modest compared to other sources, private foundations have been key sources of innovation, since the early 20th century.

While private foundations, particularly those based in the United States, are quite widely researched in general,[3] there has been little systematic assessment about private foundations' involvement in

[1] http://news.bbc.co.uk/2/hi/business/4524046.stm.

[2] http://seattletimes.nwsource.com/html/localnews/2003687791_webmgates30.html.

[3] See for instance Fleischmann 2007, Berndtson 2007 (book review), Vogel 2006 and Nielson 1985.

global health and international development.[4] This chapter analyses private foundations' contribution to global health, their catalytic role, strengths and weaknesses, drawing on case studies of different foundations.

1. An Overview of Private Foundations

Private foundations are a diverse group of organisations. Given the sheer numbers of private foundations, this diversity is not surprising. U.S. registered private foundations have increased from 50 000 in the year 2000 to 67 000 in 2007 (Foundation Centre 2008a). The European Foundation Centre listed some 95 000 public-benefit foundations in 2007 (European Foundation Centre 2008).

An often cited definition of a private foundation has been established by the U.S. foundation centre (Text Box 1).[5] We will use this definition throughout the chapter as the world of global philanthropy has been strongly shaped by U.S. foundations. Two important aspects can be read from it: a foundation is principally a grant-making and not an implementing entity; and grants are awarded for charitable purposes and not for activities that help to accumulate private wealth. Two additional aspects are that private foundations are somewhat hybrids between the public and

Text Box 1: Foundations' Definition

'*A foundation is an entity that is established as a non-profit corporation or a charitable trust underlaw, with a principal purpose of making grants to unrelated organizations or institutions or to individuals for scientific, educational, cultural, religious or other charitable purposes*' (http://foundationcenter.org/getstarted/faqs/html/foundfun.html). Furthermore, a foundation is usually governed by a board and by-laws.

---

[4] See literature list for references of preceding statements.

[5] In the United States, the term 'foundation' is not a legal term.http://foundationcenter.org/getstarted/faqs/html/foundfun.html.

the private sectors: They are private entities engaged in reaching public goals. Moreover, private foundations are, as the name already implies, private institutions. They enjoy great freedom to award grants as they see fit with very limited public reporting requirements or accountability.[6]

Within the group of foundations', a distinction needs to be made between private foundations and grant-making public charities. Private foundations usually have their own source of funding, a family, an individual or a corporation. A grant-making public charity, sometimes called a public or a community foundation, does not have funding of its own. They receive funding from other sources such as the public sector. This chapter focuses on private foundations that derive their money from a family or an individual. Foundations that derive their funds from corporations, companies and public charities are not covered.

The history of private foundations. The first private foundations as we know them were founded at the beginning of the nineteenth century. Historically, foundations have been mirrors of the time they were established in. Their source of wealth reflects what business one could make money, or better millions, at the time (Nielsen 1985, p. 11): The foundations of the early nineteenth century were based on oil (such as the Rockefeller) coal or steel. At the beginning of the twentieth century, wealth was derived from the mass production of cars (Ford), tobacco, cornflakes (Kellogg's) and chain stores, followed by pharmaceutical, construction (Kaiser), real estate and mass media. In the twenty-first century, wealth shifted from manufacturing to areas of computer electronics (Gates), investment banking (Soros) and telecommunications (Slim). Most recently, celebrities have also started engaging in philanthropy (Wyclef Jean), and the geographic sources have increased, for example the Carlos Slim Foundation from Mexico.

The reasons for establishing a private foundation. There are many different reasons for why the wealthy would decide to establish a foundation. In fact, the motives for establishing foundations are as individual as their founders and have changed over the years. The decision for the early foundations of the nineteenth century was often taken near the deathbed

[6] See the discussion part for more detailed information on their transparency and accountability.

(Nielsen 1985, p. 15). This pattern has changed. For people such as Bill Gates, Carlos Slim or George Soros that have achieved everything and more in the business world, establishing a foundation is more of a second-career option to use their skills for public benefit (Fleischmann 2007, p. 40). Today's foundations are, therefore, bringing the skills of their founders to issues they feel strongly about. There are also financial incentives for establishing a foundation. In the United States, for example, private foundations are exempt from taxes if these organisations meet certain requirements. In countries where the state plays a greater role and does not provide similar tax benefits, such as in Northern Europe, the role of private foundations is less prominent.[7]

2. Private Foundations in Global Health

'So the question is Can the relatively small contributions of foundations make a difference? I think the answer is yes. If funders have a vision, pick their niche carefully by looking for gaps, and if they are comfortable taking on some hard or risky projects, they can make a big difference.' (Interview with Elaine Gallin, Program Director for Medical Research at the Doris Duke Charitable Foundation in J Investig Med. 2005 Sep;53(6):275–278).

Private foundations are international actors. Private foundations have been active beyond the borders of their nation-state since the beginning of the nineteenth century. Institutions such as the Rockefeller and the Ford Foundation are older than the United Nations. With the growing recognition that additional sources of finance to public funds are needed, their importance has been growing. The private sector, including private foundations, holds great potential for bringing additional money to the table. Therefore, how can private foundations be positioned within the international aid architecture and what is their financial contribution?

Private-sector contribution to international development. Development funding from the private sector is gradually becoming more significant (OECD 2010, Murray 2009, Marten and Witte 2008). One reason is the current global recession which affects funding from donor governments, though will also affect private sources. During the preceding

[7] http://foundationcenter.org/getstarted/faqs/html/np_pro_con.html.

Table 1. OECD estimates of non-governmental aid flows in 2007 (OECD 2010).

1	Annual Foundations giving for development:	US$5 billion
	— US Foundations (international grants)	*US$3 billion*
	— European Foundations (international grants)	*US$600 million*
	— Asian Foundations (include local activities)	*US$400 million*
2	Private flows at market terms[8]	US$312 billion
3	Official Overseas Development Assistance[9]	US$103 billion

period of rapid economic growth from 1980 to 2000, considerable private endowments had been created. While some of these rely on stock market valuations, they present a major source of funding available over the coming years. In addition, the scale of private flows of funding (which are greater than public sources of aid) are also increasingly recognised. Table 1 gives the Organisation for Economic Co-operation and Developments (OECD) estimates for non-governmental aid flows for the year 2007, highlighting the figures for foundations.

According to the OECD, figures on private aid flows are not readily available because of their diversity, lack of commonly agreed definitions and mechanisms for capturing data. Most likely, the figures for voluntary agencies, private flows and official development assistance through non-governmental organisations (NGOs) are under-reported. Despite their inaccuracy, these estimates show that non-government aid flows are significant resources. Foundations are estimated to have provided US$5 billion in 2007, of which the majority is from U.S. foundations. While foundations' share of aid flows is growing, their total contribution of US$5 billion in 2007 was still limited compared to private flows at market terms or the estimated US$103 billion official Overseas Development

[8] Private flows consist of flows at market terms financed out of private sector resources (i.e. changes in holdings of private long-term assets held by residents of the reporting country) and private grants (*i.e.* grants by **non-governmental organisations** and other private bodies, net of subsidies received from the official sector) (see OECD 2010a, p. 274).

[9] Official Development Assistance (ODA) is defined as grants or loans to countries and territories on the DAC List of ODA. Recipients and multilateral agencies that are undertaken by the official sector at concessional terms (i.e. with a grant element of at least 25%) and that have the promotion of the economic development and welfare of developing countries as their main objective. In addition to financial flows, technical co-operation is included in aid. Grants, loans and credits for military purposes are excluded (OECD 2010a, p. 273).

Assistance. For the future, they provide a significant untapped potential for international development. In the United States, the total assets of foundations are estimated at US$950 billion with US$30 billion of annual grant giving. However, only approximately 10% of their grants support international activities (World Bank 2007).

Private foundations contribute roughly 10% to global health. Total development assistance for health was estimated at US$21.8 billion for the year 2007 (Murray 2009). This estimate includes funds of public and private origin. For the same year, the U.S. Foundation Center estimates that U.S. private foundations contributed roughly US$2 billion to global health, implying that their share would be 9–10%. The Bill & Melinda Gates Foundation alone contributed 3.9% of the US$21.8 billion in the same year, thereby exerting influence on other private foundations' orientation towards global health.

In 2008, aid provided for global health by private U.S. foundations amounted to roughly US$2.4 billion (Table 2). The Gates Foundation tops the list by accounting for more than half of the total. Overall, in the area of global health, family foundations are clearly bigger donors than the corporate sector in the United States; the first corporate foundation was seventh largest (ExxonMobil).

Private foundations' recipients. Grants to developing countries seem to be the exception: 84 countries have received roughly US$732 million

Table 2. Top 10 U.S. foundations awarding international grants for health, 2008.

Foundations	**US$ millions**
1. Bill & Melinda Gates Foundation	1,985
2. The Susan Thompson Buffett Foundation	168
3. The Ford Foundation	63
4. William and Flora Hewlett Foundation	38
5. David and Lucile Packard Foundation	36
6. Rockefeller Foundation	23
7. ExxonMobil Foundation	18
8. John D. and Catherine T. MacArthur Foundation	14
9. Abbott Fund	13
10. Bristol-Myers Squibb Foundation	12
Total for the top 10 foundations	***2.4 billion***

Source: Foundation Centre (2008).

in 2008. The three countries that received the most funding were India (104 grants worth US$165 million), Viet Nam (26 grants worth US$88 million) and Bangladesh (6 grants worth US$77 million). On average, grants awarded directly to countries had a size of US$8.7 million (high-middle income countries excluded). The rest of the funding was awarded to develop countries without specifying a location and to global programmes such as GAVI or the Global Fund (U.S. Foundation Center).

Critical innovations private foundations have brought to public health. Private foundations' financial contributions to development are of growing significance and with a focus on health. However, they also make important additional contributions. They have helped to foster innovations in research and development, introduced innovative ways of management and innovated in global health governance through their direct influence and the creation of other important actors. Examples of these innovations as well as the challenges will be given in the following sections.

3. The Value Added by Private Foundations

'Foundations are not only free to take risks; they are expected to do so'
(Bell 1971, p. 472)

This section looks at private foundations in more detail: the way they have made a difference, how their role depends on the context they work in and their specific strengths and challenges. We aim to bring out the differences between private foundations, while giving examples for the innovations they brought to the health sector. Three foundations are portrayed in case studies, selected because they represent the following distinct groups of private foundations[10]:

1. The classic foundations such as the Rockefeller Foundation or the Ford Foundation;
2. The twenty-first-century foundations such as the Soros Foundation or the Bill & Melinda Gates Foundation and

[10] This classification focuses on portraying today's three most important groups of private foundations. It has the disadvantage that there is a certain time gap between the Rockefeller Foundation and the Gates Foundation. Other important foundations that were established in the meantime are, for instance, the MacArthur Foundation, Kaiser Family Foundation or the Hewlett Foundation.

3. The emerging foundations such as the Carlos Slim Foundation and the Carlos Slim Health Institute.

4. Tradition and Innovation: The Rockefeller Foundation

Ford, Rockefeller and Carnegie are amongst the oldest American foundations and are generally referred to as the prototypes for U.S. private foundations (Nielsen 1985)[11] or the Big Three (Arnove 2007). The Rockefeller Foundation is portrayed here in more detail, as it has made important contributions to global public health long before the advent of the World Health Organization. Typically, the Rockefeller Foundation is described as the embodiment of the modern, scientific approach to philanthropy: attacking root causes rather than alleviating symptoms, advancing basic knowledge, training leaders, and creating needed new scientific and educational institutions (Nielsen 1985, p. 83). It has to be noted, however, that the Ford Foundation's spending for health is currently greater than that of the Rockefeller Foundation (Table 3), related to the fact that the Ford Foundation is still the third largest U.S. Foundation.[12] Carnegie does not focus on health.

> '...few can equal the prestige and goodwill it (the Rockefeller Foundation) has garnered by funding the most eminent scientists and institutions in medicine, public health, biogenetic, agricultural research, reproductive technologies and environmental studies.' (Arnove 2007, p. 404)

The Rockefellers' philanthropic interest. Founded around 1913 by John D. Rockefeller and John D. Rockefeller, Jr., the Rockefeller Foundation's wealth is based on the profit generated by the Standard Oil Company. The foundation has been strongly involved in public health since its beginning. Health was declared a priority at the first meeting of the board on 22 May 1913, when Frederick Gates, longtime advisor to

---

[11] Nielsen only sees Ford and Rockefeller as the prototypes and lists Carnegie under liberal activists (Nielsen 1985).

[12] In addition, the Ford Foundation has a somewhat different approach to health than the Rockefeller Foundation. It is not a separate programme area, but mainstreamed across to promote empowerment, democracy and equity. However, it should be noted that they fund a special Global HIV/AIDS initiative. For more information on the Ford Foundation, see Bell 1971, Arnove 2007 and Nielsen 1985.

John D. Rockefeller, Sr., argued that *'disease is the supreme ill in human life.'* (http://www.rockefellerfoundation.org/who-we-are/our-history/1913–1919). Shortly, thereafter, in June 1913, the foundation created the International Health Commission (later called Board), which was responsible for the Foundation's international public health services.

The Rockefeller Foundation acquired worldwide prestige by the end of the 1920s, which was around the same time as separate philanthropic institutions, such as the Rockefeller Sanitation Commission, were folded into the foundation. In its early years, the Rockefeller Foundation focused on fighting three diseases: hookworm, malaria and yellow fever (Text Box 2). These quite successful programmes may have been amongst the earliest international vertical health initiatives, long before the advent of Global Programs. Rockefeller took a distinct approach with these initiatives. The foundation focused on controlling one disease at a time, using science as the basis together with a strong focus on results. This approach itself may have been one of the major innovations that Rockefeller has brought to the health sector, at a time when state-supported global public health was very limited or did not exist.

Text Box 2: The Rockefeller Foundation's early successes (builds on Stapleton, p. 206ff and Nielsen 1985)

- Hookworm: National campaign in 1909, followed by an international campaign in 1913. Programmes in 62 countries on every continent. Managed to eradicate hookworm in the Southern States of the United States.
- Yellow fever: Campaign in 1915 in Latin America and Africa. Supported research to develop a vaccine. Eventually successfully developed by the South African microbiologist Max Theiler at the Rockefeller Institute in the 1930s.
- Malaria: Started around the same time as the yellow fever campaign. Gained more importance after 1920s. Big worldwide campaign to control malaria, building on wide-spread use of DDT in Latin America and other places. Faced with criticism that malaria interventions would take place in locations where Rockefeller-related companies had strategic interests (Agueldo 1983).

The Rockefeller Foundation's more recent initiatives. Today, the Rockefeller Foundation has five main issue areas, of which global health is one. The other four are: basic survival safeguards, climate and environment, urbanisation, social and economic security (Rockefeller Foundation website). In 2008, the Rockefeller Foundation ranked sixth in international giving for global health with US$23 million awarded to 81 grants. No information could be found on the share of global health in their total portfolio.

The objective of their global health programme is to create *'accessible, affordable and equitable health services and systems'*, with a clear focus on technology, infectious diseases and involvement of the private sector.[13] Another important area of their work has been sexually transmitted diseases including HIV/AIDS, where the Rockefeller Foundation has provided catalytic funding to new initiatives, of which some examples are provided below:

- Around 1990, Rockefeller united a number of major donor agencies and international organisations to form the **International HIV/AIDS Alliance.** The International HIV/AIDS Alliance was established in 1993 and their original goal was to transfer more funds from donors to developing countries' non-governmental organisations for HIV/AIDS prevention and care (Arnove 2007, 407ff). The Alliance has become a focus for the development of the HIV/AIDS NGO movement internationally.
- In addition, around 1990, Rockefeller convened a meeting of HIV/AIDS experts at the Bellagio Center in Italy to discuss how to progress in finding an AIDS vaccine. Out of these efforts emerged the **International AIDS Vaccine Initiative (IAVI)** in 1996 as well as partnerships to develop and manufacture safe, effective, affordable treatments for HIV/AIDS and other tropical diseases. Today, the initiative is funded by

[13] The Rockefeller Foundation has supported research to improve crops such as rice, wheat, sorghum and maize. These efforts to improve food security were carried out in collaboration with the Ford Foundation (Arnove 2007, p. 406 and Fleischmann 2007, p. 115ff).

major donor agencies as well as corporate and private foundations, including the Rockefeller Foundation (Rockefeller and IAVI website).

- Since 2002, the Rockefeller Foundation supports, among other foundations, the **MTCT (Mother to Child Transmission) Plus Initiative**. This initiative by Columbia University transformed the conventional approach to prevention of mother to child transmission (PMTCT) by linking PMTCT with comprehensive programmes focused on the health of mothers and their families (ICAP and Rockefeller website).

In addition to disease-specific interventions, Rockefeller has also influenced global health governance. For instance, in 1998, the Rockefeller Foundation awarded a US$2.5 million grant to WHO for a Global Health Leadership Fund to be spent over two years (Arnove *et al.* 2007, p. 409 and Press Release WHO/56). At this time, WHO's executive director was Gro Harlem Brundtlandt. One of her major undertakings was a management reform of the organisation.[14] The Global Health Leadership Fund was meant to support the reform process. The Fund gave Brundtlandt the financial freedom to recruit top level experts from a variety of fields to serve during a two-year transition period to infuse the organisation with fresh approaches to global health challenges (1998). No information could be obtained about the success or failure of the Global Health Leadership Fund. However, these catalytic activities supported significant period of change and a key shift in WHO's orientation to health and development.

In conclusion, the Rockefeller Foundation is a good example of a scientifically inspired foundation that has early on declared health as one of their priorities. Furthermore, through its scientifically targeted approach, it has managed to achieve important results in the first half of the century. In addition, as shown in the examples listed above, the foundation has also taken a catalytic role in health governance, starting and supporting new initiatives in global health.

[14] On the management reform, see for instance Lerer and Matzopoulos 2001 and Yamey 2003.

5. The Twenty-First-Century Foundations: Private Thinking for Public Goals

This section looks at the newer foundations that have emerged at the end of the twentieth century. Rather than carrying the legacy of the past founders, modern day foundations are personified by their founders that are actively involved in the management. The Soros' and Gates' foundations are two examples.

Open Society Institute. Investment banker George Soros' Open Society Institute was founded in 1994. It serves as a hub of the Soros network of foundations, which is comprised of 33 distinct private foundations, operating in more than 60 countries around the world. (Fleischmann 2007, p. 134). The Open Society Institute is somewhat different to other foundations portrayed in this chapter. Although it is an American-based foundation, OSI has many close ties to Europe. Soros itself was born in Hungary and Eastern Europe was the primary region in which the foundation intervened. Furthermore, the Open Society Institute represents a foundation whose *raison d'être* is politically inspired. Soros was strongly influenced by Austrian-British philosopher Karl Popper's concept of the open society. Its mission is to build vibrant and tolerant democracies whose governments are accountable to their citizens. This approach has extended to health, which is seen as one factor within the overall objective of establishing a pluralistic and empowered open society. In this sense, for Soros, health is a means to a wider goal. Although the Open Society Institute has supported many important public health interventions in Eastern Europe such as needle-exchange programmes for drug users, it is not covered here in more detail because the Gates' Foundation has comparatively more engagement in global health.

> 'Although there is a long history of private philanthropic funding in global health — notably by the Rockefeller Foundation and the Ford Foundation — the influence of the Gates Foundation is of a different order' (McCoy *et al.* 2009, p. 1645).

Rockefeller 2.0. Bill Gates, owner of Microsoft, has been engaged in philanthropy through the William H. Gates Foundation since 1994. He established the Bill & Melinda Gates Foundation together with his wife in the year 2000. At the end of 2009, Bill Gates retired from his business to fully devote himself to the foundation. Interestingly, the Gates Foundation has important similarities with the Rockefeller Foundation: They too have a strong focus on health and treat it mainly as a scientific-technological issue (as evidenced in their guiding principles). In fact, on the announcement that Bill Gates would leave his day job, MSNBC published an article titled: '*Rockefeller 2.0: Bill Gates relaunches philanthropy.*' (MSNBC 2008).

Similar to Soros, the Gates Foundation is formed by the convictions of its founders, Bill and Melinda Gates. The foundation's mission statement states the following: *'Guided by the belief that every life has equal value, the Bill & Melinda Gates Foundation works to help all people lead healthy, productive lives. In developing countries, it focuses on improving people's health and giving them the chance to lift themselves out of hunger and extreme poverty. In the United States, it seeks to ensure that all people — especially those with the fewest resources — have access to the opportunities they need to succeed in school and life.*' (http://www.gatesfoundation.org/about/Pages/foundation-fact-sheet.aspx). The Gates Foundation has therefore determined health as their primary area of engagement for developing countries. Despite the foundation's large financial assets, the foundation has a very lean structure with three main programme areas at present: Global Health, Global Development and United States as well as special initiatives such as emergency relief.

The Gates Foundation is not the big fish in the pond, it is a whale. As of fiscal year 2008, the foundation has an estimated asset of US$30 billion, thereby making it the biggest U.S. foundation. In fact, it is three times as large as number two on the list, the J. Paul Getty Trust which has total assets of roughly 10 billion. Its influence over global health is even more pronounced; in 2008, the Gates Foundation awarded grants worth US$2 billion. This is 11 times as much as the second largest private foundation in global health, the Susan Thomas Buffet Foundation (see Table 3). In the future, the Gates Foundation's funding will continue to grow through their own but also through donations by others. In 2006, Warren Buffet, at that time the richest man of the world, donated roughly US$10 million to the Gates Foundation, to be disbursed over the coming years. Reportedly, he chose the Gates Foundation because of the results achieved to date and the management capacity brought by its founders.[15]

The activities and organisations it funds. Because of the enormous size of the Gates Foundation, we attempt to give an overview over its funding portfolio rather than selecting specific initiatives. This overview is based on a previous analysis for the years between 1998 and 2007 (McCoy *et al.* 2009). It was shown that most of the financing went into research and development and science (36%). For instance, it supports the 'Grand challenges in global health' initiative, which provides research funding for tropical diseases. The rest of the financing was spent on health care delivery (24%), enabling supply and purchasing (18%) and applied health research (11%). This distribution reflects the Foundation's approach to health as a technological issue, bringing innovations to "market", while trying to strengthen health service delivery.

Most of the Gates' Foundation financing goes to other organisations. Due to its flexibility, it can play something of a "venture capital" role in global health. Major recipients were non-governmental organisations such as PATH; Global Health Partnerships such as GAVI or the Global Fund to Fight AIDS, Tuberculosis and Malaria; universities such as Columbia and intergovernmental organisation such as WHO (in this order). Again, the choice of organisations is in line with the Gates Foundation guiding principles of focusing on science and technology. For instance, the organisation PATH builds on technology to improve health outcomes. Similar to many other foundations, it acts as a catalyst by funding institutions that are in line with the Gates' vision for development. In fact, the Gates Foundation is known to keep a close eye on its grants (financially and in terms of their management). Furthermore, the Gates Foundation is said to have a very business-oriented approach to health with many of its senior officials coming from the private sector.

Net of influence. Because most of its funding goes to other organisations, the Gates Foundation has a significant influence on global health governance beyond its own governance. Not only has it shaped global public health by helping to establish new global health initiatives, it also funds well-established organisations such as the WHO (McCoy *et al.*

[15] http://news.cnet.com/Buffett-donates-his-billions-to-Gates-foundation/2100–1022_3–6087682.html.

2009, p. 1650). For instance, the Gates Foundation provides a significant amount of funding to the WHO's Polio Eradication Initiative, speeding up its progress. It is represented in the governance structures of global health initiatives, such as the Boards of GAVI and the Global Fund, and has the possibility to fairly directly influence strategic decisions. Because it also engages in other advocacy and media-initiatives, Global Health Watch even goes as far as saying that '*the Foundation has become the dominant actor in setting the frames of reference for international health policy*'(Global Health Watch 2008, p. 251). This is probably an overstatement, but its influence on global health governance and innovation go beyond its financing.

Contribution to global public health. The foundation's contribution to global public health has been widely recognised: Gates Foundation has '*raised the profile of global health*' (Global Health Watch 2008, p. 256); '*revived funding & research for neglected diseases*'; and '*has brought a fresh and deep political commitment to health*'. Some even go as far as saying that Gates Foundation has set an example for others (Lancet 2003). However, the Gates Foundation has not only brought unprecedented interest to global health,but also received significant criticism for its engagement, particularly of its own and distinctive governance (Text Box 3).

Text Box 3. Points of criticism at the Gates Foundation (based on McCoy *et al.* 2009, Black *et al.* 2009 and Global Health Watch 2008)

- Governance structure and lack of transparency: The Gates family ultimately takes all funding decisions (guiding principles). It is unclear on what grounds grants are awarded and results of completed grants are not readily available, though this is an increasing priority.
- Allocation of funding: The Gates Foundation is perceived to allocate their funding on criteria other than disease burden, which can lead to distortions in the health sector. In addition, the foundation has been criticised as not having the necessary expertise to prioritise health interventions. However, they do state their funding is innovative and catalytic.

(*Continued*)

(Continued)

- Approach to health: The Gates Foundation takes a very scientific-technological approach to health, primarily aiming to find technical solutions. The foundation has been criticised to neither sufficiently explore the social dimension of health, nor to explore how existing cost-effective interventions could be made more accessible.
- Mode of collaboration: The Gates Foundation is not well represented in global donor coordination efforts and works largely outside government structures. Most funding goes to U.S.- and European-based organisations, meaning that the control over the Gates' financing mainly remains in the North. This may lead to beneficiaries in the South being excluded from decision-making processes that concern their own public health.

In comparison with Rockefeller, Ford or Soros, Gates is a much more active foundation. It is a driver of change. It has brought change to global public health through the amount of financing it brings. It has changed global health governance by supporting the establishment of new and prominent actors instead of intervening directly. However, its most important contribution might have been to have stimulated the global health debate: The Gates Foundation has forced other actors to think equally big, to come up with equally creative solutions, and to find counterarguments to the Gates Foundation, e.g. why its scientific-technological approach to health is insufficient. Business as usual has become more difficult with the Gates Foundation intervening in the global health arena.

6. New Actors and New Money: Carlos Slim Helú

The philanthropic landscape is changing. In March 2010, Forbes published their annual list of billionaires (Forbes 2010). The list counted 1,011 billionaires from 55 countries, up from 793 last year.[16] More and more billionaires come from countries other than the United States and

[16] Despite this growth, the number of billionaires for the year 2010 is still lower than it was before the crisis (1,125 in 2008). See http://www.dnaindia.com/world/report_carlos-slim-tops-annual-list-of-billionaires_1358163.

Europe. For the first time, China had more billionaires than any other country except the United States. India increased its number of billionaires from 24 to 50 compared to the year before. Africa had 4 billionaires on the list, of which two each came from South Africa and Egypt. This growing accumulation of private wealth beyond the traditional geographical limits of the United States and Europe will also have implications for global philanthropy. Carlos Slim Helú is currently leading the way, in developing his foundations from Mexico.

Carlos Slim Helú.[17] Carlos Slim Helú may not be very well known outside Latin America, but as of 2010, he is the wealthiest person in the world. Mexican in nationality and of Lebanese descent, his net worth is around US$53.5 billion. He has reportedly overtaken Bill Gates by US$500 million. In 2011, and following the financial crisis, Carlos Slim further increased his wealth compared to those in the North to US$74 billion now significantly ahead of Bill Gates on US$56 billion. With telecommunication companies such as America Móvil, Telmex and Telmex International, Carlos Slim has a substantial influence over the industry in Mexico and much of Latin America (www.dnaindia.com press release). Over recent years, he has passed on the daily operations of its companies to his three sons and is devoting himself to philanthropy through the Fundación Carlos Slim. Similar to recent foundations, the founder provides management and leadership during his life, rather than just finance.

Slim's network of social investment. Carlos Slim Helú is widely engaged in social activities, yet he does not see himself as a philanthropist that gives money away to the poor. Rather, he considers himself to be engaged in 'social investment', as he invests in people, seeing the number of beneficiaries as a social return of investment (Interview Saucedo). Slim's social investment started as early as 1986 with Asociación Carso A.C., later renamed into the Fundación Carlos Slim. Slim has established several social investment initiatives since then. According to his website, the total number is not less than 11 (see Table 3).[18] Most of the initiatives

---

[17] Interview with Carlos Slim Health Institute representative, 12 May 2010.

[18] http://www.carlosslim.com/responsabilidad_ing.html#tmx, see Table 3.

Table 3. Philanthropic initiatives by Carlos Slim Helú.

Name of the Initiative	Sectors	Endowment
Fundación Carlos Slim	Education, health, justice and personal and community development	US$3.5 billion
Carlos Slim Health Institute	Health	US$500 million
Aid to Latin America (ALAS)	Various, some funding for early childhood education	US$4 billion
Fundación Telmex	Education, health, culture, justiceand social well-being	US$1.5 billion
Casa TELMEX	Education	Not available
Ciudad Jardin TELMEX Bicentenario	Sport	Not available
Fundación del Centro Histórico de la Ciudad de México	Culture	Not available
Museo Soumaya	Culture	Not available
Centro de Estudios de Historia de México Carso	Culture	Not available
Socially Responsible Company Award	Social development	Not available
Asociación de Superación por México, A.C.	Human Development	Not available

are focused on Mexico and cover a wide range of sectors. Due to a recent change in the Mexican legislation, Slim is now able to expand its activities to other countries. These initiatives and their results are all the more important given the few philanthropic initiatives in Latin America (Alleyne *et al.* 2008).

The Carlos Slim Health Institute. One of the main organisations for public health is the Carlos Slim Health Institute (ICSS), an initiative of the Fundación Carlos Slim and financially linked to it. The Carlos Slim Health Institute was inaugurated in Mexico City in 2008 with an endowment of US$500 million, donated by Carlos Slim's son, Marco Antonio Slim, who now also serves as the Chair of the Board. The Carlos Slim Health Institute is working in different areas such as maternal and child health, chronic diseases, decreasing indoor pollution, the use of wireless health technologies and education in health and strengthening of human resources. Their general focus is on improving the public health of the Mexican and Latin American population. Health priorities and decisions on interventions are made by the leadership of the Health Institute (Interview Saucedo). Interestingly, when established, the Carlos Slim Health Institute was faced with scepticism within Mexico; was it just another way for Slim to make money?

The Slim way of working. The Carlos Slim Health Institute has its specific way of working. As a foundation from an emerging market economy that primarily works within national boundaries, the Institute has close relationships with the government. The Carlos Slim Health Institute would typically pilot and refine interventions over a period of 6 to 24 months, after which it seeks federal and state governments to appropriate the interventions and incorporate them into their public health programmes. By acting as a non-profit service-provider to the government, the Carlos Slim Health Institute aims at strengthening the government's capacity. This mode of collaboration may well be an innovation in itself. The Carlos Slim Health Institute also reports its results quite transparently. For example, the 2009 annual report states that 630,265 persons have been reached by their interventions in the past three years. Similar figures have been more difficult to obtain for other foundations. Examples for interventions include[19]:

Wireless Health. The wireless health initiative makes use of an integrated platform in which the mobile phone, internet and the fixed phone converge to support people in achieving self-management of health. Currently, there are three programmes which focus on HIV/AIDS, diabetes and cardio-vascular diseases. Patients register both online and through the cell phone for free and can interact with the system to have personalised education protocols, receive appointments, lab and medicine reminders, and they can also register their biomarkers and monitor them online. Wireless health services are run in collaboration with the telemobile company Telcel, which is owned by Carlos Slim.

The Mesoamerica Health 2015 Initiative. Launched in June 2010, the objective of the Mesoamerica Health Initiative is to reduce the gap in

[19] These examples are based on Saucedo 2010; Feder 2010; Lanval News 2010; Tapia-Conyer 2009; Instituto Carlos Slim de Salud 2009.

health equality faced by the poorest 20% of the population living in Central America and Southern Mexico. This initiative is a joint collaboration among the Carlos Slim Foundation, the Bill & Melinda Gates Foundation and the Spanish government. Each partner contributes US$50 million over five years.

The Carlos Slim Health Institute is an emerging foundation in an emerging market economy that still needs to overcome the hurdles that young foundations are faced with. Similar to Rockefeller's interventions in Latin America, the public is learning to understand that the objective of the Carlos Slim Health Institute is public benefit. It is quite obvious that innovations play a key part in the Institute's work. When asked about the role of innovations, a representative of the Carlos Slim Health Institute answered: '*Why would we engage in something if it is not innovative?.*'[20]

7. Private Foundations' Contribution to Global Health

Private foundations have experimented and invested in areas that have later been taken over by public interventions (Rockefeller), have acted as catalysts for new initiatives (Gates) and have emerged as new South-South funding streams (Carlos Slim). First, we look at the positive contributions they have made to global public health. Second, we discuss them more critically.

A. Their positive contributions

Introducing innovative management

Social entrepreneurship, venture philanthropy and philanthrocapitalism are all terms used to describe private foundations' business-oriented management style. Sometimes criticised, private foundations' management style is also an innovative way of approaching public health. They are often influenced by the role of the founder in leadership and management as well as in providing funds.

[20] Interview with Carlos Slim Health Institute representative, 12 May 2010.

While venture philanthropism and philanthrocapitalism have a slightly negative connotation and emphasise an intensive personal engagement of donors in the decision-making processes of the recipient (Fleischmann 2007, p. 271), social entrepreneurship may be the most neutral term to describe private foundations' management and methods. Social entrepreneurship can be defined as '*the productive efforts of an individual, team or organization that reform or revolutionize the patterns by which private sector resource relationships are mobilized and deployed to effect social change*' (Dees, in Fleischmann 2007, p. 181). Social entrepreneurship also means that private foundations '*embrace strategies and tactics drawn from the for-profit sector*' (Fleischmann 2007, p. 181), including a strong focus on results, impact, effectiveness and efficiency.[21] The assumption is that a focus on results will lead to quick and tangible improvements (ebd.).

To give examples, private foundations have implemented business thinking by funding non-traditional recipients that can deliver fast results, such as public-private partnerships, global initiatives, think-tanks or academic groups. Another example is the area of microfinance, which has been promoted by foundations such as Ford. Microfinance very strongly follows a business approach by granting microcredits to the normal villager, thereby treating them as entrepreneurs. Private foundations also tend to hire staff from the private sector who can apply their skills for the public goals of the foundation such as the current CEO of the Gates Foundation who was a member of Microsoft's senior leadership team.

Social entrepreneurship is most often raised in relation with the newer foundations. However, it dates back as far as the Rockefeller Foundation (Fleischmann 2007, p. 181). In fact, it was John D Rockefeller III who first used the term venture philanthropy during a 1969 Congressional Hearing in the simple but compelling meaning of '*the adventurous funding of unpopular causes*' (John, in Edwards 2008, p. 22).

As stated earlier, social entrepreneurship is not only a great strength but also a much criticised feature of private foundations. One downside is that little attention may be paid to the process and governance of how

[21] On social entrepreneurship or philanthrocapitalism, see also Witte and Marten 2008, p. 14ff.

results are achieved. This may mean that not enough attention is being paid to involving a wide range of stakeholders in the decision-making process, and this may jeopardise sustainability.

Supporting innovative approaches

Research and development is probably the most traditional support area for private foundations. Their independent decision-making provides them with a comparative advantage to support unconventional projects and underfunded areas (Aschwanden 2007). This is also true for funding research and development for neglected diseases,[22] in which the pharmaceutical industry has had less interest because of low expected commercial returns (Matter and Keller 2008).

In supporting research and development, private foundations can act quicker than public actors and are more likely to take risks. Because they have only a few stakeholders and do not need to justify their decisions to the public, it is easier for them to take unpopular decisions. Hereby, the credibility of the researcher is a paramount criterion for funding.

There are several prominent examples of private foundations successfully supporting medical research, such as the Rockefeller Foundation funding the development of the yellow fever vaccine or the Doris Duke Foundation support of inexpensive monitoring of CD4 counts and HIV viral load (Gallin 2005). A more recent example is the Grand Challenges in Global Health Programme, funded by the NIH, the Gates Foundation, the Wellcome Trust and the Canadian Institutes of Health Research. Launched in 2003, the programme aims at improving and inventing new vaccines and limiting drug resistance. With a total amount of US$436 million for 43 grants in 33 countries, this initiative is quite significant.[23]

---

[22] Most tropical diseases are neglected diseases. Examples include malaria, tuberculosis, buruli ulcer, dengue fever, leishmaniasis, trypoanosomiasis, diarrhoeal diseases and others. See Matter and Keller in Drug Discovery Today, Vol 13, April 2008, p. 347.

[23] In 2008, the Gates Foundation launched a related initiative, called Grand Challenges Explorations, a $100 million programme to encourage even bolder and less conventional solutions. See www.grandchallenges.org/about/Pages/Overview.aspx.

Despite the general positive acknowledgement, there is also some criticism related to private foundations' support to medical research. Their willingness to fund may in fact allow corporate and public funding to withdraw. Private funding may stop at any time, creating an instable relationship and strong dependency between the researcher and the foundation (Aschwanden 2007). In addition, there has been criticism that private foundations' providing funding to selected research areas has narrowed down the scope of research and development, limiting it to primarily technologically oriented research that promises quick results.

New actors in global health governance

Global health governance can be defined as the manner in which stakeholders make and implement decisions to promote and protect good health. As such, it includes not only the roles of public and private organisations, but also the formal and informal rules and traditions through which these institutions relate to each other and to the people whose health they seek to defend.

Through bringing additional funds to the table, private foundations have bought a certain amount of influence in global health governance. In addition, private foundations have further influenced global health governance through the organisations and initiatives they have established and are currently supporting. For example in 2007, seven global health programmes relied entirely on the Gates Foundation for funding and at least nine global health programmes listed the same foundation as their single largest donor (Buse *et al.* 2007, p. 267). Because private foundations mainly provide funding to organisations that represent the private foundations' spirit, they have managed to multiply their influence in global health governance. Combining private and public approaches, private foundations also often become the voice of the private sector in various fora, further extending their influence.

B. Subject to debate

Governance and transparency

While private foundations have brought new thinking into global health governance, the governance, transparency and decision-making of private foundations themselves have been subject to criticism. The minimum level of transparency required for US-based private foundations is to report who they support in a given year and the amounts provided. For foundations outside the United States, even this standard is not uniformly applied. It is actually quite interesting that while private foundations' strongly focus on achieving results, they do not always openly share their results.

The achievements and the shortcomings of private foundations stem from their unique independent governance structures. A private foundation is governed by its board of trustees which is guided by the will and wishes of the financing entity. It can make financing decisions quite freely, unconventionally and relatively fast. On the other hand, when the funds are invested to foster public goods, the lack of any public accountability in decision-making and the volatile nature of the funding are raising concerns and direct critique. In addition, private foundations are also questioned for having opaque decision-making processes when it comes to assessing potential grant recipients (Global Health Watch 2008, p. 250).

Harmonisation and coordination

Even though private foundations form relations with other actors and engage in discussion on global health, there are issues around insufficient integration of private foundations. There is a global dialogue on equitable and balanced aid allocation; however, this is not comprehensive as private foundations are not fully part of it (see also Witte and Marten 2008). International aid databases, such as the OECD's Creditor Reporting System, do not cover private foundations.[24] Initiatives to improve aid transparency, such as the recent International Aid Transparency Initiative, have so far not extended to private foundations.[25]

[24] The Creditor Reporting System intends to capture all aid disbursed to developing countries by OECD member states, which cover most industrialised nations. For more information and to access the CRS, see http://stats.oecd.org/Index.aspx?DatasetCode=CRSNEW.

[25] IATI's aim is to make information about aid spending easier to access, use and understand. It was set up in 2008 to help implement the transparency commitments in the Accra Agenda for Action (AAA). IATI is a temporary coalition of donor governments, governments of developing countries and NGOs (non-governmental organisations). For more information on IATI, see www.aidtransparency.net.

There are also issues around coordination at the country level. Private foundations usually work outside government structures and hence outside the national development frameworks (Witte and Marten 2008, p. 23ff). This can lead to tense relations between the private foundation and the government, e.g. in the case of the Open Society Institute and former states of the Soviet Union. They are also absent from country-led donor harmonisation exercises, such as development round tables. With the growing size of the foundations, the risk of overlap and duplication of efforts is increasing.

Independence and neutrality

Foundations are generally seen as independent decision-makers, in particular of decisions that are regarded as risky or unpopular. However, the degree of independence of private foundations is influenced by home country legislation, their freedom of scope can be circumcised through national law: such as the anti-terrorism act; their grantees, who may not follow what has been agreed; other donor aid; the mother company: e.g. only Ford cars were used in the very early years of the Ford Foundation; and the host government: there have been cases where private foundations have had to leave because of non-receptiveness of the host government (Bell 1971).

Independence does not mean neutrality. Due to the multiple layers of stakeholders in the involvement of private foundations in global health, the criteria for selection may be scientific or professional, but there are many other influences which affect the implementation of their programmes and the role they can play.

Accountability and ethics of investments

Due to their largely private decision-making, private foundations do not have a direct and wider public counterpart they would be accountable to (Fleischmann 2007, p. 53). In today's globalised world, the watchdog function has been assumed by a variety of non-governmental organisations, such as *Global Health Watch*. This dialogue is new and different to when the classic foundations such as Ford were the largest private actors.

Other organisations are also accountable to private foundations who are part of their boards, as the example of the Gates Foundation shows: '*The fact that the Gates Foundation is a funder and board member of the various new global health initiatives* (e.g. *the Global Fund; GAVI, Stop TB Partnership; and Roll Back Malaria) means that other global health actors are accountable to the Gates Foundation, but not the other way round.*'(Global Health Watch 2008).

8. The Way Forward: Private Foundations as Partners in Global Health

The classic private foundations were some of the first important actors in global health and have influenced the way they have developed. They were seeking to provide aid in a scientific manner, looking for evidence of what worked and looking for results. The focus on managing aid for results is equally in line with the twenty-first-century private foundations, which have also influenced modern aid in health combining private funds and management approaches for public goals.

The private foundations have important differences in focus and scope, which are largely defined by their founders. However, their independence offers them a comparative advantage in the global health scene today. Although they are criticised for non-accountability to the public, the freedom of independent decision-making enables them to take risks, and to be innovative on a different scale than other players in global aid.

Private foundations bring the ability to look into new solutions and innovations to global health. They have a track record of finding and trying out new approaches, which are later adopted or used by the nation-state or other public entities. That has been shown by the influence of the Rockefeller Foundation in the WHO reform programme under Brundtland, and by the Gates Foundation in providing catalytic funding to create new global initiatives such as GAVI.

To ensure that private foundations' aid is provided effectively, developing countries should assume stronger leadership and ownership in shaping the partnerships that directly affect the health of their citizens. A stronger leadership role for developing countries would e.g. mean that they include private foundations and initiatives funded by private foundations in their donor coordination efforts.

The role and focus of private foundations and Overseas Development Assistance donors is quite distinct. Private foundations look for new ways of working which are complimentary to bilateral, multilateral and global health initiatives. They play an important direct and catalytic role as innovative health partners, which needs to be better incorporated into global health governance.

Chapter 17 assesses an innovative HIV prevention programme in India supported by the Gates Foundation. Chapter 18 describes characteristics of the NGO response in Russia with a focus on activities supported by the Soros Foundation. Chapter 12 assesses further innovations introduced directly by the role of the private sector.

References

Agudelo CA (1983) "Community Participation in Health Activities: Some Aspects and Appraisal Criteria", Bulletin of the Pan American Health Organisaiton, 17(4):375–86.

Alleyne G, Aninat E, de Ferranti D, de Quadros C, Chen L, Freire M, Guerrero R, Langer A, Rodríguez JG (2008) "Instituto Carso de la Salud: A Boost for Health Philanthropy", *Lancet* 371(9607):100–101.

Arnove R, *et al.* (2007) "Revisiting the 'Big Three' Foundations", *Critical Sociology* 33:389–425.

Aschwanden C (2007) "Freedom to fund", *Cell* 128(3):421–23.

Associated Press (2006) "Gates: Buffett Gift May Help Cure Worst Diseases", Press Release 26/6/2006, http://www.msnbc.msn.com/id/13541144/ (last accessed 20/7/2010).

BBC News online (2005) "Anita Roddick's New Wealth Agenda", http://news.bbc.co.uk/2/hi/business/4524046.stm (last accessed 20.7.2010).

Bell D (1975) "The Future of Philanthropic Foundations. The Next Twenty-Five Years", *Ciba Found Symp* 30:151–78.

Bell D (1971) "The Ford Foundation as Transnational Actor", *International Organization* 25:465–78.

Berndtson E (2007) "Power of Foundations and the American Ideology", *Critical Sociology* 33:575–87.

Bill & Melinda Gates Foundation (2009) Press Release 21/01/2009, http://www.gatesfoundation.org/press-releases/Pages/rotary-international-effort-in-eradicating-polio-090121.aspx.

Bill & Melinda Gates Foundation (2009) Avahan. The India AIDS Initiative. Fact Sheet, Seattle, http://www.gatesfoundation.org/avahan/Documents/Avahan_FactSheet.pdf (last accessed 22/07/2010).

Black R, *et al.* (2009) "Accelerating the Health Impact of the Gates Foundation", *Lancet* 373(9675):1584–85.

Buse K, Harmer HM (2007) "Seven Habits of Highly Effective Global Public-Private Partnerships: Practice and Potential, *Soc Sci Med* 64(2):259–71. Epub 2006 Oct 20.

Casalonga S (2008) "Private Research Foundations: New Stakes for Europe and France", *BIOFUTUR* 288:52–55.

Chapman S (2008) "Group Carso, Health Philanthropy, and Tobacco", *Lancet* 371(9620):1243.

Cohen J (2006) "Global Health. Public-Private Partnerships Proliferate", *Science* 311(5758):167.

Dees G (2008) "Philanthropy and Enterprise: Harnessing the Power of Business and Entrepreneurship for Social Change", *Innovation* 3(3)119–32.

Desai R, Kharas H (2009) Do Philanthropic Citizens Behave Like Governments? Wolfensohn Center for Development, Working Paper 12, Washington, http://www.brookings.edu/papers/2009/10_kiva_global_giving_kharas.aspx.

DNA India Online (2010) Carlos Slim tops annual list of billionaires, http://www.dnaindia.com/world/report_carlos-slim-tops-annual-list-of-billionaires_1358163 (last accessed 20/07/2010).

Dyer O (2006) "In Search of a Sustainable Philanthropy", *Bull World Health Organ* 84(6):432–33. Epub 2006 Jun 21.

Editorial (2009) "What has the Gates Foundation Done for Global Health?" *Lancet* 373(9675):1577.

Edwards M (2008) Just another emperor? The Myths and Realities of Philanthro-Capitalism, Demos: A Network for Ideas & Action, The Young Foundation, http://www.nonprofitquarterly.org/images/fbfiles/files/Just_Another_Emperor.pdf.

European Foundation Centre (2008) Foundations in the European Union. Facts and figures. Brussels.

Fleischmann JL (2007) The Foundation: A Great American Secret: How Private Wealth is Changing the World, Public Affairs, New York.

Forbes (2010) Forbes' List of Billionaires, http://www.forbes.com/lists/2010/10/billionaires-2010_The-Worlds-Billionaires_Rank.html (last accessed 20/7/2010).

Ford Foundation (2008) Annual Report, New York, http://www.fordfoundation.org/about-us/annual-reports.

Foundation Centre (2008) International Grant-Making Highlights, New York, http://foundationcenter.org/gainknowledge/research/pdf/intlgmiv_highlights.pdf.

Foundation Centre (2008a) Number of Grantmaking Foundations, 1975 to 2007, New York, http://foundationcenter.org/findfunders/statistics/pdf/02_found_growth/2007/03_07.pdf.

Foundation Centre (2009) Philanthropy Annual, New York, http://foundation-center.org/philanthropyannual/2008.html.

Foundation Centre (2009a) Highlights of Foundation Yearbook, New York, http://foundationcenter.org/gainknowledge/research/pdf/fy2009_highlights.pdf.

Fox DM (2006) "Foundations' Impact on Health Policy, *Health Aff* (Millwood) 25(6):1724–29.

Franco-Agudelo S (1983) "The Rockefeller Foundation's Antimalarial Program in Latin America: Donating or Dominating?" *Int J Health Serv* 13(1):51–67.

Frenk J (2009) "Response from Instituto Carso de la Salud. Comment on Group Carso, Health Philanthropy, and Tobacco", *Lancet* 371(9620):1243–44.

Galaskiewicz J (2001) "Private Funds, Public Purpose: Philanthropic Foundations in International Perspective", *Administrative Science Quarterly* 46(2):356–58.

Gallin E (2005) "Interview with Elaine Gallin, Program Director for Medical Research at the Doris Duke Charitable Foundation", *J Investig Med* 53(6):275–78.

Global Health Watch (2008) "The Alternative World Health Report", Zed Books, London.

Gunzburger LK (1994) "Foundations that Support Medical Education and Health Care: Their Missions, Accomplishments, and Unique Role", *Acad Med* 69(1):8–17.

Gupta S, Patillo C, Wagh S (2006) Are Donor Countries Giving More or Less Aid? IMF Working Paper, WP/06/01, Washington, http://aideffectiveness.zunia.org/uploads/media/knowledge/AidEffectiveness/wp0601.pdf.

Instituto Carlos Slim de Salud (2009) Que mas Personas Vivan mas e mejor, Informe, Mexcio D.C.

John R (2002) *Venture Philanthropy: The Evolution of High-Engagement Philanthropy in Europe*, Cambridge: Skoll Center for Social Entrepreneurship.

Joint Working Group of the Council of Foundations and the European Foundation Centre (2007) Principles of Accountability for International Philanthropy. An aspirational tool for international donors, Brussels, http://www.efc.be/SiteCollectionDocuments/EFC_COF_PrinciplesAccountabilityUKV.pdf.

Lancet (2003) "Philanthropic Gifts for Health: The Stage is Set", *Lancet* 362(9390):1087.

Lancet (2005) "Bill Gates: a 21st century Robin Hood?" *Lancet* 365(9463):911–12.

Lanval News (2010) Slim, Gates and the Spanish government together for Salud Mesoamerica 2015, http://lanval.com/news/slim-gates-and-the-spanish-government-together-for-salud-mesoamerica-2015/7141142/ (last accessed 20/7/2010).

Lerer L, Matzopoulos R (2001) "'The Worst of Both Worlds': The Management Reform of the World Health Organization", *Int J Health Serv* 31(2):415–38.

Lester Feder J (2010) Cell-phone Medicine Brings Care to Patients in Developing Nations, *Health Affairs* 29(2):259–63.

Marten R, Witte JM (2008) Transforming Development? The role of philanthropic foundations in international development cooperation, GPPi Research Paper Series No. 10.

Matter A, Keller TH (2008) "Impact of Non-profit Organizations on Drug Discovery: Opportunities, Gaps, Solutions", *Drug Discov Today* 13(7–8):347–52.

McCoy, *et al.* (2009) "The Bill & Melinda Gates Foundation's Grant-Making Programme for Global Health", *Lancet* 373(9675):1645–53.

MSNBC (2008) Rockefeller 2.0: Gates Relaunches Philanthropy Through His Foundation, Microsoft Founder is Aiming to Change Charity, Online article, 24/06/2008, http://www.msnbc.msn.com/id/25332025/ (last accessed 22/07/2010).

Murray C (2009) Financing Global Health: Tracking Development Assistance to Health, ICMHE, Seattle.

Nielsen W (1985) *Golden Donors: A New Anatomy of the Great Foundations*, New Brunswick and London: Transaction Publishers.

Organization for Economic Development and Cooperation (2010) The Role of the Private Sector in the Context of Aid Effectiveness. Draft Strategy, Paris.

Organization for Economic Development and Cooperation (2010a), Development Co-operation Report 2010, Paris.

People's Health Movement (2008) *Global Health Watch 2: An Alternative World Health Report*, London: Zed Books, http://www.ghwatch.org/ghw2.

Ravishankar N, Gubbins P, Cooley RJ, Leach-Kemon K, Michaud CM, Jamison DT, Murray CJ. (2009) "Financing of Global Health: Tracking Development Assistance for Health from 1990 to 2007", *Lancet* 373(9681):2113–24.

Reich M (2000) "Public–Private Partnerships for Public Health", *Nat Med* 2000 Jun; 6(6):617–20.

Saucedo R (2010) The Carlos Slim Health Institute, Power Point Presentation; available under http://www.slideshare.net/rosaucedo03/icssinstitutionalpresentation.

Seattle Times Online (2007) Melinda Gates Shares the Lessons She's Learned in 10 Years of Philanthropy http://seattletimes.nwsource.com/html/localnews/2003687791_webmgates30.html.

Stapleton D (2004) Lessons of History? Anti-Malaria Strategies of the International Health Board and the Rockefeller Foundation from the 1920s to the era of DDT", *Public Health Rep* 119(2):206–15.

Tapia-Conyer R, Saucedo R (2009) "Last Mile Delivery in Health Care and Patient Empowerment Through Technology: The Case of 'Telecommunication for Health'", *Global Forum Update on Research for Health* 6:10–13.

Vian T, *et al.* (2007) "Public-Private Partnerships to Build Human Capacity in Low Income Countries: Findings from the Pfizer Program", *Hum Resour Health* 2(5):8.

Vogel A (2006) "Who's Making Global Civil Society: Philanthropy and US Empire in World Society", *Br J Sociol* 57(4):635–55.

Walt G, Buse K (2000) "Partnership and Fragmentation in International Health: Threat or Opportunity?" *Trop Med Int Health* 5:467–71.

Widdus R (2005) "Public-Private Partnerships: An Overview", *Trans. R. Soc. Trop. Med. Hygiene* 99S:S1–8.

Witte and Martens (2008) "New Philanthropy and International Development", Alliance Magazine, 1 September, 2008.

World Bank (2007) Philanthropic Foundations and Their Role in International Development Assistance, World Bank, Washington.

Wyn Owen J, *et al.* (2009) "The role of Foundations in Global Governance of Health", In Making Sense of Global Health Governance, eds. Buse, Hein, Drager, Palgrave Macmillan, New York.

Yamey G (2003) "Education and Debate: WHO's Management: Struggling to Transform a 'fossilised bureaucracy'", *BMJ* 326(7382):217–18.

12

Private Sector: New Ways of Doing Business

Dida Connor, David Evans and Brian Brink

Summary

As the private sector increases its involvement in global public health, it is fostering innovation and having an impact on the ways in which international health programmes are financed and implemented. Through the example of the Global Fund, this chapter provides an overview of the private sector and its contribution to global health, and introduces some of the key players. The chapter also highlights some innovative global health initiatives, such as (PRODUCT)$^{RED TM}$, and offers other examples of new partnerships between private-sector actors and international organisations. The chapter concludes with a discussion of the benefits and challenges of incorporating the private sector into global health and its governance.

1. Introduction

There is growing evidence that improving healthcare, fighting disease and increasing life expectancy are all essential for supporting economic growth, which, in turn, is crucial to long-term business success (UNDP, IBLF 2003; Over 2009; Gupta 2006). AIDS, tuberculosis (TB) and malaria are major infectious disease burdens, with impacts on development and the economy. Together, the diseases kill more than five million people annually, perpetuating a cycle of sickness and poverty and stifling economic growth, education and life expectancy in many of the poorest economies in the world. Beyond the tragic human costs, these epidemics have significant impact on businesses in the areas of significant HIV and malaria burdens. Increased worker illness and health costs, insurance premiums, larger expenditure on welfare benefits, declines in productivity and increases in hiring and training costs are among the added costs of doing business in the areas with high prevalence rates of AIDS, TB and malaria (Lancet Infectious Diseases 2007). Although losses in skill base and institutional knowledge, and potential conflict in the workplace because of stigmatisation are more difficult to measure, they are also important.

The private sector — in particular businesses and corporations operating in some of the hardest hit countries — has been slow to enter the fight against the three diseases (Feeley *et al.* 2007; Ridley 2001). In the 1980s and early 1990s, cooperation between the public and private sectors on health was limited, largely because both sectors were slow to recognise the benefits that could be derived from applying private sector know-how and strategies to public health. In the late 1990s, the idea of public-private partnerships took hold globally during reform of the WHO and in countries. Many of these partnerships had been in the form of social investment opportunities where businesses were asked to use their financial resources to help underwrite programmes that were providing healthcare services to those in need. The public-private partnership model has evolved significantly, however, in recent years. Businesses are now being called upon not only to provide financial resources in the scale up of the fight against disease, but also to share their expertise in business areas that are critical to the effective delivery of public health services. This has resulted in a more partnership and collaborative approach in health and economic development work.

According to the Global Business Coalition on HIV/AIDS, Tuberculosis and Malaria (GBC), a collection of more than 200 companies, the partnership approach is, in most instances, the preferred method of operation for business leaders. GBC notes that partnerships are conceived and developed in many different ways, for example:

- Companies identify non-profit programmes that are aligned with their corporate social responsibility goals and then work with those programmes with their business resources.
- Companies interested in making a difference on a specific problem seek out partners who can advise and/or work together with them.
- Potential partners approach companies with possible joint programmes or seek to leverage business skills to fill execution gaps in their programmes.
- Companies put together collective actions: cross-industry and cross-sector action teams to focus together on a critical issue.

2. Components of Private-Sector Health Partnerships

The Global Fund to Fight AIDS, Tuberculosis and Malaria is one organisation that has established long-standing partnerships with the private sector, both at the global and at the local levels. The organisation has found that private-sector partners play a significant role in filling gaps in governance, implementation, advocacy and procurement, so that Global Fund-supported programmes can continue to reach the people who are in need of their services. The private sector engages with the organisation in four distinct ways:

1. Making a cash or in-kind donation,
2. Implementing a programme that receives Global Fund support,
3. Providing commercial goods and services in a socially responsible way and
4. Serving as a public advocate and contributor to good governance globally and in countries.

Financial contributions to the Global Fund go directly to the programmes it supports in the field with no administrative costs deducted. Major private-sector donors have the choice of giving to the general pool of funds used to finance grants or making a "restricted contribution" to support particular grants or activities. Restricted contributions do not affect the available funds of the targeted grant or the programme objectives, work plans or reporting requirements.

The Global Fund does not implement programmes itself and does not have a physical presence in the countries it supports. To halt or reverse the spread of AIDS, TB and malaria, it requires a significant scale up in programmes aimed at fighting the three diseases. Governments cannot do this independently. To solve this problem, the Global Fund actively encourages countries to engage non-governmental organisations — including the private sector — as implementers of programmes and principal recipients and sub-recipients of Global Fund grants. In fact, the Global Fund explicitly recommends in its grant application package the routine inclusion of both government and non-government implementers. This approach, known as "dual-track financing", has increased the involvement of both civil society organisations and the private sector in the implementation of programmes. Together these groups are now responsible for implementing 35% of programmes receiving support from the Global Fund.

Many businesses that have offices in countries that carry a heavy disease burden operate internal programmes aimed at preserving the health of their employees and have, in some cases, such as with Anglo American expanded those programmes to cover entire communities. In many cases, this provides a medium-term solution, especially in the areas where weak health systems make it imperative for companies to develop programmes of their own. The long-term solution, however, is for country health systems to become stronger and tackle the diseases. Businesses are also using the competencies they have developed in the competitive marketplace to contribute to the delivery of health care services and to help organisations use limited resources more efficiently and effectively.

Private-sector organisations, in fact, may be particularly wellsuited to take the lead in some situations because they may be the only viable source for delivery of services in locations where other networks and resources are insufficient. For example, in 2006, international shipping giant DHL, in partnership with the United Nations Children's Fund (UNICEF), used its capacity in distribution and logistics to deliver long-lasting insecticide-treated bednets in Kenya's remote Kwale district, where road infrastructure is poor and malaria-related child mortality rates are among the highest in the country. Following the pilot phase, DHL expanded its efforts nationwide to support the bednet campaign and the Ministry of Health. With the support of DHL and UNICEF, the programme initiated national "Child Health and Nutrition Weeks" in June 2007. Communication materials such as posters and leaflets were distributed using the road transportation network that DHL established. DHL also funded a short advocacy film on integrated child survival projects.

The GBC cites the following as the types of resources businesses have brought to global health partnerships:

- Planning, management, marketing or financial expertise and assistance.
- Experienced and dedicated experts to work on specific projects.
- Infrastructure, such as distribution channels.
- Access to employees and customers.
- Strong local, national and global brand power.
- Marketing and communications channels, such as television stations and networks.
- Relationships with suppliers, governments and other businesses.
- In-kind contributions of products and other resources.

Business can also use their influence in advocacy and in making contributions to good governance to protect health and treat people who become sick. As employers, companies are important to communities and nations — and their voice can be a powerful one in support of public health. At the global level, effective communication and advocacy stimulate public interest and contributes to commitment to the investments in health. Companies and business coalitions are engaging in dialogue with consumers, suppliers and distributors, and policy makers to advocate for increased support in the fight against disease. The Global Fund, for example, has partnered with a number of leading media organisations, such as VH-1, in order to create and distribute advocacy tools. At the same time, influential private-sector representatives play a leading role in the global network of "Friends" organisations which, while remaining independent, exist to advocate for continued and increased support for the Global Fund around the world.

At the local level, companies often help set community standards. Many are active, for example, in the de-stigmatisation of HIV status. Stigma is a major obstacle to people accessing testing and treatment. Workplace policies and public communication of a company's position can be a major tool in the de-stigmatisation battle. Businesses in many parts of the world — from Russia to Kenya — have organised public testing of their CEOs to send a strong signal that testing is both necessary and socially acceptable.

The following sections discuss different types of partnerships with the private sector, using examples from the Global Fund, including examples of those related to innovative financing, management and capacity building and country implementation.

2.1 Innovative financing to mobilise additional resources: PRODUCT(RED)™

The Global Fund partners closely with a social enterprise with an innovative approach to raise additional funding for development. In 2006, (RED), a private-sector consumer marketing initiative developed by rock musician Bono and activist Bobby Shriver, was launched with the idea of supporting the Global Fund through the sale of popular brand name products bearing the PRODUCT(RED)™ logo. Current partners include American Express (UK), Apple, Converse, Dell, Emporio Armani, Gap, Hallmark, Microsoft, Starbucks and most recently Bugaboo and Nike. Up to 50% of their gross profits from the sale of these products are directed to the Global Fund. As much as 100% of the money earned for the Global Fund through (RED) is invested in Global Fund-financed grants and no overhead is charged by the Global Fund or (RED), ensuring that all funds raised have the greatest impact possible. The concept has made an important contribution, raising US$140 million by December 2009 to support programmes that provide prevention, treatment and care services for people living with HIV and AIDS in four African countries: Rwanda, Ghana, Lesotho and Swaziland.

(RED) has also helped to strengthen awareness and advocacy for AIDS in Africa among ordinary consumers in North America and Europe. By communicating with ordinary citizens and consumers through brands they know and trust, (RED) has been able to engage millions in the fight against

AIDS in Africa. Through its marketing partnerships, (RED) has provided the Global Fund and implementing partners with exposure in media coverage and advertising. Online, (RED) has been able to connect young people to the fight against AIDS in Africa, helping to create networks of concerned citizens, who may contribute to keeping AIDS in Africa on the agenda of governments, and advocate for global health and development issues.

(RED)'s partnership with the Global Fund serves as a successful model of both an innovative financing initiative and effective public-private partnership. What makes the partnership a success is that all parties, while united by a common goal, nevertheless focus on their discrete areas of expertise. (RED) and its partners contribute marketing and communications competencies from the commercial sector globally. The Global Fund and implementing partners provide a grant-making and management capability with the transparency and accountability mechanisms required to build for (RED)'s public advocacy. The continuing flow of funds from the (RED) partnership into 2010, two years into an economic downturn, show the sustainability of the business model and suggest companies may actually benefit from the increased allegiance of a significant cohort of customers who identify with the (RED) brand and mission. One critique of (RED) which has been voiced, contrasts a perceived moderate share of margins provided by partner companies with the considerable marketing budgets with which they drive sales of (RED) products. However, the marketing itself is an important contribution, and Michael Madnick, one of the contributors to a recent survey of global philanthropy, argues (MacDonald, Tayart de Borms (2010)):

> For some this model is controversial because companies are not merely donating money. I view it as a highly creative approach to sustained revenue for the Global Fund, in a manner core to the competency of the private sector. The US$140 million (RED) has generated (at no material cost to the Global Fund) in its three years of life is to me the best response.

2.2 Corporate investment of mixed resources: Chevron

In 2008, the Global Fund launched its Corporate Champions Program and welcomed Chevron as the inaugural partner. The Corporate Champions

Program provides a way for multinational corporations to make a substantial financial investment in the fight against the three diseases and gives them the opportunity to collaborate with the Global Fund on advocacy and public relations projects at the global level and to work more closely at the country level with implementers of Global Fund-supported programmes. Chevron was appropriate as the first Global Fund Corporate Champion because of its highly successful community engagement programmes tackling AIDS and malaria and its award-winning HIV and AIDS workplace programmes. As part of the partnership, Chevron agreed to invest US$30 million over three years into Global Fund-supported programmes in six countries in Asia and Africa. In addition to the financial contribution, Chevron has committed to support selected Global Fund grant recipients in each of the targeted countries. This support comes in the form of capacity development initiatives, joint advocacy and communications campaigns, or other local engagements to strengthen programme performance and reach.

Chevron decided to take on such a commitment to the fight against the diseases because AIDS, malaria and TB are critical health issues in many countries where Chevron operates. The company sees its work in global health as an opportunity to improve community health significantly in those locations and believes that improving the health status of the whole community has direct and positive effects on its workers and their families, as well as on its potential future workforce. It provides both social and business returns on its investments.

Chevron's approach to community health continues to evolve and take advantage of synergies between many existing programmes. A major focus has been on developing a holistic approach that responds to community needs, including bringing efforts in HIV and AIDS, malaria and TB together in a coordinated way that addresses local needs and includes environmental, social and economic aspects. In this way, they aim to provide sustainable health support to communities.

For example, since 2001, the company has conducted HIV and AIDS awareness, prevention and treatment campaigns around its Nigerian operations. In some locations, anti-malaria efforts have been supported through community medical clinics. During 2008, Chevron worked with partners in the Corporate Alliance on Malaria in Africa to develop a strategic business plan based on a vision of integrated support for sustainable community health. Chevron is also participating in local governance of programmes to help achieve results. As part of its role as a corporate champion, the company is becoming involved in the Global Fund's Country Coordinating Mechanisms (CCMs), which are the main governance structure for administering Global Fund grants at the country level. Chevron plans to leverage its involvement in the CCMs to test the feasibility and effectiveness of its integrated community health approach.

The partnership and the projects coming out of it are innovative in the way that they are furthering the work of Chevron, the Global Fund and the programmes that the Global Fund supports. In Thailand, for example, increasing AIDS awareness among Thai youths is one of Chevron's key partnership strategies with international non-governmental organisation, PATH, a grant sub-recipient. PATH, a local youth group and Chevron have partnered to organise regular HIV awareness and sex education road shows with the participation of more than 100 young people in each event. A programme called "Parents Network" has also been developed which equips parents and guardians with the knowledge and skills necessary to communicate with children about sexual health and HIV. In addition, 13 Caltex stations in Bangkok are helping build awareness of HIV and AIDS by distributing 30,000 AIDS information brochures to young drivers of public transportation motorcycles. Clinics near the Caltex stations reported an increase in visits during the awareness campaign.

In Angola, together with the Angolan Ministry of Health, USAID and the Corporate Alliance on Malaria in Africa and other supporters, Chevron co-sponsored a three-week training workshop on entomology, which started in February 2010. The workshop is aimed at front-line malaria-control personnel from the public and private sector.

In Nigeria, Chevron and the National Agency for the Control of AIDS (NACA — a principal recipient of Global Fund resources) have partnered to deploy a small- and medium-scale enterprises' (SME) Workplace Wellness Education Programme. The project is facilitating technical support, increasing advocacy and awareness and establishing a system for helping manage HIV, malaria and TB in the workplace. Although the overall contribution of private resources to the Global Fund is limited compared to public funds, this section has highlighted some of the innovated partnerships that can develop.

2.3 Country management and capacity: Standard bank and Marathon Oil

In December 2008, Standard Bank, Africa's largest banking group in terms of assets, geographic spread and market capitalisation, and the Global Fund to Fight AIDS, Tuberculosis and Malaria entered into a pro bono partnership through which Standard Bank offers financial and management expertise to Global Fund grant recipients in selected countries in Africa.

Through this partnership, Standard Bank is helping to ensure that Global Fund resources are distributed inside the country in a timely manner and is also assisting with reporting requirements. Standard Bank provides a range of financial advisory services to principal recipients, sub-recipients and country coordinating mechanisms on a pro bono basis.

Standard Bank's support is currently available in selected African countries for grant recipients who request it and is tailored to fit their needs and requirements. It is entirely demand-driven and free of any conditionality. The partnership is currently ongoing in Uganda, Nigeria, Swaziland and Lesotho and will spread to more African countries in the near future.

In Swaziland, Lesotho and Nigeria, Standard Bank has already organised financial and management training workshops for principal recipients and sub-recipients of Global Fund grants. In addition, Standard Bank has installed financial management software for five sub-recipients in Swaziland.

One of the trainees in Lesotho says the training has been an eye-opener: "The workshops and trainings provided by Standard Bank help us to manage our donors' money more effectively and helps us to deliver on the Global Fund's reporting requirements."

The private sector has many skills to support implementation which go beyond and are complimentary to the technical focus of traditional assistance. Companies are also contributing their expertise in large-scale initiatives that are achieving results. In 2003, Marathon Oil, in collaboration with its business partners, the Government of Equatorial Guinea, and international non-profit and research organisations, launched a five-year US$15.8 million effort to reduce the transmission of malaria on Bioko

Island. The innovative approach to malaria eradication developed for the Bioko Island Malaria Control Program (BIMCP) went beyond focussing on a single cause and addressed a number of diverse factors leading to malaria transmission. Project interventions include:

- Indoor residual spraying provided to every house on the island.
- Door-to-door bednet distribution providing coverage to more than 111,000 beds.
- Malaria testing and treatment provided free of charge at local health centres.
- Improved national health information systems to monitor health risks.
- An innovative information, education and communication campaign to educate the public on malaria and prevention strategies.
- A surveillance and monitoring system to provide real-time data on the programme and to serve as a warning against future outbreaks.

While the malaria control efforts benefitted the island's population as a whole, particular focus was given to those at highest risk on Bioko, especially children under five years of age and pregnant women. In its first two years, the project succeeded in reducing malaria transmitting mosquitoes by 95% and the presence of malaria parasites in children by 44%. As of 2008, BIMCP has reduced the presence of malaria transmitting mosquitoes by 99% and has decreased the presence of malaria parasites in children to 49% below pre-project levels.

There are nevertheless challenges to sustain this level of impact. In the Fall of 2008, Marathon Oil and partners, including the Government of Equatorial Guinea, announced the extension of BIMCP for an additional five years, carrying the programme through 2013. A major focus of the second phase of the project will be to develop capacity within the Equatorial Guinea National Malaria Control Program. This will ensure local capacity and project management skills are in place to sustain the programme beyond 2013.

Marathon and partners also helped the Equatorial Guinea Government apply the project's interventions to mainland Equatorial Guinea through a multi-year US$26 million grant from the Global Fund and an additional Marathon Foundation grant of US$1 million. This has enabled the

Equatorial Guinea Government to establish one of the first nationwide integrated malaria control projects in Africa.

2.4 Country implementation: Anglogold Ashanti

In 2005, AngloGold Ashanti (AGA), a major gold-mining company, implemented a comprehensive integrated malaria control programme in the Obuasi Municipal District in Ghana, with the aim of achieving a 50% reduction in malaria incidence in two years. The programme includes vector control interventions such asindoor residual spraying, targeted larviciding (a preventive method used to interrupt the development of larvae or pupa into adult mosquitoes), community lifestyle change, prompt and effective case detection and distribution of insecticide-treated bednets to targeted groups. The programme has reported a significant impact — as of December 2009, reported malaria cases had declined by 75%, with an average reduction of 5,800 cases per month. AGA has implemented similar programmes at their Siguiri mine in Guinea; Geita mine in Tanzania and plans to follow suit in their other operations in Africa.

The Government of Ghana wanted to benefit from AGA's expertise and experience and included the company in a proposal to the Global Fund for a US$130 million Round 8 malaria grant which would be implemented through a Public-Private Partnership model in 40 districts throughout Ghana.

Ghana's application was successful and AGA was selected as the Principal Recipient of a US$30 million Global Fund grant for an initial two years. The grant was signed and activities initiated in November 2009. In line with the Global Fund's "dual track financing" policy which promotes diversity among recipients within the context of a national disease strategy, AGA will focus on indoor residual spraying under the grant, while working in tandem with the government recipient working on the scaling-up of home-based care. As principal recipient of the grant, AGA receives Global Fund financing directly, and then uses it to implement the programme. An objective is to mentor other organisations to become subrecipients, thus building capacity in Ghana.

In addition to being the principal recipient of the grant, AGA is contributing material and management resources. Under the programme, the

Malaria Control Centre in Obuasi, set up by AGA, will serve as the headquarters and a training centre for the expanded national programme. The centre has an existing insectary (for keeping, breeding or observing living mosquitoes), an entomological laboratory, training facilities as well as extensive administrative infrastructure. AGA's existing vehicles, spray pumps and other equipment will be incorporated into the national programme at no charge and AGA's existing Malaria Information System will be used to improve the national malaria data collection and reporting system.

AGA staff's collective expertise and technical skills in operational management, planning, training and implementation, acquired during the planning and implementation of the programme in Obuasi will be of benefit to the newly expanded government programme. With the support of Global Fund resources and hand in hand with in-country partners such as the Ministry of Health, Ghana Health Services and the National Malaria Control Program, AngloGold Ashanti is contributing to the national fight against malaria in Ghana.

3. Challenges and Benefits of Private-Sector Partnerships

For all of the innovation in thinking and know-how that the private sector can bring to bear on public health problems, there remain some real challenges for establishing partnerships between actors in global health and those in the private sector (USAID 2009; Ridley 2001). First, there is often historical mistrust between the two parties that seems to stem from a lack of dialogue about the issues, which can make forming partnerships at both the global and local levels difficult. There is sometimes a lack of understanding among public sector actors with regard to the added value of engaging the private sector. In a similar fashion, the private sector is not always fully informed about its potential role. Businesses also often prefer funding projects that have a direct impact on their markets, workforce and surrounding communities as opposed to support national programmes. In addition, quite often businesses have a suspicion of collective and multi-sector engagement due to the perceived long-lead times, and opt to implement their own projects, or act only with pre-selected partners. They have, therefore, not fully leveraged their contribution to governance and global health.

For companies such as those that manufacture drugs and other products used in the fight against disease, health programmes are a major source of business revenues. Business interests have at times created potential conflicts of interest and tensions that have made establishing partnerships particularly difficult. However, that way of thinking is beginning to change towards a partner approach. Increasingly institutions such as the Global Fund are seeking to collaborate with manufacturers to create and develop programmes and policies which can reduce costs and promote access to life-saving prevention, treatment and care.

The global health community is also opening its eyes to the fact that many of these companies are taking on significant financial risk in developing and producing the products that will be needed to continue to treat the diseases as they mutate and resistance is developed to treatments currently available. Examples include companies which make commitments to not-for-profit pricing of key commodities, notably drugs; companies which continue to develop new products such as paediatric drug formulations, even where these may not be justified commercially; companies which license intellectual property to encourage low-cost manufacture and companies which commit to continue to invest in research into new ways of fighting the diseases.

Sometimes market forces and the social commitments of providers are not enough to secure optimal outcomes for patients in the field. In such cases, the Global Fund has an interest in working to overcome such market failures. In 2008, the Global Fund Board approved a pilot for a new innovative financing mechanism, designed to ensure that people suffering from malaria have access to inexpensive and quality-assured antimalarial treatment, in the form of artemisinin-based combination therapies (ACTs). The programme, known as the Affordable Medicines Facility for malaria (AMFm), will promote the use of effective antimalarials and drive out ineffective medicines from the market by reducing consumer prices to an affordable level through price negotiations, a buyer co-payment, and ensuring safe and effective scale-up of ACT use by introducing in-country supporting interventions.

4. Conclusion

Partnerships between the public and private sectors, whether at the global or local level, are often challenging but vital to achieve the results necessary to meet the Millennium Development Goals related to health. The Global Fund shows the different partnerships possible with the private sector from governance and innovative financing through to implementation. We have illustrated these and highlighted some of the challenges, which include the historical mistrust between the public and private sectors; the potential conflicts of interest that arise when companies that manufacture products used in the fight against the diseases consider taking on other roles; and the effects of the business cycle and financial crises on both the private and public sectors. The Global Fund has benefited from the inclusion on its board of a member of the private sector (as well as private foundations) supported by a wider delegation of interested companies. Furthermore, the Global Fund was chaired, 2007–2009, by a private-sector representative Rajat Gupta, formerly Managing Director of McKinsey and Company. This kind of receptivity to private-sector perspectives and engagement has enabled the Global Fund to create partnerships with the private sector to raise money, to implement programmes, to provide commercial products and services in a socially responsible way and to raise awareness of the fight against AIDS, TB and malaria through effective advocacy and communications campaigns.

Chapter 11 assesses the contribution of private foundations.

References

Feeley F, Connelly P, Rosen S (2007) "Private Sector Provision and Financing of AIDS Treatment in Africa: Current Developments", *Current HIV/AIDS Reports* 4:192–200.

Gupta A (2006) "Public-Private Partnerships in Health", *Health for the Millions* 32(6):7–13.

Lancet Infectious Diseases (2007) "Engaging the Private Sector in Global Health", *Editorial* 7(12):757.

MacDonald N, Tayart de Borms L eds (2010) Global Philanthropy, Mercator Fund.

Over M (2009) "AIDS Treatment in South Asia: Equity and Efficiency Arguments for Shouldering the Fiscal Burden When Prevalence Rates Are Low." Center for Global Development Working Paper 161. Washington: Center for Global Development. Available at www.cgdev.org/content/publications/detail/1421119/.

Ridley GR (2001) "Putting the Partnership into Public-Private Partnerships", *Bulletin of WHO* 79(8): 694.

UNDP and IBLF (2003) "Business and the Millennium Goals: A Framework for Action", UNDP, New York.

USAID (2009) "Private Sector Involvement in HIV Service Provision", Washington, USA.

13

Civil Society Partners — Claiming Spaces for Civil Society in Global Health

Josh Galjour and Asia Russell

Summary

Civil society is a critical actor in global, national and local efforts to improve health outcomes. As a diverse stakeholder, civil society plays a role in the delivery of services; ensuring communities are mobilised to reach people at risk; and in governance. In some countries, resistance to the inclusion of civil society as equal partners remains a challenge. Weak or uneven capacity as well as accountability within civil society can also challenge the effectiveness of the sector. The chapter assesses the challenges and opportunities of robust civil society engagement in working for improved health outcomes. First, the development and diversity of civil society as a key stakeholder in global health is described.The chapter then focusses on examples of securing the strategic involvement of civil society in policy setting around global health.The chapter concludes with an exploration of the added value of civil society and the challenges and recommendations of claiming spaces for civil society in global health.

Press conference transcript between reporter and President Reagan's Press Secretary Larry Speakes, 15 October 1982.

Reporter: Larry, does the President have any reaction to the announcement made by the Centers for Disease Control in Atlanta, that AIDS is now an epidemic and have (sic) over 600 cases?

MR. SPEAKES: What's AIDS?
Reporter: Over a third of them have died. It's known as "gay plague."(Laughter.) No, it is. I mean it's a pretty serious thing that one in every three people that get this has died. And I wondered if the President is aware of it?

MR. SPEAKES: I don't have it. Do you? (Laughter.)
Reporter: No, I don't.

MR. SPEAKES: You didn't answer my question.
Reporter: Well, I just wondered, does the President —

MR. SPEAKES: How do you know? (Laughter.)
Reporter: In other words, the White House looks on this as a great joke?

MR. SPEAKES: No, I don't know anything about it, Lester.
Reporter: Does the President, does anyone in the White House know about this epidemic, Larry?

MR. SPEAKES: I don't think so. I don't think there's been any —
Reporter: Nobody knows?

MR. SPEAKES: There has been no personal experience here, Lester.

***

"I am happy to be part of the Global Fund Board as a person living with HIV/AIDS, because I have a voice now! When I vote, my voice is equal to that of the United States of America. That is something I have hardly seen before! That if I manage to argue my case well, my point of view will even outweigh that of the United States — that is a big thing and it began with the Global Fund; I have never seen it elsewhere, which is what I keep repeating... If these decisions are made without our input, they may end up working against us." — Dr Françoise Ndayishimiye, former member of the Global Fund Board.

1. Introduction

The spread of HIV among societies' most marginalised communities — along with the stigma that arises once a person is infected with HIV — has shaped political, social and economic aspects of the response to the AIDS crisis. Since the emergence of the AIDS pandemic, civil society in its many forms — from activist organisations, to direct service providers, to grassroots self-help networks — has played crucial roles in securing changes to health, funding, governance and human rights policies at local, national and global levels. Civil society has been a central and innovative partner in AIDS, with one foot inside and one foot outside its governance.

This chapter argues that concerned individuals, fellow activists and their supporters were the first people to respond to devastatingly high rates of HIV in marginalised communities in US cities in the early 1980s. In the absence of an evidence-based government response and with extreme stigma towards AIDS patients, activists united disparate networks and began to agitate for prevention, treatment, care and support. As the first treatment for AIDS entered the market and was made available to patients in the developed countries, civil society groups loudly condemned global inequity and advocated for the provision of AIDS drugs in the developing countries. In the first decade of the twenty-first century, the HIV epidemic — and the profound inequities in health care access that it exposed — led to a resurgence in global health awareness, advocacy and funding. At the same time, civil society groups took advantage of opportunities of the global health architecture — much of it caused by the creation of new programmes around HIV — and thereby institutionalised their role in global health governance.

Since the report of the first diagnosis in 1981 of what would become known as AIDS, civil society's engagement in the AIDS response was catalysed by outrage over neglect, bigotry, greed, homophobia, racism and exclusion. It has also shaped a vibrant civil society sector increasingly engaged in health governance and advocacy of health priorities beyond HIV. Progress and lessons learned by AIDS activism have contributed to cross-fertilisation among a range of health issues and between allied social movements and activists. At the same time, they established an important set of global best practices on engagement of directly affected consumers in shaping and evaluating health policy.

Civil society has filled gaps in the absence of a government response, but has also increasingly worked in partnership with government. This partnership has been one of the most distinctive and innovative elements of the AIDS response. Civil society has advocated vociferously against government policy decisions ranging from benign neglect to outright disgrace, while at other times, it has worked alongside government in new forms of partnership and collaboration. In the last 10 years, civil society has mobilised for substantially expanded HIV prevention and treatment services worldwide while carving out an increasingly powerful position in global health governance.

In 1982, President Reagan's Press Secretary, quoted above, responded with crude bigotry and homophobia to some of the first questions on record about AIDS, during a now-infamous press conference. His responses prefigured decades of deliberate and deadly political neglect by the U.S. and other governments. Twenty-nine years later, the transformative action of some of the communities most directly affected by the AIDS crisis, along with the "personal experience" of HIV positive people that so disconcerted Press Secretary Speakes, has become central to national and global AIDS policy debates. Their voice is now heard and recognised locally, nationally and in global health governance.

In the early days of the HIV epidemic in the United States, AIDS activists and AIDS service organisations were concentrated in urban areas with a high burden of HIV and an existing network of LGBT (Lesbian, Gay, Bisexual, Transgender) activists and their allies. In New York City, San Francisco, Washington D.C., Philadelphia, Chicago and other cities, LGBT activists and their allies were the first to respond to the epidemic. From 1996 on, as regimens of life-prolonging triple combination antiretroviral therapy — some of the most expensive medicines ever approved — came into widespread use in developed countries, AIDS advocacy focussed on winning reductions in medicine prices, ensuring equal access for marginalised groups such as low-income people, prisoners, drug users and homeless people, and advocating for the development of less toxic and more powerful antiretrovirals.

Initiating people with HIV on life-long, multiple daily doses of antiretroviral therapy — often with significant side effects — was unprecedented at the time in public health. Civil society developed and implemented innovative programmes designed to improve antiretroviral treatment "literacy" while increasing treatment adherence. These efforts both prolonged the benefit of treatment for people with HIV while reducing the risk of developing viral resistance — providing an individual and public health benefit.

Despite the fact that 60% of men, 80% of women and 90% of children living with HIV in 1998 were in sub-Saharan Africa, at that time access to the antiretroviral treatment that had revolutionised the AIDS response in wealthy countries was virtually nonexistent in developing countries.[1] As a result, by 1998, activist organisations in developed and developing countries began to form alliances of civil society organisations focussed on securing access to life-saving HIV treatment in resource-poor settings.

These alliances developed into sustained campaigns challenging national governments to guarantee access to HIV treatment in Thailand, Brazil, South Africa and elsewhere in the global South. In 1998, the consensus statement of an international seminar for AIDS NGOs on access to treatment for HIV in developing countries concluded, "Adequate infrastructure to deliver care safely is needed, but the lack of infrastructure should not be used as an excuse not to advocate better care and treatment."[2] Civil society efforts also focussed on the pricing practices of the multinational pharmaceutical industry[3] and the refusal of Western donors to invest in anything other than HIV prevention and palliative AIDS care in the developed world — essentially leaving millions to die from a condition

[1] *The status and trends of the HIV/AIDS epidemics in the world.* Joint United Nations Programme on HIV/AIDS, *Provisional Report*, June 1998, Available at:http://search.unaids.org/Html.aspx?q=PUB$CP&u=http://data.unaids.org/Publications/IRC-pub03/map_en.pdf [Accessed 6 October 2010].

[2] "Consensus Statement. Access to treatment for HIV in developing countries; statement from international seminar on access to treatment for HIV in developing countries, London, June 5 and 6, 1998", *The Lancet*, 1998, **352**:1379–1380.

[3] McNeil DG Jr. (2000) "Companies to cut cost of AIDS drugs for poor nations", *The New York Times*. Available at http://www.nytimes.com/2000/05/12/world/companies-to-cut-cost-of-aids-drugs-for-poor-nations.html[Accessed 6 October 2010].

that had become a long-term and chronic illness in wealthy countries.[4] These campaigns, led by people with HIV demanding an end to "medical apartheid", developed into a powerful new global social movement for AIDS treatment access.[5]

Alongside these developments, civil society both catalysed and benefited from changes in global health governance. Civil society played a critical role in the development and launch of the Millennium Development Goals at the Millennium Summit in New York in September 2000.[6] Civil society continued to pressure global leaders to create new multilateral global health financing institutions, which led to the creation in 2002 of the Global Fund to Fight AIDS, Tuberculosis, and Malaria.[7] In the United States, progressive and conservative activists found rare common ground to encourage the Bush administration to create a large development assistance programme focussed on HIV, which led to the President's Emergency Plan for AIDS Relief (PEPFAR).[8,9] In this way, civil society helped create innovative global health programmes and ensured they then had a central role in defining, implementing, and governing them.

Civil society participation and representation in global health governance has become institutionalised in the context of the HIV response. Such an innovative feature has been adapted by other health advocates in related institutions and partnerships, such as the International Health

---

[4] *AIDS, Drug Prices, and Generic Drugs*. Avert website. West Sussex, UK [online] Available at http://www.avert.org/generic.htm [Accessed 6 October 2010].

[5] Act Up: AIDS Coalition to Unleash Power (2000)*AIDS Drugs for Africa March and Rally*. [online] Available at http://www.actupny.org/reports/march5.html [Accessed 6 October 2010].

[6] United Nations Millennium Summit (2000) United Nations website. Available at http://www.un.org/millennium/[Accessed 6 October 2010].

[7] Civil Society and Private Sector. Global Fund to Fight AIDS, Tuberculosis, and Malaria. Available at http://www.theglobalfund.org/en/civilsociety/?lang=en[Accessed 6 October 2010].

[8] Dietrich JW (2007) "The politics of PEPFAR: the President's Emergency Plan for AIDS Relief", *Ethics and International Affairs*. [Online] Available at http://www.carnegiecouncil.org/resources/journal/21_3/essay/001.html [Accessed 14 February 2011].

[9] Allen M, Blustein P (2003). "Unlikely allies influenced Bush to shift course on AIDS relief",*Washington Post* 30 January. As accessed on Harvard Law School blog. Available at http://cyber.law.harvard.edu/blogs/gems/politicshiv/Unlikely AlliesInfluencedBush.htm [Accessed 6 October 2010].

Partnership (IHP+).[10] However, the increasing influence of civil society is not without risks, particularly in the areas of legitimacy, accountability, conflict of interest and capacity. The future of this innovative partnership will depend on the ability of civil society to negotiate the tensions in their new and developing roles.

2. Defining Civil Society in the Health Sector

Civil society is a diverse and complex sector, comprising non-state actors from an array of interest groups, networks, organisations and institutions. As such, "civil society" is difficult to define precisely. Identifying elements common to a "global civil society" is also a challenge. Members of civil society organisations typically share certain goals, such as achieving concrete policy change, leading them to coalesce around a demand, organising themselves and their communities, while creating alliances with like-minded communities through agitation for non-remunerative purposes. Other common principles around which civil society organises may be the notion of global solidarity, a focus on the right to health care as a fundamental human right and an insistence on the involvement of those affected by the disease in basic decision-making.

An expansive definition would include all non-state actors, including trade unions, foundations, universities, research institutions — even Parliamentarians and the media. Diversity in civil society leads to practical difficulties when referring universally to a "civil society" in global health governance. Under an inclusive definition, civil society equally includes a poor woman in a remote village providing home-based care services for a neighbour through a local women's group, and an international development organisation with an annual budget roughly equivalent to the size of a poor country's annual gross domestic product. Some academics reject the notion of a monolithic "global civil society", arguing instead that the notion of a "global civil society" is a weak analogy of a more authentic civil society, defined as "an entity built on a history of trust

---

[10] International Health Partnership: Partners — Civil Society. [Online] Available at http://www.internationalhealthpartnership.net/en/partners/civil_society [Accessed 6 October 2010].

or coexistence between people living in physical proximity and sharing a common culture".[11] Such sceptics have explored the "undeserved democratic legitimacy on policy decisions" conferred by the notion of civil society.[12]

Focussing instead on shared function can prove more useful. For the purposes of this chapter, we choose a restricted, functional definition of civil society organisations in the health sector: those organisations in the global North and South that agitate for equal, meaningful participation in global health governance, with a particular focus on those civil society groups engaged in activism, service delivery, policy development and independent oversight in support of increased access to prevention, treatment, care and support services.

3. The Development and Diversity of Civil Society in Health

Social and political injustices have long outraged individuals and led them to mobilise and unite in advocacy to defend and advance the rights of certain groups of people. These groups sometimes coalesced into organisations which today would be understood as civil society. Public health is an inherently political discipline — its discourse often distills into questions of who does and does not have access to life — and its history has been shaped by cases of individuals and networks organising and agitating to correct inequities through collective action. Examples of health-related activism can be traced from public hygiene and sanitation movements of the nineteenth century, to the anti-infant formula campaigns of the 1970s to the contemporary contributions of civil society to global health governance.[13] Civil society involvement in health

---

[11] Doyle C, Patel P (2008) "Civil society organisations and global health initiatives: problems of legitimacy", *Social Science and Medicine* **66**:1928–1938.

[12] *Ibid.* Doyle references Seckinelgin H (2003) Time to stop and think: HIV/AIDS. In Anheier H, Glasius M, Kaldor M eds, *Global Civil Society 2002/3.* London: Sage.

[13] Berridge V, Loughlin K, Herring R (2009) Historical dimensions of global health governance. In: Kent Buse *et al.* ed. *Making Sense of Global Health Governance: A Policy Perspective.* Hampshire: Palgrave Macmillan, pp.28–46.

matters is not new, but the primacy and participation of civil society involvement in decision-making structures of global health institutions is — along with the standard expectation of full and meaningful inclusion in those institutions.

An historical analysis reveals how civil society's contribution to global health governance developed and diversified through its response to the AIDS epidemic. In the early 1980s, the HIV epidemic exploded in American cities with the first diagnosed case of AIDS in 1981. Gay men were catastrophically affected, along with injecting drug users and their sex partners and haemophiliacs. Among gay men, shared social stigma and experience in major LGBT activist movements in the 1960s and 1970s laid the foundation for solidarity in response to the AIDS epidemic. Aware that local and national authorities were refusing to respond proportionately, accurately or effectively, activists built public and underground networks almost overnight. They established trusted channels for dissemination of literally life-saving safer sex and harm reduction information and materials to prevent HIV transmission, such as condoms and sterile injecting equipment. Fury ignited over the absence of a comprehensive government response to the AIDS crisis. Civil society had little opportunity to channel the collective voice of the most affected populations into the existing health policy and governance mechanisms of the time.

Against deep-seated fear and prejudice, early AIDS activists were public health pioneers, demanding respect and dignity as people with agency in their own health care, and a reliance on fact and evidence rather than hysteria and bigotry. In 1983, people with HIV in the United States published the "Denver Principles", a landmark declaration defining the human rights of people with HIV, and demanding the involvement of HIV positive people at every stage of health decisionmaking as a non-negotiable element of health policy and service delivery.[14] AIDS activists from this early period were literally campaigning for their lives — and the lives of their communities.

[14] Denver Principles Project. [online] Available at http://www.denverprinciplesproject.com/ [Accessed 6 October 2010].

3.1 Early civil society responses to HIV

In 1981, the Gay Men Health's Crisis was created by six concerned men in New York City. An answering machine set up in Rodger McFarland's house received over 100 calls the first night. The organisation was to be the first to provide information, advocacy and care to the most affected populations.[15]

In March of 1987, the AIDS Coalition to Unleash Power (ACT UP) was created in New York City "as a diverse, nonpartisan group of individuals united in anger and committed to direct action to end the AIDS crisis". The group argued that AIDS was a political and social as well as a medical crisis, and used direct action, community organising and media savvy to challenge decision makers with concrete policy demands. Early ACT UP actions demanded comprehensive leadership and investment by the U.S. government, accelerated regulatory approval for promising experimental HIV treatments, and other efforts to challenge policies that obstructed an effective response to the epidemic.[16]

At the same time, thousands of kilometres away in East Africa, an HIV positive leader named Noerine Kaleeba — one of the first in the country to openly declare her status — along with her colleagues founded The AIDS Support Organization (TASO) in Uganda. TASO's founding emanated from individuals who "were unified by common experiences faced when encountering HIV/AIDS at a time of high stigma, ignorance and discrimination. The founders met informally in each other's homes or offices to provide mutual psychological and social support. Cohesion among these was strengthened by the fact that they were either directly infected with HIV or affected because their very close familial associates were infected."[17]

---

[15] Gay Men's Health Crisis: About Us. [online] Available at http://www.gmhc.org/about-us [Accessed 6 October 2010].

[16] AIDS Coalition to Unleash Power: NYC Information. [online] Available at http://www.actupny.org/indexfolder/NYC.html [Accessed 6 October 2010].

[17] The AIDS Support Organization: About TASO (2008) [online] Available at http://www.tasouganda.org/index.php?option=com_content&view=article&id=51&Itemid=61 [Accessed 6 October 2010].

In the developed and developing world, grassroots home-based care services for the sick and/or dying first emerged out of necessity — where hospitals, hospices, clinics and other facilities refused to touch or admit HIV positive people, a diverse range of compassionate and outraged volunteers responded, including members of religious networks, LGBT community organisations and HIV positive health professionals. Over the years these informal practices became integrated into mainstream AIDS programmes. Often their service delivery efforts cut across political issues and they became increasingly institutionalised into mainstream AIDS programmes. With their success and recognition as a key component of service delivery, grassroots organisations in sub-Saharan Africa slowly moved from working outside government structures to become an indispensable partner of government. The civil society movement in several countries had emerged from an organic response to governmental exclusion into a steadfast deliverer of critical services and a recognised political counterpart.

3.2 The rise of the international treatment access movement

In the mid-1990s, effective and life-prolonging combination antiretroviral treatment first became widely available in developed countries, providing for the first time a hope that people with HIV could live with a chronic manageable illness rather than face a death sentence. Even in the West, antiretroviral treatment was first available only to those with private insurance but eventually became part of public entitlement programmes, and was — as a result of activism — eventually made available to inmates, the homeless and drug users.

By 1998 activists in developed countries began publicly describing the inequity of HIV treatment access — that the majority of people with HIV live in developing countries and, therefore, experience HIV as a death sentence, while people in developed countries experience HIV as a chronic, manageable illness. At that time virtually no one in the developing world with HIV had access to triple combination therapy — apart from those wealthy enough to pay out of pocket or who were participating in clinical trials or as part of a small number of pilot projects.The rapid pace of globalisation and democratisation of technology strengthened linkages between Northern and Southern activist movements. By 1999, organised protests, in the tradition of what has been dubbed "confrontational modes of action" for social justice, rose up in a concerted fashion against national governments and the multinational pharmaceutical industry.[18] The fight against AIDS had turned into a fight for universal access to treatment.

In developing countries, civil society organisations were mobilising to demand investment in treatment. One case is that of South Africa, the country with the highest burden of HIV in the world, where the activist organisation Treatment Action Campaign (TAC) played a crucial role in securing investment in HIV treatment. TAC's early activism included a range of important campaigns, from challenging the South African government to break patent monopolies on overpriced, essential medicines such as fluconazole (used to treat the life-threatening opportunistic infection cryptococcal meningitis) to forcing 39 multinational pharmaceutical companies to abandon a lawsuit against South Africa, brought about because of national efforts to promote access to generic medicines.

In 2001 — the same year — TAC sued the South African government as part of a campaign to ensure access to medicine to prevent transmission of HIV from pregnant women to newborns. In December 2001, a South African judge ruled that pregnant women with HIV should be provided nevirapine, the standard of care at the time for the prevention of mother to child transmission, calling it an "ineluctable obligation of the state."[19] The government appealed in a lengthy court battle, until the Constitutional Court finally ruled in 2002 that poor pregnant women with HIV in public hospitals must be provided nevirapine.[20,21] Civil society activists, led by

---

[18] McCoy D, Hilson M (2009) Civil society, its organization, and global health governance. In: Buse K *et al.* ed., *Making Sense of Global Health Governance: A Policy Perspective.* Hampshire: Palgrave Macmillan, pp.209–231.

[19] Cauvin HE (2001) "South African court orders medicine for HIV-infected mothers. *The New York Times.* [online] 15 December 2001. Available at http://www.nytimes.com/2001/12/15/world/south-african-court-orders-medicine-for-hiv-infected-mothers.html [Accessed 15 February 2011].

[20] Cauvin HE (2001) "South Africa to appeal ruling ordering access to AIDS drug. *The New York Times.* [online] 20 December 2001. Available at http://www.nytimes.com/2001/12/20/world/south-africa-to-appeal-ruling-ordering-access-to-aids-drug.html [Accessed 15 February 2011].

[21] Sidley P (2002) "South African government forced to give mothers antiretroviral drug", *British Medical Journal* website, 20 July 2002. [online] Available at http://www.bmj.com/content/325/7356/121.2.full [Accessed 15 February 2011].

TAC, waged a successful fight for access to ART for all adults and children in South Africa, and national roll out of ART finally began, after initial delays and what was perceived as a continued lack of political commitment, only in 2004.[22] Despite these delays, the South African government has rolled out one of the most comprehensive treatment programmes in Africa.

In North America and Europe, a small network of civil society organisations developed high-profile treatment access campaigns. New organisations including Health Global Access Project (Health GAP) along with the Médicins Sans Frontières (MSF) Campaign for Access to Essential Medicines and existing organisations such as ACT UP worked together to overcome the impact of pharmaceutical company patent protection and to secure expanded access to treatment in developing countries. Health GAP was formed by American activists to respond to treatment barriers for millions of people in need of life-saving medicines. MSF's Campaign for Access to Essential Medicines works to reduce the high cost of existing drugs, challenge the use of outdated treatment guidelines and encourage new research into drugs for neglected tropical diseases. In 1999, MSF, an "early, vocal leader in demanding AIDS treatment for the world", was awarded the Nobel Peace Prize for its efforts.[23]

These campaigns used a variety of activist techniques to garner public support, spread their message, and publicise barriers to treatment scale-up. Initial efforts by Health GAP and other US allies focussed on overcoming the Clinton Administration and pharmaceutical company opposition to efforts to produce generic versions of antiretroviral medicines in India, Thailand, Brazil and elsewhere. These efforts were compliant with national obligations under the World Trade Organisation's Agreement on Trade Related Aspects of Intellectual Property Rights (TRIPS) but were nevertheless considered by the Clinton Administration to constitute "barriers to trade." Activists challenged U.S. Trade Representative Charlene Barshefsky with a series of massive protests,

---

[22] LaFraniere, Sharon. "South Africa is criticized for delay in AIDS treatment." *The New York Times*. [online] 20 February 2004. Available at: <http://www.nytimes.com/2004/02/20/world/south-africa-is-criticized-for-delay-in-aids-treatment.html?src=pm>. [Accessed 15 February 2011].

[23] D'adesky, Anne-Christine, 2004. *Moving Mountains: The Race to Treat Global AIDS*. London: Verso.

office takeovers and other direct actions; Vice President Al Gore — the Co-Chair of the US-South Africa Bi-National Commission on Trade and a point person on implementing the pharmaceutical industry's demands to thwart generic competition in South Africa — was challenged on national television when he announced his candidacy for President. A group of activists interrupted his inaugural address as a candidate, shouting "Gore's Greed Kills, AIDS Drugs for Africa" — and interrupted him again two more campaign stops over the next 48 hours.

Within months, the Clinton Administration directed the U.S. Trade Representative to change its trade policies, and by December 1999 had issued an Executive Order stating that it would no longer punish countries that were attempting to increase access to affordable AIDS medicines through use of generic competition. Clearing political space for companies to begin manufacturing generic versions of antiretroviral medicines at a fraction of the cost was a critical step in securing HIV treatment as a fundamental aspect of the response to HIV in resource-poor countries. This success by activist health groups not only highlights one of civil society's great achievements in the AIDS response but also illustrates their important role in catalysing and accelerating issues related to access to health care.

3.3 HIV as civil society's entry point into global health governance

The recognition of vast inequities in treatment access dovetailed with the turn of the millennium, global leadership that favoured new attention and resources for health and a series of new global campaigns. In 2000, the international community agreed to the Millennium Development Goals, eight goals for poverty reduction, three of which are health-related and one of which is focussed on fighting infectious diseases including HIV. In addition, in 2000, the Global Alliance for Vaccines and Immunizations (GAVI) was launched. A critical milestone for the inclusion of civil society in global health governance occurred when civil society representatives were included on the GAVI Board of Directors.

Support for roll-out of anti-retroviral therapy was not universal, however. In January 2001, the then-Director of the U.S. Agency for International Development Andrew Natsios testified before the US House

Committee on International Relations and expressed his scepticism of ART provision in developing countries:

"So the biggest problem, if you look at Kofi Annan's budget, half of the budget is for antiretrovirals. If we had them today, we could not distribute them. We could not administer the programme, because we don't have the doctors, we don't have the roads, we don't have the (inaudible).

This sounds small, and some people, if you've travelled to rural Africa, you know this. This is not a criticism, just a different world. People do not know what watches and clocks are. They do not use Western means for telling time, they use the sun. These drugs have to be administered during a certain sequence of time during the day. Moreover, when you say, "Take it at 10:00," people will say, "What do you mean by 10:00?" They don't use those terms in the villages to describe time. They describe morning and the afternoon and the evening."[24]

Such initial resistance was in time overcome through advocacy based on evidence, which at times provoked opposition by mainstream public health experts who insisted that life-saving HIV treatment was neither "cost effective" nor "sustainable". A few months later, in April 2001, at the Organization of African Unity meeting in Abuja, the then-U.N. Secretary General Kofi Annan called for substantial new resources in the fight against HIV/AIDS, TB and malaria, declaring, "The war on AIDS will not be won without a war chest, of a size far beyond what is available so far."[25]

In April 2001, multinational drug companies dropped their lawsuit against the South African government, and the production and distribution of generic ART made the roll out in the global South financially possible. As competition increased, the price of ART reduced. These global campaigns and new initiatives were important in creating a well-resourced and favourable policy environment for increased scale-up. Later that summer,

---

[24] Transcript of the U.S. House of Representatives, International Relations Committee Meeting, 7 June 2001. [Online] Available at http://democrats.foreignaffairs.house.gov/archives/107/72978.pdf

[25] Transcript of the Address by Kofi Annan to the African Summit on HIV/AIDS, Tuberculosis, and other Infectious Diseases. United Nations website. [Online] Available at http://www.un.org/News/ossg/sg/stories/statments_search_full.asp?statID=8 [Accessed 15 February 2011].

heads of state gathered at the U.N. General Assembly Special Session on HIV/AIDS to recognise the severity of the HIV epidemic and highlight the urgent need for action.[26]

In early 2002, the Global Fund to Fight AIDS, Tuberculosis, and Malaria was formed as a public-private partnership that included three seats on its Board of Directors for civil society representation — one from a developed country NGO, one from a developing country NGO and one from communities living with and affected by the three diseases. With a new stream of funding in place, the policy space to produce low-cost generic versions of antiretroviral treatment and an organised and vocal global network of treatment activists to hold national governments and donors accountable, treatment campaigns in developing countries finally rolled out globally seven years after the first protease inhibitor, Saquinavir, received Federal Drug Administration approval.

In 2003, two major initiatives highlighted the success of the international treatment access movement. First, the launch of the World Health Organisation's 3x5 initiative, a campaign to put at least three million people on ART by 2005, lent urgency to ART roll out.[27] In January 2003, in his State of the Union speech, President George W. Bush announced the creation of the President's Emergency Plan for AIDS Relief (PEPFAR) and asked Congress for $15 billion for the next five years to scale up prevention, treatment, care and support in 15 focus countries, mostly in sub-Saharan Africa.[28] Treatment scale-up has proceeded at a rapid clip through the first decade of the new millennium. In South Africa, in 2004, only 55,000 people were estimated to be receiving ART; in 2005, the number had nearly quadrupled to 207,000, and by 2007, the number had

---

[26] 2001 Declaration of Commitment on HIV/AIDS, UNAIDS website. [Online] Available at http://data.unaids.org/publications/irc-pub03/aidsdeclaration_en.pdf [Accessed 15 February 2011].

[27] The 3 by 5 Initiative. [Online] World Health Organization website. Available at http://www.who.int/3by5/en/ [Accessed 15 February 2011].

[28] Transcript of President Bush's Second State of the Union Address, January 29, 2003. [Online] CNN website. Available at http://edition.cnn.com/2003/ALLPOLITICS/01/28/sotu.transcript/ [Accessed 15 February 2011].

grown to 460,000.[29] For its part, by December 2010, the Global Fund was supporting ART for three million people worldwide.[30] According to WHO and UNAIDS estimates, however, of the 14.6 million people in need of antiretroviral therapy in 2009, in that same year only 5.25 million in low- and middle-income countries had access to the lifesaving medications.[31]

Following the finding in the Global Fund 2007 Results Report "that civil society organisations are strong implementers" and they can "improve the speed of finance and add additional capacity", the next year, the Global Fund Board of Directors endorsed the concept of "dual track financing" in which applicants are recommended to request funding for government as well as non-governmental implementers.[32] By December 2009, 35% of the Global Fund portfolio was allocated to implementers from civil society organisations, reflecting the important service delivery role that CSOs perform.[33]

The experience of the International HIV/AIDS Alliance in the Ukraine illustrates one of the earliest and most successful examples of civil society implementation of Global Fund grants. In January 2004, the Alliance Ukraine (a foundation that is part of the international Alliance family) was invited to take over implementation of the Round 1 HIV/AIDS grant following mismanagement by the original PRs, becoming one of the first civil society PRs. In an example of effective North-South civil society partnership, the UK-based International HIV/AIDS Alliance provided

[29] Epidemiological Fact Sheet on HIV and AIDS: Core data on epidemiology and response, 2008. [Online] UNAIDS website.Available at http://apps.who.int/globalatlas/predefinedReports/EFS2008/full/EFS2008_ZA.pdf [Accessed 15 February 2011].

[30] Fighting AIDS, Tuberculosis, and Malaria. [Online] The Global Fund website. Available at http://www.theglobalfund.org/en/fighting/?lang=en [Accessed 15 February 2011].

[31] HIV/AIDS: Antiretroviral therapy. [Online] World Health Organization website. Available at http://www.who.int/hiv/topics/treatment/en/index.html [Accessed 15 February 2011].

[32] The Global Fund to Fight AIDS, Tuberculosis, and Malaria (2007) Annual Report. [Online] Available at http://www.theglobalfund.org/documents/publications/progressreports/ProgressReport2007_en.pdf [Accessed 15 February 2011].

[33] The Global Fund to Fight AIDS, Tuberculosis, and Malaria (2009) Key Performance Indicators. [Online] Available at http://www.theglobalfund.org/en/performance/kpi/2009/?lang=en [Accessed 15 February 2011].

capacity building and technical support to local implementers.[34] A U.N. evaluation of the national AIDS response in Ukraine observes: "The impressive performance of the Alliance as a PR demonstrates that direct financing of Global Fund grants to civil society recipients can improve the speed of grant implementation and help to mobilize additional implementation capacity."[35]

Despite the success of the treatment access movement, some donors have reduced investments in HIV/AIDS, pointing to the global financial crisis and other emerging global health priorities.[36] In May 2010, the *New York Times* reported that AIDS patients were being turned away from access to free treatment in Uganda, jeopardising the progress that has been made to date and increasing the risk of treatment resistance.[37] "It is regrettable that we don't have enough resources to pay for the unmet need anywhere — in Uganda or anywhere on the planet," U.S. Global AIDS Ambassador Eric Goosby said to CNN.[38] In June 2010, activists in South Africa took to the streets to protest what they called the retreat by donors from the commitments they have made, as well the failure of African governments to provide sufficient funding to health, as agreed in the Abuja Declaration of 2001.

In the wake of the financial crisis, civil society organisations attempted to hold donors and national governments accountable, while donors

---

[34] Hoover J (2008) Civil Society Success on the Ground: Community Systems Strengthening and Dual Track Financing: Nine Illustrative Case Studies. [Online] Available at http://www.theglobalfund.org/documents/publications/progressreports/Dual-Track_Report_en.pdf [Accessed 15 February 2011].

[35] Comprehensive External Evaluation of the National AIDS Response in Ukraine, Consolidated Report (January 2009) [Online] Available at http://www.un.org.ua/files/20090522_ee_en_5.pdf [Accessed 15 February 2011].

[36] Winslow R (2010) "AIDS funding flat in 2009", *The Wall Street Journal* [Online] Available at http://online.wsj.com/article/SB10001424052748704196404575375373124308764.html?KEYWORDS=hiv [Accessed 15 February 2011].

[37] McNeil DG (2010) "At front lines, AIDS war is falling apart", *The New York Times* [Online] Available at http://www.nytimes.com/2010/05/10/world/africa/10aids.html [Accessed 15 February 2011].

[38] McKenzie D, Swails B (2010) "Funding threat to Uganda's winning AIDS program", *CNN* [Online] Available at http://edition.cnn.com/2010/WORLD/africa/ 06/18/uganda.aids/ [Accessed 15 February 2011].

increasingly emphasised that national governments, along with donors and other partners, must increase investments in HIV/AIDS. The U.S. ambassador to Uganda wrote in the Ugandan *Daily Monitor* in September 2010: "Addressing Uganda's long-term HIV and Aids [sic] needs requires a renewed commitment from the people of Uganda, the Government of Uganda, the Global Fund and other donors. The US Government is not — and cannot — be the only source of funding for Uganda's HIV and Aids [sic] prevention, care, and treatment efforts."[39] Thus, despite the formidable gains in increasing treatment access in the last eight years, the sustained rate of scale up remains ambitious.

3.4 The institutionalisation of civil society participation in global health governance

The contribution of civil society to global health governance has become increasingly recognised. In 2009, the medical journal *TheLancet* published an editorial by the Maximizing Positive Synergies Collaborative Group, which stated, "Civil society has crucially important roles ranging from advocacy, demand creation, and service delivery, to policy-setting and providing oversight by emphasizing accountability to service users. These more inclusive partnership arrangements, which put countries in the driving seat, represent important innovations that should be supported as an integral part of systems strengthening, especially in the context of the current discussions around global health architecture."[40]

As debates in global health shift and new priorities emerge, it appears that civil society's role in global health governance will endure. Indeed at this time, civil society engages with U.N. agencies, including the World Health Assembly, and is represented on the UNAIDS Programme Coordinating Board and the Global Health Workforce Alliance.

---

[39] Lanier JP (2010) "Addressing HIV/AIDS requires renewed commitment", *Daily Monitor* [Online] Available at http://www.monitor.co.ug/OpEd/Commentary/-/689364/1020632/-/13vb93oz/-/index.html[Accessed 15 February 2011].

[40] Atun R *et al.* (2009)"Venice statement on global health initiatives and health systems", *The Lancet* **374**(9692):783–784.

A fierce struggle to ensure that a rights-based approach defines the global response to HIV/AIDS has characterised the rise of civil society representation and participation in global health governance. From early grassroots responses in small affected communities across the world to efforts to humanise the epidemic by lifting the voices of those living with HIV, civil society has often had an adversarial relationship with the established power structure. Confronting stigma, deep-seated prejudices, and religious views that blamed the victim for his or her HIV status, civil society activists have organised, agitated and ultimately succeeded in capturing a chair at the global health table.

However, now that civil society representation has become a part of the public health establishment against which in its early years it protested, what now is the appropriate role for civil society in global health governance? Despite all of civil society's gains, there may be a tension between the unique perspective of civil society as partners *outside* of the government-business structure and their unique voices *in* the global dialogue.What then should be the role of civil society — protesting in the street or negotiating in the boardroom? Can civil society be empowered to do both, and if so, how? In the next section, we address some of the main challenges facing civil society in their new roles.

4. Challenges and Recommendations for the Way Forward: Legitimacy, Accountability and Capacity

Civil society has achieved policy victories in the areas of HIV, tuberculosis and malaria, alongside representation and participation in decision-making structures of new multilateral initiatives such as GAVI, the Global Fund and the IHP+. These structures contribute to what some describe as a "global health architecture", referring to the multiple health financing, normative and policy-setting institutions operating at the global level. While civil society has demonstrated its ability to achieve impact and tens of millions of people in need of essential services in the developing world have benefitted and continue to benefit from their efforts, civil society faces emerging challenges of legitimacy and accountability in their larger role in global health policy making.

4.1 Legitimacy — whom do you represent?

Public queries regarding the legitimacy of civil society have historically been used by state actors as "red herrings" to weaken, distract and confuse civil society representatives. Nevertheless, there are reasonable questions regarding legitimacy arising from within and outside the sector. Civil society members can claim legitimacy based on their proximity to the population or community in question, their membership in a vulnerable community or population whose interest their organisation represents, or from those constituents whom they claim to serve and represent. Civil society organisations themselves have suggested legitimacy derives from their "knowledge and local experience, technical skills, innovation, ability to influence public opinion, internal democratic governance, and a capacity to mobilize people for social change."[41] Other sources of legitimacy and accountability which have been suggested, and criticised, include civil society's "moral authority,[42] non-profit generating role, or appeals to a rights-based approach. Indeed if civil society did not represent communities affected by the diseases, who would?

Representation is a political process, and representation by its nature includes as well as excludes certain views and agendas. Representation within the civil society constituency and of the constituency itself has heretofore been achieved through a process of soliciting the views of other constituency members, developing a coherent, justified position based on those views, arguing and lobbying for that position and finally reporting it back to the constituency. Unfortunately, some CSOs, particularly those operating at the national or regional level, still lack the technical capacity, financial resources and access to power structures to complete this feedback loop.

A key goal of civil society involvement is engagement that moves beyond representation, instead insuring active, ongoing participation — in

---

[41] Tomlinson B (2008) Civil society and aid effectiveness: a synthesis of advisory group regional consultations and related processes.[Online] Available at http://siteresources.worldbank.org/ACCRAEXT/Resources/4700790–1208545462880/AG-CS-Synthisis-of-Consultations.pdf [Accessed 15 February 2011].

[42] Kovach H *et al.*(2003) Power without accountability? The Global Accountability Report 2006. [Online] One World Trust.Available at http://www.wto.org/english/news_e/news03_e/gar2003_e.pdf [Accessed 15 February 2011].

debates, policy development, in gathering and evaluating evidence and in service delivery. Barriers to this sort of participation are substantial — and civil society often lacks the capacity and resources to engage beyond the level of basic, pro forma representation. In the case of the Global Fund, Coordinating Mechanisms (CCMs) are mandated by eligibility requirements to include representatives from civil society and individuals affected with and by the three diseases. However, the quality of contribution and engagement continues to vary widely.

4.2 Accountability — to whom do you report?

With increasing levels of responsibility for decision-making come heightened levels of accountability. If civil society's role is to hold government and the private sector accountable, it is much less clear whose role it is to hold civil society accountable. Unlike the democratic state, which receives its legitimacy from its citizens' votes, "global civil society" has only members or stakeholders, or interested parties; it does not have overarching mechanisms for regulation, coordination or governance. Some argue that this very dissonance within civil society is critical to an effective role as watchdog and enriches the debate within the sector. Global coordination efforts imply that civil society should speak with one voice — an unrealistic and undesired goal.

Some civil society advocates argue that accountability should be "self-regulated" within civil society.[43] Given the fragmentation and diversity of civil society, efforts to self-regulate within the sector may remain aspirational. However, at local levels, some civil society networks have in fact developed and implemented accountability and consultation mechanisms. Defining to whom civil society is accountable, as well as mechanisms to ensure accountability, is an important feature of maturing civil society participation in global health governance. Attempts to coordinate within the sector have not kept up with

[43] Tomlinson B (2011) Civil society and aid effectiveness: a synthesis of advisory group regional consultations and related processes. [Online] Available at http://siteresources.worldbank.org/ACCRAEXT/Resources/4700790–1208545462880/AG-CS-Synthisis-of-Consultations.pdf [Accessed 15 February 2011].

the proliferation of civil society organisations operating at local, national and international levels.

4.3 Capacity — how do you perform?

As civil society takes on new roles, new skills and capacities are required. Building capacity for advocacy, service delivery and oversight will be paramount, as civil society receives increasing shares of funding from donors and governments and becomes a reliable contributor to global health governance. In turn, civil society must be able to document the achievement of quality results. Global decision-making bodies should include civil society organisations in the measurement, monitoring and dissemination of development results. Attempts to ensure civil society participation in country-level Paris Declaration monitoring processes are an example of a recent effort to improve transparent results monitoring.

Donors are increasingly focussing on national health sector and disease-specific strategies as priority instruments for funding. Civil society has had very little experience in "speaking the language" of developing, evaluating and implementing such health plans. Civil society must quickly expand its capacity to influence and contribute to these planning processes — using internal and external pressure — while challenging national governments and donors to fund and implement quality plans once they are developed. It is hoped that the International Health Policy Action Fund, supported by IHP+ and related initiatives and operationalised in 2010, will help to build civil society capacity in national health planning processes.[44]

5. Conclusion: the Promise and Possibility of Civil Society

In this chapter, we have described how civil society developed as an innovative partner in HIV in a few cities, and expanded to a global HIV

[44] Civil Society Health Policy Action Fund 1. [Online] Available at http://www.healthpolicy-actionfund.org/joomdr/ [Accessed 15 February 2011].

movement and one which has extended into other health areas. From acting on the outside, it has now become an essential partner in global health governance, though one not without its internal and external challenges. We traced the historical rise of civil society participation and representation in global health and have highlighted the early spread of HIV in stigmatised populations in the U.S. in the early and mid-1980's as a moment of profound change for civil society engagement in health. There is no question that in the last 10 years, civil society has gained an increasingly prominent role in the decision-making apparatuses of the highest level of global health governance.

At the turn of the century, civil society worked both outside the structures of the government-international organisation complex, but also increasingly shaped new initiatives and programmes and meaningfully contributed to decisionmaking within them. Through this paradox in partnership, civil society played a unique role by working alongside government, but not completely with it, maintaining its traditional distance and scepticism, and when necessary, provoking, pushing and holding government accountable. This innovative partnership changed the nature of civil society and offered it new roles and responsibilities in the reconstructed global health architecture of the new century.

Critical engagement by civil society has ranged from reactive, emotional and subversive activism to the newer responsibilities of contributing to governance of global health. Civil society participation in policy development is not necessarily new. Since the beginning of the epidemic, civil society has fought for — and won — seats at policy setting tables, from the Internal Review Boards and community advisory boards of clinical trials, to Ryan White planning councils, to HIV clinical guidelines development committees, and most recently to the Global Fund Board of Directors. What is innovative, however, is the dual role that civil society has recently negotiated — working both *inside* global health agencies in oversight, resource mobilisation, and policy development, and on the *outside* of agencies through its traditional activist role.

Historically, civil society has taken on a more reactive, rather than proactive role, by taking to the streets and mounting global campaigns against inequitable policy decisions; civil society's contemporary contribution to global health policy making is forcing its members to learn new skills, build additional capacities, and experiment in novel forms of partnerships. The proliferation of civil society organisations, the strengthening of civil society networks, and their increased coordination has catalysed the global health architecture, and has afforded civil society the opportunity to agitate in the street as well as simultaneously negotiating in the boardrooms of global health governance.

The successes of civil society are clear: seats at the tables of the major international health funders, norm-setting agencies and foundations; the provision of services to millions of vulnerable people; and financial resources and global attention to health inequities. However, how then does civil society consolidate these early successes, maintain a focus on improved health outcomes and continue to raise the voices of the most disadvantaged? These are the questions that civil society faces, and that civil society alone will answer. United, angry, everyday people have coalesced to form groups that have narrated to the world the private tragedies of "personal experience" which the Reagan White House lacked; the images have entered our collective imagination and today guide our response to global health inequities. The force and power with which civil society has responded to the global HIV epidemic — and their acceptance by the international community as innovative partners — suggests that civil society engagement in global health has just begun.

The authors wish to thank Daniel Low-Beer and Prerna Banati for their guidance and support.

> Chapter 18 assesses in detail the civil society response in Russia. Chapter 20 assesses the importance of community partnerships for effective health programmes.

Section 3

Integrating New Partnerships at Country Level

14

Governance and Sustainable Financing in Southern Africa: Swaziland, a Case Study

Alan Whiteside[1]

Summary

This chapter focusses on issues of health governance and sustainable financing, illustrated with the health situation in Swaziland. It describes the current health status of the country, looking at how health programmes are negotiated within the country and in relation to international partners. Inevitably the HIV/AIDS epidemic will be at the centre of the discussion since Swaziland has the worst epidemic in the world. It looks at how Swaziland has responded to the epidemic and addresses some the main challenges they face. It shows how the response developed and how AIDS challenged governance models in country and in relation to international aid. Central to this will be the issue of sustainable financing and governance internally and in relation to donors. The chapter will examine the development of the domestic and international responses in a critical manner. The conclusion looks beyond Swaziland to some of the big challenges faced by the region and will suggest that there are lessons for the countries of the region and for global health governance more broadly.

[1] Professor Alan Whiteside is the Director of the Health Economics and HIV/AIDS Research Division of the University of KwaZulu-Natal.

1. Introduction

The story of global health and its governance has generally been one of success and progress. Across most of the world life expectancy has risen, people are living longer and are healthier. In the 1950–1955 period, global life expectancy was 46.6 years; between 2005 and 2010, it was estimated at 67.6 years. Over the same period, there have been reductions in infant mortality, which fell from 151.9 per 1000 live births between 1950 and 1955 to an estimated 47.3 between 2005 and 2010 (United Nations Social and Economic Affairs 2008). If the problems and challenges raised in the WHO Commission on Social Determinants of Health are addressed with resources and courage, then the world can expect continued progress. The United Nations Population Division predicts infant mortality could drop to 22.9 in 2045–2050 and life expectancy rise to 75.5 in the same period.

People are living healthier lives. A 2006 article (Mathers and Loncar) analysing global mortality and the disease burden from 2002 to 2030 noted:

> Global DALYs lost are projected to increase from 1.48 billion in 2002 to 1.54 billion in 2030, an overall increase of only 3%. Since the population increase is projected to be 27% during the same period, there is actually a decrease in the global per capita burden. Unlike deaths, where the overall global death rate is projected to increase by 1%, the DALY rate decreases because the increasing number of deaths is offset by the shift in age at death to older ages. (Mathers and Loncar 2006, p. 2021).

The number of deaths from communicable disease will decline, while the proportion of people dying from non-communicable diseases will increase (from 59% in 2002 to 69% in 2030 under their baseline scenario). Lifestyle diseases and especially tobacco use are projected to be the major killers.

This is the global picture. Unfortunately, there are bleak areas in this generally optimistic world view. The biggest communicable disease burden will come from the AIDS epidemic. Although deaths from infectious diseases decrease overall, AIDS deaths continue to increase. The scale of this will be determined, in the short term, by access to antiretroviral drugs both first and second line, and in the longer term by how effective prevention efforts are.

AIDS is not a global problem though. Across most of the world the epidemic has been controlled and is located in specific at risk populations such as injecting drug users, men who have sex with men and commercial sex workers. In some instances, it seemed that HIV might spread but was brought under control (Thailand, Cambodia and Senegal provide examples). In other areas, despite the fears in the 1980s, it may never have had the potential to become a generalised epidemic (in the rich world, for instance, and most of Latin America and North Africa and the Middle East). The areas where the epidemic is having a significant impact on health indicators are eastern and Southern Africa with a few outlier countries in the Caribbean, Central Africa and Papua New Guinea, in Oceana.

The global response to health issues is addressed elsewhere in this volume. Specifically with regard to AIDS, in 1996, the UNAIDS, the new agency charged with harmonising and coordinating the UN response to HIV/AIDS, opened for business having been established in terms of an Economic and Social Council of the United Nations (UNECOSOC) resolution (1994/24). In 2001, the then UN Secretary General, Kofi Annan called for spending on AIDS to be increased ten-fold. In 2002, the Global Fund for AIDS, TB and Malaria was established. In 2003, President George W. Bush pledged \$15 billion towards his Presidential Emergency Programme for AIDS Relief (PEPFAR) and the World Health Organisation (WHO) launched the "3 × 5" campaign aiming to place three million people on treatment by 2005. In 1996, there was about \$300 million available for HIV/AIDS in low- and middle-income countries; by 2008, this increased to \$13.7 billion (UNAIDS 2009).

This chapter focusses on issues of AIDS and its impact on governance, including health governance, in countries with high HIV prevalence and is illustrated with examples from Southern Africa and in particular Swaziland. It begins by describing the evolution of the epidemic in the region and the responses that have been seen. The article then looks at the governance issues — the impact AIDS has on service delivery and governance, and that governance has on AIDS. I suggest the impact of AIDS on governance is central to both lack of response and its failure to be fully effective. As part of the review, I look at health financing and the particular challenges AIDS brings to this. Included in this section is the problem of the hyper-endemic countries of being defined as "middle-income".

2. HIV/AIDS in Southern Africas

The first cases of AIDS were reported in the USA in 1981. As the reports of this new disease spread, African physicians made the world aware that they had been seeing cases for some years and numbers were increasing rapidly. In Zambia, a significant rise in cases of Kaposi's sarcoma had been recorded; in Kinshasa in the Democratic Republic of the Congo, there was an upsurge in patients with cryptococcosis; and the Ugandan Ministry of Health was receiving reports of increased and unexpected deaths in Lake Victoria fishing villages (Whiteside 2008). The history of HIV has been well documented — the early years by Randy Shilts (1988); for Africa by John Iliffe (2006); and the global response by Lindsay Knight (2008). The early fears that HIV/AIDS would be a rampant unstoppable epidemic sweeping uniformly across the entire world were soon seen to be unfounded.

Sadly, for parts of Africa, the reality has proven to be different. By the end of the 1980s, there was the evidence of a serious epidemic in central and eastern Africa. The country that was most open about the disease was Uganda. It consequently became known as the "ground zero" or centre of the epidemic, received much donor support and has been held up as an example of how HIV can be controlled. There was evidence of high and growing prevalence in East Africa and a fear that HIV might explode across the rest of the continent.

The data for Africa in the early 1990s found a gradient of HIV prevalence, high in the north and declining to the south. In Malawi, HIV prevalence was 25.9% among antenatal clinic attendees in the Blantyre hospital in 1991; in Zimbabwe, it was estimated to be 18% in the same group in Harare in 1991 (Iliffe 2006, p. 38). In Southern Africa (defined as the area south of the Limpopo river), up to 1990 all the data suggested that HIV prevalence was very low and that there was not (yet) an epidemic. There was a narrow window of opportunity which sadly was missed. The first antenatal surveys, in South Africa in 1990 found national prevalence of just 0.7% nationally (Whiteside and Sunter 2000), while in Swaziland in 1992 ANC prevalence was 3.9% (Whiteside and Wood 1994).

Across Southern Africa (with the puzzling exception of Angola), there is a generalised hyper-endemic that began spreading in about 1990. Incidence may have peaked by 2000, but remains unacceptably high and the nature of the disease means the numbers infected and affected will continue to climb. By 2007, adult prevalence ranged from 12.5% in Mozambique to 26.1% in Swaziland. There were 1.4 million infected adult Mozambicans and 5.4 million South Africans. Key indicators for selected Southern African countries are shown in Table 1.

Across the region, more females than males are infected, 58–42% in Mozambique and 61–39% in Botswana. Women are infected at a younger age. In Swaziland, the Demographic and Health Survey data (Swaziland Central Statistical Office 2007) show once girls reach age 15, the number of infections begins to rise rapidly, peaking at 49% in the 25–29 age group. Males are infected later and the peak is slightly lower, at 45% in the 35–39 age group. In South Africa, female prevalence peaks at 32.7% in the 25–29 age group and at 25.8% in men of 30 to 34 (Shisana *et al.* 2009).

There has been a global dispute around whether AIDS is exceptional. The reason for this debate may be the amount of funding AIDS receives or because detractors believe it is prioritised above other health issues. The strongest argument against exceptionalism, claims that AIDS has undermined health systems in developing countries and created a vertical programme that diverts human resources away from the public health sector and weakens government efficiency (England 2008). The epidemic, it is said, has been overstated and resources poured into inappropriate responses. An alternative view is that those who see AIDS as unexceptional are in the words of Stephen Lewis (2009): "the pinched bureaucrats and publicity-seeking academics who advocate exchanging the health of some for the health of others — who propose robbing Peter to pay Paul rather than arguing, in principled fashion, that money must be found for every imperative, including maternal and child health, and sexual and reproductive health, and environmental health as well as all the resources required to turn the tide of the AIDS pandemic." This

Table 1. HIV, health and population data for Southern African countries.

Indicator	Date/Date Range	Data Type	DATA: Botswana	Lesotho	Mozambique	South Africa	Swaziland
HIV/AIDS							
Adults Living with HIV/AIDS	2007	#	280,000	260,000	1,400,000	5,400,000	170,000
Adult HIV/AIDS Prevalence Rate	2007	%	23.9%	23.2%	12.5%	18.1%	26.1%
AIDS Deaths	2007	#	11,000	18,000	81,000	350,000	10,000
AIDS Orphans	2007		95,000	110,000	400,000	1,400,000	56,000
ARV Need	2007		120,000	85,000	370,000	1,700,000	59,000
ARV Treatment	December 2007	#	93,000	22,000	90,000	460,000	25,000
ARV Coverage Rate	December 2007	%	79%	26%	24%	28%	42%
Program, Funding & Financing							
Financial Development Assistance for Health	2007	$	$45.46	$19.11	$296.04	$320.56	$19.99
Financial Development Assistance for Health Per Capita	2007	$	$24.16	$9.52	$13.84	$6.60	$17.51
Health Expenditure Per Capita	2006	$	$815	$98	$36	$715	$300
Total Expenditure on Health	2006	%	7.1%	6.8%	5.0%	8.0%	6.3%

(*Continued*)

Table 1. *(Continued)*

Indicator	Date/Date Range	Data Type	DATA				
			Botswana	Lesotho	Mozambique	South Africa	Swaziland
Government Health Expenditure as Percent of Total Health	2006	%	76.5%	58.90%	70.8%	37.7%	65.8%
Health Workforce & Capacity							
Physicians	Most recenty year data	Rate Per 10,000	4	1	<1	8	2
Demography & Population							
Under Five Mortality Rate	2007	Rate Per 1,000	40	84	168	59	91
Maternal Mortality Ratio	2005	Rate Per 100,000	380	960	520	400	390
Population Growth Rate	2009	%	1.94%	0.12%	1.79%	0.28%	–4.46%

debate has been addressed in a number of recent articles (Whiteside 2009).

For Southern Africa, AIDS must be exceptional. The absolute numbers infected and affected are huge, and in terms of the relative disease burden, it is the most important health issue the governments face. If the epidemic is exceptional, then the response should also be exceptional.

In South Africa, the number of AIDS-related deaths rose from just over 180,000 in 2000 to over 350,000 in 2007. It is projected that by 2015, some six million South Africans may have died of AIDS — 13% of the population (UNAIDS 2008). In Swaziland, life expectancy rose from 54 in 1980 to 58 in 1990, but fell to 40 in 2007. South African life expectancy fell from 62 years in 1990 to 50 in 2007. Infant mortality in South Africa in 2007 was 46 per thousand live births (the average for all upper-middle-income countries is just 21); in Swaziland it is 66 but the average for lower-middle-income countries (Swaziland is categorised as an LMIC) is 38. Maternal mortality is 400 per 100000 live births in South Africa, and 390 in Swaziland compared to averages of 97 and 300 in upper-middle- and lower-middle-income countries, respectively (WHO 2009). In terms of demographic and development indicators, AIDS is having a devastating impact and means these countries are unlikely to achieve the millennium development goals around child mortality (goal 4); maternal health (goal 5) and combating HIV/AIDS TB and malaria (goal 6) (United Nations Development Programme Swaziland 2009 and UNDP South Africa 2009).

Despite the well-documented impact of the disease, it seems that the region is not getting to grips with it in the way we would expect or hope. The reasons are three fold: first, it is difficult for political leaders to get to grasp a catastrophe of this magnitude, especially since they would have to look to their own behaviours; second, there is little ownership of the disease in the region; and third, the scale of resources required to respond are so daunting as to be demoralising.

3. AIDS and Governance

AIDS leads to increased mortality and morbidity which have long-term intergenerational impacts (Barnett and Whiteside 2006). Where prevalence is high, the demographic consequences of increased deaths and fewer births will change the structure of societies and negatively impact development. Illnesses and their consequences are harder to measure but are probably more devastating for AIDS than for most other diseases. With AIDS, in the absence of treatment, the periods of sickness increase in severity, duration and frequency. Given that most patients are normally healthy, young and middle-aged adults, the consequences for a society are bleak and the demand on health care systems are additional to what would normally be seen.

AIDS deaths and illnesses will affect the capacity for development and service delivery. The degree to which this will happen will vary according to the level of human and financial resources in a nation and the location and size of the epidemic. The paper "Is AIDS exceptional?" attempts to categorise countries, arguing AIDS is exceptional in some places and must be treated as such. The exceptionality is determined by prevalence, demographic dynamics of the country and availability and domestic affordability of treatments. In countries with prevalence of over 3% and less than 10%, the exceptionality "rule" will be a function of prevalence and wealth. If people access domestically supported treatment, then we cease to regard AIDS as exceptional. If treatment is dependent on outside resources and the expenditure per patient exceeds per capita health expenditure, AIDS is exceptional. However, AIDS is always exceptional in countries with high prevalence due to increased mortality and morbidity and/or the challenges of providing treatment. Additionally, AIDS is a long-wave event, in 20 years, there will be people infected in 2009 living on treatment. There will be children who have grown up without parents. The demographic, social and political repercussions will still be being felt (Whiteside 2009).

It has been noted the loss of teachers, coupled with their absenteeism will become an issue for the education sector (Boler and Archer 2008); in agriculture HIV and AIDS is implicated in lower production in Swaziland (de Waal and Whiteside 2003; Naysmith *et al.* 2009) and industry will face lower output and growth (Barnett and Whiteside 2006). Political scientist Nana Poku criticises past analysis of the epidemic's impact on national GDPs for not considering the reduction of welfare caused by the loss of family members. He argues if a broader analysis is taken, "the combined economies of Africa actually shrank by two percent in the 12 months up to the end of 2004" (Poku 2006, p. 347). There will be fewer workers: "by 2010 the labour force of the 39 most affected countries will be nine percent smaller.... The remaining workforce will contain a greater proportion of younger workers who are less experienced and less well educated than the present cohort" (Poku 2006, p. 346).

However, there is a conundrum in assessing the impact of AIDS. Most countries in the region are labour surplus economies where unemployment rates are high, especially among young people. In South Africa, 21.9% of work seekers are unemployed (Mail and Guardian online 2009). Unemployment in Swaziland in 2004 was estimated at around 30% of the economically active population, if the definition included discouraged job seekers, the rate would be over 40% (FAO/WFP Crop and Food Supply Assessment Mission to Swaziland 2005). Each year brings a new cohort of job seekers into the market. What does it mean for a country to have high levels of unemployment in the formal sector but face increased morbidity and mortality in the adult population? One way forward might be to move towards more of a care economy and including looking to grants or cash transfers.

Impacts are felt worst at the household level. In the poorest households, there is no recovery from the shock of illness and death and households simply vanish, unrecorded and uncounted. The burden of care is felt here particularly by poor women, already battling against other stressors such as poverty, inequity and lack of access to services. UNAIDS estimates that 90% of HIV and AIDS care is done in the home. In the context of inadequate social and health services, the social, emotional and economic burden is great (Akintola 2008). This is especially the case for older women (Chazan 2008).

The issue of orphans is important. Predictions of masses of child headed household and feral bands of orphans roaming the capital cities have not materialised. This is because in the first instance families do their utmost to absorb children. It was reported by UNICEF Swaziland (2006) that communities in Swaziland stated they had "no orphans". However, with the evolving epidemic and as numbers of AIDS orphans increased and caregivers fell the situation has changed and orphan support is now high on Swaziland's agenda. Second, this type of support is an "easy sell" to the global community and there are many NGOs involved in this. This is not say that resources are adequate or that people are exploitative — but rather to realise the instinctive need to care for and nurture children.

Research in Swaziland shows deterioration across sectors. This includes flows of foreign direct investment, agricultural output and economic growth. A compelling case can be made for AIDS being a reason for this, but assigning causality is difficult (Whiteside and Whalley 2007). By contrast, prior to the recent global economic crisis, South Africa, Botswana and Mozambique experienced strong economic growth, confounding the predictions of severe impact from AIDS. It may be that this is specific to the shape of the epidemic, the size and nature of the economies, including capital labour mix and the robustness of skills stock, but these are areas for future research.

With regard to actual governance: the running of the country by civil servants, traditional leaders and the election of representatives, the situation is more complex. In September 2009, the AIDS, Security and Conflict Initiative (ASCI) research report was launched. This project was convened by the Netherlands Institute of International Relations "Clingendael" and the U.S. Social Science Research Council with support from the Netherlands Ministry of Foreign Affairs, the Australian Agency for International Development, the Canadian Department of Foreign Affairs, the Swedish Ministry of Foreign Affairs and UNAIDS (de Waal *et al.* 2009). This project brought together researchers, policy makers and practitioners across geographic regions and specialist fields in an attempt to come up with a definitive response to the belief that fragile states and conflict would spur the spread of HIV, while an unchecked AIDS epidemic would increase the likelihood of state collapse.

The work was carried out by both northern and southern researchers and stemmed from the securitisation of HIV/AIDS of the period from 1998 to 2004. The prime example of this was two U.S. National Intelligence reports which warned of dire scenarios in which AIDS could lead to economic, political and social collapses. The first in 2000 (National Intelligence Council 2000) suggested armies would become unmanageable, there would be increased armed conflict and humanitarian emergencies would be exacerbated. Their 2002 report (National Intelligence Council 2002) extended this analysis to "second wave" countries: Russia, China, India, Ethiopia and Nigeria.

The ASCI research confirmed HIV/AIDS is a long-wave event with the result that causal links between the epidemic and state fragility are hard to pinpoint. This is due to inadequate indicators but, and hardly surprisingly, responses to the epidemic will reduce impact. AIDS is not as prevalent among armies as previously thought and command-centred approaches to HIV prevention are effective in reducing risk of HIV infection and impact. However, the role of the police and other law enforcement and uniformed services has been neglected and they are important in setting the framework in which in epidemics occur and may be prevented.

AIDS does not lead to state fragility in the sense of governments collapsing, but it increases poverty and reduces wellbeing. It means in Southern Africa millennium development goals 3, 4, and 5 will not be met. At the national level, governments appear resilient: however, ASCI research identified measurable, though not yet catastrophic, impacts on local government structures, and the ability to represent constituencies and deliver services (de Waal *et al.* 2009, p. 18). It is at the local level that pressures on human capacity and increased demand for services are most apparent, particularly in the health sector.

In South Africa work commissioned for ASCI and partially funded by HEARD found hyper-endemic HIV creates stress and attrition for local government institutions, which in turn contributes to poor-quality services and less responsive and effective local government (Chirambo and Steyn 2008):

> Local government in South Africa was showing definite 'cracks', which contribute to the problem of poor service delivery to the general public. In a sample of 12 municipalities throughout the country, most councillors surveyed thought that disclosing HIV status would be ruinous for a political career. The study also found a consistent pattern of elevated death rates among councillors aged 29–42 and increased sick leave and lower productivity among councillors at low pay grades.... fear of stigmatization and discrimination has influenced wider social attitudes towards HIV and AIDS and may account for the underutilization of HIV services, including treatment, and the unexplained withdrawal of councillors from public duties. Practically, it has affected the representation of some communities in local government, thereby limiting the potential for the effective

> decentralization of service delivery.... Increased cost burdens, staff turnover and representational ruptures may not in the short term cause acute crises in local government. But they are severe enough to warrant intervention and targeted support to ensure that local government can function more efficiently under the impacts of the epidemic (de Waal *et al.* 2009, p. 30).

There has been little measurement of this, but perhaps the initiative in South Africa to reduce the power and responsibility of the provinces might be seen as symptomatic. What is deeply interesting is that at the same time as we have argued that HIV/AIDS would cause a deterioration of governance the response to the epidemic has built capacity. This ranges from additional central government staff through to the development of an articulate and vibrant civil society. This has been seen in many countries. Two examples are the South African Treatment Action Campaign (TAC), a lobby group, and the Swaziland budget process. The TAC was established with a vision of a "unified quality health care system which provides equal access to HIV prevention and treatment services for all people" and a mission to ensure that everyone living with HIV had access to care through providing treatment in select districts and advocacy to mobilise people around health and HIV (TAC 2009). The organisation has been willing and able to mobilise and at times was very critical of the government to the extent that they launched a civil disobedience campaign in 2003 to push for access to treatment. In Swaziland, where civil society is very much weaker, in every government department budget there is a significant provision for addressing AIDS.

The ASCI report argues for capacity-constrained governments to do a few simple things and do them well. "For such states, the priority is to implement policies that have clear goals, ideally bring universal benefit and command popular support" (de Waal *et al.* 2009, p. 30). The question is whether or not AIDS is one of those things and in particular if prevention and treatment are priorities.

3.1. Challenges to providing care and treatment

The political effect of decisions on who lives and who dies (in terms of who gets treatment) has not been assessed. Despite the resources poured into health systems most sub-Saharan African countries are unable to meet the demands resulting from HIV and AIDS related illness and treatment needs. In countries with high prevalence, providing anti-retroviral therapies (ART) on a largescale is a massive undertaking for already struggling health systems. Kober and Van Damme argue that lack of health system capacity is the single most serious obstacle to ART scale-up. In reference to ART programmes in some of the countries with the highest prevalence (South Africa, Malawi, Mozambique and Swaziland): "These national treatment plans would seem ambitious for most of the world's health systems, yet there are to be realized in countries where health systems are already struggling with severe constraints" (Kober and Van Damme 2004, p. 104).

While it is quite hard to obtain consistent data on the numbers of people on treatment, or even needing it, for the sake of consistency I use the data sheets from the Kaiser Family Foundation (Kaiser Family Foundation 2009). Botswana began its programme in 2001 as a partnership between the Government, the drug company, Merck and the Gates Foundation (The African Comprehensive HIV/AIDS Partnership). It is estimated that of the 120,000 people who needed treatment in 2007 some 93,000 or 79% were receiving it. In the same year, Swaziland had 59,000 people needing treatment of whom 42% (25,000) were receiving it.

The failures in South Africa's treatment policy have been well documented (Nattrass 2007; Cullinan and Thorn 2009). Under the cold hand of President Mbeki and his lackey Minister Tshabalala-Msimang at a national political level the programme was not rolled out, although provincial governments did press ahead. In 2007, only 28% of the 1,700,000 needing drugs were getting them (460,000 patients) (UNAIDS 2009a). Under the interim government of President Motlanthe (September 2008 to May 2009) and the newly elected President Zuma, the country was in the process of implementing the largest ART programme in the world with about 700,000 receiving medications currently, and another 760,000 in need, under current treatment guidelines, but not yet receiving ART.

The TAC recently pointed out that to start an additional 285,000 people on ARVs in 2009, as the country's national strategic plan aims to do, would require about R1 billion (US$122 million) more than was budgeted for (IRIN News 2009). News in September 2009 indicated that South Africa has run into severe challenges. A Budget and Expenditure Monitoring Forum (BEMF) has been established by civil society and this noted that following rapid expansion of the ARV programme in 2008 this slowed significantly in 2009. Some 40% of HIV-positive people in need are not getting treatment and sustained access to treatment is under threat. There have been reports of long waiting lists, drug stock-outs and mismanagement of health budgets in six of the nine provinces. Additionally, there is a lack of publicly available information. An emergency fund of R5-million (US$676,550) was established for provinces struggling to provide ARVs, but the shortfall was estimated at R1-billion ($123 million) (aidsmap news 2009).

It should be noted that the costs and challenges of getting people on treatment were based on starting treatment at a CD4 cell count of 200. New research advocates starting treatment when CD4 counts are 350. This would mean the number of people "in need" of treatment would be even greater along with the costs and the demands on the health service.

Once treatment begins, medication must be taken for life and patients will, after a period of time, need to move from first-line treatment to second-line treatment. As governments increase the portion of the health budget going to treatment, questions arise as to what is sustainable. For example, in Malawi, a programme implemented by Medicines Sans Frontiers reported that the annual recurrent cost for direct care per patient on ART was $237 (Jouquet 2009). However, the national health expenditure per capita was just $132 per person per year. For countries with higher prevalence this challenge is even greater. In 2006, in South Africa, the per capita health expenditure was $715 and government accounts for 37.7%; and in Swaziland it was $300 and government accounted for 65.8%. In both countries, expenditure is below the Abuja target of 15% of government expenditure (9.1% in South Africa and 11.2% in Swaziland).

In 2010, Universal Access targets were supposed to have been reached. In their report on "Monitoring progress towards universal access" in 2008 WHO, UNAIDS and their partners recognise that even high-income countries with well-developed infrastructure have difficulty in reaching 100%

of the people who need interventions. Accordingly, they are playing with the concept of access.

> "Access" is a broad concept that measures three dimensions of key health sector interventions: availability, coverage and outcome and impact. Availability is defined in terms of the reachability (physical access), affordability (economic access) and acceptability (socio-cultural access) of services that meet a minimum standard of quality. Making services available, affordable and acceptable is an essential precondition for universal access. Coverage is defined as the proportion of the people needing an intervention who receive it. Coverage is influenced by supply (provision of services) and by the demand from those who need services. Outcome and impact are defined in terms of behavioural change, lower infection rates or higher survival rates. Outcome and impact are the result of coverage, modulated by the efficiency and effectiveness of interventions. (WHO, UNAIDS and UNICEF 2008).

What does this mean for the worst affected countries and for their health governance? The answer is really that choices will have to be made — and then plans developed and executed. There is a view that admitting we would not reach universal access targets means giving up on treatment completely, and that this is in some way a betrayal. Ignored is that if we do not succeed in reaching prevention targets, we will continue to see increases in the number of people living with HIV. The reality that we cannot do everything now for everyone does not mean we should do nothing for anyone. It is time for activists, politicians and those concerned with all forms of health provision to engage with economists.

3.2. The response: Swaziland

In this section, I will focus on the response in Swaziland. This little country followed the recommendations of the World Health Organisation's Global Programme for AIDS in the early years. A National AIDS Prevention and Control Programme was established in 1987; the first three-year plan was completed in 1992 and extensive education programmes were put in place. As early as 1993, the Cabinet held briefings on the epidemic and its potential wider implications. In 1999, the King declared HIV/AIDS a "national disaster".

As early as 1992, the government began considering HIV/AIDS as a developmental issue. The potential effects of the epidemic were recognised in the 1992/93–1994/95 Development Plan. In 1993, the government carried out an exercise looking back at the first 25 years of independence and forward to the next 25 as part of a National Development Strategy. In 1993, a report on "The Socio-Economic Impact of HIV/AIDS" (Whiteside and Wood 1994) was commissioned as part of this, and was the first such study done anywhere in the world.

There was little "hard" data on the impacts of infection, so government found it difficult to develop innovative responses to this "invisible" disease. As would be expected, the burden on the health sector was increasing. In 1998, it was estimated that 46% of hospitalised patients were HIV positive. This, however, did not inspire any exceptional reaction, even from the Ministry of Health. The Swaziland National AIDS Programme (SNAP) was located within the health ministry but found it hard to lead in this setting, as it lacked authority and status. The government recognised more was needed.

In December 2001, the National Emergency Response Committee on HIV/AIDS (NERCHA) was established, with a mandate to coordinate and mobilise resources. In 2003, it was placed under the Prime Minister's Office and elevated to the status of being a Council by an Act of Parliament. The functions include overseeing the coordination of the multi-sectoral response; reviewing and adopting appropriate policies and strategy recommendations; approving funding allocations to implement agencies and advising the minister and government on issues relating to the epidemic.

Effectively, NERCHA coordinates and facilitates the national multi-sectoral response to HIV and AIDS through the National Strategic Plans. It acts as a conduit for funding to implement agencies; and is tasked with mobilising, receiving, managing and allocating resources, from government and other sources. It is also expected to facilitate information sharing on local and international best practices and to monitor and evaluate both its projects and those it funds.

NERCHA has gone about its business in a professional business like manner and has scored a number of successes. The availability of anti-retroviral therapy (ART) in 2003 meant that public health facilities began offering treatment. The roll-out was not as rapid as hoped. There have been a range of impressive programmes to provide support for orphans and vulnerable children and their carers. Of particular importance is that NERCHA has looked at Swazi culture and has incorporated some aspects to advance the response to the epidemic. There have been a range of prevention activities some of which have been controversial such as the "secret lover" campaign, when billboards appeared warning "Makhwapheni Uyabulala", which translates as "Your secret lover can kill you". None have had an immediate impact in bringing prevalence down.

Interestingly, one of the challenges in Swaziland is to give the right messages. For example, the trends in HIV prevalence need interpretation. In 2004, the national HIV ANC prevalence peaked at 42.6; in 2006, it fell to 39.2% but in 2008,it was up to 42.1% again. A close analysis shows prevalence has fallen in the cohort of 15–19-year-olds, the greatest increase is among women aged 35–39. Does this mean that there are enough people getting treatment to push up prevalence? If this were the case, it would be good news.

However, national government spending on health has declined in both relative and absolute terms. General government expenditure on health as percentage of total government expenditure peaked at 13.2% in 2003 and fell to 9.4% in 2006 (Lievens *et al.* 2009). The relative decline is not a major issue — there were huge quantities of donor funding flowing into the country — a sign of the success of NERCHA being able to mobilise international support. Swaziland put proposals to four rounds of Global Fund calls. The country requested $195,386,808 and was awarded $134,944,918. The absolute decline is an issue. It points to the real danger that the epidemic is seen as a concern that will be dealt with people outside the country, and to a lack of national ownership.

In 2003, public health facilities began offering anti-retroviral therapy (ART). The roll-out meant that by June 2006, there were 14,009 people being treated, 26.5% of the 52,909 estimated to need it. By 2007, it had risen to 42% of the population in need. It was somewhat stalled and the issue is capacity, rather than funding.

The challenge was, and remains, prevention. In 2003, the report "What is driving the HIV/AIDS epidemic in Swaziland and what more can we do about it?' (Whiteside *et al.* 2003) was completed. This was supplemented in 2006 by the report "The socio-economic impact of HIV/AIDS in Swaziland" (Whiteside *et al.* 2006). Despite this research and the efforts of NERCHA, HIV prevalence climbed.

In early 2007, the terms of reference for a study to assess the impact of the AIDS epidemic across the nation were drawn up. The ideas were developed primarily by Dr von Wissell, Head of the National Emergency Response Council on HIV/AID in Swaziland (NERCHA) and Professor Whiteside, Director of the Health Economics and HIV/AIDS Research Division (HEARD) at the University of KwaZulu-Natal. The research was partly funded by HEARD and lead by Amy Whalley, a former Overseas Development Institute Fellow who had worked with NERCHA and the Ministry of Health. Whalley's task was to gather and analyse information on exactly what was going on across the nation using available data sets; to compare Swaziland's situation with other countries and thus build advocacy material for use inside the country and with the international community. In October 2007, the report "Reviewing 'Emergencies' for Swaziland: shifting the paradigm in a new era" (Whiteside and Whalley 2007) was published. It was widely distributed and presented. The conclusion was that Swaziland faces an emergency and the mortality rates alone should lead to the declaration of an emergency by the international community. The report noted, "*While, in many ways, Swaziland's response has been admirable and unique, it is clear that the HIV prevention programmes have not worked thus far*" (Whiteside and Whalley 2007).

In March 2009, NERCHA, working with UNAIDS and the World Bank Global HIV/AIDS Programme, produced the Swaziland HIV Prevention Response and Modes of Transmission Analysis (NERCHA *et al.* 2009). The report noted "it was agreed that Swaziland would participate in the MOT process with the **purpose** of '*contributing to the ongoing efforts to understand the epidemic and response in Swaziland and thus help the country improve the scope (doing the right kind of activities), relevance (with the right populations) and comprehensiveness (reaching all members of target populations) of HIV prevention effort.*'"(NERCHA *et al.* 2009, p. 3). This work will be translated into policy and interventions over the next year.

3.3. The lower-middle-income country conundrum

Of the nine hyper-endemic countries of Southern Africa, five are classified as middle-income countries — namely Botswana, Lesotho, Namibia, South Africa and Swaziland; the other four Mozambique, Zambia, Malawi and Zimbabwe are low-income countries. The World Bank classifies countries into three broad categories, low-, middle- and high-income countries using the gross national income (GNI) per capita as the criteria. This measure is used to determine assistance and at what level a country can access it. Low-income countries can access International Development Association or IDA support while lower- and upper-middle income countries access support through the IBRD. Both IDA and IBRD are part of the World Bank. There are also issues of perception. Once a country is classified as middle-income country, it tends to get a lower priority in global consciousness. While this is not measured, it is nonetheless an important concern.

It can be argued that GNI is not a suitable measure anyway.[2] GNI per capita is a proxy measure for poverty and there are reasons why it is particularly weak in certain countries. There are three specific conditions identified.

Countries may be resource-rich but the citizens not benefit. It is worth remembering Adam Smith's book was called the "Wealth of Nations", not the "Income of Nations". Countries which are simply selling resources may give an appearance that they are getting better off (or developing), as aggregate income rises, but in the long term, they are becoming worse off. Income may rise quickly, but few jobs will be created, so a small proportion of the population benefits from that income. Government's revenues may rise rapidly but is no reason to assume that their ability to prioritise and execute spending, or redistribute income, will improve. African examples abound and include Angola and Gabon. This applies to some extent in Botswana although the government there has been deeply aware of this issue.

Small countries may have volatile exchange rates. Swaziland, Lesotho, Namibia and South Africa form the Common Monetary Area and

[2] I am grateful to Andrew Ockenden who was with DFID Pretoria for sharing his ideas on this. However, this is my interpretation of our discussion.

the currency is pegged to the South African Rand. This means that, as the Rand changes value — for reasons which are beyond the control of the smaller countries, so their income changes. Worst hit was Lesotho which was recently reclassified from low- to middle-income country. Its GNI per capita rose 30% in just one year. In contrast, its actual GDP growth was 3%. This reflected the rise in the value of the South African Rand between 2002 and 2003 which in turn was caused by the shift in commodity prices. The shift to middle-income status did not represent any real change for the people of Lesotho, who remain desperately poor. This also has implications for donor dependency because loans tend to be denominated in dollars. In February 2009, a dollar was worth R10.27; in October, R7.71 and in 2005, it was worth R5.54. This level of volatility is hard to manage (Rainbow Nation 2009).

In the region what is considered the "average income" has little relation to the actual incomes of the vast majority of the population. The Gini coefficient is a measure of income inequality. It ranges between 0, which represents everyone having the same income, and 100, which represents one person holding all of the wealth. All Southern African countries have higher Gini coefficients than Brazil (54) and Argentina (52.8), societies which are generally thought of as unequal. In Southern Africa, the Gini coefficient is extremely high: Namibia (74.3), Lesotho (63.2), Botswana (63), Swaziland (60.9) and South Africa (57.8).

Swaziland faces a particularly extreme conundrum. The 2006 population was estimated at 1,126,000. The GNI per capita in 2006 was $2430, giving a total gross national income of $2,736,180,000. In 2007, the preliminary census found that the population had dropped to 912,229. If the existing GNI is simply divided by the new population, the per capita income rises to $3,000, an increase of 23%. This may also happen in Botswana and Lesotho. Clearly, this issue needs action on a global level.

4. Conclusion and Lessons

The poorer the country is, the greater will be the disease burden and the more they will be dependent on assistance. Where international funding is required to provide treatment, domestic governments lose control over their citizens' lives. Citizens living with HIV and AIDS become dependent on international aid, and countries become dependent on the same aid in order to maintain a healthy and productive society. On the other hand, donor countries have to provide ongoing aid. This international dependency has been documented by Over (2007 and 2008), who examined it from an international entitlement viewpoint, asking if a global welfare paradigm is appropriate.

There are a number of points raised in this chapter to which we return. The first is that HIV/AIDS in Southern Africa is catastrophic for the populations. This disease is a major development challenge. The debates about AIDS exceptionalism are absolutely irrelevant in this region. It is quite possible that a number of these countries will see their populations fall. The levels of impoverishment and psychological "disease" are enormous, and as usual the bulk of the burden is be borne by the poor, and in particular poor and older women.

Despite the enormity of the issue, we have not seen clear links between AIDS and governance at a national level. There is no evidence that AIDS is political deal maker, but it continues to be stigmatising and for minority groups, especially men who have sex with men are discriminated against (legally in some countries). The work of the ASCI project shows that AIDS and politics are linked, especially at local government. Unfortunately, AIDS does not generally mobilise populations (TAC is an exception rather than the rule), the disease and its effect is background noise, something we cope with. Perhaps the next example of this type of issue may be environmental change. Having said that, the resources that have been poured into HIV/AIDS have made a difference, and have led to action at all levels. There are many mobilisations and perhaps in the future we will see AIDS was a catalyst although it may not be recognised as such. The key issue of vertical versus horizontal programmes — or as was being talked about in 2009 — diagonal programmes is not covered in this chapter, but is discussed elsewhere in the book. This is important and the ideology/methodology that is dominant will shape health delivery in HIV-affected countries for decades to come.

AIDS certainly has mobilised huge quantities of money. At the end of 2009, the key issue was that what had seemed an unstoppable upward trajectory of funding will plateau and may even fall. It is a different world dealing with restricted rather than expanding funding and that is the challenge for those engaged in health for the next few years. As Dr Bertozzi said at the July 2009 International AIDS Society Pathogenesis Conference in Cape Town, we need more health for the money as well as more money for health.

At the international governance level, the emergence of UNAIDS, the Global Fund, PEPFAR and the Gates Foundation has been a mixed blessing. There is a Kiswahili saying that "when elephants fight, it is the grass that suffers". The trouble for those who constitute the "grass" over which the fighting is taking place, is there are too many elephants battling. Moreover, these elephants require the grass to report on the fight. Health governance needs to evolve. If WHO can provide the leadership that is so desperately needed (and which it is mandated to), and 30 years on there seems little sign of commitment or ability, then one lesson from AIDS is we need reform.

Chapter 17, 18 and 20 further assess issues of HIV governance at community level in India, Russia and Uganda, respectively.

References

Aidsmap News (2009) "South Africa: Budgeting Failures Threaten ARV Programme", 23rd Sepetember 2009,http://aidsmap.com/en/news/245008FA-B836-4C99-990F-685430B361E6.asp.

Akintola O (2008) "Unpaid HIV and AIDS Care in Southern Africa: Forms, Context, and Implications," *Feminist Economics* 14(4):117–47.

Barnett T, Whiteside A (2006) *AIDS in the Twenty-first Century: Disease and Globalization*. Basingstoke: Palgrave.

Boler T, Archer D (2008) *The Politics of Prevention: AGlobal Crisis in AIDS and Education.* London: Pluto Press.

Chazan M (2008) "Seven 'Deadly' Assumptions: Unravelling the Implications of HIV/AIDS Among Grandmothers in South Africa and Beyond", *Ageing and Society* 28:935–58, doi:10.1017/S0144686X08007265.

Chirambo K, Steyn J (2008) AIDS and local government in South Africa: Examining the impact of an epidemic on ward councillors. New York: ASCI (ASCI Working Paper No. 25). Available at http://asci.researchhub.ssrc.org/working-papers/ASCI%20Research%20Paper%2025-IDASA.pdf.

Cullinan K, Thorn A eds. (2009) *The Virus, Vitamins and Vegetables*. Johannesburg: Jacana.

de Waal A, Whiteside A (2003) "New Variant Famine: AIDS and the Food Crisis in Southern Africa," *The Lancet* 362(9391):1234–37.

de Waal A *et al.* (2009) HIV/AIDS, security and conflict, new realities, new responses. New York: SSRC and Den Haag: Netherlands Institute of International Relations. Available at http://asci.researchhub.ssrc.org/rdb/asci-hub.

England R (2008) "Writing is On the Wall for UNAIDS," *British Medical Journal* 336:1072.

FAO/WFP Crop and Food Supply Assessment Mission to Swaziland (2005) Special report Swaziland. Available at http://www.fao.org/docrep/008/J5512e/J5512e00.htm.

Iliffe J (2006) *The African AIDS Epidemic: A History*. Oxford: James Currey.

IRIN News (2009) South Africa: No simple formula for universal access. IRIN News. 3 August 2009. [Online] Available athttp://www.irinnews.org/Report.aspx?ReportId=85555 [Accessed 3 September 2009].

Jouquet G *et al.* (2009) Cost analysis of an ARV care programme reaching universal access in Thyolo, Malawi. The International AIDS Society Conference on Pathogenesis, Treatment and Prevention: 19 July 2009, Cape Town.

Kaiser Family Foundation Global Health Facts (2009) Customized Data Sheets. Available at http://www.globalhealthfacts.org/factsheets_custom.jsp.

Knight L (2008) *UNAIDS the First 10 Years*. Geneva:UNAIDS.

Kober K, Van Damme W (2004) "Scaling Up Access to Antiretroviral Treatment in Southern Africa: Who Will Do the Job?"*Lancet* 364:103–7.

Lewis S (2009) Presentation at *the International AIDS Society Conference on Pathogenesis, Treatment and Prevention*, 19 July 2009, Cape Town.

Lievens T *et al.* (2009) *Sustainable Financing for HIV and AIDS in Swaziland*. Oxford Policy Management Group. Mail and Guardian (Online) (2009, 2 March) "Stats SA: Unemployment rated down"Available at http://www.mg.co.za/article/2009-03-02-stats-sa-unemployment-rate-down.

Mathers CD, Loncar D (2006) "Projections of Global Mortality and Burden of Disease From 2002 to 2030," *PLoS Med* 3(11):e442. doi:10. 1371/journal.pmed.0030442 *Ibid* page 2021.

National Intelligence Council (United States) (2000) *The Global Infectious Disease Threat and Its Implications for the United States*. Washington, DC, US NIC (NIE 99–17D).

National Intelligence Council (United States) (2002) *The NextWave of HIV/AIDS: Nigeria, Ethiopia, Russia, India, and China.* Washington, DC, US NIC (ICA 2002–04D).

Nattrass N (2007) *Mortal Combat: AIDS Denialism and the Struggle for Antiretrovirals in South Africa.* Pietermaritzburg: University of KwaZulu-Natal Press.

Naysmith S *et al.* (2009) "Rethinking New Variant Famine: The Case of Swaziland", *Food Security* 1(3):251–60.

NERCHA, UNAIDS and the World Bank Global HIV/AIDS Programme (2009) *Swaziland HIV Prevention Response and Modes of Transmission Analysis.* Mbabane: NERCHA.

Over M (2007) AIDS treatment as an international entitlement: Are we ready for a global welfare paradigm? Blog, 28 September 2007. Washington: Center for Global Development. [Online] Available athttp://blogs.cgdev.org/globalhealth/2007/09/aids_treatment_as_an.php [Accessed 3 September 2009].

Over M (2008) Prevention failure: The ballooning entitlement burden of US Global AIDS treatment spending and what to do about it. Washington: Center for Global Development. Working Paper No.144.

Poku N (2006) "HIV/AIDS Financing: The Case for Improving the Quality and Quantity of Aid", *International Affairs* 82(2):345–59.

Rainbow Nation (2009). "South Africa Rand vs US Dollar," Available at http://www.rainbownation.com/usa/compare/index.asp.

Shilts R (1988) *And the Band Played On*. London: Viking.

Shisana O *et al.* (2009) *South African National HIV Prevalence, Incidence, Behaviour and Communication Survey 2008: A Turning Tide among Teenagers?* Cape Town: HSRC Press.

Swaziland. Central Statistical Office (2007) *Demographic and Health Survey*. Central Statistical Office, Mbabane.

Treatment Action Campaign. (Online) Available at http://www.tac.org.za/community/about [Accessed 9 October 2009].

UNAIDS (2008) *Report on the Global AIDS Epidemic*. Geneva: UNAIDS.

UNAIDS (2009) *What Countries Need: Investments for 2010 Targets*. Geneva: UNAIDS.

UNAIDS (2009a) *South Africa: Progress towards Universal Access and the Declaration of Commitment on HIV/AIDS*. [Online] Geneva: UNAIDS. Available at http://cfs.unaids.org/country_factsheet.aspx?ISO=SOA [Accessed 22 October 2009].

UNICEF, Swaziland (2006) *Report on the Assessment of Neighborhood Care Points*. Geneva: UNICEF.

United Nations Development Programme, South Africa (2009) Available at http://www.undp.org.za.

United Nations Development Programme, Swaziland (2009) Available at http://www.undp.org.sz.

United Nations Economic and Social Affairs. Population Division homepage. World population prospects (2008) Available at http://esa.un.org/unpp/p2k0data.asp.

Whiteside A (2008) *HIV/AIDS: A Very Short Introduction*. Oxford: Oxford University Press.

Whiteside A (2009) *Is AIDS Exceptional?*Available at http://www.aids2031.org/working-groups/programmatic-response?view=papers#105.

Whiteside A *et al*. (2003) What is driving the HIV/AIDS epidemic in Swaziland? And what more can we do about it? Report prepared for the National Emergency Response Committee on HIV/AIDS and UNAIDS, Mbabane.

Whiteside A *et al*. (2006) *The Socio-economic Impact of HIV/AIDS in Swaziland*. Mbabane: NERCHA; Durban: HEARD.

Whiteside A, Sunter C (2000) *AIDS: The Challenge for South Africa*. Cape Town: Human and Rousseau/Tafelberg.

Whiteside A, Whalley A (2007) *Reviewing Emergencies in Swaziland: Shifting the Paradigm for a New Era*. Mbabane: NERCHA; Durban: HEARD.

Whiteside A, Wood G (1994) *Socio-economic Impact of HIV/AIDS in Swaziland.* Ministry of Economic Planning and Development, Government of Swaziland.

World Health Organisation (2009) WHO Statistical Information System, Health indicators from the WHO data base accessed 9 October 2009. Available athttp://apps.who.int/whosis/data/Search.jsp?countries=%5bLocation%5d.Members.

WHO, UNAIDS and UNICEF (2008) Towardsuniversal access: Scaling up priority HIV/AIDS interventions in the health sector Progress Report 2008. Geneva: WHO. Available at http://www.who.int/hiv/pub/2008progressreport/en/index.html.

15

Negotiating Aid Reform in Viet Nam: Unpacking "Country" Ownership[1]

Rebecca Dodd and Jean-Marc Olivé

World Health Organization, Viet Nam

Summary

Viet Nam is a good place to examine the influence of the aid effectiveness agenda: high levels of aid mean the agenda is relevant, but low levels of aid-dependency create an even "balance of power" between donors and recipients. The country has a reputation for taking a strong lead in disciplining its donors and pushing for more efficient and effective forms of aid delivery, both at home and internationally. The chapter suggests that behind the concept of "country ownership" are a range of different forces influencing implementation of the aid effectiveness agenda in Viet Nam. The various actors engaged in the provision and receipt of aid are influenced by different incentives and there are differing rationales and logics underlying their actions. The concept of policy networks offers a useful framework to understand this situation. The broader point is that the health community needs a better understanding of the interests and incentives that affect the aid relationship and "country ownership". Aid reform should be understood as a political issue with all the associated tensions, incentives and challenges.

---

[1] An earlier version of this article was published in the journal: *Global Public Health* **6**(6): 606–20 September 2011.

"Even in the most aid-dependent countries, no amount of aid is going to make governments do what they don't want to do."[2]

Viet Nam is one of the brightest stars in the constellation of developing countries. Its remarkable achievements in reducing poverty and improving health and education outcomes are well known, and as result it has enjoyed generous aid programmes. The country also has a reputation for taking a strong lead in disciplining its donors and pushing for more efficient and effective forms of aid delivery, both at home and internationally.

This chapter discusses how efforts to improve the effectiveness of aid intersect with policy-making processes in the health sector. By aid effectiveness efforts, we mean processes and activities inspired by the Paris Declaration on Aid Effectiveness (OECD 2005), a global agreement signed by over 100 developed and developing countries.

Our analysis reveals a web of incentives influencing the implementation of the aid effectiveness agenda in the health sector in Viet Nam, and resulting in decisions that run counter the perceived wisdom on "what kind of aid government's want". We suggest that these apparent paradoxes make more sense if we conceptualise health governance as multiple, overlapping "policy networks" which cut across organisations and across the traditional donors — government divide. The principles of aid effectiveness make sense for some of these networks, but for others they are irrational and may lead to a loss of influence and resources, and are, therefore, resisted.

Nevertheless, the aid effectiveness agenda can help to promote "diplomacy amidst diversity". By providing a common language and shared principles, aid effectiveness can facilitate interactions *within* different policy communities and build bridges between them. These strategic coalitions can in turn help to overcome individual and institutional incentives. However, there is a limit to this influence: as we discuss below, the focus of aid effectiveness efforts in Viet Nam has been predominantly technocratic yet aid reform is fundamentally a political process with all the associated tensions, perverse incentives and challenges.

---

[2] Development partner, Viet Nam, 2009.

Country context

According to the World Bank, Viet Nam is one of the most successful developing countries (World Bank 2009). Remarkable gains have also been made in health, with under-five child mortality more than halving between 1990 and 2008 (from 58 to 14 deaths per 1000 live births) and infant mortality reducing by almost two-thirds in the same period (from 12 to 39 deaths per 1000 live births) (WHO 2010), though there remain significant inequalities in access to health care and health outcomes across Viet Nam, with ethnic minority groups particularly disadvantaged (Axelson *et al.* 2009).

Donors have rewarded this success with generous aid programmes. According to the Organization of Economic Cooperation and Development (OECD) Viet Nam received US$2487 million in official development assistance in 2007; this makes it one of the top 10 aid recipients in the world (OECD 2008).

It also has well-developed structures for donor coordination and dialogue (Alcaide and Sanz-Ramos 2007). It was one of the first countries to adopt and localise the Paris Declaration, with the agreement of the Hanoi Core Statement in 2005 (Government of Vietnam 2005), and requested to be a pilot country for UN Reform, which aims to streamline and harmonise the operations of UN agencies working at country level.

1. Tracking of Key Aid Effectiveness Processes — Methodological Issues

The analysis presented in this chapter is based on a quantitative review of health aid flows in Viet Nam and a qualitative analysis of the aid environment using event analysis, participant observation and key informant interviews.

The quantitative analysis uses a review of health aid flows to Viet Nam commissioned by the World Health Organization and first published in September 2008 (Martinez 2008). This review was limited by the fact that health partners in Viet Nam do not systematically report their health aid contributions to a common format. An *ad hoc* survey of the main health partners was, therefore, conducted: an electronic questionnaire was circulated, and follow up contacts were made to verify the data.

Locally collected data were compared against those published by the Development Assistance Committee (DAC) of the OECD. However, comparison was limited by two factors. First, DAC data are provided by agencies at *headquarters level* (i.e. not the country offices) so tend to under-represent the real figures, as many aid decisions are made at country level based on unspent aid resources. Indeed, National Health Accounts (NHA) record that US$ 56 million of donor support was spent on health in 2007 compared to OECD figures of US$143 million for the same year. Second, DAC reports on an annual basis, while our survey covers different multi-year periods, corresponding to the different project or programme cycles of different donors.

The qualitative analysis was carried out by the authors and employed a recognised research method: events analysis (Sofaer 1999). Two aid effectiveness processes were tracked over an 18-month period, from January 2008 to June 2009. One located in the health sector: the development of a *Statement of Intent on improving the effectiveness of development assistance for health* (hereafter Statement of Intent). The other, the Poverty Reduction Support Credit (PRSC), was examined from a health perspective. These processes were chosen because of their relevance to the study question — i.e. the influence of aid effectiveness processes on health policy making — and their proximity to the work of the lead authors, which facilitated access to key informants and the events analysis. It should be noted that they are not the only aid effectiveness processes underway in Viet Nam; others include UN Reform, the Partnership Group on Aid Effectiveness and the Paris Declaration Monitoring Survey.

This paper is also informed by discussions with a range of key stakeholders in the donor community and in government, including Ministry of Health; counterparts in MOH were given the opportunity to review this paper prior to publication.

2. Findings from the Quantitative Analysis: Overview of Health Aid Flows in Viet Nam

Following *Doi Moi*, the period of economic reform that began in the late 1980s, many Western countries re-established diplomatic relations with

Viet Nam, and donor aid soon followed. The first World Bank loan for health was provided in 1996: US$123 million for infrastructure. Over the following decade, health aid grew significantly in real terms, though as a proportion of government health expenditure it remained steady, at 8–10%. In 2007, aid's share of government health spending dropped markedly, to 3.4%, reflecting recent increases in government's allocation to the sector.

The growth in health aid has coincided with the government policy of "socialisation" which aims to attract resources from donors, the private sector and individuals to supplement government spending (state spending on health remained at just under 5% of total government spending between 2002 and 2007) MOH (2008).

According to the OECD DAC, disbursements of official aid to Viet Nam in the categories of "health" and "population policy and reproductive health" (which covers HIV) totalled US$143 million in 2007. Some 35% of health aid to Viet Nam is in the form of investment projects (infrastructure, etc.); 25% is technical cooperation and just 0.8% is recorded as sector programme support — this low level of un-earmarked funding in health is in stark contrast to the high levels of general budget support.

DAC figures also suggest a fairly high degree of fragmentation, with 58% of health aid provided to Viet Nam between 2002 and 2006 in the form of small projects of less than US$500,000. Only 5% of the health projects were for amounts equal or above US$10 million (Figure 1). This finding is confirmed by a separate OECD study which found that 11 out of 24 health donors in Viet Nam represent less than 10% of total health funding (OECD 2008a), and by our in-country survey of donors which recorded over 107 separate health projects, of which just 8 (7%) involve some kind of co-financing.

Communicable disease control is a major priority for health donors in Viet Nam, reflecting a global trend (Piva and Dodd 2009). In HIV, in particular, there is a significant donor presence: our survey found 12 major donors and five UN agencies each running their own HIV projects. Much of this support is relatively recent, with donor funding for HIV increasing from US$7–8 million in 2002–2004 to US$52 million in 2006. This is equivalent to 80–90% of total HIV spending, a level of donor dependence that is much higher than in other disease programmes and in the sector

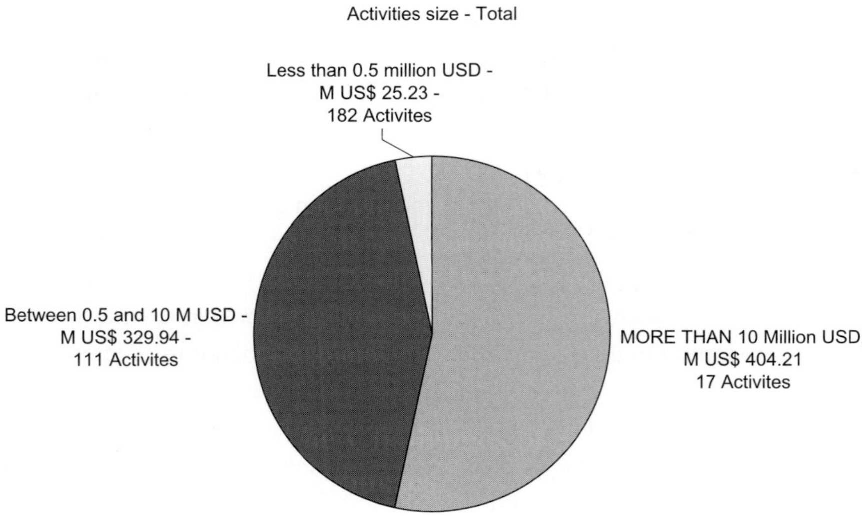

Figure 1. Size of donor-supported activities — cumulative total 2002–2006.

Source: OECD DAC.

more broadly (Martinez 2008). As Viet Nam continues to develop economically, it is likely that many donors will scale back their support to health and to HIV. This has led to concerns about sustainability, particularly in relation to the provision of anti-retroviral therapies (ART), which are heavily funded by donors, and which will become increasingly costly as coverage expands and patients move on to second and third line regimens. WHO's 2008 survey suggests that this is unlikely to be a problem in the medium-term as no HIV donors have immediate plans to pull out, but anticipates that there will be significant uncertainty after 2012, particularly if the US government moves away from supporting HIV as global priority (Martinez 2008).

Examined from an aid effectiveness perspective, health aid to Viet Nam has a number of "ineffective" attributes. Data on financial flows are poor and reported irregularly; aid fragmentation is high; there is an over-reliance on project aid with little experience of other aid modalities; and, in certain sub-sectors there is significant donor dependence.

Our key informant discussions suggest that many partners are aware of the short-comings but feel unable to move towards more flexible forms of financing — such as sector programme support — until a prioritised and costed health sector plan and associated monitoring framework are in place. The next section reports on efforts to move in this direction.

3. Findings from the Qualitative Analysis: Programmatic vs. Project Approaches

This section summarises key events and draws out significant points from the two aid effectiveness processes tracked for this paper: the Statement of Intent and the negotiation of a health trigger for the Poverty Reduction Support Credit.

The Statement of Intent, developed by the Ministry of Health and health partners in Viet Nam, sets goals for government and partners in relation to improve the effectiveness of health aid. It has a narrative text setting out commitments, and milestones (Table 1) which summarise

Table 1. Milestones from the statement of intent.

1	Matrix of donor activities produced on annual basis, to an agreed format. First, matrix to be prepared by WHO, thereafter MOH.
2	A study is carried out to assess the degree to which technical assistance in the health sector is harmonised and aligned.
3	Guidance issued on provision of budget support in the health sector.
4	Review of the approval, procurement and disbursement procedures for the use of health aid.
5	Government approves the TOR for the HPG set out in Annex 2, a dedicated funding mechanism for HPG secretariat is established and supported by interested partners. Procedures to formally link the Health Partnership Group and other health-related partnerships agreed.
6	Review of transparency, accuracy and timeliness of financial information provided by partners.
7	Finalisation of expenditure framework linked to the 5-Year Plan which documents all external and domestic revenues for health.
8	Completion of a viable 5-Year Plan with costs estimated for the health sector, and associated monitoring framework.
9	Assessment of the degree to which partner support is aligned with the 5-Year Plan and associated annual plans.
10	Joint Annual Reviews carried out, involving all levels of government, CSOs and donor partners, and disseminated.

these commitments and set a deadline for their achievement. In this sense, it is similar to the *Codes of Conduct* or *Memoranda of Understanding* which have been used in other developing countries to improve donor coordination (Walt *et al.* 1999).

The original impetus for the Statement of Intent was the desire of a small number of donors to establish a programme-based approach in the health sector. (A programme is defined as donors coordinating their support behind a single, comprehensive programme and budget framework which government has taken the lead in designing (OECD 2003).) Previous studies (Bijlmakers *et al.* 2006) had highlighted the desirability of moving towards a more programmatic approach in Viet Nam, and some local partners — particularly those that had made a commitment to aid effectiveness at global level — saw this as the way forward, and initiated the process. As summarised in Box 1, the range of actors engaged in the process expanded over time as coalitions or "networks" formed around the Statement of Intent process; these networks then engaged with or influenced other networks engaged in aid effectiveness processes.

Box 1: Key events in the development of the statement of intent

In February 2008, an informal meeting of **EU health partners** agreed to work towards a Programme-Based Approach (PBA) in the health sector. The following month they write formally to the Ministry of Health expressing their commitment to harmonisation and alignment, and requesting a meeting. While waiting for the MOH response, **WHO** carries out round of consultations with all partners (not only EU) on how to take forward the PBA commitment. A "code of conduct" or "statement of intent" (SOI) is suggested — WHO prepares a first draft and circulates among development partners.

In June 2008, **the World Bank, Asian Development Band, EC (representing the EU) and Aus AID plus WHO** — meet with Minister of Health. This grouping represents a new and expanding coalition of the major health donors interested in aid effectiveness, though with the significant absences

(*Continued*)

Box 1: (*Continued*)

of the United States and Japan. Partners request MOH collaboration in developing a Statement of Intent. The Minister agrees and nominates the **Department of International Co-operation** to lead the process.

Over the following months, text is reviewed and re-drafted following several rounds of consultation. Partners agree to establish a "core group" comprised of one representative from each of the following groups **UN, EU/EC, development banks, NGOs and other major bilaterals (Australia, Japan and the United States).** This illustrates a further widening of the circle and suggests that a strong network is forming around the SoI process.

In September, the **Ministry of Planning and Investment (MPI)**, which has overall responsibility for Aid Effectiveness in Viet Nam, gets involved. They comment that the SoI is duplicative of the Hanoi Core Statement and suggest that it be transformed from a statement of principles to an "action plan" indicating how the health sector will implement the Accra Action Agenda (AAA). Ministry of Health argues successfully against this, though the encounter suggests that the SoI network is now overlapping with the networks responsible for aid effectiveness in higher levels of government, creating some tension.

In November, the United States announces that it is unable to sign because it does not have clearance from its HQ to do so. In December 2008, the SOI is presented to a Consultative Group meeting of **Ambassadors** — an indication of its influence beyond its own network or "policy community" — and in March 2009 is formally adopted at a meeting of the health partnership group.

One specific challenge identified in discussions around the Statement of Intent was that the basic elements of a programme, notably a prioritised and costed sector plan linked to an expenditure framework and monitoring and evaluation framework, did not exist. Further, Viet Nam's complex legal structure for managing aid and limited experience of using aid modalities such as programme-based approaches left many in government unsure as to *how* — from an administrative viewpoint — such a funding modality might be established.

At face value, the Statement of Intent addresses these challenges by establishing a timeline to get the key elements of a programme in place (see Table 1). At the same time, though, the Ministry is wary of alienating development partners that work mainly through projects and has — to the surprise of some donors — said openly that it does *not* favour programmatic approaches over projects. This suggests that the Ministry of Health wants to ensure that its commitment to aid effectiveness principles does not in any way jeopardise its access to donor resources.

In addition, project aid allows the Ministry of Health to establish programme management units (PMUs). These are beneficial for at least two reasons: first, they allow Ministry staff to bypass some of their own administrative rules, thus allowing a faster rate of implementation. Second, they offer opportunities for income: donors pay an overhead charge to establish the PMU, and staff working within it are entitled to additional financial rewards. Projects — and the PMUs they create — are thus a means of attracting and retaining staff in the public service, where base salaries are very low. Aid that flowed through the budget could not be used in this way. One informant explains: "[Until now] aid has been in the form of project support which follows donor norms, which are much higher than government norms and create important incentives for recruiting good people."

Given the high number of projects in Viet Nam (Alcaide and Sanz-Ramos 2007) and the importance of project resources to the day-to-day functioning of individual departments (Kotoglou *et al.* 2008), there is a risk that any move to reduce projects in favour of programmes will be resisted by at least some Government staff. A recent study comments,

> "Line ministries [in Viet Nam] appear to be content with stand-alone project modalities, which are usually the preferred aid modality. In part, this may be a desire to accommodate donors who prefer to remain with traditional projects. However, there are also deeper incentives at play." (Kotoglou *et al.* 2008)

Nevertheless, both partners and Government recognise the downside of financial incentives associated with donor projects: they pull staff away from their regular jobs resulting in disproportionate levels of attention to donor priorities, and create accountability systems oriented towards donors rather than government.

A related issue reported by key informants is that the Ministry favours projects of less than US$500,000 because this is the threshold at which approval from the Ministry of Planning and Investment is required, a lengthy and complex process which many line ministries would prefer to avoid. Thus, the fragmentation of aid into a large number of small projects, while ineffective from the perspective of the Paris Declaration and global aid effectiveness processes, is both rational and effective from the perspective of MOH.

While the Statement of Intent began as an initiative of a select group of health donors, over time the involvement of other donors, and of the Ministry of Health itself, increased. However, Ministry engagement remains limited to two departments: the Department of Planning and Investment and the Department of International Cooperation. Other technical departments did not comment on the document nor attend meetings. This suggests that the notion of "country ownership", or even "MOH ownership", is problematic: some sections of the MOH saw value in the Statement of Intent and took ownership of the process, but others did not.

3.1 Negotiating the health trigger of the poverty reduction support credit

The budget support mechanism in Viet Nam, called the *Poverty Reduction Support Credit* or PRSC, provides another example of some of the tensions inherent in applying the aid effectiveness agenda. The mechanism is managed by the World Bank, and brings together funds from a number of bilateral donors, as well as revenues from the World Bank itself, into a single pool. Funds are transferred from the World Bank directly to the State Bank of Viet Nam where they are mixed with general government revenues.

PRSC disbursement is linked to (though not conditional on) the achievement of a set of policy actions or "triggers". Each PRSC contains around 10 triggers and 20 associated benchmarks covering all sectors, which form the focus of a series of *policy dialogue* meetings between donors themselves, and between donors and the government. The triggers are linked to Viet Nam's socio-economic development plan, and in practice tend to focus on specific actions — such as the passing of a new law — which can be easily measured and achieved within the timeframe of the annual PRSC cycle. Though there is no formal relationship between achievement of the triggers and disbursement of funds, it is understood that failure to achieve triggers may lead donors to reconsider their financial contribution to the PRSC.

In Viet Nam the PRSC process began in 2001 (PRSC 1) and by 2009 was up to its eighth round (PRSC 8). In that time, the size and balance of disbursements has changed significantly, from US$177 million in 2002, of which US$145 million was provided by the World Bank and just US$32 million by other donors (in 2007 prices), to US$334 million in 2007, with the World Bank providing US$175 million and partners US$159 million.

In health, there is typically a single trigger with perhaps one or two associated benchmarks. Box 2 describes the short process of negotiation around the PRSC 9 health trigger (in 2009–2010). It illustrates the limitations of the PRSC mechanism as a forum for dialogue: the principle role of the PRSC is to make sure that existing commitments are honoured; it is not a mechanism through which to pursue reform nor to negotiate difficult issues. Indeed, if partners try to use the PRSC to influence "real-time" policy discussions — as with the health trigger in 2009 — they are likely to fail.

Box 2: Negotiation of the PRSC health trigger

At the beginning of the PRSC 9 negotiations, donors proposed a trigger related to the establishment of an independent medical council with disciplinary powers. At the time, establishing a medical council was on the Ministry of Health policy agenda as part of a bundle of reforms associated with the accreditation and licensing of health professionals. By including this trigger in the PRSC, donors hoped to send a strong and positive signal to Government encouraging this reform direction.

(*Continued*)

Box 2: (*Continued*)

However, at a Cabinet meeting soon after, it was decided to delegate the task of licensing health professionals to provinces, and to de-link the accreditation and disciplinary systems. The relevant law was revised accordingly, and sent to the National Assembly for debate.

The implication for the PRSC was that the health trigger flipped from being in line with government policy, to being at odds with it. In response, health partners removed reference to a disciplinary council from the trigger. However, reference to a national and independent accreditation system was maintained, though partners were fully aware that this would be at odds with the Cabinet decision. Partners opposed the decision, as they felt that provinces lacked the capacity to carry out accreditation and because of potential difficulties associated with standardising a single system across 63 different provinces.

In essence, donors attempted to use the PRSC mechanism to express their opposition to the Government's new policy direction, and force it back on the original reform path. Unsurprisingly, this approach failed and the final wording of the trigger reflected the government's decision to keep control of the licensing system.

It is interesting to compare health triggers with another non-economic issue: gender. A European Union review (EC 2008) found that a total of nine gender triggers and benchmarks were included in Viet Nam's PRSCs between 2000 and 2008. Of these, only two were met, with others being reported as "not implemented" or off track. These failures had no impact on donor funding of the PRSC. Similarly, the 2008 health trigger (which focussed on classification of private health facilities) was reported as "unmet" but this had no impact on the level of PRSC financing. This point is important because it goes to the heart of the budget support "contract" — i.e. that donors provide resources directly to government in return for access to and influence over strategic policy discussions (ODI 2007). This analysis suggests that in Viet Nam, this "contract" is not functioning well, i.e. budget support "buys" only limited leverage over policy decisions.

A final point to emerge from the PRSC analysis is around the importance of timing: the PRSC timeline is short and rigid, while Government policy development processes are lengthy and unpredictable, in part because of Viet Nam's tripartite governance structure involving the Communist Party, the National Assembly and the Government itself. In theory, each entity has a distinct role: the party sets the broad strategies and directions for social and economic development and the road map to achieve these strategies. The National Assembly, which represents all sections of the population including minorities, approves the socio-economic development plan and budget. In addition, government's role is to implement. In practice, all three entities engage in policy development again making the notion of a single "country view" or position problematic.

4. Making Sense of the Complexity: Can Aid Effectiveness Promote Diplomacy Amidst Diversity?

Ultimately, aid givers are interested in whether aid contributes to the improvement of development outcomes: reducing poverty, making people healthier, better educated and so on. Even so, there is increasing recognition that the ways in which aid is provided are also important, and may impact on the results aid achieves. Are donors coordinating effectively with each other, or pulling in different directions? Does aid support locally developed plans and strategies, or follow donor priorities? Are aid monies delivered in a timely and predictable fashion? A concern for such issues lies at the heart of the OECD's work on aid management, which has became known as the "aid effectiveness" agenda, and which culminated in the signing of the Paris Declaration in 2005.

As a social sector with clear links to human well-being and poverty reduction, health has long been popular with donor agencies. Accordingly, it captured a significant share of new aid resources delivered post-Millennium (Piva and Dodd 2009), and attracted a range of new partnerships and initiatives. The large number and diversity of partners, along with the inherent complexities of the health sector itself, mean that health is particularly affected by challenges linked to the provision of aid. These challenges have been recognised for over a decade: problems such as donor coordination and supply-driven aid are a recurrent theme in the literature on health development (Buse and Walt 1996; Cassels and Janovsky 1995; Walt *et al.* 1999).

The Paris Declaration and the associated aid effectiveness agenda attempt to address these shortcomings. Yet five years on from its signing, many problems persist. Based on the experience in Viet Nam, our analysis attempts to provide some insight into the reasons. The next section presents themes emerging from the study and the following section suggests recommendations based on these.

4.1 Unpacking "country" ownership

A strong theme to emerge from the study is that the aid effectiveness principle of "country ownership" may be too simplistic. This principle is that "countries" set their own development agenda and coordinate development partners in support of this agenda. Yet, the quantitative and qualitative analyses both reveal a wide diversity of actors with a stake in the aid relationship in Viet Nam, often with different approaches and opinions, pointing to the difficulty of conceptualising "countries" or even ministries as a single entity. The Statement of Intent and the PRSC process show that these differences are not only donors vs. government (as often characterised by the aid effectiveness literature (Deutscher and Fyson 2009)) but also within donor agencies, between government ministries, and between the government, the Communist Party and the National Assembly.

Similarly, aid effectiveness principles are valued differently by different actors depending on where they "sit" institutionally. For instance, the Paris Declaration has more weight among European donors than in the United States, as evidenced by the U.S. decision not to sign the Statement of Intent. However, even within agencies, there are differences: for example, we found that staff working on vertical programmes are less engaged than those working on sector reform. Equally, within government, certain actors have greater interest in the aid effectiveness agenda. The Department of International Cooperation within the Ministry of Health has a formal mandate to improve donor harmonisation in health (MOH 2008a), while the Ministry of Planning and Investment has been tasked with implementing the Paris Declaration and the AAA in Viet Nam. Unsurprisingly, these were the actors on the government side most engaged in developing the Statement of Intent. Conversely, other technical departments in the health ministry were much less involved.

The third theme to emerge is that policy development processes are complex and *nonlinear*, particularly when there are many actors involved. This has implications for the implementation of aid effectiveness measures. The emergence of different interest groups in the negotiations around the Statement of Intent, and the evolution of the PRSC health trigger are both illustrations of this. It is accepted that donors provide aid for a variety of reasons — development, political and strategic (Picciotto 2007). It follows — and our analysis suggests — that recipients will also be influenced by a range of motivations in their acceptance of aid. Some recipients may want to maximise their resource base, others will be more concerned about ability to use aid flexibly (for example, as salary top-ups), while others will value that leverage the projects provide over spending decisions at provincial level (Kotoglou *et al.* 2008). The point here is not to argue about whose perceptions are right or wrong, but to acknowledge that a diversity of views exist.

4.2 Policy networks: a framework to make sense of diversity

The idea of "Policy networks" or "policy communities" borrowed from the literature on governance provides a useful theoretical framework for conceptualising this diversity. Shiffman describes policy communities as "networks of individuals (including researchers, advocates, policymakers and technical officials) and organisations (including government, non-governmental organisations, United Nations agencies, foundations and donor agencies) that share a concern for a particular issue". When policy networks develop strong "institutions", they can have an important influence on policy development (Shiffman 2009). By "institution" we mean — in the political economy sense — the informal and formal rules and structures as well as the explicit and underlying incentives and constraints through which governance is exercised, and which make organisations and individuals behave the way they do (Menard and Shirley 2005; Acemoglu 2008).

The growth of issue-specific networks of influence which cross borders and — critically — organisational boundaries has transformed global health governance (Kickbusch 2000). In some cases, these networks have resulted in the establishment of distinct organisations, such as the Global Fund and GAVI; in others, partnerships such as the Partnership on

Maternal Newborn and Child Health and the International Health Partnership have been formed. Informal groups such as the "Like-Minded"[2] have also flourished, providing an intellectual and information network for individuals working on similar issues across organisations.

The aid effectiveness agenda describes itself — and is commonly understood — as an approach that can help recipient countries to negotiate across competing policy communities and deliver a more integrative and rational approach to health development (Shiffman 2009). However, we would argue that aid effectiveness should be understood as a policy community in its own right: it is one of the players, not the referee, competing with other policy communities for influence, resources and institutional space in the governance of health policy. Certainly, it has all the institutional arrangements common to policy communities: it is supported by a network of government and non-government actors which interact through formal, inter-governmental mechanisms (the OECD/DAC) as well as informal networks; and it generates its own literature and knowledge base, as well as its own norms, standards and agreements, such as the Paris Declaration.

Nevertheless, the aid effectiveness agenda does provide some common ground on which the conflicting agendas and incentives of different policy networks can be negotiated. It is worth noting that, during the discussions on the Statement of Intent, there was never any disagreement that the Paris Declaration and the AAA were appropriate frameworks for discussions on aid management; rather the areas of tension were around who should lead the reform process and what shape it should take.

In this sense, global-level agreements are important: not only because they give legitimacy and "weight" to local process, but also because their content helps to set the parameters of the debate and creates a common language around things such as programmatic approaches, harmonisation and alignment. The Statement of Intent uses the leverage of the Paris Declaration and the Hanoi Core Statement to focus donor support on developing a sector-wide planning and budget framework. Equally, the PRSC provided a forum to address one of the most pressing issues in sector development: how to regulate health practitioners. This suggests that aid

[2] Provide Footnote

effectiveness processes are most likely to be more successful when they make substantive links with other development agendas. The offer of budget support as an incentive for reforming public financial management systems is one example. In health, the importance of such a link has been recognised since the early days of sector-wide approaches (SWAps), when aid management reforms inherent in SWAps were seen as a key vehicle for pursuing broader reform in the health sector (Lake and Musumali 1999; Bodart *et al.* 2001). By contrast, if aid coordination processes do not make such a link, they run the risk of becoming marginalised, parallel processes that further complicate an already crowded policy-making arena at country level (Dodd *et al.* 2009).

Yet, the diverse contexts in which aid effectiveness advocates now operate set limits on what they can achieve. In addition to constituting a separate policy network, it is arguable much aid effectiveness activity goes on within policy networks rather than between them. In other words, the locus of "diplomatic activity" (in the sense that it is used in this volume, i.e. coordination, cooperation and negotiation) is increasingly based around policy communities. As a consequence, over-arching "diplomatic" structures such as the Paris Declaration — which attempt to coordinate across networks — are likely to enjoy only partial success.

5. Conclusion and Recommendations

Viet Nam is a good place to examine the influence of the aid effectiveness agenda: high levels of aid mean the agenda is relevant, but low levels of aid-dependency create a "balance of power" between donors and recipients. In this sense, it provides a unique perspective, as most countries that invest in aid reform are donor dependent, and any analysis is thus distorted by this asymmetry of power.

Our analysis suggests that there is a range of different forces influencing implementation of the aid effectiveness agenda in Viet Nam. The various actors engaged in the provision and receipt of aid are influenced by different incentives and there are differing rationales and logics underlying their actions. The concept of policy networks offers a useful framework to understand this complexity. The broader point, though, is that the health community needs a better understanding of the interests and incentives that affect the aid relationship. The importance of "understanding the politics" has long been recognised in relation to health sector reform (Walt and Gilson 1994) and broader development agendas. Aid reform should be understood in the same light: as a political issue with all the associated tensions, incentives and challenges (ODI 2008).

For example, "government" should not be regarded as a single entity, nor assumed to be an ally in pushing for more "effective" donor behaviour. Indeed, from the perspective of (some parts of) government the potential gains associated with aid effectiveness do not always outweigh the potential difficulties associated with implementing the agenda, particularly when it comes to introduce complex and new administrative procedures (such as pooled funding) or approaches that may upset existing distribution of aid resources (such as programmatic approaches).

Regardless of the level of aid-dependency, it is clear that in Viet Nam — as in other developing countries — reform cannot be imposed from the outside. This in turn highlights the limited interface between global policy agendas (such as aid effectiveness) and the local processes. Global processes may be very relevant to country realities, but they are unlikely to have any impact without active local champions, sustained local engagement and resonance in local political debates. Indeed, this chapter has described genuine problems in the delivery of aid which provide a legitimate mandate for the existence of the aid effectiveness agenda. However, it has also shown the continuing slow progress in implementing that agenda.

Can anything be done? A clear understanding of the various tensions inherent in aid governance, as provided by this chapter, is hopefully a good start. This should lead to more realistic expectations about what can be achieved through aid effectiveness processes. Building on this understanding, some tentative recommendations for advancing the aid effectiveness agenda at global and country level are provided in the following paragraphs.

At global level, international health policymakers need to recognise that while the principles of aid effectiveness are important and meaningful, attempting to implement those principles through the establishment of a single global process — at sector level or in general — is likely to fail.

As a result, global actions need to be much less prescriptive and much more flexible — efforts to improve aid governance need to be designed and implemented locally, according to local timetables and adapted to local circumstances. This in turn means that country actions will be non-standardised and non-comparable, which may create difficulties for global advocacy and monitoring, but this is a limitation that global stakeholders must accept.

At ***country level***, policy makers should beware of adopting an overly simplistic concept of "ownership". To this end, it may be useful for development partners to engage a political scientist familiar with the "networks of influence" approach to map the different policy communities and interest groups relevant to the governance of aid, and try to establish their incentives and disincentives in relation to aid effectiveness reforms.

Equally, aid effectiveness efforts are most powerful and meaningful if linked to a substantive policy reform agenda. Aid effectiveness measures cannot on their own deliver gains for sector development, but they do have the potential to catalyse (or help maintain momentum for) efforts to improve health sector planning, budgeting and so on. Accordingly, an exercise to map the possible points of intersection between aid effectiveness reforms and relevant policy-making processes may be useful.

A related recommendation is that introducing new approaches (aid reforms) requires both sustained engagement and the identification of local champions, recognising that there will often be differences of opinion within government. This is one of the first rules of good development practice, and it also applies to the introduction of aid effectiveness reforms: just because they make sense and are for the benefit of recipient governments, does not mean they can be imposed "from the outside". Even so, partners can play an important role in supporting local reform processes, as described above.

A final recommendation is to collect and publish data on aid flows at country level. As aid effectiveness reforms need to be tailored to local circumstances and synergise with local policy processes, detailed and specific knowledge of local aid flows is required. The findings of such analysis should not only provide an entry point for discussions on aid challenges but also be welcomed by staff working on health sector planning and budgeting (who often lack detailed information on what donors are doing), helping to create local champions for aid reforms. Information should be organised in a way that makes most sense for local planning processes, rather than according to global templates.

In conclusion, aid effectiveness is not an agenda that is going to go away, and action on aid effectiveness challenges will always be needed — particularly in the health sector. However, making progress on aid effectiveness challenges will mean learning to accommodate a variety of tensions. In particular, the international health community needs to recognise that global health governance is inherently dynamic and diverse. This diversity creates challenges for countries and cannot be regulated through further global processes. It also creates opportunities for countries — in particular opening up space for policy dialogue and giving countries a legitimate mandate to make demands of the development partners that support them. Harnessing these "diplomatic" opportunities to manage the diversity that global health creates at country level has to be led by recipient countries themselves, according to their timetable, and in a way tailored to their own context and circumstances.

Chapter 5 draws on this chapter and other cases to assess the issue of health systems more generally. Chapter 2 tackles issues of negotiating aid effectiveness at global level, while Chapter 7 assesses negotiating aid effectiveness among global programmes.

References

Acemoglu D (2008) *Lecture Notes for Political Economy of Institutions and Development (Spring 2008)*. Massachusetts Institute of Technology, Department of Economics.

Alcaide MD, Sanz-Ramos S (2007) *Vietnam's Laboratory on Aid: Donor Haromonisation: Between Effectiveness and Democratisation. Case Study 1*, in Working Paper 42. Madrid: FRIDE.

Axelson H *et al.* (2009) "Health Financing for the Poor Produces Promising Short-Term Effects on Utilization and Out-of-Pocket Expenditure: Evidence from Vietnam," *Int. J. Equity Health* 8(20):1–17.

Bijlmakers L *et al.* (2006) *Feasibility of the programme approach in the health sector in Vietnam*. Independent Report Commissioned by the Swedish Embassy in Hanoi: Hanoi.

Bodart C *et al.* (2001) "The Influence of Health Sector Reform and External Assistance in Burkina Faso," *Health Policy & Planning* 16(1):74–86.

Buse K, Walt G (1996) "Aid Coordination for Health Sector Reform: A Conceptual Framework for Analysis and Assessment", *Health Policy* 38(3):173–87.

Cassels A, Janovsky K(1995) "Better Health in Developing Countries: Are sector-Wide Approaches the Way of the Future?" *The Lancet* 352(9142):1777–9.

Deutscher E, Fyson S (2009) *Committing to Effective Aid: Why Can't Donors Walk Their Talk?* in *Development Outreach*. Washington DC: World Bank Institute.

Dodd R *et al.* (2009) "Paris on the Mekong: Using the Aid Effectiveness Agenda to Support Human Resources for Health in the Lao People's Democratic Republic," *Human Resources for Health* 7(16):1–11.

EC (2008)*PRSC 6–10 Mid-Term Review*. Hanoi: EC Delegation to Viet Nam.

Goverment of Vietnam (2005) *Hanoi Core Statement on Aid Effectiveness*. Hanoi: Government of Viet Nam and Development Partners.

Kickbusch I (2000) "The Development of International Health Policies — Accountability Intact?" *Social Science & Medicine* 51(6):979–89.

Kotoglou K *et al.* (2008) *Independent Monitoring of the Implementation of the Hanoi Core Statement at Sectoral and Sub-National Level in Viet Nam*. Hanoi.

Lake S, Musumali C (1999) "Zambia: The Role of Aid Management in Sustaining Visionary Reform", *Health Policy & Planning* 14(3):254–63.

Martinez J (2008) *How External Support for Health and HIV will Evolve as Viet Nam Becomes a Middle-Income Country*. United Nations Country Team Viet Nam.

Menard C, Shirley MM (2005) What is New Institutional Economics? in *Handbook of New Institutional Economics*, Menard C, Shirley MM (eds). The Netherlands: Springer 1–18.

MOH (2008a) *Decision on the Functions, Responsibilities, Authorities and Organisational Structure of the Department of International Cooperation under the Ministry of Health*, 52/2008/QD-BYT, 30 December 2008. Hanoi, Vietnam: Ministry of Health.

MOH (2008) *Joint Annual Health Review: Health Financing in Vietnam*. Hanoi: Minstry of Health of the Socialist Republic of Vietnam and the Health Partnership Group.

ODI (2007) *Budget Support to Ghana: A risk worth taking?* in *Briefing Paper 24*. London: Overseas Development Institute.

ODI (2008) *Aid Effectiveness After Accra: How to Reform the 'Paris agenda'*. Briefing Paper 39, July. London: Overseas Development Institute.

OECD (2003) *Harmonising Donor Practices for Effective Aid Delivery*, in *DAC Guidelines and Reference Series*. Paris: OECD.

OECD (2005) *Paris Declaration on Aid Effectiveness*. Paris:OECD.

OECD (2008) *Survey on Monitoring the Paris Declaration Volume 2 Country Chapters: Viet Nam*. Paris: OECD.

OECD (2008a) *Scaling Up: Aid Fragmentation, Aid Allocation and Aid Predictability — Report of the 2008 Survey of Aid Allocation Policies and Indicative Forward Spending Plans*. Paris: OECD Development Assistance Committee.

Picciotto R (2007) "Book Review of '*Does Foreign Aid Really Work?*' (Roger C. Riddell) & '*Foreign Aid: Diplomacy, Development, Domestic Politics*' (Carol Lancaster)", *Annual Journal of the Carnegie Council on Ethics and International Affairs* 21(4 (Winter)), p.477–80.

Piva P, Dodd R (2009) "Where Did All the Aid Go? An in-Depth Analysis of Increased Health Aid Flows Over the Last 10 Years", *Bulletin of the World Health Organization* 87(12): 930–39.

Shiffman J (2009) "A Social Explanation for the Rise and Fall of Global Health Issues", *Bulletin of the World Health Organization* 87(8):608–13.

Sofaer S (1999) "Qualitative Methods: What are They and Why Use Them?" *Health Services Research* 34(5 Part 2):1101–18.

Walt G *et al.* (1999) "Health Sector Development: From Aid Coordination to Resource Management", *Health Policy & Planning* 14(3):207–18.

Walt G *et al.* (1999) Managing External Resources in the Health Sector: Are There Lessons for SWAps (sector-wide approaches)? *Health Policy & Planning* 14(3):273–84.

Walt G, Gilson L (1994) "Reforming the Health Sector in Developing Countries: The Central Role of Policy Analysis", *Health Policy & Planning* 9(4):353–70.

World Bank (2009) *Viet Nam and the World Bank*. Available at http://go.worldbank.org/2QUQ2023L0 [Accessed 20 June 2009].

World Health Organization (2010) *World Health Statistics 2010* Geneve, WHO.

16

Ethiopia: Aligning Stakeholders Behind National Health Plans

W Lemma, N Kedir,† G Azene,‡ B Abdosh,‡ J Aliy‡ and O Bushen**

**Center for Global Health Equity, Tulane University School of Public Health and Tropical Medicine. New Orleans, LA, USA*
†Plan Monitoring and Evaluation Directorate, Federal Ministry of Health of Ethiopia, Addis Ababa Ethiopia
‡Tulane University Technical Assistant Program Ethiopia, Addis Ababa Ethiopia

Summary

This chapter assesses the importance of mechanisms for coordinating partners at district and local levels in Ethiopia, to compliment the earlier chapter on national leadership (Chapter 3). The practical diplomacy behind planning and tracking results at district level to coordinate donor activities is highlighted as important. The chapter provides evidence of the integration of disease and general health services, which has been the backbone of the Ethiopian response. The extent and depth of such coordination at the district level has been instrumental towards achieving significant strides in stakeholders' alignment at operational levels within the country's decentralization framework. The challenges faced by the health sector of Ethiopia in aligning stakeholders behind national plans especially in its process of gaining support from all health development partners, global programmes for the principle of "one plan, one budget and one reporting" is also summarised.

1. Introduction

1.1 Background

Ethiopia has been a major recipient of funding support from Global Health Initiatives (GHI's) such as — GFATM, GAVI and PEPFAR. The health system of Ethiopia has taken a series of measures to successfully align these important funding streams within the successive National Health Sector Development Programs and Plans (HSDP I, II, III, IV). Such harmonization and alignment have allowed Ethiopia to manage global programmes to deliver HIV/AIDS, TB and malaria services, strengthen the health delivery system, and also focus donor funding on achieving meaningful country results. This chapter assesses the extent and depth of such coordination that has been instrumental towards achieving significant strides in stakeholders' alignment both at the national as well as at key districts and operational levels within the country's decentralization framework. The chapter also describes the stages and processes of negotiations that the health sector pursued for improving health delivery with diverse health partners both at the national and local levels.

The challenges faced by the health sector of Ethiopia in aligning stakeholders behind national plans especially in gaining support from all health development partners to the principle of "one plan, one budget and one reporting" is also summarised.

1.2 Country profile

Ethiopia is located in the horn of Africa with diverse peoples of over 80 ethnic groups. It is a developing country with an estimated annual per capita income of US$810 (PPP). According to the 2007 census, the total population has reached 73.9 million with 85% of the population living and working in rural areas. This shows the country is the least urbanised amongst developing countries. The population is growing at an annual rate of 2.7%.

The 1994 Constitution of the country has introduced a federal government structure composed of nine regional states: Tigray, Afar, Amhara, Oromia, Somali, Benishangul-Gumuz, Southern Nations and Nationalities and Peoples Region (SNNPR), Gambella and Harari and two city administrations: Addis Ababa and Dire Dawa. The national regional states and city administrations are further sub-divided into approximately 801 woredas, which are the basic decentralised administrative units representing 125,000–150,000 people governed by an administrative council composed of elected members. The woredas are further divided into around 15,000 kebeles (each representing about 5,000 people).

1.3 Health profile

The health status of the population of Ethiopia is low even by the average measures within the Sub-Saharan Africa (SSA) countries. The major health problems are attributable to preventable infectious and communicable diseases including nutritional disorders that account for about 60–80% of the disease burden of the people. The average life expectancy at birth is 53.4 years for men and 55.4 years for women and maternal mortality is 673/100,000 live births (PPD, 2006/07).

According to the MOH/FHAPCO, the national HIV prevalence for the year 2009 is 2.3% and a total of 1,116,216 adults and children are living with HIV/AIDS in Ethiopia. In 2009 alone, there are an estimated 131,145 new HIV infections and 44,751 AIDS deaths. The country also has one of the largest populations of children orphaned by AIDS in SSA, currently estimated at 855,720 (FMOH/FHAPCO, 2007). AIDS has become the leading cause of mortality in the 15–49 age groups, accounting for an estimated 43% of all adult deaths in this group. In urban areas, nearly two-thirds of adult deaths are estimated to be attributable to AIDS (FMOH, 2006) in this age group.

Estimates show that 75% of the Ethiopian land is malarious (altitude <2000 metre) andmore than 50 million (68%) people are at risk. In 2005/06, malaria has been reported as the first leading cause of outpatient visits (17.8%) and death (21.8%) and second cause of hospital admission (14.1%) in health facilities across the country. In addition, TB is also another major public health problem in the country. The incidence and prevalence of all forms of TB is estimated at 378 and 641 per 100,000 populations, respectively (WHO, 2008). As noted in the HSDP (FMOH, 2005), the ultimate goal of the health sector is to improve the health status of the Ethiopian people through provision of adequate and optimum quality of promotive, preventive, basic curative and rehabilitative health services to all segments of the society. Towards achieving these ultimate goals, the focus has been on high value interventions specifically to reduce child mortality, improve maternal health and combat HIV/AIDs, malaria, TB and other diseases of public health importance.

One of the major strategies of the Ethiopian health sector has been progressive expansion of primary health care services at community level aimed at universal health coverage by covering rural Ethiopia through rapid development of primary health care units (PHCU) (health centres and health posts). Ethiopia's resolve to effectively use disease-specific financing support for health systems strengthening has been instrumental for the implementation of HSEP in rural Ethiopia, expansion of PHCU including the institutionalization of the community health services in largely underserved and hard-to-reach areas of the country.

The health systems strengthening initiative involved considerable expansion in the PHCUs through new construction, rehabilitation and upgrading of existing facilities throughout the country. As shown in Table 1, there have been rapid increases in health posts, health centres and hospitals. This increase has enabled the potential health service coverage to reach 92%, showing a cumulative growth rate of 25% over the last five years (FMoH, 2007/8). Currently, there are about 149 hospitals, 1,338 health centres and 12,446 health posts operating in Ethiopia (FMoH, 2006/07).

In terms of human resource for health (HRH) development, there is significant improvement in the trainings and deployment of mid- and community-level health extension workers (HEWs). Two accelerated training of community-level HEWs and mid-level HEWs (non-physician clinicians or health officers) were initiated since 2003/04. As a result, to date there are 31,831 HEWs and about 5,000 Health officers trained and deployed to serve at various levels of the public health sector (see Table 1).

As a result of these HRH and physical expansion initiatives, there has been significant progress in the area of health systems strengthening, improvements in maternal and child health as well as in the prevention and control of major communicable diseases, especially HIV/AIDS, tuberculosis (TB) and malaria.

The malaria prevention and control programme in Ethiopia is guided by a five-year strategic plan that has been developed in the context of HSDP and the objectives of the international movements of Roll Back

Table 1. Trend in health infrastructure, human resource and potential health service coverage: 2004/5–2008/9.

Indicators	2004/5	2005/6	2006/7	2007/8	2008/9
No. of facilities					
Hospital	131	138	143	149	
Health centre	600	635	690	732	1,338
Health posts	4,211	5,955	9,914	11,446	12,488
Human resource					
Physicians	2,453	2,115	2,085	1,806	2,486
Health officers	776	715	1,151	1,242	2,518
Nurses	18,809	17,845	16,765	18,146	16,765
Para medicals	6,259	5,431	3,863	7,731	
Health extension workers	2,737	9,900	17,653	24,571	31,831
PHS coverage (%)					
PHS coverage (public facilities)	72.1	76.9	86.7	89.6	92

(*Source*: FMOH indicator report)

Malaria. HSDP III has put a target of reducing malaria morbidity and mortality from 22% to 10% and from 5% to 2% by 2010, respectively. FMoH is implementing a three pronged approaches namely; selective vector control, early diagnosis and treatment of cases and epidemic prevention and control. Distribution of long-lasting ITNs is one of the major approaches of vector control with a cumulative total distribution of more than 22 million ITNs to date using the HSEP (Figure 1).

HEWs are playing a major role in early diagnosis and treatment of cases. To this effect, 4.1 million rapid malaria diagnosis tests (RDT) and 6.1 million doses of Coartem have been procured and distributed. With these, the country has made remarkable progress in the fight against malaria over the last few years. The recently completed malaria indicator survey has reported that in malarious aresas, 66% of households were protected by at least one ITN, ITN use by children under five years and pregnant women increased to nearly 42% and to over 60%, respectively in those households that own at least one net, and the parasite prevalence was very low (0.7%) in malarious areas (Ethiopian National Malaria Indicator Survey 2008). Furthermore, the FMOH report shows a declining trend of malaria cases and deaths in recent years (Figure 2).

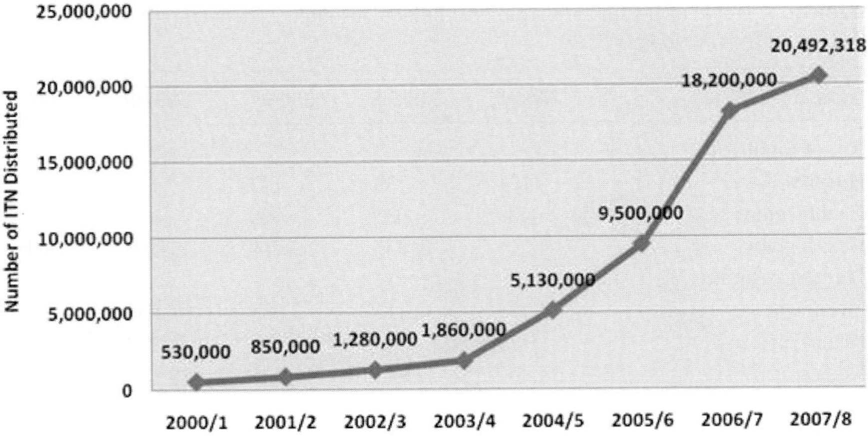

Figure 1. Number of ITN distributed over the past 2001–2007/8.

Source: Annual Performance Report of HSDP III (Ethiopian Fiscal Year 2000, 2001).

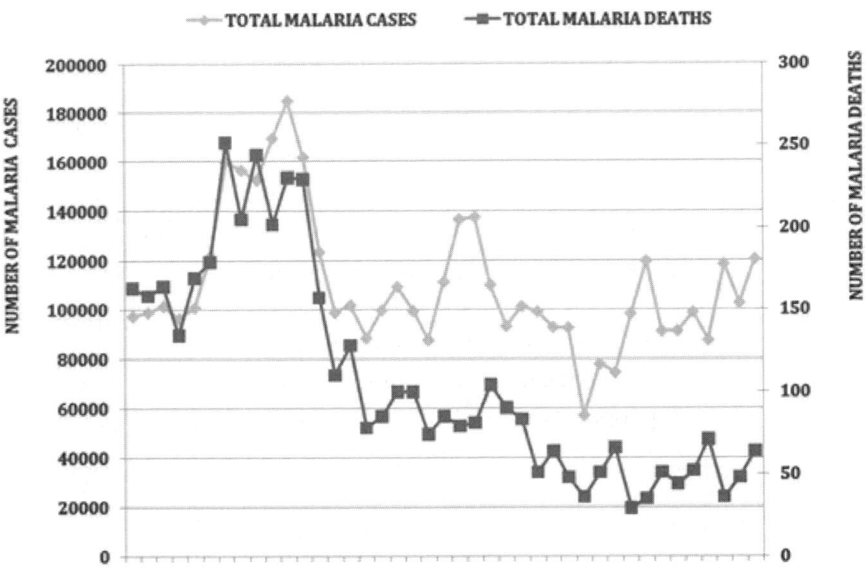

Figure 2. Trend of malaria cases and deaths (Ethiopia, January 2005–May 2008).

Source: Annual Performance Report of HSDP III (Ethiopian Fiscal Year 2000, 2001).

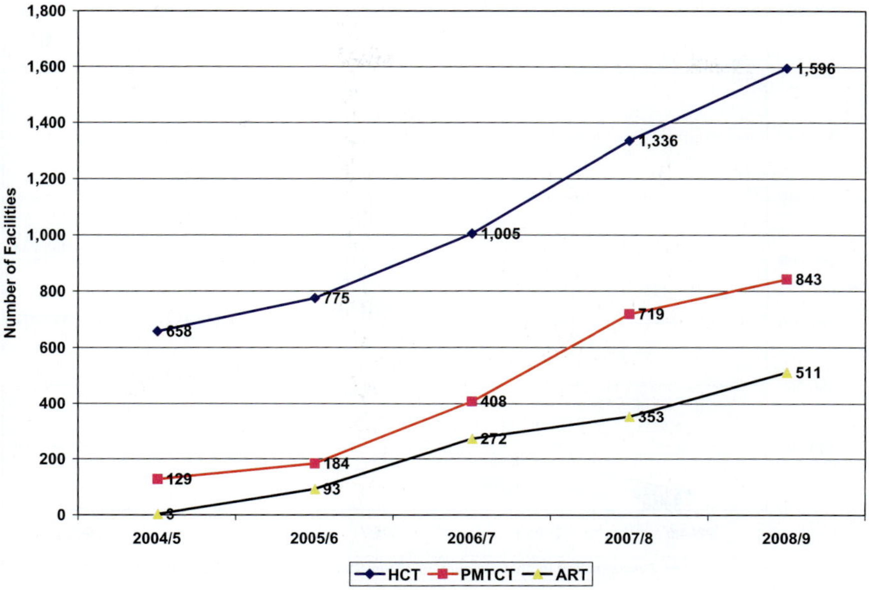

Figure 3. Trend in HIV/AIDS-related health service provision sites, 2004/5–2008/9.
Source: Annual Performance Report of HSDP III (Ethiopian Fiscal Year 2000, 2001).

Prevention and control of HIV/AIDS is the other focus area which showed significant improvement in the last five years both in service site expansion and service uptake. The trend in the number of public and private health facilities providing HIV counselling and testing (HCT) services, prevention of mother to child transmission of HIV (PMTCT) and anti-retroviral therapy (ART) over the past five years is summarised in Figure 3.

In line with the expansion of facilities providing HIV/AIDS services, the number of people who utilised these services has significantly increased. The number of people who have been counselled and tested for HIV has increased over 13-fold from 436,854 in 2004/5 to 5,853,472 in 2008/9. Similarly, the number of people who benefited from chronic HIV care and ART has shown remarkable increase over the past five years (Figure 4)

Three indicators are used to monitor and assess the overall TB prevention and control programme: TB case detection rate, TB treatment success rate and TB cure rate. The progress so far shows that the TB case

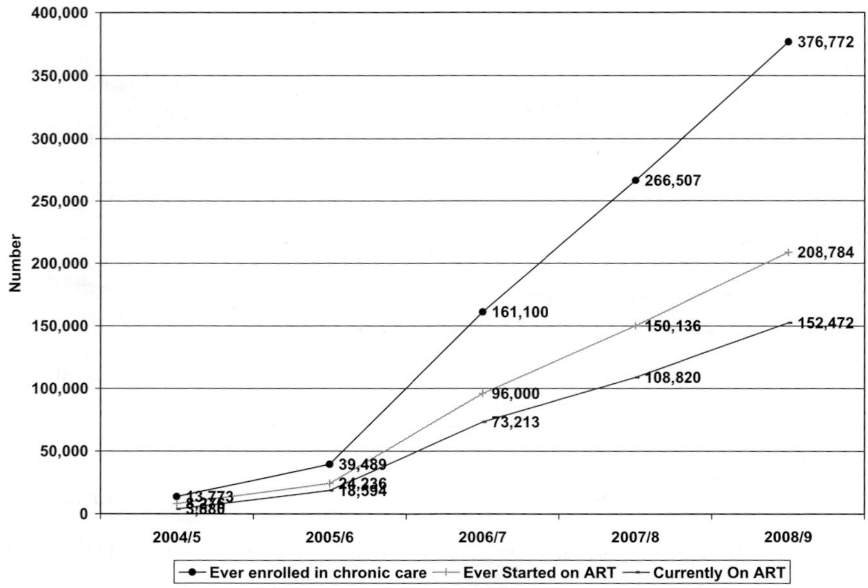

Figure 4. Trend in number of people enrolled in "chronic HIV care, ever started on ART and currently on ART", 2004/5–2008/9.

Source: Annual Performance Report of HSDP III (Ethiopian Fiscal Year 2000, 2001).

detection rate at 34% in 2007/8 still remains low; while the treatment success rate is almost equal to the WHO recommended rate at 84%.

Over the last five years, there is also improvement in the coverage of MCH services. According to service statistics of the FMOH (2008/09), for there is an increasing trend in the coverage of expanded programme of immunization (EPI), contraceptive acceptance rate, antenatal care and delivery attended by health personnel.

There has been an increasing trend in the funding availability to the health sector of Ethiopia over the last five years. According to the third National Health Account (NHA 2007), the national health expenditure has increased from US$356 million in 1999/2000 and reached US$522 million in 2004/05. Distribution of the total health expenditure by source of funding showed that external funding contributed 37% to the total health expenditure followed by government (31%) and households (30%). While government expenditure on health has increased by 37% over the five year

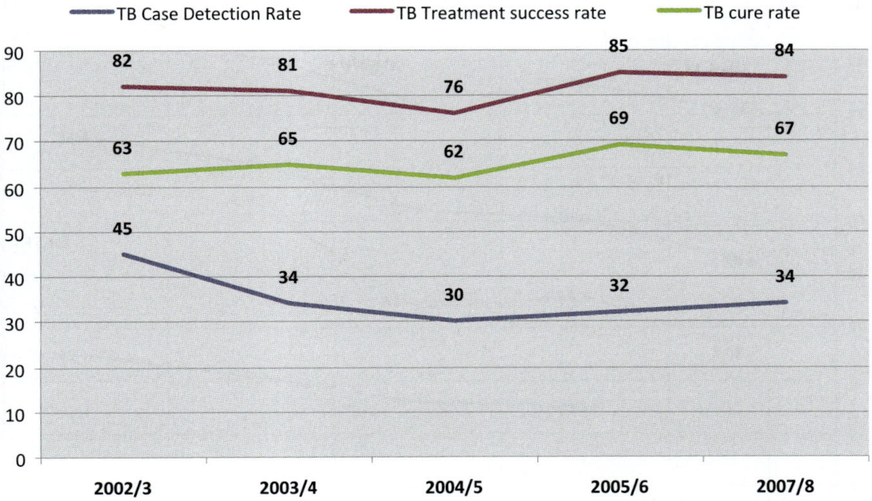

Figure 5. Trend in TB detection rate, treatment success rate and cure rate, 2002–2007/8.
Source: Annual Performance Report of HSDP III (Ethiopian Fiscal Year 2000, 2001).

period, the increment of external funding is significant — two-and-a-half times greater — which is mainly attributed to the flow of funds from new initiatives such as Global Fund to Fight AIDS, Tuberculosis and Malaria; the Global Alliance on Vaccines and Immunizations; and others such as PEPFAR (HCF/PPD 2007). Furthermore, based on the data available from the Ministry of Finance and Economic Development (MoFED), there has been also an increasing trend in per capita public expenditure on health from an average of ETH Birr 11.3 in 2001/2 to ETH Birr 23.1 (more than double in seven years, Figure 7).

2. Policy and Planning Analysis

The following section outlines the history and the recent experiences of Ethiopia in the innovative health partnerships between the health sector and its partners in the planning and alignment behind the national health plan. This chapter uses different methodologies to illustrate this experience including desk review of the available national health sector data and in-depth expert interviews.

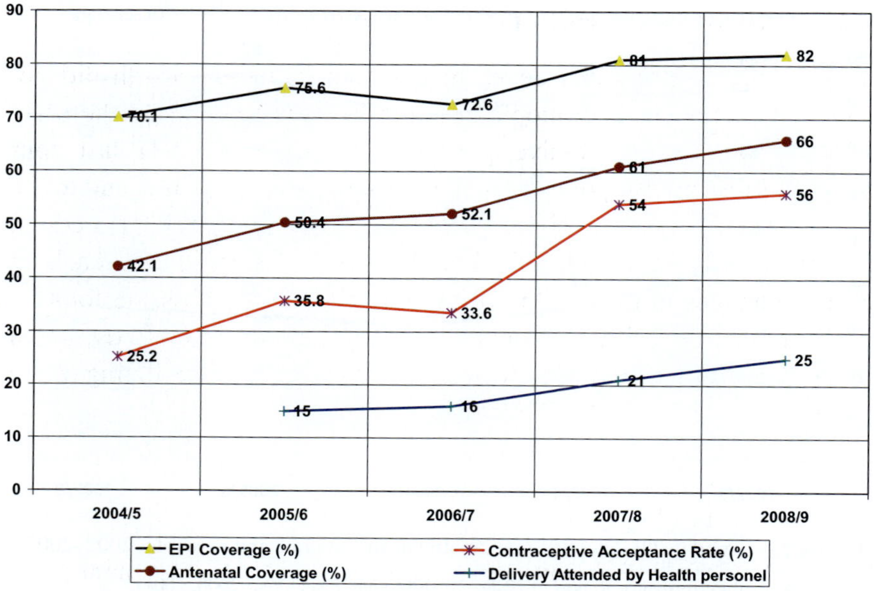

Figure 6. Trend in coverage of maternal and child health services, 2004/5–2008/9.

Source: Annual Performance Report of HSDP III (2008/09).

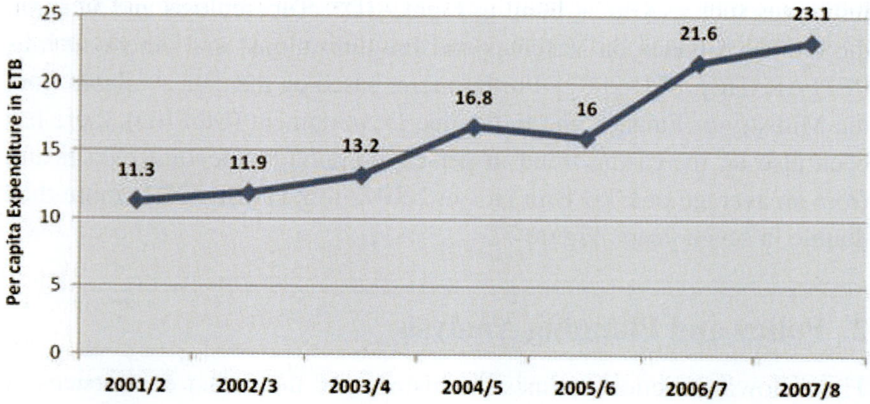

Figure 7. Trend on per capita public health expenditure, 2001–2007/8 (1 US$ = ETH Birr 11.50 in 2007/08 exchange rate).

Source: Annual Performance Report of HSDP III (Ethiopian Fiscal Year 2000, 2001).

2.1 The history of health policy and planning

The advent of a national development plan including health did not have a long history in Ethiopia and it only started as late as the early 1960s. However, successive government changes in the last four decades from imperial rule to socialist-oriented military rule, and to the present transformation of the governance structure into the Federal System have brought with it the initial concept of planning far reaching radical changes in the health policy of Ethiopia providing the foundation for further health care development and more importantly, as an integral part of socio-economic development policy and planning of the country.

2.2 General policy guide

The turn around and the intimate linkage of health development planning with the general socio-economic development plan of the country only became possible shortly after the Transitional Government of Ethiopia (TGE) published in September, 1993 its 20 year health policy, the first of its kind in the country. The policy statement in the document states that "'...health development shall be seen not only in humanitarian terms [but] also as an essential component of the package of social and economic development as well as being an instrument of social justice and equity'. The major features of the health policy were democratization & decentralization of the health service system; development of the preventive and promotive components of health care; development of an equitable and acceptable standard of health service system that will reach all segments of the population within the limits of resources; development of appropriate capacity building based on assessed needs; promotion of the participation of the private sector and NGOs in health care" (Health Policy of TGE 1993).

The translation of the health policy into actual implementation was to be divided into four phases of planning each for five years through what was to be called planning phases of Health Sector Development Programs (HSDPs).

2.3 Health sector development program phase I (HSDP I)

The first phase known as HSDP I emerged in 1997/98 for a planning period of 1997/98–2001/02. HSDP I was the result of a broader consultation among the FMOH, the Regional Health Bureaus and Health Development Partners including the private and the NGO sector. It was developed in the context of a strong government commitment to democracy and decentralisation, and was designed explicitly to respond to the needs of the rural population who constitute about 85% of the total population. HSDP I proposed long-term goals for the sector, and the means to attain them by way of a series of phased, medium-term plans. The sectoral programme demonstrated the priority that the government accorded to health and was backed by a commitment to allocate the necessary internal and external resources to facilitate HSDP implementation. The specific objective of the first phase of HSDP was the development of a health system which would: (a) improve the coverage and quality of health services; (b) to be primarily implemented and managed by regional, zonal and woreda-level health officials and (c) strive to be financially sustainable. The document had contained a resource allocation of capital and recurrent plans and provided estimated costs based on eight components for health systems strengthening and development. These components were: health service delivery & quality of care; facility rehabilitation & expansion; human resource development; strengthening pharmaceutical services; IEC; HMIS; health care financing and monitoring and evaluation (M&E).

The document also defined the governance for the implementation of HSDP I. At the top, the Central Joint Steering Committee (CJSC) chaired by the Minster for the Social Affairs at the Prime Minister's Office with membership from heads of major donor agencies including WB, USAID, UN agencies and EU. CJSC meets quarterly to make decisions on oversight. Regional Joint Steering Committees at the regional level, a joint consultative forum meeting every two months between the FMOH Health and Population Donor Group for discussion, dialogue and making implementation recommendation to the CJSC were also created.

HSDP I was phased out with remarkable results and learning experiences which has contributed to the planning and implementation of the second phase or HSDP II. It was evaluated by a mixture of local and expatriate experts who were independent of both the development as well as the implementation of the plan. A number of important lessons have been learned during the implementation of HSDP I. As the evaluation report confirmed, "HSDP I has made very important contributions to comprehensive planning of the whole health sector. For the first time, the design of HSDP I with its various components permitted to look at the sector in an integrated way and thus plan the various components according to the need of the sector". In particular, the review reported that "the HSDP has permitted encouraging improvements in the relation with the various stakeholders, like donor agencies and NGO's that now are fully on board and contribute in a more coordinated way to the development of the national health plan" (Final Evaluation of HSDP I Vol. I; 2003).

However, there were also a number of challenges that its implementation has faced through the planning period. One of the major problems was lack of proper harmonisation of the HSDP I with the government socio-economic development planning and withmonitoring cycles. The HSDP failed to integrate into the general government planning and monitoring processes. Regional health bureaus (RHBs) were used to preparing two separate plans — one as part of the regional development plan, and one as their contribution to the HSDP, each of which required reporting both on an annual and on periodic bases. Budget codes, reporting formats and processes differ, doubling the administrative burden on management entities at regional level. There was also weak ownership of the HSDP at the implementation level, including limited familiarity with and understanding of the HSDP at lower levels of the health system.

2.4 Health sector development program phase II (HSDP II)

In recognition of the problems caused by developing a five-year health sector planning cycle which was not synchronised with the overall government development planning process, the health sector has revised the duration of the second phase of HSDP (2002/03–2004/05) reducing the planning period to three years in order to make it consistent with the overall government socio-economic development plan.

The development of HSDP II conveniently coincided with the deepening of decentralisation and devolution not only from the centre to the regional level but also to the woreda/district level. As clearly stated in the HSDP II, "The primary objectives of the political, administrative and economic decentralization policy are to increase government services, to improve efficiency in resource allocation, and to improve accountability of government and the public service to the population" (HSDP II, p.23). It also saw finalisation of the process of development of the country's poverty reduction strategy paper (PRSP), as a means of articulating a broad-based and national strategy to refocus activities and resources towards reducing the level of poverty in the nation. Another important reform initiative that helped shape both the design and implementation of HSDP II was the Civil Service Reform Program (CSRP). This was introduced in February 2002 in order to create a civil service which needed to be efficient and competent to achieve the economic, social and political missions of the government, and to promote a culture of administration which reflects direct participation by the people's representatives. The CSRP has five sub-programmes: expenditure management and control; human resources management; service delivery; top management systems and ethics. Other global health initiatives such as roll back malaria, and most importantly, the dire need to accelerate the prevention and control of HIV/AIDS and the beginning of significant support from GFATM and PEPFAR to the country have greatly enhanced the shape and the deepening planning of HSDP II.

In recognition of the HIV/AIDS crisis in the country, the government had already declared a five-year HIV/AIDS strategic plan covering periods 2000–2004, which has become a major and priority intervention focus in the HSDP II. Another health initiative which was unique to HSDP II was the introduction of health extension programme (HEP) which has aimed at universal basic health coverage through, for the first time, institutionalisation of village health care delivery. The HEP was to be provided as a package of essential services focussing on preventive health measures targeting households particularly women/mothers and children at the kebel level. The health professionals chosen were HEWs who are all female, to be recruited from their localities and to be trained for one year after completing 10-grade high school education.

Targets to be achieved in HSDP II were similarly organised to HSDP I under eight components with a relatively strong built-in M&E

mechanism. The governance structure to the implementation of HSDP II was also broadly similar to HSDP I. However, in response both to changes in government structures and the lesson learned from HSDP I, some changes have been made in the second phase. Some of the major changes were: a separate CJSC for the health sector, an additional woreda (district) Joint Steering Committee (WJSC), a separate Annual Review Meeting (ARM), a FMOH-HPN Donor Group Joint Consultative Meeting (JCM) to be held every two months. The estimated cost of implementing HSDP II was nearly 2 billion birr in 2002/03, and reaching around 2.3 billion birr in 2004/05 with the capital cost around 43% and the remainder for financing the recurrent costs.

HSDP II was evaluated between 31 January and 6 March 2006 by a multidisciplinary team of 33 national and international consultants. The report in its executive summary indicated that "Ethiopia has achieved a remarkable reduction in infant and under five mortality rates as evidenced in the recent preliminary Demographic and Health Survey" (DHS 2005). Many factors including improvements in the health sector may account for this remarkable progress. Within the health sector, access to health services — as measured by the potential health service coverage — has improved. Similarly, the coverage of some key health service indicators has improved. These include coverage of family planning, antenatal and postnatal cares, DPT3 and measles. However, limited to no progress is being made in the control of some communicable diseases such as TB, malaria and HIV/AIDS and in the births attended by skilled staff (Evaluation report of HSDP II, pp. x and xiv).

The report further stated that "progress made in the health service coverage is still below the targets proposed in HSDP II. Increased access to health services has not been translated into improved outpatient visits, TB case detection rates and supervised deliveries". The evaluation report in the governance section indicated that "HSDP II was ambitious in trying to address most weaknesses of the Ethiopian health system in three years. In that regard, HSDP II posed a real challenge for managers to perform within the set framework. However, it also explains why most HSDP II targets have not been met, because HSDP II was overly ambitious given the available time and human resource capacity in the country".

2.5 Health sector development program phase III (HSDP III)

The most refined generation of health development planning was HSDP III. There are a number of features that distinguish HSDP III from the previous series of HSDP I and HSDP II. The document defines its motto as "Health care is one of the crucial components of basic social services that has a direct linkage to the growth and development of a country" (HSDP III, p. 43). The general policy framework as a guide was roughly similar to the previous two phases of planning. However, the emergence of new policy initiatives within and outside the health sector brought new outlooks and a sense of urgency in the implementation of priority health interventions. The formulation of HSDP III was to be for five years from 2005/06 to 2009/10. According to the document, "the main policy contexts that are considered during the design and implementation of HSDP III are a commitment towards the achievement of MDGs by aligning HSDP III with PASDEP; institutionalisation of community health services through the implementation of HSEP, accelerated expansion of PHC services; implementation of HRH development plans, the health care financing strategy, the national HIV/AIDS policy, essential health service package, child survival strategy, the national reproductive health strategy, and the national health communication strategy, last but not least, the deepening and wide ranging implementation of the CSRP."

HSDP III was both ambitious and very practical in setting heath targets to be achieved by each year and by the end of the five-year planning cycle aiming towards reaching MDGs by the year 2015. One of the major targets was reaching universal PHC coverage by 2010 through the expansion programme of health posts at the community level and health centres as a first curative care referral centre serving a satellite of five health posts to cover a population of 25,000, and most importantly, through the accelerated training of HEWs for the management of health posts and non-clinician physician assistants or what they are popularly known as health officers to serve at the health centre and primary hospitals. Moreover, the planning document contained a remarkable costing model that provided three costing scenarios for different levels, target achievements in both priority health intervention and other health care deliveries.

HSDP III articulated its goals by narrowing down to three focus areas: *reducing infant and child mortality; improvement in maternal health and combating HIV/AIDs, malaria, TB and other communicable and preventable diseases.* Most of all, the design and implementation of HSDP III marked the beginning and further articulation of the need for a full-fledged woreda-based planning with wider participation by both health development partners, community participation, harmonisation and the integration of central, regional, zonal and woreda health planning based on top-down and bottom-up planning processes. HSDP III reaffirmed the importance of this process by stating that "the preparation of HSDP III is meant to serve as a blue print and as a guiding framework for further Regional and Woreda detailed planning and implementation of the Health Sector activities for the coming five years" (HSDP III, p. 137).

HSDP III from the onset of its development has become not only a vehicle by which the National Health Policy of 1993 is implemented, but also a live document that continued to be enriched with complementary strategies such as the HRH strategy (2009–2020), the first of its kind in the country. Implementation manuals such as the HSDP Harmonization Manual that sought a clear direction towards one plan, one budget and one report (HHM 2007) and the New HMIS that is creating one M&E system all brought benefits to local level. To affirm these commitments, partners not only endorsed HSDP III and Harmonization Manual, but also signed an MOU promising to work together to achieve the objectives clearly described in HSDP III. It brought aid effectiveness commitments from national to local coordination.

3. Woreda-Based Health Sector Planning

3.1 Planning approach

In the years preceding Woreda-Based Health Sector Planning (WB-HSP), stakeholders at various levels were used to prepare separate plans which were not harmonised and aligned with the national priorities. For instance, Regional Health Bureaus (RHBs) prepared two separate plans — one as part of the regional development plan and the other as their contribution to the national HSDP. Budget codes, reporting formats and processes differ, doubling the administrative burden on management entities at regional level. There was also weak ownership of the HSDP at the implementation level including limited familiarity with and understanding of the HSDP at lower levels of the health system (FMOH 2003).

To overcome this problem, the Ethiopian woreda-based annual health sector planning was initiated, for the first time during HSDP III in the 2007/2008, with the "One Plan" principle of harmonisation (FMOH 2007b). The preparation of the 2007/8 WB-HSP is different from the previous planning approaches in that it promotes integrated priority setting and also takes into account the objective reality of the different localities to align HSDP goals and targets with the MDGs (FMOH 2007/8).

The major principle underpinning woreda-based planning is ensuring vertical and horizontal linkages of annual plans. The former serves to make sure that national priorities are addressed at all levels as well as national targets are the sum of sub-national targets; while the latter ensures that priorities and targets of all stakeholders are aligned and resources are channelled primarily towards those priorities.

3.2 Focus areas

The focus areas of the WB-HSP conform to the priority areas of HSDP III, which are aimed at making primary health care services accessible to the general population. These major focus areas include: improving maternal and child health, prevention and control of communicable diseases (HIV/AIDS, malaria and TB) and to establish systems that potentially influence the development of the sector in line with the implementation of newly redesigned business process reengineering (BPR). The core plan comprises the following 10 priority health care delivery issues:

1. Health system development and capacity building;
2. Expanding primary health care services;
3. Strengthening hospital-based services;
4. Strengthening maternal and youth health services;
5. Improving child health;
6. Increasing the coverage of health-related nutrition services;
7. Improving hygiene and environmental health services;

8. Prevention and control of major communicable diseases;
9. Prevention and control of non-communicable health problems and
10. Strengthening monitoring and evaluation and health systems research.

3.3 Development process of the WB-HSP

The Ethiopian health sector planning process emerged from the need to address health problems through harmonised and aligned health service priorities that answer and satisfy the needs and expectations of the general public through iterative and participatory planning. The aim is to develop an evidence-based plan that will be used as a blueprint and as a single-point of reference for all implementers. The development of the WB-HSP encompasses top-down and bottom-up planning principles and passes through the following major stages. The first is the national consultative process that involves the FMOH, the RHBs and health development partners to develop the indicative planning direction on priority health interventions and capacity building. The second is a regional consultation between the regional government, the RHB, the woreda health offices and regional/national health development partners. In the third stage, woreda health offices consult with woreda administration and local health partners and then develop woreda-based health planning. The following sections briefly describe some of these processes.

National-level joint planning with partners

The development process of the WB-HSP starts with the establishment of a technical working group (TWG) from the MoH & Development Partners. The TWG included members from FMoH and partner organisations: UNICEF, WHO, WB, UNFPA, USAID/Essential Services for Health in Ethiopia (ESHE), and the Tulane University Technical Assistance Program Ethiopia (TULANE UNIVERSITY). This technical committee, under the leadership of the FMoH Executive Committee and the Joint Core Coordinating Committee, is responsible for the preparation of the Indicative Core Plan and annual planning materials and for overall technical coordination. The indicative plan consists of

Figure 8. Capacity building on WB-HSP.

priority HSDP III indicators with numerical targets at federal level which have been agreed upon by the Joint Steering Committee. The annual planning tools include evidence-based planning & budgeting tool (an excel-based customised MBB tool), training materials, facilitators' guide, planning formats, references. The prepared indicative plan and the planning toolkit are communicated to the lower tiers of the health system (regions and woredas); where local priorities will be identified and included.

Coordinating development partners

There has been progress in terms of a framework for alignment and harmonisation that involved health development partners who were active in the health sector. A step forward in this regard was the finalisation of the IHP road map and the signing of its compact. To date, seven development partners namely WHO, UNICEF, UNFPA, World Bank, Spanish Cooperation, DFID and Irish Aid have signed the Joint Financing

Agreement (JFA) for the MDG performance fund. In addition to the MDG performance fund, there are also other pooled funding arrangements such as the Technical Assistance Health Pool Fund managed by UNICEF and Protection of Basic Services (PBS) pool fund which is a contribution from six development partners. There are also other partners such as Global Fund and GAVI alliance who have made considerable contributions to the health sector through other funding arrangements and aligning their funded activity to the new *WB-HSP*. PEPFAR in this WB-HSP year is aligning its support and activities. Hence, major global health Initiatives (GHI) in the country are working to support this WB-HSP initiative in order to strengthen harmonisation in the spirit of the Paris Declaration. Overall, the commitment and contribution of the development partners towards the health sector plan *WB-HSP* is encouraging.

Local (woreda)-level planning

After completion of the woreda-level training, woredas collected health and health-related information relevant for planning. With the technical assistance, they also identified stakeholders and undertook Woreda-level resource mapping. Based on these, all woredas developed their annual plans using evidence-based planning andbudgeting tools (a modified WB MBB module). Woreda plans were collected and aggregated by zones and regions culminating in national aggregation. This constitutes the basis for bottom-up consolidation of the revised core and comprehensive plans, enabling the sector to produce a vertically and horizontally aligned plan. Finally, the WB-HSP is endorsed by the official signed contractual agreement between the FMoH and RHB at the annual review meeting (ARM). This was again signed between the RHBs and the woreda health offices.

The top-down and bottom-up planning approaches not only helped to harmonise and align health intervention priorities from the national to the woreda levels, but also to bring up the final plan that can be handled and implemented by the actual implementers. This approach has been instrumental in adjusting the targets in the indicative plan based on the local realities (Box 1).

Box 1: Best practice in adjusting the targets in the indicative plan based on the local realities

In EFY 2001 (2008/9), the indicative target for the number of households graduated after completing the health extension package training was 2,299,464; while the target for the number of deliveries attended by HEWs was 878,304. However, the final agreed targets after aggregating the woreda plan have been adjusted to 6,120,360 and 844,761, respectively. This shows that the final target was taken from the woreda plans because the responsibility for implementation of the plan is at the woreda/facility level (Bekuretsion et al. 2008).

Figure 9. Signing of contractual agreement between the FMoH and RHB on WB-HSP.

3.4 Progress and lessons learnt

WB-HSP has shown progressive improvement of both the planning process and its quality over the last three years. The Joint Review Mission (JRM) report both at federal and lower levels have indicated the progress with regard to the development and use of evidence-based planning and budgeting as well as capacity building for all woredas (FMOH 2009). The ownership of the woreda-based plan is increasingly strengthened at lower levels. Moreover, the WB-HSP has led to a better coordination between the health and finance government offices at woreda level in actual planning and budgeting (Box 2).

Box 2. Progress in the WB-HSP development process

The planning process is evolving and maturing over time. The annual plans developed in the past did not incorporate the functions and interventions at the hospital levels. Furthermore, they focussed more on setting the targets for service delivery and articulating the resource gaps without sufficiently linking these to action. The exercise in EFY 2002 (2009/10) has helped in making corrections to these weaknesses through the development of hospital plans as part of the woreda planning process and ensuring the inclusion of activity plans in the annual plan at all levels. Furthermore, costing of the annual woreda-based plan with resource mapping and gap analysis has been included in the third WB-HSP. This has proven effective especially for development partners who require activity-based planning for their funding to align and reduce the transaction cost of developing vertical plans (FMoH 2009).

Similarly, the in-depth interviews with five RHB planning heads have also highlighted this progress; although there have been variations in views among the regions. All the interviewed RHBs have reported that there have been marked improvements in the stakeholders' involvement (both government and health development partners), ownership at lower levels, resource mapping and mobilisation. They have also mentioned that the WB-HSP has contributed towards the "one plan and one report" principles of harmonisation (Box 3).

3.5 Major challenges in the woreda-based planning

Despite encouraging progress, there are some challenges in the planning and implementation of the WB-HSP. Some of the major challenges come both within and outside the public health sector. Within the public sector, the major challenge is lack of capacity in planning and management including high staff turnover at all levels. There is also a resource limitation for the financing the initial capacity building as well as for replacement training to replenish the sometimes excessive staff turnover. On the technical side, there is still unresolved scarcity in the availability of the required baseline information at woreda level as an input for the full-fledged bottleneck analysis to produce accurate evidence-based planning (FMOH 2009).

The main challenges coming from the donor and implementing partners include inadequate cooperation by some of them in terms of transparently providing their commitment and relevant disbursement data when needed, and constraints to align their planning and fund disbursement calendar with the woreda planning. There are also a significant number of health development partners who have not yet endorsed the one plan initiative and who have not signed the IHP compact that are both needed for the accelerated implementation of harmonisation and alignment initiative. On the funding side, the challenge also involves delays in the commitment and when it is available, in the disbursement of funds. Overall, much remains to be done on the health partners' side in terms of a commitment for the global initiative of "one plan, one budget and one reporting". Although there are practical challenges in the implementation of the "one budget" principle, government and health partners in the interim should agree on functional integration including supporting the provisions of the IHP compact and also improving the predictability of funding.

Box 3. Progress and challenges in the "*One plan, One Budget and One Report*" principle of harmonisation

There is good progress in the implementation of one plan and one reporting principle. However, there is a long way ahead to address the issue of one budget. One of the interviewed RHB planning heads said *"In the previous years, all the regional and woreda health partners were using their own plan, budget and reporting channels and indicators. This year, the regional health partners have agreed and accepted the regional and woreda level priorities and targets; and to use the same indicator and reporting in the region. But the issue of one budget is still very difficult. Some of the partners were able to provide only crude budget for the region and not for the Woredas while majority were not willing to talk about their budget"* (Harari RHB Planning Head).

4. Conclusion and Recommendation

The chapter has shown the progress and challenges of taking coordination of partners from national to local planning. The WB-HSP is an important tool for realising the "one plan" principle of harmonisation and alignment to further enhance the development of the Ethiopian health care system. The practice so far shows that the WB-HSP has proven an excellent instrument for enhancing ownership at the local woreda level and in strengthening the partnership between the federal, regional and woreda health offices. It also helped to build the planning capacity at the local level, promoted evidence-based planning and decision making at local level, to prioritise health financing and resource mapping.

However, it also poses some challenges and shows the issues of coordinating national and local policies. Initially, local districts prepared two plans; one for national level and the other for local implementation. They were not aligned. Some of the major challenges at local level include shortage of experts to engage in planning from national to woreda level. This requires extensive capacity building and mentorship. The other challenge is the requirement for both material and financial resources to do the actual planning. Lastly, not all partners are on board to support "one plan, one budget and one reporting."

Although major health partners in Ethiopia in principle accept the "three ones", the implementation has been slow and especially, major difficulties still remain to fully align funding support from development partners including PEPFAR and Global Fund in order to make a major stride in the development of evidence-based planning required at local level. With greater harmonisation and alignment down to local level, the health care system of Ethiopia willmake major improvements, in the fight against HIV/AIDS, TB, malaria, including reductions in child and maternal morbidity and mortality.

Chapter 3 further assesses aid effectiveness issues at national level in Ethiopia.

References

Ayalew S (1991) The Social Context of Health Care Planning in Africa: Ethiopian Case Studies and Perspectives. PhD Thesis; Karolinska Institute, IHCAR, Stockholm, Sweden.

Azene G (1995) Developing Basic Bealth Care Services in Ethiopia: An explanatory Model for Providing and Financing a Sustainable National Health Care System. PhD Thesis; Department of Public Health and Policy, London School of Hygiene and Tropical Medicine; Faculty of Economics, University of London.

Central Statistical Agency (2006) Ethiopia Demographic and Health Survey of 2005. Calverton, Maryland, USA: CSA, ORC Macro.

Central Statistical Agency (2009) The 2007 Population and Housing Census of Ethiopia: Analytic report. Addis Ababa: CSA.

Donaldson C, Gerald K (1993) *Economics of Health Care Financing: The Visible Hand. The Macmillan Press Ltd. London.*

Federal Ministry Health (2009) HSDP-III Woreda Based Annual Core Plan for 2009/10. *Planning and Programming Department (PPD), FMOH, Addis Ababa.*

Federal Ministry of Health (2005) Health Sector Strategic Plan, HSDP III (2005/06–2009/10. *FMOH, Addis Ababa, Ethiopia.*

Federal Ministry of Health (2005) National Strategy for Child Survival in Ethiopia. Addis Ababa: Family Health Department, FMOH.

Federal Ministry of Health (2006) Protection of Basic Services Project: Project Operational Manual, Revised Draft. Addis Ababa: FMOH.

Federal Ministry of Health (2006/07) Health and Health Related Indicators. Addis Ababa: Department of Planning and Programming (PPD), FMOH.

Federal Ministry of Health (2007) Accelerated Access to HIV/AIDS Prevention, Care and Treatment in Ethiopia: Road MAP 2007–2008/10.

Federal Ministry of Health (2007) HSDP-III Core Plan for 2007/08. Addis Ababa: Planning and Programming Department (PPD), FMOH.

Federal Ministry of Health (2007) The HSDP Harmonization Manual (HHM), First Edition. Addis Ababa: FMOH.

Federal Ministry of Health (2007/08) Health and Health Related Indicators. Addis Ababa: Department of Planning and Programming (PPD), FMOH.

Federal Ministry of Health (2008) HSDP-III Core Plan for 2008/09. Addis Ababa: Planning and Programming Department (PPD), FMOH.

Federal Ministry of Health (2008) Ethiopian National Malaria Indicator Survey. Addis Ababa: FMOH.

Federal Ministry of Health (2009a) Woreda-Based Health Sector Planning (WB-HSP): Training Material. Addis Ababa: Planning and Programming Department, FMOH.

Federal Ministry of Health (2009b) Annual Performance Report of HSDP III EFY 2001 (2008/9). Addis Ababa: Planning and Programming Department, FMOH.

Figueras J (1993) Effective Health Care Planning: The Role of Financial Allocation Mechanisms. PhD thesis; Department of Public Health and Policy; London School of Hygiene and Tropical Medicine, University of London.

FMOH/FHAPCO (2007) Single Point HIV Prevalence Estimate. Addis Ababa, Ethiopia.

Gertler P, Van der Gaag J (1990) The willingness to Pay for Medical Care: Evidence from two Developing Countries. Baltimore, Maryland, U.S.A.: A World Bank Publication; The John Hopkins University Press.

Gilson L (1988) Government Health Care Charges: Is Equity Being Abandoned? Evaluation and Planning Center for Health Care; London School of Hygiene and Tropical Medicine (LSHTM), EPC Publication No. 15.

Government of Ethiopia (2004) Ethiopia HIV/AIDS Five-Year Plan for 2004–2008. Addis Ababa: Ministry of Health-HAPCO, Health Programs Department.

Green A (2007) *An Introduction to Health Planning for Developing Health Systems*. Third Edition, Oxford University Press.

Health Care Financing Team, Planning and Programming Department, Federal Ministry of Health. September 2006. Ethiopia's Third National Health Accounts 2004/05. Bethesda, MD: The Partners for Health Reform plus Project, Abt Associates Inc.

HSDP I Evaluation Team (2003) Report of the Final Evaluation of HSDP I: 30 January to 3 March, 2003; Volume I. Addis Ababa: Federal Ministry of Health.

HSDP II Evaluation Team (2006) Report of the Final Evaluation of HSDP II: 31 January to 6 March, 2006; Volume 1. Addis Ababa: Federal Ministry of Health.

JRM Team (2009) The 3rd Joint Review Mission Report of HSDP II. Addis Ababa: Federal Ministry of Health.

JRM Team (2009a) The Joint Review Mission Report of HSDP III. Addis Ababa: Federal Ministry of Health.

Lee K, Mills A (1982) *Policy-Making and Planning in the Health Sector*. Croom Helm, Ltd.

Mills A, Gilson L (1988) Health Economics for Developing Countries: A Survival Kit. Evaluation and Planning Center for Health Care; London School of Hygiene and Tropical Medicine (LSHTM), EPC Publication No. 17.

MoFED (2006) Ethiopia: Building on Progress: A Plan for Accelerated and Sustained Development to End Poverty (PASDEP), 2005/06–2009/10; Volume I, Main Text. September, 2006. Addis Ababa: Ministry of Finance and Economic Development (MoFED).

Montoya-Aguilar C, Marin-Lara M (1986) "International Equity in Coverage of Primary Health Care: Examples from Developing Countries", *World Health Statistics Quarterly* 39:336–44.

Mooney G (1987) "What does Equity in Health Mean", *World Health Statistics Quarterly* 40:296–303.

Musgrove P (1986) "Measurement of Equity in Health", *World Health Statistics Quarterly* 39(40):325–35.

Office of the National Committee for Central Planning (1984) Ten-year Perspective Health Development Plan. Addis Ababa: The Provisional Military Administrative Government of Ethiopia.

The Federal Democratic Republic of Ethiopia (1998) Program Action Plan for the Health Sector Development Program. Addis Ababa: Ministry of Health.

The Federal Democratic Republic of Ethiopia (2002) Health Sector Development Programme II. Addis Ababa: Ministry of Health.

Transitional Government of Ethiopia (1993) Health Policy of the Transitional Government of Ethiopia. Addis Ababa: TGE.

Whitehead M (1992) "The Concepts and Principles of Equity and Health", *International Journal of Health Services* 22(3):429–45.

Williams A (1988) "Priority Setting in Public and Private Health Care: A Guide Through the Ideological Jungle", *Journal of Health Economics* **7**:173–183.

World Development Report (1993) *Investing in Health: World Development Indicators*. The International Bank for Reconstruction and Development, The World Bank. Washington, D.C.: Oxford University Press, Inc.

World Health Organization (2008) *Global Tuberculosis Control: Surveillance, Planning, Financing*. Geneva, Switzerland.

17

India: Scaling HIV Prevention Through Partnerships — The Avahan Experience

Aparajita Ramakrishnan[1], *Sema K. Sgaier*[2] *and Ashok Alexander*[3]

Summary

This chapter presents an innovative partnership model to scale up health programmes, focussing on the Avahan HIV programme in India funded by the Bill & Melinda Gates Foundation. This programme attempted to bring to scale community-based approaches to HIV prevention. It faced twin partnership challenges. First, the programme needed to negotiate the implementation of a new HIV prevention model in India, based on community partnerships. Second, the sustainability of the programme required partnership and transition into the government programme, as part of the routine response to HIV. The chapter describes the establishment of an innovative business model to scale up HIV prevention, and the challenge of increasing integration as part of the national programme to ensure

[1] Aparajita Ramakrishnan is a senior program officer with the Bill & Melinda Gates Foundation.

[2] Sema K. Sgaier is a program officer with the Bill & Melinda Gates Foundation.

[3] Ashok Alexander is the head of the India Office of the Bill & Melinda Gates Foundation.

sustainability. This chapter documents the birth, evolution and current status of Avahan, with the intention of highlighting Avahan's partnerships with four critical stakeholders: implementing partners, community, government and other stakeholders from scale to transition. We also reflect on the lessons that could be relevant to other large-scale public health programmes, which attempt to bridge the gap between community and government partnerships.

"Through Avahan, we have learned how important it is to get local communities involved in delivering effective public health interventions at a large scale. The next challenge will be passing on all that we've learned and transitioning Avahan to the government and other partners. We look forward to continuing that collaboration."

— Bill Gates, acceptance speech delivered to the President, Prime Minister and Congress President of India after being awarded the Indira Gandhi Prize, 25 July 2009

Introduction

The Bill & Melinda Gates Foundation was created in the mid-1990s with the guiding principle that all human lives have equal value. Born of the passions and commitment of the Gates family, the foundation believes in harvesting technological advances to solve large-scale and complex development challenges in global health, education and poverty reduction. Currently, the largest private grant-making foundation in the world (McCoy *et al.* 2009), the foundation has over $30 billion in assets under endowment, has committed over $20 billion since its inception, and has an annual payout of $3 billion (The Bill & Melinda Gates Foundation 2009).

The foundation's India AIDS Initiative, Avahan (Sanskrit, meaning "a call to action") was launched in 2003, at a time when experts predicted a rapidly accelerating HIV/AIDS epidemic in India (Nagelkerke *et al.* 2002; The Economist 2004), creating an understandable sense of urgency and concern around HIV prevention. Given India's concentrated HIV epidemic, Avahan was designed to rapidly scale up coverage of most-at-risk populations (MARP) with prevention services to help halt and reverse the epidemic (Avahan 2008).

Historic evidence showed that a multilevel governance, or partnership, is needed for an effective HIV response including formal (such as government) and informal (such as community) actors (Dodgson *et al.* 2002; Low-Beer and Sempala 2010). The scaling up and sustaining of prevention services and their impact in India were highly dependent on the partnerships that Avahan was able to foster and nurture. From its inception, Avahan established partnerships with multiple stakeholders including implementing partners, communities of MARP, government and other advocates and technical experts. The nature of the partnership with each stakeholder is unique and has evolved over time. This chapter documents the birth, evolution and current status of Avahan, with the intention of highlighting Avahan's partnerships with four critical stakeholders: implementing partners, community, government and other stakeholders (Figure 1) from scale to transition. We also reflect

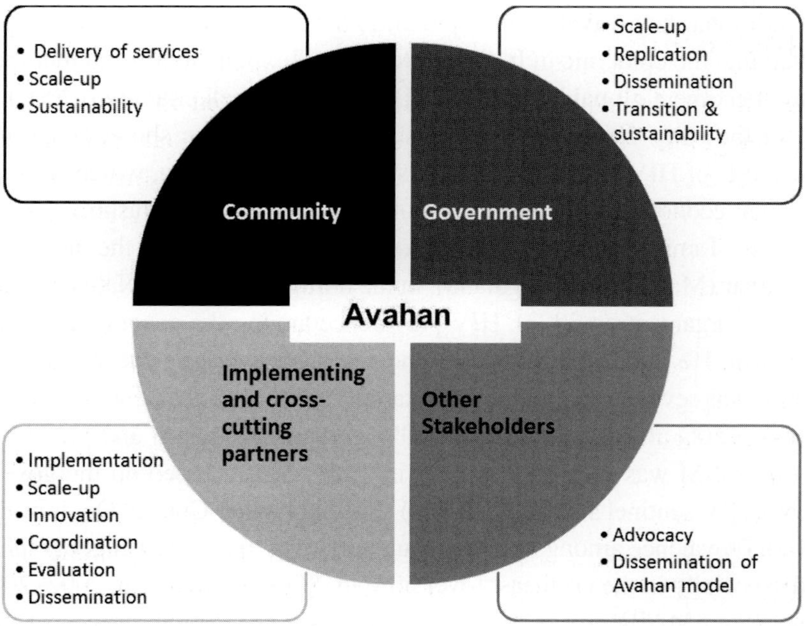

Figure 1. Avahan partnerships.

on the lessons that could be relevant to other large-scale public health programmes.

1. Avahan — The Early Years

1.1 The market: The HIV/AIDS epidemic in the early 2000s

HIV sentinel surveillance data and other studies conducted in the early 2000s classified the Indian epidemic as a "concentrated" one (National AIDS Control Organization 2000, 2003). Most of the infections were accounted for by sexual transmission through unprotected sex between MARPs (female sex workers [FSWs], men who have sex with men [MSM] and transgenders [TGs]) and their male clients and partners (Moses *et al.* 2006). Male clients and partners of MARPs act as a bridge population for the spread of HIV to the lower risk general population as they can transmit HIV to their regular female and male partners. In certain pockets of the country, such as northeast India, injecting drug use (IDU) was found to be an additional key driver of the epidemic. Modelling and other studies predicted that the epidemic in India would take off exponentially and that India could become a global hot spot for HIV/AIDS (Nagelkerke *et al.* 2002).

In the early 2000s, the data on the Indian epidemic showed that over two-thirds of HIV infections were in six states within India, which included the four economically advanced southern states of Maharashtra, Andhra Pradesh, Tamil Nadu and Karnataka, and two states on the border of Myanmar (Manipur and Nagaland), in the northeast of India (National AIDS Control Organization 2003). HIV prevalence among the general population was over 1% in all the six states and prevalence among the highest risk groups was several fold higher. For example, FSW prevalence was estimated at above 50% in Maharashtra and 20% in Andhra Pradesh and prevalence among MSM was estimated at 20% in Maharashtra (based on the government's HIV sentinel surveillance data) (National AIDS Control Organization 2003). Prevalence among injecting drug users was high in select geographies and especially in the northeast (over 50% in 2000). However, in 2002–2003, coverage of MARP groups with any kind of HIV prevention service was low across India, even in the six high prevalence states that had a history of some HIV interventions (Chandrasekaran *et al.* 2006).

Despite alarming projections, emerging country-wide data on the epidemic, and growing awareness that HIV/AIDS could be a potential public health problem of unprecedented scale in India, the national response was limited in the early 2000s. This was the period during which the National AIDS Control Programme's second phase (NACP-II) was being implemented, and its early phase had been severely under-resourced, thinly staffed and without sufficient focus on high-risk groups as warranted by the epidemic at this stage (Claeson and Alexander 2008). Most important, political will to tackle the HIV/AIDS epidemic with full force was still relatively low.

1.2 Entering the market: Avahan's initial approach

In 2002, Bill Gates announced the foundation's intention to invest $100 million in HIV control in India, to launch the foundation's India AIDS Initiative. The foundation team, along with McKinsey & Company, started a detailed exercise to design and plan the foundation's approach to HIV in India. The initial investment of $100 million was quickly expanded to over $200 million after the design exercise, and as of 2009, the foundation has committed over $338 million in the area of HIV/AIDS prevention in India.

These early days were critical to Avahan's direction and strategic approach. Technical experts cautioned the foundation design team against attempting scaled prevention in a country as vast and complex as India. Instead, they suggested first piloting programmes and then scaling after proof of concept. The foundation team, however, believed that unless a scaled approach was taken from the start, the desired impact of halting and reversing the epidemic would not be possible. Furthermore, there was a sense that "re-piloting" a widely proven package of prevention interventions with MARPs was not necessary. Therefore, eliciting expert peer advice, the chosen approach aimed to be innovative and develop a new strategy for a scaled HIV prevention initiative in India. The team chose to build the concept of scale into the DNA of the programme at all stages — designing, organising, executing and sustaining for scale (through transition). A strong evaluation design was also developed. The design team also highlighted the importance of a strong local presence and strong local partnerships to ensure results in a short period of time in the challenging Indian setting. Using experience and success models from the private sector, it was during this period that the team brought in management as well as technical expertise and the approach of "business unusual" developed (Alexander and Ramakrishnan 2006).

Avahan made the following critical strategic choices in its early stages and during its subsequent evolution:

1. Focussing on prevention efforts with MARPs (FSWs, MSM, TGs and IDUs) and their male sexual partners and concentrating efforts on the six states[4] with the majority of HIV cases at the time (2003).
2. Basing the initiative on globally known solutions and best practices in HIV prevention.[5]
3. Engaging the communities at risk as equal partners in the implementation of the programme, addressing their needs beyond HIV, and building their collective and institutional capacity for longer-term sustainability of the response.
4. Building strong partnerships with civil society, government and opinion leaders to build momentum around HIV/AIDS interventions in the country, and to facilitate scale-up of the programme to pave the way for sustainability.
5. Rapidly scaling up the delivery of services across intervention geographies to contain the spread of the epidemic.
6. Creating the foundation's first in-country office to facilitate rapid scale-up.
7. Investing in knowledge-building, evaluation and dissemination.
8. Articulating an explicit goal to transfer the funding and management of the programme to natural owners including government and communities.

---

[4] Andhra Pradesh, Karnataka, Maharashtra, Tamil Nadu, Manipur and Nagaland.

[5] The Avahan prevention package included outreach through peer educators, behaviour change communication, distribution of commodities (condoms and clean needles and syringes), provision of safe spaces in the form of drop-in centres (DICs) for the community, counselling and management of sexually transmitted infections through programme and referral clinics, referral to TB, ART and HIV testing services, local- and high-level sensitization and advocacy with power structures (such as police), crisis response, and community mobilization.

From the outset, the Avahan programme adopted a business approach to scaling up HIV in India (Alexander and Ramakrishnan 2006). The first six hires within Avahan were from the private sector. The team chose to apply standard business principles to the programme — know your customer, focus, maintain flexibility, integrate across moving parts, use data at every opportunity and "feel the need for speed" when it comes to execution. The benchmark for the team was, how fast would a large scale corporate giant such as Reliance[6] deliver a similar product? One year? Two years? The pace set by the team reflected the collective urgency to build, operate and ultimately transfer and replicate the Avahan programme over a 10-year time frame. The responsibility of delivering a scaled HIV prevention programme for highest risk groups in India was upon the foundation's Avahan team.

2. The Operating Model and Partnership with Key Implementers

The Avahan programme had three goals:

1. Build an HIV prevention model at scale in India.
2. Catalyse others (such as the government and communities of MARPs) to take over and replicate the model.
3. Foster and disseminate learnings within India and worldwide.

While the first five years (Avahan Phase I, 2003–2009) focussed on goal 1, the next five years (Avahan Phase II, 2009–2013) focussed on goals 2 and 3 in addition to consolidating impact on goal 1. In order to execute these goals, Avahan organised itself into a virtual implementation pyramid to ensure it was scaled from the national to the community level (Figure 2). The implementation pyramid facilitated the disbursement of the $258 million budget through over 20 grantees (large NGOs and universities) with extensive management and technical capacity, many of whom in turn contracted over 130 smaller, grassroots NGOs to deliver

---

[6] Reliance Industries is one of India's largest conglomerates with a record of fast scale-up of product delivery.

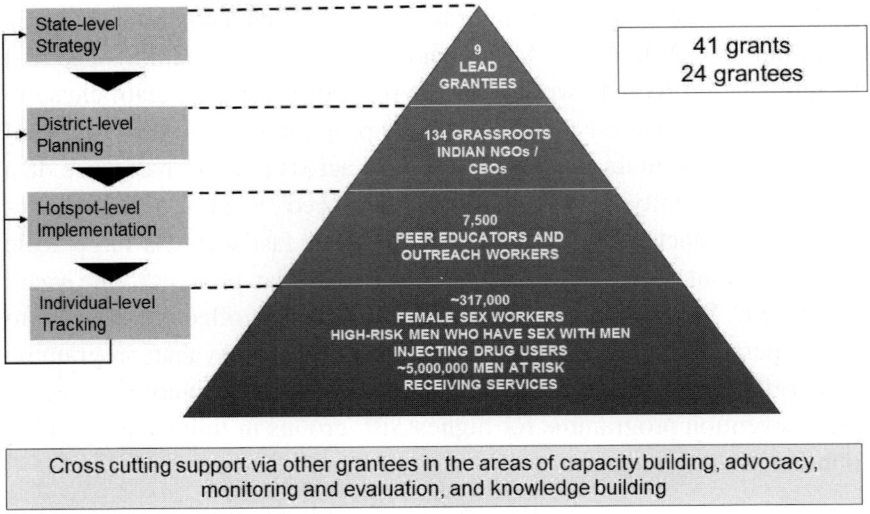

Figure 2. Avahan's organization, a virtual pyramid.

Source: Avahan routine monitoring data. July 2008.

the HIV prevention services to the populations in need. This virtual organisation structure was designed with the explicit intent of enabling rapid and simultaneous scale-up across geographies, facilitating standardisation of key elements, and sharing of best practices across all implementation programmes. The partners within Avahan included:

1. Lead implementing partners for prevention implementation.[7]
2. Capacity-building partners in the areas of advocacy, communications, clinical services and other areas.[8]

[7] University of Manitoba/Karnataka Health Promotion Trust, Population Services International, Voluntary Health Services, Australian International Health Institute/ Emmanuel Hospital Association, Transport Corporation of India Foundation, Family Health International, International HIV/AIDS Alliance, Hindustan Latex Family Planning and Promotion Trust, and Pathfinder International.

[8] PATH for communications support, PSI for social condom marketing, CARE for community building, Family Health International for technical support of STI delivery, The Futures Group for advocacy support, INP+ for capacity building of positive networks, Center for Advocacy and Research for media advocacy, and Heroes Project for advocacy with opinion leaders.

3. Communications for social norm change partners.[9]
4. Monitoring and evaluation partners.[10]
5. Knowledge building partners.[11]

A wider governance and partnership structure was needed to support this scale-up (Text Box 1). The governance structure was put in place in order to ensure the highest level of coordination with government (Health Secretary as co-chair of the Avahan Board), to involve key opinion leaders (Mrinal Pande from a leading national newspaper, Ratan Tata who heads the Tata Group), policy makers (Anand Grover — Supreme Court lawyer, Kapil Sibal — Member of Parliament), and celebrities (Rahul Dravid, the then captain of the Indian cricket team) in the cause, and to provide robust programme and technical oversight and direction (Rajat Gupta — head of McKinsey & Company as co-chair of the Board, Richard Steen from WHO, David Wilson from the World Bank, and others on the Technical Panel).

Text Box 1. Avahan's advisory and technical partners at key levels

National level

***Board of directors*:** A board of 23 members provides high-profile advocacy and oversight of the initiative.
***Technical panel*:** A technical panel consisting of 17 national and international experts in HIV programming provides technical counsel for programme design, reviews grant proposals and provides ongoing input and advice as the programme is implemented.
***WHO evaluation advisory group*:** A World Health Organization-convened team provided technical input for the evaluation design and continues to

[9] BBC World Service Trust for condom media campaigns.
[10] Family Health International, Indian Council of Medical Research, London School of Hygiene and Tropical Medicine, University of Laval, PRAXIS, John Hopkins University, and Amaltas.
[11] Population Council, Nossal Institute, University of Melbourne.

provide ongoing advice on evaluation issues and analysis as data become available.

State level

***State advisory committee*:** Foundation staff, State AIDS Control Societies, programme directors of lead implementing partners in the state, and major state-level HIV stakeholders meet regularly to exchange ideas and experiences and coordinate activities.

Partner/NGO level

***Community advisory committees*:** Partners have created fora for community members to provide input into the project activities in their respective communities, both at start-up and during the life of the project.

Avahan's first goal, scaling up the nuts and bolts of a "known" HIV prevention package in over 600 towns of Maharashtra, Tamil Nadu, Karnataka, Andhra Pradesh, Manipur and Nagaland, was the focus for the first three years. To illustrate the scale-up of implementation, let us take an example of one state, Karnataka, and within that state, one district, Belgaum.[12] The first step was to understand the denominator: how many FSWs, MSM and TGs are there in the district of Belgaum? These are the basic customers in the business model and important to know their numbers, locations and networks very well in order to deliver the services effectively. In order to answer this question, a mapping and size estimation exercise was conducted, yielding geographic and numerical distributions of MARPs across the district. Further data on MARPs, such as patterns of mobility, time and location of solicitations, services available to them, location and nature of violence faced by power structures, were also collected. Once this baseline was identified, the local NGOs began to build their infrastructure to deliver services: renting safe spaces called "drop-in centres" or DICs, setting up STI management facilities

[12] The district is an administrative unit in India — there are over 600 districts in India, each with an average population of 1.5–2 million.

within these DICs, and hiring an army of peer educators.[13] Meanwhile, a separate grant for condom promotion among the clients of sex workers was also scaled up in the same locations. The grantee utilised the size estimation and mapping data mentioned above to open condom social marketing outlets in the same locations. Finally, as the project scaled up its HIV prevention service delivery, the communities of MARPs started strengthening their collective identity through group formation and community-based organisation (CBO) development. While this activity was being conducted by the grantee in Karnataka in Belgaum district, the grantee was also doing the same set of activities across Karnataka, through a set of other grassroots NGOs simultaneously in 18 districts, and other grantees were doing the same thing across 83 Avahan districts simultaneously in 2004 and 2005. Simultaneity was a critical component of this scale-up. Scale in terms of coverage and quality was achieved by the third year (Ramakrishnan *et al.* 2010).

The above-described rapid and simultaneous programme scale-up was possible through partnerships performing strong supporting functions: communications and advocacy at the national, state and grassroots levels; knowledge building and dissemination of best practices; monitoring and evaluation; and capacity building in key technical areas (STI management, interpersonal communications, community mobilisation, advocacy and other related technical fields). Of particular importance was the advocacy programme that set out to tackle stigma and create a sense of urgency around focussed prevention in India against the political and epidemiological background mentioned above.

3. Partnership with Communities Most at Risk

In addition to financial and human capital, an effective HIV prevention programme relies on tapping into social capital (Putnam 2000) to influence behaviour, communication and norms (Low-Beer and Sempala 2010). Social

[13] Peer educators (peer outreach workers) are members of the core group who work part time on the project, are hired by the NGO and are paid an honorarium for their time which they spend providing testimonials, information, commodities and services to other community members to improve health seeking behaviour and reduce risky behaviour.

capital can be fostered through social movements and the collective action and behaviours of community groups and networks (Low-Beer and Sempala 2010). The Avahan programme realised early on the importance of the social capital residing within communities and coordinated the delivery of services to MARPs with interventions to mobilise a community-led response by establishing a cadre of staff from the community and fostering community-led committees, groups, organisations and networks.

When Avahan first entered the HIV prevention "marketplace" in 2003, it became clear from extensive field visits and study tours to places such as Sonagachi[14] and Bangladesh that the consumer (MARP community member) of HIV prevention services needed to be the keystone of the programme to scale up successfully, achieve impact and sustain the programme beyond the lifetime of Avahan. From being a recipient of services, to participating actively in service delivery, to beginning to own the interventions, partnership with the communities of MARP was a central aspect of Avahan. Avahan programme managers quickly recognised that involving peer educators from the MARP community in delivering outreach and services was far more effective than the model on the ground at the time which used non-community outreach workers to perform the peer function. Peer educators from the community were able to tap into and mobilise their social capital and networks, unlike non-community members. In fact, when Avahan switched to a community-led service delivery model, contacts with MARPs quadrupled (Figure 3) (Avahan 2009a).

Listening to the community was central and allowed Avahan to generate demand for HIV prevention services. When Avahan first started, HIV and health were not even in the top 10 priorities for a marginalised community member. Making health and HIV relevant to this community required a unique trust-based partnership and addressing the pertinent issues first. It became evident that the community members were facing considerable violence and harassment from police, clients, partners and other power structures. The environment in which they lived and worked was not enabling them to adopt safe behaviours. How could an FSW, for example, negotiate for condom use with her client when she was beaten by him and had no support to protect her or address this violence? To

[14] Sonagachi is the largest red-light district in Kolkata, India and one of the largest in Asia. It is an area with several hundred multi-story brothels and some 10,000 sex workers.

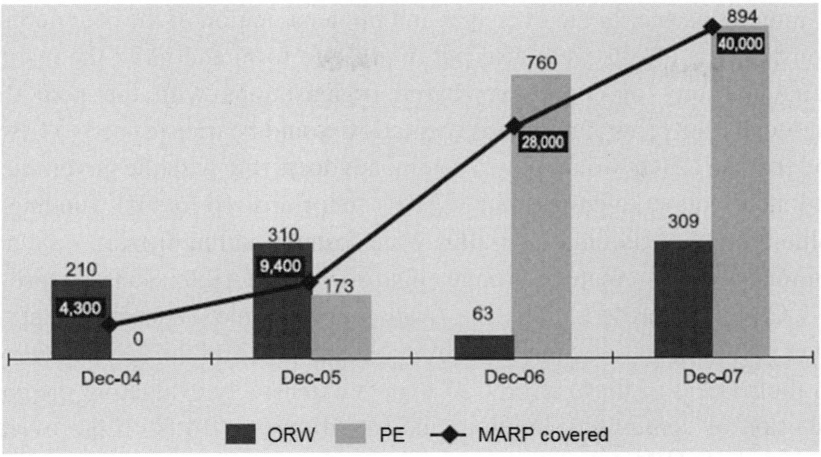

Figure 3. Community-led outreach and service delivery.

Data from one Avahan implementing partner shows how MARPs covered dramatically increased when peer educators (members of the MARPs community) replaced non-community member outreach workers. ORW, outreach worker who is a non-community member; PE, peer educator and member of the MARP community.

Source: Managing HIV Prevention from the Ground Up: Avahan's Experience with Peer Led Outreach at Scale in India. New Delhi: Bill & Melinda Gates Foundation, 2008.

create an enabling environment, Avahan along with the community quickly realised that setting up a system to address crises should be a central component of the programme. Community-led crises response teams were established across all Avahan interventions and as a result crises are being addressed actively (Avahan 2009b,c). This not only led to trust building with the community but also ensured that health and HIV moved up the priority list for the community. As a result, communities are now demanding and accessing HIV prevention services.

Midway into Phase I, Avahan also realised that there was a need to foster and build strong community-based organisations (CBOs) as part of its sustainability plan. This required a lot of support and capacity building from both the Avahan implementing and cross-cutting partners as building and strengthening community-based organizations requires tremendous facilitation. Community-based committees were fostered across the programme to monitor the delivery of services (such as in the formation of outreach committees or STI committees) and hence became an integral partner in the oversight and implementation of the programme. Considerable efforts were also put in place to form and build the institutional capacity of community-based organisations with the goal that eventually the programme implementation would be transitioned to CBOs and that the CBOs would play a central advocate role with the government and other donors to ensure that MARPs are prioritised for HIV funding in India. Finally, networks for CBOs were fostered at the district, state and national level to create a stronger platform for MARPs. Today, close to 185 CBOs are present under the Avahan programme. District- and state-level networks have begun to form in all states. While the jury is still out on the success of these efforts, Avahan is extensively evaluating the contribution of community building and mobilisation efforts on the overall impact of its HIV prevention programme.

4. Partnership with Government

Avahan's partnership with government has evolved extensively over the years and can be divided into three distinct phases: (1) limited partnership (primarily at the state level) in the early years of design and scale-up (2003–2005), (2) strengthening of the partnership at national and state levels during the design and execution of NACP-III (2005–2007) and (3) robust partnership during the design and execution of transition of the Avahan programme to government (2007 onwards). Challenges along the way included limited commitment of political leadership at certain times, engaging without being seen as agenda-driven, scepticism from other donors who had been working in the Indian HIV/AIDS arena well before Avahan, and working with government who initially had a very different culture than the foundation managers.

When Avahan first started its programme, partnership with government was not as strong as the foundation would have liked. This was partly because political will in India to tackle the HIV/AIDS epidemic was relatively low with some level of denial among key stakeholders, and because Avahan wanted to move fast. While less at the national level, Avahan did engage at the state level with the State AIDS Control Societies (SACS), which are the state arms of the National AIDS Control Organization (NACO). By working with the SACS, the prevention landscape with MARPs within the six states was reviewed closely and the districts where Avahan was to operate selected in order to fill in the coverage gap. Furthermore, both the foundation team and implementing partners engaged with SACS and NACO to provide regular updates on project progress and to gain political acceptance of Avahan's efforts. At the district level, engagement was less because in the early years of NACP-II, HIV testing and treatment services were minimal so linkages to government services were minimal as well.

The political landscape around HIV/AIDS changed considerably in the mid-2000s as a result of a change in government leadership, which led to a change in the nature and level of partnership between Avahan and the government. By that time, Avahan and its extended team[15] were beginning to work to disseminate the Avahan experience, model and results and the project was gaining national acceptance and attention. In 2005, NACO embarked on a nationwide, consultative process to develop the NACP-III strategy and implementation plan for the period 2007–2012. The government had an ambitious goal to scale up prevention programmes with MARPs and bridge groups (male clients of MARPs) during NACP-III, and aimed to reach two million FSWs, 0.3 million high-risk MSM and 200,000 IDUs (National AIDS Control Organization 2007). It also planned to spend $100 million to triple condom sales by increasing outlets and creating demand. Other notable features of NACP-III include: significant increase in money allocated to the national plan — up four times to $2.5 billion[16]; ART availability increased significantly to achieve national coverage; less effective interventions (e.g. slum dwellers, short-distance truckers) severely curtailed; and surveillance, voluntary counselling and testing and treatment to prevent mother-to-child transmission scaled up. With this plan, NACP-III placed appropriate and substantial resources into prevention through focussed programmes for MARP and bridge groups, and also decentralised and expanded infrastructure for care and support. The strategic collection, synthesis and use of data to inform programme planning, and

[15] Such as the board, technical panel and state advisory committees.

[16] Including external resources. The NACP-III envelope for the project excluding external aid was $1.8 billion.

the need for state-level capacity building also gained increased attention in the design of NACP-III (Claeson and Alexander 2008).

The foundation and its grantee staff, among other players involved, made contributions (in terms of time and technical expertise) to the design of NACP-III strategies in the following ways: being involved in developing the prevention strategy and guidelines for MARP and bridge populations, condoms, M&E, sexually transmitted infections (STI) and several other areas; highlighting the need for the increase in funding, emphasising the need for focus on prevention among MARP, and condoms for sexual partners of MARPs; and helping to highlight the centrality of communities to the design and implementation of targeted intervention programmes.

The design and rollout of NACP-III saw a sea change in the policy backdrop of HIV in India. With the government's own programme well funded, well designed and well focussed, Avahan and the Government of India engaged in discussions on the long-term sustainability of the Avahan-funded interventions and the quick scale-up and high-quality implementation of government programmes, since Avahan was the largest partner implementing prevention programmes with MARPs in the six high prevalence states. As a result, the Avahan team repositioned the programme to fit within the national rubric, with the intention of handing over the programme to natural owners such as the government and communities and helping strengthen policies and agencies to achieve the smooth handover. Within the first few years of its launch, Avahan conducted a planning exercise with a team that included members of other donors and government representatives in India to shape the contours of Avahan's next five years — Avahan II, 2009–2013. Avahan's goals were recalibrated through this exercise to focus on goals 2 and 3 (as mentioned above).

During this second phase of Avahan, partnership with government was stronger and the initiative had a more formal engagement with NACO, which required doing things differently. A $23 million, three-year Memorandum of Understanding (MOU) was entered into by NACO and the foundation in 2006 for Avahan to provide technical and management assistance to NACO in order to strengthen NACO's prevention programmes with MARPs and bridge populations (including truckers), STI, M&E and condom programming across the country. NACO also requested Avahan to help develop guidelines for the national programme for prevention programmes with MARPs, STI, condoms and truckers. Through this MOU, Avahan made two major grants — to the Public Health Foundation of India (PHFI) and the Condom Technical Support Group (through Hindustan Latex Family Planning and Promotion Trust, HLFPPT). Appreciating the value of bringing "business principles" into a public health implementation, the government decided to strengthen its implementation capacity by setting up technical support units at the national level (National Technical Support Unit, NTSU) and enhancing and streamlining state-level structures (State Technical Support Units, TSU). These technical support units consisted of contractual staff that brought extensive management and technical expertise and whose role was primarily "managerial" — to ensure supervision of quality and scale-up. Avahan helped set up the NTSU by seconding a team of experts from within the foundation and its grantees to support NACO. The nine-member team was led by a member of the foundation, and included grantee technical experts in the areas of programme management of targeted interventions (TIs — prevention programmes with MARPs), community-based organisations, monitoring and donor coordination. This team worked closely with the newly hired TI division at NACO — which had grown from a staff of one to almost 15. The goal of the NTSU was to: (1) draw on existing experiences with TIs including within Avahan to assist NACO with the development of operational guidelines; (2) work closely with the newly hired TI to mentor them in methods of scaling HIV prevention with MARPs and (3) assist this team with programme management in the scaling up of TIs across India based on existing best practices. This entire structure was important for the scale-up of NACP-III and for further consolidation of learnings from scaled HIV prevention into the national programme.

At the state level, Avahan supported TSUs in Karnataka and Maharashtra to help the SACS in these two states scale up and manage their prevention programmes. Additional state support for trainings, module development and materials/communications were also provided on an ongoing basis.

Avahan signed a second MOU with the Government of India in 2009 to outline the process of handover of prevention programmes funded by Avahan to NACO. The process of handing over the programmes started in 2009 and is ongoing. Overall, this is a phase that requires intense engagement of Avahan and its implementing partners at the national, state and district levels for smooth handover.

5. Partnership with Other Stakeholders

In addition to partnering with implementers, government and communities of MARP, Avahan engaged with external stakeholders along the same trajectory as with government: a slower start at the beginning, limited engagement in the first few years of implementation and extensive engagement thereafter. Feedback from the Avahan mid-term review in 2005–2006 highlighted that Avahan needed to engage more with other donors. The foundation team began to focus on this through the course of helping develop NACP-III and beyond. Whether the UN system, the World Bank, other bilaterals or other advocates and voices in the Indian landscape, Avahan considers partnerships with stakeholders a key determinant of the success of Avahan's transition. Engagement through joint/collaborative meetings (e.g. jointly sponsored trainings for NACO's technical support units with USAID, co-sponsoring a "Learning Forum" to disseminate community best practices with the World Bank and NACO), participation in key committees and groups (e.g. the Joint Implementation Reviews conducted by the pooling partners of NACO), and bilateral discussions with specific donors on mutual agendas are some of the ways in which Avahan engaged with key stakeholders in the external environment.

6. Lessons and Implications for Partnerships in HIV Prevention and Beyond

Avahan is often referred to as "an experiment of scale", and at the centre of this scaled approach is a "new way of doing business" in the world of public health. The programme highlights not only the need but also the challenge of a response based on collective governance and partnerships with diverse groups, ranging from the formal, such as government and other donors, to the informal, such as the MARP community. Similar to other successful HIV prevention efforts (Low-Beer and Sempala 2010), the success of Avahan relies heavily on a community-led response. While it is too early to declare success for the Avahan programme, the programme has achieved scale, coverage and impact (Verma *et al.* 2010). For example, self-reported condom use has increased dramatically (Lipovsek *et al.* 2010; Pickles *et al.* 2010) and prevalence of STIs and HIV has declined (Ramesh *et al.* 2010; Reza-Paul *et al.* 2008). The process is also underway to ensure the sustainability of the Avahan programme by transferring the elements of the approach, tools and management to government and communities. Important partnership and governance lessons can be drawn from the eight-year life span of Avahan.

First, the objectives of each partnership should be clear and an agenda with well-defined milestones should be developed since negotiating and building relationships with diverse players is challenging. For example, the partnership with government and other donors in India was only clearly defined midway into Phase 1; however, an earlier start in building this relationship could have been beneficial for the programme. Second, nurturing any kind of relationship, whether it is with government or implementing partners, is an ongoing and time intensive process that requires considerable skills in listening, management, capacity building and diplomacy. The Avahan operating model is based on intense management along its implementation pyramid, which enabled rapid scale-up of the programme. Listening to the needs of the community, on the other hand, formed the basis of the community-led response as it allowed the programme to tap into the social capital within the community. The programme also placed considerable resources and efforts to "formalise" the community-led response by helping build community-based groups, organisations and networks across the six states in which it operates. Third, partnership with government and community, a dual challenge in itself, is the principal route to scale and sustainability. The transition of funding and management of the Avahan programme to government poses a particular challenge — its success will be evident only in the coming years.

The Avahan experience shows that partnerships play a critical role in (1) ensuring appropriate oversight and supportive supervision of implementing partners, (2) building a sustainable platform, (3) strengthening communities and fostering a community-led response, (4) enabling advocacy and (5) ensuring impact.

Chapter 11 assesses the role of private foundations, more generally. Chapters 17, 18 and 20 assess the role of community approaches in HIV prevention in India, Russia and Africa, respectively.

References

Alexander A, Ramakrishnan A (2006) "Practicing Theory: Management in HIV Intervention", *Harvard International Review* 28(2):5–16.

Avahan (2008) *Avahan — The India AIDS Initiative: The Business of Prevention at Scale*. New Delhi: The Bill & Melinda Gates Foundation.

Avahan (2009a) *Managing HIV Prevention from the Ground Up: Avahan's Experience with Peer Led Outreach at Scale in India*. New Delhi: The Bill & Melinda Gates Foundation.

Avahan (2009b) *The Power to Tackle Violence: Avahan's Experience with Community Led Crisis Response in India*. New Dehi: The Bill & Melinda Gates Foundation.

Avahan (2009c) *Community Led Crisis Response Systems: A Guide to Implementation*. New Delhi: The Bill & Melinda Gates Foundation.

Chandrasekaran P, Dallabetta G, Loo V, Rao S, Gayle H, Alexander A (2006) "Containing HIV/AIDS in India: The Unfinished Agenda", *Lancet Infectious Diseases* 6(8):508–21.

Claeson M, Alexander A (2008) "Tackling HIV in India: Evidence-Based Priority Setting and Programming", *Health Aff (Millwood)* 27(4):1091–102.

Dodgson R, Lee K, Drager N (2002) *Global Health Governance: A Conceptual Review.* Geneva: World Health Organization.

Lipovsek V, Mukherjee A, Navin D, Marjara P, Sharma A, Roy KP (2010) "Increases in Self-reported Consistent Condom Use Among Male Clients of Female Sex Workers Following Exposure to an Integrated Behaviour Change Programme in Four States in Southern India", *Sex Transm. Infect.* 86(Suppl 1): i25–i32.

Low-Beer D, Sempala M (2010) "Social Capital and Effective HIV Prevention: Community Responses", *Global Health Governance* 4(1), p. 1–17.

McCoy D, Kembhavi G, Patel J, Luintel A (2009) "The Bill & Melinda Gates Foundation's Grant-making Programme for Global Health", *Lancet* 373(9675):1645–53.

Moses S, Blanchard JF, Kang H, Emmanuel F, Paul SR, Becker ML, Wilson D, Claeson M (2006) *AIDS in South Asia: Understanding and Responding to a Heterogeneous Epidemic*. Washington, DC: World Bank.

Nagelkerke NJ, Jha P, de Vlas SJ, Korenromp EL, Moses S, Blanchard JF, Plummer FA (2002) "Modelling HIV/AIDS Epidemics in Botswana and India: Impact of Interventions to Prevent Transmission", *Bull. World Health Organ.* 80(2):89–96.

National AIDS Control Organization (NACO) (2000). *Report on Round 2000 HIV Prevalence Levels, State-wise*. New Delhi: M.o.H.a.F.W., Government of India.

National AIDS Control Organization (NACO) (2003) *Sentinel Surveillance Data*. New Delhi: Government of India.

National AIDS Control Organization (NACO) (2007) *NACP III: To Halt and Reverse the HIV Epidemic in India*. New Delhi: M.o.H.a.F.W., Government of India.

Pickles M, Foss AM, Vickerman P, Deering K, Verma S, Demers E, Washington R, Ramesh BM, Moses S, Blanchard J, Lowndes CM, Alary M, Reza-Paul S, Boily MC (2010) "Interim Modelling Analysis to Validate Reported Increases in Condom Use and Assess HIV Infections Averted Among Female Sex Workers and Clients in Southern India following a Targeted HIV Prevention Programme", *Sex Transm. Infect.* 86(Suppl 1):i33–i43.

Putnam R (2000) *Bowling Alone: The Collapse and Revival of American Community*. New York: Simon and Schuster.

Ramakrishnan L, Gautam A, Goswami P, Kallam S, Adhikary R, Mainkar MK, Ramesh BM, Morineau G, George B, Paranjape RS (2010) "Programme Coverage, Condom Use and STI Treatment Among FSWs in a Large-Scale HIV Prevention Programme: Results from Cross-Sectional Surveys in 22 Districts in Southern India", *Sex Transm. Infect.* 86(Suppl 1):i62–i68.

Ramesh BM, Beattie TS, Shajy I, Washington R, Jagannathan L, Reza-Paul S, Blanchard JF, Moses S (2010) "Changes in Risk Behaviours and Prevalence of Sexually Transmitted Infections Following HIV Preventive Interventions

Among Female Sex Workers in Five Districts in Karnataka State, South India", *Sex Transm. Infect.* 86(Suppl 1):i17–i24.

Reza-Paul S, Beattie T, Syed HU, Venukumar KT, Venugopal MS, Fathima MP, Raghavendra HR, Akram P, Manjula R, Lakshmi M, Isac S, Ramesh BM, Washington R, Mahagaonkar SB, Glynn JR, Blanchard JF, Moses S (2008) "Declines in Risk Behaviour and Sexually Transmitted Infection Prevalence Following a Community-led HIV Preventive Intervention Among Female Sex Workers in Mysore, India", *AIDS* 22(Suppl 5):S91–S100.

The Bill & Melinda Gates Foundation (2009) *Foundation Fact Sheet*. Seattle: The Bill & Melinda Gates Foundation.

The Economist (2004) When Silence is Not Golden — Could AIDS Explode in India? *The Economist*. April 15.

Verma R, Shekhar A, Khobragade S, Adhikary R, George B, Ramesh BM, Ranebennur V, Mondal S, Patra RK, Srinivasan S, Vijayaraman A, Paul SR, Bohidar N (2010) "Scale-up and Coverage of Avahan: a Large-Scale HIV-Prevention Programme Among Female Sex Workers and Men Who Have Sex with Men in Four Indian states", *Sex Transm. Infect.* 86(Suppl 1):i76–i82.

18

Russia: Key Characteristics of the NGO AIDS Response: Assertive Leadership, Professional Reputation, and Broad Partnerships

Alexey Bobrik

Summary

This chapter describes the inclusion of "hard-to-reach" populations in health responses, with a focus on the work of the innovative partnership of the Open Health Institute in Russia. The first section describes the establishment of the Open Health Institute, the role of private foundations including the Soros Foundation, and subsequent access to wider funding to coordinate a national HIV prevention response. It describes how this response ensures the inclusion of groups often excluded from health. The second section assesses the challenges of incorporating these networks into the AIDS response in Russia, at two levels implementation and governance. The AIDS response in Russia illustrates a number of key themes in health partnerships. It shows the importance of NGOs in identification of neglected issues, attracting seed funding, advocating and piloting the interventions needed. This helps extends the health response to hard-to-reach populations. It also illustrates the difficult diplomacy of scaling the

NGO response, the complex political and programmatic issues, and the challenges of creating this wider partnership for health, which incorporates all stakeholders affected by AIDS.

1. Background

The first case of HIV-infection was diagnosed in Russia in 1985 and initially the country's response was shaped by the attempts to isolate those with the disease and by the legacy of the Soviet health system. The response was characterised by a range of highly specialised vertical programmes with very little horizontal integration even between closely related sub-fields. It involved a very traditional approach to health issues with little involvement of patients or affected communities in decision making on clinical or public health issues. Institutionally, the Soviet Ministry of Health created a separate centralised network of AIDS-centres that bore sole responsibility for health care for HIV-infected people, and instituted a system of mandatory testing for a wide number of groups deemed to be at risk. As a result of these institutional choices, in the early stages of the country's experience with HIV/AIDS, the Soviet health system was able to prevent active transmission of infection through the introduction of blood safety measures and infectious control in hospitals (with the exception of two tragic outbreaks in paediatric facilities in the late 1980s). However, as a result of these decisions, HIV prevention and treatment were not integrated into primary health care, with the result that general health care providers remained untrained and uninformed about the disease. In the absence of links to civil society, the health system's ability to reach most at risk groups was undermined.

The traditional focus of the Russian health system on biomedical measures coupled with the relative weakness and lack of experience in behavioural interventions, was not suited to an effective HIV prevention response to HIV, for which there is no vaccine and whose transmission happens mostly through hidden forms of behaviour. The vertical structure of AIDS-centres and HIV surveillance based on systematic testing of large population groups was also quite expensive. This became evident when a newly democratic but chaotic Russia emerged in the early 1990s and the financing available for medical care plummeted both in absolute terms and as a percentage of state budget and of GNP. For many years, AIDS-centres suffered from universal underfunding, aggravated by an inappropriate allocation of scarce resources to mass screening rather than on targeted interventions among high risk groups. This practice continued even after the explosive outbreaks of HIV among injection drugs users (IDUs) and the significant deterioration of the epidemiologic situation in the second half of the 1990s. This can be explained by a tendency to view the Russian population as a general mass, rather than made up of constituent groups, and a very limited view of health partnerships.

2. NGOs Taking the Lead in Fighting AIDS in Russia

Given the inadequacy of the government response, since the end of the 1990s,the first non-governmental organisations, both international and Russian, have started working in Russia in the field of HIV/AIDS. They were not always welcomed by the local decision makers or medical community, taking into account the traditional lack of cooperation of the health system with representatives of broader society, and especially given NGO's involvement in sensitive human rights issues. The early diplomacy was strongly related to the political changes in Russia, and the slow development of civil society more generally. The first AIDS-service NGOs in Russia were funded exclusively by international donors that focussed their efforts on advocacy activities and on the implementation of prevention programmes, which did not receive proper attention from governmental institutions. For example, MSF-Holland, MDM-France and especially the Soros Foundation, a private American charity operating in Russia since the breakup of the USSR, were the first who launched harm reduction projects in Russian cities hit by the outbreaks of HIV among IDUs. The Soros Foundation in particular was an interesting force, benefiting from the rise in private foundations in the USA, but with its emotional roots in Eastern Europe. Its involvement in HIV/AIDS and health came mainly from its general ideological focus on promoting "Open Society" with broad human rights values that imply attention to the needs of vulnerable and marginalised population groups. It became an important force behind a more open approach to health partnerships.

Figure 1. Needle-exchange project run by an NGO in St. Petersburg.

USAID supported a couple of regional projects on HIV prevention among men having sex with men as well as a programme on strengthening prevention of mother-to-child HIV transmission. Several projects on sentinel surveillance of HIV infection at sites or in population groups with high-risk behaviour were supported by the Canadian International Development Agency (CIDA), the Department for International Development of UK (DFID) and other donors. While all these interventions helped raise awareness about the problem of HIV/AIDS and were significant as pilots, they were not sufficient to prevent or control the HIV epidemic because of the short time in which they functioned and inability to reach a sufficient coverage of the target groups. The gap between available resources and existing needs was becoming more and more obvious. What was required was a more comprehensive partnership and source of funding to support significant levels of coverage in Russia.

Given the lack of political will in the country to deal with HIV/AIDS, the leadership was taken by NGOs. In 2003, five non-governmental organisations formed a Consortium led by the Open Health Institute and submitted a non-CCM proposal to the Global Fund. The process of negotiating the consortium was quite simple. After repeated failures to convince the government to either allocate the required funding or launch a formation of the CCM for the application to the GFATM, the leaders of the strongest NGOs decided that in such a desperate situation, even an unsuccessful application to the Global Fund can be useful, as it would attract attention to the need to address HIV/AIDS in Russia. The distribution of areas of responsibility went seamlessly as all five NGOs having been previously funded by different international donors developed the capacity in different sectors of HIV control with very little programmatic overlap, while together covering all the major sectors — from HIV prevention among IDUs and other vulnerable groups to youth mass-media campaigns and condom social marketing in the general population. The Open Health Institute, being a spin-off of the Soros Foundation, had a proven track-record of managing numerous and substantial grants, and thus was the best candidate for the role of the Principal Recipient. The availability of financing in this situation became an important catalyst for a more ambitious consortium and partnership approach to fight AIDS in Russia. However, at this stage, it developed outside of a wider partnership with government.

The application of the Consortium to the GFATM became a turning point in fighting HIV/AIDS in Russia. On the one hand, it resulted in the award of an $88 million grant to a project later called GLOBUS, which was unprecedented in Russia in terms of scope and scale. On the other hand, it stimulated a lot of interest in the topic of HIV/AIDS, with the resulting frank discussion of major stakeholders on existing priorities and opportunities, which soon led to the formation of the CCM by the initiative of the Federal AIDS-centre, with the next successful Russian application to GFATM already in the following Round 4. The creation of this Consortium challenged and drew in the government further to the AIDS response (and through the channel of the CCM). This showed the importance of an activist diplomacy in AIDS, which can at times provoke as well as harmonise between partners. At last, the country went out of denial of the HIV epidemic!

3. From Activism to Professionalism

The GLOBUS project had to start in a pretty complex environment, programmatically and politically. In order to reach ambitious targets, quite sensitive interventions had to be launched within tough deadlines. Given the size of the country multiple components of the project had to be implemented by about 150 sub-sub-recipients in five time zones, where often there was a short supply of necessary skills and capacity. The limited influence of the principal recipient was often complicated by conflicting interests of a diverse range of stakeholders, starting from hostile Federal officials opposed to a "non-authorised" GFATM grant, to some regional AIDS-centres interested just in getting new lab equipment but not in providing care, and occasionally even NGOs trying to renegotiate grant conditions. Russia provides an extreme but important example of health diplomacy between diverse partners, whose interests are not always fully aligned.

This situation has required from the principal recipient a specific management style shaped by realities around three key elements. First, assertive leadership necessary for reconciliation of competing interests and resistance among various stakeholders was developed. Second, maximal standardisation of procedures and protocols was needed for the rapid scale up of the interventions. Moreover, third, decentralised operational management through four sub-recipients and using existing regional systems was established.

This allowed the PR team to remain small and split the overall project into manageable pieces assigned to empowered implementers accountable for results. Regular meetings provided the management team

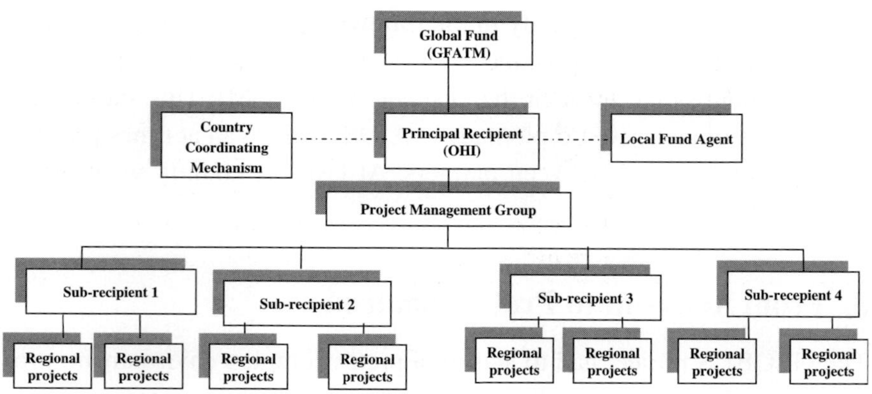

Figure 2. Organisational structure and management of GLOBUS projects.

Table 1. Key interventions and results of GLOBUS project.

Major Target Groups	**Major Interventions**	**Coverage by the End of the 5-Year Project**
IDUs	Syringe exchange Condom distribution Informing on HIV and risk reduction VCT Referrals for STI and TB treatment, ART, treatment of drug dependency, social support, etc.	• 34 thousand IDUs (or 47.2% of the target group in the regions) reached by syringe-exchange, outreach and other HIV prevention activities
CSWs	Condom distribution Informing on HIV and risk reduction VCT Referrals for STI and gynaecological treatment, ART, social support, etc.	• 15.2 thousand CSWs (or 56.9% of the target group in the regions) reached by outreach and HIV prevention activities
MSMs	Outreach Condom distribution Informing on HIV and risk reduction VCT Referrals for STI treatment, ART, social support, etc.	• 22.7 thousand MSMs (or 15% of the target group in the regions) reached by outreach and HIV prevention activities
Youth and general population	Mass media HIV awareness campaigns Condom social marketing HIV & STI school curriculum	• 3 million people aged 15–29 (or 56%) reached by safer sex mass media campaigns • 4.3 million condoms distributed
People living with HIV/AIDS (PLWHA)	VCT and PIT ART Palliative care Self-support groups	• 3.4 thousand people received life-saving ART • 980 PLWHA received palliative care and support

with the rigorous control needed to ensure that changes to the project are identified and processed properly. Such a strong business-like approach to project management helped NGOs quickly launch dozens of projects on HIV prevention among IDUs, CSWs, MSMs and other hard to reach groups, ensure mobilisation of the community of people living with HIV/AIDS, and deliver all the planned project results. It represented an important transition in the NGO response from advocacy and pilot projects to a professionalised, programme approach that could be scaled. This has been a challenge to NGOs in many situations in the AIDS and health response — yet is necessary to create a sustained response with sufficient coverage to fight HIV.

While at the beginning of the GLOBUS programme, the regions selected for the projects had a higher HIV registration rate than the national average, by the 5th year of implementation the HIV rate in these regions declined significantly below the average Russian figures.

Table 2. New HIV cases in GLOBUS regions vs. all Russia from 2003 (the start of the project) until 2009.

	31.12.2003	**31.12.2004**	**31.12.2005**	**31.12.2006**	**31.12.2007**	**31.12.2008**	**31.12.2009**
Buryatia	196	233	233	287	342	372	349
Tatarstan	666	647	636	773	945	879	985
Krasnoyarsk	685	468	615	639	873	1,434	1,351
Vologda	113	115	111	134	112	152	143
N.Novgorod	434	438	440	441	578	749	862
Tver	500	496	472	586	607	623	651
Orenburg	1,512	1,320	1,432	1,493	1,488	1,505	1,907
Pskov	31	42	34	58	45	53	72
Tomsk	65	61	59	79	71	113	124
St.Petersburg	3,357	3,388	3,668	4,022	3,434	3,385	3,513
Total	7,559	7,208	7,700	8,512	8,495	9,265	9,957
Annual increase (%) in GLOBUS regions		–5%	6.8%	10.5%	–0.2%	9.1%	10.5%
New HIV cases in Russia	36,345	33,760	35,697	39,688	44,800	54,046	58,448
Annual increase (%) in Russia		–9%	5.7%	11.1%	12.8%	20.6%	15.3%

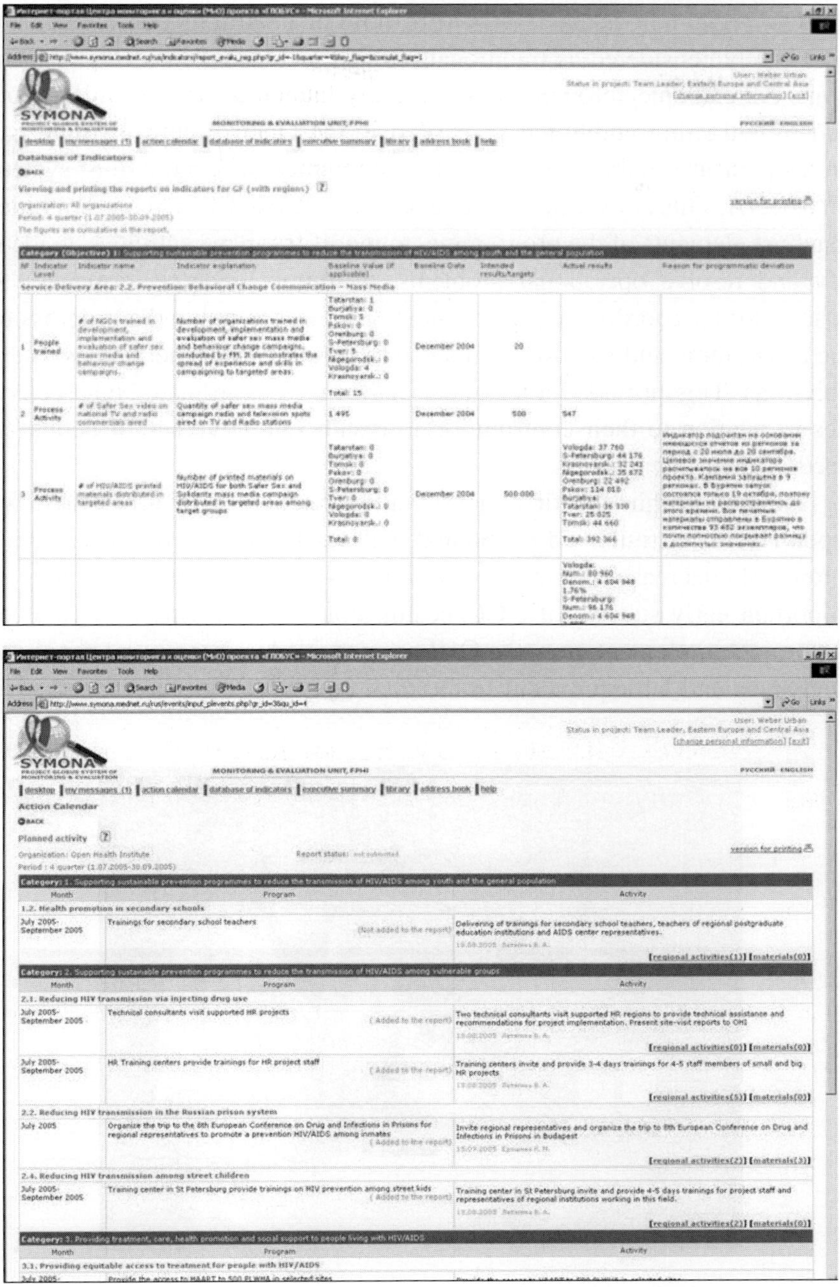

Figure 3. M&E web-based system SYMONA.

Of special note is that NGOs were quite successful in areas, which are not usually considered as traditional ones for non-governmental organisations. For example, through cooperation with the leading research institutes and by attracting additional IT expertise, the Open Health Institute has developed a reliable web-based monitoring and evaluation system SYMONA. This allows easy on-line access to project data needed in order to adjust elements of the programme, to modify/reshape activities, to identify and resolve operational problems, to correct underperformance, to ensure proper coordination of the sub-recipients, to judge the progress of the programme and its correspondence to the plan and other management decisions. This provided a technical platform to coordinate NGO activities in relation to their contribution to results and coverage of people in need of their interventions.

Already within the first months after the launch of GLOBUS, the Open Health Institute had negotiated with the pharmaceutical companies a four-fold decrease in prices for antiretroviral (ARV) drugs. This was an important early success of NGO health diplomacy. During five years of the project implementation, the OHI has provided uninterrupted supply of medicines and lab equipment to the total cost of $20 million, conducted

Figure 4. Health Extension Workers (HEWs) in AIDS-centre in Kazan dispense ARV drugs procured by NGOs in the GLOBUS project.

trainings for over 5,000 regional medical specialists and launched the first mass-scale ARV-treatment programme that provided medications to more than 3,300 patients in 10 regions of the Russian Federation where 20% of the country's population live.

The implementation of such a complex project became possible through the constant focus of the principal recipient on results and openness of the consortium to partnerships with a broad range of stakeholders. There were no iron cast rules, e.g. some regional harm reduction projects could be run by NGOs, some by AIDS-centres and some by drug-dependence treatment facilities. The choice of the partner was always based on a pragmatic consideration of the regional situation, existing capacity, and demonstrated reliability. The focus on results provided a common currency for diplomacy among diverse partners in a very politically charged context. The success of GLOBUS as well as consistent adherence of the principal recipient to high standards of governance and transparency helped the consortium build its nation-wide professional reputation. By representing the groups they served, the NGOs were crucial for meaningful coordination and building bridges across civil society and government.

Following a period of confrontation, there were signs of an operational partnership with government. First, the government implicitly recognised the importance and relevance of the NGO's response by paying back the Global Fund one dollar for every dollar disbursed to the NGO Consortium. They showed clearly the additionality and value to the programme beyond the financial contributions of the Global Fund, reaching groups the government could not do on its own, for both political and operational reasons. Another direct indication of the recognised role of the NGOs became their participation in the National Priority Health Project that started in Russia in 2006 and currently is the major source of HIV-related funding in Russia. AIDS-service NGOs and organisations of people living with HIV became involved in all national HIV coordination bodies and are able to actively influence practice through expert opinion and direct funding. Very often NGOs are the first ones who bring the attention to existing problems, attract funding and start innovative programmes. This process is not always easy and sometimes may include internal arguments in the NGO community around the priorities, or isolated episodes of tensions based on the competition for resources, etc.

However, without any doubt non-governmental organisations are one of the key players in fighting HIV-infection in Russia today.

4. New Challenges

It is hard to overestimate the importance of international influences and the role of NGOs in shaping HIV/AIDS control in Russia. Probably without them, the country would still have questioned the relevance of HIV/AIDS to the national public health agenda, trying not to pay attention to the most marginalised patients, and ignoring the real needs for ARV treatment. Without the non-governmental organisations, large populations they represent would not be included in the AIDS response. Over the last several years, local capacity to fight AIDS became incomparably stronger, successful models of HIV prevention among hidden population groups were developed to the stage of reproducible technologies, the HIV/AIDS problem became widely recognised in the country, the Russian CCM was formed, several GFATM grants totalling $210 million were awarded, and Russian domestic funding for HIV control increased 60-fold, from $5 million to about $300 million. It is exactly the leadership and professionalism of NGOs combined with the courage of the Global Fund to pay serious attention to non-standard situations that made this possible and mobilised the Russian government's response to AIDS.

Unfortunately, the major progress in government programmes is seen mostly on the treatment side, which enjoyed massive procurement of ARV drugs and lab equipment from the National Priority Health Project. HIV prevention among highly vulnerable groups remains heavily dependent on external funding, because realistic approaches, such as harm reduction, are still very sensitive and vulnerable groups are not generally perceived as important constituencies.

Another important issue is related to a specific Russian feature. Current policy is mostly determined by the opinion of an individual decision maker currently in office. As a result of administrative changes in 2009, a significant share of power and control of HIV funding passed from the Federal Health Service to the Ministry of Health and Social Development. With new people in charge of fighting HIV/AIDS in Russia came an unexpected development. All funding previously earmarked for

HIV prevention among vulnerable population groups was directed for health promotion in the general population. It immediately put at risk a significant portion of the GFATM achievements in Russia and led to another unprecedented decision of the Board of the Global Fund to "provide additional 2-year funding for the OHI project in order to continue life-saving prevention activities." This has brought to the front the crucial issue of health diplomacy between NGOs and government, to create a sustainable partnership to deliver services to those most at risk.

5. Lessons Learned

In a nutshell, the history of fighting HIV/AIDS in Russia over the last 10–12 years can be traced by how NGOs supported by international donors earned respect from the government, developed strong managerial expertise, and progressed from small pilot projects to successful implementation of big programmes that strongly influenced the national HIV/AIDS policy. The scale and speed of that transformation are remarkable. Arguably it is exactly AIDS-service NGOs that represent the most vivid example of development of civil society in the Russian Federation, with wider political implications. It is a strained yet important example of diplomacy among diverse partners in health, which does not always lead to an easy resolution.

On the downside, however, there are many concerns about the sustainability for both NGOs and some most needed interventions. This illustrates the challenges of sustaining an overall health response between government and civil society, which at one level is synergistic, yet important tensions may exist which need to be worked through over time.

Despite significant increases in domestic funding for HIV control over the last five years, radically improved laboratory capacity, and undisputable progress in the provision of lifesaving ARV treatment, the institutional response of the Russian health care system remains implemented through the vertical system of AIDS-centres that have very limited access to high risk groups, i.e. the driving forces of the HIV epidemic. Although the key prevention interventions are well developed and professionally implemented in a number of Russian territories, their sensitivity and lack of integration in established budgeting, makes their continuation possible only with external support. In a relatively wealthy country, large vulnerable populations and key aspects of the health response can remain neglected.

The same goes for Russian NGOs that in the absence of the administrative procedures and the long-term commitment of the government, they cannot count on regular internal funding and become very vulnerable. Altogether, it shows that general formal characteristics such as membership of G8 or G20, growing GDP, or even substantial increases in HIV-related funding, may not necessarily mean that a country is ready to effectively deal with HIV/AIDS on its own. Within these countries, large populations can remain excluded from the health response. While ARV treatment, VCT, PMTCT, blood safety and other biomedical measures are easily accepted by health facilities and relatively ensured by a rapid improvement in infrastructure, many other key interventions, especially those targeting vulnerable population groups, still represent a serious challenge for traditional thinking, rigid bureaucratic systems and entrenched funding mechanisms. They thus may require from the international community somewhat longer support until they are fully institutionalised, and a sustainable health partnership formed.

The development of the AIDS response also reflects that of civil society in Russia. Initially, the NGO response played an advocacy role in supporting and provoking the AIDS response. The NGO response received limited amounts of external support in keeping with this role. Once they received larger programme funding, this led to rapid consolidation and coordination within the NGO response but also challenges. The NGO response was transformed and with its new responsibilities had to negotiate leadership, procedural and decentralised management systems. The longer-term sustainability of the response required a stronger partnership with government. While there have been major developments in the Russian AIDS response, this remains an unfinished agenda. Even in relatively wealthy countries, critical populations can remain excluded if external support is not extended. This support can be catalytic in stimulating a national AIDS response. However, it also needs to acknowledge an extended political period of diplomacy between government and civil society to create a sustainable response. The NGO response in Russia shows the value of innovative partnerships to reach most at risk populations, and the challenges of building a sustainable health response — which in many political contexts cannot rely solely on NGOs or on government.

> Chapter 11 assesses the role of private foundations in health more generally. Chapter 17 also assesses community responses, in India.

19

State Fragility: Working with Partners to Achieve Health Results in African Countries

Erling Høg

Summary

This chapter examines how the relation between "state fragility", "state capacity" and "global health" influences the strengths and weaknesses for establishing and maintaining transnational "partnerships for health". Such analytical differentiation promotes understanding how and why current approaches to "health development", "humanitarian intervention" and "medical relief" complicate the relation between local governments and their international partners. Following this, it provides policy guidance at the local level by emphasising three areas that influence health partnerships: (1) political context, (2) global priorities in health and (3) relations between donors, governments and non-governmental organisations (NGOs). Case illustrations serve to improve our understanding of health partnerships in terms of fragility, capacity, and government politics. This chapter, therefore, brings out the major challenges of engaging with innovative health partnerships in difficult contexts.

1. Introduction: Partnerships in Health

> *"We are the first generation to possess the resources, knowledge and skills to eliminate poverty. Experience shows that where there is strong political resolve, we see progress. And where there is partnership, there are gains."*
>
> United Nations Secretary-General Ban Ki-Moon (United Nations 2009)

Lester Pearson originally defined partnerships in development as an exclusive donor–recipient relationship between governments in which no other bodies were considered partners (Pearson 1969). Since then, a proliferation of partnerships has emerged between recipient and donating governments, bilateral and multilateral donors, international and local NGOs, communities and private enterprises. The background to partnerships has been dealt with elsewhere (Brinkerhoff 2002; Buse and Walt 2000a, 2000b, 2002; Johnson and Wilson 2006), as well as its history and diversity (see Manning; Isenman and Shakow; Thalwitz, this volume). Principles of "agreement, mutuality, equality and respect" characterise an ethics of collaboration, which implies how partnerships *ought* to succeed. In particular, a new partnership paradigm emerged from the Paris Declaration of Aid Effectiveness (OECD 2005), which listed five core principles of "ownership, harmonisation, alignment, results and accountability" (see Adhanom and Fassil; Banati and Low-Beer, this volume). This chapter looks at "fragile states" with a wider analysis of "global fragility", meaning the accountabilities of local and foreign governments, donors and non-state actors for the effectiveness of partnerships. Mozambique, considered an "easy partnership" country, provides the main case story, complemented by examples of "difficult" partnerships cases (Sudan, Somalia and Zimbabwe).

2. Fragility, Capacity and Global Health

> *"This is what I usually say: I cannot get a shrimp to transform into a lobster just because it's hungry. One thing is to define the objectives and*

> *another is to see whether I have the resources to realize these objectives. This is happening bit by bit, considering the country's capacity".*
>
> National AIDS Council Deputy, Mozambique

The relation between state fragility, state capacity and global health improves our understanding of key obstacles to successful partnerships in health. "State fragility" primarily concerns security and political stability (The Fund for Peace 2009b; Transparency International 2008; World Bank 2006) and "state capacity" the power and capabilities of government (Ikpe 2007; Price-Smith 2002). Fragility and capacity pertain to *risk* and *performance* which is influenced by a partnership beyond the concept of "fragile states. 'Global health' has been a useful approach to understand health inequalities yet there is limited common understanding of its definition, content and implications for research and practice (Macfarlane *et al.* 2008). The 'global' dimension relates to an increasing awareness of how globalization affects health and health delivery (Brown *et al.* 2006). This can be accounted for in three ways: (1) proliferation in funding channels, (2) growth in pharmaceutical and clinical research, and (3) renewed concern for 'biosecurity' (Adams *et al.* 2008). 'Biosecurity', in particular that of the United States, underlies much of the 'fragile states' approach particularly in relation to the HIV epidemic"(Barnett and Dutta 2007; Barnett and Prins 2006; Elbe 2005, 2006; Garrett 2005; Ingram 2007; Prins 2004).

Normative definitions of weak and fragile states are found in the Failed States Index, FSI (The Fund for Peace 2009b), the Corruption Perceptions Index, CPI (Transparency International 2008) and the Low-Income Countries Under Stress approach, LICUS (World Bank 2006) (Table 1).

The Fund for Peace applies social, economic and political indicators to qualify "state failure". Examples include refugee migration, internal displacement, inequality, poverty, corruption, deteriorating public services, disrespect for the rule of law, human rights violations and elite formation (The Fund for Peace 2009b). The 2007–2009 ranking of state failure has been rather consistent (years with full data from all sub-Saharan African

Table 1. State failure, corruption and fragility in sub-Saharan Africa.

Country	State Failure FSI 2009	Corruption CPI 2008	State Fragility LICUS 2006
Somalia	1	1	Severe
Zimbabwe	2	7	Severe
Sudan	3	3	Core
Chad	4	4	Marginal
Dem. Rep. of the Congo	5	6	Core
Central African Republic	6	14	Severe
Guinea	7	2	Core
Ivory Coast	8	15	Core
Kenya	9	16	—
Nigeria	10	25	Core
Ethiopia	11	22	—
Uganda	12	20	—
Niger	13	28	—
Burundi	14	9	Core
Cameroon	15	17	—
Guinea-Bissau	16	12	Core
Malawi	17	29	—
Republic of Congo	18	11	Core
Sierra Leone	19	8	Marginal
Liberia	20	18	Severe
Burkina Faso	21	39	—
Eritrea	22	23	Core
Rwanda	23	31	—
Mauritania	24	27	—
Equatorial Guinea	25	5	—
Togo	26	24	Core
Comoros	27	19	Severe
Angola	28	10	Core
Zambia	29	30	—
Swaziland	30	40	—
Lesotho	31	36	—
Madagascar	32	38	—
Tanzania	33	32	—
Mozambique	34	21	—
Djibouti	35	—	—
Gambia	36	13	Marginal

(*Continued*)

Table 1. (*continued*)

Country	State Failure FSI 2009	Corruption CPI 2008	State Fragility LICUS 2006
Mali	37	35	—
Cape Verde	38	45	—
São Tomé and Príncipe	39	26	Marginal
Namibia	40	42	—
Benin	41	33	—
Gabon	42	34	—
Senegal	43	37	—
Botswana	44	47	—
Seychelles	45	43	—
South Africa	46	44	—
Ghana	47	41	—
Mauritius	48	46	—

Sources: (The Fund for Peace 2009b; Transparency International 2008, World Bank 2006).

countries). Somalia, Zimbabwe and Sudan have failed the most and Mauritius, Ghana and South Africa have failed the least. Those countries that fall above the black 2009 line have worsened between 2007 and 2009, while those that fall below this line have improved. For example, state failure has worsened in Kenya (17 to 9) and the Comoros (35 to 27). State failure has decreased in Sierra Leone (13 to 19) and Cape Verde (30 to 38) (Figure 1).

The Corruption Perceptions Index measures how business people and country analysts perceive corruption in their country. "Failed states" are also among the most corrupt states. Corruption in the 47 sub-Saharan countries divides into *pervasive* (1–30), *serious* (31–44) and *low* (45–47) (Transparency International 2008).

The World Bank characterises "Low-Income Countries Under Stress" by their "weak policies, institutions, and governance" and their "lack of capacity or inclination to use finance effectively for poverty reduction"(World Bank 2002). Such countries may undergo various degrees of stress, such as deterioration, prolonged political crisis, post-conflict or political transition and gradual improvement. The World Bank assesses state fragility in terms of economic management, structural policies,

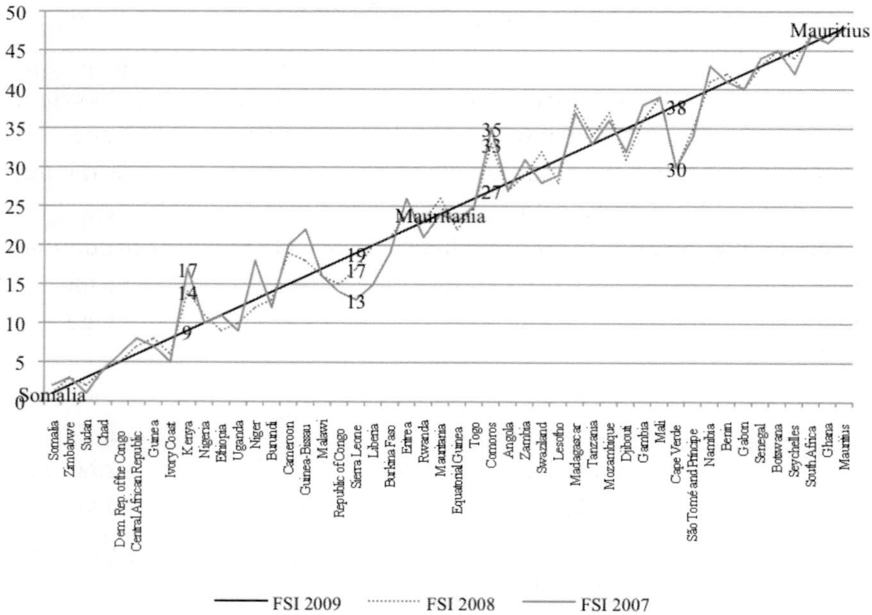

Figure 1. Ranking of state failure in sub-Saharan Africa, 2007–2009.

Sources: The Fund for Peace 2007, 2008, 2009b.

policies for social inclusion/equity and public sector management and institutions. Countries are then classified as *marginal*, *core* or *severe* fragile states. Notably, the term *fragile states* replaced the LICUS term retaining the same criteria to identify these countries (World Bank 2006).

The three sets of indicators measure lack of success, in particular towards the partnership goal of poverty reduction. Moreover, they measure deviations from normative state administration, since the 1990s called "good governance". However, there is now a tendency to measure state fragility and failure in operational terms, meaning "*the difficulty that a state has in utilizing international assistance for its stated goals*" (de Waal 2009: 100). This is about *absorptive capacity* and *absorption capacity* (see later discussion).

Three interpretations stand out across state failure, corruption and state fragility. First, there is regular *correspondence* among state failure, fragility and corruption (e.g. Somalia, Zimbabwe, Sudan, South Africa, Ghana and Mauritius). Second, some states maintain *state resilience*, despite being highly corrupt (e.g. Gambia, Equatorial Guinea, Sierra Leone and Angola). In other words, relatively "good governments" and relatively "successful states" may simultaneously be highly corrupt. Third, *discordance* primarily shows between the level of governance — a proxy for state fragility — and the levels of corruption and state failure. Highly fragile states may not necessarily be particularly corrupt and lead to state failure (e.g. Comoros, Angola and Togo). On the other hand, relatively "good governments" may simultaneously be relatively corrupt and show indication of state failure (e.g. Chad, Ethiopia, Kenya and Uganda) (see Table 1).

State capacity concerns performance maximisation in terms of prosperity, stability, capacity and resilience (Ikpe 2007; Price-Smith 2002). Capacity relates to how a state must be able to withstand internal and external threats and shocks and simultaneously be able to take advantage of external support (Donovan *et al.* 2005). Resilience pertains to the management of social relations and political risks (Ikpe 2007).

Other factors than state failure, corruption and fragility may indeed account for the reason why some states seek to be "strong" in the name of sovereignty. Specifically, a "sovereignty gap" exists between *de jure* sovereignty afforded to states by the international system and *de facto* state capabilities (e.g. service provision and responsible membership of the international community) (Ghani and Lockhart 2008: 3–4). Therefore, my fragility/capacity typology initially looks at how "weak states" relate to state capacity. This has been done by dividing weak states into four categories: relatively good performers; weak but willing states; states that have the means but not the will and states with no means and no will (Patrick 2006) (Table 2).

Table 2. Capacity and will as dimensions of state weakness.

	Strong Will	**Low Will**
High capacity	Relative good performers (e.g. Senegal, Honduras)	Unresponsive/corrupt/repressive (e.g. Burma, Zimbabwe)
Low capacity	Weak but willing (e.g. Mozambique, East Timor)	Weak and not willing (e.g. Haiti, Sudan)

Source: (Patrick 2006).

Low growth and inability to realise the Millennium Development Goals, MDGs, primarily characterise weak states. They fail to eradicate extreme poverty, provide primary education and reduce child mortality. They face malnutrition, endemic diseases, low life expectancy, high illiteracy and lack of access to health care. Weak states have often experienced civil war and large numbers of refugees and internally displaced peoples. Weak states are also unable to comply with human rights (Patrick 2006).

However, my perspective on fragility and capacity has also been influenced from long-term fieldwork in Mozambique (Høg 2008a). First, there is an important difference between *absorption* capacity and *absorptive* capacity. Absorption capacity concerns the state ability to digest and consume financial resources. Problems of liberating incoming financial resources and the time-consuming operational process once the money has been disbursed pose an intrinsic dilemma for many poor countries receiving donor aid.

The World Bank fragile states index relates to conflict status in three ways: non-conflict-affected, conflict-affected and post-conflict (World Bank 2006). In particular, lasting peace explains a country's marginal or absent position to the fragile state definitions. Capacity, willingness and resilience in Mozambique, a post-conflict country since 1992, can be explained in terms of lasting peace, political reform and economic growth. This is a different development history compared to other sub-Saharan African countries. Instability contributes to state fragility as defined in the conflict and security sense. Mozambique's democratisation process since the end of the civil war and its exceptional economic growth in the African context also explains its relative good performance (Høg 2008b).

The efforts needed to engage in partnerships seem to depend more on a given country's fragility, less on its capacity. Difficult partnerships are more likely found in countries with "high fragility" and "low capacity". Easy partnerships are most likely found in countries with "high capacity" and "low fragility". However, it is important to remember that there are many reasons why states fail, and it has been noted that "every failing state is failing in its own way" (The Fund for Peace 2009a).

Critically fragile states with weak capacity are due to weak to non-existent government and recurring conflict (e.g. Somalia, DRC). Critically fragile but strong capacity states are governed by a small group of people who ignore the needs and rights of their citizens (e.g. Zimbabwe, Sudan). They are not necessarily conflict-affected. Somalia is the extreme case of non-existing government, below what is considered minimal government, though several other states meet this criterion. The failing state of Zimbabwe differs by its extreme coercive power and malevolence against its people. The results in the Zimbabwean state failure to provide basic goods to its citizens (Collier 2009).

Democratising states during periods of stable peace characterise "marginally fragile states". They have weak capacity, but they are nevertheless willing and able to improve their statehood through "physical security, legitimate political institutions, economic management, and social welfare" (Patrick 2006: 29) (e.g. Mozambique, Sierra Leone). Finally, relatively strong democratic governments characterise robust peaceful states with strong capacity and continuous willingness to improve (e.g. Botswana and Mauritius) (Table 3).

3. Asymmetric Power Relations

"The donors keep saying that we need ambitious indicators. It's not enough to have ambitious indicators, when I know that I will not be able to realize them. This is the same as dreaming about going to the moon, when I don't even have a bicycle. Have a dream ambition that doesn't become reality."

National AIDS Council Deputy, Mozambique

Table 3. Capacity/fragility correlation.

Fragility	Capacity	Government	Conflict	Partnership	Examples
Severe/core	Weak, *not willing*	Weak/non-existent	Yes	Difficult	Somalia, DRC
Severe/Core	Strong, *not willing*	Oligarchic	No/Yes	Difficult	Zimbabwe, Sudan
Marginal	Weak, *willing*	Democratising	No	Easy	Mozambique, Sierra Leone
—	Strong, *willing*	Strong, democratic	No	Easy	Botswana, Mauritius

Concurrently, a growing international concern for "global health" and "global partnerships" has emerged with stronger motivation by foreign governments, donors and research funding channels to find solutions how to engage with fragile states. Key examples illustrate this trend during the late 2000s. Governmental development agencies engage in fragile states (e.g. Australia, USA, UK and Denmark). The World Bank and the OECD maintain their own fragility and conflict forums. Agencies and donors across a wide spectrum created the Health and Fragile States Network in 2007. In 2009, Sussex Institute of Development Studies launched a health and fragile states dossier and the European Commission initiated a conflict prevention implementation plan. The Center for Global Development and the London School of Economics host their own fragile states research centres (see Resources). They commonly aim to find solutions how to organise and finance development including health services in fragile states. They ask pertinent questions how to meet the MDGs and how the international aid effectiveness agenda can be implemented to deliver basic services.

The global health agenda relates to the realisation of the MDGs envisioned by the world's richest countries and the United Nations including their main directing and coordinating authority for health (G8 2005; United Nations 2000b; WHO 2005a, 2005b, 2006). Difficult partnerships pose a particular challenge for the successful realisation of such goals. Indeed, there is growing recognition, both at the local and global levels, of the need to build or rebuild health systems. However, the lack of consensus on *how* this should be achieved reveals both political and organisational challenges (Pfeiffer and Nichter 2008; Low-Beer, this volume). Which entity or entities should receive incoming development aid? Do governments have the capacity to coordinate the activities of the many co-existing partners and projects? What are the implications of partnerships for governance and state sovereignty? How can the private sector, the public sector and NGOs be held accountable in specific political contexts? The implications of the opposite meanings of "agreement, mutuality, equality and respect" become questions of inequality and asymmetric power relations.

"Global governance" can be defined as "*the exercise of power, persuasion, or authority by organizations and networks over a jurisdiction that spans at least two national states*" (Lieberman 2009: 65). The proliferation of bilateral, multilateral and NGO funding channels makes such governance diffuse. This creates *indirect* challenges to state authority, unlike other sources of transnational governance that involve *direct* military challenges to state authority, e.g. imperialism and occupation (Lieberman 2009: 66).The global governance agenda adds to the dilemma of *de jure versus de facto* sovereignty. The bypassing of governments by foreign partners may be an implicit sign of resignation by the international community that some states remain too unwilling to live up to the standards of state building.

Several countries choose not to follow the mandate of authorities beyond the national boundaries, claiming their political power to govern their internal affairs (Keohane 2002; Lieberman 2009). When weak states reinforce their call for independent governance, this may simultaneously compromise the welfare of their peoples. This is an extremely delicate question of responsibility that reaches beyond the normative measurements of state fragility and state failure. The international community must understand its share of responsibility sidestepping governments in the name of humanitarianism.

State governance may become a matter of when and why sovereignty precludes solidarity. An example remains Republic of Guinea President Touré's famous dictum, when he claimed sovereignty and independence from French rule in the 1950s: *"We will not renounce and we will never renounce our legitimate and natural right to independence. We prefer poverty in liberty to riches in slavery"* (Chaffard 1965: 197). In contemporary times, Médecins Sans Frontières, MSF, has experienced different levels of admonition for inadvertently challenging the role of local governments in places otherwise considered "easy partnership" countries (e.g. Mozambique, South Africa) and in "difficult partnership" countries (e.g. Sudan, Zimbabwe).

The most fragile low-capacity states would normally enjoy highest donor priority to engage in health partnerships. However, state fragility causes "difficult partnerships" and, therefore, a *selective* donor approach to development. In other words, fragile states tend to get excluded from donor aid, even though several factors would recommend their inclusion: (1) aid is lower than their policy and institutional quality qualify, (2) donor aid is more inconsistent compared to other low-income countries, (3) fragile states encompass the most severe levels of poverty and (4) aid drops rapidly in post-conflict situations, when aid is most needed (OECD 2008). In fact, measures of "performance" and "effective governance" in aid allocation may deny countries with "bad governance" and "poor performance" sufficient access to resources needed under such circumstances (Jones, *et al.* 2005; McGillivray 2005).

As much as 75% of the 2006 Official Development Assistance for 38 fragile states benefited just five countries: Nigeria, Afghanistan, Sudan, Democratic Republic of Congo and Cameroon. Half the total assistance remained debt relief (OECD 2007). McGillivray and Feeny looked at what would happen to absorptive capacity in fragile states, if they were not supported by donor aid. Growth would have been 1.4% lower, compared to 2.5% in other countries. Moreover, the *most* fragile states can only efficiently absorb about a third of the amounts of aid compared to other countries and would, therefore, seem to be *over*-aided (McGillivray and Feeny 2008).

Good timing is important for donor aid to fragile states. Collier and Hoeffler analysed aid and policy reform in post-conflict countries and concluded that absorptive capacity increases significantly during the decade after peace has been obtained. Specifically, absorptive capacity is no greater than normal during the first three years after peace, but then it doubles its normal level during the next seven years (Collier and Hoeffler 2004). Thus, they recommend increased aid in the post-conflict decade congruent with the OECD finding that this is the period when aid is most needed (OECD 2008). Indeed, bad governance worsens outcomes in "difficult partnership" countries by increasing the volatility of aid inflows (Levin and Dollar 2005), but this may be caused by unstable flows of donor aid. Cross-country variation in sector aid volatility may reflect donor characteristics more than recipient characteristics (Fielding and Mavrotas 2008). The fact that "difficult partnership" countries receive disproportionately less aid than their policy and institutional quality qualify (OECD 2008) suggests that *"donors could modestly increase aid to the group as a whole without challenging the performance basis of aid allocations"* (Levin and Dollar 2005). This means more efficient use of donor aid through improved partnerships paying attention to both donating and recipient partners.

The OECD created its own state fragility based index to capture "Difficult Partnership Countries" with weak states and weak capacity (Levin and Dollar 2005). Somalia, Sudan and Zimbabwe are prime examples of "difficult partnerships", ranked as the most corrupt and failed states in the world (The Fund for Peace 2009b; Transparency International 2008).

Experiences of "bad governance", "conflict" and "difficult partnership" may produce donor withdrawal or avoidance in search of "good governance" and "easy partnership". However, international organisations may also experience expulsion. For example, in early 2009, the Sudanese president Bashir expelled 13 INGOS after being accused by the International Criminal Court for crimes against humanity and war crimes (ICC 2009). In addition, the 2008–2009 cholera outbreaks in Zimbabwe resulted in an accusation game whether it was "Brown's cholera" (colonial control by the United Kingdom) or "Mugabe's cholera" (denial and an attempt to stay in power).

Rather than general "standard" agreements, it seems more likely that a series of locally defined priorities would benefit poor countries. Indeed, the new partnership paradigm — including the MDGs and the Global Fund public-private partnership — rests upon national plans and priorities (see Isenman and Shakow; Thalwitz, this volume), and are, therefore, prone to state fragility.

4. AIDS Exceptionalism and Dependency

> *"AIDS is a cross-cutting issue! As it is, AIDS is certainly not a cross-cutting issue. We need a multi-sector approach. But in fact, agencies continue to do other things. UNICEF works with children, WFP works with food, WHICH works with health. There is no substance to this. How can we evaluate this in relation to reality?"*
>
> UNAIDS Advocacy Officer, Mozambique

The introduction of antiretroviral treatment in the Mozambican public health system provides an important partnership example. The government and its partners considered three financing paradigms: health development (state budget), medical relief (donor aid) and *exceptional funding* (donor aid) (Ooms 2008). The Mozambican government developed a Mozambican model for the introduction of AIDS drugs based on government priorities and international funding (Høg 2008a).

The health development paradigm implies sustainability, the use of domestic resources, self-determination and sovereignty. The medical relief paradigm implies dependency, foreign aid, humanitarian assistance and an exceptional response (Ooms 2008). The government and its partners debated whether the HIV epidemic was a structural problem (state budget) or an emergency problem (international aid). There was no third way. Ooms eloquently poses this dilemma as a deadlock for many poor countries:

> But what if a problem is structural or chronic, and therefore not exceptional and does not justify a medical relief approach? What if the appropriate response is technically feasible for the affected state, but too expensive? The medical relief paradigm would not be appropriate, but neither is the health development paradigm. This is precisely the conundrum the AIDS crisis created in Mozambique, and other affected states (Ooms 2008: 87).

"AIDS exceptionalism" sets the need for a wider response to poverty, public health and underdevelopment in sharp contrast. At first, the Mozambican government aimed for "emergency relief" under the given circumstances, which is common practice in a country with recurrent natural disasters. Calamity funding relates to *exceptional* events with no limit to foreign assistance (Ooms 2008: 93). However, disaster funding produces foreign aid dependency. On the one hand, MSF had been using the medical relief paradigm for decades to support the fight against cholera, which thereby would justify the use of relief money for AIDS drugs. On the other hand, the Mozambican government saw the HIV epidemic as a long-term structural problem and it therefore favoured the health development paradigm under its sovereign governance. Thus, funding had to come from the national health budget, which the government could ill afford (Ooms 2008: 120). The government did not have the "fiscal space" within the state budget to finance AIDS drugs, defined as "*... the availability of budgetary room that allows a government to provide resources for a desired purpose without any prejudice to the sustainability of a government's financial position*" (Heller 2005: 3). Money for AIDS drugs would take away scarce resources from other expenditures. Moreover, the government was not in a position to borrow the money or to raise taxes to create financial space for AIDS drugs, neither in the short-term perspective, nor in the long-term perspective.

Such negotiations reveal much about partnerships in action. First, governments remain ambivalent whether to avoid or embrace foreign aid. Partnership negotiations exemplify government appropriation of how and what qualifies as "normal" and "exceptional" in terms of development and relief. Governments may opt for a "calamity compromise", which allows relief money though this means more aid dependency, on the basis that state budgets cannot promise access to basic health care for all or access to specialised health care for some.

Partnership negotiations vary in specific contexts, but the majority of cases from the example of AIDS intervention may turn out to be both politically and practically decided by foreign actors (governments, donors) to the extent it becomes *government-by-exception* (Nguyen 2009). The *new* health paradigm defined sustainability in a new way that honours the long-term goals of poor countries, but on the condition that international aid would have to pay virtually all expenses in a sustained manner (Ooms 2008: 130). This may sound contradictory to a government policy that attempts to reduce donor dependency. However, AIDS treatment programmes became *exceptional* in those countries that appropriated this solution, which adds a new dimension to AIDS exceptionalism (Swaziland: see Whiteside, this volume).

AIDS exceptionalism brings out many of the paradoxes in international development driven by partnerships. In the case illustrated above, partners negotiated biomedical drugs as one essential and exceptional expenditure. Money for drugs could not be spent on health care components. The need for infrastructure and human resources came on the partnership agenda after the negotiation over AIDS drugs concluded in 2004. This created a new situation: emergency funding could not pay for HEW training, since it could not be defined in exceptional terms. Moreover, the state budgets in developing countries could not pay for it either. This first of all created the *Medicines without Doctors Paradox* (Ooms 2008: 140), but it also revealed the lack of a wider response to underdevelopment.

5. Looking Beyond AIDS and Health

> *"We are standing with our arms crossed, waiting for foreigners to give us money. When you give money to people on the street, it will take them away from there, but they will be back on the street soon again. What we need is economic investment and development! We need to change our attitude. We need autonomy and sovereignty as a people and as a nation."*
>
> Health worker, Mozambique

> *"The challenge is even bigger, when we go to the interior, where access is most difficult, communication is most difficult, electricity is most difficult, and access to water is most difficult, infrastructure is most difficult. This is where we need a lot of coordinated aid and we need to repeat this to our partners of the international community."*
>
> Senior Member, Ministry of Health, Mozambique

The analysis of health financing says much about *sustainability* and *capacity*. Relief aid is temporary for temporary crises. Therefore, it raises difficult questions for chronic underdevelopment and how to respond to chronic diseases and persistent disease epidemics. *Sustainable* health care, narrowly defined as independent from international aid, is illusory in the world's poorest countries (Ooms 2006). Exceptional and sustained funding for AIDS illustrates the point. As physician anthropologist Vinh-Kim Nguyen points out, massive intervention into populations defined by their medical condition increasingly and indelibly rests on foreign economic commitment, foreign responsibility to deliver life-long treatment, and foreign unprecedented intervention on entire populations (Nguyen 2009).

> *"The message that we send to our partners is the following: sometimes we are poorly understood. Partners are here to complement, to improve what the health system doesn't have the capacity to do. They are not here to compete with our system or to create a structure, which is unsustainable for the country or the National Health Service after they leave."*
>
> Senior Member, Ministry of Health, Mozambique

Dependency controversies are central to considering "partnership" and "ownership" (de Waal 2002; Jerve 2002; Schmidt 2002). The New Partnership for Africa's Development, NEPAD, was established in 2001 to develop an African integrated socioeconomic development framework for Africa. Initially, African governments would decide their own locally appropriate policies and keep the promises of "good governance". However, the NEPAD initiative has sparked a series of critical questions related to the possibility, probability and feasibility of its realisation (Schmidt 2002). The meaning of "good governance" remains unclear, but it may minimally imply a series of commitments: multiparty elections; a judiciary; a parliament; protection of human rights; non-discriminatory laws; efficient, impartial and rapid judicial processes; decentralisation and citizen participation (Weiss 2000). Political theorist John Dunn provides a more succinct definition:

> As a concept good government is holistic and consequentialist rather than specific or procedural. It implies, *ceteris paribus*, and in relation to the policies that it actually pursues, a high level of organisational effectiveness; but it certainly does not imply the choice of a particular ideological model of state organisation ... Good government is best defined ostensively rather than by semantic prescription. It is what Sweden and Singapore enjoy, and what Zaire and Ethiopia distressingly lack (Dunn 1986: 169).

The analogy of country ownership to the slogan "recipient countries must be in the driver's seat" is striking in partnerships since the late 1990s (Abrahamsen 2004; Brinkerhoff 2005, 2008; Buchert 2002; Buse and Walt 1997; Jerve 2002; Mercer 2003). The "driver's seat" metaphor originated in World Bank president James D. Wolfensohn's 1997 speech in which he outlined the Bank's changes in its development approach by calling upon the need for local participation (Wolfensohn 1997).

The partnership contracts, commonly known as "Memorandums of Understanding" and "Codes of Conduct", repeatedly emphasise the ownership principle. However, in my experience, reaching such agreements are highly time consuming processes that precisely hinge on issues of power, trust and distrust, misunderstanding and mistranslation, and ultimately the "too many cooks are going to spoil the broth" phenomenon. It is common to see a memorandum between a government and its partners, for example "Irish Embassy; DFID; The Government of the Kingdom of Norway; European Commission; Swiss Agency for Development and Co-operation; Ministry for Foreign Affairs of Finland; Danish Embassy; The Netherlands Embassy; Canadian International Development Agency". Local governments are *assumed* to be in the driver's seat, while partners are *assumed* to act in the interest of local governments, to cooperate rather than compete, to listen rather than direct (Buchert 2002: 76). As a Mozambican citizen explained, "you can never feel comfortable in a borrowed suit. There will always be conditions attached to such a loan and this is the problem with ownership. It is not *my* suit. I want my own."

6. Discussion: Sovereignty, Diplomacy and Solidarity

> *"Countries do not have the time to get organized: they hear about 'UNGASS', '3 by 5', 'Universal Access'. This creates such confusion for the man on the ground. He doesn't know what to do. There is no time for us to learn. People don't know how to differentiate one thing from another. It is not people's language. How can I stuff my stomach with UNGASS? How can I improve my life? These guidelines don't exist."*
>
> Advocacy Officer, Mozambique

This chapter has discussed some of the most delicate issues how to engage in partnerships with fragile and failed states in sub-Saharan Africa. The diversity of how and why states fail and become fragile is the most striking feature of this analysis. "Difficult partnership" countries are indeed difficult and there are no easy solutions. We know this from Somalia, Sudan and the Democratic Republic of Congo. As Collier reminds us, the traps of conflict, the unused potential of natural resources, being landlocked and bad governance keep the "bottom billion" down (Collier 2008). There is much concern for global provision of public goods, including, as we have seen, global health. However, the issues discussed here, sovereignty and state failure in particular, make such ambition difficult to realise.

The basic tenet reading the statements by Mozambicans throughout this chapter concerns the need for comprehensive partnerships that look beyond health. In fact, this remains enshrined in the goals for development in the new millennium and normatively in the right to health as an inclusive right. The right to health covers health care and those circumstances necessary to maintain health, such as access to water, sanitation, food, nutrition, housing, working conditions, a healthy environment and access to education and information related to health (United Nations 2000a).

The diversity of state failure at the minimum calls for unique localised negotiations to establish strong partnerships. Reading Patrick Chabal, Alex de Waal and Paul Collier (Chabal 2002; Collier 2009; de Waal 2002), they following themes related to political change and governance history remain relevant at the end of this decade for the future of partnerships:

Historical factors: Look into the reasons that have previously prevented development.

Good governance: Critical evaluation of the "new set of circumstances" for the exercise of power.

Ownership: Analyse how the reform agenda is driven by internal and external factors.

Democratisation: Consider the ways in which political competition in emerging multi-party states enhances or worsens accountability and good governance.

Participation: Examine the ways by which the new partnerships embrace or exclude popular inclusion.

Sovereignty: Respect recipient government priorities.

Sovereignty: Look into the implications of shared sovereignty.

Sovereignty: Consider the possibility of temporarily limited sovereignty of post-conflict governments.

Partnerships for health are combined human rights and public health issues. The main policy implication of this analysis is, therefore, to recommend fortifying partnerships that seek to build the foundations of a society. The most basic task for health partnerships will be to insist on comprehensive preventive public health provision: water, sanitation and proper housing to protect against vector borne diseases. The next step is to continue to strengthen local health systems to improve curative health. The factors that influence international partnerships discussed here provide the challenges for the diplomacy and implementation of global health governance that extends beyond the sovereign nation-state.

Chapter 14 further assesses questions of AIDS exceptionalism raised in this chapter

References

Abrahamsen R (2004) "The Power of Partnerships in Global Governance," *Third World Quarterly* 25(8):1453–67.

Adams V, Novotny TE, Leslie H (2008) Global Health Diplomacy. *Medical Anthropology* 27(4):315–23.

Agamben G (1998) *Homo Sacer: Sovereign Power and Bare Life*. Stanford: Stanford University Press.

Barnett T, Dutta I (2007) *HIV and Fragility: Is HIV a Security Risk?* P. 18.

Barnett T, Prins G (2006) "HIV/AIDS and Security: Fact, Fiction and Evidence — a Report to UNAIDS", *International Affairs* 82(1):1–19.

Brinkerhoff DW (2005) "Rebuilding Governance in Failed States and Post-Conflict Societies: Core Concepts and Cross-cutting Themes," *Public Administration and Development* 25(1):3–14.

——— (2008) "The State and International Development Management: Shifting tides, Changing Boundaries, and Future Directions," *Public Administration Review* 68(6):985–1001.

Brinkerhoff, JM (2002) "Government-Nonprofit Partnership: A Defining Framework," *Public Administration and Development* 22(1):19–30.

Brown TM, Cueto M, Fee E (2006) "The World Health Organization and the Transition from International to Global public Health," *American Journal of Public Health* 96(1):62–72.

Buchert L (2002) "Towards New Partnerships in Sector-Wide Approaches: comparative Experiences from Burkina Faso, Ghana and Mozambique," *International Journal of Educational Development* 22(1):69–84.

Buse K, Walt G (1997) "An Unruly Melange? Coordinating External Resources to the Health Sector: A Review," *Social Science & Medicine* 45(3): 449–63.

——— (2000a) "Global Public-Private Partnerships: Part I — A New Development in health?" *Bulletin of the World Health Organization* 78:549–61.

——— (2000b) "Global Public-Private Partnerships: Part II — What are the Health Issues for Global Governance?" *Bulletin of the World Health Organization* 78:699–709.

——— (2002) The World Health Organization and Global Public-Private Health Partnerships: In Search of "Good" Global Governance. In *Public-Private Partnerships for Public Health*. M.R. Reich, ed. pp. 169–196. Harvard Series on Population and International Health. Cambridge: Harvard Center for Population and Development Studies, Harvard University Press.

Chabal P (2002) "The Quest for Good Government and Development in Africa: is NEPAD the Answer?" *International Affairs* 78(3):447–+.

Chaffard G (1965) *Les Carnets Secrets de la Décolonisation, II*. Volume 2. Paris: Calmann-Lévy.

Cheru F (2001) The highly indebted poor countries (HIPC) initiative: A human rights assessment of the Poverty Reduction Strategy Papers (PRSP). Geneva. United Nations Economic and Social Council. Electronic document. Available at http://www.unhchr.ch/Huridocda/Huridoca.nsf/e06a5300f90fa0238025668700518ca4/d3b348546ad5fb91c1256a110056aca4/$FILE/G0110184.pdf[Accessed 7 October 2009].

Collier P (2008) *The Bottom Billion: Why the Poorest Countries Are Failing and What Can Be Done About It*. Oxford: Oxford University Press.

——— (2009) "The Political Economy of State Failure", *Oxford Review of Economic Policy* 25(2):219–40.

Collier P, Hoeffler A (2004) "Aid, Policy and Growth in Post-Conflict Societies", *European Economic Review* 48(5):1125–45.

de Waal A (2002) "What's New in the 'New Partnership for Africa's Development'?" *International Affairs* 78(3):463–75.

——— (2009) "Mission Without End? Peacekeeping in the African Political Marketplace", *International Affairs* 85(1):99–113.

Donovan *et al.* (2005) “Emergency Needs Assessment and the impact of food aid on local markets”, MSU study for World Food Program, Rome.

Dunn J (1986) The politics of representation and good government in post-colonial Africa. In *Political Domination in Africa: Reflection on the Limits of Power*. P. Chabal, ed. Pp. 158–74. Cambridge: Cambridge University Press.

Elbe S (2005) “AIDS, Security, Biopolitics”, *International Relations* 19(4):403–19.

——— (2006) “Should HIV/AIDS be Securitized? The Ethical Dilemmas of Linking HIV/AIDS and Security”, *International Studies Quarterly* 50:119–44.

Fielding D, Mavrotas G (2008) “Aid Volatility and Donor-Recipient Characteristics in ‘Difficult Partnership Countries’”, *Economica* 75(299):481–94.

Foucault M (1981) *The History of Sexuality, 1. An introduction*. Harmondsworth: Penguin.

——— (2003) *Society Must Be Defended. Lectures at the Collège de France, 1975–76*. D. Macey, transl. London: Penguin Books.

G8 (2005) Gleneagles Communiqué. London. Electronic document.Available at http://www.unglobalcompact.org/docs/about_the_gc/government_support/PostG8_Gleneagles_Communique.pdf[Accessed 7 October 2009].

Garrett L (2005) HIV and National Security: Where are the Links? A Council on Foreign Relations Report. New York. Council on Foreign Relations. Electronic document.Available at http://www.cfr.org/content/publications/attachments/HIV_National_Security.pdf[Accessed 7 October 2009].

Ghani A, Lockhart C (2008) *Fixing Failed States. A Framework for Rebuilding A Fractured World*. Oxford: Oxford University Press.

Heller PS (2005) Understanding Fiscal Space. IMF Policy Discussion Paper. Washington DC. International Monetary Fund. Electronic document. Available at http://www.imf.org/external/pubs/ft/pdp/2005/pdp04.pdf [Accessed 7 October 2009].

Høg E (2008a) The Process: Experiences, Limitations, and Politics of ARV Treatment in Mozambique. Ph.D. dissertation, LSE Health, Department of Social Policy, London School of Economics and Political Science.

——— (2008b) States of HIV Fragility: Capacity, Vulnerabilities, and Epidemic Evolution in Mozambique. ASCI Research Report No. 11, April 2008, AIDS, Security and Conflict Initiative, HIV/AIDS, Fragile and Crisis States, Social Science Research Council, New York & Clingendael Institute, the Hague. New York. Electronic document.Available at http://asci.researchhub.ssrc.org [Accessed 7 October 2009].

ICC (2009) Situation in Dafur, Sudan in the Case of the Prosecutor vs. Omar Hassan Ahmad Al Bashir ("Omar Al Bashir"). The Hague. International Criminal Court. Electronic document.Available at http://www.icc-cpi.int/iccdocs/doc/doc639078.pdf[Accessed 6 October 2009].

Ikpe E (2007) "Challenging the Discourse on Fragile States," *Conflict, Security & Development* 7(1):85–124.

Ingram A (2007) "HIV/AIDS, Security and the Geopolitics of US-Nigerian Relations," *Review of International Political Economy* 14(3):510–34.

Jerve AM (2002) "Ownership and Partnership: Does the New Rhetoric Solve the Incentive Problems in Aid?" *Forum for Development Studies* 2(29):389–07.

Johnson H, Wilson G (2006) "North-South/South-North Partnerships: Closing the 'Mutuality Gap,'" *Public Administration and Development* 26(1):71–80.

Jones S, Riddell R, Kotoglou K (2005) Aid Allocation Criteria: Managing for Development Results and Difficult Partnerships. Oxford Policy Management. Electronic document.Available at http://www.opml.co.uk/publications/client_reports/aid_allocation_c.html[Accessed 28 September 2009].

Keohane RO (2002) Global Governance and Democratic Accountability. London. Miliband Lectures, London School of Economics & Political Science. Electronic document.Available at http://www2.lse.ac.uk/publicEvents/events/2002/20020321t1112z001.aspx[Accessed 22 September 2009].

Levin V, Dollar D (2005). The Forgotten States: Aid Volumes and Volatility in Difficult Partnership Countries (1992–2002). DAC Learning And Advisory Process On Difficult Partnerships. Electronic document.Available at http://siteresources.worldbank.org/INTLICUSSPANISH/Resources/34687926.pdf[Accessed 7 October 2009].

Lieberman ES (2009) *Boundaries of Contagion: How Ethnic Politics Have Shaped Government Response to AIDS*. Woodstock, Oxfordshire: Princeton University Press.

Macfarlane SB, Jacobs M, Kaaya EE (2008) "In the Name of Global Health: Trends in Academic Institutions," *Journal of Public Health Policy* 29(4):383–401.

McGillivray M (2005) Aid Allocation and Fragile States. Electronic document.Available at http://www.wider.unu.edu/publications/working-papers/discussion-papers/2006/en_GB/dp2006-01/_files/ 78091766212527657/default/dp2006-01.pdf[Accessed 7 October 2009].

McGillivray M, Feeny S (2008) Aid and Growth in Fragile States. Unu-Wider. United Nations University, World Institute for Development Economics Research. Electronic document.Available at http://www.wider.unu.edu/publications/working-papers/research-papers/2008/en_GB/rp2008-03/[Accessed 5 October 2009].

Mercer C (2003) "Performing Partnership: Civil Society and the Illusions of Good Governance in Tanzania," *Political Geography* 22:741–63.

Nguyen V-K (2009) "Government-by-Exception: Enrolment and Experimentality in Mass HIV Treatment Programmes in Africa," *Social Theory & Health* 7:196–217.

OECD (2005) Paris Declaration on Aid Effectiveness. Ownership, Harmonisation, Alignment, Results and Mutual Accountability. Joint Progress toward Enhanced Aid Effectiveness: Harmonization, Alignmnet, Results. High Level Forum, Paris, 2005, p. 12.

——— (2007) Ensuring Fragile States Are Not Left Behind. Factsheets. Electronic document.Available at http://www.oecd.org/dataoecd/34/24/40090369.pdf[Accessed 28 September 2009].

——— (2008) Monitoring Resource Flows to Fragile States: 2007 Report. Resource Flows to Fragile States. Paris. Organisation for Economic Co-operation and Development, OECD. Electronic document.Available at http://www.oecd.org/dataoecd/4/21/41680220.pdf[Accessed 28 September 2009].

Ooms G (2006) "Health Development Versus Medical Relief: The Illusion Versus the Irrelevance of Sustainability," *PLoS Medicine* 3(8):e345.

——— (2008) The right to health and the sustainability of healthcare: Why a new global health aid paradigm is needed. Ph.D. dissertation, Ghent University.

Ooms G, Schrecker T (2005) "Expenditure Ceilings, Multilateral Financial Institutions, and the Health of Poor Populations," *Lancet* 365:1821–23.

Patrick S (2006) "Weak States and Global Threats: Fact or Fiction?" *Washington Quarterly* 29(2):27–53.

Pearson LB (1969) *Partners in Development: Report of the Commission on International Development*. New York: Praeger Publishers.

Pfeiffer J, Nichter M (2008) "What Can Critical Medical Anthropology Contribute to Global Health?" *Medical Anthropology Quarterly* 22(4):410–15.

Price-Smith AT (2002) *The Health of Nations. Infectious Disease, Environmental Change, and Their Effects on National Security and Development*. Cambridge, Massachusetts: The MIT Press.

Prins G (2004) "AIDS and Global Security," *International Affairs* 80(5):931–+.

Schmidt R (2002) Ownership and Partnership in Africa's Development Strategy. Ottawa. The North-South Institute. Electronic document.Available at http://www.nsi-ins.ca/english/pdf/nsi_g8_briefing.pdf[Accessed 28 September 2009].

The Fund for Peace (2007) The Fund for Peace Failed States Index 2007. The Fund for Peace. Electronic document.Available at http://www.fundforpeace.org/web/index.php?option=com_content&task=view&id=229&Itemid=366 [Accessed 7 October 2009].

——— (2008) The Fund for Peace Failed States Index 2008. The Fund for Peace. Electronic document.Available at http://www.fundforpeace.org/web/index.php?option=com_content&task=view&id=292&Itemid=452[Accessed 7 October 2009].

——— (2009a) "The Failed States Index," *Foreign Policy* (173):80–3.

——— (2009b) The Fund for Peace Failed States Index 2009. The Fund for Peace. Electronic document.Available at http://www.fundforpeace.org/web/index.php?option=com_content&task=view&id=391&Itemid=549[Accessed 7 October 2009].

Transparency International (2008) Transparency International Corruption Perceptions Index 2008. Berlin. Transparency International. Electronic document.Available at http://www.transparency.org/policy_research/surveys_indices/cpi/2008[Accessed 7 October 2009].

United Nations (2000a) The right to the highest attainable standard of health: CESCR General Comment 14. New York. United Nations, Economic and Social Council. Electronic document.Available at http://www.unhcr.org/cgi-bin/texis/vtx/refworld/rwmain?docid=4538838d0&page=search[Accessed 7 October 2009].

——— (2000b) United Nations Millennium Declaration. New York. United Nations General Assembly. Electronic document.Available at http://www.un.org/millennium/declaration/ares552e.pdf[Accessed 14 September 2009].

——— (2009) The Millennium Development Goals Report. New York. United Nations. Electronic document.Available at http://www.un.org/millenniumgoals/pdf/MDG%20Report%202009%20ENG.pdf[Accessed 14 September 2009].

Weiss TG (2000) "Governance, Good Governance and Global Governance: Conceptual and Actual Challenges", *Third World Quarterly* 21(5):795–14.

WHO (2005a) Building Stronger Health Systems Key to Reaching the Health Millennium Development Goals. World Health Organization. Electronic document.Available at http://www.who.int/mediacentre/news/releases/2005/pr35/en/print.html[Accessed 7 October 2009].

——— (2005b) Health and the Millennium Development Goals. World Health Organization. Electronic document.Available at http://www.who.int/mdg/publications/mdg_report/en/[Accessed 7 October 2009].

——— (2006) The World Health Report 2006: Working together for Health. Geneva. World Health Organization. Electronic document.Available at http://www.who.int/whr/2006/en/[Accessed 7 October 2009].

Wolfensohn JD (1997) The Challenge of Inclusion: 1997 Annual Meetings Address. Hong Kong. World Bank. Electronic document.Available at http://go.worldbank.org/CW114BRXH0[Accessed 6 October 2009].

World Bank (2002) World Bank Group Work in Low-Income Countries under Stress: A Task Force Report. Washington. World Bank Independent Evaluation Group. Electronic document.Available at http://go.worldbank.org/KBS5WOCE60[Accessed 7 October 2009].

World Bank, Independent Evaluation Group (2006) Engaging with Fragile States. An IEG Review of World Bank Support to Low-Income Countries Under Stress. Washington. World Bank Independent Evaluation Group. Electronic document.Available at http://www.worldbank.org/ieg/licus/download.html [Accessed 29 September 2009], World Bank, Washington.

Additional Sources

Addressing Situations of Fragility, European Commission
http://ec.europa.eu/development/policies/9interventionareas/governance/fragile_states_en.cfm

Center for Global Development, Washington
http://www.cgdev.org/section/topics/fragile_states

Conflict and Fragility, OECD
http://www.oecd.org/dac/fragilestates

Corruption Perceptions Index, Transparency International
http://www.transparency.org/policy_research/surveys_indices/cpi

Crisis States Research Programme, London School of Economics & Political Science
http://www.crisisstates.com

Failed States Index, The Fund for Peace
http://www.fundforpeace.org/web/index.php?option=com_content&task=view&id=391&Itemid=549

Fragile States, DFID
http://www.dfid.gov.uk/Global-Issues/How-we-fight-Poverty/Government/Fragile-States

Fragility and Conflict, World Bank
http://go.worldbank.org/VG5203PSD0

Health and Fragile States, Eldis
http://www.eldis.org/go/topics/dossiers/health-and-fragile-states

Health and Fragile States Network
http://www.healthandfragilestates.org

High-Level Forum on the Health MDGs
http://www.hlfhealthmdgs.org

Low-Income Countries Under Stress, LICUS, World Bank
http://www.worldbank.org/ieg/licus

Political Instability Task Force, PITF
http://globalpolicy.gmu.edu/pitf

Principles for Good International Engagement in Fragile States, OECD
http://www.oecd.org/fsprinciples

20

Health Communities: Social Capital and Effective Partnerships – Building on Community Responses

Daniel Low-Beer

Summary

Most work on health partnership has been concerned with global and national coordination; this chapter starts with community responses. It argues that successful HIV prevention has occurred where health partnerships and programmes have built on community responses. This is because the majority of the resources needed for HIV prevention reside in social networks, as social capital. The chapter focusses on AIDS but assesses the general importance of mobilising community responses for health. The critical resources to achieve health outcomes are often not financial but occur in communities, villages, workplaces and populations at risk, and we need to mobilise responses in these contexts. Many innovative health partnerships include an important new mix of partners which could mobilise such a wider response. The challenge is to leverage this innovative mix of partners in programmes to reach into communities, workplaces, and most at risk populations. New approaches to health diplomacy are required, focussed on engaging village meetings as much as high-level coordination meetings. As with the growing understanding of aid and development, health partnerships need to leverage a much greater source of resources than their own finances to deliver desired health outcomes.

1. Introduction

In 1981, in New York and San Francisco, gay men began to notice a new condition was appearing in their community. Already as it was diagnosed in teaching hospitals, communications on AIDS were spreading rapidly through gay networks. Mobilisation of these networks initiated care, support and community responses (like the Gay Men's Health Crisis established in January 1982). As formal public health projects were established, risk and behavioural patterns were changing, and declines in HIV incidence occurred first in white, and then in black and Hispanic gay men (Low-Beer and Stoneburner 2003; Stoneburner *et al.* 1996; Low-Beer and Sempala 2010).

At the same time, on the banks of Lake Victoria, Ugandans identified and started talking about a new disease. They gave it the evocative name "SLIM," communicating more than the split acronym HIV/AIDS used later and elsewhere. In 1983, SLIM was "discovered" by epidemiologists in these Ugandan villages (Serwadda *et al.* 1985) and by the government who initiated its HIV programme as early as 1986 (Iliffe 1998). Yet in this very different setting, similar community responses were already developing, changing communications, behaviours and the epidemiology of HIV (Figure 1).

As the village chief told me, they talked very directly about SLIM in village meetings, households and bars. They discussed openly how it spread — and how to respond — and they organised care networks for young people, the dying and orphans (later formalised into the AIDS Support Organisation, TASO). What disturbed the village chief most was that SLIM went against nature: the elders were caring for the young who should not die first. By the time, medical and development projects moved into these districts in Southern Uganda, HIV incidence had declined by 50%. These initial community responses had a greater impact than

(a)

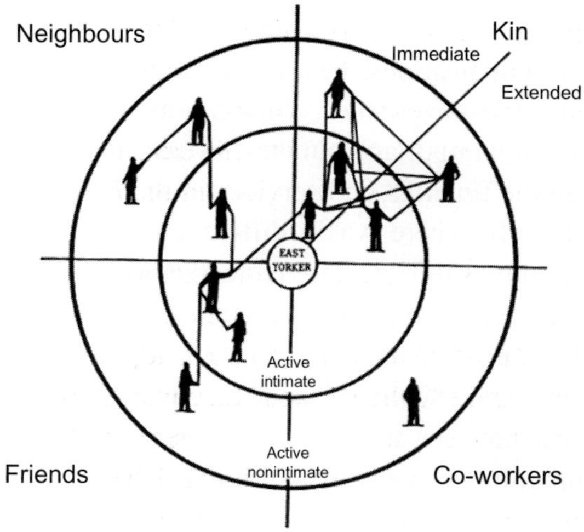

(b)

Figure 1. Uganda villages by Lake Victoria where "SLIM" was first identified by communities and their responses developed (a). Illustrative social network from the East York community, Toronto (b).
Source: adapted from Wellman (1979).

subsequent health programmes, as shown by two decades of randomised control trials (Low-Beer and Stoneburner 2004).

While most work on health partnerships and governance has been concerned with global and national coordination, this chapter starts with community responses (Buse *et al.* 2009; Roseneau 1995; Lee 2003; Burris *et al.* 2005). It argues that successful HIV prevention has occurred where health governance and programmes have built on community responses. The chapter provides examples where such success has been achieved and HIV prevention has been amplified. It compares to situations where coordination between HIV programmes and community responses has not occurred, and relatively fragile community responses have often been confused and smothered. In these situations, despite the delivery of financial and technical resources, HIV prevention has been much less successful. The chapter also assesses the barriers to leverage social capital and community responses missing in many HIV prevention responses.

First, community responses precede many health programmes, and with AIDS they named, diagnosed and organised the most effective HIV prevention responses seen so far. Community responses have a primary role in health communications, behaviours and outcomes — and, therefore, partnerships and governance. This is not to say that formal health programmes were not important, but they leveraged and built on resources much wider than the finances and services in their programmes that they could deliver directly. There was a different intensity to effective HIV prevention programmes in Uganda, Thailand, Cambodia, Kenya and New York and San Francisco, which partnered and went deeper into communities in very different contexts. They had a deliberate and central public health strategy to engage with and mobilise communities. This innovative health partnership between the vertical delivery of programmes and the horizontal community response was critical to HIV prevention success (and defined its limits, for example, compared with modest progress in Thailand among drug users and gay men, in the USA with Hispanic and black gay men, and in Uganda over time as the community response was not renewed).

Second, the chapter is focussed on AIDS but assesses the general importance of mobilising community responses for health partnerships. To achieve many health outcomes, partnerships need to work through social capital, as well as coordinate finances and programmes. These resources reside in social networks and are mobilised not delivered directly as health services. This level of agency is critical to health outcomes — for chronic conditions such as smoking, diabetes, heart disease and road accidents as well as infectious diseases such as HIV, TB and malaria (Wilkinson 1996;

Radelet 2004). Health outcomes are determined in communities, bars, villages, bedrooms as importantly as in clinics, and we need to mobilise resources in these contexts to tackle health risks. Health governance and programmes can play a critical role as they can engage the population and community response. Yet community responses are also fragile. They are easily confused with misinformation, marginalised politically or diverted with technical solutions to behavioural issues. Similar to the growing understanding of aid and development, many health programmes need to leverage a much greater source of capital than their own to deliver health outcomes.

Finally, this chapter argues that an important test of innovative partnerships and health diplomacy is beyond international meetings and national strategies but in communities. Coordination mechanisms and health diplomacy need to engage with resources that go deep into communities and social networks. There should be a greater focus on mobilising and aligning the last 10 metres of the health response, which engages the community networks, social behaviours and situations where health risks occur. Many innovative health partnerships include an important new mix of partners in their governance at global and national level. The potential is to leverage these partners in programme implementation to reach into communities, workplaces and most at risk populations.

New approaches to health diplomacy are required, focussed on engaging village meetings as much as high-level coordination meetings. In very diverse settings, these community responses have been key to successful HIV prevention, and amplified health programmes and the uptake of services. Where they have not been mobilised, despite greater financing and technical services, progress towards health outcomes has been more limited. The chapter concludes with the challenges of including community responses and social capital as part of our approach to health partnerships, governance and diplomacy.

1.1. Innovative health partnerships for prevention: What is missing?

Health indicators in Europe, United States and Japan illustrate that health outcomes are not closely related to health spending and the delivery of services (Wilkinson 1996). This is both a limitation of health programmes and an opportunity. Health spending on its own does not buy health outcomes. However, programmes to tackle health issues such as smoking, obesity, road accidents and heart disease which leverage resources at the broad population-wide level rather than at the project level, can have significant impacts (Wilkinson 1996).

In Africa, community responses present health programmes with even more of a limitation and opportunity. First, if we compare the successes of HIV prevention in Uganda, Malawi, Rwanda, Ethiopia and Kenya to limited progress in Botswana and Southern Africa which have spent many times more on prevention projects, the limitations of health programmes and financing become apparent (Low-Beer 2003). Some have argued this is due to health systems, stage of the epidemic (in the 1990s, yet we are now 15 years on) or political leadership. No doubt these are important, but we need to take a step further into the community — the extent to which formal programmes have mobilised, aligned and not confused a community response.

There is also an opportunity — if programmes can build on the resources in African communities, HIV prevention can work in the poorest situations, with the weakest health systems and technical resources. Museveni, the president of Uganda, always fought what he called AIDISM — mocking ministers who looked only to foreign aid and programmes from outside to combat AIDS. He went around Ugandan villages, talked to leaders, churches and with cultural leaders, created a space where people could respond to what he called a fearful, "routinely avoidable disease".

Botswana provides the example of the best funded, advanced technical programme (which looks very good on PowerPoint) to fight HIV, designed with the support of McKinsey consultants and Gates. It has a multi-sectoral national aids coordination committee (established in 1999) and significant funding from the government, PEPFAR, Gates Foundation, Merck Company Foundation, and the Global Fund. It is delivered through a well-developed health system with local clinics in remote areas. When I visited the community level, everything was scaled up — all the acronyms — routine ARV treatment, PMTCT, adult and youth friendly clinics, STD treatment, VCT, even ABC (abstinence, be faithful, condom use). There were even professional community mobilisers, young professionals not linked to the community. The health governance, diplomacy and coordination to bring these services and health systems to community level were truly extra-ordinary. Yet the HIV infection rate has remained stubbornly above 20%.

Here was a remote, rural community where everything was scaled up. Yet many of the local officials I talked to were desperate, despite spending 10 times programmes such as those in Uganda since 1991. I asked the local health worker "do you talk to a patient who comes in with AIDS about AIDS, do you confront it in your community and clinic?" He said "No," as a six-week counselling course had told him not to. He had a tick box on a sheet of paper for notifiable conditions that did not include AIDS (but included leprosy and syphilis). I asked about the village chief — he does not feel qualified to talk about AIDS. I asked about the church, no one mentions it at funerals. AIDS had not gone beyond the headspace of awareness, education and counselling to a lower centre of gravity between the gut and the heart of behaviours.

What was missing in this situation? Much needed services had been delivered, but the community response had remained switched off. Coordination occurred in terms of strategies, financing, technical assistance, health systems, but programmes had not been coordinated with the community. Yet the majority of the prevention resources needed to fight AIDS came from within the community, and not from outside. The opening of social networks to AIDS was necessary for the flow of communications, behaviours and care needed to fight AIDS. Interventions which could be delivered (with finance and technical cooperation) had not as yet mobilised the basic resources in the community to fight AIDS.

2. The Role of Social Capital

Social capital is the resource that resides in social networks (Putnam 2000; Woolcock 1998). It assumes that society is built from social groups rather than just individuals, and, therefore, the agency of these groups is significant. There is an interesting analogy with traditional societies, where the basic units or tribes were often groups of 200–400 people (in hunter and gatherer societies). These social networks may still be an important intermediary level of social organisation. Between the state and the individual, they provide significant social resources for coping, caring, communications, norms, and behaviours (Figure 1).

There is a long history of social capital from sociology, economics and politics (Jacobs 1961; Wilkinson 1996; Coleman 1998; Woolcock 1998; Putnam 2000). It is recently defined by Putnam as "features of social organization, such as trust, norms and networks that can improve the efficiency of society by facilitating coordinated actions" (Putnam 2000). The strength of this definition is its focus on "coordinated actions" and the components of networks, norms and trust which facilitate such actions and create what Putnam terms "sociological glue". HIV prevention in Uganda, Thailand and the United States actively engaged with community norms and networks and the trust of community leaders, brothel owners and gay groups to facilitate "coordinated actions" between the health programme and community members.

Putnam distinguishes social capital from other forms of capital "whereas physical capital refers to physical objects and human capital refers to properties of individuals, social capital refers to connections among individuals" (Putnam 2000). For HIV, these are the connections which open up communications, negotiate behaviour norms and provide care. Coleman concludes that the working of the economy requires recognition of four types of capital: Bio-physical capital (land and the environment), financial, human and social capitals (Coleman 1998). Furthermore, social capital has a number of interesting features that distinguish it:

- It resides in groups rather than being owned by individuals.
- Stocks of social capital increase rather than decrease with use.
- Social capital is easier to destroy than create.
- It improves the functioning of human and physical capital (complementary rather than a substitute or allocative issue).
- It has intrinsic as well as instrumental values: health, education and friendship.

In terms of health programmes, it can be mobilised but not delivered in programme mode. It is complementary to other forms of capital, and can amplify the demand for and functioning of health services (as seen by the close collaboration between health departments and Gay Men's Health Crisis in the USA). Furthermore, it increases with use as shown by the development of care networks into TASO, and has intrinsic value for health, education, friendship and support. Yet, of equal importance, it is easier to destroy than create, and to exclude, marginalise and switch off social networks from important issues such as AIDS. Vibrant community networks in South Africa were confused by the mixed messages on AIDS; MSM and IDU groups in Thailand were marginalised; and the local chiefs in Botswana were excluded feeling unqualified to talk about AIDS (Low-Beer 2003).

Critics have argued that social capital is too diverse a concept and functions so differently from other forms of capital, as not to be well captured by the term (Fine 1999). Others have pointed to its perverse properties as in crime organisations, the mafia, excluding those not part of networks, and stigma in relation to AIDS (Portes and Landolt 1996). As a resource, its value depends on the uses to which it is put (and in AIDS it is often a source of stigma as well as care). Social capital has concrete relevance for AIDS in terms of support, care, demand for services and is of primary relevance if it influences communication and behaviours. A feature of successful HIV prevention is coordination, diplomacy and empowerment of social networks, in Uganda, Thailand, Kenya or the gay community in the United States social networks were switched onto AIDS. In other situations with strong social networks, for example in South Africa (which engaged with Apartheid, poverty and social communications about other risks such as crime), they were not.

3. Successful Community Responses

There have been successful community HIV prevention responses in very different settings in Africa, Asia, the USA and Australia (Low-Beer and Stoneburner 2004; Clements *et al.* 2004; Low-Beer and Sempala 2010). In these situations, HIV programmes have built on, supported and empowered this response, with very distinctive health diplomacy and programming. They have been aware that 80% of the resources for HIV prevention are in the community and 20% are financial and services brought from outside. This has not limited these programmes, but given them substantial leverage to extend to situations where health risks occur.

The important distinction is not between a bottom up community response and a top down programme delivering resources. A diagonal approach to HIV prevention has ensured services are carefully articulated with the community response, and amplifies HIV prevention. Research with Rand Stoneburner has shown a distinctive factor behind HIV prevention success — wide social communication leading to declines in risk by 65%. Where this did not occur, despite greater financing, HIV prevalence did not decline substantially until much later in the epidemic.

In each of the situations noted above where HIV prevention has been successful, there has been an intensity and directness to community mobilisation to ensure that HIV communication takes root in social networks. This has not just been national media, but conversations and diplomacy with local leaders and most at risk populations. The focus and intensity of programming in social networks have been distinctive, empowering a communication and behavioural response.

Table 1 shows the diversity and scale of HIV prevalence declines. Each situation has shown a combination of HIV prevention programmes and community responses (Low-Beer and Stoneburner 2003). How programmes were linked to and leveraged the community response through innovative partnerships was, therefore, critical. Three elements were important: (1) intense and focussed social communications on AIDS from the national level which opened up the agenda; (2) governance and partnerships which engaged systematically through social networks of local leaders, community groups and most at risk populations to leverage a wider response and (3) official recognition and local diagnosis so AIDS became an official and social fact, and care and community networks could respond. These provide only the basis for HIV prevention and services, but in most countries, they have not been put in place.

3.1 Communication and behaviour responses in Uganda

Uganda remains the best example of changes in population behaviours and communications reducing HIV. The data is relatively clear and conclusive. HIV prevalence declined nationally from 21.1% to 9.7% from 1991–1998 across 15 antenatal clinic sites, supported by trends in data from urban and rural areas, population cohorts and sentinel HIV surveillance (Stoneburner and Low-Beer 2004). These declines are repeated in other national datasets, army recruits and blood donors, as well as data from all strata of

Table 1. Epidemiological and behavioural changes in situations where HIV prevalence has declined significantly in diverse populations and stages of the epidemic.

Country	Decline (with range)		Years	Population	Indicator Used	Data
Uganda	54%	(21.1%–9.7%)	1991–1998	Antenatal clinical attendes (ANC)	HIV prevalence	Sentinel surveillance
	55%	(18%–8%)	1991–1996	Army military recruits	HIV prevalence	Sentinel surveillance
	58%	(7.6–3.2 per 1000)	1990–1998	Adults, male and female	HIV incidence	Population cohort
Kenya	38%	(16%–10%)	1997–2003	Adults	HIV prevalence	Estimated from ANC & DHS
	25%	(12%–9%)	2001–2003	ANC, urban, age 15–49	HIV prevalence	Sentinel surveillance
Rwanda	19%	(16.3%–13.2%)	1998–2003	ANC, Kigali, age 15–49	HIV prevalence	Sentinel surveillance
	39%	(9.5%–5.8%)	1998–2003	ANC, other urban, age 15–49	HIV prevalence	Sentinel surveillance
	25%	(2.8%–2.1%)	1998–2003	ANC, rural, age 15–49	HIV prevalencee	Sentinel surveillance
Ethiopia (Urban)	38%	(24.2%–15.1%)	1995–2001	ANC, urban, age 15–24	HIV prevalence	Sentinel Surveillance
	14%	(14%–12%)	2001–2003	ANC, urban, age 15–49	HIV prevalence	Sentinel Surveillance
Malawi (Urban)	38%	(26.9%–16.7%)	1999–2003	ANC, urban, age 15–49	HIV prevalence	Sentinel Surveillance
Haiti (Urban)	45%	(5.5%–3%)	2000–2003	Women, age 15–44	HIV prevalence	Sentinel Surveillance
Thailand	88%	(4%–0.5%)	1993–2002	Male conscripts, age 21	HIV prevalence	Surveillance, male Conscripts
	56%	(28.2%–12.27%)	1996–2002	Female sex workers	HIV prevalence	Surveillance, sex workers
	45%	(2.8%–1.5%)	1995–2002	ANC, Northern and Central	HIV prevalence	Sentinel Surveillance
Cambodia	35%	(4%–2.6%)	1999–2002	Adults	HIV prevalence	Surveillance
	32%	(42.6%–28.8%)	1998–2002	Female sex workers	HIV prevalence	Surveillance, sex workers
	55%	(2%–1.9%)	1998–2006	Adults	HIV prevalence	Surveillance, modeling

(*Continued*)

Table 1. (*Continued*)

Country	Decline (with range)	Years	Population	Indicator Used	Data
			Epidemiological		
Australia	29% (194–138)	1995–1998	Homosexual men	HIV incidence	Surveillance, modeling
	8.1% per annum	1996–2000	Homosexual men, age 15–65	HIV notifications	Surveillance, HIV notifications
Zimbabwe	47% (29.3%–15.6%)	1997–2007	Women, age 15–49	HIV prevalence	Surveillance
			Behavioural		
Uganda	60% decline casual sex	1989–1995	Adults, urban and rural, age 15–55	Non-regular partners	Behavioural surveys
	62% decline casual sex	1989–1995	Men, rural, age 15–55	Non-regular partners	Behavioural surveys
	72% decline casual sex	1987–1992	Adult men, 15–49	Two or more partners	Population cohort study
Thailand	55% decline	1990–1993	Men	Men visiting sex workers	Behavioural surveys
	46% decline	1990–1993	Men	Non-regular partners	Behavioural surveys
			Behavioural		
Cambodia	58% decline	1997–2001	Police, urban	Men paying for sex	Behavioural surveys
Haiti	20% decline	1994–2000	Urban	Multiple partners	Behavioural surveys
Kenya	43% decline	1998–2003	Men	Multiple partners	Demographic Health Surveys
	50% decline	1998–2003	Women	Multiple partners	Demographic Health Surveys
Malawi	67% decline	1996–2004	Men, urban	Multiple partners	Demographic Health Surveys
Ethiopia	64% decline	2000–2005	Men, urban	Multiple partners	Demographic Health Surveys

Sources: Stoneburner and Low-Beer (2004); Clements *et al.* (2004); Commission on AIDS in Asia (2008); UNAIDS (1998); Sullivan *et al.* (2009); Bello *et al.* (2006); Hallett *et al.* (2006); Potts *et al.* (2008); Kayirangwa *et al.* (2006).

society, urban and rural. The major mechanism was a reduction in non-regular sexual partners by 60% over the period 1989–1995, and an associated contraction of sexual networks. The scale of these changes is equivalent to a "social vaccine" of 75% efficacy (Stoneburner and Low-Beer 2004).

What does it tell us about HIV prevention? First, that it can be highly successful, changing the course of an epidemic over a matter of years, even in resource poor settings. Second, it is built on behaviour changes, a response at the broad population level to the epidemic and to avoid risk. This can be supported and catalysed, but cannot be delivered as a traditional intervention. Yet how programmes leverage this population response is critical. Other interventions, for example, the demand for voluntary counselling and testing services (VCT) and care networks, are greatly enhanced if this basic population response is mobilised.

Communication is often reduced to the provision of messages, media campaigns or transferring knowledge. More fundamentally, how we talk about AIDS and people with AIDS reflects and influences how a population responds. The response in Uganda was catalysed by a distinctive communication process, discussing AIDS through social networks and knowing someone with AIDS (Low-Beer and Stoneburner 2004). Personal channels dominated for communicating about AIDS (in urban and rural areas, men and women), and there was a shift from 1989 to 1995 and from impersonal to personal channels. There was a particular and unique quality to the response and communications in Uganda: trusted conversations through personal sources, transparency to the consequences of the epidemic and attitudes of care. This was much more than a lack of stigma or just conversation, but a real and difficult involvement with AIDS and people with AIDS.

The Ugandan response was not just talk. It was a clear policy implemented with local conviction, to mobilise a community response (Low-Beer 2003). There were three direct messages: AIDS is AIDS and it is fearful; casual sex has consequences, love carefully, "zero graze"; do not point fingers, care for people with AIDS. Crucially, prevention messages were converted into social communications working through local networks of chiefs, churches, musicians and village meetings. Awareness campaigns began with the beating of a drum, the basic and traditional method of mobilising a community against imminent danger. Every politician was required to talk about AIDS when going to a community, even if the meeting was for education, economic or other issues. Museveni, the president, went around Ugandan villages, talked to leaders, churches and with cultural leaders, created a space where many individuals could respond.

Second, AIDS was notifiable, so it became a medical and social facts in communities. This allowed health personnel and communities to talk and deal with AIDS as AIDS (Low-Beer and Stoneburner 2004). AIDS became a social fact in communities and care networks developed, formalised into TASO in 1987. Prevention was expressed with genuine fear of AIDS and the feasibility of avoidance. AIDS was people in your community, fear, care and not a little stigma, it was Philly Lutaaya the musician giving his farewell concert, an army major, a priest, a friend with AIDS. The response was based on the understanding that Africans have many of the unique resources and local networks to achieve the population response, compared to the awareness and counselling services from outside.

Third, care networks supported people with AIDS and brought communities "face to face" with AIDS. The role of the AIDS support organisation (TASO) and other NGOs were essential in creating these social networks and resources for care (Kaleeba *et al.* 2000). The AIDS support organisation (TASO) was formed in 1987 by a group of 16 volunteers in Kampala, 12 of whom had HIV/AIDS. They debated hard whether or not to use the word AIDS in their name (due to stigma). In the end, they decided not to compromise on the open approach symbolised by the word "AIDS". Initially, people asked them not to park their vehicles marked with TASO on them near their houses, so as not to be associated with AIDS. However, their commitment to promote openness and "living positively with AIDS" increasingly involved people with AIDS in their communities, and mobilized social networks of support, counselling and care. They promoted "shared confidentiality," openness about HIV status with a limited circle of trusted people, opening up channels of support and care.

TASO grew rapidly, and worked in developing other NGOs. The approach of organisations such as TASO is apparent in the quality of the communication process (trusted personal communications, transparency, attitudes of care) and the basic behavioural response.

The range of behavioural responses reported by Ugandans is shown in Figure 2 (Low-Beer and Stoneburner 2004). The public health programme was focussed on going face to face with AIDS, not on a prescriptive response, either A, B or C. Stigma was also part of the response (and a key message — do not point fingers, care for people with AIDS — was critical). However, stigma could not be fully avoided, and the most dangerous situations can be where there is no stigma and no response. There were a range of responses, including condom use, sticking to one partner and stopping sex. In the Ugandan situation, sticking to one partner was the most widespread community response. Interestingly, stopping all sex was a significant response among young men (aged 15–19, the only group in which it was the predominant response) but not young women (as had been programmed and used to explain the declines by many international organisations). Starting using condoms was important among young men (though not the major response) but declined significantly with age. The direct Ugandan HIV programme was critical as it mobilised a much wider response than the resources and services it delivered.

Social networks also provide the basis for a rapid communication and behaviour response to HIV, as shown by the modelling in Figure 3. Where there is extensive openness about AIDS, over 90% of the population will have come "face to face" with AIDS before peak HIV incidence (Low-Beer and Stoneburner 2004). The response through social networks can multiply more quickly than the epidemic, as shown by the early changes in behaviours and declines in HIV prevalence in gay men in the USA, Thailand and Uganda. However, communication programmes have to take root at the level of social networks, working through local networks of meetings, chiefs, churches and community groups.

If communications in social networks are restricted, the community response can be displaced much later in the epidemic. The behavioural impact will be less significant. In the most restricted situations, even with very high HIV prevalence and mortality, a very limited number of people know someone with AIDS and go "face to face" with AIDS. Given identical epidemic conditions (HIV prevalence and mortality), over 90%, 45% or under 20% of people know someone with AIDS at peak HIV incidence, depending on the mobilisation and

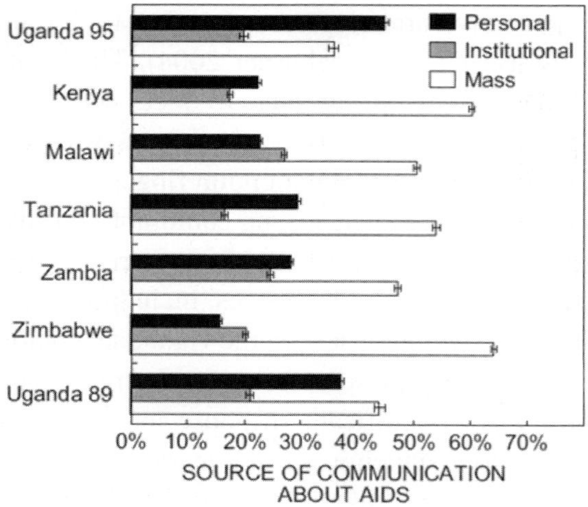

(a)

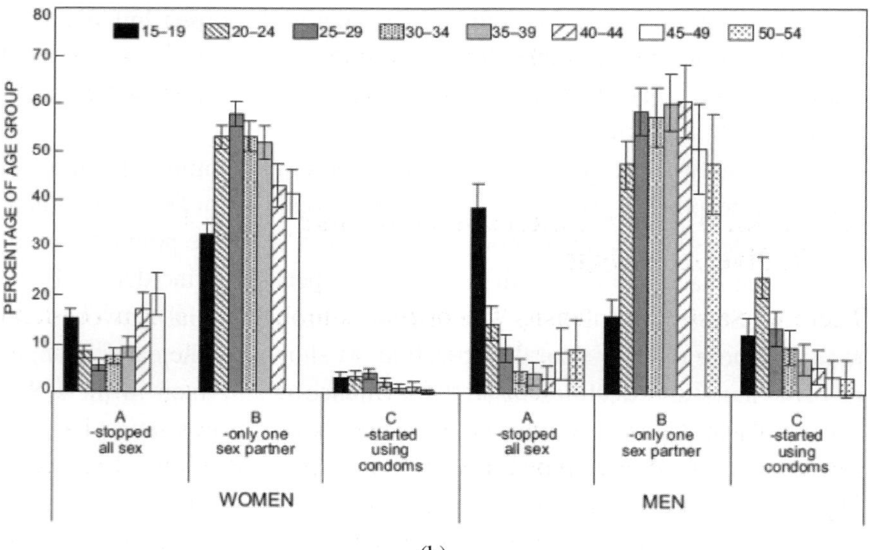

(b)

Figure 2. (a) Differences in source of communication about AIDS: classified by personal networks, institutional and mass sources. *Source*: DHS surveys in Uganda (1995); Kenya (1998); Malawi (1996); Tanzania (1996); Zambia (1996); Zimbabwe (1994); Uganda (1989) AIDS survey, WHO, 95% confidential limits shown. (b) Reported behavioural changes due to AIDS in Uganda — Self-reported response by five year age and sex, Uganda DHS 1995. *Source*: DHS survey in Uganda (1995), 95% limits shown.

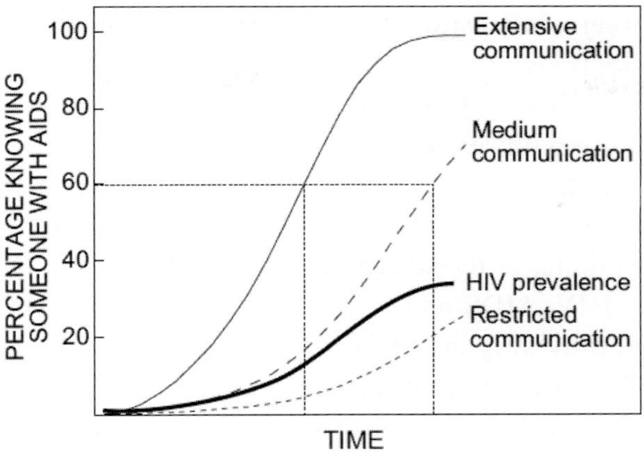

Figure 3. Modelling of communication networks and HIV prevalence.

Source: Low-Beer and Stoneburner (2004).

openness of social networks. The community response in social networks may be a necessary resource (alongside services and finance) to scale HIV prevention.

3.2 Social communication and behaviour changes in diverse settings

There was a similar intensity and openness to the response in Thailand and Cambodia. There were important programmes for delivery of services to individuals — condom distribution and testing (type 1 prevention — services to individuals) as well as interventions to mobilise a community response (type 2 prevention — population social change). Type 2 prevention was deliberately and successfully programmed where HIV prevention was successful. These included direct mobilisation of social networks — NGO outreach in factories and villages, national self-help groups of people with HIV, intensive prevention with army recruits, in private work places, and with taxi drivers in Thailand. The response was supported by widespread social communication — AIDS messages presented every hour on all the major 500 radio and 7 TV stations (with hourly 15-second slots). A large range of behaviour changes occurred beyond the programme goals of 100% condom use with sex workers. Interestingly, in both countries, declining risk behaviours and infections (e.g. STI and HIV prevalence trends in Thailand) preceded the high-level coverage of discrete interventions (for example, condom use with sex workers) (see Figure 4).

According to surveillance data, HIV prevalence in Thailand increased rapidly in the late 1980s in quick succession among drug users, sex workers, army recruits and pregnant women (Mason *et al.* 1995). Early HIV, AIDS and behavioural surveillance were central to the response, providing information politically and publicly. In particular, the 1990 national behaviour survey showed 22% of men visited sex workers and 28% had non-regular partners, resulting in extensive public, media (and probably domestic) debate. Detailed Thai data (HIV surveillance data, army cohort data and repeated behavioural surveys) show that from 1990 to 1993, there was a wide range of reported behaviour changes far exceeding the policy interventions to which the success is attributed. The programme worked carefully with the networks related to sex workers, including brothel owners, taxi drivers and clients themselves. The focus and intensity of the programme helped support increasingly consistent condom use with sex workers during this period.

There was an equally important population response, with visits by men to sex workers decreasing by 55%, and any non-regular partners decreasing from 28% to 15% in repeated national surveys from 1990 to 1993. The much publicised graph showing declines in STD rates and success of the "100% condom policy," actually confirms the importance of the wider social response. The initial rapid declines in STD rates occur when condom use with clients was too low to explain them (20–40%, when much higher levels of consistent use were shown to be needed for protection (Low-Beer and Stoneburner 2004)). In addition, the declines occur early on. STD rates had already declined 50% before condom use reached 50% (see Figure 4). This suggests that social changes in key populations may be catalysed early and account for the initial 50% decline in risk behaviours (although they are certainly sustained as health programmes are delivered which build on this response). These population responses precede and exceed the aims of health programmes, for example Thailand's "100% condom use

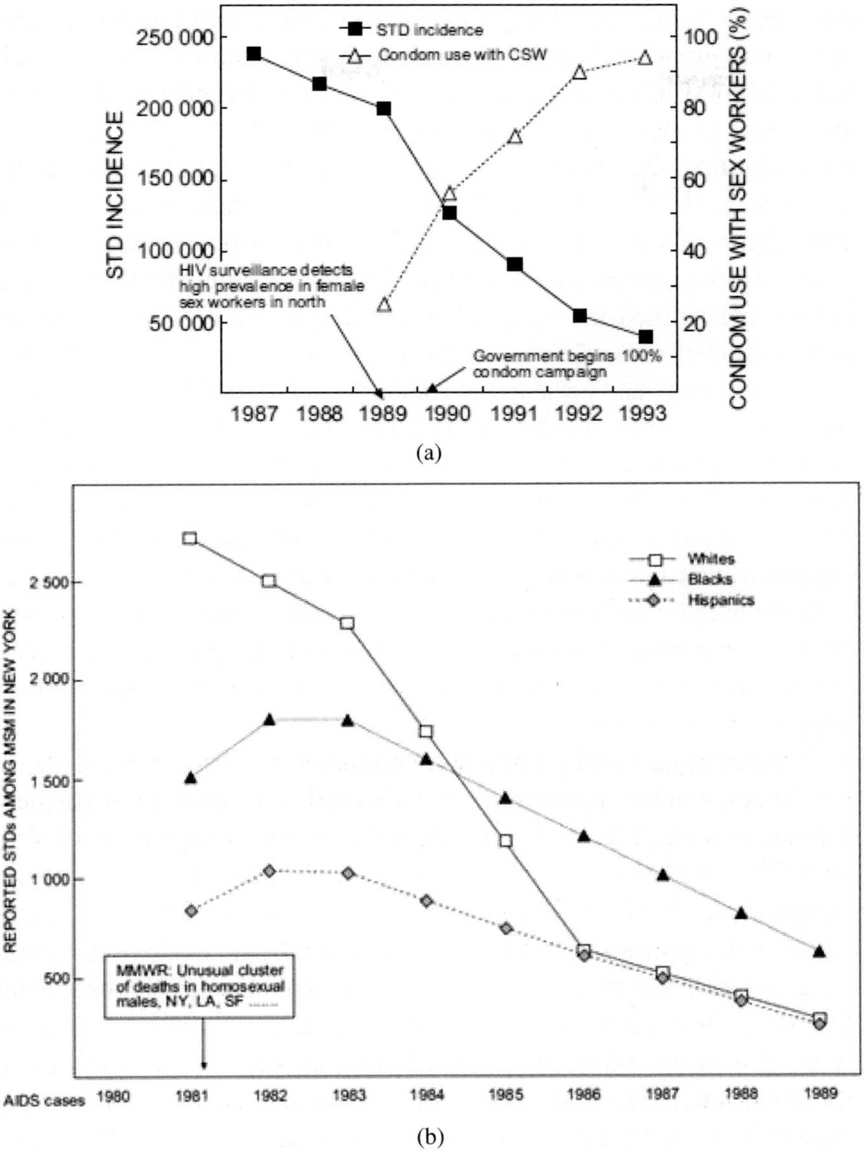

Figure 4. (a) Thailand: trends in reported STDs and condom use among sex workers among Thai males, 1987–1993. *Source*: All reported STDs at government clinics, Thai ministry of public health, VD division. (b) White, black and hispanic gay males in New York city. Changes in HIV prevalence among MSM in New York city.

Source: Stoneburner *et al*. (1996); Low-Beer and Stoneburner (2004).

programme". Similarly, in Cambodia, HIV prevention combined services to individuals and social change at population level (Low-Beer and Sempala 2010; Commission on AIDS in Asia 2008). There was a distinctive focus on social communication from 1998 across all radio and TV stations, and working through over 90 NGOs among street children, the military, men who have sex with men, injecting drug users and over 400 support groups for HIV-positive people. In both situations, governance ensured vertical social communication to ensure AIDS was on the agenda and worked through horizontal social networks of community groups, brothel owners, taxi drivers and NGOs.

A community and behavioural response which preceded and exceeded health programmes is also apparent in a very different setting, the gay community in the USA (Stoneburner *et al.* 1993). Public health programmes were crucial in providing initial information, but only went so far. However, public health departments worked very quickly to coordinate communication and support through gay community organisations. In New York, the Public Health Department provided an early sub-contract with the gay men's health crisis (GMHC) to ensure health prevention information entered into social networks, with credibility and connections inaccessible to government. This gave them the critical last 10 metres to their interventions to ensure they were present where HIV was.

The community response was spearheaded by community organisations such as the GMHC, which was established in January 1982, two years before HIV was identified as the cause of AIDS, by eighty men who gathered in a New York apartment. GMHC provided a crisis counselling hotline initially from a home telephone number, legal aid, volunteers, buddy systems and social workers. Coordinating closely with the health department it was able to provide community communications reaching out personally to 15,000 gay men, and through activities in community sites to many more. One of the founding members who left in 1983 formed ACT UP which subsequently had a wide political impact in the USA and internationally. By 1984, the Centers for Disease Control (CDC) had requested GMHC assistance in delivering HIV prevention, as had the New York Public Health Department. The close coordination between public health programmes and community groups was essential for the wider community response.

Already as more formal public health projects were established, risk and behavioural patterns were changing, and declines in HIV incidence occurred first in white, then in black and then in Hispanic gay men (Martin 1987; Van Griensven 1989; Torian *et al.* 1996). Some have argued that as the medical and financial responses have intensified from the 1990s, the community response has not been maintained, and increases in HIV incidence in young cohorts have occurred (Sullivan *et al.* 2009). A social communication process preceding and exceeding formal interventions, spread rapidly through gay social networks. However, this community response did not extend to the same extent to black and Hispanic gays, with both a lag in declines in biological markers in these groups and smaller overall HIV prevalence declines (Martin 1987; Van Griensven *et al.* 1989; Torian *et al.* 1996).

There is evidence of a similar community communication and behaviour response in other less well-documented examples of HIV prevalence declines. In urban Malawi, recent declines in HIV prevalence from 27% to 17% have been associated with reduction in risk behaviours by two thirds (Bello *et al.* 2006). In Kenya, HIV prevalence declined from 16% to 10% from 1997–2000 associated with similar declines in risk behaviours (Hallett *et al.* 2006; Potts *et al.* 2008). This coincided with a significant governance change to the programme in 1999 to link it to the community response. Parliamentarians realised that the AIDS programme was not working and organised an emergency parliamentary session on AIDS in Mombassa. The president, who had planned to go to an international coordination meeting in Djibouti, cancelled his plans to attend at the last minute at the request of the speaker of parliament. Here, they were told that despite public health programmes AIDS required their leadership, as these programmes had not reached into schools, local meetings and communities (Low-Beer and Sempala 2010).

The politicians declared AIDS a national security emergency and communicated this nationally. Most ministers tested themselves publicly for HIV, as well as local leaders and CEOs of companies. All 221 members of parliament were also trained in AIDS information to work through local networks. Each weekend, they returned to their communities throughout Kenya and were required to talk about AIDS (similar to in Uganda), show videos and mobilise their communities. AIDS was brought into the school curriculum, recognised in communities and care organised, and STI treatment widened. In November 1999, 210 local constituency AIDS committees were established, using the MP's constituency office, but independently bringing together local leaders, schools and committees of elders to fight AIDS at community level. A whole community response was added to the AIDS programme, working through local leaders, politicians and community meetings. It shows that a response can be built in at a later stage of the epidemic, even after initial failures.

There have also been declines in HIV prevalence in Rwanda (Kayirangwa *et al.* 2006) and Ethiopian cities (Tsegaye *et al.* 2002) and in Australia MSM. Both of the African examples have had strong national AIDS programmes building on community responses and Australia in particular is a leading example of strong coordination between the health programme and most at risk populations (Kippax and Race 2003).

4. Fragile Partnerships — Switching Community Responses Off

Yet the community response can also easily be confused or switched off. In South Africa, there are powerful social networks which were mobilised against Apartheid, and where stories of crime and other community risks are discussed openly. However, the community response to AIDS has not been mobilised, and has been confused by national discussions on whether HIV causes AIDS, and the failure to diagnose AIDS medically. This is a transcript of conversations after a funeral of someone with AIDS collected with the HSRC and CADRE in South Africa as part of the Communicating AIDS Needs Project:

Social communication after a community funeral in South Africa

"Then the neighbour [T's best friend] came over as we were talking. She came asking for washing powder soap.
My mother-in-law asked her, "How did the funeral go?"
The neighbour said, "It went well."

(*Continued*)

(*Continued*)

My mother-in law asked, "What did she die from?"
The neighbour said, "She had piles."
My mother-in-law said, "Oh shame she had piles. Why didn't she consult a doctor?"
The neighbour said, "She went to the doctor but she still died."
My mother-in-law said, "Shame now who will look after the child, at least the grand mother is still alive it won't be such a big hassle."
Then the neighbour went.
That's when my mother-in-law said,
"AIDS is killing children."

Source: Communicating AIDS Needs Project, CADRE.

Although there is recognition of AIDS among the immediate family, the powerful secondary social communications around AIDS are switched off. This makes HIV prevention and the communication and behaviour adjustments much more difficult.

HIV is also not routinely reported on medical records (as was required in Uganda) and doctors use a series of terms which patients do not understand to refer to AIDS among themselves. This prevents AIDS becoming a medical and social fact within communities. The following box is a transcript from a South African clinic in a key period of HIV spread in 2001.

Communication concerning HIV reporting and diagnosis in clinics.

TLB: *How many of your patients are affected by HIV?*
IS: *About 1/3rd of patients in gastroenterology have HIV.*
TLB: *Do you talk to the patient about their condition?*
IS: *No, although both the patient and doctor may know that he or she has HIV, we do not mention it, or mark HIV on the medical records. Partly this is due to insurance but also mistrust.*
TLB: *So how do patients know what condition they have?*
IS: *Often they do not, often they do, but we don't talk about it.*

(*Continued*)

(*Continued*)

TLB: *Is there not an ethical responsibility of a doctor to talk about the patient's underlying condition with him or her?*

IS: *I suppose so, but the patients themselves don't want it in their records, and for the doctor there is so much paperwork in mentioning AIDS compared to other conditions (testing, counselling etc.), and although both know it is HIV, they do not talk about it.*

Source: Communicating AIDS Needs Project, CADRE; Soweto (2001).

The Communicating AIDS Needs project undertaken by the Centre for AIDS Research and Evaluation (CADRE) in South Africa has assessed some of the important links between health programming and community networks in more detail (Birdsall *et al.* 2007; Makhubele *et al.* 2007). In some key community settings, it shows how fragile social communications and the community response can be — it is easier to destroy than create social capital.

Table 2 illustrates the barriers to social communications and programme delivery when a gap opens between national coordination and the community response. The gap in social communications and trust is apparent in the comments that HIV prevention "is a strategy devised by the government," and that "people who are infected who go out and educate people about HIV are being bought by the government". There is a gap at provincial level which "is multi sectoral and multi departmental ... but they don't come, they don't attend those meetings (at community level) … they don't feel they have the right to stand on platforms and talk about HIV if they are the government".

The partnership gap between programmes and the community response presents serious barriers for service delivery. Some of the basic links between community communications and service outcomes are illustrated in Table 2. In these communities, HIV is generally not diagnosed "Even the doctor doesn't say he died of AIDS" nor mentioned in community events "Meningitis is used because people do die from it without having contracted HIV". Similarly, HIV prevention has many activities but lacks the intensity of effective HIV prevention programmes which have taken root at community level "One organisation is doing a lot of things within HIV but there is no intensive focus on one area".

Table 2. Selected community quotes on HIV governance and community programs.

National governance	"We even dismiss its existence by developing the myth that the people we see everyday who claim to be HIV positive are lying, and it's all a strategy devised by the government to scare people from having sex, thereby decreasing the population level." "So that myth is still dominant in the community, that the people who are infected who go out and educate people about HIV are being bought by the government ... That myth is still there, especially amongst school going youth." "You can have lots and lots of funding but if it's not servicing the people it's supposed to be servicing, then it's like throwing water into the ocean."
Local governance	"The provincial government is multi-sectoral and multi-departmental on those grounds, but they don't come, they don't attend those meetings. Even if they say they will come they change their minds at the last minute. So you start to wonder whether they really take this thing of HIV seriously... Also on a personal level maybe, they don't feel they have the right to stand in platforms and talk about HIV if they are part of the government." "The NGO coalition is busy embarking on that profile of the region, so that we know who is doing what, where, the organizations dealing with aids should have formed their consortium a long time ago ... They should have had their own big platform or common ground." "The AIDS councils it's something that comes from government. It's not because we the people involved with HIV wanted to have that in the first place."
Community events and activities	"He says because there are so many other illnesses that AIDS can come from, meningitis will be identified as the cause of death and not AIDS. Meningitis is used because people do suffer from meningitis and die from it without having contracted HIV ... I don't want to lie to you, not even once have I been to a funeral where people actually disclosed." "Her answer is that we need to focus on the issue of prevention thoroughly, because you find that one organization is doing a lot of things within HIV but there is no intensive focus on one area."
Communication programmes	"This AIDS thing is something that should take priority even on TV. I think that we should be shown so much of it that a person would rather switch off their television sets. Maybe let's say at 3pm in every channel... Now we don't really take it serious." "I think that Nkosi Johnson made a great impact. He brought great change in our communities when it comes to changing behavior (was this sustained?) not in every situation. Maybe out of ten people, four people will change their behavior while six will remain with the same attitude."
HIV testing and diagnosis	"But I had a lot of difficulties about getting tested, I won't lie. I would go to the clinic, look around and see someone I know and pretend as if I am enquiring about something important from the receptionist, then I would quickly get out of there. I would walk my girlfriend to the clinic, and while I was there I would ask about this HIV test, the nurse would explain, I would say no I have not personally come for that, I'm just accompanying the lady." "It's a rumour so to speak, because nobody has the actual testimony unless you were a close family friend. Even the doctor doesn't say he died of AIDS."
Condoms	"There are condoms and they have names or labels there is trust, lovers plus. Then a girl will tell you that she does not want you to use "Manto's condoms" .. They call them Manto's condoms because they are provided by the government and they are free, and the person who introduced them is Manto the Minister of health ... You see if she doesn't like the free ones that I have access to, then we might as well not use any."
HIV treatment and care	"You see most people don't even want to take this treatment, so then the doctors just end up dealing with just opportunistic diseases rather than the root cause of all these other diseases." "Care there is not enough and it is the major thing that is needed, their families don't help them, their parents took them here and they won't visit them again ... I do not even tell my friends I am a carer, if I told them, they would think it is a very bad thing."

Partnerships can become formal and closed. They can lack the "network governance" which reaches out to social networks and community sources of authority, to more effectively steer the HIV response. This makes HIV testing more complicated ("I would go to the clinic, see someone I know and pretend and then quickly get out of there"), free condom distribution ("a girl will tell you she does not want to use "Manto's condoms" provided by the government), and care ("I do not even tell my friends I am a carer, if I told them, they would think it is a very bad things"). As well as a primary factor in behaviours and HIV incidence, the community response is important for the basic delivery of health services.

There is a whole area of health diplomacy to better engage community leaders and networks. This is important to ensure health programmes build on and coordinate with a population response, alongside coordination of financing and programmes.

5. Conclusion — The Challenges of Building in Community Responses

Sometimes, community responses are noticeable on the ground, before you encounter them in the data. In the 1990s, when visiting Uganda, I would mention I worked in AIDS in a taxi, and there would follow a stream of opinions, stories and questions, personal ones about families and communities, sometimes outrageous even with a bit of stigma, but also a sense of reality and care. Without getting a word in edgeways, I would open the door of the taxi at my destination, already having gone face to face with the AIDS response. When I took a similar taxi ride in Kenya, and said I worked on AIDS, there would be silence and a swift change of subject. In Southern Africa, there would be questions about whether HIV causes AIDS, then silence, occasionally taking you to the side at the end of the trip to ask you what can be done for a relative who has tuberculosis. The difference in the community response was striking but not something that was often included in analysis or programmes.

This chapter has argued that health programmes need to build on community responses — which often precede and exceed their HIV prevention goals. A critical area of governance and partnership is not coordination at international and national levels, but ensuring sufficient diplomacy and connection to community responses. There has been close coordination between the vertical delivery of services and the horizontal mobilisation of social networks and community responses where HIV prevention has been successful. A similar process has occurred in very different settings in Asia,

Africa and America, and at all stages of the epidemic. This relies on the diagonal coordination of the service delivery and community responses. Where they are well articulated, HIV prevention is amplified. However, the community response can be easily confused and marginalised. This has significant implications for health governance: there is an intermediary constituency of local leaders, community groups and most at risk populations which it is important to include not just for representation but to support the basic effectiveness of health programmes.

This is both a limitation and an opportunity for health programmes. If the resources in social networks (social capital) can be mobilised, health programmes can have a much greater impact than the financial and technical resources they provide. In particular, social networks can provide the critical last 10 metres of an intervention, to ensure services, communications and support are matched with people who are most at risk. Mobilisation of this community response has been a deliberate and priority component of effective health programmes. There is an increasing danger that as we scale up treatment and prevention options, if the basic community response is not mobilised, HIV prevalence will not decline. A fundamental lesson from many HIV prevention successes, is that HIV prevention can work in the poorest situations, with the least financial and health system resources. It does require significant mobilisation of social capital.

There are several important components to mobilise these responses. However, they are not easy, and require focus, persistence and engagement to mobilise social capital to fight AIDS. First is the importance of vertical, political communications, to engage networks and open up communications, to put AIDS on the agenda. Second is the importance of engaging and working through horizontal community networks — a critical extension of any health programme. Third is the need for the persistent focus to talk about AIDS and social behaviours, not prescriptively but to address risks. Fourth, care networks are needed which provide support and draw in and involve people with HIV. There are strong links between care networks and prevention. Finally, local surveillance and analysis are needed — so the reality of AIDS is diagnosed and becomes a social fact at community level. These are not easy, packaged services, but require real engagement and mobilisation of social capital. They have been a deliberate and highly successful component of effective HIV prevention programmes. Most countries have not included these basic components of HIV prevention, and it makes the response more difficult.

There are many critiques and barriers to community approaches at country level. The chapter suggests community responses are an important constituency between the individual and state, but they often lack legitimacy and representative points of contact. In addition, community responses cannot replace the provision of essential health services, particularly for treatment. The approach here is that they are an essential component of a partnership, particularly to deliver effective HIV prevention. Social capital can also be interpreted in a static way, that some communities have more or less social capital. The approach of this chapter has been more active with a focus on how "coordinated actions" can be mobilised in very different settings. However, there are critical barriers, such as the legal status of many most at-risk populations, gender issues for young and married women, and structural migration which fragments communities in Southern Africa (Gupta *et al.* 2008). Nevertheless, community responses have occurred despite significant barriers, often in the most difficult situations. There are important recent changes over time not captured in this chapter, particularly in South Africa (Rehle *et al.* 2009). Community responses have changed with the advent of treatment and the "business of the AIDS response" focussing on delivering an increasing range of individual services. In many situations, the community response has also adapted to this role. As these interventions are scaled up, it will be particularly important that HIV programmes build in a strong community process of communication and behaviour change.

Finally, innovative health partnerships have provided a constituent role for community movements and people living with the diseases. In its first stage, this has largely been at the level of governance and coordination, in Boards and country coordinating mechanisms. The next stage is to ensure an innovative mix of implementing partners which reach into communities, workplaces, and most at risk populations. This could combine the delivery of services with the community responses needed to achieve health impact. There are many challenges — to bring together the right partners, coordinate their activities, ensure basic government and community roles are not overwhelmed, and measure community responses alongside service delivery. To accompany the focus on coordination mechanisms, new techniques of health diplomacy are required focussed on engaging community meetings as much as high-level meetings. However, in very diverse settings in Asia, Africa and America, innovative partnerships between communities and health programmes have been required to deliver effective HIV prevention and health outcomes. They have provided some of our most innovative and effective health partnerships. Our formal partnerships and health governance need to better support, mobilise and reflect these real, ground-level and innovative partnerships.

Chapter 13 assesses civil society partners more generally and Chapters 17 and 18 provide further country examples in India and Russia, respectively. The themes of the chapter are also further developed by Low-Beer and Stoneburner (2004), and in relation to AIDS governance by Low-Beer and Sempala (2010).

References

Bello G, Chipeta J, Aberle-Grasse J (2006) "Assessment of Trends in Biological and Behavioural Surveillance Data: Is There Any Evidence of Declining HIV Prevalence or Incidence in Malawi?" *Sex Trans Infect* 82:9–13.

Birdsall K, Ntlabati P, Kelly K, Banati P (2007) *Models for Funding and Coordinating Community-level Responses to HIV/AIDS*. Johannesburg, South Africa: CADRE.

Burris S, Drahos P, Shearing C (2005) "Nodal Governance," *Australian Journal of Legal Philosophy* 20:20–58.

Buse K, Hein W, Drager N eds. (2009) *Making Sense of Global Health Governance*. Basingstoke: Palgrave.

Clements M, Prestage G, Grulich A *et al.* (2004) "Modeling Trends in HIV Incidence Among Homosexual Men in Australia, 1995–2006," *JAIDS* 35:401–6.

Coleman J (1998) "Social Capital in the Creation of Human Capital," *American Journal of Sociology* 94:S95–120.

Commission on AIDS in Asia (2008) *Redefining AIDS in Asia; Crafting an Effective Response*. New Delhi: Oxford University Press.

Communicating AIDS needs Project (2001) CADRE, Johannesburg, South Africa.

Fine B (1999) "The Development State is Dead — Long Live Social Capital," *Development and Change* 30:1–19.

Gupta GR, Parkhurst JO, Ogden JA, Aggleton P, Mahal A (2008) "Structural Approaches to HIV Prevention," *Lancet* 372(9640):764–5.

Hallett T, Aberle-Grasse J, Bello G *et al*. (2006) "Declines in HIV Prevalence can be Associated with Changing Sexual Behaviour in Uganda, Urban Kenya, Zimbabwe, and Urban Haiti," *Sex Trans. Infect* 82:1–18.

Iliffe J (1998) *East African Doctors: A History of the Modern Profession*. Cambridge, UK: Cambridge University Press.

Jacobs J (1961) *The Life and Death of Great American Cities*. New York: Random House.

Kaleeba N, Kadowe J, Lalinaki D, Williams G (2000) *Open Secret, People Facing up to HIV and AIDS in Uganda*, Strategies for Hope Series No. 15. London, ACTIONAID.

Kayirangwa E, Hanson J, Munyakazi L, Kabeja A (2006) "Current Trends in Rwanda's HIV/AIDS Epidemic," *Sex Transm. Infect* 82:7–31.

Kippax S, Race K (2003) "Sustaining Safe Practice: Twenty Years on," *Social Science & Medicine* 57:1–12.

Lee K eds. (2003) *Health Impacts of Globalization: Towards Global Governance*. Basingstoke, Palgrave.

Low-Beer D, Stoneburner R (2003) "Behaviour and Communication Change in Reducing HIV: Is Uganda unique?" *African Journal of AIDS Research* 2(1):9–21.

Low-Beer D, Stoneburner R (2004) "AIDS Communications Through Social Networks: Catalyst for Behaviour Changes in Uganda," *African Journal of AIDS Research* 3(1):1–13.

Low-Beer D, Stoneburner R (2004) Uganda and the Challenge of AIDS, in Whiteside A, Poku N eds. *The Political Economy of AIDS in Africa*. Aldershot, UK: Ashgate Press.

Low-Beer D (2003) "This is a Routinely Avoidable Disease," *Financial Times*, November 28.

Low-Beer D, Sempala M (2010) "Social Capital and Effective HIV Prevention: Community Responses," *Journal of Global Health Governance* IV(1), p. 1–17, (open access).

Makhubele M, Parker W, Birdsall K (2007) *Strengthening Community Health Systems: Perceptions and Responses to Changing Community Needs.* Johannesburg, South Africa: CADRE.

Martin J (1987) "The Impact of AIDS on Gay Male Sexual Behaviour Patterns in New York City," *American Journal of Public Health* 77:578–1.

Mason C, Markowity L, Kitsiripornchai S *et al.* (1995) "Declining prevalence of HIV-1 Infection in Young Thai Men," *AIDS* 9:1061–65.

Nelson K, Celentano D (1996) "Decline in HIV Infections in Thailand," *New England Journal of Medicine* 335(26):1998–9.

Portes A, Landolt P (1996) "The Downside of Social Capital," *The American Prospect* 26:18–23.

Potts M, Halperin D, Kirby D *et al.* (2008) "Reassessing HIV Prevention," *Science* 320(5877):749–50.

Putnam R, Alone B (2000) *The Collapse and Revival of American Community.* New York: Simon and Schuster.

Radelet S (2004) "Aid Effectiveness and the Millennium Development Goals," Working Paper #39. Washington: Center for Global Development.

Rehle T, Hallett T, Shisana O *et al.* (2009) "A Decline in New HIV Infections in South Africa: Estimating HIV Incidence from Three National HIV Surveys in 2002, 2005 and 2008," *PLOS One* 5(6):1–8.

Rosenau J (1995) "Global Governance in the Twenty-First Century," *Global Governance* 1(1):13–43.

Serwadda D *et al.* (1985) "Slim Disease: A New Disease in Uganda and its Associations with HTLV-III Infection," *Lancet* 326(8460):849–2.

Stoneburner R, Low-Beer D (2004) "Population-Level HIV Declines and Behavioural Risk Avoidance in Uganda," *Science* 304:4–8.

Stoneburner R, Lessner L, Fordyce E *et al.* (1993) "Insight into the Infection Dynamics of the AIDS Epidemic: A Birth Cohort Analysis of New York City AIDS Mortality," *American Journal of Epidemiology* 138(12): 1093–2004.

Stoneburner R, Low-Beer D *et al.* (1996) "HIV Infection Dynamics in East Africa Deduced from Surveillance Data," *Am J Epidemiol.* 144(7):682–95.

Sullivan P, Hamouda O, Delpech V *et al.* (2009) "Re-emergence of the HIV Epidemic Among Men Who Have Sex with Men in North America, Europe and Australia 1996–2005," *Annals of Epidemiology* 19:423–1.

Torian LV, Weisfuse IB, Makki HA (1996) "Trends in HIV Seroprevalence in Men Who have Sex with Men: New York City Department of Health Sexually Transmitted Disease Clinics, 1988–1993," *AIDS* 10:187–2.

Tsegaye A, Rinke de Wit T, Mekonnen Y *et al.* (2002) "Decline in Prevalence of HIV-1 Infection and Syphilis Among Young Women Attending Antenatal Care Clinics in Addis Ababa, Ethiopia, 1995–2001," *JAIDS* 30:359–2.

UNAIDS (1998) *Relationships of HIV and STD Decline in Thailand to Behavioural Change*. Best Practice Series. Geneva: UNAIDS.

Van Griensven G, de Vroome E, Goudsmit J, Coutinho R (1989) "Changes in Sexual Behaviour and the Fall in Incidence of HIV Infection Among Homosexual Men," *British Medical Journal* 298:218–1.

Wellman B (1979) "The Community Question: The Intimate Networks of East Yorkers," *American Journal of Sociology* 84(5):1201–31.

Wilkinson R (1996) *Unhealthy Societies*. London: Routledge.

Woolcock M (1998) "Social Capital and Economic Development: Towards a Theoretical Synthesis and Policy Framework," *Theory and Society* 27:151–208.

Conclusions — Towards an Innovative Global Health Partnership

Daniel Low-Beer

> *"In our consultation with African leaders, Korea was reminded of the scepticism we once met from donors (on what) we proposed ... acknowledged as successes today ... we recognize that developing countries must choose their own priorities for the future. The development path we have chosen embraces complexity and hard choices."*
>
> President of South Korea, 2010, in preparation for the G20 summit

A **10-year perspective** shows the remarkable growth in global health financing and new partners. A diverse range of health constituencies have emerged, asserted themselves, and worked together in innovative partnerships. This has changed the governance of health, at global and country level. Yet they have also faced many of the traditional challenges of development, coordination, alignment with country plans and accountability for health results. This book analyses the emergence of new health partnerships, how they can work together effectively, and the implications for health governance.

A **two-year perspective** shows some of the challenges ahead. The rising curve of health and development spending has crested and broken into a severe financial crisis. There is an associated change in focus — towards the effectiveness of partnerships. Having mobilised more money for health, the focus is how to achieve among partners more health for the money. This is the challenge of the book: recommendations and actions to make innovative health partnerships more effective. They are provided from diverse perspectives, the private sector, civil society, ministers of health, multilaterals, those working in global programmes, and those working in communities delivering health services. What brings them together is the will to work together for health results.

A **six-month perspective** shows some of the conflicting trends. Their resolution will determine the key period of health progress towards the MDGs in 2015. The Global Fund for AIDS, TB and Malaria completed a largely successful replenishment of its funds at the end of 2010. It attracted commitments of US$11.7 billion over three years, an increase of 20%. Similarly, GAVI and the World Bank have undertaken replenishments of their funds. GAVI was able to fully replenish its funds in a difficult financial climate, raising US$4.3 billion from donors in June 2011. A report in September 2011, emphasised "an era of consolidation, not expansion", characterised by renewed focus on financial safeguards, value for money and sustainability (High Level Panel Independent Review, 2011). This emphasises the focus of the book on effectiveness, identified in health before the financial crisis but given impetus by it. It has not been easy to hold donors to these global health commitments over the subsequent months, as reflected in the difficult negotiations of the Global Health Initiative in the US Congress in 2011. This is most reflected in AIDS funding, where UNAIDS reported a 10% decline in 2010, with very divergent trends by donor countries (some increases but declines by 38% from Spain, 23% from Germany, and 10% from USA). However IHME suggests overall development assistance for health continued to increase in 2010 and 2011.

The **decisions made in the coming months of 2012 will be critical**. They will determine whether the MDGs can be achieved by 2015. Progress will depend on our ability to forge an innovative global health partnership to respond to global challenges. Alternatively, we will retreat into national and fragmented responses. Even if the financial crisis heightens the awareness of global challenges, the political trade-offs are very difficult. As a politician commented to me "*When you are knocking on people's doors for votes in the rain in Coventry, England, it is difficult to explain the need to increase support for global development or global action to tackle the financial crisis, when you are cutting funding in their community*." However, our ability to develop a global development partnership to tackle financial, environmental or health challenges will characterise the period 2010–2015. This is maybe why it is the final MDG, MDG 8 — a global partnership for development. Maybe MDG 8 should have been the first, but it will be a major achievement if a global partnership is an outcome of this innovative period in global health.

The last decade has seen an innovative, almost tectonic period in global health, with fissures forming in old structures and an eruption of new partners to create a new landscape of global health. The next period to 2015 will be important in how this landscape is shaped by the more gravitational forces of financing, global governance and diplomacy.

1. From Innovative Partners to an Innovative Global Partnership for Health

This conclusion looks forwards towards 2015 — to assess whether or not we can build on individual innovative partnerships to create an overall global partnership for health. This partnership will need to recognise diversity, as well as the complimentary roles of partners, traditional and new. Health partners will need to show the wider public (who does not distinguish between multilaterals, bilaterals, global programmes, foundations, health systems or diseases) that they can work as a team to tackle global challenges.

The conclusion asks three questions — what are the expectations of this partnership, what global health governance and diplomacy will support it, and how will new partners, like the G20 and South Korea, change the axis of development. South Korea moves from the first emerging country chair of the G20 in 2010, to host the high-level forum on development aid in December 2011. South Korea provides an important opportunity to refresh the global partnership and governance of aid. Development was a priority South Korea brought to the G20, as a recent recipient of aid and now a donor. South Korea reflects a new axis in development (distinct from the Paris-Accra axis of previous declarations) — including the aim for a Korean compact or refreshed development partnership.

Yet, there are just a few, brief years to 2015 when we will be held to account for the MDGs. The decisions made now will provide the momentum for the final push towards these goals. Governments have responded to the financial crisis in very different ways. Some countries have been forced to reduce spending on development aid. Others like the UK have increased aid but focussed it more carefully. They have distinguished explicitly and publicly between the effectiveness of development programmes. The review of UK multilateral aid published on 1 March 2011, based future funding on a ranking of the effectiveness of aid organisations (admittedly towards UK goals). Overall aid was increased. DFID also exited from 16 countries, 4 of the 43 international organisations it reviewed, and placed "special conditions" on a further four organisations seen as poorly performing.

In Germany, there has been a rebalancing of bilateral and multilateral aid channels. In the United States, both the domestic and development government budgets are still heavily contested. There remains uncertainty on how the proposed US$1.1 trillion general government budget cuts over 10 years will affect global development and health.

At the same time, China is increasing significantly its investments in trade, aid and health in Africa. China combines a mixed emphasis on "reciprocity and mutual benefit," economic benefits, and the political interest and obligations of a "big country" (Xiaoyun 2009). China views development as two-way cooperation rather than one-way aid, and brings its own aid principles to the debate, see Figure 2. A new axis of development to Paris-Accra (described in the Paris Declaration and the Accra Action Agenda) is nevertheless emerging. It stretches further east. It is focussed on the future challenges of global development rather than aid tied to a particular historical, cold war or colonial past. Yet, it is certainly political and economic and brings new approaches to development, including donors with a very direct and recent experience of development aid.

2. Expectations of a Global Health Partnership

Why is such a global partnership needed? First, the book shows that global programmes, civil society, private sector and private foundations have evolved beyond just innovative partners. They have become constituencies in global health, and "claimed a space" in health diplomacy and decision making. Yet global health governance has not yet built on this constituency model, on this diversity, to facilitate diplomacy and draw in constituencies to make collective decisions. Second, there are limits to the effectiveness of individual innovative partners. No innovative partnership provides the answer to global health. The book suggests they work best as part of an overall partnership at country and global level. Bill Gates will not have the answer to global health, but can provide considerable innovation alongside existing partners as shown in the chapter on India. Civil society has an important role to play alongside government programmes, provoking or working with them. Global Programs work best alongside the policy leverage of bilateral partners, the long term, systems building of development banks, and the unique technical coordination of WHO. Finally, a period of global risks will require global not fragmented responses. Innovative partnerships will only contribute global responses, as one part of a global health partnership. This will require a two-way adaptation — by partners to define their roles as part of this partnership, and by global health governance to better incorporate them.

What do those working in countries expect of this partnership? First, they do not underestimate the progress made in health in the last decade; the declines in adult mortality in many countries in Africa for the first time in 20 years due to HIV treatment; and in child mortality due to malaria, immunisation and integrated childhood interventions. As the Ministry of Health in Rwanda comments "*in fighting malaria in the last ten years we found child mortality declined by 50 percent due to many aspects of the health programmes ... during the malaria season previously if you went to the health centres there were always two people ill for every bed, now for the first time there are not more people than beds, there are free hospital beds.*" At the same time, there are major gaps in progress towards health goals, in particular MDG 5 to reduce maternal mortality.

Second, countries see many of the key partners present in health. They do not see them yet working effectively as a partnership. Yet each partner brings a unique element of this wider partnership, if this diversity is fully recognised and built into health governance. Bilateral partners have a privileged policy dialogue with many countries (and a network of ambassadors and advisers to support this. It is probably no coincidence that the head of PEPFAR in the country was the US ambassador. She is likely to be heard at a different level than a USAID, WHO or Global Fund health director). Development banks can integrate health into planning and to the ministry of finance. They have a strong role in fiduciary responsibility, with their presence in countries. Other multilaterals have key roles, UNICEF in procurement, UNDP in implementation in many difficult situations (it is used by the Global Fund in many fragile states, where government capacity is very limited). In health, we are privileged to have WHO, a potential default point of coordination, a partner with the Ministry of Health (very few other multilaterals map so clearly into a country ministry, and are trusted and owned by them. The only other equivalent relationship is maybe the World Bank with country ministries of Finance, though the ownership is more limited). Diplomacy among health partners rarely starts with an acknowledgement of these complimentary roles. They compete on the margins of their roles, rather than cooperate based on their core competences.

Yet, countries do not see these individual partners, traditional and innovative, well combined as a team. Some countries have been able to define partner roles, rooting them firmly in the country health plan. As the Minister of Health in Ethiopia comments "*we are cultivating a healthy diversity of partners with different approaches and comparative advantages*" yet ensuring that "*both domestic and external resources are well-aligned with a costed national strategy.*" In negotiating manageable diversity "*two things are key — country commitment and results and more importantly the link between the two*" (Chapter 3). Finally, there is anxiety about the sustainability of aid flows to health. Countries are looking to new sources of funding from China and the G20, private foundations, as well as domestic resources, tax and insurance based. They are also spurred to take actions to improve effectiveness, and ensure scarcer resources are focussed on sustainable country priorities.

The challenge of this book — how to make the most of innovative health partnerships — is, therefore, likely to be a central question in the period to 2015. There is an increasing diversity of sources of funding — from the new G20 countries including China, India, Brazil, Mexico and South Korea. Private foundations, from Carlos Slim in Mexico to Bill & Melinda Gates, are emerging, with 34 billionaires pledging to give away at least 50% of their wealth to charity as part of "The Giving Pledge" campaign launched in 2010. There are also diverse implementing partnerships, shown in the book at community level in Uganda, among sex workers in India, or most at risk populations in Russia. The Global Health Partnership will need to become more inclusive, and incorporate a greater rather than lesser diversity of partners in the future.

The book has drawn lessons from two unique periods — the creation of innovative health partnerships (from 2000) and of concerted actions to improve their effectiveness (from 2005). A consistent historical pattern can be identified: "*International cooperation for better health outcomes has developed through a number of periods of creativity ... usually followed by periods of consolidation as participants sought to rationalize the architecture they had created. A feature of the creative periods is the innovative nature of the partnerships*" (Richard Manning, Chapter 1). The book shows how different partners worked to improve their effectiveness, individually and through collective actions. They have introduced considerable innovation — in their governance bringing together constituencies in new ways, and in how they implement programmes with results based funding. The country-level chapters have highlighted innovations and challenges: to negotiate national strategies to coordinate partners in Ethiopia, Rwanda, Malawi; and incorporate excluded partners in Russia supported by the Open Society, and India by the Gates Foundation.

3. The Diplomacy of Diversity and Global Health Governance

The **diplomacy of diversity** aims to challenge as well as find consensus — "*It also pays off to challenge partners, occasionally with bold requests, to put the country and its health system at the centre of their funding considerations*" (Minister of Health, Ethiopia, Chapter 3). Each chapter in the book has, therefore, provided recommendations and actions to improve effectiveness which cut across partners. They aim to provoke more effective health partnerships. The recommendations show the importance of developing national policies which provide a common platform for the work of diverse partners. Firsthand advice was provided on how to negotiate with partners, at national and local level, from Ethiopia, Vietnam to India.

Equally, reform within health partnerships is needed to open policies to directly fund national health strategies. Global programmes need to develop operating systems which are open to country plans and partners, not closed proprietary grant mechanisms. To achieve this, the stages of learning and engagement were described in relation to global programmes. Some frustration was expressed on the speed of these reforms from countries, particularly in relation to health systems. Two key points of entry were recommended. First, partners should "think twice" when setting up new health partnerships, so that the right funding channels are used and best practice is built into their governance. Second, partners should promote consistent stakeholder behaviour across their Boards, to provide clear incentives for the partnerships to become more effective.

Donors should use a portfolio approach to ensure balanced support of development channels, to fund disease programmes, health systems and technical assistance. This portfolio approach should take into account evidence of effectiveness. A significant example is DFID's multilateral review published on 1 March 2011 (Figure 1). Finally, the book shows the investments required in health diplomacy at country level, the policy networks, the strategies, the monitoring frameworks, as well as the results possible when the diplomacy of diversity is successful. As well as formal coordination in meetings, there needs to be much greater informal coordination using the "invisible hand" of results and transparency of programmatic and financial information (as supported by the International Aid Transparency Initiative).

Looking forward, the challenge to 2015 will be to forge an innovative global health partnership. This will need to define how partners work effectively, not just individually, but collectively as a team (with respective roles, competencies and dependencies). Many of the groups in this book, civil society, global programmes, private sector, private foundations, have evolved beyond just innovative partners. They have become constituencies in global health, as reflected in the chapter on civil society "claiming a space in global health". Much can be learnt from the way their voice has been incorporated in innovative health partnerships, for example their roles in the Board and the country coordinating mechanisms of GAVI or the Global Fund. However, the global-level inclusion of these constituencies is unlikely to be a macro model of global health partnerships. Global health governance is unlikely to be the sum of the chapters in this book, or its recommendations. It will require something new. To create a global health, partnership raises difficult questions of global governance and diplomacy, themes of this book, of this series, and of the final MDG 8 goal.

Global health governance may develop beyond recognition of innovative health partnerships, of extending consultations, including their networks, organising side-meetings or special sessions of existing governance mechanisms. Global health may need to internalise their role not just as partners but as new constituencies into its structure, decision making and

INDEX	COMPONENTS
Contribution to UK development objectives*	• Average of: o Critical role in meeting international development and humanitarian objectives • Average of: o Adaptation to fragile contexts o Promotion of gender equality o Ensures activities are low carbon, climate resilient and environmentally sustainable o Focus on poor countries o Contribution to results
Organisational strengths	• Cost and value consciousness • Partnership behaviour • Strategic/performance management • Financial resources management • Transparency and accountability

* includes humanitarian objectives

Very good	Good	Adequate	Poor
AsDF	AfDF	CDB	CommSoc
ECHO	CERF	EC'ion Budget	FAO
EDF	CIFs	EFW	HABITAT
GAVI	EBRD	IADB	ILO
GFATM	FTI	OHCHR	IOM
ICRC	GEF	UNAIDS	ISDR
IDA	GFDRR	UNEP	UNESCO
PIDG	IFAD	UNFPA	UNIDO
UNICEF	IFC	WHO	UNIFEM
	IFRC		
	OCHR		
	PBF		
	UNDP		
	UNHCR		
	UNITAID		
	WFP		

Note: Organisations are listed in alphabetical order.

Figure 1. Summary of criteria used to assess value for money and classification of multilateral organisations supported by DFID (DFID 2011, pp.13, 80). The individual organisations are not the focus of this figure, but acronyms are described in the original DFID document.

governance. This will not be just for representation. As shown in this book, governance should extend the available resources, the available implementers on the ground, and widen and deepen the development partnership to achieve health outcomes. At global level, it will need to incorporate new players, in particular the G20. The G-20 currently represents approximately 90% of the world's wealth, 80% of the world's trade and two-thirds of the world's population. They will bring not only new players (Brazil, Russia, India, China, South Africa and South Korea) but "*new stakes and rules of the game*" (Garrett and Alavian 2010). There is likely to be a continuing period of innovation in health partnerships, which will need to be responsive to new partners, ways of doing business, and global risks.

Second, forging, strong collective actions will require renewed health diplomacy. It will be health diplomacy, not diplomat to diplomat, but diplomacy that can form common actions with the private sector, communities, reach out to private foundations, and most importantly those affected by health issues. It will be a health diplomacy of diversity, recognising the different constituents of health, and able to reach into village meetings, company board meetings, engage most at risk populations, as much as health assemblies. As suggested in this book, "*a new type of diplomacy is needed which uses the "soft power" of negotiations, networks and incentives*" (Isenman and Shakow, Chapter 2). This diplomacy will need to be a network model to forge consistent actions across very different fora, contexts, boards and organisations.

As Dodgson notes "*an essential element of global health governance is the need to involve, both formally and informally, a broader range of actors and interests*" (Dodgson 2002). Rosenau furthermore stresses the "*variety of steering mechanisms and institutions which have come into being as instruments of governance*" (Rosenau 2003). He adds that to exert "*a modicum of control over affairs*" requires internalising the "*numerous steering mechanisms found in NGOs, and still others consist of informal spheres of authority that may never develop formal structures*". Health governance will require a renewed health diplomacy of diversity, as described by the Minister of Health in Ethiopia in this book "*formal coordination forums need to be matched with direct diplomacy ... a culture of candid dialogue to jointly address challenges, leverage positive peer pressure on partners to keep promises.*"

4. The Korean Contribution — A New Axis for Development

The year 2012 is an important year to forge this global development partnership. This global partnership is seen as one of the important inputs and outcomes of the MDGs, in MDG 8. The new axis of development is reflected in South Korea hosting the important high-level forum on aid in December 2011. The forum will draw together development and finance ministers, countries receiving aid, and new development partners, to review the effectiveness of aid. It will formally be the end of the accountability structure based on the Paris Declaration and principles, which set targets to 2010.

South Korea is a new member of the G20 group of nations, a new donor and recent beneficiary of aid. It has close ties with China, India and Japan. South Korea will provide an important bridge to a refreshed development partnership. The South Korean President Lee Myung-bak already introduced development as an integral part of the G20's mission for the first time, stating "*We must not let the needs of the world's poorest countries be obscured by preoccupation with the major economies. In fact, helping the poorest of the poor can contribute to the global rebalancing and growth we seek, instead of being seen as a subsidiary issue*" (he noted that economic growth in sub-Saharan Africa from 2002–2008 averaged greater than 7%) (Lee Myung-bak 2010). There is a possibility of a refreshed "Korean consensus, charter or compact" for development, to build on the Paris principles and the Accra Action Agenda. The draft outcome document for the South Korean High Level Forum stresses "a new global development partnership" that is "broader and more inclusive than ever before ... embraces diversity" and is grounded in "transparent, country-led results frameworks". It also suggests actions to reduce proliferation of new instruments and embed them in a more cohesive country and global development partnership.

There may be at least three important contributions from this Korean perspective. First, the South Korean support of a "***fresh development partnership***" which is more inclusive, open, innovative and draws contributions from all constituencies. In a concept paper preparing for their role in 2011, the Koreans describe "*an opportunity to provide a "turning point" ... which would reflect a more inclusive, effective, development paradigm, that focuses on enabling effective governments, productive businesses and* *engaged citizens. The outcome … would be a fresh global development partnership*" (South Korean Ministry of Foreign Affairs and Trade 2010). This partnership reflects Korea's development experience and role as member of the G20 group of nations. It presents the opportunity for new roles and responsibilities for countries such as Brazil, South Africa, China, India and South Korea in a development partnership (many with long experiences of aid as donors, China since 1956, and as recipients). These countries also support a strong centre to the partnership, certainly in country governments, but also globally with the role of the United Nations and G20 (and have discussed a Secretariat and more formal governance for the G20). These partners bring different principles of aid and cooperation with similarities and differences to the Paris principles, see for example Figure 2. There will need to be acknowledgement of diversity, of the need for collective actions, and a two-way adaptation, to negotiate a refreshed partnership. However, there is also a risk of very divergent models of aid emerging, if the Korean compact cannot be shaped.

Second, **South Korea assumes country ownership, often in a quiet but firm and determined way**. It is the basis of engagement with partners. Country ownership is based on mutual accountability and contribution to results. Commitments to country results provide an "invisible hand" to coordinate partners, beyond more formal coordination and harmonisation meetings. There is a rebalancing of the Paris principles on aid effectiveness towards country ownership, mutual accountability and results. As the president of South Korea commented as chair of the G20 summit in 2010, "*In our consultation with African leaders, Korea was reminded of the scepticism we once met from donors and some multilateral agencies when we proposed to build the Seoul-Busan Expressway or to set up the Pohang Iron and Steel Co., both acknowledged as successes today. Accordingly, we recognize that developing countries must choose their own priorities for the future — infrastructure, quality of human capital for jobs, private investment. Having chosen the hard path itself, Korea could not choose the easy road for the Seoul Summit — picking one isolated development issue, creating a flashy new donor fund, moving on after the photo opportunity. The development path we have chosen embraces complexity and hard choices.*" (President of South Korea, Lee Myung-bak 2010).

The Eight Principles of Chinese aid to foreign countries:

1. The Chinese Government always bases itself on the principle of equality and mutual benefit in providing aid to other countries. It never regards such aid as a kind of unilateral alms but as something mutual.
2. In providing aid to other countries, the Chinese Government strictly respects the sovereignty of the recipient countries, and never attaches any conditions or asks for any privileges.
3. China provides economic aid in the form of interest-free or low-interest loans and extends the time limit for the repayment when necessary so as to lighten the burden of the recipient countries as far as possible.
4. In providing aid to other countries, the purpose of the Chinese Government is not to make the recipient countries dependent on China but to help them embark step by step on the road of self-reliance and independent economic development.
5. The Chinese Government tries its best to help the recipient countries build projects which require less investment while yielding quicker results, so that the recipient governments may increase their income and accumulate capital.
6. The Chinese Government provides the best-quality equipment and material of its own manufacture at international market prices. If the equipment and material provided by the Chinese Government are not up to the agreed specifications and quality, the Chinese Government undertakes to replace them.
7. In giving any particular technical assistance, the Chinese Government will see to it that the personnel of the recipient country fully master such technique.
8. The experts dispatched by China to help in construction in the recipient countries will have the same standard of living as the experts of the recipient country. The Chinese experts are not allowed to make any special demands or enjoy any special amenities.

Figure 2. Chinese guiding principles of aid to foreign countries developed in the 1960s and still influential today (with similarities and differences to the Paris Declaration).

Finally, **South Korea may bring an Asian model of human development** based on capacity investments in education, health and infrastructure (Sen 1999). As countries graduate from aid, they tend to forget the capacity building and social investments which catalysed economic growth (and there is also the possibility of promotion of a narrow economic model of aid and development). Countries at all stages of development make heavy investments in capacity, often from 25% to 50% of their GDP. The G20 countries bring experiences as recipients and donors of health aid, and of recent graduation between the two. They break up the traditional axis of donor-recipients and bring a wider and more recent experience of the impact and challenges of aid (China, for example, is a donor, a recipient and even a donor to some countries wealthier than itself; for example, Botswana and South Africa). Many G20 members still rely on aid for domestic health, three of the top 10 recipients of health aid are G-20 countries (India the largest recipient, Indonesia 6th and China 10th), and three more are in the top 20 (South Africa, Brazil and Argentina) (Garrett and Alavian 2010). The question is how to best finance country capacity, so it can act as a catalyst for development. South Korea could bring important new experiences to define a Korean compact for development in 2012. If this does not occur, it will need to be negotiated in the following years before 2015.

The last decade has seen an innovative period in global health partnerships. A diverse, lively, sometimes slightly disorganised social movement for health goals emerged drawing in new partners. These partners have worked together in the many global and country contexts assessed in this book. They have emerged not just as partners, but as constituents in a refreshed global health partnership. The next period to 2015 is unlikely to see such an eruption of new health partnerships. The focus will be on how to shape the landscape that has emerged, the governance and diplomacy to effectively respond to country needs and global crises. Chapter 3 concluded "*It is often from difficult situations, with open, clear dialogue that strong partnerships can be created ... tough love (is needed), development partners must move forward with a new spirit of candor*". As the president of South Korea adds it will be "*a development path which embraces complexity and hard choices,*" but which may lead to a more inclusive, innovative, health governance. A number of characteristics have been shown in the hard choices and partnerships in this book:

1. **The dividends of development still come from social investments:** by educating a new generation, the health dividend of the removal of infectious diseases of poverty, and the removal of the fear of poverty to allow people to focus on wealth creation. Individuals and families prioritise these investments, and it is important that governments also do.
2. **This has been the basis for a social movement for global health since 2000:** which has gone beyond the traditional governance and institutions. It has reflected a new partnership between the public,

private sector, civil society, private foundations, and multilaterals. This has created innovative health partnerships, globally and in countries.

3. **Global risks require a renewed global partnership:** a linear model of development has been replaced by a period of global risks since 2007: financial, food, environmental and health. Global risks will require global not fragmented responses, mobilising responses to health similar to those to global financial risks.
4. **New constituency model of health governance:** the new actors have evolved beyond just innovative partners. They have become constituencies in global health, and "claimed a space" in health diplomacy and decision making. This is changing governance mechanisms.
5. **Results based diplomacy:** a renewed health diplomacy is appearing — not diplomat to diplomat, but a diplomacy of diversity which can build common actions across governments, civil society, the private sector. Commitments to country results may provide an "invisible hand" to coordinate partners, beyond formal, political, coordination mechanisms.
6. **Shift East and South in development partnership:** the importance of new players, the G20, China, India and South Korea provides the opportunity to refresh the axis of development from donors and recipients towards a more mutual, structured, inclusive global compact.

The few years to 2015 will be critical to achieve the health MDGs. It will require a strengthened global development partnership, as an important input and outcome of the MDGs. This innovative global partnership will need to move beyond principles, actions (and the Paris-Accra, donor-recipient axis) to a more mutual, structured, sustained and inclusive compact. The partnership will require an enhanced health diplomacy which can listen to the different voices, situations, interests, challenges and recommendations presented in the chapters of this book, and which can shape collective actions. The short period to 2015 will need to build on the individual innovative partnerships described in this book, to forge an equally innovative global partnership for health to achieve MDGs 4, 5, 6 and ultimately MDG 8 — a sustained global partnership for development.

References

DFID (2011) "Multilateral Aid Review: Ensuring maximum value for money for UK aid through multilateral organisations," London, UK.

Dodgson R, Lee K, Drager N (2002) "Global health governance: A conceptual review," WHO, Geneva.

Garrett L, Alavian E (2010) "Global Health Governance in a G-210 World", *Global Health Governance* IV(1):1–14.

High Level Independent Review Panel (2011), *Final Report on Fiduciary Controls and Oversight Mechanisms of the Global Fund: Turning the Page from Emergency to Sustainability*, The Global Fund for AIDS, TB and Malaria, Geneva. http://www.theglobalfund.org/en/highlevelpanel/

Korean Ministry of Foreign Affairs and Trade (MOFAT) (2010) "Concept Paper for the Evolving Global Aid Architecture", Seoul, Republic of Korea.

Lee Myung-bak (2010) "G20 Summit shouldn't Overlook the Poorest Countries" November 10, *Washington Post*.

Pang T, Daulaire N, Keusch G, Leke R, Piot P, Reddy S, Rys A, Szlezak N (2010) "The New Age of Global Health Governance Holds Promise", *Nature Medicine* 16(11):1181.

Rosenau J (2003) *Distant Proximities: Dynamics beyond Globalization*. Princeton, New Jersey: Princeton University Press.

Sen A (1999) *Development as Freedom*. Oxford: Oxford University Press.

The Guardian (2010) "South Korea put Development on the Agenda for Seoul G20 Summit", October 4.

Xiaoyun Li (2009) "China's Foreign Aid to Africa," presentation to OECD, Paris.

Appendix of Additional Study Resources

In addition to the references in each chapter, below are selected resources for further information on innovative health partnerships, health constituencies and health governance:

Selected Health Partnerships and Foundations

Carlos Slim social and philanthropic work, www.carlosslim.com/responsabilidad_ing.html, including Carlos Slim Institute of Health, information, interviews and philanthropic activities.

FIND — Foundation for innovative new diagnostics, http://www.finddiagnostics.org/ — including resource centre, reports, articles and documentation.

GAVI Alliance, www.gavialliance.org — and independent evaluations of the GAVI Alliance, www.gavialliance.org/performance/evaluation.

Global Fund to fight AIDS, TB and malaria, www.theglobalfund.org, including Evaluation library of independent evaluations, www.theglobalfund.org/en/library.

Health Metrics Network, www.who.int/healthmetrics, includes tools and resources.

International Health Partnership (IHP+), www.internationalhealthpartnership.net, including reports, initiatives and IHP+ results on partner data and progress.

International HIV/AIDS alliance, www.aidsalliance.org, supporting community actions on AIDS, best practice guides, resources, projects, technical support hubs, and publications.

Open Society Foundations supported by Soros Foundations network, www.soros.org/initiatives/health. Information on their public health programs, articles, multimedia and program descriptions.

Partnership for Maternal, Newborn & Child Health, www.who.int/pmnch/, including resources, journals, notes from the field, publications, www.who.int/pmnch/topics/.

(RED) — innovative financing to support AIDS programs, www.joinred.com/red/ list of commercial companies, products and business model.

Rockefeller Foundation, www.rockefellerfoundation.org/who-we-are/our-focus/global-health — including history, grants and resources on innovations in global health, e-health, market models.

Roll Back Malaria Partnership, www.rollbackmalaria.org, including resource centre of publications and multimedia resources, www.rollbackmalaria.org/multimedia/.

Stop TB Partnership, www.stoptb.org, including reports, technical publications, and independent evaluations.

The Bill & Melinda Gates Foundation, global health program, http://www.gatesfoundation.org/global-health/, including strategy overview and case studies.

UNITAID, www.unitaid.eu, includes resources, projects for innovative financing to scale up treatment access for malaria, TB and HIV.

US President's Emergency Plan for AIDS relief, www.pepfar.org, includes all progress reports, www.pepfar.org/progress — and latest indicators and results on progress.

Wellcome Trust, www.wellcome.ac.uk/, including education resources, information on investments and the welcome library with online catalogue and resources — library, www.wellcome.ac.uk/.

Selected Journals, Networks and Other Open Access Resources

Bulletin of WHO — open access, peer reviewed, with many articles and issues on global health, health systems and governance issues — www.who.int/bulletin.

Center for Global Development, www.cgdev.org/, includes Global Health Policy Research Network, HIV/AIDS Monitor, resources, interviews, publications and research.

Centre for AIDS, Development and Research, www.cadre.org.za, including programs, research, resources, *African Journal of AIDS Research, and Community Communication Materials.*

Global Business Coalition on HIV/AIDS, TB and malaria, www.gbcimpact.org/, case studies, expert interviews, e-learning, and resources on business activities in the fight against disease.

Global Health Council, www.globalhealth.org/, resources, trainings and links for largest global organization of professionals, NGOs, foundations, corporations working for global health.

Global HIV/AIDS Initiatives Network — research network of national and sub-national effects of global HIV/AIDS initiatives at the country level — http://ghinet.org/index.asp.

Health Economics and HIV/AIDS Research Centre, www.heard.org.za, includes knowledge centre, publications, and materials on evidence of impact in health and HIV.

Health Gap, www.healthgap.org/, resources, fact sheets, global campaigns, and stimulating materials on global campaigns for access to health, support of health workers and human rights issues.

Institute of Health Metrics and Evaluation (IHME), University of Washington. Development Assistance for Health Database, www.healthmetricsandevaluation.org/resources/datasets/2010/dah/dah.html.

Journal of Global Health Governance — open access, peer reviewed journal with individual articles and themed issues on global health and governance — www.ghgj.org.

Medecins Sans Frontieres — www.msf.org, country fact sheets, publications, resources, position papers on its activities providing emergency medical assistance in more than 60 countries.

Organisation for Economic Cooperation and Development. Statistics and reports on aid and other resource flows to developing countries — www.oecd.org/dac/stats/data.

Overseas Development Institute, www.odi.org.uk, includes discussions, resources libraries, working papers and publications on aid and development.

PLOS Medicine — open access, peer reviewed journal including global health — www.plosmedicine.org.

World Bank, Data and Research, www.worldbank.org — including data, tools and journals and development impact evaluations including database of ongoing impact evaluations.

World Health Organisation — www.who.int — including WHO statistical information system presenting most recent health statistics from members.www.who.int/whosis/- and general research and data on health — www.who.int/research.

Index